Practical Aspects of Rape Investigation

A Multidisciplinary Approach

Third Edition

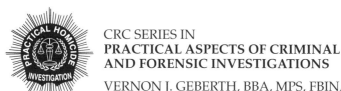

CRC SERIES IN
**PRACTICAL ASPECTS OF CRIMINAL
AND FORENSIC INVESTIGATIONS**

VERNON J. GEBERTH, BBA, MPS, FBINA *Series Editor*

Practical Aspects of
Rape Investigation
A Multidisciplinary Approach
Third Edition

Edited by
Robert R. Hazelwood
Ann Wolbert Burgess

CRC Press
Boca Raton   London   New York   Washington, D.C.

Library of Congress Cataloging-in-Publication Data

Practical aspects of rape investigation : a multidisciplinary approach / edited Robert R. Hazelwood, Ann Wolbert Burgess.—3rd ed.
    p. cm.— (Practical aspects of criminal and forensic investigations)
  Includes bibliographical references and index.
  ISBN 0-8493-0076-2 (alk. paper)
    1. Rape—Investigation. 2. Rape—United States—Investigation. I. Hazelwood, Robert R. II. Burgess, Ann Wolbert. III. CRC series in practical aspects of criminal and forensic investigations.

HV8079.R35 P7 2001
363.25'9532—dc21   2001025118

Visit the CRC Press Web site at www.crcpress.com

© 2001 by CRC Press LLC

No claim to original U.S. Government works
International Standard Book Number 0-8493-0076-2
Library of Congress Card Number 2001025118
Printed in the United States of America   4 5 6 7 8 9 0
Printed on acid-free paper

Series Editor's Note

This textbook is part of a series entitled *Practical Aspects of Criminal and Forensic Investigation.* This series was created by Vernon J. Geberth, a retired New York City Police Department Lieutenant Commander, who is an author, educator, and consultant to homicide and forensic investigations.

This series has been designed to provide contemporary, comprehensive, and pragmatic information to the practitioner involved in criminal and forensic investigations by authors who are nationally recognized experts in their respective fields.

Preface

Despite the increased focus on criminal investigation of rape and sexual assault crimes, only slightly more than half of the reported rape cases result in the arrest of a suspect — a figure that has not changed over the past three decades. These figures become even more critical when realizing that less than half of all rapes believed to occur are reported to law enforcement; and of those assailants arrested, even fewer are convicted of rape. It is impossible to determine whether increases in rape and sexual assault are due to better reporting methods or due to the possibility that sex offenders who are not arrested or convicted repeat their behaviors. The problem is now being addressed by all professionals whose work brings them into contact with the victims or the offenders.

Concurrent with the increasing numbers of rape victims, there has been a burgeoning of research into myriad factors interwoven with sexual violence and its aftermath. Substantial contributions have been made to advancing the state of knowledge for law enforcement agents, health professionals, rape crisis staffs, and criminal justice staffs.

Although most people working with sexual crimes see *either* the victim or offender, the investigator and prosecutor frequently encounter *both* the victims and the offenders of sexual assaults. Thus, it becomes crucial that these two groups have the benefit of research results in the fields of victimology, criminology, behavioral sciences, forensic sciences, and criminal justice. Such information can substantially impact the effectiveness of the investigative interview, the collection of forensic evidence, and the prosecution of cases.

The aim of this Third Edition of *Practical Aspects of Rape Investigation* is to present current research findings, new forensic techniques, and recent data about special populations of victims and offenders.

The book is divided into four sections. Section I includes four chapters specific to the victim of rape and sexual assault. In the first chapter, Ann W. Burgess reviews contemporary issues in the field of sexual violence. In the second chapter on the victim's perspective, Ann W. Burgess and Robert R. Hazelwood capture both the thoughts and reactions of victims going through an assault and its distressing aftermath. Myths about the victim are interspersed as we outline the investigator's approach to interviewing the victim as a method to help the officer understand the wide range of behaviors that relate to rape. Such understanding benefits the victim in his or her recovery and the officer in the investigation. Chapter 3, by Ann W. Burgess and Robert R. Hazelwood, discusses prototypes for victim care services and provides a data collection instrument for rape and sexual assault. A new chapter on sexual abuse of elderly and cognitively handicapped persons is presented by Ann W. Burgess, Elizabeth B. Dowdell, and Robert A. Prentky. A study of 20 cases provides the data for this chapter and includes suggestions for the interviewing and care of elderly victims.

Section II includes 10 chapters on the investigation of rape and sexual assault cases. Chapter 5, *The Relevance of Fantasy in Serial Sexual Crime Investigations,* by Robert R. Hazelwood and Janet I. Warren, proposes that fantasy is the link between the underlying motivation for sexual assaults and the behavior exhibited during the crime. In companion Chapter 6, Robert R. Hazelwood and Janet I. Warren contrast impulsive and ritualistic behavior in the sexually violent offender and illustrate by case example. In Chapter 7, *The Behavioral-Oriented Interview of Rape Victims: The Key to Profiling,* Robert R. Hazelwood and Ann W. Burgess describe interviewing the victim to determine the verbal, physical, and sexual behavior exhibited by the offender during the commission of the crime. The purpose of this interview is to elicit information from the victim that will aid in the preparation of a profile of an unidentified offender. In Chapter 8, *Analyzing the Rape and Profiling the Offender,* Robert R. Hazelwood presents an initial categorization of rapists from a profiling standpoint. It then sets forth a detailed case history followed by an analysis of that case history and the resultant profile derived from the analysis. Chapter 9, *Classifying Rape and Sexual Assault,* by Ann W. Burgess, Robert R. Hazelwood, and Allen G. Burgess, presents categories derived from decades of research on rapists.

One of the thorniest problems in rape investigations is false allegations. An inherent conflict arises between the investigator's obligation to accept the victim's complaint as legitimate and his duty to develop the facts of the case. Chapter 10, *False Rape Allegations,* by Ann W. Burgess and Robert R. Hazelwood, reviews the literature on rape allegations, proposes a model to understand the concept, and includes discussion on motivation and red flags for false allegations. Cases of false allegation fall on a long continuum from the extreme of obscene telephone calls to the other extreme of self-mutilation and/or amputation to substantiate a claim of rape. In Chapter 11, Kenneth V. Lanning describes a typology of offenders who assault children. This typology includes incest offenders and pedophiles as well as psychopathic character disordered offenders. Cyberstalking by pedophiles is a new section to the chapter. This carefully designed typology is derived from cases investigated from the law enforcement perspective. Chapter 12, *Collateral Materials in Sexual Crimes,* by Robert R. Hazelwood and Kenneth V. Lanning, defines the concept of collateral material and identifies its uses by investigators.

Chapter 13, *Interrogations and False Confessions in Rape Cases,* is new and written by criminologist attorney Richard Leo, who has studied how and why innocent people confess to crimes that carry lengthy prison sentences, life imprisonment, or execution. Interrogation tactics are discussed. New Chapter 14, by Kenneth V. Lanning and Robert R. Hazelwood, on the maligned investigator of criminal sexuality, provides a perspective on difficulties experienced by the sexual assault investigator.

Section III deals with Forensics and the Court. Chapter 15, *Physical Evidence in Sexual Assault Investigations* and its companion Chapter 16, *Evidence Recovery Considerations in Sexual Assault Investigations,* by Robert P. Spalding and P. David Bigbee, are new and revised chapters that provide a solid background and framework for recovering and processing physical evidence in rape and sexual assault cases. The forensic scientists discuss the collection and observation of physical and trace evidence of the victim, the offender, and the scene of the crime. These chapters also discuss the presentation of this evidence in court. In Chapter 17, William Heiman, Ann Ponterio, and Gail Fairman describe the standard processing of rape cases in the criminal justice system. Difficult cases discussed include identification issue cases, consent issue cases, and the imperfect victim. The use of expert testimony is also discussed. Chapter 18, *Forensic Examination of Sexual Assault Victims,* by nurse–practitioner Kathleen Brown, orients the sexual assault forensic examiner and the rape investigator to the conduct of a medical examination and the manner in which evidence should be collected. Medical treatment for the victim is also outlined.

Section IV is on special populations. New Chapter 19, *The Sexual Crimes of Juveniles,* by forensic psychologist John Hunter, provides insights on the latest research on juvenile sex offenders, especially in the area of classification. New Chapter 20, *Female Sex Offenders: A Typological and Etiological Overview,* by Janet I. Warren and Julia Hislop, presents research on a little understood population of women who sexually offend. Chapter 21, *The Serial Rapist,* written by Robert R. Hazelwood and Janet I. Warren, includes findings from their study of 41 serial rapists. Major findings contradict popular stereotypes. For example, most serial rapists are not carefully stalking a particular woman; rather, their choice of victim is more dependent on general proximity, the victim's availability, and access to her residence. Chapter 22, *The Criminal Sexual Sadist,* by Robert R. Hazelwood, Park Elliot Dietz, and Janet I. Warren, contains findings from their study of men who sadistically raped and/or murdered their victims. New Chapter 23, *Sexual Sadists: Their Wives and Girlfriends,* by Robert R. Hazelwood, discusses findings from interviews with the partners of the sexual sadists. And Chapter 24, *Sexual Predators in Nursing Homes,* by Ann W. Burgess, Robert A. Prentky, and Elizabeth B. Dowdell, reports on a sample of offenders against nursing home residents, the majority of whom were between the ages of 70 and 94. Classification of the offender by motivation is discussed.

This book represents a major commitment by its authors to present the most current knowledge for the investigation and prosecution of rape and sexual assault cases. We wish to thank the many people who helped in the first, second and third editions.

Acknowledgments

The editors wish to acknowledge the following individuals, without whose efforts this book would not have been possible.

For their encouragement and support: Peggy Driver-Hazelwood, Allen G. Burgess, Retired Assistant Director James D. McKenzie (FBI), Retired Deputy Assistant Director James A. O'Connor (FBI), and Retired Unit Chief Roger L. Depue (FBI).

Others deserving special thanks are Retired Supervisory Special Agent Howard D. Teten (FBI) and Professor Emeritus Carol R. Hartman (Boston College) for their insight and professional advice over the years.

A special word of thanks to CRC Editor Becky McEldowney and manuscript editor Madeline Leigh for their patience and scrupulous attention to detail.

The Authors

P. David Bigbee has been an FBI agent since 1980. He is currently the supervisor of the Miami-based Violent Crimes/Fugitive Task Force of South Florida and the Caribbean. Prior to that he served in the Albuquerque and Tampa field divisions as an examiner in the Serology Unit of the FBI Laboratory, as an instructor in forensic science at the FBI Academy, and as chief of the DNA Analysis Unit of the FBI Laboratory. Special Agent Bigbee was the recipient of the U.S. Attorney General's Award for Excellence in Law Enforcement in 1990 as well as the University of Virginia–FBI National Academy Thomas Jefferson Award for Excellence in Law Enforcement Education in 1989.

Kathleen Brown, R.N., Ph.D. is a nurse–practitioner in women's health. She is on faculty at the University of Pennsylvania School of Nursing, where she directs the Sexual Assault Nurse Examiner Program and coordinates the forensic science courses. Educated at the University of Pennsylvania, Dr. Brown has been in a private women's health practice since 1979. Through a state grant, she has trained nurses in the Commonwealth of Pennsylvania to conduct sexual assault examinations in their counties. Dr. Brown has testified throughout Pennsylvania and has published her research on domestic violence, forensic interview, and evidence collection.

Allen G. Burgess, D.B.A. is president of Data Integrity, Inc., a software manufacturing firm in Waltham, MA. He earned his B.S.E.E. at Massachusetts Institute of Technology and his M.B.A. and D.B.A. from Boston University. He has been in the computer industry for over 30 years. He was the designer of a Y2K solution and has also developed TraceIT and CodeIT, software tools that detect errors in large data sets. Dr. Burgess has been on faculty at Boston University, Babson University, and Northeastern University, where he lectured on business administration, crime classification, statistics, and research methodology.

Ann Wolbert Burgess, R.N., D.N.Sc., C.S., F.A.A.N. is professor of nursing at Boston College School of Nursing. Educated at Boston University and the

University of Maryland, she and Lynda Lytle Holmstrom cofounded one of the first hospital-based crisis intervention programs for rape victims at Boston City Hospital in the mid-1970s.

She has been principal investigator on 12 funded research projects and has coauthored 21 books and over 135 articles on crime victims and their offenders. Dr. Burgess maintains a private clinical practice; she also serves as an expert witness in criminal and civil cases. She has testified before congressional committees and served on the U.S. Attorney General's Task Force on Family Violence. She was elected to the Institute of Medicine in 1994 and chaired the 1996 National Research Council's Task Force on Violence against Women. Currently she serves as the research partner to the CDC-funded National Sexual Assault Resource Center, directed by the Pennsylvania Coalition against Rape.

Elizabeth Burgess Dowdell, R.N., Ph.D. is an assistant professor at Villanova University School of Nursing. Educated at Vanderbilt University, Boston College, and the University of Pennsylvania, Dr. Dowdell has studied and published in the areas of caregiver stress, crime victims, and elder sexual abuse. Her current research is on school safety and family response to nursing home abuse.

Park Elliot Dietz, M.D., M.P.H., Ph.D. is president of Threat Assessment Group, Inc., in Newport Beach, California, clinical professor of psychiatry and biobehavioral sciences at UCLA School of Medicine, forensic psychiatry consultant to the FBI's National Center for the Analysis of Violent Crime, and president of the American Academy of Psychiatry and the Law. Educated at Cornell, Johns Hopkins, and the University of Pennsylvania, Dr. Dietz was previously a professor at Harvard and the University of Virginia. He served as the government's chief expert in the trials of John Hinckley, Jr. and Jeffrey Dahmer and has testified in hundreds of trials throughout the U.S.

Gail Fairman is an assistant district attorney in the city of Philadelphia. Ms. Fairman earned her A.B. at Franklin and Marshall College and her J.D. from the National Law Center of George Washington University. She was in private practice and a deputy district attorney in Bucks County, Pennsylvania, before her assignment to the Rape Prosecution Unit in the Philadelphia District Attorney's office. She is currently assigned to the homicide unit.

Robert R. Hazelwood is a retired supervisory special agent of the Federal Bureau of Investigation, currently with the Academy Group, Inc., in Manassas, Virginia. He earned his undergraduate degree at Sam Houston State College and his master's degree at Nova University. Mr. Hazelwood also attended a one-year fellowship in forensic medicine at the Armed Forces Institute of Pathology. Before joining the FBI in 1971, he served 11 years in the U.S. Army's Military Police Corps, attaining the rank of major. His works have been published by the *Journal of Police Science and Administration, Social Science and Medicine, American Registry of Pathology, Journal of Forensic Sciences, FBI Law Enforcement Bulletin,* and other professional journals. He co-authored the book *Autoerotic Fatalities* and has lectured extensively on criminal sexuality throughout the U.S., Europe, Canada, and the Caribbean. He has consulted for law enforcement agencies throughout North America, Canada, Europe, and the Caribbean in the investigation of sexual assaults and homicides.

William Heiman, Esq. graduated from the Wharton School of the University of Pennsylvania and Temple University School of Law. He was an assistant district attorney in the Philadelphia District Attorney's office from 1972 to 1985. He served as chief of the Rape and Child Abuse Unit from 1978 to 1984. In 1981, he received the Program of Excellence Award from the National Organization of Victim Assistance, recognizing the Philadelphia District Attorney's Rape Unit as the most outstanding unit of its type in the country. Mr. Heiman is the author of several articles on rape prosecution issues and is currently in private practice.

Julia Hislop, Ph.D. is currently affiliated with The Children's Advocacy Center at the Children's Hospital of the King's Daughters in Norfolk, Virginia, where she completes psychological testing and evaluation of children alleged to have been abused and their caretakers. She is also associated, in private practice, with the Clinical Associates of Tidewater in Virginia Beach, Virginia. Previously, she was a psychologist with the Kennedy Krieger Institute in Baltimore, Maryland, where she provided therapy and evaluation for foster care children and their caretakers. She co-authored *Female Sexual Abusers: Three Views,* which was published in the Safer Society Press. She is expecting her book (working title *Female Sexual Offenders*) to be published by Idyll Arbor Press in early 2001.

John A. Hunter is an associate professor of health evaluation sciences and psychiatric medicine at the University of Virginia in Charlottesville, Virginia. He has published over 35 articles or book chapters and has been the recipient of five federal research grants on the subject of juvenile sexual offenders and sexual trauma. He has directed both community-based and residential treatment programs for juvenile sexual offenders and is a former member of the board of directors for the Association for the Treatment of Sexual Abusers (ATSA). Dr. Hunter served on the National Task Force on Juvenile Sexual

Offending and has been a frequent lecturer for the FBI and the Department of the Navy on juvenile sexual offenders and their effective management. Dr. Hunter is a member of the editorial boards of the *Review of Aggression and Violent Behavior* and the *Journal of Family Violence.* He serves on clinical and research advisory committees for the Center for Sex Offender Management and the U.S. Office of Justice Programs. He was recently awarded a grant from the Office of Juvenile Justice and Delinquency Prevention to continue his research on the development of a juvenile sex offender typology.

Kenneth V. Lanning is a retired supervisory special agent formerly assigned to the Behavioral Science Unit at the FBI Academy in Quantico, Virginia. He has made presentations before the National Conference on Sexual Victimization of Children, the National Conference on Child Abuse and Neglect, and the American Orthopsychiatric Association. He has testified before the U.S. Attorney General's Task Force on Family Violence, the President's Task Force on Victims of Crime, and the U.S. Attorney General's Commission on Pornography. He has also testified before the U.S. Senate and the U.S. House of Representatives and, as an expert witness, in state and federal courts. Mr. Lanning has lectured and trained thousands of police officers and criminal justice professionals.

Richard A. Leo, Ph.D., J.D. is an assistant professor of criminology, law, and society and an assistant professor of psychology and social behavior at the University of California, Irvine. Dr. Leo is widely recognized as a leading national authority on the subject of police interrogation practices, coercive influence techniques, and false confessions. In the last decade, Dr. Leo has observed, analyzed or evaluated more than 500 interrogations; and he has authored more than two dozen publications on the subject of interrogations and confessions. Dr. Leo is the recipient of the Ruth Shonle Cavan Award from the American Society of Criminology as well as the Shaleem Shah Career Achievement Award from the American Psychological Association and the American Academy of Forensic Psychology.

As part of his research, Dr. Leo has received advanced interrogation training from several law enforcement organizations, including the Federal Law Enforcement Training Center and Reid and Associates. Dr. Leo has served as a consultant on approximately 200 criminal and civil cases. He has testified in state, federal, and military courts on numerous occasions; and he is actively involved in various professional organizations in the academic, legal, and law enforcement communities.

Ann Ponterio was appointed an assistant district attorney in the Philadelphia District Attorney's Office in 1984. She earned her B.A. at St. Bonaventure

University, her J.D. at New England School of Law, and an M.G.A. at the University of Pennsylvania in 1994. Since her appointment in 1984, Ms. Ponterio has been assigned to the Rape Prevention Unit, the Juvenile Unit where she prosecuted child physical and sexual abuse cases, the Major Trial Unit where she prosecuted robbery, aggravated assault, burglary and arson cases, and the Municipal Court Unit where she prosecuted misdemeanor cases.

Robert A. Prentky, Ph.D. is director of assessment at the Justice Research Institute in Bridgewater, MA. He has received funding from the National Institute of Justice for a wide range of studies including research on developmental antecedents of sexual aggression, classification models for sexual offenders, juvenile sexual offenders, risk assessment, and female offenders. He has published extensively in the field of sexual aggression; and his most recent book, *Forensic Management of Sexual Offenders,* was co-authored with Ann Wolbert Burgess.

Robert P. Spalding, M.S. retired from the Federal Bureau of Investigation in 1999 as a supervisory special agent. He joined the FBI in 1971 as an investigative agent in the Cleveland and Washington field offices. Upon transfer to the Laboratory Division in 1973, he was assigned to the Serology Unit. He examined evidence and presented expert testimony in criminal matters in local, state, federal and foreign courts. From 1975 to 1989 he taught forensic serology at the Forensic Science Research and Training Center (FSRTC), FBI Academy, Quantico, Virginia, teaching a graduate-level course through the College of Continuing Education at the University of Virginia. During this time, he developed expertise in bloodstain pattern analysis. Mr. Spalding was later assigned to the newly formed Evidence Response Team Unit, where he taught crime scene investigation to FBI field office evidence response teams throughout the U.S. He also taught a course in bloodstain pattern analysis at the FBI Academy to FBI evidence response team personnel.

Mr. Spalding earned his B.S. and M.S. in biochemistry at the University of Maine in 1965 and 1968, respectively. He is currently a member of several professional forensic science organizations and is the owner of Spalding Forensics, LLC, a consulting and training firm specializing in casework involving bloodstain patterns and crime scene reconstruction.

Janet I. Warren, DSW, LCSW is an associate professor of clinical psychiatric medicine at the University of Virginia. She is on faculty at the Institute of Law, Psychiatry, and Public Policy, where she evaluates criminal defendants and conducts research on serial and violent crime. Dr. Warren also serves on faculty for the diverse training offered through the institute and maintains the Forensic Evaluation Information System, an information-management system containing all court-ordered forensic evaluations conducted in Virginia each year. Dr. Warren has published extensively in the areas of serial rape, sexual sadism, and serial murder, and has been a research consultant to the FBI Behavioral Science Unit since 1986.

Table of Contents

Section II: Investigation

7   The Behavioral-Oriented Interview of Rape Victims: The Key to Profiling   115

Robert R. Hazelwood and Ann Wolbert Burgess

8 Analyzing the Rape and Profiling the Offender   133

Robert R. Hazelwood

9 Classifying Rape and Sexual Assault   165

Ann Wolbert Burgess, Robert R. Hazelwood, and Allen G. Burgess

12 Collateral Materials in Sexual Crimes   221

**Robert R. Hazelwood and
Kenneth V. Lanning**

13 Interrogations and False Confessions in Rape Cases   233

Richard Leo

Section III: Forensics and Court

16 Evidence Recovery Considerations in Sexual Assault Investigations   299

Robert P. Spaulding and P. David Bigbee

17 Prosecuting Rape Cases: Trial Preparation and Trial Tactic Issues   347

William Heiman; Revised and Updated by Ann Ponterio and Gail Fairman

18 Forensic Examination of Sexual Assault Victims   365

Kathleen Brown

Section IV: Special Populations

19   The Sexual Crimes of Juveniles   401

John A. Hunter

22   The Criminal Sexual Sadist   463

**Robert R. Hazelwood, Park Elliot Dietz,
and Janet I. Warren**

23 Sexual Sadists: Their Wives and Girlfriends   477

Robert R. Hazelwood

24 Sexual Predators in Nursing Homes   487

Ann Wolbert Burgess, Robert A. Prentky, and Elizabeth B. Dowdell

Section I: The Victim

Contemporary Issues

1

ANN WOLBERT BURGESS

Introduction

Thirty years ago, when police departments and rape crisis centers began to address the crime of rape, little was known about rape victims or sex offenders. The issue of rape was just beginning to be raised by feminist groups, and the 1971 New York Speak-Out on Rape had been held. Contemporary feminists who raised the issue early were Susan Griffin (1971) in her now-classic article on rape as the "all-American" crime, and Germaine Greer (1973) in her essay on grand rapes (legalistically defined) and petty rapes (everyday sexual rip-offs). Susan Brownmiller (1975) wrote the history of rape and urged people to deny its future. The general public was not particularly concerned about rape victims; very few academic publications or special services existed, and funding agencies did not see the topic as important.

Rape emerged as a major issue with the 1976 funding and establishment of the National Center for the Prevention and Control of Rape. Rape crisis centers were opened in Washington D.C. and San Francisco. Hospital-based rape counseling services started in Boston and in Minneapolis. These centers were replicated and services flourished. Kilpatrick (2000) summarizes the major accomplishments over the 30 years as follows:

- Widespread reform of rape statutes and other legislation for crime victims — stalking laws
- Improvements in the way criminal justice officials treat victims — victim impact statements
- A better understanding of the scope and impact of rape — protocols for health care providers
- Improved medical, nursing, and mental health services — sexual assault forensic examiners
- Improved funding for rape crisis services

The closing of the National Center for the Prevention and Control of Rape in the late 1980s, however, left a void for funding until 1994. The importance of violence against women as a national problem was once again recognized by Congress in its 1994 passage of the Violence Against Women Act (VAWA) (as part of its Violent Crime Control and Law Enforcement Act) and by President Clinton's establishment of an Office on Violence against Women in the U.S. Department of Justice. A panel on Research on Violence against Women was established by the National Research Council in 1995 to fulfill a congressional request to develop a research agenda to increase understanding and control of violence against women. This report (see Crowell and Burgess, 1996) highlights the major literature on the scope of violence against women in the U.S., the causes and consequences of that violence, and the interventions for both women victims of violence and male perpetrators.

As we enter the 21st century, we acknowledge the progress made as well as the old and new problems that continue. In this chapter we review some of the contemporary issues involved in the understanding of rape and its victims. Issues covered include incidence and prevalence of rape; evidentiary examination of the rape victim; sexual crimes against the elderly; the psychobiology of rape; cyberstalking; and issues in the forensic management of sexual offenders.

The Size of the Problem

Incidence

We still do not know how many rapes occur in the United States each year. The problems of estimating the frequency of sexual violence still plague epidemiologists. Part of the problem is in defining the term. From a legal perspective, rape is a criminal act. The Federal Bureau of Investigation (FBI) Uniform Crime Report (UCR) defines forcible rape as "the carnal knowledge of a female forcibly and against her will." Because the legal definition of forcible rape is so restrictive, the term *sexual assault* has been used to cover a wider range of sexual crimes. Most states define any type of sexual behavior with a child as illegal. Rape charges may also occur where victims cannot consent due to mental deficiency, psychosis, or altered consciousness induced by sleep, drugs, illness, or intoxication.

The manner in which rape is defined affects incidence and prevalence rates. *Incidence*, which refers to the number of behaviors of a particular type, may, at the present time, be more reliable than *prevalence*, which refers to the proportion of people who engage in a particular behavior.

To count rape and sexual assault (incidence) depends on the victim and the police perception and interpretation of what occurred. Victims must: (1) perceive a rape has occurred; (2) decide it was an illegal act; (3) decide whether or not to disclose it; and (4) the police (or researcher) must decide whether the act meets the definition of an illegal act. For that act to come before a court of law, the prosecutor must decide that the evidence meets the charge. Only if the authority's classification concurs with that of the victim does the incident become recorded and counted.

A second problem in determining the number of sexual assaults is underreporting. Most rape cases go unreported (Kilpatrick, Edmunds and Seymour, 1992; Crowell and Burgess, 1996). Of those responding to a telephone survey and who answered they had been sexually assaulted in 1995, only 32% reported the incident (Bureau of Justice Statistics, 1996). Guilt, fear of retribution, humiliation, lack of knowledge and trust in the legal and medical system, and impaired cognitive processing that occurs following intense trauma are some reasons why persons may not report (Burgess, Fehder, and Hartman, 1995). In the original Burgess and Holmstrom study (1983), in more than half of the cases, someone other than the victim reported the sexual assault to police. Those statistics have not varied in 20 years. A study of nonincarcerated sex offenders found that 126 men admitted they had committed a total of 907 rapes involving 882 different women, with an average of seven different victims per rapist (Abel et al., 1987).

Contrary to popular belief, rape is not a rare event; it affects hundreds of thousands of people (females and males) each year. When compared with other types of serious crimes, rape has a number of unique characteristics. First, as already noted, it is difficult to know how many rapes occur because of the low reporting rate. Second, in contrast to other crimes, there is a subjective element in determining whether the sexual act occurred against the victim's will. If the victim is of unquestioned chastity and if considerable force was employed by the assailant, then the act is usually considered to be a "real rape." However, if the woman was dating the man or met the man in a bar or over the Internet and said she was forced to have sex with him, some may not perceive the act as rape. Third, rape is the only serious crime in which victims may be held responsible for their own assaults. The belief is still held that women like to be overpowered sexually and say *no* when they mean *yes*. Rules of evidence accepted in the courtroom may be stringent; for example, signs of resistance or an immediate report are required as proof of nonconsent.

There were 93,103 forcible rapes reported to the FBI Uniform Crime Report in 1998, which does represent decreased reporting for the sixth consecutive year. There were 97,464 forcible rapes reported to law enforcement agencies in 1995 and 96,122 in 1997. Although rape occurs in all age, race, and cultural groups, rape is highest among 20- to 24-year-old black females (Bureau of Justice Statistics, 1995). Females ages 16 to 19 are the age group next at risk.

Of the 93,000 reported rape cases to law enforcement, only half of the rape offenses were cleared with an arrest (UCR, 1999). Clearly, law enforcement needs help to improve its clearance rates as well as its classification of rape cases in contrast to unfounded cases.

Philadelphia is a case in point. When DNA from two previously unfounded rape cases in Philadelphia matched the DNA of a rape-murderer of a University of Pennsylvania graduate student, a reporter for the *Philadelphia Inquirer* began re-interviewing victims whose files had been tossed in the unfounded category. The series of articles pressured the Philadelphia police department to set up a special committee of victim advocates and women attorneys to help review its unfounded cases (called inactive by that time).

Prevalence

Prevalence rates reflect the number of individuals who have been raped at any time in their lives. There are no available federal estimates, but individual researchers have estimated prevalence on the basis of victimization surveys. Koss (1993) estimated that rape/sexual assault prevalence among adult women generally ranges between 14 and 25%. The *National Women's Study* (*NWS*) found that approximately 13% of adult women had been victims of completed rape during their lifetime (Kilpatrick, Edmunds, and Seymour, 1992; Resnick, Kilpatrick, Dansky, Saunders and Best, 1993). During the year between interviews, 0.6% of adult women, or an estimated 683,000, were victims of rape (Kilpatrick et al., 1992). In the two years between the first and third interviews, 1.2% of the adult participants in the *NWS* were raped. The results were that an estimated 1.1 million women were raped in the United States during this two-year period (Kilpatrick, Resnick, Saunders, Best, 1998). Of note, as in the federal data bases, methodological differences between studies affect the estimates.

The National Survey of Adolescents (NSA) is a National Institute of Justice-funded study of national household probability. In a sample of 4023 adolescents aged 12 to 17, 8.1% had been victims of at least one sexual assault (Kilpatrick and Saunders, 1997; Kilpatrick, Acierno, Saunders, Resnick, Best and Schnurr, 2000). This indicates that an estimated 1.8 million adolescents in the 12 to 17 age range have been sexually assaulted. This figure suggests that more than 52% of all rape/sexual assault victims were females younger than 25. Women who suffered physical injury in addition to the injury suffered from the rape or sexual assault reported 37% of those crimes, while only 22% of rapes and sexual assaults without an additional physical injury were reported (Kilpatrick, 2000).

The national incidence of rape in females 65 years of age and over was 10 per 100,000 in 1990 (Federal Bureau of Investigation, 1993). The only study found on rape in an institutional setting, Nibert, Cooper and Crossmaker (1989) reported that, out of 190 people invited to participate in a survey, 58 patients agreed to participate. Of those 58 participants, 22 reported sexual assault either by another resident or a staff member while in an institution. Twenty-five percent were over age 50.

Underreported Crime

Sexual abuse is an underreported crime, and victims of all ages do not readily identify themselves. The extent of nondisclosure ranges from over 50% (Burgess and Holmstrom, 1986) to as high as 68% (Bureau of Justice, 1996). Koss (1993), Resnick and colleagues (1996), and Acierno, Resnick, and Kilpatrick (1997) have identified several reasons for nondisclosure, including (1) fear of retribution by an offender, especially if the assailant is proximate or known to the victim; (2) fear of the stigma attached to being a victim of rape; (3) fear of being blamed; (4) history of negative outcomes following previous disclosure (court involvement leading to acquittal); (5) lack of encouragement to discuss abuse; and (6) fear of psychological consequences of disclosure (anxiety or depression upon revisiting the event).

In a community survey of rates of sexual assault in 3132 adults from two Los Angeles communities, Burnam et al. (1988) reported approximately half of the respondents were female, half were Caucasian, and half were Hispanic. More women (16.7%) than men (9.4%) and more Caucasians (19.9%) than Hispanics (8.1%) reported histories of sexual assault. Most initial assaults (80%) happened when the victim was between 18 and 25 years of age, while almost 7% of the respondents reported that they experienced their first sexual assault after the age of 65.

Victims of sexual abuse suffer in silence, actively avoid recalling their trauma, seek help reluctantly, and do not volunteer information about their traumatic experience (Kolb, 1989; McFarlane, 1989; Scurfield, 1993). Because most rape cases go unreported (Kilpatrick, Edmunds, and Seymour, 1992; Crowell and Burgess, 1996), surveys indicate that only a minority of victims who sustain rape-related mental or physical problems obtain effective treatment (Kilpatrick, 2000; Tjaden and Thoennes, 1998). Of those sexually assaulted in 1995, only 32% reported the incident (Bureau of Justice 1996). In the Burgess and Holmstrom study (1986), in more than half of the 146 cases, someone other than the victim was involved in reporting the rape to police.

Relationship of Victim and Offender

The national surveys indicate that most women are raped by persons they know. The *National Women's Study* found only 22% of rape victims were assaulted by someone they had never seen before or did not know well. The National Violence against Women survey used different designations for victim–perpetrator categories but reported similar findings. A minority (23.2% of the victims) reported a stranger assaulted them, while 76% of perpetrators were intimate partners (current and former spouses, cohabitating partners, dates, and boyfriends).

The national surveys obtain data through telephone contact and may include victims who did not report. The FBI Uniform Crime Reports shows only a 51% clearance rate of forcible rapes, which suggests that women report stranger assaults to police.

Evidentiary Examination of the Victim

Physical injury, including genital injury, is not an inevitable consequence of rape and does not provide proof of consent (Cartwright 1987; Slaughter and Brown, 1992). The absence of genital injury in the sexually assaulted patient may be explained by many possibilities including the lack of vaginal contact by the perpetrator, delayed reporting, the lack of magnification, the lack of training or experience by the examiner, known sex partner rape, and a non-aggressive perpetrator with a nonresistive victim. False allegation may also be a consideration (Girardin, Faugno, Seneski, Slaughter & Whelan, 1997).

The victim's body is the primary crime scene in sexual assault cases (Kilpatrick, 2000). Two critical parts of an investigation are the interview of the victim and the evidentiary examination. Based on the interview, the forensic exam collects evidence that can establish: (1) sexual activity occurred; (2) the sexual act produced injuries consistent with a history of forced sex; and (3) a given person committed the acts as confirmed by DNA analysis. With an identified suspect, the only legal defense can be consensual sex.

However, most sexual assault evidentiary examinations do not include magnification or state-of-the-art procedures and equipment for detecting physical injuries to the victim's vulva, vagina, or anus. The colposcope, used by nurse practitioners and gynecologists, magnifies an area over 30 times the actual size, permitting detection of bruises, tears, or abrasions not visible to the naked eye. Conventional sexual assault exams without colposcopes have typically reported evidence of genital injuries in only 19–28% of cases (Slaughter and Brown, 1992). However, examiners using colposcopes find evidence of genital trauma in up to 87% of cases (Slaughter and Brown, 1992). A major correction to this problem has been the advent of the sexual assault nurse examiner programs that have served to set protocol and guidelines for the collection of forensic evidence using colposcopes (Burgess, Dowdell, and Brown, 2000; Ledray, 1997).

A final advantage of the colposcope is that technology exists to take color photographs or make videotapes of the injuries detected. This documentation is useful in court as visual evidence for jurors and defendants who often enter guilty pleas when confronted with this evidence (Kilpatrick, 2000).

Crimes against the Elderly

Crimes against the elderly are of concern to law enforcement (Safarik, Jarvis and Nussbaum, 2000) and health practitioners. Although official statistics are elusive, population data show that an increasing number of the baby-boom generation will be aging into the elderly population in the first part of the 21st century. Coupled with the fact that people are living longer, it stands to reason that the risk of violent victimization of the elderly is likely to increase. In addition, nearly 75% of people older than 65 are women (U.S. Bureau of the Census, 1999). Thus, this information suggests the merit of examining any factors related to crimes against the elderly that may assist health practitioners for case identification (Burgess, Dowdell and Prentky, 2000) and law enforcement in rapidly identifying and apprehending responsible offenders and protecting potential elderly victims (Safarik, Jarvis and Nussbaum, 2000).

A review of the literature on the general problem of crime against the elderly has been addressed in the literature (Lent and Harpold, 1988), specifically addressing robbery (Faggiani and Owens, 1999); and homicide (Fox and Levin, 1991; Nelson and Huff-Corzine, 1998).

Homicide

Of the 16,914 homicides reported to police in 1998 (FBI, 1999), approximately 855 victims were determined to be 60 years of age or older; and less than half of this total (414) was identified as female. Therefore, elderly female homicides constituted about 2–3% of all homicides in 1998. It is difficult to determine how many of the homicides were sexual in motivation. Some of the difficulties involve lack of proper identification, lack of noting the subordinate offense of sexual assault (Brownmiller, 1975), poor communication among investigators and other personnel relative to the sexual nature of the offense, and classification errors in official data entries (Burgess et al., 1986).

Although the criminal investigative analysis process as applied to elderly female sexual homicides has relied heavily on experiential data as reported by the FBI and FBI-trained profilers (Ressler, Burgess, and Douglas, 1988), two axioms are evident in particular. First, the ages of the victims and offenders appear to be negatively correlated. That is, elderly victims are most often killed by younger offenders. The second axiom is that the intraracial nature of violent crimes seems to be conditional. That is, the general intraracial character of violent criminal offenders appears, to profilers, to be dependent on specific case factors rather than on the general expectation that the offenders are of similar race (Safarik, Jarvis and Nussbaum, 2000).

Elder Sexual Abuse in Nursing Homes

Indeed, the decade of the nineties catapulted sexual assault from relative obscurity to high profile in the legal and public health arenas (Goodman et al., 1993; Koss, 1993; Prentky and Burgess, 2000). Despite the considerable attention given to the diversity and ubiquity of sexual assaults, it is all the more noteworthy that one of the most vulnerable groups of victims, the residents of nursing homes (estimated by Gabrel (2000) to be 1.5 million persons in 1997) remain in obscurity. Although the reasons for our failure to tackle the problem of elder and nursing home resident sexual abuse are unclear, we can certainly posit two explanations: (1) the incomprehensibility, and hence rejection, of claims of sexual assault of nursing home residents, and, perhaps most importantly, (2) ageism — generalized, negative attitudes, if not outright hostility — for older and cognitively impaired people (Butler and Lewis, 1973).

All other vulnerable target populations for sexual assault — children, adolescents, the developmentally delayed, and patients with physical and/or mental impairments — have been the subject of varying degrees of clinical and empirical scrutiny. As with the elderly, when members of these populations reside in an institutional setting, the risk for abuse increases simply as a function of their dependence on staff for safety, protection, and care. Although there are no estimates of the incidence or prevalence of elder sexual abuse in residential care (Lachs and Pillemar, 1995), The National Citizens' Coalition for Nursing Home Reform (Holder, 2000) has confirmed that its agency receives an increasing number of reports of sexual abuse in nursing homes. And, in the reporting statistics from state ombudsmen offices (who have only recently been documenting sexual abuse as separate from physical abuse), the number of reported sexual abuse cases has increased from 548 in 1996 to 666 in 1998.

While no data are available on institutional elder abuse, there are a few descriptive studies of rape in the elderly (Tyra, 1993). Ramsey-Klawsnik (1991) surveyed social workers as to suspected elder sexual abuse cases and identified 28 cases of women assaulted in the home primarily by family members (predominantly sons and husbands). In a study of 760 inner-city hospital victims, 2.7% of the sexually assaulted victims were 60 years and older (Cartwright and Moore, 1989). In a Texas study, 2.2% (109) of the reported sexual assault victims over a 5-year period involved women over 50 (Ramin, Satin, Stone and Wendel, 1992).

The few studies on elderly rape victims are equivocal regarding injury. Genital trauma, evident even without colposcopy, is more evident in post-menopausal sexually assaulted women than it is in their younger counterparts (Cartwright, 1987). However, as with those 65 and younger, rape may occur without obvious injury (Cartwright and Moore, 1989; Tyra, 1993). Medical and forensic records were reviewed between 1986 and 1991 from 129 women 50 years or older and 129 women from a comparison group ages 14 to 49. Trauma, in general, occurred in 67% of the older group and 71% in the younger group. Genital trauma was more common in older than in younger women (43% vs. 18%). In contrast, extragenital trauma was more common in younger victims (66 vs. 49%). Forensic findings were similar in both groups; however, in the older group, motile spermatozoa were seen only in those examined within 6 hours of the assault (Ramin, Satin, Stone and Wendel, 1992).

While considerable research has been conducted on memory and trauma in adults and children, only a few case reports have dealt with elderly victims (McCartney and Severson, 1997). In elder sexual abuse cases, a question arises as to whether the person can truly remember a sexual assault. McCartney and Severson (1997) remind us that the emotional meaning of an experience may be retained when the cognitive meaning is not present. Their case report indicates that the elderly, despite cognitive impairments, can develop neuro-chemical and physiological symptoms of hyperarousal and post-traumatic stress disorder (PTSD). More importantly, if the elderly victims go without proper diagnosis, there cannot be proper treatment.

A pilot study of 20 sexually abused nursing home residents identified barriers to effective health care interventions (Burgess, Dowdell and Prentky, 2000). First, delayed reporting of the sexual abuse resulted in failure to obtain a timely medical evidentiary examination; delayed treatment for injuries and infection; and an absence of medical or psychological follow-up care. Second, there was difficulty in performing an evidentiary rape examination due to leg contractures and cognition/memory problems. Indeed, in a number of the victims, fetal position and muscular rigidity made examination impossible. Third, there was evidence of wide variation in sexual assault evidentiary examination such as lack of colposcope photographs for evidence. And fourth, the offenders (who were arrested) were either employees of the nursing homes or residents; and, without prompt victim identification, the offenders were suspected to have abused more than one victim (Burgess, Dowdell, and Prentky, 2000).

The 20 predominantly elderly victims (18 women and 2 men) presented with rape-related trauma symptoms (urinary tract infections, nightmares, and repeated reference to the event); general symptoms of traumatic stress (fear, confusion, hypersomnia, lack of appetite, and withdrawal); and an exacerbation of symptoms related to their primary diagnoses. Preliminary findings suggest that the presence of a preexisting cognitive deficit such as dementia markedly delayed information processing, impaired communication, and compounded the trauma of the sexual assault. These victims simply were not equipped — physically, constitutionally, or psychologically — to defend against and cope with the proximal effects of assault. Perhaps the single most profound result of the sexual assaults against these victims was that 11 of the 20 victims died within 12 months of the assault.

Over the past several decades our awareness of the magnitude and the impact of sexual victimization has increased considerably. Sexual abuse has become an acute problem, manifested in ever-increasing costs to society as well as to its victims. The costs incurred by society include medical and psychological services to aid victim recovery, the apprehension and disposition of offenders, and the invisible climate of fear that makes safety a paramount consideration in scheduling normal daily activities. In addition to the monetary costs associated with sexual abuse (Prentky and Burgess, 1990), the impact of such abuse on the victim has been well documented (Crowell and Burgess, 1996).

History

The concept that a person may develop symptoms following an accident is not new; psychological trauma has been noted in literature as far back as the writings of Homer (van der Kolk, McFarlane and Weisaeth, 1996). In Shakespeare's *King Henry IV*, Lady Percy described the nightmares that Hotspur suffered, particularly dreams of war. Samuel Pepys' *Diary* chronicles the effects of the September 2, 1666, great fire of London (Daly, 1983). Pepys outlines the gradual progression of the fire toward his home and the terror he sees in other people fleeing their homes; and he subsequently develops "dreams of the fire and falling down of houses." Six months later he was still unable to sleep "without great terrors of fire." Charles Dickens was involved in a railway accident on June 9, 1865, and later documented the horrifying scene of the dead. He wrote of feeling slightly off-kilter, developing a phobia of railway travel, and feeling weak as if recovering from a long illness (Forster, 1969).

The Psychobiology of Trauma

The mental health field has long been interested in the aftermath of trauma; the debate focuses on whether trauma is biophysiologically based or psychologically based. As early as 1859, French psychiatrist Briquet described symptoms of hysteria that he linked to childhood histories of trauma in 381 out of 501 patients. However, his belief was that the symptoms reflected personal weaknesses in the patients' abilities to deal with traumatic events. This notion continued and came to characterize soldiers suffering from post-trauma stress during World Wars I and II (van der Kolk et al., 1996). In fact, the term *shell shock*, as coined by British military psychiatrist Meyers, could be explained as part of the soldiers' makeup. Even Freud supported the notion and argued that trauma symptoms were a "flight into illness by subconscious intentions ... [and] that at the end of the war the war neurosis would disappear" (van der Kolk et al., 1996, p. 55). Freud believed that the symptoms were consciously incited and motivated by the soldiers' unconscious desires to get out of the war and that the symptoms would disappear once the war was over. This amelioration of symptoms, of course, did not occur (van der Kolk et al., 1996).

In 1889, Pierre Janet noted the psychobiological link to trauma response. He suggested that the psychological effects of trauma are stored in somatic memory and expressed as changes in the biological stress response. To quote psychiatrist van der Kolk (1994), "the body keeps score." Janet emphasized that intense emotional reactions make events traumatic by blocking the usual information processing into existing memory paths (Janet, 1889). He also observed that traumatized patients reacted to environmental cues reminiscent of the traumas, were unable to put the traumas behind them, had trouble learning from their experiences, became fixated on the past or obsessed with the traumas, and behaved and felt as if they were traumatized all over again without being able to determine the origins of the feelings (van der Kolk and van der Hart, 1991).

Psychiatrist Kardiner (1941) examined returning soldiers and noted that they were extremely sensitive toward external factors that could provoke a fear response. For example, a patient riding a subway train through a tunnel would get a flashback of the trenches in wartime. Kardiner's analysis was that the patient acted as if the original trauma were recurring and suggested that the soldier's view of the world and of himself had been permanently altered. In *Men Under Stress*, Grinker and Spiegel (1945) described the physical symptoms of soldiers as flexor changes in posture, hypermovements, a violent propulsive gait, tremor at rest, mask-like faces, rigidity, stomach distress, urinary incontinence, mutism, and a hyperstartle reflex.

Another group of researchers looking at stress and its physiological effects contribute to the knowledge base of trauma. Hans Seyle (1956) suggested that some stress experiences are growth enhancing. In contrast, repetitive, continuous, escalating, and uncontrollable stressful experiences may put the person at risk for illness. Stress has been shown to be mediated by the hypothalamic-pituitary-adrenocortical (HPAC) biologic stress systems. Stress that challenges homeostasis stimulates secretion of glucocorticoids, which are catabolic hormones that help mobilize stored energy to support the body's physiologic response to stress for use in the "flight or fight" response (Cannon, 1932; Seyle, 1956; van der Kolk and Fisler, 1995).

More recently, neurophysiologist Bruce McEwen (1998, 2000) has described a theory of the dynamic interplay between stress and physical illness. McEwen's allostatic load model accounts for psychological impact of accumulated stress or trauma on physical tissue over time. As chronic stress affects neuroendocrine and neurophysiological functions, the dynamic between genetic background and allostasis drives the expression of medical and psychiatric illnesses. Catecholamines and glucocorticoids have both protecting and damaging effects. McEwen (2000) suggests in the short run they are essential for allostasis; however, over the long run they exact a toll (the allostatic load). These concepts of allostasis and allostatic load center around the brain as interpreter and responder to environmental challenges. Allostatic load takes the form of chemical imbalances, alterations of diurnal rhythms, and, in some situations, atrophy of brain structures (McEwen, 2000).

Early childhood experiences of abuse and neglect, major risk factors for these conditions, increase allostatic load in later life and may lead to major health concerns (Fellitti et al., 1998). Studies of allostatic load have identified primary mediators (Seeman et al., 1997).

With the focus on rape in the late 1960s and early 1970s, a new group of trauma patients emerged. Early work on trauma of rape victims began with a study that coined the clinical term 'rape trauma syndrome' (Burgess and Holmstrom, 1974). Rape trauma syndrome, which includes both acute and long-term symptom responses to traumatic sexual assault, has two distinct variations — compounded rape trauma and silent rape trauma (Burgess and Holmstrom, 1974). Rape trauma syndrome is a clustering of varying degrees of biopsychosocial and behavioral responses to the extreme stress and fear of death that victims experience during an assault. The ability to cope with the incidents depends on the type of assault, preexisting functioning, coping skills, and available support systems. In compounded rape trauma, victims have past and/or current histories of psychiatric, psychosocial, or physical problems that compound the effects of the sexual assaults. In silent rape trauma, expression of assault-related symptomotology is muted, undetected, or absent (Burgess and Holmstrom, 1974). Rape and sexual assault are more likely to lead to post-traumatic stress disorder, a DSM-IV diagnosis, than other traumatic events affecting civilians.

In conclusion, too few victims who sustain rape-related mental or physical problems obtain effective treatment (Kilpatrick, 2000). In many persons who have experienced extreme stress, the post-traumatic response fades over time,

— whereas in others it persists. van der Kolk (1994) emphasizes that much work needs to be done to spell out the issues of resilience and vulnerability; but magnitude of exposure, previous trauma, and social support appear to be important predictors for development of chronic PTSD (McFarlane, 1989).

Memory

Memory formation involves encoding, storage (or consolidation), and retrieval. Encoding is the initial laying down of the memory trace. Storage involves the keeping of the memory trace over time. A related concept is consolidation, which refers to the process — which can occur over several weeks or more — of establishing the permanence of a memory trace, during which time the memory trace is theoretically susceptible to modification. Retrieval is the process of bringing out a memory from storage into consciousness (Bremner, Krystal, Southwick and Charney, 1995).

Memory can also be categorized by memory type. Squire and Zola-Morgan (1991) have divided the different types of memory function into declarative or explicit and procedural or implicit. Further, the role of hormones in the modulation of memory has been linked to memory alterations (Squire, 1994).

The importance of trauma lies not only in the way it affects memory structure and presentation but also in the method by which it affects the brain — in particular, the key regulatory processes that control memory, aggression, sexuality, attachment, emotion, sleep, and appetite. The particular location of interest in the brain is the limbic system. It is also the seat of the alarm system that protects the individual in the face of danger. It is the location where all sensory information enters the human system and is encoded.

Declarative memory functioning has been affected by lesions of the frontal lobe and of the hippocampus, which also has been implicated in the neurobiology of post-traumatic stress disorder (van der Kolk, 1994; 1995). Implicit memory refers to memories of skills and habits, emotional responses, reflexive actions, and classically conditioned responses. Each of these implicit memory systems is associated with particular areas in the central nervous system (Squire, 1994). According to van der Kolk and Fisler (1995), an individual's memory depends on his existing memory structure. Once an event is processed (integrated into one's mental schemes), it is no longer available as a separate entity but is liable to be altered by associated experiences, demand characteristics, and emotional state at the time of recall. To paraphrase Schachtel (1947), Memory … is the capacity for the organization and reconstruction of past experiences and impressions in the service of present needs, fears, and interests.

Stalking

The National Violence against Women Survey emphasized that stalking is a significant social problem. Using a definition that requires victims to feel a high level of fear, the survey found that stalking is much more prevalent than previously thought: 8% of surveyed women and 2% of surveyed men said they were stalked at some point in their lives; 1% of surveyed women and 0.4% of surveyed men said they were stalked in the previous 12 months. Based on U.S. Census estimates of the number of women and men in the country, these findings equate to approximately 1,000,000 women and 371,000 men who are stalked annually in the U.S. (Tjaden and Thoennes, 1998). The definition used in the survey was defined as a course of conduct directed at a specific person that involves repeated visual or physical proximity; nonconsensual communication; verbal, written, or implied threats; or a combination thereof that would cause fear in a reasonable person.

Cyberstalking

In the last two decades of the 20th century, the terms *stalking* and *cyberstalking* have become part of the American vocabulary as well as a new classification of crime. Stalking, in contrast to a direct physical attack, involves pursuit of a victim and includes the acts of following, viewing, communicating with, or moving threateningly or menacingly toward another person. Stalking behavior has many dimensions that include written and verbal communications, unsolicited and unrecognized claims of romantic involvement on the part of victims, surveillance, harassment, and loitering — all of which produce intense fear and psychological distress to the victim. In addition, these behaviors can take the form of telephone calls, vandalism, and unwanted appearances at a person's home or workplace. When perpetrated through the Internet (electronic stalking or cyberstalking), the acts include unsolicited E-mail, negative messages in live chat rooms, hostile Internet postings, vicious rumors, leaving abusive messages on site guestbooks, impersonating another online and misrepresenting him, and electronic sabotage (sending viruses, scamming, etc.)

While the Internet is viewed as an information superhighway and an invaluable communications tool, it also provides a new environment for harassers and criminals to target victims. As U.S. Attorney General Janet Reno noted in the report prepared by the Department of Justice (Reno, 1999), many of the attributes of this technology — low cost, ease of use, and anonymous nature — make it an attractive medium for fraudulent scams, child sexual exploitation, and cyberstalking. She also noted that, while some conduct involving annoying or menacing behavior might fall short of illegal stalking, such behavior may be a prelude to stalking and violence and should be treated seriously.

Cyberstalking, also called online stalking or online victimization, shares important characteristics with offline stalking. The similarities are that: (1) the majority of cases involve stalking by former intimates, although stranger stalking certainly occurs in the real world and in cyberspace; (2) most victims are women and most stalkers are men; and (3) stalkers are believed to be motivated by the desire to control the victim. Major differences include (1) offline stalking requires the stalker and victim to be located in the same geographic area, whereas cyberstalkers may be located in the same city or across the country; (2) technologies make it easier for a cyberstalker to encourage third parties to harass and/or threaten a victim; and (3) technologies lower the barriers to harassment and threats, and a cyberstalker does not need to physically confront the victim (Reno, 1999).

Understanding cyberstalking is to understand stalking in general. Cyberstalking may be viewed as simply another phase in an overall stalking pattern or it may be viewed as a regular stalking behavior using new, high-technology tools. In some reported studies, both offline and online behaviors are surveyed, making it difficult to separate the behaviors.

Youth Online Victimization

The United States Congress became aware of the misuses of the Internet to prey upon children and quickly took action, implementing the Child Online Privacy Protection Act to help safeguard children from unsavory advertising practices and the registration of personal information without parental consent. Congress also enhanced federal law enforcement resources such as the Federal Bureau of Investigation's Innocent Images Task Force and the U. S. Customs Service's Cybersmuggling Unit, both of which have successful records of investigating and arresting online predators. One of the most important tools for law-enforcement staff and families has been the development of the National Center for Missing and Exploited Children's Cyber-Tipline, a resource that has initiated numerous investigations and arrests of child predators. However, Congress's strong message of intolerance for online predators was not enough without information regarding the number of children victimized on the Internet and the various ways in which they are approached. Thus, Congress commissioned a study to identify the threats, incidence rates, and victim responses to online predators and illegal content. This initial report, *Online Victimization: A Report on the Nation's Youth,* provides a starting point in better understanding what children face online (Gregg, 2000).

Nearly 24 million youths aged 10 to 17 were online regularly in 1999, and millions more are expected to join them shortly. But not every online adventure is stress-free. The Internet has a seamier side that young people can encounter. A telephone survey (the Youth Internet Safety Survey) yielded a representative national sample of 1501 youths aged 10 to 17, who reported using the Internet at least once a month for a six-month period on a computer at home, at school, at someone else's home, or some other place. This definition was chosen to exclude occasional users, while including both heavy and light users. The survey asked about three different types of online victimization — sexual solicitations and approaches, unwanted exposure to sexual materials, and harassment. The key conclusions of the Youth Internet Safety Survey findings are cited as follows (Finkelhor, Mitchell and Wolak, 2000):

- A specific fraction of youth are encountering offensive experiences on the Internet.
- The offenses and offenders are diverse and include males and females.
- Most sexual solicitations fail, but their quantity is potentially alarming.
- The primary vulnerable population is teenagers.
- Sexual material is very intrusive on the Internet.
- Most youths brush off these offenses, but some are quite distressed.
- Many youths do not tell anyone.
- Youths and parents do not report these experiences and do not know where to report them.

Internet friendships between teens and adults were not uncommon and appeared to be mostly benign. Little is still known about the incidence of traveler cases (where adults or youths travel to physically meet and have sex with someone they first came to know on the Internet), or any completed Internet seduction and Internet sexual exploitation cases including trafficking in child pornography.

Collegiate Stalking and Cyberstalking

Critical to the study of any behavior is definition. Meloy (1996) made one of the first attempts to define *stalking* as obsessive following. Using a similar concept, Cupach and Spitzberg (1997) define obsessive relational intrusion (ORI) as "repeated and unwanted pursuit and invasion of one's sense of physical or symbolic privacy by another person, either stranger or acquaintance, who desires and/or presumes an intimate relationship."

Definition aside, what is the impact on the victim of stalking, whether online or offline? In the limited studies on stalking, Mullen and Pathe (1994) noted victims feel compelled to alter their lifestyles by moving, changing addresses, or giving up social activities. Hall (1996) found that 83% of victims surveyed report their personalities change as a result of being stalked. Hall's study also found that 85% of the respondents are more cautious, 40% often feel paranoid, 53% feel more easily frightened, and 30% are much more aggressive. Indeed, being stalked over a period of time has been described as psychological terrorism (Spitzberg, Nicastro and Cousins, 1998) and has been suggested to be a cause of post-traumatic stress disorder (Wallace and Silverman, 1996).

College and university student health and counseling staffs have reported on changes in student mental health issues (Koplik and DeVito, 1986), coercive sex on campuses (Miller and Marshall, 1987), drug and alcohol abuse (Bowen, 1987), and problems related to stalking (Gallagher, 1988). In a 1992 survey of counseling center directors, Gallagher (1992) found that 26% of the directors reported a definite increase in collegiate stalking, while 74% reported the incidence of such cases was about the same as in the previous year. However, no director reported a decrease.

A study of offline and online stalking was undertaken on a college population of 656 students in an east coast university (Burgess, Alexy, Baker and Smoyak, under editorial review). Seventy-two (or 10.98%) of the students responded *yes* to the question, *have you ever been stalked*? The majority (44 or 61.1%) were female, with 28 (38.9%) male. Ages ranged from 17 to 42, with 54.9% age 20 or younger. Students were undergraduates (91.7%), and the majority were Caucasian (70.4%).

The profile characteristics of these 72 students reveal the students to be undergraduates, average age of 20, who began using the Internet at age 15 $^1/_2$, and who currently use it about 5 hours a week but do not enter chat rooms. The majority of students had come across inappropriate material on the Internet, and over half had received inappropriate E-mail; a small number had received threats of physical violence, and about half had been solicited for sex online. The majority agreed that sexually explicit material on the Internet was a growing problem and it was too easy to access sexually explicit material, but they were divided as to whether the government should regulate Internet content.

The profile characteristics of the pursuer, noted the majority, were age 20 or younger and were white males. The students being pursued usually first told a friend within a month of the stalking. Students tried to both reason with and then ignored the pursuers. They had telephone calls screened. The majority did not feel threatened or fearful of being in great danger, suggesting that the acts could be termed cyberharassment rather than cyberstalking. A number of male targets in this sample were high school or college atheletes, suggesting the stalking was because of their celebrity status.

Adult Cyberstalking

The earliest publication that was found concerning the area of cyberstalking was a brief note by Christina Carmody in the *ABA Journal* in 1994. She noted that women were complaining of relentless E-mails and jammed fax machines with messages from obsessive admirers. Writing in the *Washington Law Review,* Gene Barton (1995) concluded that computer abuse was advancing as quickly as computer technology; but the laws addressing the problems of harassment by computer were lagging. At that point in time, he noted that the federally subsidized Internet connected more than 5000 networks and 1.7 million computers throughout the U.S. and abroad and was frequented by more than 20 million users. Growth on the Internet was estimated to be as high as 15% a month. However, E-mails were being sent for improper purposes, and Barton cited *flaming,* a general term describing vitriolic E-mail. Flaming is a massive mailing of vituperative, sexually suggestive, or meaningless messages by a group acting either in concert or not and which is designed to intimidate one or more other users. Another form of E-mail abuse is the mail bomb or letter bomb, a long E-mail message that ties up a recipient's system by consuming its computer memory.

Concerning the application of law to this problem, Barton (1995) concluded that bills not specifically tailored to the nature and scope of E-mail harassment were insufficient. He spelled out four standards for effective, enforceable cyberstalking laws:

- Specific intent
- Recognition of technological differences in means of communication
- Proscription of anonymous E-mail and single, identified contact in mass flaming
- Provision of a combination of harassment by telephone and other electronic communication to constitute repeated harassment

It became apparent that the use of the Internet to engage in these behaviors presented unique legal questions, and the first cyberstalking provisions were enacted in Michigan law in 1992 with the first successful prosecution in that state in 1995 (Ross, 1995). Andrew Archambeau pleaded no contest to having sent 20 E-mails over a two-month period to a woman after he had been asked by the victim and the police to stop. He claimed that he was pursuing the

woman for romantic reasons and that the communication was non-threatening since the victim could have ignored it. Archambeau was sentenced to
a year's probation, and a psychiatric evaluation was ordered.

The best compilation of information concerning the phenomenon of
cyberstalking can be found in *Cyberstalking: A New Challenge for Law Enforcement and Industry* (Reno, 1999), a report from the Attorney General to the
Vice President of the United States published on the web in August, 1999. The
report explored the nature and extent of cyberstalking; surveyed the steps law
enforcement, industry, victims' groups, and others were taking to address the
problem; analyzed the adequacy of current federal and state laws; and provided
recommendations on how to improve efforts to combat this growing problem.
One large study cited by Reno was done on a random sample of 4446 college
women. Fisher et al. (1999) reported that 25% of stalking incidents among
college women could be classified as involving cyberstalking. The report also
noted that the majority of police agencies had not investigated or prosecuted
any cyberstalking cases. However, some agencies, particularly those with units
dedicated to stalking or computer crime offenses, have large cyberstalking
caseloads, i.e., New York City and Los Angeles. On the matter of jurisdiction
and statutory limitations, Reno urged the need for state, local, and federal
officials to work closely together in addressing these questions. She also made
recommendations to the Internet industry and to victims and their support
groups concerning how they could assist in dealing with cyberstalking.

Cyber Child Pornography

In *U.S. vs. Reinhardt* (97-60030-01) the court granted the government's
motion for pretrial detention. The defendant was charged with producing
and distributing child pornography. On the government's motion for pretrial
detention under the Bail Reform Act, the District Court held that: (1) the
defendant's case involved a crime of violence; (2) there were no conditions
of release which could reasonably assure safety of the community and appearance of defendant; and (3) the defendant also posed risk of flight.

This case is critically important for its illustration of the use of the
Internet as a tool for pedophiles and child pornographers. This case clearly
links a pedophile's use of technology to access children for sexual purposes,
to gain control over the child and his family, to recruit new victims, and to
communicate with other pedophiles. The amount of detail, care, and com-
pulsiveness that is demonstrated in the profile of a career pedophile is exemplified in this case.

Pedophiles' social networks are other pedophiles. They socialize, telephone, write letters, E-mail, network, and share strategies for continuing

their deviant relationships with children, even when in prison. In Florida, one convicted child pornographer used his prison post office box number to expand his distribution of child pornography until he was discovered.

Pedophiles can move from an isolated position of a solo operator into a network of perpetrators; i.e., Reinhardt had a co-defendant. It is no wonder that we now see the elaborate and organized networking that is well under way on the Internet both nationally and internationally. This case emphasizes the Internet pedophile as an entrepreneur having a product line on his own home page. Reinhardt provides advice to a chat room correspondent on how to build a long-term relationship with a young boy, how to manipulate parents so they will not cause problems, and taught his victims how to answer questions about the ongoing sexual relationship. Reinhardt videotaped a session in which he instructed his victim on how to type in responses to sexually-oriented questions sent from a chat room. His home page contained images of nude children and his victims as well as an image of his own penis. A minor assisted in scanning his genitalia — an act serving as a permanent document of his sexual entrapment of the boy.

Pedophiles are totally preoccupied with their sexual interest in children. The probation office identified nine jobs Reinhardt had held between 1986 and 1997 in four states. His obsession with the Internet was evidenced by his owning several computers while living in a trailer. The reason for his job instability may be due to whether the job was in the service of sexual deviation or whether his compulsion for children interfered with his work productivity.

This case reveals the inner workings of pedophiles and child pornographers. The general public can now access all dimensions of child sexual exploitation through the Internet. They can call up a pedophile's home page or talk with him in a chat room. Although Internet pedophile activities will lose their clandestine nature, the pedophile can be more discriminating in selecting and testing his victims by remaining anonymous (Burgess, 1998).

References

Abel, G., Becker, J., Mittleman, M., Cunningham-Rathner, J., Rouleau, J., and Murphy, W. (1987) Self-reported sex crime of nonincarcerated paraphiliacs, *J. Interpersonal Violence*, 2(1), 3–25.

Acierno, R., Resnick, H.S., and Kilpatrick, D.G. (1997) Prevalence rates: case identification and risk factors for sexual assault, physical assault, and domestic violence in men and women, *Behav. Med.*, 23(2), 53–64.

Barton, G. (1995) Taking a byte out of crime: E-mail harrassment and the inefficacy of existing law, *Wash. Law Rev.*, 4465, 841.

Bowen, O. (1987) Campus alcohol uses, paper presented at the National Conference on Alcohol Abuse and Alcoholism, Washington, D.C.

Bremmer, J.D., Krystal, J.H., Southwick, S.M., and Charney, D. (1995) Functional neuroanatomical correlates of the effects of stress on memory, *J. Traumatic Stress,* 8, 527–553.

Brownmiller, S. (1975) *Against Our Will: Men, Women, and Rape,* New York, Simon & Schuster.

Bureau of Justice Statistics (1995; 1996; 1998) *National Crime Victimization Survey,* Washington, D.C., Department of Justice.

Burgess, A.W. (1988) Predator on web, molester tangled, *The Forensic Echo,* New York, The Forensic Panel.

Burgess, A.W., Hartman, C.R., Ressler, R.K., Douglas, J.E., and McCormack, A. (1986) Sexual homicide: a motivational model, *J. Interpersonal Violence,* 1, 251–272.

Burgess, A.W. and Holmstrom, L.L. (1974) Rape trauma syndrome, *Am. J. Psychiatr.,* 131, 981–986.

Burgess, A.W., Dowdell, E.B., and Prentky, R.A. (2000) Sexual abuse in nursing homes, *J. Psychosocial Nursing,* 38(6), 11–18.

Burgess, A.W. and Holmstrom, L.L. (1986) *Rape: Crisis and Recovery,* Newton, MA, Awab, Inc.

Burgess, A.W., Fehder, W., and Hartman, C, (1995) Delayed reporting of the rape victim, *J. Psychosocial Nursing,* 33(9), 21–29.

Burgess, A.W., Dowdell, E.B., and Brown, K. (2000) The elderly rape victim in the ER, *J. Emergency Nursing,* 26(10).

Burgess, A.W., Alexy, E., Baker, T., and Smoyak, S. (2001) *Stalking of College Students,* (ed. review).

Burnam, M.A., Stein, J.A., Colding, J.M., et al. (1988) Sexual assault and mental disorders in a community population, *J. Consulting Clin. Psychol.,* 56, 843–850.

Butler, R.N. and Lewis, M.I. (1973) *Aging and Mental Health: Positive Psychosocial Approaches,* St. Louis, Mosby.

Cannon, W.B. (1932) *The Wisdom of the Body,* New York, Norton.

Carmody, C. (1994) Stalking by computer, *Am. Bar Assoc. J.,* 80, 70.

Cartwright, P.S. (1987) Factors that correlate with injury sustained by survivors of sexual assault, *Obstet. Gynecol.,* 70, 44–46.

Cartwright, P.S. and Moore, R.A. (1989) The elderly victim of rape, *South. Med. J.,* 82(8), 988–989.

Crowell, N. and Burgess, A.W. (1996) *Understanding Violence against Women,* Washington, D.C., National Academy of Sciences.

Cupach, W.R. and Spitzberg, B.H. (1997) *The Incidence and Perceived Severity of Obsessional Relational Intrusion Behaviors,* paper presented at the Western States Communication Association Conference, Monterey, CA.

Daly, R.J. (1983) Samuel Pepys and post-traumatic stress disorder, *Brit. J. Psychiatr.,* 143: 64–68.

Faggiani, D. and Owens, M.G. (1999) Robbery of older adults: a descriptive analysis using the national incident-based reporting system, *J. Justice Res. Stat. Assoc.*, 1, 97–117.

Federal Bureau of Investigation Crime in the United States, *Uniform Crime Reports* (1993; 1997; 1998; 1999) Washington D.C., U.S. Government Printing Office, p. 26.

Fellitti, V.J. et al. (1998) Relationship of childhood dysfunction to many of the leading causes of death in adults; the adverse childhood experience (ACE) study, *Am. J. Prev. Med.*, 14: 245–258.

Finkelhor, D., Mitchell, K.J., and Wolak, J. (2000) *Online Victimization: A Report on the Nation's Youth*, Alexandria, VA, National Center for Missing and Exploited Children.

Fisher, B.S., Cullen, F.T., Belknap, J., and Turner, M.G. (1999) Being pursued: stalking victimization in a national study of college women, *Report to the National Institute of Justice*, U.S. Department of Justice, U.S. Government Printing Office, Washington.

Forster, J. (1969) *The Life of Charles Dickens*, 2, London, J.M. Dent and Sons.

Fox, J.A. and Levin, J. (1991) Homicide against the elderly: a research note, *Criminology*, 29, 317–327.

Gabrel, C.S. (2000) Characteristics of elderly nursing home current residents and discharges: data from the 1997 National Nursing Home Survey, *Vital and Health Statistics of the Centers for Disease Control and Prevention*, National Center for Health Statistics, No. 312.

Gallagher, R.P. (1988) *National Survey of Counseling Center Directors*, Pittsburgh, PA, University of Pittsburgh.

Gallagher, R.P. (1992) *National Survey of Counseling Center Directors, (Monograph Series)*, Alexandria, VA, International Association of Counseling Services.

Girardin, B.W., Faugno, D.K., Seneski, P.C., Slaughter, L., and Whelan, M. (1997) *Color Atlas of Sexual Assault*, St. Louis, Mosby.

Greer, G. (1973) Seduction is a four-letter word, *Playboy*, January.

Gregg, J. (2000) Foreword to *Online Victimization: A Report on the Nation's Youth*, D. Finkelhor, K.J. Mitchell, and J. Wolak, Eds., Alexandria, VA, National Center for Missing and Exploited Children.

Griffin, S. (1971) *Rape: The All-American Crime*, Ramparts, 10.

Grinker, R.R. and Spiegel, J.P. (1945) *Men under Stress*, Philadelphia, Blakiston.

Goodman, L.A., Koss, M.P., Fitzgerald, L.F., Russo, N.F., and Keita, G.P. (1993) Male violence against women: current research and future directions, *Am. Psychol.*, 48, 1054–1958.

Hall, D. (1996) *Outside Looking In: Stalkers and Their Victims*, Unpublished.

Holder, E. (2/2000) *Personal Communication*.

Janet, P. (1889) *L'automatisme Psychologique*, Paris, Alcan.

Kardiner, A. (1941) *War Stress and Neurotic Illness*, New York, Hoeber.

Kilpatrick, D.G. and Saunders, B.E. (1997) The prevalence and consequences of child victimization, *National Institute of Justice Research Preview,* Washington, D.C., U.S. Department of Justice.

Kilpatrick, D.G., Acierno, R., Saunders, B., Resnick, H., Best, C., and Schnurr, P. (2000) Risk factors for adolescent substance abuse and dependence: data from a national survey, *J. Consulting Clin. Psychol.,* 68(1), 19–30.

Kilpatrick, D.G. (2000) *Rape and Sexual Assault,* National Violence against Women Prevention Research Center, Medical University of South Carolina, Charleston.

Kilpatrick, D.G., Edmunds, C.N., and Seymour, A.K. (1992) *Rape in America: A Report to the Nation,* Arlington, VA, National Victim Center and Medical University of South Carolina.

Kilpatrick, D.G. et al. (1998) Rape, other violence against women, and post-traumatic stress disorder: critical issues in assessing adversity-stress psychopathology relationships, in Dohrenwend, B.P., Ed., *Adversity, Stress, and Psychopathology,* New York, Oxford University Press, pp. 161–176.

Kolb, L.C. (1989) Chronic post-traumatic stress disorder: implications of recent epidemiological and neuropsychological studies, *Psychol. Med.,* 19, 821–824.

Koplik, E.K. and DeVito, A.J. (1986) Problems of freshmen: comparison of classes of 1976 and 1986, *J. Coll. Stud. Personnel,* 27(2), 124–130.

Koss, M.P. (1993) Detecting the scope of rape: a review of prevalence research methods, *J. Interpersonal Violence,* 8, 198–222.

Lachs, M.S. and Pillemar, K. (1995) Current concepts: abuse and neglect of elderly persons, *New Engl. J. Med.,* 332(7), 437–443.

Ledray, L. (1997) SANE program locations: pros and cons, *J. Emergency Nursing,* 23(2), 182–186.

Lent, C.J. and Harpold, J. (1988) Violent crime against the aging, *FBI Law Enforcement Bull.,* 57, 11–19.

McCartney, J.R. and Severson, K. (1997) Sexual violence, post-traumatic stress disorder and dementia, *J. Am. Geriatr. Soc.,* 45, 77–79.

McEwen, B.S. (1998) Protective and damaging effects of stress mediators, *New Engl. J. Med.,* 338, 171–179.

McEwen, B.S. (2000) Allostasis and allostatic load: implications for neuropsychopharmacology, *Neuropsychopharmacology,* 22, 108–124.

McFarlane, A.C. (1989) The treatment of post-traumatic stress disorder, *Br. J. Med. Psychol.,* 62, 81–90.

Meloy, J.R. (1996) Stalking (obsessional following); a review of some preliminary studies, *Agressive Violent Behav.,* 1, 147–162.

Mullen, P.E. and Pathe, M. (1994) Stalking and the pathologies of love, *Austr. New Zealand J. Psychol.,* 28, 469–477.

Nelson, C. and Huff-Corzine, L. (1998) Strangers in the night: an application of the lifestyle routine activities approach to elderly homicide victimization, *Homicide Stud.,* 2, 130–159.

Nibert, D., Cooper, S., and Crossmaker, M. (1989) Assaults against residents of a psychiatric institution, *J. Interpersonal Violence,* 4(3), 342–349.

Prentky, R.A. and Burgess, A.W. (1990) Rehabilitation of child molesters: a cost-benefit analysis, *Am. J. Orthopsychol.,* 60, 108–117.

Prentky, R.A. and Burgess, A.W. (2000) *The Forensic Management of Sexual Offenders,* New York, Kluwer Academic.

Ramin, S.M., Satin, A.J., Stone, I.C., and Wendel, G.D. (1992) Rape in postmenopausal women, *Obstet. Gynecol.,* 80(5), 861–864.

Ramsey-Klawsnik, H. (1991) Elder sexual abuse: preliminary findings, *J. Elder Abuse Neglect,* 3(3), 73–84.

Reno, J. (1999) Cyberstalking: a new challenge for law enforcement and industry, *A Report from the Attorney General to the Vice President,* Washington, D.C., U.S. Government Printing Office.

Resnick, H.S., Kilpatrick, D.G., Dansky, B.S., Saunders, B.E., and Best, C.L. (1993) Prevalence of civilian trauma and PTSD in a representative national sample of women, *J. Consulting Clin. Psychol.,* 61, 984–991.

Resnick, H.S., Falsetti, S.A., Kilpatrick, D.G., and Freedy, J.R. (1996) Assessment of rape and other civilian trauma-related PTSD: emphasis on assessment of potentially traumatic events. In Miller, T.W., Ed., *Theory and Assessment of Stressful Life Events,* Madison, CT, International Universities Press, 235–271.

Resnick, H.S., Saunders, B.E., and Best, C.L. (1998) Rape, other violence against women, and post-traumatic stress disorder: critical issues in assessing adversity-stress-psychopathology relationships, in B.P. Dohrenwend, Ed., *Adversity, Stress and Psychopathology,* pp. 161–176, New York, Oxford University Press.

Ressler, R.P., Burgess, A.W., and Douglas, J.E. (1988) *Sexual Homicide,* New York, Free Press.

Ross, E.S. (1995) E-mail stalking: is adequate legal protection available? *John Marshall J. Comp. Inf. Law,* 23(3), 405.

Safarik, M.E., Jarvis, J., and Nussbaum, K. (2000) Elderly female serial sexual homicide, *Homicide Stud.,* 4(3), 294–307.

Schachtel, E.G. (1947) On memory and childhood amnesia, *Psychiatry,* 10, 1–26.

Scurfield, R.M. (1993) Posttraumatic stress disorder in Vietnam veterans, in Wilson, J.P., and Raphael, B., Eds., *International Handbook of Traumatic Stress Syndromes,* New York, Plenum Press, 285–295.

Seeman, T.E., Singer, B.H., Rowe, J.W., Horowitz, R.I., and McEwen, B.S. (1997) Price of adaptation — allostatic load and its health consequences, *Arch. Intern. Med.,* 157, 2259–2268.

Seyle, H. (1956) *The Stress of Life,* New York, McGraw Hill.

Slaughter, L. and Brown, C.R.V. (1992) Colposcopy to establish physical findings in rape victims, *Am. J. Obstet. Gynecol.,* 166(1), 83–86.

Squire, L.R. and Zola-Morgan, S. (1991) The medial temporal lobe memory system, *Science,* 153, 2380–2386.

Squire, L.R. (1994) Declarative and nondeclarative memory: multiple brain systems supporting learning and memory, in Schacter, D.L., and Tulving, E., Eds., *Memory Systems*, 203–231, Cambridge, MA, MIT Press.

Spitzberg, B.H., Nicastro, A.M., and Cousins, A. (1998) Exploring the interactional phenomenon of stalking and obsessive relational intrusion, *Comm. Rep.*, 11(1), 33–47.

Tjaden, P. and Thoennes, N. (1998) Prevalence, incidence, and consequences of violence against women, Findings from the *National Violence against Women Survey*, U.S. Department of Justice, National Institute of Justice, and Centers for Disease Control, Washington.

Tyra, P.A. (1993) Helping elderly women survive rape using a crisis framework, *J. Psychosocial Nursing*, 34(12), 20–25.

U.S. Bureau of the Census (1999) *1999 Census of Population: Characteristics of the Population*, Washington, D.C., U.S. Government Printing Office.

van der Kolk, B.A. (1987) *Psychological Trauma*, Washington, D.C., American Psychiatric Press.

van der Kolk, B.A. (1994) The body keeps score: memory and the evolving psychobiology of post-traumatic stress, *Harv. Rev. Psychol.*, 1(5), 253–265.

van der Kolk, B.A. and Fisler, R. (1995) Dissociation and the fragmentary nature of traumatic memories: an overview and exploratory study, *J. Traumatic Stress*, 8(4), 505–525.

van der Kolk, B.A. and van der Hart, O. (1991) The intrusive past: the flexibility of memory and the engraving of trauma, *Am. Imago*, 48(4), 425–454.

van der Kolk, B.A., McFarlane, A.C., and Weisaeth, L., Eds. (1996) *Traumatic Stress: The Effects of Overwhelming Experience on Mind, Body, and Society*, New York, Guilford Press.

Wallace, H. and Silverman, J. (1996) Stalking and post-traumatic stress syndrome, *Police J.*, 69, 203–206.

The Victim's Perspective

2

ANN WOLBERT BURGESS
ROBERT R. HAZELWOOD

Introduction

Victims confront endless new situations as they wend their way through the criminal justice system. The police are often the first on the scene and are therefore the first source of protection to whom the victim turns. Police should be mindful that, in fulfilling their obligations to solve the crime and apprehend the criminal, they must also treat the victims with the attention due them. The manner in which police officers treat a victim affects not only an immediate and long-term ability to deal with the event but also a willingness to assist in the prosecution. This chapter describes the emotional aftermath of rape. It is intended to describe the stress response of rape trauma syndrome in order that the police officer and prosecutor are aware of the basic response pattern many victims experience and the attendant effect on trial preparation.

Rape Trauma Syndrome

> It's been three years and I still won't get in an elevator alone or go out alone unless it is very necessary. When I enter my apartment I don't dead bolt it till I get my knife out and check everywhere — under the bed, in the shower, in the closets. Then I deadbolt the door. I do this two or three times a night. I don't enjoy walking anymore. I never had these problems before I was raped ... I'm scared I will be like this forever.
>
> **Rape Victim**

In the early 1970s Burgess and Holmstrom (1974) published a study of reported cases of rape and sexual assault in which 146 victims were interviewed at the emergency ward of a Boston hospital. They were contacted 4 to 6 years later to follow up on the problems they experienced as a result of having been attacked. The term *rape trauma syndrome* is used to describe an acute phase and long-term reorganization process that occurs as a result of forcible rape or attempted forcible rape. The syndrome of behavioral, somatic, and psychological reactions is deemed an acute stress reaction to a life-threatening situation.

The above quote by a rape victim captures some of the distressing and repetitive symptoms that a victim continues to experience long after the rape. The symptoms of this victim highlight the fears and phobias that have developed and the terror from which she may not recover.

The Acute Phase: Disorganization

Immediate Impact Reaction

A prevailing myth about rape victims is that they are hysterical and tearful following a rape. To the contrary, victims in the Boston study described an extremely wide range of emotions in the immediate hours following the rape. The physical and emotional impact of the incident may be so intense that the victim feels shock and disbelief. As one victim said, "I did some strange things after he left such as biting my arm … to prove I could feel … that I was real."

The emotional demeanor of the victim during the initial interview may be one of two types — expressive or guarded.

In the expressive style, the interviewer will be able to observe either on the face or through the body language the feelings experienced by the victim. Fear, anger, and anxiety can be visibly noted on the expression of the victim. Victims will express these feelings during the interview by becoming tense when certain questions are asked, or crying or sobbing when describing specific acts of the assailant. Interviewers should be aware that some victims may smile when certain statements are made. Such a reaction is not uncommon and denotes anxiety, not amusement, on the victim's part. Practically everyone associated with the identification, arrest, and prosecution of the rapist is reassured if the victim exhibits the expressive demeanor initially. However, this is not always the case and should not be expected.

In the guarded style, the feelings of the victim cannot be observed directly. The victim may appear very composed and able to calmly discuss the rape. The feelings are controlled, masked, or hidden. The composed victim is not lying but rather is able to control her true feelings, is in a state of shock, or is physically exhausted. Silence does not usually mean the victim is hiding facts but rather that she is having trouble talking and thinking about the assault. This victim typically talks in a calm, subdued manner.

The interviewer may note a change between the expressed and guarded style; and it may be related to time, place, and length of the interview. For example, one victim who was expressive during the initial interview was very guarded the next day when the police officer came to talk to her at work. As an office manager, the victim was aware that her employees noted the presence of the police; and she did not want them to know about the rape. Thus, her demeanor was significantly different. The police officer had not telephoned prior to his arrival, and later the victim refused to proceed with charges. In another case, a victim who was guarded during the initial interview later became less anxious when talking in her home; and she was able to provide additional information for the police. It is clear that interviewers can influence the amount of cooperation provided by the victim by showing due regard for the victim's privacy.

Physical Reactions to Rape Trauma

Rape is forced sexual violence against a person. Therefore, it is not surprising that victims describe a wide range of physical reactions in the days following the assault. Many victims will describe a general feeling of soreness all over their bodies. Others will specify the body area that has been the focus of the assailant's force such as the face, jaw, throat, chest, arms, or legs. In one case, a 29-year-old woman was attacked in her bed by a 16-year-old male who hit her on the hand and head with a heavy lamp prior to the rape. The victim later reported the following:

> At the hospital I had 19 stitches in the back of my head, and my hand was so swollen I couldn't move it for a week. I had bad eye problems — lines zagging in my vision. For months I had headaches; and even now, when I'm under stress, a headache starts and I think back to the rape.

Sleep Pattern Disturbances.   Victims have difficulty sleeping in the months following the rape. They complain that they cannot fall asleep or, if they do, they wake up during the night and cannot fall back asleep. Victims who have been attacked while sleeping in their own beds may awake each evening at that same time. It is not uncommon for victims to cry out or scream in their sleep, with or without the presence of nightmares.

Eating Pattern Disturbances.   The eating patterns of victims may be affected. Some victims report marked decrease in appetites and complain of stomach pains or nausea. There are some victims who report increases in eating and weight gain; however, the eating is often a coping response to stress rather than a genuine appetite increase.

Physical Symptoms.   Victims also report physical symptoms specific to the area of the body which has been a focus of attack. Throat and neck symptoms may be reported by victims who have been strangled or forced to have oral sex. Victims forced to have vaginal sex may complain of vaginal discharge, a burning sensation on urination, and generalized pain. Those forced to have anal sex may report rectal bleeding and pain in the days immediately following the rape.

Emotional Reactions

Prevailing stereotypes of rape are that the main reactions of victims are to feel ashamed and guilty after being raped. To the contrary, one of the primary feelings reported by victims is fear — fear of physical injury, mutilation, and death. It is this main feeling of fear that explains why victims develop the range of symptoms called the *rape trauma syndrome.* Their symptoms are an acute stress reaction to the threat of being killed. Most victims feel they had a close encounter with death and are lucky to be alive.

Victims express other feelings in conjunction with the fear of dying. These feelings range from humiliation, degradation, guilt, shame, and embarrassment to self-blame, anger, and revenge. Because of the wide range of feelings experienced during the immediate phase, victims are prone to experience mood swings. The following quote is from a 31-year-old singer who was attacked shortly after entering her apartment.

> I moved immediately from the apartment. I was unable to return to work. I felt I was being watched and followed. My panic was unbelievable. I could not sleep at night and had to cat-nap during the day. I hugged the walls walking down the street. I could not concentrate, would break out crying for no reason. I threw out every reminder of the rape — my bed, mattress, sheets, pillows, and clothes. I became a hermit and stayed in and stared at the television set for months.

Many victims do realize that their feelings are out of proportion to the situation. They report feeling angry with someone, later realizing that the anger was unfounded. Women become quite upset over their behavior which, in turn, produces more stress for them.

One young woman reported feeling on the verge of tears constantly. In a situation involving her child, one mother reported her distress after realizing that she was disciplining her children more severely after the rape.

Victims also report feeling irritated with people during the first few weeks when the symptoms are acute. Victims are very sensitive to the reactions of people when they learn of the rape. Perceived lack of concern as well as insensitive remarks will devastate a victim who already feels on an emotional rollercoaster. As one professional woman said, "My supervisor told me to take time off but not to come back till I had my feelings about this under control."

Thoughts

A continual stream of thoughts relating to the rape haunts many victims. Victims usually try to block the thoughts of the assault from their minds. However, the thoughts — called intrusive imagery — continue to break through into consciousness (*It's the first thing I think of when I wake in the morning*). Day images are common (*Something will trigger in my head and it all comes back*). The victim may feel as though the traumatic event is recurring (*I panicked at work when two people came into the store and acted suspicious*).

There is a strong desire on the part of the victims to try to think of how they might have escaped from the assailant or how the situation might have been handled differently. Generally, the outcome of such thinking is that they would have been beaten or killed if they did not comply with the demands of the assailant.

Victims vary as to the amount of time they remain in the acute phase. The immediate symptoms may last a few days to a few weeks. More often than not, the acute symptoms overlap with the symptoms of the long-term recovery process.

The Long-Term Process: Reorganization

> I feel embarrassed that I have not gotten over the rape … it has been 3 years, and my self-confidence is still shattered. I find it unacceptable in me that an event of l0 minutes could so interfere with my entire life.

48-year-old rape victim

A rape represents a disruption in the lifestyle of the victim — not only during the immediate days and weeks following the incident — but well beyond that to many weeks, months, and years. On the surface the victims often appear to function well, resuming work and family/social activities. The well-hidden psychological scars may remain undetected unless someone takes the time to really listen to the path of reorganization.

Various factors influence how the victims reorganize their lives — personality styles, the people available for support, or the way they are treated by people who learn of the rape. This section identifies four lifestyle areas most vulnerable to disruption following rape — physical, psychological, social, and sexual.

Physical Lifestyle

As previously discussed, immediately following rape, victims report many physical symptoms related to musculoskeletal pain, genitourinary difficulties, gastrointestinal upset, general distress, and disruptions in eating and sleeping patterns. The health areas with which victims have most difficulty over a long-term period include (1) body areas where injury caused interference to functioning — broken bones, lacerations, or organ trauma; and (2) gynecological and menstrual functioning. Victims with the latter problems report chronic vaginal problems and changes in menstrual cycle functioning.

Psychological Lifestyle

Dreams and nightmares are major symptoms of rape victims and occur during both the acute phase and the long-term process. The 48-year-old victim quoted earlier reported three dreams that recurred frequently during the third year of the reorganization process. First, she reported waking up suddenly and feeling someone was in the room. Her fright, in response to such a dream, is that the assailant will come back to kill her. Second, in a dream she is walking down a hallway and a stranger grabs her. She wakes up with the same feeling she experienced when the assailant grabbed her while she was jogging. Third, she dreams that she is being drowned in a boat. This dream triggers her memory of the location where the rape occurred — along a jogging path by a river.

Dreams may be of three types: (1) replication of the state of victimization and helplessness (*I use my mace and it turns to water*); (2) symbolic dreams which include a theme from the rape (*I am grabbed from behind and raped*); and (3) mastery dreams in which the victim is powerful in assuming control (*I took the knife and stabbed him over and over*). Non-mastery dreams dominate until the victim is recovered.

Phobias

A common psychological defense in rape victims is the development of fears and phobias. Fears are normal and protective devices used by people to warn them of danger. Phobias may become maladaptive because they prevent a person from acting in a situation. Victims described fears and phobias of a wide variety of circumstances: fears of indoors if the rape occurred inside; fears of outdoors if the rape occurred outside the home; fears of being alone (*I just can't stand it if no one else is home*); or fears of elevators or stairs or people behind them (*I won't go in some buildings because I am terrified of elevators and stairwells*). There are a wide variety of activities that can trigger a flashback (*Violence on television really upsets me*).

The victim may develop specific fears related to characteristics of the assailant such as the odor of beer on the assailant's breath. A facial feature, such as a moustache, may trigger a reaction in a victim raped by an assailant with a moustache. Some victims describe a very suspicious, paranoid feeling (*I felt everyone on the bus knew I was a victim*).

The occurrence of a second upsetting victimizing situation following a rape can produce additional fearful feelings. One victim was involved in a car accident the day following the rape and re-experienced the fright and fear of dying.

Social Lifestyle

Rape holds the potential for disrupting the victim's normal social routine. In some cases, several areas of social functioning are disrupted.

Many victims are able to resume only a minimal level of functioning even after the acute phase ends. These women go to work or school but are unable to be involved in anything beyond business-type activities. Other victims respond to the rape by staying home, by only venturing out of the house accompanied by a friend, or by being absent from or quitting work or school.

A common response is to seek support from family members who are not normally seen on a daily basis. Often this means a trip home to another city and a brief stay with parents in their home. In most cases, the victim tells the parents what happened. Occasionally the parents are contacted for support, although the victim does not tell why she is visiting. The decision to tell or not to tell seems to be based on how the victim predicts the parent would respond to the news (*I didn't tell mother because I knew she would be very upset and worry about me that I might be raped again*).

There is often a strong need to get away (*I thought I'd go stir crazy if I didn't get out of the city*). Victims who are able to will move — sometimes to another city if practical. Another change victims make in their lifestyles is to change their telephone numbers. Many victims request unlisted numbers. The victim may do this as a precautionary measure or after receiving threatening calls. Victims fear that the assailants may gain access to them through the telephone. They are also hypersensitive to obscene telephone calls which may or may not be from the assailants.

The need of victims to become anonymous serves a protective purpose; it is their way of trying to gain control over a terrifying experience. Sometimes police officers incorrectly interpret the victim's behavior as a desire not to prosecute. For victims with this need for protection, the officer should talk with the victims about ways to increase their safety environments as a strategy to be sure the victims keep in contact with the office.

Sexual Lifestyle

Many female victims report a fear of sex after the rape. The normal sexual style of the victim becomes disrupted following a rape. The rape is especially upsetting if the victim has never had any sexual experience before the rape — when there is no experience with which to compare it. For victims who have been sexually active, the fear increases when their boyfriends or husbands want to resume their sexual patterns.

Partner Reactions

Rape can precipitate a crisis not only for the victim but for family, friends, and others in her network of social relationships. Police officers and attorneys very likely will have to deal with these family members; and a good under-standing of the impact the rape has on their lives may help develop a more cooperative victim and partner.

One crucial dimension to observe is whether male partners see the victim as a victim. In other words, who do they perceive to be the victim of the rape — the woman herself, her parents, her husband/boyfriend? Do they see her as a person in her own right who has been hurt by the assault, or do they view her more as their possession whose value has diminished? Do they see the rape as an unfortunate incident that was externally inflicted upon her, or do they see it as evidence of her bad character? Whom do they blame — the assailant, the woman, or themselves? Perhaps the most crucial underlying and typically unstated issue is whether the family member sees the rape primarily as sex or primarily as violence.

The rape of a wife or girlfriend has an enormous psychological impact on the male partner. News of the violation brings forth a great surge of emotion on his part, and he often experiences many conflicting feelings. The process of sorting out what the rape means to him has two major compo-nents. The first component is dealing with his feelings. In his reactions, three issues predominate: (1) perceptions and feelings about who is hurt, (2) the desire to get the rapist, and (3) the "if-only" reaction. The second component is having to cope with his wife/girlfriend — a woman who now is very upset and in a state of crisis — and to cope with the impact that the event has had on their relationship. The second component also involves dealing with three main issues: (1) their discussions of the rape, (2) the woman's new phobias, and (3) the resumption of sexual relations. In addition, for those cases that go to court, the man must deal with the court process and with a wife/girl-friend who is as upset by going to court as she was by the rape (Holmstrom and Burgess, 1983).

The first issue is, who is the victim? The view that rape is an act with a victim seems to be widely accepted. Where there is a difference of opinion, however, is in regard to who is hurt by the rape. A traditional view would be that the woman's husband is injured because the wife's value is diminished by the rape. The violation makes her worthless, or it reflects badly on him that he should have such a wife. She is stigmatized and possibly to blame as well. One such husband clearly was wrestling with the issue of whether his wife had betrayed him by having sex with another man. Although she was quite bruised, he implied she should have resisted the assailant more:

> I can't understand her reaction at the time. I can't understand why she did what she did ... I don't think the whole truth will come out even in court. But I haven't had any trouble with her in 15 years of marriage with other men, so I'll stick by her now.

Another husband said he was ashamed and blamed his wife for the incident. She was a cocktail waitress who was raped as she went to her car after work. She described his response:

> I am having problems with my husband. He doesn't want me around his family. He told his mother on Sunday he was ashamed of me. He said I shouldn't have been working there, that it was my fault that I had been working there.

And in still another case, the boyfriend was worried whether he would be sexually repulsed by the woman now that she had been raped. The girlfriend's account follows:

> That night, as soon as we got back to the apartment, he wanted to make love ... He admitted he wanted to know if he could make love to me or if he would be repulsed by it and unable to.

A more modern view would be that the woman has been hurt as a human being, but that this in no way diminishes her value as a wife or reflects badly on her character or her husband. In one such case, the woman spoke as follows:

> My boyfriend has been so wonderful about it. He is the reason I got through it. His concern was for me. He was just glad to have me alive and well.

Getting the Guy.   Strong feelings of wanting to "get the guy" are common among male partners. This desire means the husband/boyfriend wants to go after the assailant and/or that he wants very much to pursue the assailant legally through the police and the courts. Sometimes police note that the male partner urges the victim not to press charges, or he harrasses the officer during the investigaton. In such cases, it might be helpful for the officer to talk with the man about his own feelings about the rape. Such a response may represent a more traditional view of rape where the partner feels victimized and does not want to deny what has happened.

Because victims experience a great deal of ambivalence over reporting a rape, it is not uncommon to see the male partner taking the initiative. Sometimes this unilateral decision then becomes an issue between the partners. One girlfriend described such a situation as follows:

> As soon as we got to the hospital, he marched up to the police car that was sitting in the emergency yard and said, "Sir, my girlfriend has just been

raped." [How do you feel about that?] I was furious. I didn't want to report it, and to have him do it really made me mad.

The "If-Only" Reaction.   Very often husbands and boyfriends indicate they wish they had done something differently and thus perhaps the incident would not have turned out the way it did. As one husband said, "If only I hadn't been working that night … maybe it wouldn't have happened."

Dealing with the Raped Woman.   While dealing with his own emotions, the male partner must also interact with the wife or girlfriend who is in a state of psychological crisis. Often the partner will say, "She is different since the rape." The woman clearly needs some psychological support during this time of crisis and most often looks to family members.

One important issue is whether the couple feels able to talk about the rape openly. The rationale is that, if they can express their feelings, they will be able to identify what issues are upsetting them and thus gain more control over these feelings. Thus, the memory of the event will not evoke the painful reaction that it once did. However, more often than not, avoidance of the topic is the norm.

The second important issue is dealing with the new phobias triggered by the rape. Often this area is where the partner is most helpful; he is able to provide for her protection and safety and is willing to be more available to her.

The third major issue is resuming sexual relations. Since sex is the means that the rapist used to attack the woman, it is not surprising that she may develop a phobia to resuming sex. And because of societal views regarding sex, it is not surprising that males have difficulty in resuming sexual relations with the raped partner.

Two interpretations may apply to this issue. The first interpretation concerns the maintenance of a double standard of behavior. For example, one husband who reported that, although he had not been an angel all his married life, he still felt betrayed when his wife was raped (i.e., "had sex with another man"). A second interpretation focuses on mutual sexual exclusiveness expectations that couples may have — expectations that apply to both partners. One example of this involves a homosexual couple. The woman was raped by a man; her homosexual partner, with whom she had lived for 3 years, was very upset. For this couple, each of the partners was very jealous over any outside relationships that the other partner might have. Further support for this interpretation is found in the case of a male victim in which the husband was raped homosexually, and the wife's reaction was to blame him. She questioned why he was out and why a big man like him could not fend off an assailant. His "unfaithfulness" during the rape was an issue for her.

Many couples have difficulty resuming sexual relations. The main problems from the woman's point of view are her: (1) temporary aversion to physical contact, (2) experience of flashbacks of the rape, (3) physical discomfort during sex, (4) changes in physical response to sexual stimulation, and (5) worry over her partner's reaction.

Dealing with the Courts.   Courts are as upsetting to the woman as the original rape. While testifying in court, the victim mentally relives the rape. Courts have their own set of pressures; there is the embarrassing public setting, the confrontation with the offender, and the difficult cross-examination by the defense lawyer. The victim finds the courtroom to be very stressful, and psychologically it often returns her to a state of crisis. The husband/boyfriend has this added responsibility to support his partner during this stressful event.

Counseling Implications

Law enforcement officers are frequently the first professionals with whom the victim interacts after the crime. It is critical to the well-being of the victim and to the criminal investigation that she can successfully resolve the emotional turmoil experienced. An emotionally healthy victim is better able to assist the police in the investigation of the crime. For that reason, officers should be aware of the value of counseling in such matters.

An understanding of the disruptive capacities of a rape attack requires a brief discussion of the concept of homeostatic balance and the relationship of coping behaviors to stable psychological functioning. The principle of homeostasis is the need for a stable balance within the body to function effectively in the world. When these psychological balances are upset, self-regulatory mechanisms (i.e., coping behaviors) are triggered to help return these balances to healthy levels for the individual. Crisis theory is based on this principle applied to psychological functioning.

We all have reasonably consistent balances between the way we think and the way we feel. Although this homeostatic balance varies from person to person, the primary characteristic of this balance is its stability for that individual — a stability that is "normal" for each individual. However, each and every day, experiences are encountered in which this balance is disrupted; and negative and uncomfortable feelings arise. These experiences may be termed emotionally hazardous situations. Such events give rise to stress and motivate the individual to bring coping behaviors into play that help to reestablish the balance. When the individual experiences an emotionally hazardous situation and is unable to effectively utilize previously learned coping behaviors, then an emotional crisis may ensue. In rape, a crisis usually develops because the event is so traumatic, unexpected, and uncontrolled that the person is unable to cope effectively.

Rape, a criminal victimization, poses a situational crisis. The victim is unprepared for the hazardous event and feels out of control and unable to cope. Crisis intervention is clearly the treatment of choice when a rape is disclosed immediately after it has occurred. The rationale for this type of treatment includes: (1) the rape represents a crisis in that the victim's style of life is disrupted; (2) the victim is regarded as normal or functioning adequately prior to the external stressor; and (3) crisis intervention aims to return the victim to his or her previous level of functioning as quickly as possible. The crisis intervention strategy is to provide or mobilize support for the victim during the acute phase of disruption. The speed of intervention is crucial. Other crisis services that may be offered to the victim include advocacy services, especially regarding legal matters; work with victim's support systems; and victim mutual support groups.

Compounded Reaction to Rape

Victims who are raped may describe past or current difficulties with psychiatric conditions, physical conditions, or behavior patterns that create difficulties for them in this society. These victims are frequently known to other therapists, physicians, or agencies. These victims need more than crisis counseling because, under the stress of the rape, they become vulnerable to prior difficulties. For example, a victim may develop increased physical problems, increased drinking or drug use, become suicidal, or exhibit psychotic behavior. A careful study of the victim's background will help in determining if the previous therapist or physician needs to be identified for referral. The referral suggestion should be made to the victim.

Silent Reaction to Rape

It seems to be a fairly well-accepted statement made by police and law officials that many victims of rape do not report the assault. This pattern alerted clinicians to a syndrome called *silent reaction to rape*. This syndrome occurs in the victim who has not reported the rape to anyone, who has not dealt with feelings and reactions to the incident, and who, because of this silence, has further burdened herself or himself psychologically. When this situation is defined, the referral should be for victim therapy.

Police Response to the Rape Victim

Victims of rape are often first seen by police officers who respond to a call for assistance. The treatment that a victim receives will influence his or her recovery process. Except for homicide, rape is the most serious violation of a person's body; it deprives the victim of both physical and emotional privacy and autonomy. The victim's response to rape primarily reflects her reaction to violation of self; it is an emotional as well as a physical assault. The officer must remember that the victim is being asked to discuss with a stranger the details of what is probably the most traumatic and personal experience of her life.

Police officers generally see victims and their families immediately after the crime, when they are most in need of help. The officer's response to these persons often has a major effect on how swiftly and how well the victim recovers.

Police officers who respond quickly after a report is made, who listen attentively, and who show concern for the victim's plight will greatly reassure the victim and help him or her overcome a sense of fear and helplessness. Rape victims who comment favorably on their initial exposures to law enforcement officers seem to feel more comfortable with police officers who project both personal concern and professional objectivity. Steps in the initial introductory phase of the police interview include the following.

Introduction

The initial interaction with the victim, the introduction, is the most critical phase of the interview process. Depending upon the victim's perception of the interview, she will or will not feel comfortable with and confident in the ability of the police to assist her. The officer should introduce himself or herself in a professional, confident, and sincere manner, using the victim's last name preceded by Ms., Mrs., Mr., or Miss. The interviewer(s) should accomplish three important tasks during this phase: express regret that the victim was assaulted (do not use the term *rape*), and assure her that she is the victim of a crime that was not her fault; assure her of her safety and that everything possible and reasonable will be done to maintain that safety; and convince her of the competence and experience of the interviewers.

An example scenario might proceed as follows:

> Good evening, Ms. Roberts. I am Bob Jackson of the Sexual Assault Unit, and I would like to discuss the crime which occurred, if you are feeling up to it at this time. I want you to know how deeply I regret your being the victim of such an assault and that I and the other members of the department will do our best on your behalf. Other officers have completely checked your residence (where the assault occurred) and have secured it. I've arranged for our patrols to increase their travel through your neighborhood, and I will also provide you with an emergency police number before I leave. I've been an investigating officer for nine years and am experienced in such matters, so please don't hesitate to ask questions during our time together.

The officer(s) should explain that the length of the interview will be as brief as possible and that, while the questions will necessarily be personal, their importance cannot be overemphasized and their answers will aid greatly in identifying the offender.

The Interview

The officer(s) would be well advised to remember that the process involved is an interview and not an interrogation. The victim has agreed to be interviewed, and this is strongly suggestive that she wants to cooperate and has faith in the abilities of law enforcement. Consequently, it is recommended that the following factors be adhered to during the interview phase:

1. Involve the victim in the interview process. Explain the procedures that have taken place and those that will follow. Provide her with a phone number which she can call to obtain information about the progress of the investigation, or advise her that you will periodically call to keep her informed. Ask for her opinions throughout the interview.

2. Allow the victim as much control as possible. Ask how she would like to be addressed, e.g., as Ms. Jones. Do not use her first name without her permission — do not presume the right. Inquire if the interview environment is agreeable to her or if she would be more comfortable elsewhere. Ask if she would prefer to describe the crime in her own words or if she would rather you ask questions. Determine if she wants anyone called.

3. Listen and respond to her wishes and requests if at all possible.

4. Pay attention to what she is saying and be alert to expressions of:
    a. guilt (*I shouldn't have gone to the market so late*),
    b. fear (*He said he would know if I called the police*),
    c. humiliation (*I didn't want to do that*), and
    d. unnecessary attempts to convince (*I know this sounds strange, but it really did happen,* or *I tried/wanted to stop him*).
    Upon hearing such phrases, the officer should reassure the victim:
    a. *You have a right to travel as you wish without becoming a victim,*
    b. *You're safe now inside your home,*
    c. *You had no choice in the matter,* and
    d. *It doesn't sound strange and I'm sure it happened,* or *You're not expected or required to become injured or killed.*

5. Balance questions having to do with humiliating acts or sexual aspects with ones relating to the victim's feelings. For example, if the victim had been asked about the occurrence of ejaculation (never ask if she "climaxed"), it should be balanced by a question such as *Do you feel*

safe now? or *May I get you something to drink?* or *Would you like to stop for a while?*

6. Begin by utilizing professional terminology. One can always lower the level of terms, but it is very difficult, if not impossible, to raise the level of terminology. An example would be questions pertaining to forced oral sexual acts. The professional interviewer will begin by using the term *fellatio*. It is quite probable that the victim might not be familiar with the term, and the officer would then use the term *oral sex*. Should the victim fail to understand at this level, the officer could ask, *Did he make you put your mouth on his penis?* To appreciate the value of such an approach, simply reverse the sequence.

7. Use language that is nonjudgmental or threatening to the victim. Instead of *Tell me about your rape,* use *Please describe the assault.* Instead of stating a bias (*What were you doing out so late?*), provide the opportunity for the victim to tell what happened (*Please describe what was happening leading up to the assault*). Rather than saying, *Why didn't you fight him?* ask, *Did you have any opportunity to resist?* The phrasing of the question can reveal the interviewer's personal bias and feelings to the victim and may impede the investigation.

8. Throughout the interview, it should become clear to the victim that the issues of power, control, anger, and aggression — not sexuality — are central to the crime. Sexuality is not the salient feature of the assault. A crime of violence has occurred and the victim should understand that it is this aspect (violence) on which the investigation will focus.

9. Obtain the facts of the crime in as factual a manner as possible. The interviewer should take precautions to ensure that the victim does not perceive the process as voyeuristic in nature. It must be remembered that the victim is most likely the only witness to the crime; and should she perceive the officer as invasive, she may withhold vital information. The victim has been, and is in, a stressful situation. The officer must attempt to decrease stress, not increase it. Dwelling on sexual activities or rushing through discussion of them may precipitate flashbacks to the rape experience. In other words, a very narrow periphery exists for the interviewer to operate within, and common sense must prevail. In general, the best information is gathered by allowing the victim to tell her story in her own words. This method will help relieve some of her emotional tensions as well as to allow the officer to listen carefully to what she is saying and to evaluate her mood, general reactions, and choice of words. When asking direct questions, the officer should be sure the victim understands what is being asked. It is important to talk on her level. Always give the reason for asking the question.

Concluding the Interview

Following the interview, the investigator should continue to include the victim in the process of the investigation. This approach is used to prevent the victim from feeling used by the system. The rapist has already conveyed such a feeling, and she must not perceive that she will be victimized by the system designed to prosecute her attacker. Therefore, it is suggested that the following information be provided to the victim:

1. Advise her of the next step in the investigative process. At this point, the victim needs to have stability in her life and to be reassured that she will not become only a statistic in some file. She is important and should be made to feel that her importance is recognized and that everything possible will be done to ensure justice is served.
2. As previously mentioned, she should be given a number to call or be told that she will be kept apprised of investigative progress.
3. The victim should be referred to, or preferably introduced to, supportive services that have advocacy systems designed to assist her through this emotionally traumatic time.
4. Ask whether the victim has any questions, and ensure that she fully understands what will happen in the future as well as her role in those events.
5. Thank the victim! Express your appreciation for the time she has taken to help in the investigation. The victim should leave feeling safe, guiltless, and confident about what will be accomplished as a result of her cooperation.

In conclusion, the investigator should be aware that the initial descriptions and interviews are likely to be colored by the trauma and crisis nature of the assault. Follow-up interviews with the victim are likely to reveal more details as the victim calms down and tries to resume her life. The investigator should be aware that the victim, in trying to return to a normal life, may want to forget the assault ever occurred; she may subsequently forget who the investigator is or refuse to talk to him or her. The victim should be alerted to the fact that she may want to forget the assault ever happened but that supressing the memory will not make it go away. Instead, it will reappear in nightmares, phobias, and other symptoms. She needs somebody to talk with until the memory can finally fade naturally.

Special Issue — Fresh Complaint

The issue of *fresh complaint* is a legitimate concern of the criminal justice system and arises quite often in matters involving sexual assault. It has been well noted that the victim may choose not to divulge the crime to anyone, including law enforcement; or, in other situations, she may delay in reporting it for hours, days, or even longer.

The issue really involves looking at the process of reporting a rape and understanding that the process means looking not only at the victim but also at her social network and at her community in general. A striking finding in the sociological study of rape victims by Holmstrom and Burgess (1983) is the degree to which people other than the victim are involved in the chain of events leading her to the police. In more than half of the 92 adult rape victims cases, someone other than the victim made the decision to contact the police, acted as intermediary at the request of the victim, or persuaded the victim to call.

The hesitation of many victims and the tendency for the family and friends to discuss whether to report the rape can be discouraging and sometimes bewildering to police. In many ways similar feelings exist among health professionals as to why patients do not report symptoms earlier and seek medical attention. However, police cannot do their work unless the rape is reported. They also know that any delay "looks bad" in court. Some members of the criminal justice system even label victims as collaborators when they do not immediately report the crimes.

Socially and psychologically, however, the need of many victims to seek out others for support or for advice makes sense. Rape victims typically experience rape as an attack that threatens their very lives and, as a result, they are in a state of psychological crisis. They have experienced an overwhelming danger that they could neither escape nor solve with their customary psychological resources. People in crisis typically have difficulty making any decisions. It is thus understandable that victims should turn to others. It may be added that some victims of rape also are physically incapable of making any decisions. The assailant may have beaten them so badly or so terrified them regarding reporting that their faculties are not completely available to them — a fact not always appreciated by professionals.

The officer needs to understand the wide range of behaviors that can occur related to reporting a rape. Rather than project a reason onto the victim for why she delayed, it is a better strategy to ask the victim to describe how she was finally able to make the decision to report — implying that the decision must have been a difficult one for her — thus acknowledging this process rather than judging it.

Summary

This chapter outlines the rape trauma syndrome as a two-phased process (acute and long-term) of physical, psychological, social, and sexual symptoms experienced by individuals following attempted or completed forcible rape.

The trauma is accompanied by immediate impact reactions as well as acute and long-term symptoms. Partner responses include emotional reactions, intent to get the assailant, dealing with his raped partner, and participating in court issues. Counseling implications are discussed as well as the police officer's response to the rape victim.

References

Burgess, A.W. and Holmstrom, L.L. (1974) Rape trauma syndrome, *Am. J. Psychiatr.,* 131, 981–986.

Holmstrom, L.L. and Burgess, A.W. (1983) *The Victim of Rape: Institutional Reactions,* Transaction Books, New Brunswick, NJ.

Victim Care Services and the Comprehensive Sexual Assault Assessment Tool (CSAAT)

3

ANN WOLBERT BURGESS
ROBERT R. HAZELWOOD

Introduction

Rape crisis centers have been providing services for victims for more than 30 years (Koss and Harvey, 1991). This systematized response evolved when it was realized that rape victims could not get the required understanding or support from family, friends, or medical and legal systems. The grass-roots movement took on the tasks of ensuring that victims had access to informed and sympathetic advocate–counselors to assist with the emotional conse-quences of rape and to deal with the appropriate systems. These centers also considered community education, system reform, and empowerment of women and victims to be central to their mission.

There is a history of victim care services in general, and the anti-rape movement in particular. Largen (1985) credits two forces for finally bringing the problem of rape to the attention of the citizens of the U.S. in the late 1960s. First, primary credit is given to the women's movement for initiating the consciousness-raising groups and then the "speakouts," where women began saying publicly what they had not dared say previously about rape. Second, in response to a rising crime rate and the growing community concern over the problem of rape, Senator Charles Mathias of Maryland introduced a bill in September, 1973, to establish the National Center for the Prevention and Control of Rape. The purpose of this bill was to provide a focal point within the National Institute of Mental Health from which a comprehensive national effort would be undertaken to conduct research, develop programs, and provide information leading to aid for the victims and their families; to rehabilitate the offenders; and, ultimately, to curtail rape crimes. The bill was passed by an overwhelming vote in the 93rd Con-gress, vetoed by President Ford, and successfully reintroduced. The National Center was established through Public Law 94-63 in July, 1975.

Parallel with these political forces, there was a push in the early 1970s for major efforts to organize services for rape victims, including community-based and hospital-based programs. Although most of the pioneer services were grass-roots self-help programs, now widely known as rape crisis centers, nurses practicing in hospital emergency departments began to develop programs to provide rape counseling services. Boston City Hospital, Boston's Beth Israel Hospital, and Santa Monica Hospital were among the first hospital-based programs; they represent the roots of forensic nursing programs (Lynch, 1993).

This chapter presents a description of the comprehensive multidisciplinary victim care service program and the sexual assault nurse examiner (SANE) programs. These programs may be viewed as prototypes for cities to consider for their own communities. The chapter also presents the Comprehensive Sexual Assault Assessment Tool (CSAAT) that was developed by the authors for forensic and/or research purposes.

Hospital-Based Victim Care Service (VCS)

In 1972, a victim counseling program was developed as a nurse-managed service at the Boston City Hospital by Burgess and Holmstrom (1974). The counseling approach developed in the early years of this program expanded in the mid-1980s into a six-phase VCS coordinated by an advanced practice psychiatric nurse (Minden, 1989). These six phases include various health-care providers and networks throughout a state and are suggested for hospital-based programs.

> Phase 1: Setting standards and training treatment providers in victim care; coordinating with other programs in the city and state
> Phase 2: Providing acute intervention with victims entering the emergency department or any other patient unit in the hospital system
> Phase 3: Providing crisis intervention follow-ups of victims by masters-prepared psychiatric nurses or social workers
> Phase 4: Providing education regarding sexually transmitted disease including HIV according to the age and verbal requests of the victims
> Phase 5: Providing ongoing therapy through referral to psychiatric clinicians
> Phase 6: Evaluating and researching sexual victimization

The Victim Care Service is organized around six fundamental assumptions as follows.

1. There is a continuum of sexual victimization. Although states and jurisdictions legally define rape differently, three criteria are generally present: (a) sexual penetration of the victim's vagina, mouth, or

rectum that (b) occurs without the individual's consent and that (c) involves the use of force or threat of force.

Sexual assault refers to a wider range of forced or pressured sexual contact, specifically, child sexual assault, incest, acquaintance rape, and marital rape. Furthermore, there are situations involving relationships of unequal power in which the person in authority violates the normal bounds of the relationship and abuses and sexually pressures or forces the subordinate. Such abusive relationships include husband/wife, therapist/patient, parent/child, teacher/student, and employer/employee.

A basic premise of the VCS is that a patient does not need to meet any stringent legal criteria for rape in order to be considered sexually victimized. The legal system bears the burden of determining the validity of a given charge of rape, whereas the primary responsibility of the VCS is to care for the patient reporting sexual victimization.

2. Sexual victimization is not a rare event. Rape is a serious public health problem. In 1997, there were 96,122 reported forcible rapes. An estimated 70 of every 100,000 females in the country were reported rape victims in 1997, a decrease of 1% from 1996 and 13% from 1993. A 1997 National Crime Victimization Survey, which includes both reported and unreported crimes, found that despite a decline of 7% in the nation's crime rate in 1997, rates of rape and sexual assault did not decline (Kilpatrick, 2000).

3. Responses to sexual assault victims have frequently been based on myths and stereotypes. The stereotype that rape victims are somehow responsible for their victimization is grounded in the belief that women have rape fantasies and that it is acceptable for men to fulfill such fantasies. This belief is also noted in the attitude that women who dress provocatively, stay out late, or frequent unsafe areas get what they deserve. Although engaging in certain behaviors may increase one's risk of victimization, the VCS maintains that it is the offender who is responsible for the victimization.

Other myths include: rape is a crime that is prone to false complaints; rape only happens to other people; and rape occurs in dark alleys at the hands of strangers. To the contrary, studies suggest that victims of rape are disinclined to make complaints under current laws and that those who do so frequently refuse to continue their testimony because of the manner in which they are treated (Schwartz and Clear, 1980). Also, contrary to popular belief, confidence rape — or assault by someone known to the victim — is a more frequent occurrence than stranger rape; and it often happens in the victim's home or another familiar place.

Furthermore, sexual assault and abuse crosses all boundaries of class and culture. The fact that victims can be of either sex helps to negate the myth that women are naturally better equipped than men to care for sexual assault victims. The clinician, whether male or female, must be accepting of the patient. A female clinician caring for a female victim might defend against her own feelings of vulnerability by rejecting the patient. In contrast, that same patient might benefit from interaction with a male clinician who acts in a caring manner. Attitude rather than gender determines a clinician's ability to provide victim care (Minden, 1989).

4. Rape or sexual assault represents a trauma or crisis that results in a disruption of the victim's physical, emotional, and social lifestyle. An individual who has been raped usually describes it as an extremely traumatic event in her life. Whether an individual is able to cope with the trauma depends on a number of factors, including the nature of the assault, the presence of other stressors, the patient's pre-crisis functioning and coping skills, and the available support system. The clinician who can communicate a sense of optimism for recovery may help nullify the chronic negative effects of sexual assault.

    Rape trauma, a clinical term, describes a clustering of biopsycho-social and behavioral symptoms exhibited in varying degrees by a victim following a rape. Most victims of forcible rape develop a pattern of moderate to severe symptoms described as rape trauma syndrome (see Chapter 2); a minority of victims report no symptom or mild symptoms. Rape trauma is an acute reaction to an externally imposed situational crisis. The trauma of the victim results from facing a life-threatening and highly stressful situation. The crisis that results when a person is raped is a form of self-preservation. The victim's reactions to the impending threat to her life are the nucleus around which such an adaptive pattern may arise.

    For many rape victims, responses during the rape and after the rape correspond to the critical symptoms of post-traumatic stress disorder (PTSD). Diagnostic criteria are found in the CSAAT (see the Appendix at the end of this chapter).

5. Rape trauma is a traumatic stressor. Crisis intervention encourages a positive resolution of the victimization experience. Patterns of coping after the assault can be adaptive or maladaptive. The purpose of crisis intervention is to direct the victim into therapeutic coping patterns rather than defensive positions.

    The forte of VCS is crisis intervention; the emphasis is moving the patient from being a victim to being a survivor. A salient feature of

victimization for the patient is a loss of control. Emergency department clinicians can easily mirror the patient's crisis and may also
experience feelings of being overwhelmed by the trauma. Consequently, the VCS implements a very structured process for providing
victim care, which has helped to reestablish a sense of control for the
clinician who can then put energies into stabilizing the patient.

Two phases of care are provided the rape victim (Minden, 1989).
The first phase of care includes implementation of the sexual assault
protocol. The second phase is victim follow-up by telephone over a 3
to 4 day period, when a counseling referral to facilitate the recovery
of the victim from the acute phase is discussed.

6. A multidisciplinary approach to victim care is required because rape
    is a complex, multifaceted problem that no one individual or group
    can resolve alone. Indeed, dealing with sexual victimization requires
    the collaborative and cooperative efforts of a network of services.
    Thus, a multidisciplinary team approach not only helps to meet the
    diverse needs of the victim but also provides the caregivers with a
    support system for dealing with the stress of victimization. The VCS
    provides continuous victim care training for various community
    agencies and joins with other programs in offering workshops to
    enhance community awareness of sexual victimization (Minden,
    1989).

7. Victim care providers experience compassion fatigue. *Compassion
    fatigue,* a term coined by trauma expert Charles Figley, describes how
    working with victims can take a psychological toll on the providers of
    care. Clinicians working in emergency departments of large city hos-
    pitals have very direct and frequent exposure to trauma. Ever-escalat-
    ing economic constraints and patient acuity result in increasing
    challenges for the care providers that are physically, intellectually, and
    emotionally stressful.

Rape Crisis Services

Rape crisis services have come to be standard fare in many communities in
the U.S. Most such services consist of 24-hour crisis lines offering information and support, advocacy in the form of information about the medical
and legal systems, accompaniment to medical and legal appointments or
court appearances, and supportive post-rape counseling. The counseling has
often been offered as a group treatment. In many cases, the services have
been delivered by trained volunteers; but increasingly, mental health professionals supervise or carry out the counseling.

The National Sexual Violence Resource Center (NSVRC)

The National Sexual Violence Resource Center (NSVRC), incubated by the Pennsylvania Coalition against Rape (PCAR) and funded by the Center for Disease Control and Prevention in 1999, is the nucleus of a national movement to prevent sexual violence and to sustain a national momentum that influences practice, research, policy, and ultimately, public attitudes and beliefs. The broad goals of the NSVRC are to: (1) strengthen the support system serving sexual assault survivors by providing competent leadership, resources, and information to develop the capacities of national sexual assault organizations, state sexual assault coalitions, community-based programs, and allied professionals; (2) provide accurate and comprehensive information and technical assistance in supporting effective intervention in the prevention of sexual violence; (3) identify emerging policy issues and research needs to support the development of policy and practice leading to the prevention of sexual violence; and (4) enhance the organizational structure and technological capacity supporting the development and implementation of NSVRC activities.

The NSVRC is housed in Enola, Pennsylvania, and provides information and resources, technical assistance, and access to research through its toll-free number and E-mail address. Organizational partners who collaborate with the NSVRC include: (1) the University of Pennsylvania as the research partner; (2) the Violence against Women Prevention Resource Center; (3) the VAWnet/National Resources Center, (4) the National Alliance of Sexual Assault Coalitions; and (5) the National Coalition against Sexual Assault.

Sexual Assault Nurse Examiner Services

Interventions in the health sector usually involve the treatment of injuries incurred in a physical or sexual assault. Besides treating the injuries of a sexual assault victim, a hospital emergency room is often critical in gathering forensic evidence to be used if legal charges are brought against an assailant.

Sexual assault nurse examiner programs (SANEs) that were developed in the late 1970s were located in Memphis (1976), Minneapolis (1977), and Amarillo (1978). In 1992 the first national meeting bringing forensic nurses together was hosted by the Sexual Assault Response Team of Minneapolis. The International Association of Forensic Nurses (Ledray and Arndt, 1994) was established as an outgrowth of that meeting.

Sexual assault nurse examiners are specially trained registered nurses who provide comprehensive care to sexual assault survivors. Certification is usually by the local institution after completing a 40-hour training program and demonstrating competence in conducting a comprehensive evidential examination. Although sexual assault nurse examiners work cooperatively with medical facilities, most are from independent nursing programs or agencies that contract with the hospital to provide the specific services on an on-call basis. Some hospitals that provide services to large numbers of rape victims have their own programs (Ledray and Arndt, 1994).

Variations in the collection procedure and treatment components exist because hospitals and SANE programs have each developed their own sexual assault protocols. Many states have developed statewide protocols, and other states have adopted a protocol developed by the U.S. Department of Justice. Most states have developed rape examination kits that allow for consistency in evidence collection and that ensure a proper chain of evidence. Although some variation is likely to continue, all forensic nursing examinations of sexual assault victims include the following five essential components:

- Treatment and documentation of injuries
- Treatment and evaluation of sexually transmitted diseases
- Pregnancy risk evaluation and prevention
- Crisis intervention and arrangements for follow-up counseling
- Collection of medicolegal evidence while maintaining the proper chain of evidence

In some states the nurse examiner collects the evidence and does the crisis intervention. In other states the nurse works in conjunction with a rape crisis counselor, who is usually a volunteer from a local crisis center. Frequently, the nurse examiner will be called upon to testify in legal proceedings.

One of the purposes of the International Association of Forensic Nurses is to coordinate research on rape. To that end, the following assessment tool, the CSAAT, has been devised and is published here for the use of law enforcement and other professionals and to create an awareness of the existing national data set being coordinated by forensic nursing investigators. The CSAAT can be used for compilation of statistics for use at an agency, program development, research data, and victim evaluation reports for clinical or forensic purposes.

Comprehensive Sexual Assault Assessment Tool (CSAAT)

The Comprehensive Sexual Assault Assessment Tool (CSAAT) is composed of four major areas for data collection. Items for the first area, Investigative Data, are identified in Chapter 8 as behavioral aspects of the offender. Items for the second area, Victim Forensic Data, are described in the Appendix to this chapter. Items for the third area, Legal/Services Information, and the fourth area, Psychosocial Assessment for PTSD, are included in this chapter. Each area of data collection may be completed separately.

I. Investigative Data

Information basic to the background of the victim includes age, date of birth, gender, race, marital status, education, occupation, employment status, presence and/or type of disability, living arrangements, primary language, and whether multiple victims were involved.

Information basic to the offense includes time of the rape, day of the week, and location (residence, place of employment, inside, outside). Data on offender characteristics include race, gender, approximate age, weight and height, unique features, and whether there were multiple offenders. Other information includes offender relationship to victim, weapon brought to the scene, telephone disabled, bindings brought to the scene, use of gloves, washing up of the scene, evidence taken from the scene, items of value taken, or victim's personal items taken.

The offender's method of approach is recorded as to whether it was a con, a blitz, or a surprise. The control of the victim is recorded as to mere presence, weapon of opportunity, threats used, victim use of alcohol or drugs, whether the victim was bound or blindfolded, battery of the victim, abduction of the victim, bribery, psychological coercion, and percentage of clothing removed from the victim. Information is requested about the offender's use of drugs or alcohol and level of physical force used. Questions are asked about the victim's resistance (passive, verbal, or physical) and offender reaction to victim's resistance (cease demand, compromise/negotiate, flee, threats, or increased force/beatings). Information is requested about the assailant's sexual dysfunction such as erectile insufficiency, premature ejaculation, retarded ejaculation, conditional ejaculation, and type and sequence of sexual acts during the offense. In addition, information is requested about the offender's verbal activity, the victim's verbal activity, the offender's initial attitude and behavior (and whether this changed during assault), and the offender's attire. These are crucial aspects of victim interviews and crime investigations.

II. Victim Forensic Data

The second area, Victim Forensic Data, includes information on height, weight, vital signs (blood pressure, pulse, temperature), and post-assault activities such as urination, defecation, vomiting, bathing, or showering. Questions are asked to determine whether the pelvic examination was performed by direct visualization, bimanual, speculum, or colposcopic exam; the number of photographs taken and areas of body; and the use of the evidence kit. Microbiology findings from the vagina, anus, or pharynx are recorded, as are the results of VDRL and HIV testing, findings about sperm presence/motility in vagina, anus, or mouth, and DNA testing results. Treatments given for sexually transmitted disease and pregnancy prevention are recorded.

In addition, rape examination findings are documented regarding genital trauma to female (labia majora, labia minora, clitoris, posterior fourchettes, fossa navicularis, periurethral, vestibule, vagina, hymen, cervix, perineum, anus, and rectum) and to male victims (penis, periurethral, perineum, anus, rectum, and scrotum).

A knowledge of the various emotional states and responses experienced by victims can facilitate additional details of the offender's behavior for suspect apprehension. Information is therefore requested about the victim's behavior during the interview as quiet or tense, trembling or tearful, agitated, or verbally upset. Victim's responses to questions are also recorded as brief, reluctant, or readily responsive; and the victim's behavior during the examination is recorded as controlled, expressed, fearful, or angry.

The prior history of a victim can be important for planning referrals and follow-up counseling. Also of import is information regarding a prior history of assault or victimization and the victim's prior psychiatric history. These data are therefore also recorded.

III. Legal and Services Information

Victims need access to a comprehensive system of services and resources. Provision of eight services, which are intended to assist victims in dealing with the short-term, long-term, and/or delayed effects of victimization, are documented in the third area of the CSAAT.

1. Emergency response: A set of services is provided by the first person(s) coming in contact with the victim after the crime, i.e., a law enforcement dispatcher, a crisis line operator, family members, or a neighbor. These services should ensure the physical safety of the victim and make him or her feel safe and secure.

2. Forensic services: Forensic services include treatment and documentation of injuries, treatment and evaluation of sexually transmitted diseases, pregnancy risk evaluation and prevention, and rape examination for the collection of medicolegal evidence while maintaining the proper chain of evidence. Forensic medical and nursing services should include victim stabilization and should immediately follow the emergency response.

3. Resource mobilization: Resource mobilization services are designed to assist the victim in his or her recovery. They include crisis intervention or other kinds of emotional support following the trauma as well as protection, shelter, food, or other emergency aid as necessary. Arrangements for follow-up counseling are included. Additionally, resource mobilization includes a broad array of help, ranging from

filling out insurance forms and filing for victim compensation to short-term counseling or long-term therapy. This stage may last for years with some victims.

4. Suspect arrest: When a suspect is arrested, a victim automatically becomes involved in the criminal justice system. The victim needs to be informed of the investigation and the arrest, the potential and actual charges that may be filed, and any bail considerations. Interaction with the victim may also include consultation with the victim over such decisions and emotional support during this period.

5. Preparation for court: Services at this stage focus on preparing the victim for his or her involvement in the court process. Examples include giving the victim an orientation to the courthouse and the courtroom, telling him or her what to expect in a hearing or trial, and what he or she will be expected to do. Victim assistance programs linked to the county prosecutor's office are best equipped for this service.

6. Court appearance: Victims who become involved in court appearances may need a number of tangible services — transportation, child care, parking, and separation from the accused while waiting for the appearance. Often overlooked is the need for an escort and supportive court counseling, both in the courtroom and after the appearance is over.

7. Sentencing process: Most states have legislation that allows the victim to be involved in the sentencing process. Services at this stage include helping with a victim impact statement or alternative expression of his or her concern; escort and support for victims wishing to provide testimony at the sentencing hearing; and short-term counseling following the sentencing outcome.

8. Post-sentencing: Often the services needed after a sentencing are ignored. Yet victims may need to be kept informed about probation revocation hearings, parole hearings, escapes, appeals, and other issues related to the criminal justice system. They also may need continued short-term counseling or long-term therapy once the case is over.

A crime classification for rape and sexual assault is found in Chapter 9. The classifications include whether the offense was criminal enterprise, felony rape, personal cause of domestic sexual assault, entitlement rape, social acquaintance rape, subordinate rape, exploitative rape, anger rape, sadistic rape, abduction rape, group cause of formal gang rape, or informal gang rape. Chapter 10 includes discussion about unfounded cases, including insufficient evidence, *nol pros,* charges dropped, sex-stress situation, and false rape accusation.

IV. Psychosocial Assessment for PTSD

Clinicians evaluating rape victims generally use the American Psychiatric Association's *Diagnostic and Statistical Manual (DSM IV)* (1994) for determining a psychiatric diagnosis. An assessment for post-traumatic stress disorder (PTSD) is defined by the following criteria:

- The experience of an event that involved actual or threatened death, serious injury, or threat to physical integrity
- Re-experiencing the trauma by external cues, memories, or dreams
- Avoidance of stimuli associated with the trauma
- Numbed responsiveness, i.e., feelings of detachment from others, constricted feelings, or diminished interest in significant activities.
- Persistent symptoms of increased arousal such as sleep disturbance, irritability, difficulty concentrating, hypervigilance, and/or exaggerated startle response

Other symptoms requested on the CSAAT and noted since the assault include increased perspiration or heart rate, changes in appetite, increased nervousness, body image disturbance, unusual body sensations, sexual problems with partner, self-blame, low self-esteem, fear of being alone, prior victimization, and prior psychiatric history.

A multiaxial evaluation report as suggested by the DSM-IV is recommended and is included after the CSAAT in this chapter. Axis I includes diagnoses, the most common of which will be post-traumatic stress disorder. Other DSM-IV diagnoses may also be used, especially if there is a pre-existing condition. Axis II includes diagnoses from the list of personality disorders and mental retardation in the DSM-IV. Axis III includes any diagnosed medical condition. Axis IV includes a list of psychosocial and environmental issues such as problems with primary support group, social environment, schooling, work, hobbies/activities, finances, health care access, and legal problems. Axis V asks for the highest level of functioning for the past year. An assessment scoring for symptoms is included.

References

American Psychiatric Association (1994) *Diagnostic and Statistical Manual,* IV, APA, Washington, D.C.

Burgess, A.W. and Holmstrom, L.L. (1974) *Rape: Victims of Crisis,* Bowie, MD, Robert J. Brady Co.

Kilpatrick, D.G. (2000) *Rape and Sexual Assault,* South Carolina, Medical College of South Carolina, Charleston.

Koss, M.P., and Harvey, M.R. (1991) *The Rape Victim: Clinical and Community Interventions,* Newbury Park, CA, Sage.

Largen, M.A. (1985) The anti-rape movement: past and present, in A.W. Burgess, Ed., *Rape and Sexual Assault,* New York, Garland Publ. Inc., pp. 1–13.

Ledray, L.E. and Arndt, S. (1994) Examining the sexual assault victim: a new model for nursing care, *J. Psychosocial Nursing,* 32(2), 7–12.

Lynch, V.A. (1993) Forensic nursing: diversity in education and practice, *J. Psychosocial Nursing,* 31(11), 7–14.

Minden, P.B. (1989) The victim care services: a program for victims of sexual assault, *Arch. Psychosocial Nursing,* 3(1), 41–46.

Schwartz, M.D. and Clear, T.R. (1980) Toward a new law on rape, *Crime and Delinquency,* 4, 129–51.

Appendix

Comprehensive Sexual Assault Assessment Tool (CSAAT)*

Facility _____ City _____ State _____
Case Number: _____ Date: _____

I. INVESTIGATIVE DATA

Victim Data

1. Age of victim: _____   2. Date of birth: _____
3. Gender: Male_____ Female_____
4. Race: Asian___ Black___ Caucasian___ Hispanic___ Other___
5. Marital status: Single_____ Married/cohabitating_____
    Divorced/separated _____ Widow_____ Other_____
6. Education by highest level completed: _____
7. Occupation: _____
8. Employment status: Full time_____ Part time _____
    Unemployed _____ Retired _____ Looking for work _____
9. Disability: No_____ Yes_____
10. Living arrangements: Self_____ Parents/relatives _____
    Spouse/partner _____ Other_____
11. Primary language: _____
12. Multiple victims: No _____ Yes _____

Offense Data

13. Time of rape: AM _____ PM _____
14. Day of week: Sun __ Mon __ Tue __ Wed __ Thu __ Fri __ Sat __
15. Date: / /
16. Location: Residence No _____ Yes _____
    Place of employment: No _____ Yes _____
    Outside: No _____ Yes _____ Describe _____
    Inside: No _____ Yes _____ Describe _____
    Other: No _____ Yes _____ Describe _____

Offender Characteristics

17. Race: Asian ___ Black ___ Caucasian ___ Hispanic ___ Other ___

18. Gender: Male ____ Female ____
19. Approximate age (in years): _____ to _____
20. Approximate weight: _____
21. Approximate height: _____
22. Unique features: No ____ Yes ____ Describe _____
23. Multiple offenders: No ____ Yes ____ No data ____

Offender Relationship to Victim

24. Known: No____ Yes____ If known, relationship
     ___ Acquaintance/friend ___ Current or former cohabitant
     ___ Dating relationship ___ Supervisor/authority figure
     ___ Relative or in-law   ___ Other _____
25. Weapon brought to scene: No ____ Yes ____ Type _____
26. Telephone disabled: No ____ Yes ____ No data _____
27. Bindings brought to scene: No ____ Yes ____ No data _____
28. Use of gloves: No ____ Yes ____ Type _____
29. Wash up scene: No ____ Yes ____ No data _____
30. Evidence taken from scene: No ____ Yes ____ No data _____
31. Items of value taken: No ____ Yes ____ No data _____
32. Victim personal items taken: No ____ Yes ____ No data _____

Offender Method of Approach

33. Con (subterfuge or a ploy): No ____ Yes ____ No data _____
34. Blitz (no warning):   No ____ Yes ____ No data _____
35. Surprise (sudden assault): No ____ Yes ____ No data _____

Offender Control of the Victim

36. Mere presence: No ____ Yes ____ No data ____
37. Weapon of opportunity: No ____ Yes ____ Type _____
38. Threats: No ____ Yes ____ No data ____
39. Victim alcohol or drug use: No ____ Yes ____ No data ____ Type___
40. Victim bound: No ____ Yes ____ No data ____
41. Victim blindfolded: No ____ Yes ____ No data ____
42. Battery/beating: No ____ Yes ____ No data ____
43. Abducted: No ____ Yes ____ No data ____
44. Bribery: No ____ Yes ____ Describe _____
45. Psychological coercion: No ____ Yes ____ Describe _____
46. Percentage victim clothed (0% for nude): _____ %

47. Offender alcohol or drug use: No ___ Yes ___ No data ___ Type ___
48. Physical force by the offender: No ___ Yes ___ If yes, type:
    ___ Minimal (little/no physical force)
    ___ Moderate (repeated slaps/hits)
    ___ Excessive (beaten, bruises, lacerations)
    ___ Brutal (sadistic torture)
49. Victim resistance: No _____ Yes _____ If yes, type:
    ___ Passive
    ___ Verbal
    ___ Physical
50. Offender reacted to victim resistance: No _____ Yes ___
    ___ Cease demand
    ___ Compromise/negotiate
    ___ Flee
    ___ Threats
    ___ Increased force/beatings

Sexual Acts

51. Sexual dysfunction: No _____ Yes _____ No data _____
52. Erectile insufficiency: No _____ Yes _____ No data _____
53. Premature ejaculation: No _____ Yes _____ No data _____
54. Retarded ejaculation: No _____ Yes _____ No data _____
55. Conditional ejaculation: No _____ Yes _____ No data _____

Type and Sequence of Sexual Acts during the Assault

56. Kissed: No _____ Yes _____ Sequence _____
57. Breasts fondled: No _____ Yes _____ Sequence _____
58. Vaginal: No _____ Yes _____ Sequence _____
59. Oral (offender to victim):   No _____ Yes _____ Sequence _____
60. Oral (victim to offender):   No _____ Yes _____ Sequence _____
61. Anal: No _____ Yes _____ Sequence _____
62. Foreign object: No _____ Yes _____ Sequence _____
63. Offender masturbates self: No _____ Yes _____ Sequence _____
64. Offender masturbates victim: No _____ Yes _____ Sequence _____
65. Condom used: No _____ Yes _____ Sequence _____
66. Experimentation: No _____ Yes _____ Sequence _____
67. Punishment: No _____ Yes _____ Sequence _____
68. Other: No _____ Yes _____
                                      Describe/sequence _____

Offender Verbal Activity

69. Apologies: No _____ Yes _____ Describe _____
70. Compliments to victim: No _____ Yes _____ Describe _____
71. Personal inquiries of victim: No _____ Yes _____
72. Reassurance to victim: No _____ Yes _____ Describe _____
73. Affectionate phrases: No _____ Yes _____ Describe _____
74. Profanity toward victim: No _____ Yes _____ Describe _____
75. Demeaning statements
      toward victim: No _____ Yes _____
76. Threats: No _____ Yes _____ Describe _____
77. Orders   No _____ Yes _____ Describe _____

Victim Verbal Activity

78. Forced to talk to offender: No _____ Yes _____ Describe ___
79. Forced to state affection for offender: No _____ Yes _____
80. Self-demeaning statements: No _____ Yes _____
81. Talk to calm offender: No _____ Yes _____
82. Negotiate out of sex act: No _____ Yes _____ Describe ___

Offender's Initial Attitude/Behavior

83. Angry: No _____ Yes _____
84. Abusive: No _____ Yes _____
85. Quiet: No _____ Yes _____
86. Offender changed during rape: No _____ Yes _____
      Describe _____
87. Offender wore mask/disguise: No ___ Yes ___ Describe _____
88. Percentage offender clothed (0% is nude): _____ %

II. VICTIM FORENSIC DATA

89. Height _____
90. Weight _____
91. Blood Pressure _____
92. Pulse _____
93. Temperature _____

Actions Post-assault

94. Urination: No _____ Yes _____

95. Defecation: No _____ Yes _____
96. Vomit: No _____ Yes _____
97. Bath/shower: No _____ Yes _____

Method of Pelvic Examination

98. Direct visualization: No _____ Yes _____
99. Bimanual exam: No _____ Yes _____
100. Speculum exam: No _____ Yes _____
101. Colposcopic exam: No _____ Yes _____
102. Photographs taken: No _____ Yes _____ Number _____
     Area(s) of body _____
103. Evidence kit collected No _____ Yes _____

Microbiology

104. Vaginal: GC _____ CT _____ Other _____ Not done _____
105. Anal: GC _____ CT _____ Other _____ Not done _____
106. Pharyngeal: GC _____ CT _____ Other _____ Not done _____
107. VDRL: Positive _____ Negative _____ Not done _____
108. HIV: Positive _____ Negative _____ Not done _____
109. Sperm presence/motility: Vaginal _____ Anal _____ Oral _____
     None present _____
110. DNA: No _____ Yes _____ No data _____

Genital Trauma Noted

111. Labia majora No _____ Yes _____
112. Labia minora No _____ Yes _____
113. Clitoris No _____ Yes _____
114. Posterior fourchette No _____ Yes _____
115. Fossa navicularis No _____ Yes _____
116. Periurethral No _____ Yes _____
117. Vestibule No _____ Yes _____
118. Vagina No _____ Yes _____
119. Hymen No _____ Yes _____
120. Cervix No _____ Yes _____
121. Perineum No _____ Yes _____
122. Anus No _____ Yes _____
123. Rectum No _____ Yes _____
124. Other site of injury/or injury to male victims _____
     _____

Victim's Behavior during Examination/Interview

125. Controlled demeanor: No _____ Yes _____ If yes,
      ___ Quiet/tense
      ___ Trembling
      ___ Brief response to questions
      ___ Reluctant response to questions
      ___ Other_____
126. Expressive demeanor: No _____ Yes _____ If yes,
      ___ Tearful/sobbing
      ___ Agitated
      ___ Anxious smiling
      ___ Angry
      ___ Responsive to questioning
      ___ Other_____

Treatment Provided

127. Pregnancy prevention: No _____ Yes _____
128. STD prevention: No _____ Yes _____
      Other _____ (describe) _____

III. LEGAL/SERVICES INFORMATION

129. Emergency response: No _____ Yes _____ Type: _____
      __ Police   _____ Crisis line
      __ Family member   _____ Friend
      __ Other
130. Forensic services: No _____ Yes _____
131. Resource mobilization: No _____ Yes _____ Type: _____
      __ Crisis intervention   __ Completing forms
      __ Victim compensation __ Counseling
132. Preparation for court: No _____ Yes _____
133. Court appearance: No _____ Yes _____
134. Sentencing of offender: No _____ Yes _____
135. Postsentencing: No _____ Yes _____
136. Assailant(s) in custody: No _____ Yes _____ No data _____
137. Crime classification — circle one of the following:
      301:   Criminal Enterprise,   312:   Domestic Sexual Assault
             felony rape   313:   Entitlement Rape
      313.01: Social Acquaintance Rape 313.02: Subordinate
      313.03: Power-Reassurance Rape   313.04: Exploitative Rape

314: Anger Rape   315: Sadistic Rape
319: Abduction Rape   331: Formal Gang Sexual
390: Sexual Assault Not Classified   Assault
      Elsewhere
399: Unfounded Case; select all that apply:
      ___ Insufficient evidence
      ___ *Nolle pros*
      ___ Charges dropped
      ___ Sex stress situation
      ___ False rape allegation
      ___ Delusional rape allegation
      ___ Other Describe _____

138. Victim testified at Grand Jury: No ____ Yes ____ No data ____
139. Victim testified in Superior Court: No ____ Yes ____ No data ____
140. Defendant convicted: No ____ Yes ____ No data ____
141. Sentence: _____
142. Civil court trial: No ____ Yes ____ No data ____
143. Settlement: No ____ Yes ____ No data ____
      Verdict amount: _____

IV. PSYCHOSOCIAL ASSESSMENT FOR PTSD

Time interval since rape _____
Item Present = Yes, Absent = No; Intensity 1 = Low to 5 = High

144. Event involving actual/witnessed threatened death
      or injury   No ____ Yes ____ 1 2 3 4 5
145. Felt intense fear, helplessness, or horror No ____ Yes ____ 1 2 3 4 5

One or more of the following reexperiencing symptoms:

146. Involuntary intrusive thoughts   No ____ Yes ____ 1 2 3 4 5
147. Recurrent upsetting dreams   No ____ Yes ____ 1 2 3 4 5
148. Flashback episodes   No ____ Yes ____ 1 2 3 4 5
149. Psychological distress to trauma cues   No ____ Yes ____ 1 2 3 4 5
150. Physiological distress to trauma cues   No ____ Yes ____ 1 2 3 4 5

At least three of the following avoidant symptoms:

151. Avoids thoughts, feelings, or talk associated
      with the trauma   No ____ Yes ____ 1 2 3 4 5
152. Avoids activities, places, or people associated
      with the trauma   No ____ Yes ____ 1 2 3 4 5

153. Amnesia to aspects of the trauma   No _____ Yes _____ 1 2 3 4 5
154. Decreased interest in activities   No _____ Yes _____ 1 2 3 4 5
155. Feeling estranged from others   No _____ Yes _____ 1 2 3 4 5
156. Restricted emotions   No _____ Yes _____ 1 2 3 4 5
157. Feeling of a foreshortened future   No _____ Yes _____ 1 2 3 4 5

At least two symptoms of increased arousal:

158. Difficulty sleeping   No _____ Yes _____ 1 2 3 4 5
159. Irritability or mood swings   No _____ Yes _____ 1 2 3 4 5
160. Difficulty concentrating   No _____ Yes _____ 1 2 3 4 5
161. Hypervigilance   No _____ Yes _____ 1 2 3 4 5
162. Exaggerative startle response   No _____ Yes _____ 1 2 3 4 5

Other symptoms since assault:

163. Increased perspiration   No _____ Yes _____ 1 2 3 4 5
164. Increased heart rate   No _____ Yes _____ 1 2 3 4 5
165. Changes in appetite   No _____ Yes _____ 1 2 3 4 5
166. Increased nervousness   No _____ Yes _____ 1 2 3 4 5
167. Body image disturbance   No _____ Yes _____ 1 2 3 4 5
168. Unusual body sensations   No _____ Yes _____ 1 2 3 4 5
169. Sexual dysfunction   No _____ Yes _____ 1 2 3 4 5
170. Blames self   No _____ Yes _____ 1 2 3 4 5
171. Low self-esteem   No _____ Yes _____ 1 2 3 4 5
172. Afraid to be alone   No _____ Yes _____ 1 2 3 4 5
173. Prior victimization   No _____ Yes _____ 1 2 3 4 5
174. Prior psychiatric history   No _____ Yes _____ 1 2 3 4 5

Multiaxial Evaluation Report Form (DSM-IV)

Axis I: Clinical Disorders _____
308.3   Acute Stress Disorder (symptoms less than 1 month)
309.81 PTSD Acute (symptoms less than 3 months)
309.81 PTSD Chronic (symptoms 3 months or more)
309.81 PTSD Delayed (symptoms begin after 6 months)
Other DSM-IV Diagnoses

Axis II: Personality Disorders _____
Mental Retardation _____

Axis III: General Medical Conditions

Axis IV: Psychosocial and Environmental Problems

__ Problems with primary support group _____
__ Problems related to social environment _____
__ Educational problems _____
__ Occupational problems _____
__ Housing problems _____
__ Economic problems _____
__ Problems with access to health care services _____
__ Problems related to legal system/crime _____
__ Other _____

Axis V: Global Assessment of Functioning Score _____ Time frame _____

GAF Scale

100–91	Superior functioning	50–41	Serious symptoms
90–81	Absent or minimal symptoms	40–31	Some impairment in reality or communication
80–71	Transient symptoms	30–21	Serious impairment
70–61	Some mild symptoms	20–11	Some danger of hurting self or others
60–51	Moderate symptoms	10–1	Persistent danger of hurting self or others

Sexual Abuse of Nursing Home Residents *

4

ANN WOLBERT BURGESS
ELIZABETH B. DOWDELL
ROBERT A. PRENTKY

Introduction

In October of 1976, the National Center for the Prevention and Control of Rape (National Institute of Mental Health) awarded a one-year grant to the Philadelphia Geriatric Center to prepare a report on the sexual assault of elderly women. In the resulting report, Davis and Brody (1979) observed that, "There was virtually no information about rape and older women, nor had specific programs been developed." What is more remarkable is that — after twenty years of progress identifying the precursors, the course, and the treatment of sexually aggressive and coercive behavior — nothing more is known today about the sexual abuse of the elderly than was known in 1979 (Crowell and Burgess, 1996). Indeed, the decade of the nineties catapulted sexual assault from relative obscurity to high profile in the legal and public health arenas (Goodman, Koss, Fitzgerald, Russo, and Keita, 1993; Koss, 1993; Prentky and Burgess, 2000). Despite the considerable attention given to the diversity and ubiquity of sexual assault, one of the most vulnerable groups of victims — the elderly — remains in obscurity. Although the reasons for our failure to tackle the problem of elder sexual abuse are unclear, we can certainly posit two explanations: (1) the incomprehensibility, and hence rejection, of claims of sexual assault of the elderly, and, perhaps most importantly, (2) ageism — generalized, negative attitudes, if not outright hostility — toward older people (Butler and Lewis, 1973; Davis and Brody, 1979).

All other vulnerable target populations for sexual assault — children, adolescents, the developmentally delayed, and patients with physical and/or mental impairments — have been the subject of varying degrees of clinical and empirical scrutiny. Like the elderly, when any of these populations reside in an institutional setting, the risk for abuse increases simply as a function of their dependence on staff for safety, protection, and care. Although there

* This chapter is reprinted with permission of Slack, Inc., from Burgess, A.W., Dowdell, E.B., and Prentky, R.A. (2000) Sexual abuse of nursing home residents, *J. Psychosocial Nursing*, 38, 10–18.

are no estimates of the incidence or prevalence of elderly abuse in residential care, The National Citizens' Coalition for Nursing Home Reform has confirmed that its agency receives an increasing number of reports of sexual abuse in nursing homes. Indeed, an increasing number of these cases is being litigated. It is clear from a forensic perspective that this is a serious problem. Sexual abuse of elderly women in residential care is analyzed through a series of forensic cases. This chapter focuses on victim impact and discusses key policy and primary prevention issues.

Method

Twenty cases were reviewed from the files of Dr. Burgess. Because several of the cases were criminally investigated and all were in the civil court system, each file had extensive information related to the nursing home experience of the resident/victim and the perpetrator. Files included admission interviews, nursing notes, physician orders and progress notes, social service notes, prior hospitalizations, nursing home policies, employee files, in-service records, reports of abuse to human service agencies, depositions of nursing home administrators and staff, defense expert reports specific to liability issues and damages, and police reports and criminal justice outcomes. Over half of the residents were interviewed by outside sources (police, therapist, or sexual assault examiner, with two interviews videotaped); and two residents were interviewed by Dr. Burgess.

The files were reviewed and data abstracted. Variables were coded directly from the file data. Coded variables fell into four discrete categories: (1) demographics (sex, race, age, and marital status); (2) victim (mental status, victim response, victim outcome); (3) perpetrator (patterns of abuse, offender characteristics); and (4) forensic (method of disclosure, forensic evidence, legal outcome). Given the size of our sample, inferential statistics were not utilized, and the data are reported in descriptive terms.

Results

Demographic Characteristics of Victims

Eighteen of the 20 sexually abused residents were Caucasian widowed females over the age of 70 years old — a profile that is consistent with nursing home populations in general. Sixteen of the residents were white, 3 were Hispanic, and 1 was black. Fourteen residents were widowed, 4 were single and never married, and 2 residents were married. Ages of the residents ranged from 16 to 94. Two residents were males over 70.

All residents were in a long-term nursing home facility and needed skilled nursing intervention. Although 5 residents were ambulatory, the other 15 residents were confined to beds or wheelchairs.

Mental Status

Although the majority of the residents suffered from a primary diagnosis of dementia or Alzheimer's disease (12), other cognitive and neurological disorders included cerebral vascular accident (3), brain trauma from gun shot wound (1) and motor vehicle accident (1), polynuclear palsy (1), amyotrophic lateral sclerosis (1), and major depression (1). Many had multiple physical diseases such as stroke, cataracts, hypertension, diabetes, and congestive heart failure.

Nursing notes also contained assessments on residents' cognitive status (indications that residents were oriented to name and place but not to time). Residents were described as confused, having long- and/or short-term memory problems, being forgetful, demented, or disoriented. It was not uncommon to read in a monthly nursing summary that a resident "communicates verbally but hard to determine if resident understands due to senile dementia." One resident communicated by blinking her eyes to yes-or-no questions.

Method of Disclosure

Because of their dependent status and cognitive limitations, residents did not have the ability to report abuse directly to law enforcement. Rather, the abuse had to come to someone else's attention or the resident had to bring it to someone's attention in order for the abuse to be noted. In the sample of 20, four major methods of disclosure were observed: (1) informing a family member — 7; (2) informing a staff person — 3; (3) abuse witnessed by staff or suspected by staff — 7; and (4) clues were detected by staff — 4. Some cases included multiple methods of disclosure.

Telling Staff or Family Member

Informing a family member either directly or in a fragmented fashion was the most common method of disclosure and noted in 7 cases. One 83-year-old widow with polynuclear palsy told her daughter that she had spilled some carrot salad and that a man came in to clean it and then came back and drew her curtains and raped her. Another woman, a 72-year-old celibate resident who was having trouble walking, told her sister that a male employee took her clothes off, threw her on the bed, and "put his man thing in my front and back." In a case of fragmented disclosure, a 78-year-old male resident told family members in segments that provided a cohesive story. He told of sex parties at night away from the nursing home, that the staff talked dirty, that a (male) nurse had hurt him, and that he and his wife were not married anymore. He also pulled down his pants to show bruises.

Since many of the victims were unable to clearly communicate the assault, observation of the resident became the critical factor. The son of an 89-year-old Alzheimer's resident said, "My mother was in extreme pain when I went to visit her. An examination revealed severe bruising around her pelvic area."

The fact that the majority of nursing home residents had difficulty communicating did not mean they were unable to verbalize their plight in some manner. One resident with ALS looked so sad and upset during a visit that her sister asked the resident's husband to see if he could find out what was wrong. She said nothing until, on the next visit, the woman, using her keyboard and eyeblink sign, spelled out that the respiratory therapist had abused her.

The nursing home resident may tell staff, but no action is taken until a family member is told as in the following case. An 83-year-old widow who had suffered a cerebral vascular accident told nursing staff in Spanish that, despite her request to do it herself, a male aide had insisted on washing her vaginal area in a rough manner, stating he knew what he was doing. Family, upon learning of the complaint, reported it to police. The resident told an investigating officer that this aide said frightening things to her, such as, "If you give me extra money like the other lady does, I'll take better care of you and make sure you don't get hurt during the night."

Witnessed

In 7 of the 20 cases, the abuse was observed by a staff person. In 2 of the 7 cases, a staff member witnessed another staff member in the act of sexually assaulting a resident. In a third case, staff became suspicious of a janitor taking an Alzheimer's patient away from a locked unit. In two cases of resident-to-resident assault, staff failed to make a timely intervention to stop the assault and failed to take the incident seriously.

In 3 cases, residents reported incidents in either a fragmented form or in a delayed manner, as in the following case. Within a month of a 72-year-old resident's admission to a nursing home, nursing notes detailed her fears of danger. A few days later, at 2:30 a.m., she informed staff that she was going to call the police. Eight days later she tearfully reported that a man came into her room, pulled the curtain, covered her mouth, rubbed her breasts, and hit her in the face. She repeated this to the nursing director, adding that when she said she would call the police, the man pulled out a knife and threatened to kill her. The administrator and doctor were notified. No bruises were noted, and a psychological consult was ordered.

Physical clues were noted and resulted in disclosure in 4 cases. A 33-year-old brain-injured resident's pregnancy was finally detected in her sixth month, even though the nursing records documented "months of chronic vomiting." Two residents, an 80-year-old widow with progressive dementia and a 16-year-old traumatic brain injury victim (who lived on the same unit), were diagnosed with venereal warts (HPV) within 6 months of each other. A fourth case involved an Alzheimer's patient who complained of pain and on whom serious pelvic bruising was subsequently noted.

Clues can confirm staff suspicion as in the case of a staff member who was observed taking a resident for a walk. When she returned she would not speak, displayed fatigue, was disoriented and barefoot, and her blouse was not buttoned correctly. Later that evening, discharge fluid was noted on her underwear, and she was taken for a rape examination.

Perpetrator Identification

Although the majority of the residents had serious cognitive deficits, only 3 perpetrators were unidentified. Some residents were able to give full descriptions. An 82-year-old resident with polynuclear palsy described the perpetrator's height and weight, and said that he had no chest hair, that he was balding and wearing a girdle (later identified as a support belt). A lineup of ten men was held at her bedside. She looked at each man; and at the sixth man she sat upright and said, "Why did you do this?"

Elderly patients may be confused about some details, and that can be used against them in court proceedings. One 72-year-old resident reported that a nursing aide assaulted her on three separate occasions. Only at the time of the third assault, however, was she able to identify him. The staff had initially disbelieved her and had referred her for a psychological consult. The consultant reported the sexual assault was a delusional story, involving some "over affection" and kissing with other residents. One month later the resident identified the nursing aide, who was then reported to the police and fired from the nursing home.

Physical and Forensic Evidence

The standard procedure in suspected sexual assault cases is to conduct a forensic rape examination. In the nursing home cases reported here, the examination often was difficult because of (1) the resistance of the resident to the pelvic exam ("legs drawn up and resists any movement of legs"); (2) not being able to visualize the pelvic area or complete the examination due to severe leg contractures ("legs contracted and would not open"); (3) difficulty in communicating and explaining the exam to demented and cognitively impaired residents ("needed daughter present to communicate with mother"); and (4) difficulty obtaining reliable and accurate victim report of the assault, injuries sustained, and regions of pain or discomfort ("when asked if she hurt anywhere or if anyone hurt her, she laughed and mumbled").

In ten cases, no examinations were conducted usually because of the delayed reporting, not believing the resident, or failing to follow protocol. Of the ten exams that were conducted, six revealed some type of positive evidence (intercourse, nondischarge); two had vaginal bleeding but no sperm were noted; and two revealed no physical or forensic evidence. The primary evidence relating to a sexual assault included presence of semen and bruising in the pelvic area. Secondary evidence included vaginal or purulent discharge, evidence of a sexually transmitted disease, or positive findings of blood.

In four cases redness and swelling were noted in the vaginal area. In four cases the force of the assault left serious bruising. Forensic examination of an 89-year-old widow revealed separation of the symphysis pubis bone, an inguinal hematoma, and swelling and bruising to the right labia. It was difficult to examine the resident because she resisted any movement of her legs. Her groin was severely bruised, and she had a purulent vaginal discharge. She remained in a fetal position, moaning in pain. She would not allow her blood pressure to be taken.

Rape exams were not completed on the two male residents. In one case, the doctor had heard rumors of abuse of the resident around the hospital but paid no attention because he did not think that the rumors were likely to be true. He had no training or experience in assessing sexual abuse of males. The second case was viewed as involving consenting sexual contact.

Resident Response

Trauma-related symptoms were noted in the residents, with the following responses:

- Expressions of fear of male staff (*she had fear in her eyes when a male approached*)
- Avoidant behavior with male staff (*she leaves the room when any male enters*)
- Withdrawn behavior (*she stopped doing many of her previous activities*)
- Staying near the nurse's station or lying in bed in a fetal position

The residents became increasingly anxious or agitated during perineal care or when bathed. Other responses included appetite changes and sleep problems, including inverted sleep patterns and hypersomnulence. Signs of hyperarousal were present in the form of agitation and anxiety. One resident, upon entering her room at night, would be startled and put her hands up to protect herself. Residents displayed clear evidence of anger and noncompliance, especially regarding medications.

Reenactment behaviors were observed. Days after being taken from the unit, an 83-year-old widow was heard to repeat a statement, "Hurry up, hurry up," known to be said by the assailant when he took her from the unit. At another time, while on a walk, this resident asked a nurse if they would be caught. Sexualized behaviors were also noted. A 95-year-old resident would hold her genital area, spread her legs and ask for her back or her "pussy" to be rubbed.

Physical signs of trauma (also noted in non-sexually abused nursing home residents) included bruising, skin tears, vaginal symptoms of bleeding, prolapsed uterus, and urinary tract infections. Over half of the residents made new complaints of feeling cold. Cue memories of the assault were common, especially when a resident was confronted with a male. In one case, a female police officer obtained considerably more information than a male police officer (a clear description of the offender and of the assault). Victimized residents were noted to be hysterical, screaming and crying when near male residents (a male walking into a bathroom). One resident talked of "that boy in the closet." Others showed fear when a male staff member talked with them.

The sister of a 72-year-old resident was outraged when she learned the administrator had not told her of her sister's two separate complaints of rape. She watched her sister deteriorate after the assaults. The sister began using a walker, developed burning on urination, exhibited anxiety, and was hospitalized for fever secondary to pneumonia. One month later she evidenced a diminished level of consciousness and alertness and was transferred to a hospital and diagnosed with urosepsis. Her condition continued to deteriorate after returning to the nursing home until she was no longer independent or ambulatory. She was taken into her sister's home. After moving in, she feared that the offender would come to the house; and she asked her sister to tell him that she lived elsewhere. Despite diagnoses of coronary arteriosclerosis, senile dementia, and mental retardation, the victim gave a consistent account of the rape.

A male resident whose assault was observed by staff refused to remove his clothes at night, instead wearing two and three layers of clothing. The resident persistently asked to go home, and on at least three occasions he escaped from the nursing home. Over time the resident became reclusive and verbally aggressive, telling family members not to visit. A 73-year-old man acted ashamed and embarrassed, cried at night, said it hurt between his legs, and that he wanted to talk to a judge. He resisted going with staff for his bath, jumped when someone came in the room, and showed rapid mental deterioration.

Patients with dementia generally have more intact past memories than of the more recent or current time period. In two cases the residents' moral upbringing, where sex was considered wrong under certain conditions, caused them to refer to the assaults as "bad." One man believed his marriage to be over. A widow talked of carrying a baby. One woman recited nursery rhymes of "snips and snails and puppy dog tails." Another resident talked of being caught or displeasing or disobeying her parents, suggesting that the trauma was accounted for at an earlier age. This resident also obsessed about drinking juices offered to her "because it will make you do something bad." It was as if she had been raped as a young girl and her current memory was interwoven into a different timeframe and age.

Family members described major clinical and behavioral changes in the residents ("She seemed to be in shock"). Protest behaviors were common. Nurses' notes documented numerous incidents of four residents who were found on the floor or lying under the bed in fetal positions. In one case, the doctor ordered that the resident's mattress be put on the floor. Residents began refusing medications, meals, having vital signs taken, or allowing the nurses to treat them. Several residents cried, moaned, asked to sit by the nurse's station, insisted on staying in a wheelchair, or asked to go home. Three residents (2 male and 1 female) developed symptoms of silent rape trauma because the assault was not acknowledged or suspected by staff. The symptoms were, however, recorded. A 71-year-old female resident was given a diagnosis of major depression with psychotherapy recommended. The recommendation was not implemented, however, because the psychologist said the resident was unable to communicate effectively.

New behaviors related to the trauma were also noted by family members. One resident would cross her legs at the ankle or knee so tightly that she was unable to walk, with the possible result of nerve damage. She sat and stared, neither watching television nor putting on makeup or costume jewelry as she had in the past. Crying spells occurred. She fatigued easily. Her speech deteriorated to mumbling, and she needed assistance with activities of daily living. She was unable to sleep well and feared the attacker would come back to kill her. She was unable to get the memory out of her mind as evidenced by her constantly looking out the window, fearing his return.

More than half of the victimized residents (11) died within one year of their assaults. Four of the residents moved into family members' homes, and five residents were transferred to different nursing home facilities.

Nursing Home Response

Nursing home staff had a range of responses to the sexual assault of their residents. Although for the most part staff minimized and ignored reports of sexual abuse, in one case an aide threatened to call the media if the abuse was not reported.

In the three cases in which a resident was the perpetrator, staff ignored the abuse, laughed about it, said it was consent, or blamed the victim in overt as well as subtle ways. In the case involving two male roommates, an aide witnessed one roommate holding his roommate against the wall with one hand under his neck and the other hand on his genitals. The victim was telling him to get away. The aide immediately attempted to find a nurse because the first roommate was known to be sexually aggressive. The victim appeared to be confused and nonconsenting; and the aide had been instructed that sexually inappropriate behaviors could not be documented unless a nurse witnessed them.

The first nurse she encountered responded that she was too busy and said to get the nurse who worked on that side of the unit. That nurse entered the room, informed the roommates that breakfast was ready, and shut the door to allow privacy. The sexual assault lasted over 30 minutes. Staff who witnessed the roommate assault subsequently observed the victim in bed, looking tired and pale. Within 30 minutes of the sexual assault, the facility attempted to transfer the male victim, a Medicaid patient, for a psychiatric evaluation. This transfer failed; and the physician transferred the agressor, a private pay patient, because the physician said that it had been known for three years that this man approached male residents for sex.

Some staff changed the nursing notes after learning of the sexual abuse charge. In one case, before the charge of abuse, the aggressor was described as pleasant, cooperative, and with good interaction. After the charge, nursing notes described him as a problem patient, that he was hard to care for because of his poor skin condition and his heavy size, and that he fantasized.

Discussion

In this study, 20 residents of nursing homes who had been sexually assaulted were examined. These residents were predominantly elderly victims who exhibited rape-related trauma symptoms, general symptoms of traumatic stress (fear, confusion, hypersomnia, lack of appetite, withdrawal), and exacerbation of symptoms related to their primary diagnoses. These preliminary findings suggest that the presence of a preexisting cognitive deficit, such as a dementia, markedly delays information processing and impairs communication in a highly vulnerable population, which potentially compounds the trauma of the sexual assault. From clinical and theoretical perspectives, there is every reason to believe that vulnerability due to physical frailty and emotional fragility places elderly victims at unusually high risk for severe traumatic reactions to assault. These victims simply are not equipped physically, constitutionally, or psychologically to defend against and cope with the proximal effects of assault. Perhaps the single most profound result of the sexual assaults against these elderly victims is that 11 of the 20 victims died within one year of the assault. Because more than half of these victims were aged 80 to 99 at the time of the assault, it cannot be asserted that the death was a distal effect of the assault. Although it is impossible to determine in each case whether the assault accelerated death, it is clearly noteworthy that more than half of the victims died not from the assault, but within months of the assault.

Rape trauma syndrome, which includes both acute and long-term symptom responses to traumatic sexual assault, has two distinct variations: compounded rape trauma and silent rape trauma (Burgess and Holmstrom, 1974). In compounded rape trauma, victims have a past and/or current history of psychiatric or psychosocial problems that compounds the effects of the sexual assault. In silent rape trauma, expression of assault-related symptomotology is muted, undetected, or absent. It was clear from a review of these 20 cases that the nursing home victims were subject to both compounded and silent rape trauma. Most of the victims had preexisting areas of weakness or vulnerability, primarily physical and cognitive, that served to complicate the assault symptom presentation. In addition, many of the victims suffered in silence, and the assault became known only after suspicious clues or evidence were noted by staff or family.

In a study of work-related rape, Brodsky (1976) reported that there is a difference in the initial reaction of the victim if the rape occurs while walking through a high-risk area where violence is expected or if the victim is attacked in what is considered home territory. Brodsky defined home and work settings as safe ground and emphasized that adults have stronger reactions when that safe ground is invaded.

In translating Brodsky's notion of territorial safety to the elderly, it easily may be argued that the nursing home is, for the resident, precisely that — a home — and that the staff functions as the residents' caregivers (in both a literal and figurative sense). The nursing home and its staff are perceived as safe, and violations represent a more profound betrayal of trust than violations committed outside the sanctity of the home.

Although this study represents a preliminary examination of what appears to be yet another area of hidden rape, the findings have obvious clinical, forensic, and policy implications. All nursing home personnel should be trained rigorously to identify signs and symptoms of assault-related trauma and to be alert to suspicious, preassault behaviors, including the same manipulation observed with most other sex offenders (Prentky and Burgess, 2000). In particular, staff must be trained to detect the emergence of symptoms, including noteworthy changes in baseline behavior in victims who are likely to exhibit symptoms in a muted or silent fashion.

A thorough physical, cognitive, and psychosocial assessment must be completed at the time of admission to the nursing home. These assessments are particularly critical because they provide nursing staff and other caregivers with a baseline from which to judge behavioral changes. The American Nurses Association standards (1991) mandate that nurses take action when a patient's condition deteriorates. A major area of litigation results from failure to assess and respond properly to untoward changes in the condition of a patient.

Perhaps the most disturbing observation made was the evident lack of sensitivity of nursing home staff to the gravity of the assaults on the residents. Responses ranged from cynical disbelief that anyone would sexually assault an elderly individual to what can be described as a perverse sense of amusement. There is a well-known pattern of bystander apathy and bystander inaction in response to crime (Shotland and Goodstein, 1984), and the same pattern appears evident in this case. However, one major difference is that these bystanders are not strangers who happen upon a victim in the street. These bystanders are professionals charged with the care and protection of the residents.

Although this study has obvious limitations, most notably a small forensic sample that may not be generalizable to nonforensic samples, the findings are disturbing. As more is learned about this new subgroup of rape victims, four critical prevention areas require focus:

- Screening procedures for hiring new staff
- Training regimens for staff
- New guidelines for conducting rape trauma examinations with elderly patients
- Recommendations for increasing the safety of the nursing home environment

In summary, this chapter reviewed some preliminary work on a new subgroup of rape victims who reside in nursing homes. Nursing home victims suffer both compounded and silent rape trauma. Innovative therapies are needed for treating elder rape victims. Policy recommendations were suggested.

References

American Nurses Association (1991) *Standards of Clinical Practice,* ANA, Washington, D.C.

Brodsky, C. (1976) Rape at work, in M.J. Walker and S.L. Brodsky, Eds., *Sexual Assault: The Victim and the Rapist,* 35–52, Lexington, MA, Heath.

Burgess, A.W. and Holmstrom, L.L. (1974) Rape trauma syndrome, *Am. J. Psychiatr.,* 131, 981–986.

Butler, R.N. and Lewis, M.I. (1973) *Aging and Mental Health: Positive Psychosocial Approaches,* St. Louis, Mosby.

Crowell, N.A. and Burgess, A.W. (1996) *Understanding Violence against Women,* Washington, D.C., National Academy Press.

Davis, L.J. and Brody, E.M. (1979) Rape and older women: a guide to prevention and protection. *U.S. Department of Health and Human Services Publication (ADM) 81-734,* Washington, D.C., U.S. Government Printing Office.

Goodman, L.A., Koss, M.P., Fitzgerald, L.E., Russo, N.F., and Keita, G.P. (1993) Male violence against women: current research and future directions, *Am. Psychologist,* 48, 1054–1058.

Koss, M.P. (1993) Rape: scope, impact, intervention, and public policy responses, *Am. Psychologist,* 48, 1062–1069.

Prentky, R.A. and Burgess, A.W. (2000) *Forensic Management of Sexual Offenders,* New York, Kluwer Academic/Plenum Publishers.

Shotland, R.S. and Goodstein, L.I. (1984) The role of bystanders in crime control, *J. Soc. Issues,* 40(1), 9–26.

Section II: Investigation

The Relevance of Fantasy in Serial Sexual Crime Investigations

5

ROBERT R. HAZELWOOD
JANET I. WARREN

Case No. 1

A 24-year-old housewife was kidnapped from her home and murdered. At the time of her death, she was four months pregnant. A search of her residence revealed that all of her panties and the bottom half of her bathing suit had been taken. Her badly decomposed body was discovered two days later. She died from paper towels being lodged in her throat. There were no other signs of physical trauma.

Four months later, a woman was abducted and raped. During the assault the offender forced her to model several sets of teddies. He forced her to ask him to make love to her and, prior to releasing her, he requested a date and obtained her phone number. Two days later he was observed leaving a Christmas tree on her porch. He was arrested and convicted for the abduction-murder as well as the abduction-rape.

A search of his home uncovered several hundred pieces of lingerie, over two thousand 3×5 cards containing information on women whose photographs and personal information appeared in soft pornographic magazines, a spiral notebook with cross-indexed information from the 3×5 cards, newspaper articles about women, lingerie catalogs, and the bottom half of the murder victim's bathing suit. His wife advised that the man utilized the materials for masturbatory acts. The subject manifested several paraphilias during this and other crimes. They included fetishism, voyeurism, exhibitionism, and telephone scatology.

Introduction

Sexuality represents one of the more complex aspects of human experience. It integrates the cognitive, emotional, sensual, and behavioral elements of the individual into a uniquely personal pattern of experience that derives from both internal fantasy and external behavior. While usually a private aspect of a person's life, it becomes relevant to law enforcement once the element of coercion or exploitation is introduced into it.

Theorists (Prentky, Knight, and Rosenberg, 1988) classify the underlying motivation for sexual assault into three main categories: aggression, sex, and power. These primary motivations are frequently expressed in complex sexual fantasies that often begin to develop shortly after puberty. Through a gradual process of enactment, they also become the template for many offenders' patterns of serial sexual offenses. They serve a complex organizing function in the behavior of the offender and frequently determine the choice of his verbal interactions with his victim, his preferred sexual acts, and his overall ritualistic patterns of behavior (see Chapter 6).

The criminal investigator and others involved in the identification, prosecution, and treatment of the offender can learn to make use of these fantasy-driven behaviors within a sexual offense. Through a detailed review of the verbal, sexual, and physical behavior of the offender, the underlying fantasy behavior can be deduced and the motivational themes formulated (see Chapter 8). This information can then be used to identify sexual assaults perpetrated by the same offender, determine future patterns of victim selection, and help to predict the scenario of future crimes.

The Human Sex Drive

There are three principal components of the human sexual drive: (1) the biological; (2) the physiological; and (3) the psychosexual. Humans share the biological component with other forms of mammalian life. It constitutes the natural or instinctual urge to engage in sexual activities with others. This instinctual component influences the basic orientation of the sexual impulse but has little influence on the individual form through which it is expressed. As such, it has limited relevance to sexual crime investigations.

The physiological component is activated when the body begins to respond to stimuli in a sexual manner. This response pattern may vary in intensity and be interrupted by a variety of sexual dysfunctions that are physiological in nature. Such information may provide rudimentary information about an offender in unique cases. The psychosexual element constitutes the most variable and individualistic aspect of the human sexual experience. It integrates the highly specific cognitive, sensory, and behavioral stimuli that are arousing to an individual and reflects his/her unique pattern of experience and development. This psychosexual aspect of the sexual experience, in its almost unending variability, provides the criminal investigator with the richest source of information about an offender and provides him with the flavor of the specific individual he is seeking.

Sex is a Sensory Act

All human beings employ their available senses to enhance their sexual arousal. A thorough review of the ways in which the various senses are manipulated in a sexual assault will ensure that a comprehensive assessment of the psychosexual component of the offender's sexual arousal pattern can be captured from the victim.

Sight has been identified as the primary component of the male's sexual response. As indicated in Case No. 1, the offender had his victim model lingerie that he had purchased as props for his fantasy. Without this visual stimuli, he tended to have difficulty becoming sexually aroused. Touch, another important sense related to sexual arousal, similarly manifested itself in the offender's fondling of his victim and in his autoerotic, masturbatory activities with several hundred pieces of lingerie. The offender's request that the victim verbalize a desire to make love to him reflects a use of auditory stimuli to enhance arousal, while his post-offense delivery of a Christmas tree behaviorally demonstrates the reciprocity that lay at the core of his sexual fantasy. These fantasy-derived behaviors were consistent across the sexual assault and murder perpetrated by this particular offender and, as indicated, were instrumental in the linking of the two offenses to him.

The Paraphilias

Paraphilia is a term used in mental health to describe what is more commonly called sexual deviation. "The paraphilias are characterized by recurrent, intense sexual urges, fantasies, or behaviors that involve unusual objects, activities, or situations." (DSM IV, 1994) Such fantasies evolve around (1) non-human objects; (2) suffering or humiliation of self or partner; or (3) children or other non-consenting partners.

Paraphilic behavior is fantasy driven and is commonly exhibited during sexual crimes. The sexual deviations recognized by the *Diagnostic and Statistical Manual of Mental Disorders*, 4th edition (DSM IV) include exhibitionism, fetishism, pedophilia, sexual masochism, sexual sadism, transvestic fetishism, and voyeurism. Abel, Becker, Cunningham-Rathner, Mittelman and Rouleau (1988) have documented that individuals tend to suffer from multiple paraphilias and that individuals identified as having one paraphilia generally suffer from one or more additional forms of sexual deviation. As indicated in Case No. 1, the offender demonstrated multiple paraphilias including exhibitionism, fetishism, and voyeurism. It is important for investigators to remain aware of this clustering of paraphilic behavior since it argues against one-dimensional descriptions of particular offenders (i.e., he's just an exhibitionist) and helps to avoid the premature exclusion of offenders from other types of unsolved sexual crimes.

Paraphilic patterns of behavior have been found to remain highly consistent over time. Research suggests that some types of paraphilic behavior can be altered through comprehensive treatment (exhibitionism, for example), while the more aggressive forms of sexual offending (sexual sadism) are unlikely to be changed regardless of the type and length of treatment offered. This stability is demonstrated repeatedly in cases involving the release of a sexual offender from prison who, within months of his release, perpetrates another paraphilic-motivated crime. In such cases it is assumed that the deviant sexual fantasy has been maintained through masturbatory reinforcement and motivates behavior as soon as external constraints are removed.

The dynamics of these sexual fantasies, their possible paraphilic underpinnings, and their behavioral enactments provide the criminal investigator and others with information that can be used to direct the investigation, prosecution, and treatment of a sexual offender. Contrary to popular belief, there are no obvious demographic characteristics that identify an individual as a sexual criminal. Indeed, the serial sexual criminal is most often found to be like the guy next door (Hazelwood and Warren, 1989). Understanding the role of motivationally driven fantasy and its interaction with the human sexual drive will provide the investigator better insight into the criminal sexual behavior with which he is confronted.

Fantasy in Sexual Crimes

It is important to note that for most individuals fantasy is sufficient to satisfy psychosexual desires and, regardless of its nature, there is no impulse to enact it in reality. For others fantasy is not satisfactory, and there appears to be a progressive desire to transform the fantasy into actual behavior. McCullough, Snowden, Wood, and Mills (1983) studied 16 sexually sadistic offenders and found that their core sexual fantasy made its appearance around the age of sixteen years; but it took a number of years to be encapsulated into the criminal behavior that led to their arrests. They found that, in the interval between the appearance and enactment of the fantasy, the offender engaged in gradual and partial re-enactments of the fantasy (i.e., buying rope, following a woman home) and used these behavioral tryouts as stimuli to enhance their masturbatory activity.

Case No. 2

A twenty-two-year-old man abducted, tortured, and raped a co-worker. He killed her by taping her nose and mouth and then watching as she slowly asphyxiated. Twenty-three months later, he abducted, tortured and raped a second woman, strangling her with his hands as he looked into her eyes.

This man had modified his vehicle and constructed a "torture platform" for use in his crimes. His criminal behavior demonstrated much more criminal sophistication than would be expected in such a young offender. Investigation determined that he had begun discussing his fantasy of capture, torture, rape and murder with others when he was only 14! From 14 until 22, he developed materials for the crimes, followed women, became familiar with the roads in his county, and modified his vehicles for criminal use.

Inanimate Objects

The use of non-living objects for sexual fantasy playacting is not uncommon. Such items are passive, non-threatening, and pose the least likelihood of criminal actions against an individual. In the experience of the authors, dolls, photographs and clothing are the most common inanimate materials utilized by sexual criminals in lending a sense of reality to their fantasies.

Dolls

The authors have seen numerous crimes in which female dolls are, in some way, involved. While such cases are frequently the subject of ridicule, it is to be remembered that such behavior is a reflection of the offender's motivationally driven fantasies. In cases observed by the authors, dolls have been subjected to burning, slashing, stabbing, binding, amputation, piercing, and a variety of other equally bizarre acts.

Case No. 3

A doll was found suspended outside a hospital operating room. Its arms had been removed, an opening had been cut between the doll's legs, and hair was glued around the orifice. A pencil protruded from the opening between the legs, and burn marks were evident over the entire surface of the doll. Sutures closed the eyes and mouth. It was determined that a medical intern was responsible for this aberrant behavior.

Photographs/Magazine Pictures

Another common means of acting out such fantasies is to alter photographs or pictures taken from pornographic and non-pornographic magazines. Such alterations include drawings (sexual bondage, mutilation, knives, guns, wounds, blood), cut and paste (replacement of faces or sexual parts), or the placement of "favorite" pictures in photo albums.

Case No. 4

A professionally employed individual died during dangerous autoerotic activities. A search of his office filing cabinets revealed over 100 bondage magazines. Without exception, each page had been altered by drawings or cut-and-pasting. He had taken such care that the alterations were all but imperceptible to the naked eye. The modification of such a large amount of material required an inordinate amount of time and effort and was significant in determining the importance he attached to such activity.

Clothing

Female clothing, particularly lingerie, is a favorite object for acting out a variety of fantasies. One of the most common activities is the slashing or removal of those portions of clothing which normally cover the sexual parts of the body. Such activities are typically classified as nuisance sexual offenses, and officers have repeatedly reported that teenagers are most frequently responsible for such acts. Age does not excuse such behavior, and recognizing that sexual behavior is predicated on fantasy should alert authorities to the need for expeditious identification and mental health intervention.

Consenting Partners

Prostitutes

Any experienced sexual crimes investigator can testify to the value of speaking with prostitutes when investigating a series of ritualistically violent crimes. Prostitutes earn money by being available to anyone for a variety of sexual behaviors. With prostitutes, men can act out their sexual fantasies without fear of rejection or ridicule.

Case No. 5

A professionally employed white male was convicted for the murder of a prostitute. He had bound her wrists behind her back and placed her in a bathtub of water, where he had intercourse with her. At the moment of ejaculation he held her head under the water, and she drowned. Investigation revealed that he had previously hired several other women for the same activity.

Girlfriends or Spouses as Partners

Stereotypically, it had been assumed that perpetrators of sexual crimes either did not have consensual sexual relationships or, if they did, that the more destructive aspects of their sexuality were kept divorced from it. Recent research, however, (Warren and Hazelwood, in press) has determined that many sexual offenders are, in fact, involved in ongoing sexual relationships and that they often act out their fantasies within this context.

Self-Composition

Some individuals choreograph their fantasies using themselves as both the subject and object of the behavior. One offender, who tortured and murdered a number of women, audiotaped in detail his descriptions of what he would do to his victims and what he would have them say and do to him. At the end of the tape, he verbalized in a falsetto voice the script he was planning to have his victims repeat to him. His remarks involved statements such as "bite my titties ..." and "fuck me in the ass," verbal behavior he subsequently forced each of his victims to repeat. Other, more dangerous autoerotic activities also often contain a ritualized enactment of fantasy.

Case No. 6

> A white male was found dead, hanging from a beam in the basement of his house. He was wearing his wife's sweater turned inside out, his wife's shorts turned inside out, and had placed her panties over his head and face. The belt from her bathrobe was wrapped tightly around his testicles. A video camera had been positioned in such a way as to record his activities. The videotape showed him accidentally dying from asphyxiation. A search of the area around the body turned up a number of sketches that portrayed sadomasochistic scenes — the hangings of a male and female — and the written script of a woman undergoing a military execution by hanging.

Investigation of autoerotic fatalities has frequently revealed transvestic behavior associated with ritualized hanging. The process of the man presenting himself dressed as a woman so as to elicit arousal from himself (he undoubtedly planned on later watching the video) seems to represent the inversion that lies at the core of this complex form of enactment.

Investigative Significance of Fantasy

Over the years the authors have consulted and conducted research on violent sexual crimes. They have also testified as expert witnesses in such crimes. This experience has led to a great appreciation for the value of understanding the significant role that fantasy plays in sexual crimes. The remainder of this chapter will focus on the practical investigative value such an understanding can provide.

Fantasy and Intelligence

Fantasy is essentially a play that is acted out in the mind of a person. This play requires a set, script, actors, a director and, in some cases, a recording device. Occasionally costumes and/or other props may be involved (see Case No. 6). This ability to fantasize is dependent upon the intelligence of the individual. Continuity of thought is needed when developing a fantasy involving multiple partners or a complex scenario, and continuity of thought requires a degree of intelligence. A person with less than average intelligence has a less complicated internal world and less ability to carry out complex criminal scenarios (see Chapter 6). Based upon this association, the investigator can assume that the more complex the crime, the more intelligent the offender.

Case No. 7

> A female realtor was found hanging by her neck in the attic of a recently built home valued at more than $200,000. She had been stabbed twice in the chest. Investigation determined that she had received a call from a man claiming to be a physician who was interested in purchasing an existing home that was located on 5 to 10 acres of land. He advised that he was relocating his family and practice to the area and was on a house-hunting trip. The realtor, thinking of a substantial fee, advised him that she would be happy to show the home. He told her that he had just arrived in town and was staying at an expensive hotel. He requested that she pick him up in front of the hotel. Investigation revealed that he had not checked into the hotel.

This offender was later arrested and was found to have committed a series of violent sexual crimes throughout the eastern U.S. An examination of the crime reveals a complex scenario designed to entice a selected victim to a remote location for torture and murder. Although his formal education was halted after one year of college, it became obvious that the perpetrator was well above average in intelligence.

Fantasy is Always Perfect

A person's sexual fantasies are always perfect. Every actor in the mental image plays his or her role to perfection. Reality, however, is never perfect and, for that reason, it never lives up to the sexual offender's expectations.

Case No. 8

> Police recovered an audiotape belonging to a professionally employed male who had died while on a business trip. On the tape, the man described the murder of a teenage couple. He recorded that he had killed the female and then dwelt, at some length, on the rape and murder of the male. He expressed disappointment over the fact that the young man's blood had saturated the bed clothes and mentioned that he should have placed a plastic sheet beneath the victim's body. He also expressed regret at having cut the

male's throat and opined that he should have stabbed the victim in the kidney so he would have lived longer.

The investigator requested one of the authors (Hazelwood) to listen to the tape and provide an opinion as to whether it was fact or fantasy. The opinion was that the tape was depicting an actual crime. As previously mentioned, fantasy is always perfect and, in this instance, the man was expressing disappointment and regret over things he had done or failed to do in reality.

It has long been recognized that certain sexual offenders record their sexual fantasies and/or their crimes. This is particularly true of the sexual sadist (Dietz, Hazelwood, and Warren, 1990) and the pedophile (Lanning, 1991). There are two widely accepted reasons for the offender doing so: (1) to enable him to relive the crime for masturbatory acts; and (2) to allow him to retain souvenirs or trophies of his crimes. The authors concur in both of these reasons but suggest a third motivation — to use the recordings of past crimes to more perfectly transform fantasy into reality. By recording the crime, the individual can critique his performance and that of his victim, thereby allowing him to correct those imperfections that are invariably present in reality.

Case No. 9

A sexually sadistic killer kidnapped a series of young women and, after photographing them during sexual acts, he murdered them. In one series of photographs recovered by the police, a young woman was kneeling on a bed while performing fellatio on the man. At his feet were several photographs of another victim seemingly performing the same act on the same bed while in the same position.

It was the impression of the authors that the offender was using the photographs to more carefully model his preferred fantasy material.

Fantasy Enactment with Wives and/or Girlfriends

Recent research (Warren and Hazelwood, in press) has focused on the wives and girlfriends of 20 sexual sadists. Through analysis of the sadists' recordings and exhaustive interviews with the former wives and girlfriends of these men, it was found that, without exception, they acted out their cruel and sadistic fantasies on the women.

Case No. 10

A sexually sadistic male, responsible for raping, torturing, and murdering ten women and young girls, would ritualistically abuse his wife in a physical, verbal, and sexual manner. He would beat her almost to unconsciousness; refer to her as a slut, whore, cunt, bitch; force her to verbally degrade herself; and force her to perform analingus, use oversized foreign objects to assault her anally, and force her to engage in sexual acts with others.

Investigators should ensure that efforts are made to locate these women and to interview them to determine whether there is a consistent pattern to the offender's criminal and consensual sexual behavior.

Fantasy and the Linking of Cases

Douglas and Munn (1990) describe the difference between the *modus operandi* and "signature" aspects of a sexual crime. Historically, law enforcement has utilized the *modus operandi* to link a series of crimes. The authors consider the *modus operandi* but rely principally on the unique combination of ritualistic behaviors to link a series of cases.

The *modus operandi* has three *primary* purposes: (1) to protect identity; (2) to ensure success; and (3) to facilitate escape. It has been the authors' experience that the *modus operandi* is only valid in sexual crimes for a period of three to four months before it begins to change or evolve. This change can result from the offender's experience gained through having committed a series of crimes, education obtained from incarceration, media coverage of similar crimes, publications or other public means of discussion, maturation of the offender, and his ability to adapt to a particular crime.

The ritualistic aspects of the crime, however, do not change. They are designed to meet the motivationally driven needs of the offender and, therefore, remain psychosexually arousing to him over time.

Case No. 11

An 18-year-old male was tried and convicted of the rape-murder of a 17-year-old female. She had been stabbed more than 30 times, her abdomen was slashed, and her throat had been cut. She was left in a ditch after having been vaginally, anally and orally raped. The man had previously been found guilty of exposing himself to college coeds and was known to have made over 100 obscene and threatening phone calls to two women when he was 15 years of age. During that series of calls, he threatened to cut the womens' throats, slash and stab them, and rape and anally assault them.

The link between the verbalization of the offender's violent sexual fantasies and the murder (by the phone calls three years earlier) was obvious. Unfortunately, the responsible social agency took no action on the phone calls when the then-15-year-old was referred to them. One of the women who had received the phone calls stated that she had personally advised the mother of the young boy that he was "going to rape and kill someone if something isn't done."

Fantasy and Search Warrants

In criminally acting out sexual fantasies, offenders often utilize materials (props) to create more psychosexually stimulating scenarios for themselves. By observing the physical, verbal, and sexual behavior acted out during a sexual crime, the investigator can determine the type of sexual fantasy being carried out. It is then a simple step to determine what type of materials, if any, the person would have accumulated to complement his fantasies. Upon identification of a person suspected or known to have committed the crime(s), the affidavit supporting any search warrant should list the materials that this type of assessment suggests. For example, in Case No. 1, the offender obviously had a fetish for teddies. It is quite reasonable, therefore, to suspect that he will have a collection of similar materials (lingerie) for his masturbatory fantasies.

Case No. 12

A young woman was kidnapped and kept in captivity for an extended period of time. She was physically, emotionally, and sexually tortured during her captivity. Her statement led the police to believe that they were dealing with a sexual sadist and, based upon research conducted by Dietz, Hazelwood, and Warren (1990), a search warrant was prepared. It listed bondage materials, recording devices, burning and pinching devices, violent pornography, and numerous other materials as items to be prioritized in the search. Items in each of these categories were recovered during the search.

A person's accumulation of materials and involvement with activities designed to enhance his sexual fantasies can contribute to a better understanding, by judge and jury, of the importance of such activities to the offender. Again, in Case No. 1, police investigation determined that the man had invested over $3,000 and inestimable time in collecting, cataloging, and preserving lingerie. In Case No. 4, the offender had recreated thousands of pictures in over 100 magazines to enhance his deviant fantasies.

Fantasy and Prosecutive Strategy

As noted previously, the authors have testified as expert witnesses in trials of sexual offenders. One of the principal functions of such testimony is to educate the jury not only about the offense but also about the role that fantasy and fantasy materials play in violent sexual crimes. It should be noted that it is often also necessary to educate the prosecution team in matters involving violent sexuality. They, like many investigators and the lay public, are often naive about the complexity of such crimes and the seeming normality of the offenders.

Case No. 13

> A 36-year-old woman disappeared after a date with her fiancee. Two years later, an ex-girlfriend advised that she had helped him bury the victim's body. The body was recovered, and the man was tried and acquitted. During the trial, the former girlfriend testified that he had brought the victim to the girlfriend's home, forced her to disrobe, and then raped her vaginally, anally and orally. He also used a dildo on the victim anally and bound her in a variety of positions using pre-cut lengths of rope. The former girlfriend testified that he had taken over 100 photographs during the crime. Over one year later, the federal government indicted him for three counts of lying about his role in the crime. Interviews of the former girlfriend and a former wife of the subject (15 years divorced) revealed that they had been subjected to similar activities by the man. Five days prior to the trial, the aforementioned photographs were located; and he pled guilty and was sentenced to 8 years in prison.

The obvious problem, had the federal case gone to trial, was having to prove that the man killed the victim. This would have been necessary in order to prove that he had perjured himself about his involvement in the crime. A prosecutive strategy, suggested by one of the authors and another FBI Agent, was to call the former wife and girlfriend to testify about the consistency of the man's sexual behavior over a fifteen-year period of time. In legal terms, this would be described as a pattern of continuing behavior. Had it been necessary, the testimony of the expert witness, the women, and others would have educated the jury about the man's long-standing fantasy involving degradation and punishment that was motivated by a deep-seated hatred of women. Similar education and testimony were necessary in other cases set forth in this chapter.

Summary

The individual involved in the investigation of sexual crimes should learn the importance of the role of fantasy. Fantasy is the link between the underlying motivations for sexual assaults and the behaviors exhibited during the crimes. Such an understanding can help to determine linkages between offenses perpetrated by a serial offender, identify materials to be sought through search warrants, and provide informed prosecutorial strategies.

References

Abel, G., Becker, J., Cunningham-Rathner, J., Mittleman, M., and Rouleau, J. (1988) Multiple paraphilic diagnoses among sex offenders, *Bull. Am. Acad. Psychiatr. Law,* Vol. 16, 153–168.

American Psychiatric Association (1994) *Diagnostic and Statistical Manual of Mental Disorders,* 4th ed., Washington, D.C., American Psychiatric Association.

Dietz, P., Hazelwood, R., and Warren, J. (1990) The sexually sadistic criminal and his offenses, *Bull. Am. Acad. Psychiatr. Law,* Vol. 18, 163–178.

Douglas, J. and Munn, C. (1990) Violent crime scene analysis: *modus operandi,* signature and staging, *FBI Law Enforcement Bull.,* Vol. 61, 1–10.

Hazelwood, R., Reboussin, R., and Warren, J. (1989) Serial rape: correlates of increased aggression and the relationship of offender pleasure to victim resistance, *J. Interpersonal Violence,* Vol. 4, 65–78.

Hazelwood, R. and Warren, J. (1989) The serial rapist: his characteristics and victims, I. *FBI Law Enforcement Bull.,* January, 11–17, 19–25.

Lanning, K.V. (1991) Child molesters, a typology for law enforcement, *Criminal and Sexual Deviance,* U.S. Department of Justice, Washington, D.C.

MacCullough, M., Snowden, P., Wood, J., and Mills, H. (1983) Sadistic fantasy, sadistic behavior and offending, *Br. J. Psychiatr.,* Vol. 143, 20–29.

Prentky, R., Knight, R., and Rosenberg, R. (1988) Validation analysis on a taxonomic system for rapists: disconfirmation and reconceptualization, in R. Prentky and V. Quinsey, Eds., *Human Sexual Aggression: Current Perspectives,* 21–40, New York, New York Academy of Sciences Annals.

Warren, J. and Hazelwood, R. (In press) Relational patterns associated with sexual sadism: a study of 20 wives and girlfriends, *J. Fam. Violence.*

The Sexually Violent Offender: Impulsive or Ritualistic?*

6

ROBERT R. HAZELWOOD
JANET I. WARREN

Introduction

Sexual violence is a complex area of human behavior and experience. It incorporates human sexuality (an already complicated and largely misunderstood area), mental disorders, and criminality. To further complicate the issue, the world of sexual violence has an ever-evolving continuum of offenses and offenders.

When one begins to investigate criminal sexuality from a legal or academic perspective (or simply out of curiosity), the diversity and variation of the phenomena rapidly become apparent. One only has to consider a few of the behaviorial dimensions of sexual crimes to appreciate the complexity and fluidity of the topic:

- Sexual crimes may or may not be physically violent.
- Sexual crimes may be committed against persons, inanimate objects, or animals.
- Some sexual offenders primarily commit sexual crimes, while other offenders commit sexual crimes as part of a much broader repertoire of crime.
- Sexual offenders may prefer to act out against children, the elderly, or age mates. There are some sexual offenders for whom age is not an issue.
- Offenders may commit exclusively homosexual crimes or commit exclusively heterosexual crimes. For other offenders, gender has no apparent effect on victim selection.
- There are offenders for whom paraphilic behavior is mandatory for psychosexual pleasure and hence an integral part of their criminal behavior, others for whom it is intermittently central to their sexual

* Reprinted with permission of *Aggression and Violent Behavior,* Vol. 5, No. 3, pp. 267–279, 2000.

arousal pattern, and others for whom the paraphilic disorders apparently play little or no role.
- There are offenders who experience remorse and guilt from the commission of their crimes, and others who are unable to experience remorse or guilt.
- There are ritualistic offenders who develop complex fantasies and act them out, and there are offenders who act out impulsively with little or no thought beyond immediate gratification.

In an effort to organize these complex elements, the authors postulate a fairly simple and straightforward typology. Hopefully this will assist in identifying and organizing many parameters of an offender's criminal behavior — including his victim selection patterns, pre-offense behavior, most likely pattern of criminal behavior, his crime scene behavior, and the motivation underlying his particular sexual offense. This typological formulation may assist law enforcement in its investigations of sexual crimes while also alerting the forensic evaluator or treatment provider to the type of offender or criminal behaviors they are encountering. This type of distinction might also help to conceptualize factors for risk assessment as well as for the types and degrees of recidivism.

Similar types of paradigms have been developed by federal law enforcement in the context of its work on violent crime — processes currently referred to as *criminal investigative analysis* (CIA) and, more traditionally, as criminal profiling. In 1980, Hazelwood and Douglas published a paradigm that differentiated between the disorganized, asocial lust murderer and the organized, nonsocial lust murderer. While both types of offenders are intent upon the perpetration of sexually motivated murders, the former are described as introverted, isolated individuals who do not possess the social qualities necessary to negotiate most types of interpersonal relationships and tend to offend in a frenzied, disorganized fashion, often in an area near their homes. In contrast, the more organized lust murderers are capable of manipulating others and tend to travel further, cruising in search of a victim. These two types of sexual murderers can be distinguished based upon various aspects of their crime scene behavior including the location of the body, the evidence of torture and mutilation prior to death, smearing of blood at the crime scene, sexual penetration of the body, and the availability and extent of physical evidence at the crime scene. This paradigm, while simple in its distinction, has been used extensively in the criminal investigative analysis of many sexually motivated murders and has, for the past 20 years, been recognized by law enforcement nationally and internationally as pertinent to both the investigation and analysis of the majority of unsolved sexual murders.

Highlighting a different type of sexual violence, Lanning (1992) identified two main types of offenders against children — the situational and preferential child molesters. Building upon a distinction identified earlier by Dietz (1983), Lanning outlines in some detail the motivational impulses, victim selection criteria, methods of operation, and related sexual activities that characterize the situational offenders who prey on children without a true sexual preference for them. Lanning delineates four subtypes within this broader category — regressed, morally indiscriminate, sexually indiscriminate, and inadequate child molesters. Lanning distinguishes the situational child molesters from the preferential child molesters, who are characterized by a pervasive erotic interest in children and who engage in highly predictable behavior designed to ensure continued sexual access to victims of the desired age. Using the same dimensional criteria, Lanning differentiates between the seductive, introverted, and sadistic types of preferential child molesters and ascribes to each distinct but motivationally consistent behavioral patterns that characterize their erotic preferences and activities. This paradigm, which was initially developed for law enforcement in its investigation of sexual crimes against children, has now gained general acceptance among mental health professionals and is frequently used in evaluation of sex offenders for pretrial, pre-sentencing and pre-release decision making.

Complementing these law enforcement paradigms is the development of rapist and child molester typologies by clinical researchers. Two of the most widely recognized paradigms — the rape typology developed by Prentky, Knight and Rosenburg (1988) and the child molester typology developed by Knight, Carter and Prentky (1989) — are multidimensional constructs that derive from the empirical analysis of the development and criminal antecedents of different types of offenders as defined by general life (social competence) and crime-specific behavior (type of aggression). Recent attempts to assess the likelihood of recidivistic behavior for rapists and child molesters have begun to encompass these dimensional distinctions with the emerging research suggesting that these paradigmatic distinctions are relevant not only to typing offenders and offense behaviors but also estimating future criminal behaviors.

Recently, the gulf between law enforcement taxonomies and clinical/treatment paradigms has begun to narrow by collaborative effort across the two disciplines. The Behavioral Science Unit of the Federal Bureau of Investigation (FBI) and the Massachusetts Treatment Center (MTC) attempted to determine whether the crime scene indices used by law enforcement could be used to make the paradigmatic distinctions contained within the empirically derived MTC:3 typology (Knight, Warren, Reboussin and Soley, 1998). The encouraging results of this preliminary research have given rise to a growing academic interest in empirically exploring the crime scene behavior of these paradigmatically determined categories of offenders. It is anticipated that this type of cross-discipline work will serve to embellish the empirical underpinning of the work that is conducted in the context of CIA while simultaneously contributing to the applied and investigative significance of these empirically derived paradigms.

The Impulsive Sex Offender

The impulsive offender is a common type of sexual offender who is generally the least successful at evading identification and apprehension. As implied by the title, he invests little or no time in planning his crimes. Instead, he acts impulsively, takes few measures to protect his identity, and is seemingly oblivious to the risks involved in committing crime. Both informal and systematic assessment of his *modus operandi* (behavior used to obtain a victim, perpetrate the crime and avoid identification and apprehension) suggests a criminally unsophisticated, reactive offender.

Case No. 1

> At approximately 3 p.m. on a Saturday afternoon, a 37-year-old woman was loading groceries into her car from a shopping cart. Several other cars were in the lot. A 24-year-old male was passing through the lot on the way to his home when he observed the woman. He walked to her location, pushed the cart away from the car, struck the victim in the face with his fist, and threw her into the rear seat. He then ripped her clothes from the lower part of her body and vaginally raped her. Knocking her unconscious, he left the victim in the rear seat of her car and casually walked from the scene. He fled to Canada but was extradited and sent to prison for 18 rapes.

Motivation

Empirically derived motivation schemes of rapists highlight four primary types of rape behavior — opportunistic, pervasively angry, sexual (sadistic and non-sadistic), and vindictive (Knight and Prentky, 1987). The opportunistic and pervasively angry offenders tend to demonstrate or report little sexual fantasy. Rather, there is either an unplanned and situationally determined opportunity, or there is a predominantly motivating diffuse pattern of anger.

Laboratory research by Barbaree and Marshall (1991) delineates six etiological models of rape. Three of these — the response compatibility, disinhibition, and augmentation models — appear relevant to this kind of offending. The response compatibility model suggests that the rapist is able to experience hostile aggression and sexual arousal simultaneously in a manner that does not occur in non-aggressive men. The disinhibition and augmentation models suggest that various factors such as anger toward women or blame toward the victim can serve as either disinhibiting or augmenting forces to the sexual arousal that can occur during sexually assaultive acts.

Fantasy

In Chapter 5, Hazelwood and Warren have identified the investigative significance of exploring the sexual fantasies underlying various types of sexual assaults. The impulsive offenders, however, seem to be largely unmotivated or at least unaware of sexual fantasies underlying their desires to rape. From the authors' experience in speaking with such men and consulting on crimes committed by these types of sexual offenders, it has become clear that their fantasies are simplistic and concrete. They include only two defining dimensions — victim characteristics/demographics and self-perception.

The demographic dimension contains little specificity and, as summarized by such offenders themselves, involves, quite simply, women. It does not appear that any particular type of woman is being sought by these types of offenders. While some of the concreteness or non-specificity of this type of preference can be attributed to either the intelligence level or youth of some impulsive offenders, the more fundamental factor seems to lie in the undifferentiated anger toward women that apparently underlies a significant proportion of this type of assaultive behavior.

Personality Style

This type of offender tends to be motivated by a sense of entitlement and the perception that anything in his environment is there for the taking. He is restrained only by circumstances in the environment that are related to his own safety. Recent research by Brown and Forth (1997) indicates that this type of opportunistic offender is often characterized by a psychopathic character style as measured by *Hare's Psychopathy Checklist (Revised)* (Hare, 1991).

Collections/Pornography

This type of offender may possess pornography, but he will lack a theme (such as bondage); and typically he will not have a collection. This type of offender uses pornography reflectively. He does not have pre-existing fantasies into which he incorporates pornography, but rather he builds fantasies around what he sees.

Pre-Offense Acting Out

This type of offender will act out most often against his spouse and an occasional prostitute since these women are most easily accessible to him.

However, because his crimes are primarily motivationally driven and not fantasy based, physical cruelty (not to be confused with sexual sadism) and the abuse of alcohol are frequently involved. Consequently, the man's consenting victim is often treated as a battered spouse; and little or no consideration is given to the sexual aspects of his cruelty. When stranger victims are targeted, they are often encountered in the context of other crimes, such as burglary, or in generic environments likely to encompass a number of potential victims (a university campus or hospital parking lot). There is no indication that a particular victim has been pre-selected through stalking or peeping activities. Further, the approach behavior of the rapist involves no complex ruses or attempts at deceptive disguises.

Criminal Behavior

The core behavior of a sexual crime includes verbal (what the rapist says to the victim or demands the victim verbalize to him), physical (injurious force), and sexual (type and sequence of sexual acts) types of behaviors (see Chapter 8, Analyzing Rape).

Because fantasy plays such a minimal role in the impulsive offender's crimes, one can expect to find that his criminal behavior is designed to accomplish two things — to obtain and to control his victim. This is because he lacks the criminal skills to control a person without resorting to violence. Consequently, this man engages in little (but profane) verbalization with his victim. His verbal activity is limited to phrases such as "shut up," "take off your clothes," and "get over here."

He frequently resorts to physical violence to control his victim as well as to act out the underlying motivation of anger. Consequently, the level of force he uses is often excessive or brutal (Hazelwood, 1983).

His sexual behavior is violent and degrading and results in medically documented injuries to the sexual areas. It should be noted that the authors have found little evidence to suggest the involvement of paraphilic behaviors (bondage, voyeurism, sadism, etc.) with this type of offender. Such behaviors are classically found to play great roles in the crimes of men who commit fantasy-driven crimes.

Past Criminal Behavior

This offender's arrest history is truly diverse and generally antisocial. To him, sexual assault is simply another crime and deserving of no special attention. Therefore, depending on his age, his history usually reflects multiple offenses with no specific theme to the crimes (auto theft, DUI, armed robbery, assault and battery, rape, possession of illicit drugs, and drunk and disorderly conduct).

Travel and Search Patterns

Research on the travel patterns manifested by serial rapists in locating their victims and perpetrating their offenses (Warren, Reboussin, Hazelwood, Cummings, Gibbs, and Trumbetta, 1998) has shown that offenders who demonstrate no ritualistic behavior as a component of their crime scene behaviors tend to travel shorter distances to offend (2.30 miles vs. 3.64 miles) and to generally rape over a smaller area (4.57 miles vs. 20.39 miles). These types of search patterns possibly reflect less specific victim selection criteria and/or less sophisticated attempts to ensure that they are not recognized and identified.

The Ritualistic Offender

The ritualistic offender is less common than the impulsive offender, but he is the most successful and most difficult to identify and apprehend. He is the offender who invests a great amount of time and effort in the planning and rehearsal of his offenses. He is typically a criminally sophisticated offender.

Motivation

Like the impulsive offender, the underlying motivation for the sexual assault is power, anger, or a combination of the two. However, it appears (using the models delineated by Barbaree and Marshall, 1991) that the ritualistic offender, in contrast to the opportunistic offender, experiences a cue response to the control and aggression contained within the rape and finds that these kinds of perceptions actually contribute to his level of sexual arousal. This type of response style reflects more of a paraphilic interest in coercive sexuality.

Personality Style

The personality style of this type of offender is more varied and is less generically exploitive. Some ritualistic offenders are withdrawn and awkward in their social interactions; others are charming and gregarious, while still others maintain lifestyles that appear conventional and rather ordinary. In some of the most extreme cases of sadistic violence, the individuals were respected members of the community with their varied, perverse sexuality remaining largely hidden from those around them.

Fantasy

Unlike the impulsive sexual criminal, the ritualistic offender invests a great amount of time in the pursuit of his fantasies. In a separate study, the authors interviewed 20 women who were married to sexual sadists or dated them exclusively. Such men were overwhelmingly ritualistic in their offending behavior; and, without exception, the former wives and girlfriends reported that these men invested a large amount of time in the pursuit of fantasy. One woman, married to such a man for eight years, reported that most of her married life was devoted to intricate games in which there were five distinct and repetitive phases — pursuit, capture, torture, the kill, and finally rape.

The fantasies of such men are multidimensional and complex. The authors have identified five common components or dimensions in the ritualistic offender's fantasy life that can be identified from a study of his criminal behavior — relational, paraphilic, demographic, situational, and self-perceptional.

Relational

Perhaps the most important dimension in the ritualistic offender's fantasy is the relationship he perceives between his partner (victim) and himself. This component evidences the underlying motivation in a most telling manner. In this regard, it is important to emphasize that there is a continuum of ritualistic sexual criminals and that the form of their overt offense behaviors can vary extensively.

The analogy of a major league baseball team can be used in explaining these distinctions. A baseball team has nine positions, each requiring different skills and having different objectives. However, each of the individuals playing the various positions is nonetheless a major league baseball player. So, too, are there many different categories of ritualistic offenders (pedophile, sexual sadist, power rapist, fetish thief). In no other dimension of the fantasy does this distinction become more apparent than in the relational component.

Case No. 2

The operator of an 18-wheel truck, a 42-year-old male, offered a ride to two teenage runaways, an 18-year-old male and his 14-year-old female companion. Shortly thereafter, he murdered the male. For the next six days, the young girl was tortured, raped, costumed, and photographed by the truck driver. Her pubic region was shaved, her hair was cropped short, a steel ring perforated her clitoris, and various areas of her body were pierced with pins. At least three rolls of film were used to take pictures of the victim bound, helpless and in various stages of dress. Almost without exception, the photographs depicted the victim bound in a variety of positions with silver-colored chain. She was also photographed while costumed in hose, high heels, an evening dress, red lipstick, and red fingernail polish. The victim was eventually strangled with bailing wire and left in the loft of a barn. Following the murder, the perpetrator called the victim's grandmother and said, "Wendy's in a barn with her hair cut off." He was later arrested with another victim in his truck. A search of his apartment revealed the victim's clothing, her spiral notebook containing her grandmother's phone number, three rolls of film, detective magazines, and several lengths of silver-colored chain.

Case No. 3

A 26-year-old woman was sleeping in her apartment when she was awakened by a 28-year-old male wearing a ski mask. He held a knife to her throat and told her that he didn't want to hurt her and that, if she cooperated, he believed that she would enjoy the time spent together. He had her disrobe and spent time visually examining her entire body. He then advised her that he felt she was tense, indicating that he would try to help her relax. From a bag he brought with him, he took a bottle of lotion and applied it to her body, massaging her as he did so. He then performed cunnilingus on the victim, kissed and fondled her, and told her that she was beautiful. The victim twice kicked him in the testicles, in response to which he asked "Why did you do that? I haven't hurt you." He vaginally raped the victim and left, taking the victim's driver's license with him. He is known to have raped six women in a strikingly similar manner. A search of his residence revealed a small video camera containing film which he had taken while peeping on women, his rape kit containing condoms, body lotion, several knives, gloves, and ski masks, several soft pornographic magazines and videotapes, and a collection of lingerie.

In both of these cases, it is clear that the assailants were ritualistic and had incorporated a relational aspect of their fantasy into the crime. In Case No. 2, the offender was angry and contemptuous of the victim and had no empathy for her plight. She had been objectified by the man, and he viewed her as his slave — and himself as the victim's master. Consequently, the relationship between the victim and her captor, as he perceived it, was master-slave.

In Case No. 3, the offender was also ritualistic and his crimes were fantasy driven. However, the assailant demonstrates no anger; and his relational fantasy is one of boyfriend-girlfriend, husband-wife — that of a consensual relationship.

Paraphilic

Almost without exception, when a ritualistic offender is involved in a sexual crime, paraphilic behavior is evidenced. Abel, Becker, Cunningham-Ratner, Mittleman, and Rouleau (1988) demonstrated that a person who suffers from one paraphilic disorder generally suffers from additional paraphilic disorders that characterize various aspects of his sexual repertoire. The authors have found this to be especially true when observing crimes committed by the ritualistic offender. In Case No. 2, the offender evidenced sexual sadism, voyeurism (photographs), sexual bondage, and fetishism (chains). In Case No. 3, the offender demonstrated voyeuristic and fetishistic interests and activities.

This type of behavior is significant in that the presence of demonstrated paraphilic behavior provides the investigator with insight into what type of behaviors the offender engages in with consenting partners and also what type of collections he likely possesses to complement the paraphilias (see Chapter 5, Relevance of Fantasy).

Demographic

The ritualistic offender invests a great deal of time in fantasy and, consequently, there is a great deal of demographic specificity in his choice of victims. Leonard Lake, a ritualistic serial killer, made a pre-offense videotape in which he elaborated on his plans and rationalizations for the extensive patterns of abductions and murders that he subsequently perpetrated. In one segment of that videotape, he set forth the preferred characteristics of potential victims as being "18 to 22, petite, small-breasted, shoulder-length hair." One of the women interviewed by the authors who had been married to another sexual sadist for 8 years reported that her husband told her that the perfect victim had shoulder-length blond hair, was thin, 18 to 22 years old and a hitchhiker, runaway, or prostitute.

Situational

This type of offender attempts to recreate a situation from his fantasies. Again, the situation is largely dependent upon the motivation for the crime. In Case No. 2, it became clear that the offense was anger motivated, the relational component was master-slave, and the victim was kept in captivity for six days — hence, captivity defined the situational aspect of the fantasized encounter. This is not an uncommon fantasy for sexual sadists and, indeed, books have been written about the captivity and enslavement of women including *The Collector* by Fowles in 1963 and *Kiss the Girls* by James Patterson in 1995. Both books were made into movies, and the latter was the number one box office hit within two weeks of release. McGuire and Norton (1989) described how Cameron Hooker and Leonard Lake constructed holding facilities to keep their sex slaves contained in the way that they preferred.

In stark contrast to the situational dimension of Case No. 2, the offender in Case No. 3 had a nonviolent fantasy situation which he was attempting to bring to reality — that of a consensual, romantic encounter.

Self-Perceptional

Intrinsic to these fantasy structures is the offender's perception of himself as experienced within this particular erotic context. This experience of himself could contribute to the immense intrapsychic sway that these repetitious sexual fantasies and eventual re-enactments exert upon his behavior. In this regard, it is important to emphasize that what is being sought in analyzing this material is the offender's self-perception as it is being acted out in the crime — not as he might describe or experience himself in everyday life.

James Mitchell DeBardeleben, an extremely well-documented and highly ritualistic criminal sexual sadist (Michaud, 1994) illustrated one extreme of fantasized self-perception when he wrote his definition of sexual sadism (Dietz, Hazelwood, and Warren, 1990):

> "*Sadism*: The wish to inflict pain on others is not the essence of sadism. One essential impulse: *to have complete mastery over another person*, to make him or her a helpless object of our will, to become her God, to do with her as one pleases. To humiliate her, to enslave her *are means to this end*, and the most important radical aim is to *make her suffer since there is no greater power* over another person than that of inflicting *pain on her* to force her to undergo suffering without her being able to defend herself. The pleasure in the complete domination over another person is the very essence of the sadistic drive."

When DeBardeleben wrote "… to have complete mastery over another person … to become her God …," he provided the reader with a concrete expression of the narcissistically embellished self-perception that is the core of his erotic pleasure as well as his destructive and sadistic criminal behavior.

Case No. 4

> A man who had raped in excess of 20 women was interviewed by one of the authors. In each of his crimes, he took his victim to a waterside environment and scripted her as to what she was to say over the period of time that she was with him. She was instructed to periodically ask a question from a list of questions such as, *Are we going to the cabin this summer? Do we have enough money to get the kid's teeth fixed? What is your bowling average this year? When are you going to call the repairman to fix the washing machine?*

Clearly, the fantasized self-perception of the offender in Case No. 4 is one of husband, provider, and lover, which certainly contrasts with the self-perception of DeBardeleben in a dramatic fashion.

Pre-Offense Acting Out

Prior to attacking strangers, the ritualistic offender invariably acts out his sexual fantasies with inanimate objects, paid partners, and/or consensual partners. Inanimate objects have no risk associated with them, while paid and consensual partners are viewed as convenient and available adjuncts to the fantasized behavior.

The three inanimate objects most commonly used for acting out fantasies are dolls, clothing, and pictures (see Chapter 5, Relevance of Fantasy).

Case No. 5

A mental health institute notified the police that a doll had been left in the front of its administration building. The police discovered that the doll's wrists and ankles were bound with wire, and a gag had been placed in the mouth. There was plastic tubing inserted into the doll. During the next few weeks, several more dolls were left at the institution, and each depicted more severe disfigurement; i.e., area between the legs burned, in excess of 50 cuts symmetrically located on the doll, abdominal incisions with surgical sutures in place, fingernail polish to depict blood, and more than 100 toothpicks inserted into the entire circumference of the doll's body.

Case No. 6

A 36-year-old woman notified the police that she had been receiving ripped, cut, and torn brassieres in the mail. These brassieres had seminal fluids and printing on them. The words conveyed threats ("I will have you, bitch!" and "Your nipples belong to me.") She had also been sent story pages from detective magazines (Dietz, Harry, and Hazelwood, 1986) and a letter the offender had written, explaining how he had prepared the location and equipment to capture, torture, and photograph the woman.

Case No. 7

A woman who was interviewed as part of another study (Hazelwood, Warren, and Dietz, 1993) reported that her sexually sadistic husband had an extensive pornography collection that depicted captivity, bondage, and torture of women. She reported that he would spend hours with his collection, drawing explicit wounds on the pictures and rearranging the anatomies of the depicted women by cutting out breasts, hands, heads, and legs from pictures and carefully pasting them over the pictures of other women.

Criminal investigators, when confronted with a sexual crime which is unique in verbal, physical, or sexual acts, often conduct interviews with prostitutes to determine if any of their customers have requested these unique sexual behaviors.

Case No. 8

James DeBardeleben tape recorded his sexual acts with consensual partners, with prostitutes, and with his stranger victims. The authors have heard one recording in which one of his paid partners is heard to say, "F**k me in the ass, Daddy." The recordings of activities with his wife and with one of his victims contain the same specific phrases.

Sexual sadists, a highly ritualized group of offenders, act out their sexual fantasies with wives or girlfriends. (Warren and Hazelwood, in press). The women serve as props for the rehearsal of sexual crimes. As seen in Case No. 8, the similarities between the activities with a prostitute and a victim are strikingly similar. The following case is another example of a wife abused in a similar manner.

Case No. 9

"Michelle," a woman married to a sexual sadist for more than 5 years, advised the authors that most of her married life was devoted to her husband's aberrant fantasies. She advised that he had a death fantasy in which he would have her walk in the dirt barefooted so that it would appear she had been running. After she came back into the house, he would capture her by choking her into unconsciousness. She would then be physically tortured, "murdered" by frontal strangulation, and raped "post-mortem." She reported that he had particular clothes for her to wear during the fantasy re-enactment, and he also had a suitcase containing his crime materials. When asked how long the subject would spend in preparation for the game, she replied, "[s]ome days, we would spend an entire day getting ready. He would tell me what I was supposed to say, how I was supposed to act, what he was going to do. Then he would say 'Okay, now you tell me what's going to happen.'"

Within the past decade, it has become apparent that violent ritualistic offenders sometimes use themselves as props for enactment of their fantasies. For example, it has long been assumed that anyone engaging in dangerous auto-eroticism (Hazelwood, Dietz, and Burgess, 1983) was masochistically oriented. However, the offender described in Case No. 8 also audiotaped himself speaking in a falsetto voice and verbalizing phrases identical to those he forced his stranger victims to speak. Another serial murderer who hung his victims photographed himself cross-dressed and suspended from a tree.

Criminal Behavior

Like the impulsive offender, the core behavior of the ritualistic offender's criminal sexual behavior is verbal, physical (force), and sexual. However, unlike the impulsive offender, fantasy plays a major role in the ritualistic offender's crimes. In fact, his fantasies provide the template for his multiple crimes.

What the offender says to the victim, or demands the victim say to him, is vital to his arousal and gratification. The amount of physical violence he uses is also determined by the reaction he wishes to elicit from his victim. In Case No. 2 the victim was killed, and therefore no record of his verbal interactions could be obtained. However, one can clearly see a motivation of anger underlying the crime. From a research interview with that man's wife, it was determined that, when he acted out his anger-motivated fantasies on her, he referred to her as a "bitch," "slut," "whore," and "cunt." It can safely be assumed that he engaged in similar behavior with the murder victim. In Case No. 3, the victim reported that his interaction with her was similar to what one would expect with a consenting sexual partner.

The level of injurious force used against the victim may be minimal, or it may be brutal enough to result in death. It depends on the underlying motivation of the offender. In Case No. 2 the offender was motivated by anger and the victim was subjected to horrendous physical trauma, resulting in her death. In Case No. 3, the offender used no injurious force even when physically resisted by the victim. He was not motivated by anger, and his fantasy of a consenting sexual relationship would have been corrupted had he resorted to physical violence.

The type and sequence of sexual acts of the ritualistic offender is also dependent upon his motivation. In Case No. 2, the offender used the victim as an object and forced her to engage in diverse sexual activities. In Case No. 3, there was behavioral evidence that the offender was attempting to engage the victim into his fantasy of a consenting relationship that included kissing, fondling, and cunnilingus.

Pornography

Fantasy plays a major role in the ritualistic offender's crimes, and these fantasies are developed to complement the underlying motivation. Consequently, he possesses theme-oriented pornography. The theme of the pornography can be implied from the manner in which he interacts with his victims. The offender in Case No. 2 possessed bondage and torture pornography. The offender in Case No. 3 possessed soft-core and non-violent pornography. The ritualistic offender uses pornography inflectively; he has pre-existent fantasies into which he incorporates selected pornography. He will often invest considerable effort in creating his own pornography that is designed to reflect the proper juxtaposition of these themes and images. This might involve cutting and pasting images from commercial pornography, sketching out the desirable scenarios, or having victims or consensual partners act out certain erotic behaviors that are then photographed or videotaped.

Criminal History

Due to the highly specific nature of the ritualistic offender's criminal behavior, he may have no criminal history prior to arrest for a series of very violent crimes. If he does have an arrest history, it will typically reflect sexual or sexually-related offenses. It is not uncommon to find arrests for nuisance offenses, attempted burglary, or breaking and entering. Attempted burglary and breaking and entering are the most common non-sexual offenses because offenders are often arrested in a potential victim's apartment before the sexual crime takes place.

Summary

All of the men mentioned in the various cases were violent and serial sexual offenders, and all of their victims were adult females. However, it appears that this broad category of serial sexual crime is best understood according to two paradigmatic distinctions — the impulsive and ritualistic offender. It is the thesis of this chapter that these two groups of offenders can be distinguished — in terms of their style of offending and the underlying motivational theme(s) — and thus provide a better understanding of these common crime patterns. The impulsive offender seems to be situationally motivated by a character style and erotic predisposition that allows for the opportunistic pairing of sexual and aggressive impulses. The ritualistic offender appears to be far more specific in his intent and criminal behavior and largely motivated by the complex re-enactment of specific sexual fantasies that pair him and the victim in an erotically repetitious and arousing interaction.

It is possible that this paradigm reflects a continuum of sexually violent behavior and not two distinct groups of offenders *per se*. It is of value, however, in the investigation of sexually violent crime to understand these differences in order to determine the type of offender being sought. Evaluators can also use these ideas to structure the information gained from a forensic examination.

Previous research (Warren, Reboussin, Hazelwood, Trumbetta, Gibbs and Cummings, 1999) indicates that the more ritualistic rapist tends to increase the amount of force he uses over a series of offenses — as contrasted with the less ritualistic rapist, who continues to use similar levels of blunt force regardless of his number of crimes. Victim selection and crime location also seem to be influenced by the amount of ritualistic preparation before the crime (Warren, Reboussin, Hazelwood, Cummings, Gibbs and Trumbetta, 1998). These distinctions might also eventually prove relevant in our attempts to better understand the different recidivism rates that exist between different types of sexually violent offenders.

References

Abel, G.G., Becker, J.V., Cunningham-Rathner, B.A., Mittleman, M., and Rouleau, J.L. (1988) Multiple paraphilic diagnoses among sex offenders, *Bull. Am. Acad. Psychiatry Law*, 15, 153–168.

Barbaree, H.E. and Marshall, W.L. (1991) The role of male sexual arousal in rape: six models, *J. Consulting Clin. Psychol.*, 59, 621–630.

Brown, S.L. and Forth, A.E. (1997) Psychopathy and sexual assault: static risk factors, emotional precursors and rapist subtypes, *J. Consulting Clin. Psychol.*, 65, 848–857.

Dietz, P.E. (1983) Sex offenses: behavioral aspects, in Kadish, S.H., Ed., *Encyclopedia of Crime and Justice*, New York, Free Press.

Dietz, P.E., Hazelwood, R.R., and Warren, J.I. (1990) The sexually sadistic criminal and his offenses, *Bull. Am. Acad. Psychiatry Law*, 18, 163–17.

Dietz, P.E., Harry, B., and Hazelwood, R.R. (1986) Detective magazines: pornography for the sexual sadist? *J. Forensic Sci.*, 31, 197–211.

Fowles, J. (1963) *The Collector*, Little, Brown & Company, New York.

Hare, R.D. (1991) *The Hare Psychopathy Checklist (Revised)*, Toronto, Ontario, Canada, Multihealth Systems.

Hazelwood, R.R., Warren, J.I., and Dietz, P.E. (1993) The compliant victims of the sexual sadists, *Aust. Fam. Phys.*, 22, 474–479.

Hazelwood, R.R., Dietz, P.E., and Burgess, A.W. (1983) *Autoerotic Fatalities*, Lexington Books, D.C. Heath and Co., Boston.

Hazelwood, R.R. (1983) The behavioral-oriented interview of rape victims: the key to profiling, *FBI Law Enforcement Bull.*, September.

Hazelwood, R.R. and Douglas, J.E. (1980) The lust murderer, *FBI Law Enforcement Bull.*, April.

Knight, R.A., Carter, D.L., and Prentky, R.A. (1989) A system for the classification of child molesters: reliability and application, *J. Interpersonal Violence*, 4, 3–23.

Knight, R.A., Warren, J.I., Reboussin, R., and Soley, B.J. (1998) Predicting rapist type by crime scene variables, *Criminal Justice Behav.*, 25, 46–80.

Knight, R.A. and Prentky, R.A. (1987) Motivational components in a taxonomy for rapists: a validation analysis, *Criminal Justice Behav.*, 1, 141–164.

Lanning, K.V. (1992) Child molesters: a behavioral analysis for law enforcement officers investigating cases of child sexual exploitation, Monograph, 3rd ed., *Nat. Cent. Missing Exploited Children*.

McGuire, C. and Norton, C. (1989) *The Perfect Victim*, Dell Publishing, New York.

Michaud, S.G. (1994) *Lethal Shadow*, Onyx Publishing, New York.

Patterson, J. (1995) *Kiss the Girls*, Warner Books, New York.

Prentky, R.A., Knight, R.A., and Rosenburg, R. (1988) Validation analyses on a taxonomic system for rapists: disconfirmation and reconceptualization, *Ann. New York Acad. Sci.*, 528, 21–40.

Warren, J.I., Reboussin, R., Hazelwood, R.R., Cummings, A., Gibbs, N.A., and Trumbetta, S.L. (1998) Crime scene and distance correlates of serial rape, *J. Quant. Criminology,* 14, 35–59.

Warren, J.I. and Hazelwood, R.R. (in press) Relational patterns associated with sexual sadism: a study of 20 wives and girlfriends, *J. Fam. Violence.*

Warren, J.I., Reboussin, R., Hazelwood, R.R., Gibbs, N.A., Trumbetta, S.L., and Cummings, A. (1998) Crime scene analysis and the escalation of violence in serial rape, *Forensic Sci. Int.,* Vol. 100, 37–56.

The Behavioral-Oriented Interview of Rape Victims: The Key to Profiling

7

ROBERT R. HAZELWOOD
ANN WOLBERT BURGESS

A police department submitted an investigative report of a rape to Hazelwood and requested that a profile of the unidentified offender be prepared. A synopsis of that report follows:

Case No. 1

Alicia B., a 21-year-old Caucasian who resided alone, was sleeping in her apartment when she was awakened at approximately 2:30 a.m., by a male who placed his hand over her mouth and held a knife to her throat. The intruder warned her not to scream or resist and advised her that if she complied with his demands, she would not be harmed. He then forced her to remove her nightgown. He kissed and fondled the victim and then raped her. After warning her not to call the police, he left. Ignoring the rapist's warning, she notified the police. The victim said nothing had been stolen; however, she could not provide a description of her assailant because he had placed a pillowcase over her head. The rapist remained in the apartment approximately one hour.

Prior to preparing a profile, Hazelwood requested that the agency reinterview the victim, using a set of questions specifically designed to elicit information about the rapist's behavior during the assault. Using the questions as a guide, the police reinterviewed the victim and obtained a nine-page typewritten statement. Based upon the new statement, a profile was prepared; and subsequently the rapist was arrested and confessed not only to the rape of Alicia B., but to other rapes as well. When the profile was compared to the offender, only the marital status was found to be incorrect.

Motivation

During the past 20 years, the authors have reviewed thousands of rape victims' statements. The statements contained details of the crime as well as a great deal of information about the offender's physical characteristics — but there was a marked absence of information that could provide clues as to the motivation underlying the rape and the offender's characteristics and traits. Over a period of time Hazelwood developed a set of questions designed to elicit the behavioral aspects of the crime:

1. Describe the manner in which the offender approached and gained control over you.
2. How did he maintain control of you during the assault?
3. Describe all physical force he used and when specifically during the attack he used force.
4. Did you resist either physically, verbally, or passively? If so, describe each instance you resisted and how you resisted.
5. What was his reaction to each act of resistance?
6. Did he at any time experience a sexual dysfunction? If so, describe what type, whether he was later able to fully function sexually, and any particular act or behavior he performed or demanded that you perform to overcome the dysfunction.
7. Describe each sexual act you were forced to participate in or that was performed by the offender on himself. Please provide the sequence in which each act occurred and any repetitions.
8. As precisely as possible, detail everything he said to you, his tone of voice, and his attitude at the time he spoke.
9. If he demanded that you answer questions, repeat phrases, or respond verbally in any manner whatsoever, please tell us specifically what he demanded that you say.
10. When, if ever, did his attitude appear to change? In what manner did it change, and what occurred immediately prior to the change?
11. What actions did he take to ensure that you would not be able to identify him? Did he take any precautions to ensure the police would not be able to associate him with the crime?
12. Did he take anything when he left? Have you carefully inventoried your personal belongings (undergarments, photographs, etc.) since the assault?
13. Did you receive any calls or notes from unidentified persons prior to (or since) the assault? Have you had any experience which would indicate that he specifically targeted you for the assault?
14. How do you believe individuals who associate with the rapist on a daily basis would describe him as a person?

It is important to obtain the offender's physical description, direction, and mode of travel, and attention should be given to these critical details.

However, it is strongly suggested that additional attention be devoted to the behavior exhibited by the offender. Profiling, as it pertains to rape cases, involves three basic steps:

1. Determine from the victim what behavior was exhibited by the rapist.
2. Analyze that behavior in an attempt to ascertain the motivation underlying the assault.
3. Set forth the characteristics and traits of the type of individual who would commit the crime in the manner described by the victim and crime, given the motive indicated by behavior.

Steps 2 and 3 are accomplished by using logic, common sense, and the experience of having reviewed thousands of rape cases over the years. The first step, however — interviewing the victim — is the most crucial in the process. Only the victim can provide the information necessary to complete an analysis of the crime. Therefore, it is essential for the investigator to establish rapport with the victim through a professional and empathetic approach, hopefully overcoming her feelings of fear, guilt, anger, and humiliation. The interviewer must also isolate his/her personal feelings and not allow them to interfere with the necessary objectivity. During the interview, the investigator will be dealing with three personalities: the victim's, the criminal's, and the interviewer's. Personal feelings about the crime, the victim, and the criminal must be put aside to ensure that biased opinions about the offender do not develop. The investigator who is able to accomplish this will find that a much clearer impression of the offender begins to take shape.

Intent becomes clear only if the crime is viewed from the motivational position of the criminal. The crime will make absolutely no sense if one attempts to understand from the perspective of the victim, a police officer, or a prosecutor. Only from the offender's point of view does it seem rational. Once a reasonably safe assumption is made as to *why* the rape occurred, it is probable that the rapist can be profiled. Behavior reflects personality. The manner in which an individual behaves within his environment portrays the type of person he or she is. One of the criminal's environments (the environment to which we have access) is his crime. Through the criminal behavior, opinions can be formed about self-esteem, educational level, ability to negotiate interpersonal relationships, and goals in life. In rape cases, the victim's description of the offender's behavior allows the investigator to form an opinion as to the type of person responsible.

Questioning for Behavior

Three forms of behavior are exhibited by most rapists: physical (injurious force), verbal, and sexual. A much less biased view of the offender emerges when his behavior is subdivided into these areas.

The interview must be conducted in a tactful, professional, yet probative manner. It is imperative that the investigator impress upon the victim that he is not only concerned with the arrest and conviction of the offender but also with the victim's welfare. She has been involved in a life-threatening situation, and the importance of recognizing this cannot be overemphasized. The investigator might inform the victim that the identification of the offender may be expedited through a profile. Her contribution of detailed and personal information regarding the assault is necessary for a profile to be prepared.

Case No. 2

> An elderly woman was raped by an unknown male and the case was sub-
> mitted for profiling. The victim, out of a sense of embarrassment, declined
> to provide the police with sufficient behavioral information. Consequently,
> the victim's statement was found to be substantially lacking in detail and
> was returned to the requesting agency, along with a reprint of an article by
> Hazelwood addressing the interview of rape victims. The police gave the
> victim a copy of the article. After reading it, she expressed her understanding
> of the necessity for complete disclosure. She then provided the police with
> a detailed description of the assault.

Each of the questions will be more fully discussed in the remainder of this chapter. It is to be noted that a profile is not based on any single response but rather upon an analysis of all responses.

What Method of Approach Was Utilized by the Offender?

When an individual decides to accomplish a task, it is human nature to choose a method with which he or she feels most comfortable. Therefore, it is logical to assume that the rapist, in choosing a method of approaching and subduing his intended victim, would do likewise. Because each aspect of a sexual assault has the potential for providing information about the person responsible, it is necessary to categorize the style of approach used by the offender. The authors have labeled the various approaches as the *con, blitz,* and *surprise.*

Con

With the con approach, the offender approaches the victim openly using a subterfuge, trick, or ruse. He may offer some sort of assistance or request directions. He is initially pleasant and friendly and may even be charming. His goal is to gain the victim's confidence and, when he is in a position to overcome any resistance she might offer, capture her. Quite often, and for different reasons, he exhibits a sudden change in attitude toward the victim once she is under his control. In some instances, the rapist alters his behavior to convince the victim he is serious. In other instances, the change is merely a reflection of inner hostility toward the victim or women in general. This style of approach suggests an individual who has confidence in his ability to interact with women and is not intimidated by them.

Blitz

A person using the blitz approach immediately employs injurious force in subduing his victim. He allows her no opportunity to react physically or negotiate verbally and will frequently gag, blindfold, or bind his victim. His attack may occur from either the front or rear. Most often, he uses his fists or some other blunt force, but he may also use disabling gases or chemicals, strangulation, or suffocation techniques. The use of this approach suggests hostility toward women, an attitude that may also be reflected in his relationships with females outside the rape environment. The offender's interactions with women in non-rape relationships are likely to be selfish and one-sided, resulting in numerous but relatively short relationships with women.

Surprise

In the surprise approach, the rapist may either approach the victim while she is sleeping or lie in wait for the victim (back seat of a car, behind a wall, in the woods). Typically, this individual uses verbal threats and/or the presence of a weapon to subdue the victim. While certainly not conclusive, this style suggests two possibilities:

1. The victim has been targeted or preselected for assault. While the preselection may occur shortly before the assault, it most often involves long-term surveillance of the victim.
2. The offender does not feel sufficiently confident to approach the victim using the con approach or does not want to employ the necessary violence to capture her using the blitz approach.

How Did the Offender Maintain Control of the Victim?

The manner in which the offender maintains control of his victim is primarily dependent upon the motivation for committing the sexual assault. Less frequently, his decision to use force may be a reaction to the resistance of his victim. Four control methods have commonly been observed: mere presence, verbal threats, display of a weapon, and use of physical force.

Mere Presence

Depending upon the passivity and fear of the victim, it is very possible that the offender's mere presence is sufficient to control the victim. This may be difficult to believe by an investigator whose personality probably differs from that of the victim. Quite often the investigator judges a victim's reaction on the basis of what the investigator believes he would do, rather than taking into account the victim's personality, the circumstances surrounding the assault, and the fear factor involved. The following case is an example of this attitude.

Case No. 3

> The victim, a 21-year-old woman with a learning disability, had parked her car near her home after having been to a yogurt shop. As she got out of the car, a man in a van pulled behind her car and pointed a gun at her, saying nothing. She put down her purse and yogurt cup and said "Please don't hurt me, I'll do anything you say." The man was surprised at this reaction and told the victim to get into the van. She walked around the rear of his van, opened the side door, got into the rear of the van, and shut the door. He sexually assaulted and killed her.

If investigators had not factored in her learning disability or found that her mother was not surprised at the reaction of her daughter, given her lack of self-confidence and natural passivity, they may have unintentionally placed some of the blame on the victim. Fortunately this was not the case, and the offender was arrested shortly after this crime occurred.

Threats

Many victims are understandably intimidated by threats of violence. Clues to the motivation for the assault often lie in these verbal threats. Investigators should elicit (verbatim if possible) the context of the threats. Of course, the investigator should also record whether or not the threat was carried out.

Many rapists display weapons to get or maintain control of their victims. It is important to ascertain not only whether the rapist had a weapon but also at what point he displayed it or indicated that he had one. Did the victim see it? Was it seemingly a weapon of choice (gun or switchblade) or of opportunity (kitchen knife, screwdriver, etc.)? Did he relinquish control of it (give it to the victim, put it down, or put it away)? Did he inflict any physical injury with the weapon? Each of these questions should be addressed during the interview.

Force

The use and amount of physical force in a rape attack are key determinants of offender motivation. The interviewer should determine the amount of force and when it was employed as well as the rapist's attitude prior to, during, and after its employment.

What Amount of Physical Force was Employed by the Attacker?

The interviewer should elicit a precise description of the physical force involved. Understandably, the sexual assault victim *may* exaggerate when describing the level of force. There are legitimate reasons why this exaggeration may occur — because she wants the investigators to believe her, because she has never been struck or physically attacked before and has no frame of reference for physical violence, or because the victim may not be able to differentiate between the sexual assault and the physical assault. For these reasons, the authors have developed four levels of force to assist the investigator in arriving at opinions as to the specific amount of force used.

Minimal Force

At this level there is little or no physical force used. While the victim may have been slapped, it is not a repetitive behavior and it becomes obvious that the force was employed more to intimidate than to punish. In such cases, the rapist is typically non-profane.

Moderate Force

When the rapist employs moderate force, he repeatedly slaps or hits the victim in a painful manner, even in the absence of resistance. He typically uses profanity throughout the attack and is otherwise verbally abusive.

Excessive Force

With this level of force, the victim is beaten, has bruises and lacerations, and requires medical attention and possible hospitalization. At this level of force, the rapist is typically profane, directing derogatory remarks toward the victim.

Brutal Force

At the ultimate level of physical force, the victim is subjected to an extreme amount of violence which may include torture. The injuries demonstrate that it is the intent of the offender to inflict severe physical trauma on the victim, and she requires long-term hospitalization or may die as a result of her injuries. The verbal behavior of such an offender also reflects anger and hostility.

Did the Victim Resist the Attacker?

The victim, when ordered to act, has two options — to comply or resist. Resistance can be defined as any action taken by the victim to preclude, delay, or reduce the effect of the attack. While most interviewers are alert to physical or verbal resistance by victims, they often tend to overlook or disregard an equally important form of resistance — passive resistance.

Passive Resistance

This type of resistance is evident when the victim does not physically or verbally oppose the attacker but *does not comply* with the rapist's demands. For example, a victim who is ordered to disrobe does not verbally or physically resist the demand of the attacker; she simply doesn't obey the demand. Passive resistance is frequently overlooked during the trial process. Prosecutors would do well to educate judges and juries about this form of resistance and emphasize that the victim, simply by not obeying the rapist's commands, did in fact resist him.

Verbal Resistance

Verbal resistance is demonstrated when the victim screams, pleads, refuses, or attempts to reason or negotiate with her attacker. While crying is a verbal act, it is not considered to be resistance in this context.

Physical Resistance

Hitting, kicking, scratching, gouging, and running are examples of physical resistance.

Investigators should not assume that *any* type of resistance has taken place. Even normally assertive people may become passive during a life-threatening situation. However, when there is no evidence of resistance, the victim's personality should be taken into consideration by the investigator. The officer should make an attempt to determine whether the victim is a passive person who is easily intimidated and controlled. Is the victim a person who has been protected and cared for during her adult life? An individual's personality will largely determine how that person will react in such a situation.

What was the Offender's Reaction?

People react to stressful situations in a variety of ways. While rape is unquestionably stressful to the victim, it also creates stressors for the attacker (fear of being identified or arrested, fear of being injured or ridiculed, or fear of being successfully rebuffed by the victim). Therefore, it becomes crucial for the investigator to learn how the rapist reacted to any resistance (passive, verbal, or physical) offered by the victim. Five offender reactions have been observed — cessation of the demand, compromise, flight, threats, and force.

Cease Demand

A rapist who encounters victim resistance may not attempt to force compliance but instead may cease his demand and move to another phase of the attack.

Compromise/Negotiate

The offender may compromise or negotiate by suggesting, or allowing the victim to suggest, alternative behaviors. For instance, the rapist may demand or attempt anal sex and, upon encountering resistance, instead demand vaginal sex with no further attempt to assault the victim anally.

Flee

Occasionally the rapist may leave the scene when resisted. This flight reaction is interesting in that it suggests the offender had no desire to force the victim against her will or was unprepared for the victim's reaction and/or the attention it might bring to the crime.

Threaten

Another reaction of the offender may be to resort to verbal or physical threats in an attempt to gain compliance. If the victim ignores the threats and continues to resist, it is important to learn how the offender reacts.

Force

A final reaction to resistance may be resorting to force. If such is the case, the interviewer should determine the degree of force used and its duration, as discussed above.

Did the Rapist Experience a Sexual Dysfunction?

The term *sexual dysfunction* is defined as an "impairment either in the desire for sexual gratification or in the ability to achieve it" (Coleman et al., 1980, p. 531). In a study of 170 rapists, Groth and Burgess (1977) determined that 34% of the offender population suffered a sexual dysfunction during the assault. In the serial rapist study conducted by the authors, it was found that 38% of the offenders reported a sexual dysfunction during their first rape, 39% during the middle rape, and 35% experienced a dysfunction during their last rape. Even today, the authors encounter cases in which the victim was either not asked whether a sexual dysfunction had occurred or the matter was simply noted without further inquiry.

The investigator should be alert to the possibility that a rape victim may not volunteer such information during the interview because she does not consider it significant, she is embarrassed about the sexual acts demanded to overcome the dysfunction, or she is ignorant of such things and did not recognize it as a dysfunction. It behooves the investigator to explain the various sexual dysfunctions affecting males and how being aware of a dysfunction may assist in the investigation.

Erectile Insufficiency

Formally classified as impotence, this type of dysfunction affects the male's ability to obtain or maintain an erection for sexual intercourse. Masters and Johnson (1970) describe two types of erectile insufficiency — primary and secondary. Males suffering from primary insufficiency have never been able to maintain an erection sufficient for intravaginal ejaculation. While this type is relatively rare and not generally of concern to the investigator, it is described for the edification of the reader. Secondary insufficiency involves those instances in which the male is currently unable to obtain or maintain an erection.

Groth and Burgess (1977) identified a third form of insufficiency termed conditional. In such cases, the rapist is initially unable to become erect, but does so as a result of forced oral and manual stimulation by the victim. The authors would suggest that the methods of gaining an erection are not limited to oral and manual stimulation, but may include any type of act demanded by the offender. Such acts may include sex (anal sex, analingus) or may involve having the victim verbalize certain words or phrases or even dress in certain clothing.

Groth and Burgess (1977) compared erectile insufficiency among rapists with a group of 448 non-rapist patients studied by Masters and Johnson. They found that in both instances it was the most commonly experienced dysfunction. In the 24 years since that comparative study, the authors (through involvement in thousands of rape cases, review of police reports, and interviews of rape victims and rapists) have found that erectile insufficiency continues to be the most common sexual dysfunction in stranger-to-stranger rapes.

Premature Ejaculation

Ejaculation which occurs immediately before or immediately after penetration is termed premature ejaculation (Groth and Burgess, 1977, p. 164). In their study, Groth and Burgess found that this dysfunction affected 3% of the rapists.

Retarded Ejaculation

This dysfunction is the opposite of premature ejaculation in that the rapist experiences difficulty or fails to ejaculate. The individual experiencing retarded ejaculation is not controlling seminal discharge and prolonging enjoyment — he is unable to ejaculate and is therefore denied sexual gratification.

Groth and Burgess (1977) reported 15% of the rapist population suffered retarded ejaculation. Masters and Johnson (1970) found it to be so rare among their patients that they did not rank it with a percentage. "When the possibility of retarded ejaculation is not taken into account, the victim's version of such multiple and extended assaults may be greeted with doubts and skepticism" (Groth, 1979, p. 88).

Conditional Ejaculation

The final type of dysfunction the authors have observed is one on which there has been no research conducted and which is not, to the authors' knowledge, reported in the literature. The rapist experiencing conditional ejaculation has no difficulty in obtaining or maintaining an erection but can ejaculate only after certain conditions are met. Most often, the conditions involve particular sexual acts, such as in the following case:

Case No. 4

A 21-year-old woman was abducted at knifepoint while walking home late one evening. Over a period of 3 hours, she was forced to engage in vaginal, anal, and oral sex. Unable to ejaculate, the offender used lipstick and drew panties and a bra on the victim. Forcing her to fondle herself while he observed, he masturbated himself and ejaculated.

This is an excellent example of conditional ejaculation; and the facts of the case should suggest to the investigator that the offender will have a collection of pornography, lingerie catalogs, and/or a long history of peeping-tom activities. What a man prefers to visualize physically, or in his fantasies, is vitally important to the psychosexual gratification process of that man. The explanation for this is that the primary sexual sense of the male is sight, explaining why men are the primary producers and purchasers of erotic literature, photographs, or films and why such a large number of rapes involve voyeuristic activity.

What Type and Sequence of Sexual Acts Occurred during the Assault?

"Documenting the kinds of sex acts that occur during rape helps us to more clearly understand rape" (Holmstrom and Burgess, 1980). It is imperative for the investigator to ascertain the type and sequence of sexual assault (including repetitions) that occurred. This may prove difficult for the victim because of the emotional trauma she experienced and/or her reluctance, because of fear, shame, or humiliation, to discuss certain aspects of the crime.

The investigator may be able to overcome the victim's reluctance through a professional and empathetic approach.

In a sample of 115 adult, teenage, and child rape victims, Holmstrom and Burgess (1980) reported vaginal sex as the most frequent act; but they also reported 18 other sexual acts. "Various socio-psychological meanings are attached to forced sexual acts" (Holmstrom and Burgess, 1980). While it is common to ask about vaginal, oral, and anal acts, the authors do not frequently review reports that include information pertaining to kissing, fondling, use of foreign objects, digital manipulation of the vagina or anus, fetishism, voyeurism, bondage, or exhibitionism on the part of the offender. These and other acts can provide information about the offender which may prove useful during interrogation, interviews of the offender's consensual sexual partners, and affidavit information for search warrants.

What Was the Verbal Activity of the Rapist?

The stereotype of the male rapist's attack is that he attains power and control over the victim through strategies based on physical force. Not only does the rapist use physically based strategies, but he also uses a second set of strategies based on language. (Holmstrom and Burgess, 1979). A rapist reveals a great deal about himself and the motivation behind the assault through verbal activity with the victim. For this reason, it becomes important to elicit from the victim what the rapist said and the manner (tone, attitude) in which it was said.

Preciseness is important. For example, a rapist who states, *I'm going to hurt you if you don't do what I say,* has, in effect, threatened the victim; whereas the rapist who says, *Do what I say and I won't hurt you* may be reassuring the victim in an attempt to alleviate her fear of physical injury and gain her compliance without force. An offender who states, *I want to make love to you* has utilized a passive and affectionate phrase that suggests he doesn't want to physically harm the victim. Conversely, a statement such as, *I'm going to fuck you* is much more aggressive language with no compassion intended.

Compliments directed toward the victim (*You're beautiful*), politeness, expressions of concern (*Lock your doors, Am I hurting you*), apologies, and discussion of the offender's personal life (whether fact or fiction) may indicate a desire on the part of the offender to act out a fantasy of consent. On the other hand, derogatory, profane, threatening, and/or abusive language is suggestive of anger and the utilization of sex to punish or degrade.

When analyzing a rape victim's statement, the investigator is advised to write down an adjective that accurately describes each of the offender's statements (*You're a beautiful person* = compliment; *Shut up, bitch* = hostile; *Am*

I hurting you = concern). The investigator will thus be able to determine the offender's motivation and obtain a verbal picture of the rapist's personality.

Was the Victim Forced to Say Anything?

While sexual activity is basically a biological function among animals, humans are dependent upon psychosexual involvement for arousal and gratification. The mind dictates what is or is not sexually arousing to the individual. The mind can also control the male's ability to function sexually. The involvement of the human senses is also an integral part of human sexual activity.

Hearing is an important sexual sense. What a person says to his/her sexual partner during intercourse can be helpful or harmful not only to the gratification process but also to the relationship. The average person enjoys hearing those things that are complimentary to the individual. Similarly, the rapist may demand from the victim certain words or phrases that enhance the act for him. What he wants to hear from his victim provides the investigator with insight into the motivation and fantasy of the offender. For example, a rapist who demands the victim verbalize such phrases as *I love you, Make love to me,* or *You're better than my husband* suggests a motivation of power and a fantasy of consent. Demands that the victim plead, verbally demean herself, or beg for abuse are indicative of an anger-motivated crime and a fantasy of absolute control and domination.

Was There a Sudden Change in the Offender's Attitude during the Attack?

The victim should be specifically asked whether she observed any change in the attitude of the rapist. Did he become angry, contrite, physically abusive, or apologetic? Was this different from his previous attitude? If the victim reports an attitudinal change, she should be asked to recall what immediately preceded the change. A sudden and unexpected behavioral change, and the knowledge of what precipitated that change, may provide the investigator with a useful piece of information for interrogation should the offender be identified (what does or doesn't make the offender angry).

Factors which may cause such a change include offender sexual dysfunction, external disruption (phone ringing, noise, a knock on the door), victim resistance, a lack of victim fear, ridicule or scorn, or even completion of the rape.

An attitudinal change may be demonstrated verbally, physically, or sexually. As previously mentioned, the rape is stressful not only for the victim but also for the offender. His ability to cope with stress may become an important factor in the interrogation room.

What Precautionary Actions were Taken by the Offender?

The answer to this question is a major factor in determining the experience level of the rapist. It may be possible to conclude from the rapist's actions whether he is a novice or an accomplished offender.

While most rapists take at least some action to protect their identity (wearing a mask or telling the victim not to look at them), some go to extraordinary lengths to protect themselves from being identified. It is the latter group for which this question is primarily designed. As in any criminal act, the more rapes a person commits, the more proficient he may become in eluding detection. If a person is arrested because of a mistake and later repeats the crime, it is not likely that he will repeat the same costly error.

A determination as to whether or not the offender is a novice or an experienced rapist may be based upon the sophistication of the measures he takes to protect his identity.

Novice

The novice rapist is unfamiliar with modern medical or forensic technology and will take minimal actions to protect his identity. For example, he may wear a ski mask or gloves; change the modulation of his voice; affect an accent; order the victim not to look at him; or blindfold and/or bind the victim. These are common precautions that a person who is unaware of DNA or hair and fiber evidence is expected to take.

Experienced

The investigator should note factors in the offender's *modus operandi* that indicate a more than superficial knowledge of forensic and medical abilities. In addition to the actions above, an experienced rapist may prepare an escape route prior to the sexual assault, disable the victim's telephone prior to entry or departure, order the victim to shower or douche, bring bindings or gags rather than using those available at the scene, wear surgical gloves during the assault, or force the victim to wash items he touched or ejaculated on (bedding or the victim's clothing).

As in all such subjective analyses, the projected experience level of the rapist is a judgmental decision based on the offender's actions and the investigator's interpretation of those actions.

Was Anything Taken?

Almost without exception, police record the theft of items from rape victims. All too often, however, investigators fail to probe the matter further unless the theft involves articles of value (pawn shop, entry in the National Crime Information Center, etc.). The investigator should be interested in not only *if* something was taken but also *why* it was taken. Items taken may be categorized as evidentiary, valuables, or personal.

Evidentiary

The rapist who takes evidentiary items (those he has touched or on which he has ejaculated) may be experienced and/or have an arrest history for similar offenses.

Valuables

What an offender takes may suggest age or maturity. Younger rapists steal items such as CD collections, speakers, and stereos, while the more mature offenders tend to take money or jewelry — items that are more easily concealed and transported.

Personal

Such items may include photographs of the victim, lingerie, driver's license, or even inexpensive items of jewelry. Such items may be of no real intrinsic value but instead serve to remind the offender of the occurrence and the victim. The next point to be raised is whether the item was taken as a trophy or as a souvenir. A trophy represents a victory or conquest, while a souvenir serves to remind a person of a pleasant experience.

To determine whether the item represents a trophy or souvenir to the offender, one must examine the physical, verbal, and sexual behavior of the rapist. The abusive, hostile, and physically assaultive rapist typically takes the item as a trophy (used to validate his success). Trophy takers tend to discard the item after a period of time. On the other hand, the souvenir taker is generally the "gentleman" (or power reassurance) rapist who utilizes minimal force and is verbally reassuring and non-violent sexually. Such an individual uses the item to relive and memorialize the relationship with the victim. He is the offender most likely to retain the items.

A final factor to consider in this area is whether the offender later returns the item to the victim. If so, why? The trophy taker may return the item as a means to intimidate or frighten the victim, while the souvenir taker may do so to convince the victim that he is really a nice guy.

Has the Victim Had any Experience to Suggest She Was a Targeted Victim?

Some rapists target or select their victims prior to the commission of the crime. The occurrence of a series of rapes involving victims within a certain geographic area who were alone or in the company of small children at the time of the attack suggests that the offender was aware of the victim's vulnerability, probably through peeping activities.

The investigator should determine whether the victim had experienced any calls or notes from unidentified persons, residential or automobile break-ins, prowlers or window peeping, or even a feeling that she was being watched or followed.

Belief as to How the Rapist's Friends would Describe Him

The investigator would be well advised to request that the victim provide a description of the rapist's personality as she believes his friends and associates would describe him. Her ability to do so is dependent on her willingness to attempt the admittedly difficult task as well as her capacity to isolate her personal feelings about the offender from how others might perceive him.

She should also be requested to list, over a period of days, any facts about the crime that later come to mind.

The victim's participation in this manner may also aid in her recovery. The rape experience has deprived her of a sense of being in control of her life. Being asked to contribute to the investigation in a rational and relevant manner gives back some degree of control.

Summary

Rape is a deviant sexual activity serving nonsexual needs. Through an analysis of the offender's verbal, sexual, and physical behavior, it may be possible to determine what needs were being served and to arrive at opinions about characteristics and traits of the unidentified offender.

It must be remembered that the only available source of information about the rapist's behavior is the victim, and it is therefore necessary to establish a rapport with the victim through empathy and professionalism.

Behavior reflects personality, and a set of questions designed specifically to elicit behavioral information is the first step in the analysis of a rape.

References

Coleman, J.C., et al. (1980) *Abnormal Psychology and Modern Life*, 6th ed., Glenview, IL, Scott, Foresman and Co.

Groth, A.N. (1979) *Men Who Rape*, New York, Plenum Press, p. 88.

Groth, A.N. and Burgess, A.W. (1977) Sexual dysfunction during rape, *New Engl. J. Med.*, Vol. 297, No. 4, pp. 764–766.

Holmstrom, L.L. and Burgess, A.W. (1979) Rapist's talk: linguistic strategies to control the victim, in *Deviant Behavior*, Vol. 1, Hemisphere Publishing Corp., Washington.

Holmstrom, L.L. and Burgess, A.W. (1980) Sexual behavior of assailants during rape, *Arch. Sexual Behav.,* Vol. 9, No. 5.

Masters, W.H. and Johnson, V.K. (1970) *Human Sexual Inadequacy,* Boston, Little, Brown & Co.

Analyzing the Rape and Profiling the Offender

8

ROBERT R. HAZELWOOD

> "What is to be expected ... is an understanding not merely of the deeds, but also the doers."

Zilboorg

> "Discovery consists of seeing what everybody has seen and thinking what nobody has thought."

Szent-Gyorgi

Introduction

Analyzing a violent crime to determine identifiable characteristics of the unknown offender is not a new technique. However, the work in this area by the members of the FBI's National Center for the Analysis of Violent Crime (NCAVC), retired members of the NCAVC, and selected law enforcement officers who have studied with the NCAVC represents continuing efforts to enhance investigative methods and abilities. Until the late 1970s, such analyses had been done primarily by clinical psychologists or psychiatrists who, while trained in matters of the mind, lacked experience in conducting investigations of violent crime. As a result, their profiles were couched in terminology largely alien to the intended audience — the criminal investigator and others in the criminal justice system.

Previously termed psychological profiling and later criminal personality profiling, the term *criminal investigative analysis* (CIA) was coined to differentiate the procedure from that used by mental health professionals. For the purposes of this chapter, the term profile applies to the characteristics and traits of an *unidentified offender*. The profile of an unidentified offender can provide the client agency with significant and useful information in its investigation.

Expertise is nothing more or less than a combination of one's own experience and what one has learned from the experience of others. The material set forth in this chapter is the result of reading; attending seminars,

0-8493-0076-2/01/$0.00+$.50
© 2001 by CRC Press LLC

lectures, and courses; exchanging data with others in the field; over 30 years in law enforcement; and, for the past six years, professionally consulting on a variety of violent crimes.

While it is impossible to categorize human behavior into specific classes that are applicable to all rape situations, it is possible to identify and analyze an offender's behavior during the attack and, in most cases, to describe the type of person who committed the crime.

The first step in profiling the unidentified offender is to ascertain the rapist's behavior from the victim. After obtaining a detailed statement, one may then proceed to the next step — analyzing what is known to determine the purpose of the assault and to extract that behavioral information which will assist in the preparation of a profile. The analysis should be as objective as possible — personal feelings about the crime, the criminal, and the victim must not be allowed to influence the analyst's judgment.

The behavior of the rapist is easier to assess if it can be seen from the perspective of the offender. To assist in accomplishing this, a valid typology has been developed that can be easily understood by others.

It must be reiterated that the following types are presented for the sole purpose of assisting the analyst in viewing the crime from the viewpoint of the offender and not from the perspective of the victim, society, mental health, or law enforcement.

Pseudo-Unselfish Behavior vs. Selfish

In behaviorally analyzing the statement of a rape victim, the first objective is to determine whether the attacker intended the assault to be selfish or unselfish in nature. To categorize a rapist as unselfish may seem contrary to everything the reader believes about sexual assault. The use of the term is not intended to portray the offender in a favorable light. The terms were selected in an attempt to establish a starting point for the analyst to begin the necessary isolation of personal feelings about the offender. It would be simple and satisfying to describe the rapist as a no-good rotten bastard. However, that would not be very analytical and certainly not professionally helpful. It must be remembered that the objective of a profile is to describe an individual in the same way as those who know him would. Of the six classifications of rapists later described in this chapter, only one exhibits pseudo-unselfish behavior.

The analyst considers the verbal, sexual, and physical (injurious force) behaviors of the rapist in studying the crime. These same behaviors will be analyzed in arriving at a conclusion as to whether the offender meant the crime to be selfish or unselfish.

Pseudo-Unselfish Behavior

To the average person, the word *unselfish* implies sharing or caring. In the context of rape it has an entirely different meaning — but one that is important in understanding the crime. Pseudo-unselfish behavior indicates a belief on the part of the rapist that his concern for the victim's comfort and welfare will win her over and a hope that she will come to believe that he is not really a bad person. Of course this is ludicrous, but remember that we are attempting to behaviorally view the crime from the offender's perspective. Therefore, he attempts to involve her in the act, both sexually and verbally. For this type of offender, it is necessary for the victim to act as though she enjoys the activity. This feeds his need for power and acceptance and brings to reality his fantasy of the victim's willing compliance.

It must be noted that most rapists will not exhibit all of the verbal, sexual, or physical behaviors set forth below but will demonstrate sufficient behavior to allow classification.

Verbal Behavior

The unselfish rapist will talk in a way that is more like a lover than a criminal. He will try to *reassure* the victim that he does not intend to harm her if she cooperates. For example, he may tell her that if she does as he says, he won't hurt her or that he doesn't want to hurt her. He is frequently *complimentary*, telling her that she's beautiful, she has nice breasts, she must have a lot of boyfriends, or that she's so attractive, he questions why she isn't married. He may talk in a *self-demeaning* manner by exclaiming she'd never go out with him or she wouldn't like him if she could see him. On the other hand, he might engage in verbal activity which would indicate *ego-building* with demands, forcing her to say she loves him or that she wants him to make love to her.

Quite often, the unselfish rapist will voice *concern* for his victim's welfare or comfort by asking if he's hurting her, warning her to lock her doors and windows, or asking if she's cold. He may engage in what appears to be unnecessary and revealing (*disclosing*) conversation of a personal nature. While the investigator is obviously interested in whether such information is true, the analyst is more interested in the fact that he is verbalizing in such an unnecessary manner during a rape. An example of this type of verbiage is present in the following case:

Case No. 1

The victim, a 27-year-old white female, reported that her assailant awakened and raped her at approximately 2:00 a.m. The sexual attack lasted no more than 10 minutes. Following the assault, the offender lay down beside her and conversed for approximately 45 minutes. While asking her questions about her personal life (job, boyfriend, etc.), he was primarily interested in discussing himself and the events of the evening. He stated that he had left his keys in his car, parked a short distance away, and that he was concerned about it being stolen. He told her that a friend of his, Jack, was outside the residence, but that he wouldn't allow him near the victim because Jack was drunk. He identified himself as "David" and stated that he had never done anything like this before. Prior to leaving, he apologized and asked her not to call the police. After he left, the victim discovered that $400 was missing from her purse.

The victim reported the sexual assault and theft to the police on the same morning. Two days later, she returned home from work and found an envelope in her mailbox addressed to her, but bearing no stamp or postmark. Inside the envelope, she found the stolen money and an accompanying note which read:

Fran:

I'm just writing to try to express my deepest apology to you for what I put you through. I know an apology doesn't help the way you must feel right now, but I am truly sorry. I found Jack when I left, sitting on the sidewalk in front of your apartment complex. He was still pretty drunk. He took some money from a purse in your kitchen. He's really an alright guy and doesn't usually steal money. I hope this is all of it. I found my car later. Luckily, it wasn't stolen because my keys were still in it. Anyway, I just want you to know that I have never done anything like this before. I wish I could blame this on Jack, but I can't. You're really a sweet person, and you didn't deserve any of this.

You can tell your boyfriend that he's a lucky guy.

Good bye,

David

Typically, the pseudo-unselfish rapist is *nonprofane*. This is not to say that he won't ever use profanity, but when he does, it is mild in nature and spoken without much conviction. As mentioned in the case presented above, he may be *inquisitive*, asking questions about the victim's lifestyle, occupation, social life, plans, or residence. Very often the victim reports that the rapist is *apologetic* or asks her forgiveness, saying he wished it didn't have to be her or that she didn't deserve this.

In summary, the rapist exhibiting pseudo-unselfish verbal behavior is most often (1) reassuring, (2) complimentary, (3) self-demeaning, (4) ego-building, (5) concerned, (6) personal, (7) nonprofane, (8) inquisitive, (9) disclosing, and (10) apologetic.

When analyzing a victim's statement on the offender's verbal behavior, the analyst should identify all instances in which the victim reported offender verbiage and offender-forced verbal behavior from the victim and place an appropriate adjective (You are beautiful = complimentary) in the margin of the statement. This provides the analyst with a verbal picture of the offender's fantasy (consensual) for the rape.

Sexual Behavior

The pseudo-unselfish rapist attempts to involve the victim in bringing his fantasy to reality. This is especially true in the sexual aspect of the crime. Interestingly, he does not normally force sexual acts when the victim verbally or physically resists him. His reluctance to force sexual acts indicates a desire not to physically harm the victim. While this reluctance may emanate from a lack of confidence, it is more likely that he is attempting to bring his fantasy of a willing partner to reality; and the use of force would corrupt that fantasy. Should the victim resist, the pseudo-unselfish rapist may cease the demand, attempt to negotiate or compromise, verbally threaten her, or leave. Very seldom does he employ injurious physical force.

He often engages in what is referred to as criminal foreplay. He may demand that the victim kiss him, fondle the sexual parts of her body, and/or insert his fingers into her vagina. He may perform cunnilingus prior to penetrating the vagina; and as he rapes, he may demand that she put her arms around him or stroke his neck or back.

If he is confronted with an assertive or resistant victim, he spends a brief amount of time with her. He is an intelligent offender and can quickly discern whether his victim is intimidated and passive; and if that is the case, he may act out all of his sexual fantasies. In such cases, the sexual acts may include fellatio, anal sex, and the insertion of foreign objects as well as vaginal rape.

It is important to note at this point that it is quite possible for the pseudo-unselfish and selfish rapists to engage in or demand the same sexual acts. The former acts out in accordance with victim resistance; and the latter does whatever he wants to do, regardless of victim resistance. To differentiate between the two types of rapists when the type of sexual acts are similar, the analyst must closely examine the verbal and physical (injurious force) behaviors, as they are seldom similar. One should also consider the sequence of the sexual acts to determine if there was a desire to degrade the victim (the pseudo-unselfish rapist infrequently does so intentionally).

Physical Behavior

The amount of physical violence used by the pseudo-unselfish rapist is typically the minimal level. It was pointed out in Chapter 7 that, at this level, force is used more to intimidate than to punish. While mild slapping may occur, the offender does not intend to physically hurt the victim. Instead, he most often relies on threats, the presence or threat of a weapon, or the fear and passivity of his victim.

From a *behavioral* standpoint, the fact that a rapist exhibits a weapon, or advises the victim that he has one, does not constitute physical force unless he uses it to inflict bodily injury. From a legal standpoint, of course, the presence or threat of a weapon is very significant and escalates the seriousness of the offense. Many instances exist in which an armed assailant put the weapon aside after gaining control of the victim. There were also a few instances in which the rapist gave his weapon to the victim. Interestingly, many victims found themselves incapable of using the weapon and returned it to the offender.* They reported that they either were afraid of the weapons, thought it might be a trick (unloaded gun), or were concerned that they might not be able to incapacitate the assailants and that they would then be killed.

Selfish Behavior

Whereas the pseudo-unselfish rapist seeks to involve the victim as an active participant and behaviorally indicates some concern for her welfare, no such actions or behavior can be expected of the selfish rapist. Instead, he uses the victim in much the same way an actor in a play uses a prop. He is verbally and sexually selfish and physically abusive. During the time he is with a victim, it is clear that he has no concern for his victim's comfort, welfare, or feelings.

Verbal Behavior

Verbally, this type of rapist will be *offensive, abusive,* and *threatening.* He is extremely *profane* throughout the attack and may call the victim derogatory terms such as bitch or cunt. He will attempt to *demean* the victim by telling her that she has no sex in her or that it is no wonder she's not married. Frequently, this type of rapist will demand that the victim talk in such a manner as to humiliate herself (calling herself slut or whore). The

---

* Invariably, when I lecture to police audiences on this subject, the attendees express amazement at the fact that the victim would not take advantage of the opportunity to shoot the rapist. This attitude quickly changes to one of empathy when I inquire as to how many of them have spouses at home who are afraid of their service revolvers and demand that they be kept out of sight.

offender may *describe*, or force the victim to describe, what sexual acts are taking place. His communications will be consistently *threatening* and *demanding*. Almost invariably, his verbiage will be *nonpersonal* and *sexual* in orientation. An example of selfish verbal behavior is set forth in the following case:

Case No. 2

A young female was kidnapped, raped, and murdered. Her killer made a tape recording of portions of his verbal interaction with his young victim. The following is a brief segment of that recording.

Rapist: What are you doing?
Victim: Nothing. I'm doing what you told me to do.
Rapist: What's that?
Victim: I'm sucking on it.
Rapist: On what?
Victim: This.
Rapist: What's this?
Victim: Your dick.
Rapist: You're sucking on my dick?
Victim: That's what you told me to do.
Rapist: Are you doing it?
Victim: Yes.
Rapist: Tell me what you're doing.
Victim: I'm sucking on your dick.

In summary, the selfish rapist is verbally (1) offensive, (2) abusive, (3) threatening, (4) profane, (5) demeaning, (6) descriptive, (7) humiliating, (8) demanding, (9) nonpersonal, and (10) sexually oriented.

Sexual Behavior

Sexually, this type of rapist will do whatever he wants to do. The victim's fear, reluctance, comfort, or feelings are of no significance to him. Physical, verbal, or passive resistance will not deter him in his desire to sexually dominate, punish, and use his victim. Seldom will he engage in kissing unless he feels it will further humiliate the woman. This man does not fondle his victims. He is much more likely to pull, pinch, twist, or bite the sexual parts of her body. He may force the victim to perform analingus, fellatio, or self-masturbation. If anal rape and fellatio are forced on the victim, the sequence is more likely to be anal assault followed by fellatio than the reverse.

Physical Behavior

The selfish rapist may utilize moderate, excessive, or brutal levels of force. The amount of force used depends largely on the motivation for the attack and is seldom related to the amount of resistance offered by the victim.* Case No. 3 illustrates this point:

Case No. 3

A 33-year-old woman and her husband returned home from an evening out and were confronted with a burglar/rapist. After binding the husband, the intruder began sexually assaulting the wife, using no force toward her and engaging in vaginal rape only. During the attack, her husband inquired as to her welfare and she stated, "It's okay, he's being gentle." At that point, the rapist began to beat and burn her breasts. As a result of the attack, the victim underwent a mastectomy of both breasts. When later interviewing the rapist involved, I asked why he had so mistreated the woman following the seemingly benign comment, and he replied, "I wanted her to know who was in charge, and she found out. Who is she to say I'm being gentle?"

Categories of Rapists

Once the rapist is broadly categorized as either selfish or pseudo-unselfish, the rape may be further analyzed in an attempt to learn the motivation for the assault. For this purpose, the author has chosen to use the rapist typologies developed by Groth, Burgess, and Holmstrom (1977). The author has

---

* What should a woman do if she is confronted by a rapist? I am of the opinion that law enforcement officers should not provide specific recommendations when answering this question. I am not suggesting this as an easy out but rather as a means of dealing realistically with an impossible task. To begin with, one who is asked this question is immediately confronted with a situation having three unknown variables: (1) environment of the attack, (2) type of rapist, and (3) victim personality. My advice to an assertive woman confronted with an unselfish-type rapist in a parking lot would be entirely different from the advice I would give to a passive individual who is confronted with a sexual sadist on a little-used roadway after midnight. Lacking the variable information, one must proceed cautiously when giving advice. I have no hesitation in providing advice on preventive measures or recommending self-defense courses, firearms training, police whistles, or disabling gases where legal. However, as law enforcement officers, we must remember that when we speak in an official capacity, we speak not for ourselves but for our organizations. If a person following our advice is brutally beaten and requires long-term hospitalization, we or our organizations could be held liable. I once heard a speaker advise women in the audience to defecate, vomit, or urinate if confronted with a rapist, as this would surely deter him. I would refer the reader to Case No. 9 of this chapter and simply state that the only person such measures would surely deter is the individual who recommended the tactic. Case No. 3 illustrates the inability to determine what may or may not diminish the probability of a victim being injured. (Hazelwood and Harpold, 1986.)

found them to be quite accurate in describing the offenders that he has personally interviewed and the style of attacks he has consulted on in over 5000 rape cases. They are (1) power reassurance, (2) power assertive, (3) anger retaliatory, and (4) anger excitation. The author has taken the liberty of modifying the Style of Attack in each classification and has briefly addressed the opportunistic rapist and the gang rape. The terms pseudo-unselfish and selfish are used to describe the various styles of attack.

A word of caution is necessary here. Seldom does a rapist commit a crime in a manner that allows the analyst to classify him clearly as one of the types discussed below. More commonly, the investigator will be confronted with a mixture or blending of types. It is at this point that common sense is to be applied. Case No. 10 is an excellent example of a mixture of rapist types.

Power Reassurance Rapist

General

This offender is a highly ritualistic offender (see Chapter 6) and, in my experience, the least physically violent rapist. He is driven by the relational component (lover) of his complex and ritualistic fantasy. He dislikes what he is doing (this is not to say he will not repeat his crimes) and is afraid that he is going to hurt a victim.

Purpose of Attack

This type of rapist commits assaults to reassure himself of his masculinity by exercising his power over women. The author asks law enforcement students to associate with this sense of power by recalling their first patrol experiences after graduation from the police academy. Entering traffic in the police cruiser, they immediately note a decrease in speed by those vehicles in proximity to them; and, although not verbalized, a sense of power and authority is felt by the new officers.

So it is with the power reassurance rapist — that same feeling of power and control over another, a woman. Finally he's in charge! This individual may experience feelings of inadequacy in his interactions with women; and through the use of forced sexual activity, he proves himself to himself. While this type of rapist certainly degrades and emotionally traumatizes his victim, he has no conscious intent to do so.

Style of Attack

The power reassurance rapist exhibits pseudo-unselfish verbal and sexual behavior and uses minimal to moderate levels of force. In police jargon, he is frequently described as the gentleman rapist, the apologetic rapist, or the polite rapist.

He must be geographically comfortable in the attack environment. Consequently, he most often attacks victims in their residences, selecting them in advance through surveillance or window peeping. Through such acts, he gathers intelligence on the women (what time they arrive home, if they have overnight guests, what time they go to bed) and the environment (proximity of neighbors, lighting, cameras, security guards). He may target several victims in advance, which explains why, following an unsuccessful attempted rape, a second attack usually occurs on the same evening in the same general locale.

The victim is either alone or in the company of small children. The offender doesn't knowingly enter a residence in which an older adult (other than the victim) is present. He commits low-risk crimes (crimes which pose little or no risk to his well-being) and typically doesn't force entry, preferring to enter through an unlocked window or door. This is not to say that he won't set up the residence for later entry by breaking glass or prying a patio door while the victim is away. However, he prefers not to force entry if the victim is home because that escalates the possibility of a confrontation and physical violence — which in turn would corrupt his fantasy of a consenting relationship.

His attacks generally occur during the late evening or early morning hours. He uses the surprise approach and may exhibit (or claim that he has) a weapon. He typically selects victims within his own age range and forces them to remove their clothing, thus fueling his fantasy of the victim's willingness to participate. If he encounters a particularly passive victim upon whom he can act out all of his sexual fantasies, he will take advantage of that situation and spend a considerable period of time with that victim. If the victim resists, this type of rapist is most likely to compromise or negotiate with the victim. If he suffers a sexual dysfunction, it is most likely to be erectile insufficiency or premature ejaculation. This offender may also engage in paraphilic behaviors such as fetishism or voyeurism during the attack.

Following the assault, and consistent with pseudo-unselfish behavior, he may apologize and ask the victim for forgiveness. Occasionally, he will take a personal item (undergarment or photograph) as a souvenir.

He may contact (not re-assault) the victim after the rape by calling or writing her. For this reason, it is strongly recommended that a tape recorder be attached to the victim's phone for as long as 15 days after the crime.

If this type of rapist is unsuccessful in a rape attempt, it can be anticipated that he will quickly strike again, possibly the same evening. A successful attack will reassure him, but this feeling rapidly dissipates and he finds it necessary to attack again for reinforcement. Therefore, his pattern of attacks will be fairly consistent and will occur within the same general vicinity or in a similar socioeconomic neighborhood. He will continue to attack until he is arrested, moves, or is otherwise stopped.

This rapist may keep records of his attacks. Such records may be as simple as retaining lingerie or other fetish items taken from his victims, or it may be as complex as the method chosen by the offender in the following case:

Case No. 4

A black male raped more than 20 black females within a period of four months. The victims were always alone or with other females who were age-mates. The offender never struck his victims but relied instead upon threats or the presence of a weapon. In several instances he left the scene rather than resort to force to obtain the victim's compliance. Upon his identification and arrest, the investigators recovered a business ledger containing the victims' names, addresses, telephone numbers, and body measurements as well as a scoring system for the victims' participation in various sexual acts. The ledger also contained similar information on fantasized victims, including movie stars and popular singers.

Power Assertive Rapist

General

This offender demonstrates low to moderate impulsivity (see Chapter 6), and fantasy plays a minor role in his crimes. While certainly involved in the rape of strangers, date, spousal, or acquaintance rape is also frequently perpetrated by this type of rapist.

Purpose of Attack

In contrast to the power reassurance rapist, this type has no conscious doubts about his masculinity. To the contrary, he is outwardly a man's man. He is, in his own mind, simply exercising his prerogative as a male to commit rape. He experiences a sense of entitlement and uses rape to express his virility and dominance over women. It is of no consequence to this man if he injures a victim. She is merely an object to be used for his gratification.

Style of Attack

The power assertive rapist is sexually and verbally selfish in his attacks. He exhibits absolutely no empathy toward his victims and has no concern for their physical or emotional welfare. This style of rapist most often assaults victims of opportunity, uses the con approach, and changes demeanor only after the victim is relaxed and at ease. He uses moderate to excessive levels of force in subduing and controlling the victim and generally relies on his fists for weapons. Like the power reassurance rapist, he selects victims who approximate his own age.

His rapes are likely to occur at any location he considers convenient and safe. Frequently, he will rip or tear the victim's clothing from her and toss it aside. The victim may be subjected to repeated sexual assaults.

If he experiences a sexual dysfunction, it is typically retarded ejaculation. Paraphilic behavior is absent from his crimes. He leaves the victim clothed as she is when he is finished with her, normally partially dressed or totally nude. While he doesn't rape as consistently as the power reassurance type, he assaults when he feels he needs a woman. The offender presented in Case No. 5 is an excellent example of this type of rapist:

Case No. 5

A female motorist was stranded when her car became disabled. A white male stopped and offered assistance. He raised the hood of her car, examined it for a few minutes, and advised her that it would have to be repaired by a mechanic. Because he was well dressed and very polite, she accepted his offer to take her to a nearby service station. Once in the car, they chatted in a friendly manner until she noticed that he had passed two exits. She inquired as to how far the station was, and he displayed a gun and told her to shut up. She screamed, and he struck her twice on the head, causing her to lose consciousness. When she awakened, she discovered her clothes had been torn off and she was being raped. When she pleaded for him not to hurt her, he cursed her, hit her again and told her to keep quiet. During the next 2 hours, he raped her three times and forced her to perform fellatio twice. Following the assault, he threw her out of the car, keeping the clothes, and told her, "Show your ass and you may get some help." The victim was treated for severe bruising and painful lacerations.

Anger Retaliatory Rapist

General

This is a highly impulsive offender who, while less common than the two previous types, is extremely violent. Fantasy plays less of a role with this offender than with any of the four major categories of rapists. He openly hates women and wants to punish and degrade them.

Purpose of Attack

This type of rapist is strongly identified with anger and retaliation. As Groth, Burgess, and Holmstrom (1977) have stated, the individuals who fall within this category are getting even with women for real or imagined wrongs. They are angry with women and use sex as a weapon to punish and degrade them. They intentionally punish their victims with brute force. When one interviews the victim of such an attack or reads her statement, it becomes quite clear that anger is the key motivational component for the sexual assault.

Style of Attack

The anger retaliatory rapist is sexually and verbally selfish and uses excessive levels of force. The analyst must recognize that the presence of such unnecessary force is the result of intense rage and fulfills an emotional need of the offender to attack, punish, and destroy.

The crime itself is not premeditated in the sense that a great deal of time is committed to planning or selecting the victim. The attack is an emotional outburst that is predicated on anger and is therefore an impulsive act.

This type of rapist uses the blitz approach, subduing the victim with the immediate and injurious application of physical force, thereby denying the victim any opportunity to defend herself. The sexual assault itself is relatively brief in duration, and the total amount of time spent with the victim is also comparatively short. The pent-up anger is vented against the female sexually and physically, and he leaves following that explosive release of emotion. Eventually the anger will begin to build again, and he will experience the desire to vent his anger once more.

The anger retaliatory rapist attacks women who are age-mates or somewhat older than he is (but not elderly). He may assault women who symbolize another woman in his life. The symbology may be the style of dress, grooming, occupation, height, weight, race, or a host of other possibilities.

As with the power assertive rapist, this offender is most likely to tear or rip his victims' clothing off. There are no geographic or time patterns to his attacks. Because his crimes are anger motivated, they are likely to occur at any time or at any location. In essence, his victims cross his path at the wrong time and place. He uses weapons of opportunity, most often his fists and feet. If he experiences a sexual dysfunction, it is most commonly retarded ejaculation. There is little likelihood of paraphilic involvement in this offender's crimes, as such behaviors would be beyond his comprehension. The following case provides an example of this type of rapist:

Case No. 6

At 2 p.m. on a bright Saturday afternoon, a woman in her early thirties was pushing a grocery cart toward her car in a grocery store parking lot. A man came from behind, hit her in the back of the head, and then struck her repeatedly in the face and stomach with his fist. He placed the semiconscious victim in her parked car and proceeded to rape her. He was unable to ejaculate; and following the assault, he got out of the car and casually walked from the parking lot.

Anger Excitation Rapist

General

This offender is more commonly known as a sexual sadist — an offender who is excited by the suffering of his victims. He is a highly ritualistic rapist, and fantasy plays a major role in his crimes. The paraphilic component of his rich and complex fantasy life is most important to him.

Purpose of Attack

This type of rapist is sexually stimulated by the victim's response to the infliction of physical and emotional pain. The desired responses are fear and total submission. This is the least frequently observed type of rapist. However, the rarity is more than compensated for by the viciousness of the attack and the physical and emotional trauma suffered by the victim. Depending on the offender's maturity, experience, and criminal sophistication, investigators can be assured that they will encounter no other sexual crime as well planned and methodically executed as that committed by the anger excitation rapist. Every detail of the crime is carefully thought out and rehearsed, either literally or in the dark and complex fantasies of the criminal. Weapons and instruments, transportation, travel routes, recording devices, bindings — virtually every phase is preplanned, with one notable exception: the victim is most often a total stranger. While she certainly meets the demographic criteria established by the rapist, she is associated with him in no way known to others.

Style of Attack

While the victims of this class of rapist are generally female (of course there are also homosexual sadists), he may attack females of varying ages and races; and he may even assault boys or men. He is truly a polymorphous offender (one who tries anything sexually). He is sexually and verbally selfish and most often uses a brutal level of force that frequently results in the victim's death. He uses the con approach to gain access to his victim and then quickly immobilizes her with bindings, taking her to a preselected location that provides him with the required privacy. He keeps his victim for extended periods of time (hours to days); and during that time, he may physically torture her with instruments and/or devices while psychologically battering her until she descends into the depths of fear.

Victims frequently report that the offenders cut the clothing from their bodies and engaged in sexual bondage. The painful insertion of foreign objects into the anus and vagina is also common. Paraphilic behaviors such as voyeurism, bondage, sadism, and fetishism are also to be expected.

The anger excitation rapist is the *most likely* offender to record activities with the victim. The method of recording is dependent upon the offender's desires, maturity, experience, and/or economic ability to afford the available technology. I have observed cases in which the rapist recorded his acts with photographs, a video camera, tape recorder, calendars, maps, notes, manuscripts, code, and sketches or drawings.

The sexual acts forced on the victim are varied and experimental in nature, intended to create suffering, humiliation, and degradation for the victim. He tends to remain emotionally detached from such acts and is almost clinical in his directions to the victim. Almost invariably, this offender will experience retarded ejaculation.

There is no apparent time or geographical pattern to the assaults. However, because of the highly ritualistic and multiple paraphilic behaviors which are expected in a sexually sadistic offender's crimes, the investigator should have no difficulty in linking the assaults committed by one of these offenders. Case No. 7 provides an example of the anger excitation rapist:

Case No. 7

The victim, a 32-year-old housewife, disappeared from a shopping center after having purchased groceries from a store. She was driving a motor home at the time of her disappearance. Her nude body was found in the motor home 5 days later. She was lying on her back on the sofa with her hands bound behind her. An autopsy indicated that she had died within the past 2 days, and her death was attributed to the continued ingestion of small amounts of arsenic accompanied by bourbon. She had been raped several times, and it was the considered opinion of those concerned with the case that she had been forced to drink the arsenic-spiked bourbon to induce convulsions of the body for the pleasure of the rapist.

Opportunistic Rapist

General

This offender is categorized as an impulsive type of sexual offender. That is not to say he is not a proficient burglar or robber; but as a rapist he has given no thought to the crime prior to its commission. Since most such rapes occur while the offender is there to commit a robbery or burglary, his arrest record will reflect those types of crimes.

Purpose of Attack

This may be the only type of rapist whose primary motivation in assaulting a woman is actually sexual. The opportunist typically assaults as an afterthought during the commission of another crime. A burglar, discovering a female alone after he enters the residence, finding her attractive, and impulsively raping her, is a good example of the opportunistic rapist. The investigator must not confuse this offender with the robber who *consistently* rapes during his crimes — that type of rapist should be categorized in one of the four major classifications set forth earlier in this chapter.

Style of Attack

As stated, the opportunist is in the midst of committing another crime (burglary, robbery, kidnapping) when he decides to assault sexually. He generally uses a minimal level of force and spends a relatively short period of time with the victim, leaving her bound when he departs. He is sexually and verbally selfish and has frequently been drinking or consuming drugs prior to the crime. An example of this type of rapist is set forth in Case No. 8:

Case No. 8

The victim, a 17-year-old, was normally in school at the time a burglar entered her residence. Surprised to find anyone at home, the criminal bound and blindfolded the young girl and, after advising her that he wouldn't harm her, he began ransacking the home. Finding the father's liquor cabinet, he consumed a large amount of alcohol and began thinking of the attractive female who was in the house. He became mildly intoxicated and attempted to vaginally assault her, but was unable to maintain an erection. He told the crying girl to be quiet, that he hadn't hurt her, and he left quickly. Upon his arrest, he expressed regret at what happened and said that he had a daughter the same age as the victim. There was no indication that he had ever attempted such an act previously.

The Gang Rape

General

This is one of the most frightening situations in which a victim can find herself. She is attacked by a group of males (3 or more) who are operating with a pack mentality. Each offender is attempting to prove *something* to his peers, and consequently the victim is likely to be traumatized for life.

When confronted with a rape involving three or more offenders, it is especially important to elicit information from the victim about the apparent leader of the group. In almost all gang rapes, one person emerges as the leader; and it is this individual upon whom the analyst should focus.

It should be noted that there is invariably a reluctant personality involved in gang rapes. This individual is easy to identify because he indicates to the victim that he doesn't want this to happen and may argue with the others or even attempt to help her escape. This individual is the weak link in the group; and if such a person is described by the victim, one should apply the profiling techniques to him as well.

In the gang rapes that I have consulted on, the assault is totally selfish in nature. While the level of force varies from minimal to brutal, the vast majority of the crimes result in extensive hospitalization for the victim. The following case illustrates such a rape:

Case No. 9

A 19-year-old female was abducted from a phone booth as she was hysterically explaining to her parents that a group a four young men were following her in a car and threatening to rape her. Four hours later, she was found and immediately transported to a nearby hospital where she was treated for a fractured jaw, a broken arm, and severe lacerations in the vaginal and rectal regions. She later reported that she had been forcibly taken from the phone booth and placed in the back seat of the car used by the gang. As a result of her extreme fear, she defecated and one of the youths suggested that she be released, whereupon a second male (the obvious leader), vetoed that suggestion and said that she needed to be taught a lesson. He twisted her arm until it broke and forced her to use her mouth to clean her soiled clothing. The youth who had objected to the rape again objected and was threatened by the leader. Following this the leader directed the others to have sex with the young woman, and two complied. The third (the reluctant participant) was sexually unable to perform. The leader anally assaulted the girl and then forced the victim to perform fellatio on him. Following these acts, he vaginally assaulted her. She was later tied to the rear bumper of the assailants' car and dragged over the roadway.

A Case Study

Now that the author's methods have been described, we will examine a rape case that was submitted to him for analysis. The case is presented as it was received, with changes made only to protect the identity of the victim. Following the case report, the reader will find the author's analysis of the crime and the offender's behavior. Finally, the offender's characteristics will be set forth. The rapist has since been identified, and the profile was found to be accurate in over 90% of the characteristics set forth.

Case No. 10

Victimology: The victim, Mary, is a white female, 24 years of age. She currently lives alone but previously resided with her parents in another part of the state. Mary attended a university and graduated two years prior to the offense. She is an active Catholic, attending church regularly and participating in church events. After graduating, she obtained a teaching job in a junior high school. According to Mary, she is popular with the students at the school and attributes her popularity to the fact that she is young, friendly, outgoing, a nice dresser, and "is on their level." Mary is friendly with both black and white students and frequently attends their athletic activities. She stated that students would visit her classroom during their free time even though she was not their teacher. She drives an older-model subcompact car, made noticeable by multi-colored fenders salvaged from other vehicles. Her personal life is fairly routine, but she has a boyfriend who lives a few miles from her residence. She visits the Catholic church almost daily after school. She also attends a Wednesday night "happy hour" at a local bar/restaurant that attracts a respectable clientele. She is active athletically and eats out infrequently. She observes regular sleeping habits and is careful to draw her curtains at night. She knows of no black male fitting the physical description of her assailant.

Attack Environment: Mary resides in an apartment complex. The complex is located in a middle-class neighborhood and is in a well-established area of the city. The complex rents to a variety of people, including elderly, singles, and young couples. Mary's apartment is located at the rear of the complex and is one of 20 apartments. Her residence and the two beside hers are secluded and face a heavily wooded area immediately behind the complex. Her apartment is on the ground floor. A person not familiar with the area would be surprised to find the three apartments in the rear of the complex. The windows of the apartment face the wooded area. The management seems sincere in trying to screen all renters and maintain the quiet environment of the complex. This is evidenced by their success in evicting a recent tenant for creating heavy traffic in and out of the complex because of suspected drug dealing.

Assault: On the evening of Thursday, June 29, 1982, Mary went to bed around midnight. The evening was cool and clear, and she left her windows open to circulate the air. She wore a nightgown and panties to bed. Sometime after 2:00 a.m. she became aware of the sensation of something tickling her leg. Thinking it was a bug, she tried to brush it off with her hand. When it continued, she tried to brush it again and felt something she believes was a hand. The room was very dark, but she could see enough to determine that a naked black male was beside her bed. When she sat up, he immediately jumped up and pushed her back down on the bed. He put a hand to her throat and told her to be quiet or he would "blow your head off." Mary began asking him to leave, and he put something, which she thought was metal, to her head and told her he had a gun. He told her he had just gotten out of prison two weeks ago and not to make any trouble since he had killed the other girls he had done this with. Mary asked him how he had gotten into the apartment, and he told her he had climbed in the window. He then grabbed the sheet, but Mary kept asking him to leave. He then said he was going to kill her if she didn't let go of the sheet, because he wasn't in the mood for fooling around. Mary let go of the sheet, and he pulled her underpants off. He then told her to spread her legs, but she refused. He again threatened her, and she held her legs up. He began to perform cunnilingus and continued this for approximately three minutes. During this time, Mary tried to talk to him about his having just gotten out of prison. She told him that she had worked in a prison and that she didn't think that he had just gotten out. He stated that he was in a prison in another state. She asked him to leave several times, but he told her to be quiet and continued to perform cunnilingus. He then inserted his penis in her vagina. Several times when he hurt her, she cried out, and he quickly put a hand to her throat and warned her not to do it again or he would kill her. Mary told him not to hurt her again and he responded by telling her to take her top (nightgown) off, which she refused to do. He pushed it up and began licking her nipple. During all this time, he was careful not to raise himself above her so she was unable, in the poor light, to get a good look at him. He "slid" up her body to lick the nipple. At one point, he bit her nipple, causing Mary to cry out. Mary told him he had hurt her, and he said, "I'll show you how I can hurt you," and inserted his penis again. He told her to "shove your ass" while he was inserting his penis, and she responded by telling him that her working was not part of the deal and that she was not enjoying this. He asked if she was only "half a woman" and she said, "Yes, that's right." At one point, he moved his penis to her anus, but she told him he was in the wrong place and he ceased the attempt. Eventually he ejaculated in her vagina and Mary began asking him to leave again.

During the rape, Mary never saw a weapon but felt a metal object pressed to her head. He continually threatened her with death, but she reported that he also seemed concerned for her during the rape. When he hurt her and she let him know, he would cease the painful activity. He never struck her during the incident and his threats were not made in an angry, but rather in a stern, voice. Mary did not think he had trouble in obtaining or maintaining an erection, although he told her that he was having trouble and compared his erection with "the others." He did not ask her to do anything to help him, apart from saying "Shove your ass," and Mary said that she did not touch him during the entire incident. She did not think that a premature ejaculation occurred, but could not be certain due to her lack of sexual experience. She felt that the actual intercourse lasted approximately 15 minutes and that he seemed to be in control of his sexual sensations during that time. He did not demand that she talk to him during the assault. He was not abusive or profane at any time and, according to Mary, seemed to care about her. His demeanor changed only when he threatened her and then it was a stern tone, something Mary likened to a father correcting a child. After the rape, he leaned over the bed, closed the open window, and told her to get out of bed. She asked why, but he just repeated the order. She got out of bed, and he directed her to the living room. He told her not to turn on any lights and placed his hand on her shoulder blade and pushed her ahead. In the living room, he made her lie face down on the rug near her stereo. Mary continually asked him if he was going to leave, but he didn't say anything and she did not hear him put his clothes on. He asked her what she was going to do after he left, and she told him she would probably call her parents and cry. He asked her if she was going to call the cops and she said no. He then asked where the phone was, and she directed him to the kitchen. She could hear him feeling against the wall but he couldn't find the phone. During the time she was on the floor, he continually ordered her to "keep that nose pressed to the floor." When he couldn't find the phone, he told her to show him where it was located. He then told her to go back and lie down. She did, and he ripped the phone out, saying he was sorry that she couldn't call her folks. He had her show him how to unlock the door (deadbolt lock, manually operated) and took her to the bathroom, keeping a hand on her shoulder. In the bathroom, he obtained a towel, telling Mary not to turn on any lights. They returned to the living room, and he made her lie down again. He ripped the towel into strips, possibly using a kitchen knife, and began to tie one strip over her eyes as a blindfold. He tied it too tight and it hurt her, so she asked him to loosen it, and he did. At this point, she noticed that he was wearing gloves, similar to those used by doctors, and work boots. He tied her hands behind her back and tied one of her ankles. Then, with a wet towel, he began wiping her vagina. He asked her if he had gotten all the semen; she answered that she didn't know, and asked when he was going to leave. He kept asking what her name was during this time, but she wouldn't tell him. He then tied her ankles together and asked her if she had any money. She replied that she only had $1. He turned on the stereo and the announcer said it was 2:50 a.m., and he told her to give him $20 or he would take her stereo. Mary told him that she didn't have $20, but that she would write him a check. He found her purse, took a dollar and change, and asked, "Is your name Mary?" She assumed he had found her driver's license. He then told her that he was going to take the stereo, and she told him he was going to look funny carrying a stereo around. He replied, "There are ways." Mary told him that she wanted the cassette tapes. He wanted to know if they were mood music and she said no, but that they had identification on them that might incriminate him if he took them.

He asked if she had any beer or wine in the refrigerator and she said no, but he went to the refrigerator and found a bottle of wine. She told him it was cooking wine, but he drank it anyway, He then told her that he was going to do it again and that he was going to do an "ass job." She refused, and he said, "Yes we are." She refused again and said it would hurt her too much. He then placed a knife to her throat hard enough to prevent her from speaking and told her he was going to kill her. He told her that he had a knife and was going to slit her throat. She asked him why, and he said that since she didn't want to "make it" with him that there was no point in her living at all. He then asked why he should let her live, and she told him that she needed to love, to love her parents, her husband, her children. He asked if she had a husband or kids and she said no, that she had meant her future husband. He asked if she was afraid and she said yes. He then told her that they were going to do it again. He directed her onto her back, but it was painful and she kept rolling on her side. He put the knife to her throat and said that he didn't want any fooling around. He asked her which way she wanted it and she told him she didn't want it any way. He pressed the knife to her throat again and asked if she wanted to live, and she replied yes. At this point, he told her that he used to be a good Christian boy with a nine-to-five job until one day he came home and found his wife in bed with another guy. From then on, he just went from one girl to another. Mary told him she was sorry. He told her that if she didn't call the cops he would be back, and she told him that she would call the police. He then told her that, even in the dark, he could tell that she had "nice features" and a "picturesque ass." Mary told him she didn't think he was from prison, and he laughed and said, "No, this is from your own neighborhood." She said she had some black friends and that she didn't know if she could treat them fairly after this. He asked what friends and she replied that they were black students. He said, "I don't hang around those punks." Mary felt that he was so strong in his denial that it seemed as if he did hang around them. Mary asked why he had picked her and he replied that he had heard that she was a "classy chick" and that he had seen her around. She said that didn't mean he had to do this to her, and he replied that if he had asked her to screw around, she would have said no. Mary heard him rip some paper and asked him to leave. He replied that he was and slid the knife down her back and between her hands. She asked him to leave a light on and he said he had. She then heard the door open and close. She began trying to get the blindfold off, and she felt him tapping her on top of the head. He placed the knife inside the blindfold and told her how lucky she was. She heard a big bang and the stereo stopped playing. She heard the door slam, waited a few minutes, and then worked the blindfold off. She hopped to the door, locked it, and worked the towel from around her ankles. She opened the door and knocked on a neighbor's apartment door, and help was summoned.

Subsequent examination by a physician revealed a small laceration on her neck and towel burns on her wrists. Police investigation revealed that the rapist had removed a screen covering the point of entry (a window). Mary described the rapist as a medium- to light-skinned black male, 20 to 30 years old, 5'8" to 5'10" in height. He had spoken in soft to normal tones and seemed to be articulate. He had been very concerned about physical evidence being left at the scene. She didn't think he had worn the gloves during the rape. The knife used by the rapist was a kitchen knife from her residence. The paper she heard being ripped was determined to be newspaper he had used to light a bowl candle, which was still burning. He had also smoked a cigarette and had taken the butt with him. The "bang" she had heard was from a blow to the stereo with what is believed to have been a metal pipe.

Criminal Investigative Analysis

The investigators in Case No. 10 utilized the questions set forth in Chapter 7 (question 14 had not yet been developed) as a guide during the interview with Mary. A great deal of interaction occurred between Mary and her assailant, and it was thoroughly elicited from her. The assault is analyzed below, and the significance of the behavior exhibited during the crime is described.

Victimology

When a case is analyzed for profiling purposes, victimology is extremely important. An absence of sufficient information about the victim may preclude an accurate analysis of the crime. Victims of violent crime are categorized as being either low-, moderate-, or high-risk victims.

Low Risk

Low-risk victims are those whose personal, professional, and social lives do not normally expose them to the threat of crime. Almost without exception, such victims are intentionally sought out by the criminal.

Moderate Risk

Moderate-risk victims are those who, while generally of good reputation, have an escalated possibility of becoming victims because of their employment (working hours, environment, location), lifestyle (meeting dates through advertisement or in singles bars), circumstances (car breaking down at night) or personal habits (shopping at all-night stores).

High Risk

High-risk victims are those whose lifestyles or employment consistently expose them to danger (drug dealing, residential location, sexual promiscuousness, prostitution, going home with strangers). If a victim is categorized as high risk, the probability of profiling her offender is greatly diminished because the number of potential offenders is extremely large.

Mary was categorized as a low-risk victim. Her assailant obviously sought her out.

Method of Approach

The rapist in this case utilized the surprise approach. He entered her residence at an hour when he had reason to believe she would be asleep and unprepared for an attack. In the author's opinion, the victim had been targeted in advance through either surveillance or window peeping. The isolated location of the apartment allowed the rapist to observe the victim undetected over a period of time. The offender felt sufficiently comfortable in the residence to remove his clothing prior to approaching the victim, and he did not inquire as to whether anyone else was in the apartment or was expected — an indication that he was familiar with Mary's routine and was aware that she lived alone.

Method of Control

Although the rapist told Mary that he had a gun, and she felt a metal object at her head, he relied primarily on threats to control her. Of particular interest is the fact that, even though he threatened physical violence, he did not carry out those threats. This suggests that the intent or desire to physically punish the victim was absent.

Amount of Force

The rapist had numerous opportunities to rationalize use of physical force against the victim and yet he never struck her. The force used consisted of (1) pushing her down on the bed, (2) putting his hand to her throat, (3) biting her nipple, (4) tapping her on the head, and (5) inflicting a slight wound to her neck. Behaviorally, it is of interest to note that when he hurt her and she told him, he would stop the painful activity. For example, when she complained of the blindfold being too tight, he loosened it.

It is apparent that a battle of wills was taking place and, even though the rapist assaulted Mary sexually, he failed to intimidate her emotionally. He was aware of his failure to psychologically control her and, instead of acting out against her in a physical manner, he chose to destroy something (the stereo) that belonged to her.

Given the circumstances reported, the level of force exhibited in this attack was minimal. Although the victim's neck was slightly injured, it was such a minor wound that she made no mention of it in her statement. Furthermore, she reported that the rapist seemed to care about her welfare.

Victim Resistance

There was a wealth of resistance in this case. Mary resisted the offender verbally by consistently rejecting him, questioning his demands, and asking him to leave. She resisted passively by not complying with his order to remove her nightgown, and she resisted him physically by changing her position to avoid intercourse.

Reaction to Resistance

There is an interesting pattern of reaction to the resistance. The rapist relied primarily upon verbal threats to overcome Mary's opposition. At one point, she refused to remove an article of clothing; and he did so himself, effectively discontinuing the demand. After refusing to comply with his order to "shove your ass," the victim was asked if she was "half a woman." Again and again, the potential for physical violence was there and yet it was not employed. The offender failed to intimidate Mary, and his lack of violent reaction supports the opinion that he had neither the desire nor the intent to physically harm the victim.

Sexual Dysfunction

Mary was not able to say with certainty whether any sexual dysfunction occurred. She did report that the rapist had no difficulty in obtaining or maintaining an erection, and that he ejaculated within an average amount of time. So, even though the rapist verbally indicated some difficulty, Mary was not aware of any such problem. Her lack of sexual experience may have been a factor in her recognition of a sexual dysfunction.

Type and Sequence of Sexual Acts

The sexual attack included the following acts in the sequence reported by the victim: (1) cunnilingus, (2) digital manipulation of the vagina, (3) vaginal rape, (4) licked nipple, (5) vaginal rape, (6) attempted anal rape, (7) vaginal rape with ejaculation, (8) threatened anal rape, and (9) attempted vaginal rape.

The acts of cunnilingus and digital manipulation of the vagina preceded the first rape. The activity and sequencing suggests an attempt to stimulate the victim. This behavior is absolutely unnecessary in a rape and its presence indicates an attempt to involve rather than simply use the victim. (Remember that we examine the crime from the offender's perspective, not our own, and certainly not the victim's.) Mary told the offender that she wasn't enjoying what was taking place, that her "working" was not part of the deal, and that she didn't want sex in any way with him. Following the vaginal rape, he attempted to enter her anally and was told by Mary that he was "in the wrong place." Verbally resisted, he stopped the attempt, entered her vaginally and ejaculated. Even though he ceased his attempt to anally assault her, the desire for this type of sexual act was strong — he later told her he was going to do an "ass job." As stated in Chapter 7, a sexual assault that includes anal sex is of interest to the analyst. His desire for this activity, combined with Mary's description of his having a muscular upper torso and his talk of prison, suggest strongly that Mary's attacker had been institutionalized. This will be more fully discussed in the offender profile presented below.

Sexually, the offender exhibits a mixture of selfish and pseudo-unselfish behavior.

Offender Verbal Activity

The victim in this case was articulate and obviously in control of her emotions. She gave a comprehensive description of the entire episode and provided an abundance of behavioral information from which to draw conclusions. Nowhere is this more evident than in the victim's recall of what the rapist said and the manner in which he spoke. When originally analyzing the statement, the author wrote adjectives to describe what the rapist said. As a result, an interesting picture of the offender began to emerge. Let us examine what he said and objectively describe it using adjectives:

1. He threatened to "blow your head off" and stated that he was "going to kill you." The adjective *threatening* is certainly appropriate for these phrases.
2. He told her to "get out of bed," "spread your legs," and to "hold your legs up." *Commanding* or *demanding* describes these phrases.
3. He related that he had just gotten out of prison, that he used to be a good Christian boy, and that he had been a nine-to-five person until he found his wife in bed with another man. I would describe this personal information as *disclosing*.
4. He spoke in a *derogatory* manner when he asked if she were "half a woman."
5. He was *nonprofane*. The victim clearly recalled that he had not used profanity during the course of the crime.
6. He was *apologetic* when he told her he was sorry she couldn't call her folks.
7. He repeatedly asked her name, if she had any kids, and if she had a husband. This would accurately be described as *inquisitive*.
8. He was *complimentary* when he told her she had nice features and a "picturesque ass."
9. He was occasionally *angry* when she wouldn't comply with his demands. In one instance, he told her he would show her how he could hurt her.
10. Finally, he was *self-demeaning* when he said she wouldn't have "screwed around" with him if he had asked her.

After examining the verbal behavior, we find that the offender exhibited a mixture of selfish and pseudo-unselfish behavior. This blending of behavior allows us to see him as those who know him see him.

Attitudinal Change

Mary stated that the rapist's attitude changed only when he threatened her. She described the change as being verbal in nature and said he became stern "like a father correcting a child." We see here that the victim is able to differentiate the sexual assault from the offender's attitude. Many investigators, victim's advocates, and mental health professionals are unable to accomplish this. Her description of his change in attitude is helpful and enlightening. The rapist is in possession of a weapon, is physically larger and stronger than Mary, and has met consistent resistance. Yet she described his threatening attitude as being "stern." Certainly not the stereotypic view of a rapist, yet typical behavior for one not desiring to physically harm his victim.

What Preceded the Attitudinal Change

The victim stated that the only time she perceived a change in his attitude was when he threatened her. In each instance, the factor preceding this change was resistance by Mary. Some rapists will use physical force in such situations, others will compromise or negotiate, and still others will leave. Yet this individual chose to threaten. Why? As has been pointed out earlier, the rapist engaged in a battle of wills with Mary and lost. I believe that he is accustomed to winning in confrontations with women; and this was a situation that the rapist felt should have resulted in a submissive woman, but it didn't. His frustrations are evident in his continued threats and finally in the physical attack on the stereo.

Precautionary Actions

This case is replete with actions taken by the offender to protect his identity, facilitate his escape, and deny investigators physical or trace evidence. These actions include: (1) removing his clothing prior to the attack, thereby ensuring that Mary would be unable to provide police with their description and also reducing the possibility of fiber evidence, (2) disabling the phone, which delayed her ability to report the crime; (3) readying his escape route by having the victim show him how to unlock the door; (4) blindfolding the victim prior to turning on a light; (5) binding her ankles and wrists prior to departure; (6) wiping her vaginal area; (7) wearing surgical gloves, which he believed would preclude the possibility of fingerprints and yet allow the sense of touch; and (8) taking the cigarette butt with him, which denies police the possibility of determining DNA evidence from the saliva residue.

While a few precautionary measures are to be expected in such matters, the care exhibited by Mary's attacker indicates a knowledge of forensic capabilities beyond that expected of an average person. This area is further addressed in the arrest history of the offender's profile.

Items Taken

The rapist told the victim he wanted $20 or he would take her stereo. When advised that she didn't have the money, he took a dollar and some change from her purse. These items would be classified as valuables, but the amount is so small as to be ridiculous. The author is of the opinion that he took this small amount, not out of need, but rather because he could. In other words, he was attempting to demonstrate his power over Mary.

He threatened to take the victim's stereo, and she put him down by telling him he would look funny carrying it around. He later destroyed it. The author doesn't believe that he ever had any intention of taking it. His behavior indicates a more sophisticated and experienced individual, one who would not take such an item. The offender also took his cigarette butt with him — which would have been classified as evidentiary material. Nothing of a personal nature was taken.

The victim reported that there were no previous calls, notes, or break-ins prior to the offense. Follow-up investigation determined that there had been no attempt by the offender to contact the victim following the assault.

Purpose of Assault

Most sexual assaults service nonsexual needs. The rapist in this instance was attempting to assert his masculinity. That is to say, he was expressing his male dominance over women, which he believes is his right. Such rapists tend to be basically selfish in their attacks. However, there was a vacillation between selfish and psuedo-unselfish behavior. The unselfish behavior exhibited by Mary's rapist was simply another means to further exploit her. If he had been successful in having the victim even feign passion or involvement, he would have believed it was due to his ability to arouse and thereby control women — a characteristic of the offender that would also be found in his noncriminal associations with women.

Offender Profile

When law enforcement officers undergo training in the art of profiling, one of the most difficult hurdles for them to overcome is their reluctance to put opinions in writing without hard facts to back them up. This is perfectly understandable, since they have been trained to never put their opinions in writing. Another one of their concerns is that they don't want to be wrong in their assessment, and this is also quite natural. It must be remembered, however, that there are no absolutes in human behavior; and it is indeed rare when an offender profile will perfectly match a criminal. In some instances the profile may be largely inaccurate, and even this is to be expected on occasion. However, in most cases, profiling is not normally requested until all major investigative leads have been exhausted and the case is virtually at a standstill.

Some students have voiced concern that an inaccurate profile may mislead the investigators or cause them to overlook or disregard viable suspects who do not match the profile. The author is unaware of a single instance in which the profile influenced an investigation in such a manner.

Profile

The following profile is based on the analysis of Case No. 10. It represents the author's best opinion as to the type of person who committed the crime in the manner described and for the purpose described.

Personality Characteristics

The purpose of the assault was to express or assert masculinity. The rapist was confident, overly proud of his manliness, and dominant in his relationships with the women in his life. His vacillation between selfish and pseudo-unselfish behavior during the assault is indicative of how he is perceived by those who know him. He presents different images to different people in his life. Some would describe him as a respectful and pleasant individual, while others would say he is often hostile and angry. His fruitless attempts to dominate Mary suggest that he considers himself to be a macho male who works at projecting this image to those around him.

He is a very self-centered person who dislikes criticism, whether constructive or not. He is a person who demands instant gratification of his needs and desires and can be described as an individual who lives for the present, tomorrow be damned. Because of this characteristic, his actions are often self-defeating and he seldom achieves long-term goals. He lacks a sense of responsibility and projects the blame for failures on others or on circumstances that he claims are beyond his control. The attitudinal changes exhibited during the attack on Mary strongly suggest that he cannot stand to lose and therefore is known as a poor loser. He dislikes authority of any kind. Law enforcement officers with whom he has had contact (see Arrest History) describe him as cocky and arrogant to the extent of antagonizing them.

He exudes confidence and considers himself to be superior to others, yet he associates with individuals he considers beneath him. His choice of associates is based on whether or not he can control them. His associates describe him as cool, sophisticated, and somewhat aloof. Recalling his behavior with Mary, it is believed that he reacts negatively when his authority is challenged. Consequently, some describe him as being easily antagonized and short-tempered.

Because of his self-centeredness, few people are allowed to get close to him. While he knows many people, few know him beyond a superficial level. Socially, he frequents those areas he considers appropriate to his station in life, primarily well-known and moderately expensive establishments. He enjoys single bars or similar establishments catering to college-age crowds. He told Mary he had seen her around. She is known to frequent locations similar to those described.

He is a glib talker and extremely manipulative. He is dominant in his relationships with women; however, if he encounters a woman he cannot dominate and totally possess, he relentlessly pursues her. Women who have dated him over a period of time report that he is initially charming and attentive, but becomes overly possessive and irrationally jealous, demanding that they account for time spent away from him.

Race

As described by the victim, the offender is a black male. While some may think this is an obvious factor, numerous rape cases have been submitted for analysis in which the victim was unsure of or unable to describe the race of her attacker. One black man had raped 62 women — 31 of his victims described him as white, and 31 described him as black. In such instances, the analyst considers the racial makeup of the assault area, victimology, racial overtones in the offender's behavior, and/or similar attacks in which one or more victims described the offender's race.

Age

Age is the most difficult characteristic to provide. Its determination is dependent upon a number of factors, including the victim's estimate, type of items taken, and the manner in which the crime is carried out.

The offender in this case is between 26 and 30 years of age. Although the victim is an educated and articulate individual, her opinion as to the age of the assailant is too general (20 to 30). Mary's attacker is confident of his abilities with women and is a macho type of person, therefore he would have selected a woman who approximates his own age range. His ego demands that he attack women he deems worthy of his time and attention. With this type of rapist (and in the absence of other information), the offender's age range is generally placed 3 to 4 years on either side of the victim's age. In this case, however, an older individual is indicated.

Arrest History

The precautionary actions taken by the rapist demonstrate a level of sophistication obtained either through study, experience, or previous arrests for similar crimes. In this instance, the offender exhibits a high degree of forensic knowledge. Thus, it is likely that he has previously been arrested for rape and/or breaking and entering. His obvious desire to assault Mary anally, coupled with a muscular upper torso, suggests that he has also been incarcerated in prison and participated in upper-body exercises.

His lifestyle (see Residence) and low income (see Employment) indicate that he is currently involved in other criminal ventures. For this reason, it is believed he may be involved in the sale of narcotics and has been arrested for such crimes in the past. He is not an addict because he didn't steal items of value from Mary's residence. In fact, he destroyed a valuable (and easily fenced) stereo.

Marital Status

The behaviors exhibited by Mary's rapist reveal that he is a macho type male with a dominant attitude toward women. Such individuals typically were married while in their late teens or early twenties. His attitude toward women is such that his relationships with them are relatively short-lived. For these reasons, it is believed that he is either separated or divorced. While living with his wife, the relationship probably involved a great deal of conflict; and friends would have been aware of the offender's marital problems. Although not physically abusive toward his wife, he would have abused her emotionally. An example of such emotional battering would be leaving her stranded at a party following a public argument.

Residence

The amount of time the rapist spent with Mary provides two especially significant pieces of information: (1) he was familiar with her routine, and (2) he felt comfortable in the socioeconomic environment in which the assault occurred. The intelligence (see Education) of the rapist is such that he would not assault within a geographic area where he would feel uncomfortable or be recognized by those who knew him. Therefore, he resides in similar-type property (rental and middle class) in another geographical area. He resides with a black female who is faithful to him but whom he regards as just one in a series of women he uses and discards. The residence is an apartment or townhouse and is rental property. It is nicely furnished and includes an array of video and audio equipment. It serves as a gathering point for large numbers of people at various times of the day or night, and this may cause suspicious neighbors to alert the police.

Education

The offender is educated beyond high school. His verbiage during the assault, the victim's ideas about him, and his strong denial of "hanging around those punks" (students) led to this opinion. It is possible that his post-high school education was obtained while he was incarcerated. As a student, he achieved above-average grades and exhibited potential for high academic achievement. Because of his dislike for authority, it is improbable that he obtained a 4-year degree or utilized his education in long-term employment. Friends and associates consider his intelligence to be well above average and often seek his advice and counsel. He is considered a leader rather than a follower.

Military History

The offender's strong dislike for authority and regimentation diminishes the possibility of his having served in the military. If he did serve, however, it would have been as a member of the enlisted ranks; and the likelihood of his having been honorably discharged is minimal. His desire to project a macho image would indicate service in the ground forces.

Employment

If employed, he is working in a job for which he is overqualified. His work performance reflects an attitudinal problem, and he complains of being bored. His supervisors report frustration with his performance because they are aware of his potential for excellence. He is frequently late or absent and takes offense if corrected. If he is employed, his job is simply for appearances; his primary source of income is from the sale of narcotics or other illegal activities.

Transportation

In keeping with his lifestyle and image, he operates a two-door vehicle that is 2 to 4 years old. It is flashy, painted in a color that attracts attention, and is well maintained. He spends a great deal of time in his car and loves to drive aimlessly. He is strongly associated with his car, and his associates describe him and his car as inseparable.

Appearance and Grooming

He is a very neat individual whose normal attire is contemporary, with designer jeans at the lower end of his dress style. He takes a great deal of pride in his personal and physical appearance and is critical of those who don't do the same. He exercises regularly and maintains a high level of physical fitness. He demands that the women with whom he associates be equally conscious of their appearance. He has an expensive wardrobe that is beyond his known financial means. He has regular appointments to have his hair styled and is meticulous about body cleanliness, often bathing or changing clothes two to three times a day.

Note that the profile is phrased in common language and in such a way that those who know the offender are able to recognize him from this description.

Summary

The first and most important step in profiling an unidentified rapist is to obtain a detailed statement from the victim. The statement is then analyzed to determine the motive for the crime and whether the offender's verbal, sexual, and physical behavior exhibits a selfish or pseudo-unselfish intent. Having formed an opinion as to his motivational intent, the author then uses the classifications developed by Burgess, Groth and Holmstrom to attempt to determine the type of rapist involved. Finally, a description of the offender is set forth in a manner which enables those who know the man to recognize him.

References

Groth, A.N., Burgess, A.W., and Holmstrom, L.L. (1977) Rape: power, anger and sexuality, *Am. J. Psychiatry*, 134, 11, 1239–1243.

Hazelwod, R.R. and Harpold, J. (1986) Rape: the dangers of providing confrontational advice, *FBI Law Enforcement Bull.*, 1–5.

Classifying Rape and Sexual Assault

9

ANN WOLBERT BURGESS
ROBERT R. HAZELWOOD
ALLEN G. BURGESS

Introduction

Rape and sexual assault include criminal offenses in which victims are forced or coerced to participate in sexual activity. Physical violence may or may not be involved. The terms rape and sexual assault are used interchangeably in this book and are not to be construed as a legal definition. Each jurisdiction will apply its own legal definition to an offense.

FBI Classification of Crime

Professionals develop and advance their sciences as they are able to organize and classify their work. To this end, working with other law enforcement agencies, the *Crime Classification Manual* (*CCM*) was developed by the FBI. The purpose of classifying crimes is fourfold:

1. To standardize terminology within the criminal justice field;
2. To facilitate communication within the criminal justice field and between criminal justice and mental health;
3. To educate the criminal justice system and the public at large to the types of crimes being committed; and
4. To develop a database for investigative research.

The classifications in the *CCM* are based on the primary motivation or intent of the offender. The current intent categories include: (1) criminal enterprise, (2) personal cause, (3) sexual intent, and (4) group cause.

The *CCM* describes each classification in terms of defining characteristics, victimology, offender characteristics, common forensic findings, investigative considerations, and search warrant considerations. The specific code is used to designate the victim as adult, adolescent, or child. Brief case examples of the attack are included. Discussion of the impact of the types of rape on the victims is included in Chapter 2.

Crime Classification Numbering System

The numbering system used to classify crimes was developed with some memory assist features. The basic code uses three digits, with the first digit representing the major crime category. All possible codes are not currently assigned. There are three major crime categories in this edition — homicide, arson, and sexual assault and threat assessment. The homicide category is identified by the number 1 (codes 101–199); arson is designated by the number 2 (codes 201–299); and sexual assault is associated with the number 3 (codes 301–399). As further major crime categories are classified, they will receive appropriate identification codes.

The second digit of the code represents further grouping of the major crimes. Sexual assault is divided into three groupings: (1) criminal enterprise, (2) personal cause, and (3) group cause. Specific classifications within these groups are represented by the third digits of the code.

Individual classifications within these groups are further divided into sub-groups, using two additional digits following a decimal point after the code. For example, entitlement rape (313) is divided into four subgroups: 313:01 social acquaintance rape; 313:02 subordinate rape; 313:03 power-reassurance rape; and 313:04 exploitative rape.

Victims of rapes and sexual assaults are generally divided into three categories:

1. Adults are defined as individuals at least 18 years of age who are almost always pubescent and usually considered capable of consent under laws proscribing sexual conduct. Some exceptions may include persons who are mentally retarded, brain impaired, or psychotic.
2. Adolescents are defined as individuals 13 to 17 years of age who are usually pubescent but whose legal status under laws proscribing sexual conduct varies from state to state and even statute to statute within the same jurisdiction.
3. Children are defined as individuals 12 years of age or younger who are usually prepubescent and who are considered minors incapable of consent under almost all laws proscribing sexual conduct.

300: Criminal Enterprise Rape

Criminal enterprise sexual assault involves sexual coercion, abuse, or assault that is committed for material gain.

301: Felony Rape

Sexual assault committed during the commission of a felony, such as breaking and entering or robbery, is considered felony rape. The classification is made as to whether the rape was primary or secondary in intent.

301.01: Primary Felony Rape.   The intent of primary felony rape is a non-sexual felony (robbery or breaking and entering). The victim is at the scene of the primary felony and sexually assaulted as a second offense. If the victim was not present, the felony would still occur.

310.02: Secondary Felony Rape.   The primary intent of secondary felony rape is sexual assault, with a second felony also planned. This implies the offender knows a person will be present for both crimes to occur.

Case No. 1

Gloria is a 27-year-old single black female who was born in South Carolina. In 1967 she moved with her family to New York and has since lived in two different projects in the Bronx. She attended public school and earned average grades. Her favorite subjects were English and physical education. She left school in the 10th grade to have her first child. Prior to the rape, Gloria was employed as a home attendant.

Gloria was four months pregnant and living with her mother and daughter in a Bronx housing project. She had gone out to dinner with two friends. After dinner, she was driven home. As she was walking to her building, she saw her brother and another friend. She went into her building, passed the mailboxes, and entered the elevator. She pressed the 5th floor button and heard someone coming, so she held the door. She recognized him as James. As James came into the elevator, someone else also entered the elevator. As the door closed, this unknown man grabbed her from behind and began choking her neck in an arm hold. She struggled and lost consciousness. When she awoke she was on the roof landing. The unknown male was on top of her, and James was pointing a gun at her. She remembers screaming but not hearing herself. The unknown male told James not to shoot, and Gloria then passed out a second time.

When she awoke the men were gone. Her clothes had been ripped off except for one pant leg. Her clothes were strewn about the area. She dressed, feeling very dizzy, sore, and in shock. She walked down about 15 flights of stairs because she was afraid the men might still be in the elevator. She reached her mother's apartment. She had trouble talking. Her daughter woke up and came to see her. Gloria then telephoned a friend. When her mother realized what had happened, she called the housing police. Subsequently an ambulance took her to the hospital.

Gloria was hospitalized for 5 days. Medical reports indicated she had trauma to the head with intracranial damage, a hematoma to her forehead, and a cerebral concussion with post-concussion syndrome. This syndrome was characterized by diminished and irregular reflexes, ataxia, equilibrium disturbance, severe pressure headaches, anxiety, nausea, confusion, depression, dizziness, apprehension, nervousness, and general debility. She had flashbacks to the rape and the gun pointed at her. She worried about damage to her unborn baby. She had rectal bleeding from an anal tear and needed further medical treatment for a sexually transmitted disease.

Gloria was unable to return to live in her mother's apartment and had to be relocated. She remembered two prior crimes in the building involving a 20-year-old friend of hers who was raped and murdered on the same rooftop, and a young 18-year-old man who was beaten and hung from an exit door. She had nightmares.

She is reminded of the rape when seeing military camouflage suits, since that was the outfit of one of the assailants. She has aches and pains from the severe bruising. She has sexual difficulties with her boyfriend. Gloria has difficulty visiting her mother in the project. The elevator triggers frightening memories. She has difficulty socially. She finds it hard to relax; she gets into deep thought and finds herself staring into space.

The rape was a surprise method of attack. There was no prior warning; Gloria held the elevator for a friend of her brother's, and an unknown man also entered. She pushed her apartment floor button and was expecting to ride to the floor when she was grabbed and choked into unconsciousness. Gloria was threatened and intimidated with a gun that was used to control, intimidate, and terrorize her. There were two assailants who caused severe physical injury, who both raped her, and who also robbed her. The motivation for the felony rape was robbery. The psychological motivation was anger. She was rendered physically unconscious during the assault, and it is clear in terms of her psychological response to the attack that fear, intimidation, and threat to life paralyzed her and made the assailant feel powerful and in charge.

310: Personal Cause

Rape and sexual assault motivated by personal cause are acts ensuing from interpersonal aggression that result in sexual victimization to persons who may or may not be known to the offenders. These rape and sexual assaults are not primarily motivated by material gain and are not sanctioned by a group. Rather, underlying emotional conflicts or psychological issues propel the offenders to commit rape and sexual assault. Although the case may be legally defined as rape, the term sexual assault is used in this classification to encompass a wide range of forced and pressured sexual activities.

312: Domestic Sexual Assault

The victim in this classification is a partner, spouse, or family member of the offender.

313: Entitlement Rape

In an entitlement rape, the offender forces the victim into sexual activity. Issues of power and control are underlying psychological conflicts.

The determining criterion for the classification of sexual assault and rape as entitlement (313), anger (314), or sadism (315) is the amount of aggression involved. Any combination of the following may be used to determine the correct classification:

1. Injuries greater than minor cuts, scratches, and abrasions;
2. Force in excess of that needed to attain victim compliance (slapping, punching, or kicking, when there is no evidence of victim resistance);
3. Specific acts in the offense (mutilation, burning, stabbing, choking to unconsciousness, biting, kicking, anal penetration, or insertion of foreign objects); and
4. Desires or attempts to humiliate a victim (derogatory and demeaning remarks, any use of feces or urine, forcing a male to observe, or evidence of forced fellatio after sodomy).

313.01: Social Acquaintance Rape.   In this offense, there is prior knowledge of or relationship between the victim and offender. Often the relationship is social; and for adults and adolescents, the assault usually occurs on a date. Other relationships include student/teacher or athlete/coach affiliations. For child cases, the relationship might include a neighbor or family friend.

313.02: Subordinate Rape.   The relationship between the victim of subordinate rape and the offender is one of subordination and status imbalance. One person has power over another by employment, education, or age. The offender uses this authority relationship to take advantage of the victim.

313.03 Power-Reassurance Rape.   Sexual assault usually occurs as a blitz-style attack or sudden, unexpected assault. Usually it is a situational assault unless the victim has been targeted. The victim is usually unknown to the offender. Low expressive aggression is used with no severe physical injuries to the victim.

313.04 Exploitative Rape.   In exploitative rape, sometimes called opportunistic rape, expressed aggression is generally low and does not exceed that necessary to force a victim into compliance. Callous indifference to the victim is evident.

314: Anger Rape

Sexual assault in the category of anger rape is characterized by high expressive aggression — unprovoked physical and verbal aggression or physical force in excess of that necessary to gain victim compliance must be present. Rage is evident in this offender. He may have manifested behaviors listed for sadistic sexual assault, but these must appear to be punishing actions done in anger, not to increase sexual arousal. The primary motive for the offense is anger and not sexual gratification. When the offender knows the victim, the assault on that victim appears to be the result of the offender's easy access to that victim. These offenses are predominantly impulse driven (opportunity alone, possibly coupled with impaired judgment due to drugs or alcohol).

314.01: Gender Anger Rape.   The category of gender anger rape is reserved for offenders who hate women and express their rage through rape.

Case No. 2

After completing a 3-day seminar with a group of friends from work, Rita, a 40-year-old single teacher, stopped at a lounge to relax before returning home. She returned to her second-floor apartment around 8:30 p.m., unpacked and changed from her traveling clothes, listened to her phone messages, made a few phone calls, invited her boyfriend over for supper, and started a tea kettle. The doorbell rang, and, thinking it was her boyfriend, she went to answer it. However, it was not her boyfriend but rather her landlord's son, Nick. He told her he had a message from his father that would upset her and therefore had to tell her inside her apartment and not in the hallway. The essence of the message was that the landlord thought someone was using her apartment when she was out.

As Rita turned to get some cigarettes, Nick abruptly hit her on her head, and she fell to the floor. The assailant held a gun to her head and threatened to blow out her brains. He demanded money and her car keys, then ordered her to disrobe. She told him she had her period and he forced her to undo his pants and fellate him. Hearing noises believed to be her boyfriend, the assailant forced Rita out of the apartment, without her clothes, through a back alley to the back steps of a church. He instructed her to begin again and to do it right this time. His language was laced with demeaning, vulgar terms. The assailant continually hit her and held the gun to her temple. He forced vaginal sex. A noise was heard; the assailant removed his tee-shirt and forced Rita to put it on. He marched her back to his father's apartment, where he ordered her to clean up her face and put on a pair of his running shorts. She was then forced out of the apartment. She saw her boyfriend, ran to him, and together they flagged down a passing truck to take them to a hospital. The assailant then ran away.

The dominating motivating dynamics of the rapist were power, control and displaced anger. It is clear in terms of Rita's response to the rape that fear, intimidation and threat to life paralyzed Rita and made the rapist feel powerful and in charge. This can be noted by the language used and the moving of the victim from location to location. The displaced anger is noted in the extreme aggression inflicted on the victim. These dynamics are not uncommon in juveniles who rape and displace anger to someone of the same age as the ambivalent person in their life. The language used by the assailant suggests a dynamic compatible with a sadistic fantasy of domination and submission. The juvenile was convicted.

314.02: Age Anger Rape. The motive of the offender in age anger rape is to seek out victims of a specific age group, usually the elderly or the young.

314.03 Racial Anger Rape. This category is reserved for what appears to be racially motivated rape.

Case No. 3

Having just returned from an evening movie, Mary walked into the apartment building where she lived with her mother and sister, pushed the elevator button for her floor, and entered. As the elevator ascended toward her floor, it suddenly stopped in between floors. Mary tried to get the elevator to move and to get help. Suddenly she saw the elevator hatch open up and a man descend. She was terrified until she realized she recognized him. She asked him for help. Then a second male came through the elevator hatch, and she then realized something was wrong. A knife was flashed, and she was threatened with death by a garrote if she screamed. Mary was stripped of her clothes, sexually assaulted by both males, and forced to endure a variety of perverse sexual acts (oral, anal and vaginal sex; urinating on her body and in her mouth; vomiting on her face; multi-layered sexual acts alternating male to female and male to male). Prayer helped her to live through the terror she was experiencing.

The assailants then forced Mary back through to the hatch of the elevator to ride to the basement. There was hesitancy by the assailants about where to take her next (outside or the woods). She was then forced to climb twelve flights of stairs to the building roof, where the sexual assaults and deviant acts were repeated (both assailants simultaneously inserted their penises into her mouth). Conversations between the assailants were interlaced with sexual questions and comments, racial slurs, orders, and threats of murder. She was held over the edge of the roof and taunted with the question, "Have you ever flown?" Both her life and her mother and sister's lives were threatened if she told of the acts.

Eventually one assailant left. The second assailant changed his behavioral style (*he acted really crazy*) as he continued the assaults. Mary managed to talk him into freeing her, and she was able to return to her apartment.

She arrived at her apartment to find her mother and sister frantic with worry. She disclosed the rape, and the police were immediately called. She was terrified to have to ride in the elevator. She was taken to the hospital where she was examined. Police followed all investigative leads and were able to apprehend the pair. Both men were convicted. However, their families live in the area, and Mary has great fear for her safety when they are released from prison.

This was classified as anger racial rape due to the clear conversation and racial slurs made by the assailants, who were white, to Mary, who was black.

314.04: Global Anger Rape.   This category is reserved for offenders who appear to be globally angry at the world. This is a high expressive aggression assault with no evidence of sadism and no evidence that the offender was focally angry at women.

315: Sadistic Rape

The level of violence in a sadistic offender's rape clearly exceeds what is necessary to force a victim into compliance; the offender's sexual arousal is a function of the victim's pain, fear or discomfort. Behavioral evidence may include sham sadism (whipping, bondage); violence focus on the erogenous parts of the victim's body (cutting or otherwise mutilating the breasts, anus, buttocks or genitals); insertion of foreign objects into the vagina or anus; intercourse after the victim is unconscious; or the use of feces or urine within the offense.

Most often there is high expressive aggression with moderate to severe injury to the victim. Frequently, the offender uses items to inflict pain and injury (cigarettes, knives, sticks, bottles, etc.). In some cases of sham or muted sadism, however, there is clear evidence of eroticized aggression (insertion of foreign objects, bondage, whipping) without extensive physical injury. Death may occur.

Case No. 4

On July 31, 1998, Gina, a 37-year-old legal secretary, met friends at a neighborhood bar in a shopping center. She was a friendly, free-spirited single mother who was playing MegaTouch™ and drinking Jack Daniels when Shane, a 28-year-old handsome, tan, muscular landscaper with blue/green penetrating eyes walked in. He began flirting with Gina, admiring her tight body and calling her pretty lady. Around 1:30 a.m., Shane asked for a ride home; and although friends tried to discourage her, Gina assured them she would be fine and left barefoot with Shane, carrying her sandals.

Around 5:30 the next morning, a man leaving on vacation glanced at the blue car next to his and saw a woman (Gina) with her head leaning against the window of the driver's side. At first he thought she was sleeping but then realized she was dead. The police were called and then the medical examiner.

Crime scene: Blood was splattered on the front seats and gear shift. The victim's skirt was pulled up to expose her buttocks.

Forensics: Feces were found under the victim's fingernails. No fingerprints of value were found, and there was no weapon. Blood washed away any DNA evidence.

Autopsy: The autopsy indicated the victim died of multiple injuries to the head and body. Her vagina was lacerated in four areas with a foreign object.

Investigation: Detectives talked with the family and determined that the victim was last seen at the pub. Detectives talked with witnesses at the pub and took a photograph of Shane for identification. Detectives knew Shane from a previous rape report. Shane was arrested. His story was that he left the bar with Gina; that they were messing around; and that he had to urinate and she came out of the car with him to have him urinate in her hair. When they returned to the car, she straddled the gear shift, gave him oral sex, and choked on his penis. He tried to wake her up by patting her face; then he tried to redress her before leaving the car.

After Shane's arrest, rape victims who had not previously reported came forward. They resisted reporting because of embarrassment, blaming themselves, and thinking they would not be believed. Many said they were not sure it was rape because he was not a stranger and they had gone with him at his request.

Shane was charged with Murder 1 and Rape. No bail was set. It was hard to reconstruct the sequence of acts in the car; but it is believed she was beaten about the head and face, forced to have vaginal sex, forced to have oral sex, and then strangled. A Consolidation of Cases Hearing was held.

Crime Dynamics: The cycle of sadistic rape behavior noted in the defendant included the following: the victims were white, attractive, outgoing young women. Shane was acquainted with his victims; he met them at a drinking establishment or at work. He gained his victims' interest by complimenting them and engaging them in superficial conversations. He asked for a date, invited himself for a ride, or asked for a ride home.

All of the victims willingly accompanied him to the location where he assaulted them. Victims did not report any threats made by Shane prior to the assaults. In all but one instance, the victims drove to the destination of the assault. Initially, none of the victims perceived any physical danger. After Shane initiated sexual contact with the victims, they resisted and struggled to get away. The victims cried and pled for him to stop. In all instances, the victims became afraid and terrified because of his increasing physical aggression. After establishing physical control, Shane forced cunnilingus and vaginal rape. Victims described the pain when he inserted his fist into their vaginas. Shane laughed at his victims, made humiliating and demeaning remarks, ejaculated on their faces, and bragged that he treated them like whores.

Shane is a sexual sadist; there is a persistent pattern of his sexual excitement in response to victims' sufferings. Callous indifference is shown. With Gina, even though he noted she was not breathing, he did not call for help. He claimed she hit her head on the steering wheel and hit the left side of her head on the driver's door. (*Put my ear to her chest, not sure I heard anything but I have bad hearing in that ear. I said to myself that this was great, my luck she would probably die.*)

Trial Outcome: Shane was convicted of Murder 1 and acquitted of the rape charge.

319: Abduction Rape

Abduction by a stranger implies transportation of an individual into a vehicle, a building, or a distance of more than 20 feet for the purpose of committing a crime.

Case No. 5

Fran, a 32-year-old single white sales manager, had made reservations to stay in a hotel during a business trip. She drove from the airport to the hotel. As she entered the hotel garage she was unable to get a ticket from the automatic machine, and no one was in the garage booth to give instructions or a ticket. She continued into the garage and found a parking space. As she was preparing to leave her car, she was aware of a man running over to her and thought he had the parking ticket. Suddenly the man forced a sharp instrument to her neck, and a second man appeared. Fran was shoved into the back seat and abducted from the parking garage.

During the time period that she was in the back seat of the car, she tried a number of strategies to get out of the situation — she talked, pled, and cried. All efforts failed, and there was increased verbal aggression (*Shut up bitch*) and physical aggression with the weapon being jabbed into her ribs. After a time, the car stopped. Fran was blindfolded, forced out of the car, and then locked in the trunk of the car. Her immediate thoughts at that time were of death. She heard her abductors talking in the car and realized she was going to be raped. The car stopped and started several times over a one- to two-hour time period. Then the car stopped again, and Fran was pulled out of the trunk. The blindfold was tightened, and she was shoved into the front seat of the car where she was then raped, vaginally and orally. She was forced to drink some type of liquor from a bottle. After the rape, Fran was shoved back into the car. The rapists lectured her about keeping her doors locked as they were going to leave her in a bad section of the city. They ordered her to count to 10 and left the car. Fran removed the blindfold, calmed herself as best she could, and began driving and looking for help. She was able to ask someone for directions to a hospital and was led by another car to a hospital. At the hospital she was seen by various staff members. The police were called, and she gave a statement to two officers. She telephoned her brother, who came to the hospital and took her back to his apartment.

330: *Group Cause Sexual Assault*

This category is used for three or more offenders. When there are two offenders, each should be classified under Personal Cause. Although there are clearly group dynamics (contagion effects, diffusion of responsibility) and social dynamics (highly developed gang cultures in particular communities or cities that foster gang rape), the factors that motivate each of the offenders may well be different.

331: *Formal Gang Assault*

A formal gang is characterized by some internal organizational structure, a name as well as other identifying features (colors, insignias, patterns of dress), and some evidence of group cohesiveness (members owe some allegiance to the gang and gather to participate in a variety of activities). The gang must have some mission or purpose other than the assault.

332: *Informal Gang*

An informal gang is a very loosely structured group that congregates, typically on the spur of the moment, with a common purpose of marauding or otherwise engaging in antisocial activity. Although the group may have one or more leaders, there is no formal organizational structure. This category also includes all other instances of multiple offender assaults in which there is no evidence that the group constitutes a formal gang.

Case No. 6

Having spent an evening with her husband and other couples at a local restaurant, 25-year-old Nan was outside waiting for her husband to pick her up in their car. She heard a car, and suddenly a man grabbed her from behind and pushed her in to a car. She was thrown to the floor of the back seat, she was ordered to stop screaming, and a foot was wedged on her chest. As the car kept traveling, she was ordered to disrobe. When she failed to comply fast enough, the clothes were pulled off by the abductor. She was then raped orally and vaginally. The three assailants then took her to a home where four additional men were waiting. Throughout the night, Nan was forced to endure multiple sexual acts including rape and sodomy. She believed she would be murdered. Her terror was heightened by the method-ical, planned manner of the assaults. She coped by being very visually aware of her surroundings and by dissociating herself from feeling what was being done to her body. For example, after being forced to bathe with one of the rapists in a bathtub, she noted blood on the towel after drying herself. Feeling horrified, she threw the towel at the man and asked, "What have you done to me?" This major outburst illustrated her dissociation from the injuries inflicted upon her. The abductor then forced her into the car again, drove to another site, sexually assaulted her, and finally drove her to another location where he released her.

This rape was classified as an informal gang rape and anger racial rape since she was white and the assailants were black.

She sought help; the police responded, and she was transported to a hospital that treated her for her physical and sexual injuries from the rapes.

Her major psychological defense in coping with the victimization was dissociation (*I just focused on the details of the house*). This strategy was key to identifying the house, leading to the arrest and conviction of three rapists. Four rapists remain at large, however.

390: Sexual Assault Not Classified Elsewhere

This category is reserved for those assaults that cannot be classified elsewhere.

Reference

Douglas, J.E., Burgess, A.W., Burgess, A.G., and Ressler, R.K. (1992) *Crime Classifi-cation Manual*, San Francisco, Jossey-Bass.

False Rape Allegations

10

ANN WOLBERT BURGESS
ROBERT R. HAZELWOOD*

Introduction

Compared with other types of serious crimes, rape has a number of unique characteristics. First, it is difficult to know how frequently rape occurs because of its low reporting rate. Accurate estimates of the incidence and prevalence of rape are not readily available as the majority of victims do not report to the police, receive medical attention from hospitals, or seek help from services agencies such as rape crisis centers (Kilpatrick, Veronen, and Best, 1985). Second, rape is the only serious crime in which victims are generally held responsible for their own assaults. It is believed by many that people like to be overpowered sexually, that women say *no* but mean *yes*, and that women issue false reports regarding rape to save face, get even, or conceal pregnancy (Burt, 1980). Third, rape is treated distinctively in the courtroom. Rules of evidence have been unique and stringent (signs of resistance required as a proof of nonconsent and the need for third-party corroboration). Fourth, rape and abuse are selectively perpetrated by the male segment of the population and are selectively borne by the female segment of the population. Fifth, rape instills fear in women and serves to limit the freedom of women by placing constraints on their activities (Riger and Gordon, 1988). And sixth, unlike other crimes, there is considerable variation in what constitutes a real rape. Law enforcement agents and child protective service workers use the term *unfounded* when there is insufficient evidence, or the term *false allegation* to dismiss the complaint of a non-believable victim.

Imprisonment of a man falsely accused of rape has been described since biblical times. Potiphar, an Egyptian captain of the Pharaoh's guard, employed Joseph to watch over his household. Potiphar's wife "cast her eyes upon Joseph ... caught him by his garment, saying lie with me."

Joseph resisted this temptation, but his rejection caused her to say that the Hebrew servant Joseph came to mock her, that she lifted up her voice

---

* Sections of this chapter are reprinted with permission from the 2nd edition of *Practical Aspects of Rape Investigation*, CRC Press, Boca Raton. We specifically acknowledge the work of Margaret Aiken, Neil Hibler, and Charles P. McDowell.

0-8493-0076-2/01/$0.00+$.50
© 2001 by CRC Press LLC

and cried, that he left his garment with her and fled. Potiphar imprisoned Joseph for two years, freeing him for his skill in interpreting the dream of the seven-year famine in Egypt (Genesis, 39).

A contemporary false rape allegation was made in Chicago. Tawana Brawley, a 15-year-old girl, was found after 4 days, huddled inside a plastic garbage bag. She was covered with dirt, and racial epithets were written on her body. She told police detectives that she had been abducted and repeatedly raped by six white men, one of whom had a police-style badge. After a 7-month investigation, a grand jury concluded Brawley had falsified the story. They found no evidence of a cover-up by law enforcement officials and charged that Brawley's lawyers and advisors tried to keep authorities from learning the truth (MacDonald, 1994).

Although most experienced investigators have taken false crime reports of one type or another, they are always sensitive to the possibility. Surprisingly, even though this phenomenon of the false rape report is well recognized, there has been little careful research into the problem. This chapter reviews the brief literature on the subject and provides some case examples.

Definition

Little is published which addresses the issue and concept of false allegation. The studies describing child sexual abuse are uniform in reporting the sparse literature in the area of false allegations (Green, 1986; Faller, 1984; Rosenfeld et al., 1979; Benedek and Schetky, 1984). These authors concur that, when child custody is a prominent issue, the frequency of false allegations rises dramatically. Vindictiveness and psychological dysfunction on the part of the parents may underlie such accusations (Faller, 1984; Benedek and Schetky, 1984). Rosenfeld et al. (1979) suggested that it is possible that the specified act did occur, but the wrong person was accused. Goodwin et al. (1978) used the terms *false accusation* and *false denial*, which suggests two variations that are in no way specified by the term *false allegation*. Peters (1976) and Goodwin et al. (1978) found that they could not substantiate allegations of sexual abuse in 6% of cases.

Katz and Mazur (1979) defined a false report as a "… deliberate lie by the alleged victim accusing a man of a rape that did not occur. It may also be a fantasy report that the female believes is true" (p. 207). The authors also write that wide discrepancies in the reported frequency of false allegations are due to differences in definitions and criteria, and due to the source of the judgments in these situations.

McDowell and Hibler, in the first edition of *Practical Aspects of Rape Investigation: A Multidisciplinary Approach* (1987), presented a sensitive treatment of the issue of false allegation that includes the role of defense mechanisms, secondary gain, and other psychological aspects. They asserted that investigators can make sense of these false claims once they discover the purpose served for the victim by such an allegation. However, a precise definition of the very phenomenon they described was omitted.

McDowell (March 1990), in another source, again failed to define the concept but described three conditions used to classify cases as false allegations:

1. Victim recants complaint
2. Victim fails polygraph
3. Investigation reveals allegation to be false

These criteria are very broad and imprecise, thereby leaving a wide margin for discretionary interpretation and action. McDowell (1990) has published a checklist for use by investigators that is intended to help determine the validity of claims of sexual assault. According to the key to this instrument, the best that a victim can do or be classified as is equivocal.

Lefer (1992) reported that the primary myth about women and sexual offense is that they lie about it. Lefer wrote, "It is as though the victim is the one on trial; every gesture ... word can be held against her" (p. 198). Further, she asserted that by reporting sexual assaults, women lose credibility; and when there is inconsistency in the reports, the validity of the entire allegation comes into question. Credibility for victims is elusive. Women who are unemotional may be conveying that they were not disturbed by the alleged event — hence, the absence of harm. Women who are overwrought come across as emotionally unstable — and hence, not credible.

Factitious disorders involve feigning, producing, or exaggerating physical and/or psychological symptoms that facilitate the individual's objective of assuming the sick role (Feldman, Ford, and Stone, 1994). Such persons do not seek recognizable external incentives of evading court proceedings or obtaining drugs, as in malingering, but instead assume the patient role (APA, 1994). Feldman and colleagues (1994) discuss the cases of four women who claimed to have been the victims of rape; the allegations were later disproven. They suggest factitious rape may be prompted by a search for nurturance; by dissociation, leading individuals to believe that trauma earlier in life is ongoing; by a need to be rescued from real, current abuse; and by projections of anger onto specific male targets. Although dramatic factitious rape is rare, argue the psychiatrists, the thorough investigations of rape claims are advocated even when patients have known histories of deceptive behavior.

Investigators suspect false allegations when victims repeatedly change accounts of the assaults. Care must be taken to distinguish a changing in the story from recollection of additional data. In both true and false claims, new facts and more detail may be added in subsequent interviews. The false claimant wishes to shore up the allegation to make it more believable, while the genuine victim may remember more detail and descriptive data in the days following the assault as composure and equilibrium are regained. This situation places investigators in very delicate positions. Worst-case scenarios are that the false claimant successfully manipulates the system for personal gain or that the legitimate claimant is further traumatized by aggressive attempts on the part of investigators to elicit the ultimate truth.

It is important to distinguish between deliberate deceit and an honest mistake. The person making a false allegation may change information from the original report to further deceive and mislead the authorities. A legitimate rape victim, in the initial stages of the investigation and because of stress and psychic pain, may offer wrong information due to her altered ability to accurately process information.

When a rape or any other crime occurs, there must be three elements — perpetrator(s), act(s), and a setting or set of conditions. One can make a false allegation with reference to any or all of these elements. To further complicate the situation, a false allegation can consist of a false accusal or a false denial (Goodwin, Sahd, and Rada, 1978).

Classification of Unfounded Rape Cases

Prosecutors and investigators find the term *false allegation* of little use unless the claimant says in some way that the account is untrue. It is more common to use general terms such as *unfounded, refusal to prosecute,* and the like. These categories allow law enforcement to close cases without completing the investigations. Cases of false allegation are included in these categories; some jurisdictions have reported that as much as 35 to 40% of all cases are so classified. This is one way in which rates of false allegation have been inflated and misrepresented. It may be reported that false allegations of rape occur at the rate of 30%, for example, when what is really meant is that 30% of cases are unfounded.

The following categories represent common reasons for unfounding a rape complaint. Careful classification by police departments would help in determining how rape complaints are categorized and whether the FBI uniform crime reports of a 50% clearance rate nationwide for rape cases are accurate.

Three of the categories represent a determination based on the psychological evaluation of a victim. Three of the classifications are determined through investigation.

Psychological Determination

Sex Stress Situations

Sex stress situations are cases where the male and female initially agreed to have sexual relations but then something went wrong. Usually, what went wrong was that a third party became aware of the situation and defined the situation as rape or caused the female to say it was rape as a way out of a dilemma. Also, in some of these sex stress cases, the person who referred to the problem as rape actually wanted some service from the hospital and felt she could not directly ask for it. For example, a young teenager, having had sex the evening before, may have feared pregnancy and needed medication to prevent pregnancy (Burgess and Holmstrom, 1974).

It is important to understand sex stress cases for several reasons. First, they greatly influence how the system deals with rape. Staff members tend to become obsessed with trying to determine whether a case is a rape. A tremendous amount of energy goes into diagnosing rather than helping the victim with the request for aid. Second, sex stress cases deserve counseling in their own right. These females are victims in their own way and have many emotional concerns over what has been an upsetting experience.

The two main types of sex stress cases are (1) mutual agreement and (2) financial gain.

In one type of mutual agreement case, both parties agree to have sex but then one person wishes to deny the act or becomes repulsed by her behavior. The following case illustrates true setting, true act, and false perpetrator:

Case No. 1

Roberta, a 27-year-old female civilian employee of a state police department, made a report of rape. She disclosed the alleged rape to a male coworker. Roberta told a very detailed and complex story. She reported that when she was walking to her car from a disco club, a known male, a police sergeant, jumped out from behind a car and grabbed her from behind. He forced her into a van and ripped her clothes off. When she refused to spread her legs, he cut her thighs repeatedly (all cuts were superficial and within the reach of the victim). He also slashed at her breasts. As she gave this account, she showed her coworker the injuries. The assailant succeeded in having vaginal sexual intercourse with her.

A formal complaint was made to internal affairs, which initiated a full investigation. The officer in question was suspended from duty. After the initial disclosure to the coworker, Roberta became markedly uncooperative and resistant to investigative efforts. She refused to submit material evidence and refused the polygraph. Eventually she did turn in her dress, which was liberally stained with semen.

The investigating police officer thought this might be a false rape allegation for two reasons. First, the alleged assailant was outraged, categorically denied everything, and readily agreed to forensic evaluation and a polygraph. Second, concurrent to this complaint was a highly publicized rape case involving a police officer who eventually was convicted of raping a woman he stopped for a motor violation. Consultation supported the investigating officer's suspicions, and suggestions for proactive interviewing techniques were made.

Roberta, on re-interview, admitted to having made a false allegation. She admitted to repeated sexual intercourse with a male previously unknown to her whom she had picked up at the disco. The acts were all consensual. When she awoke the next morning she felt dirty. Additionally, she had overslept and was consequently late for work. She then inflicted the mutilating injuries and fabricated her story. The falsely accused officer was a believable suspect because he had shown considerable interest in Roberta at work. Fortunately for Roberta, no charges were brought against her. She was referred for counseling and to date remains in therapy.

In another type of sex stress mutual agreement case, the woman agrees to have sex and the male becomes violent or perverted and frightens the woman. Sex is agreed upon, but the setting and/or acts cause the victim to seek protective assistance through the police.

A third type of mutual agreement is where parental intervention may occur. A parent may suspect that sex occurred, perceives some danger to the daughter's reputation, and assumes responsibility in the matter. Or the teenager reports the sex to the parent as rape in order to receive pregnancy prevention advice.

The following is such a case where the setting and perpetrator were false and the act was true:

Case No. 2

Samantha was a pretty 15-year-old girl. She arrived home well past her curfew on a Friday night. She tearfully and reluctantly told her parents that she had gone to the skating rink with her friends. At closing time, she and her friends left the building with the intention of walking home. According to Samantha, a young man who worked at the rink called her aside and offered to drive her home. She allegedly accepted his offer and went willingly with him to his car. Samantha reported that he drove to a deserted area and forced her to have intercourse with him. The parents immediately contacted the local police (they lived in a small town in the south). Samantha and her parents were brought to the regional rape crisis center by the local police. The nurse was summoned. She completed the examination and evidence collection without incident.

The case was evaluated as a possible sex stress situation. A female supervising officer conducted a second interview. At this time, Samantha retracted her allegation, stating that she had had consensual sex with her boyfriend and was late arriving home. Because of her fear of punishment from her parents, she created this fiction.

In sex stress cases involving a money motive, prostitutes may encounter a situation in which the customer does not live up to the contract. The customer may become perverse, become violent, rob her or him, or not pay for services obtained. As a result, prostitutes often feel they are in danger and, as a result, sometimes turn to police for protection. The police, in turn, bring the woman to the hospital for medical attention.

False Rape Allegation

In false rape allegations, generally all three components of an allegation are false — the act, the perpetrator, and the setting. These are situations in which the complainants deceive due to psychological needs for attention or for financial motives. The complainants are aware that the complaints are false.

In the following false rape allegation case, the act was false but the setting and perpetrator were true:

Case No. 3

Julie, a 16-year-old, arrived at the trauma center having been severely beaten in the head and face. She reported having been abducted from the street in her neighborhood by an unknown male. She reported that he dragged her into a park and raped her vaginally and orally repeatedly. He detained her in his apartment for two days. When the rape crisis nurse arrived at the trauma unit, the staff nurses asked repeatedly whether she really had been raped. Thinking this to be strange, the forensic nurse inquired further into their concerns. The staff nurses reported that Julie's mother had called several times saying that Julie deserved a good beating. After all, she had been missing from home for 5 days.

The examination revealed no vaginal trauma. Microscopic examination of a slide prepared from vaginal secretions revealed no sperm. When confronted with the discrepancy between her mother's report of her missing for 5 days and her statement of 2 days, Julie changed her story. She actually knew her assailant. In fact, she had had consensual sex with him several months before the alleged rape. She further admitted that there had been no rape nor even sex, but that he had beaten her as she had previously reported.

The following case illustrates false act, false perpetrator, and false setting. The motive was financial:

Case No. 4

Dorina was a single mother who lived in public housing. She brought her two young girls to the rape crisis center for evaluation following allegations of child molestation. No physical evidence of the allegation was found in either child. The child advocate informed her of victim's compensation. Under this provision, victims of violent crime could apply to the state for compensation in amounts up to $3,000. The only requirement was that a police report be filed. Dorina was awarded $2,000 for each child. Approximately 6 months later, Dorina presented at the center stating that 2 unknown males had broken into her home, raped her, and left. She was unable to provide a viable description, and neither trauma nor physical evidence was found. She was again advised of the availability of victim's compensation. She made application and was compensated in the amount of $3,000.

Approximately 18 months later Dorina again reported a rape to the police. She was transported to the rape crisis center where she was again evaluated. As before, she was unable to adequately describe her assailant, and again neither trauma nor evidence was found. Under the provisions of the victim's compensation program, compensation can only be awarded one time per individual. Several months after the second assault, Dorina brought suit against the city public housing authority, seeking punitive damages in the amount of $150,000. Her claim was that both criminal assaults occurred because of a faulty lock on her door. She claimed to have made a formal report requesting appropriate repair. No record of such a report was ever found. The determination was that all of the allegations made by Dorina were false, motivated financially.

The following false rape allegation case is a false act, false setting, and false perpetrator with a financial motive:

Case No. 5

Micaela, a single teenage mother, was brought to the rape crisis center by a police officer. She claimed to have been abducted from the street in her neighborhood by an unknown assailant who dragged her into a vacant house and forced her to have vaginal sex. During this commentary, she mentioned several times that her food stamps had been stolen from her by the assailant. She seemed more concerned about the missing food stamps than about the rape. Micaela was unable to give a meaningful description of the assailant. Although she had reported the crime promptly, neither trauma nor physical evidence was identified.

While Micaela was dressing, the nurse asked the police officer if he knew about the theft of the food stamps. He said that that had been her primary concern since she had first made the complaint. He went on to say that there was a lively black market in food stamps for drugs. The officer explained that lost or stolen public subsidies can only be replaced if a police report is made.

After several attempts to complete the investigation, the case was designated as unfounded. The police were of the opinion that it was a false allegation made to obtain additional food stamps.

Delusional Rape Allegation

In delusional rape allegations, all three components of an allegation are false (the act, the perpetrator, and the setting). These are situations in which the complainant is psychotic and/or delusional. The complainant may not be consciously aware of the multiplicity of complaints made since the delusion is a continuous part of his or her thinking. It is important to carefully evaluate the complaint since it is obvious that the person is suffering a major mental illness. There may be an ongoing abusing situation that the person is trying to communicate. The problem is that it becomes repetitious in nature and represents a chronic ongoing unresolved trauma as in the following case:

Case No. 6

Ann, a 37-year-old white homeless woman, was admitted to a large, busy emergency department for the sixth time in a 3-month period, reporting she had been sexually assaulted. She had dirt and leaves in her vagina, superficial cuts and scratches on her inner thighs, and a vague description of the man who raped her, stating he had been stalking her for awhile. When the nurse examiner came into the examining room, Ann cried and reached for her hand, saying she just wanted to talk to someone who understood and cared. While waiting to be seen by the nurse, Ann was angry and volatile with severe mood shifts and little control over her anger.

Ann claimed six times that this man had stalked and raped her. The nurse examiner's assessment was that Ann was probably an incest victim who had not dealt with or resolved her incest issues. Her reports of rape were seen as a cry for help for the incest she could not yet address. The goal was to get Ann into counseling where, over time, the incest or childhood abuse issues could be discussed (Ledray, 1994).

Investigator Determination

Problematic Life Style

These are situations in which it is determined that the attributes of a person will be perceived negatively by juries. Lifestyle stereotypes may be of sexual preference or the type of work, as with a prostitute. The person may have a long history of alcoholism or mental illness, or the behavior may be perceived as influencing the credibility of the person and deemed to be viewed negatively by a jury. For various reasons, the decision is made not to move forward with the case.

Insufficient Evidence

Law enforcement and prosecutors may close an investigation because of insufficient evidence or lack of corroborative evidence. The complainant may have been unable to provide adequate information as to the assailant's physical description, or there is no workable description of an assailant. A delayed report may also account for minimal evidence.

There may be no collaborative evidence — the complainant states the assailant ejaculated or injured her, but there is no collaborating forensic evidence. The forensic examination does not match the statement of the individual.

Nol Pros

Nol pros comes from the Latin term *nolle prosequi. Black's Law Dictionary* defines *nol pros* as a formal entry upon the record by the prosecuting officer in a criminal action that states he will not further prosecute the case.

The victim may not be able to be located. She may have moved and failed to leave a forwarding address. There may be a host of other reasons which impede or prevent completion of the investigation.

Victim Drops Charges

Often, the victim will drop charges when the assailant is known. She does not want the consequences of following through with the case to court. Sometimes, the victim does not want to go through the lengthy aspects of a trial, wanting to move on with her life. The victim may refuse to testify and charges are dropped. Dropping charges does not mean the allegation was false.

The Motive for False Rape Allegations

Those who make false allegations may have legitimate problems worthy of attention in their own right. Yet if their false allegations are accepted at face value (rather than as symptoms of psychological needs), the actual problems may go untreated and result in future difficulties. It goes without saying that a false allegation, especially when it is based on malice, can result in a grievous injustice. Only by understanding the psychology of those making false allegations can investigators hope to increase the possibility of convicting rapists while also providing needed assistance and protection for everyone involved.

Study of False Rape Allegations

With the cooperation of the police agency of a small metropolitan community, 45 consecutive, disposed false rape allegations covering a 9-year period (1978–1987) were studied by sociologist Eugene Kanin. These false rape allegations constituted 41% of the total forcible rape cases (109) reported during that period. The cases were declared false when the women admitted that no rape had occurred. Consideration was given to the possibility of a rape recantation due to the woman's desire to avoid the legal process. However, in the majority of cases, the women were suspect at the time of the complaint or shortly thereafter, and the investigating detectives believed the charge was false.

While there was very little information on the demographics of these complainants, the women were all white, largely of a lower socioeconomic background, and modestly educated. The mean age of the women was 22 years.

Kanin (1994) identified three major motives for false allegations — providing an alibi, seeking revenge, and obtaining sympathy and attention.

Alibi Function

Over one half of the 45 cases of false charges (27, or 56%) needed a plausible explanation for a consensual encounter, usually sexual, with a male acquaintance. For example, the women feared they might be pregnant. In such cases, the women may have been having extramarital affairs, or their condoms broke.

Revenge

This category represents women who sought to retaliate against a rejecting male. Twenty-seven percent (12) of the cases seemed to serve this function. These rejections ranged from cases where the women were sexually and emotionally involved with males to situations in which the women were unilaterally involved with males. Because the suspect is always identified, the false allegations pose the greatest danger for a miscarriage of justice.

Attention/Sympathy

While there are several reasons for a person to falsely claim to have been raped, one motive is a need for attention. Approximately 18% (8) of the false charges served this function. The entire charge is, by and large, a fabrication without base.

Persons making false complaints for this reason usually have overwhelming feelings of inadequacy. They desperately want and need attention, usually in the form of concern and support. In their suffering, a claim of rape may seem a likely method to force a favorable response from friends and relatives as well as the authorities. Besides, they have probably tried a number of lesser methods of getting attention that have failed. Although false reports for this reason are relatively rare, it is important for the investigator to be aware of the possibility. The most significant fact in these cases is their reaction to the concern and support exhibited by friends, relatives, and the criminal justice community. In most rapes, even the most compassionate and supportive response from all concerned cannot fully alleviate the horror experienced by the victims. However, for the individuals desperately seeking attention, this solicitude may very well fill their needs.

False Allegations and the Adaptation Continuum

The creation of a factitious crime to avoid personal responsibility for some act or failure obviously represents an extreme departure from the way mature people normally deal with their problems. The extent to which false claims capitalize on actual events is unknown. However, there appears to be a rough continuum of inaccurate claims, ranging from a slightly distorted report of an actual event to the completely false report of an assault or rape. In its most extreme manifestation, the report can include bizarre scenarios supported by self-inflicted injuries and even self-mutilation. There have actually been incidents in which elaborate props, such as threatening letters or even messages written in blood, were used. Cases such as this at the far end of the continuum are extremely rare. Factitious claims of criminal victimization at the more normal end of the continuum may be more frequent.

   While the pathology involved in self-mutilation to support the false claim of rape is extremely rare, factitious claims of illness or injury on a much lower level are well-recognized phenomena in medical literature.

Munchausen's Syndrome

Severe cases of self-inflicted injuries or illnesses in which medical attention is sought have been termed Munchausen's syndrome (Asher, 1951). The name derives from the central figure in a book of tall tales and fabulous adventures who was named after Hieronymous Karl Friederich, Freiherr von Munchausen, a retired soldier known for his generosity and graphic conversations that took the form of the "serious narration of palpable absurdities." The key to understanding Munchausen's syndrome is that the patient is trying to use hospitals and clinicians in the service of pathologic psychological needs under the guise of seeking medical treatment for an ostensibly legitimate illness.

Munchausen's syndrome is based on a preoccupation with manipulation. These patients appear to be compulsively driven to make their complaints. As Gawn (1955) has noted, "While he is aware he is acting an illness, ... he cannot stop the act." Therefore, reports may capitalize on circumstances and occur only occasionally, or they may be a well-developed means of adapting and part of an extensive history. The degree to which Munchausen's patients defend their claims is in direct proportion to their need to be seen as victims. Dramatic, extreme cases are not likely to confess to the hoax, and those who present such cases are prone to become enraged at the suggestion that their illnesses are anything but genuine (Nadelson, 1979; Pankratz, 1981).

Mental States

In much the same way that Munchausen patients manipulate hospitals and doctors, a fraudulent claim of rape might be interpreted as a form of manipulation directed at the criminal justice system. This kind of manipulation is conceptually similar to other kinds of behavior (malingering, hysterical conversion reactions, and self-mutilation) that are well documented as medically achieved coping mechanisms (Ford, 1973). In Munchausen patients there is also a continuum, ranging from exaggerated claims of infirmity to actual self-induced illness (Grinker, 1961). At the extreme end of this continuum, life-threatening injuries are masqueraded as being legitimately contracted (Carney, 1980; Carney and Brown, 1983). Even child abuse, disguised as natural illness, is suspected of being an under-recognized means of gaining attention (Hodge et al., 1982; Kurlandsky et al., 1979; Meadow, 1982; Waller, 1983; Vaisrub, 1978).

Although police officers and investigators are used to seeing people who have been harmed or injured by others, they are less accustomed to seeing those who have harmed themselves. Most such instances involve a suicide or attempted suicide. However, since self-inflicted injuries used to support a claim of rape or assault are rare, it is logical for police to accept them at face value, at least initially. Where self-inflicted injuries are recognized as such and either are serious or appear to be very painful, it is understandable that police officers may look upon the victim as being mentally ill; yet, even those who reinforce their claims with severe self-inflicted injuries are seldom insane. Nevertheless, these individuals are psychiatrically impaired and should be assisted in obtaining professional help. The following case illustrates this phenomenon:

Case No. 7

A 25-year-old housewife reported receiving obscene phone calls and threatening letters that were made out of words cut from magazines and newspapers and pasted on a blank sheet. A short while later, she reported being raped by an unidentified intruder who threatened to come back and kill her in a particularly brutal manner if she reported the rape to the authorities. She had numerous bruises and a bite mark on her left breast. During the course of a subsequent polygraph examination, she admitted to fabricating the entire series of events. She also inflicted rope burns on her hands, bit her own breast, and ran face-first into a support post in her basement in order to acquire the injuries she thought would support her claim of rape. She said her husband did not understand her or pay attention to her, and she wanted to test his love.

As one proceeds along the continuum, the amount of violence the individual claims was used against her can reach fantastic levels, and the presenting dynamics of the case can become increasingly extraordinary. Keep in mind, however, that legitimate rapes may also incorporate varying levels of misperception. Because of this, every aspect must be scrutinized. For example, physical evidence and patterns of injury are always vital aspects in rape cases, and they require their own careful analysis. Appropriate support and assistance can only be given by a careful, objective examination of both the information and the physical evidence available.

This woman's self-esteem had been eroded over time by her insensitive and uncaring husband. By claiming to be the recipient of obscene phone calls and letters, and by claiming to have been raped, she was effectively making a desperate statement of her worth, both as a person and as a sexually desirable partner. Her willingness to engage in self-injurious behavior to support her claim underscores the seriousness of her emotional problems.

Red Flags of False Rape Allegations

There is no simple way to determine the legitimacy of any criminal complaint. This is true whether the report concerns the commission of a rape, a burglary, or any other offense. All complaints must be taken at face value and, unless there is some specific reason to believe otherwise, handled accordingly. False criminal reports are a relatively common reality in law enforcement. It is well known that victims frequently exaggerate the value of items taken in burglaries, and robberies are occasionally reported to explain the absence of money and other valuables to the victim's family. In most instances, it is impossible to determine whether the crime actually occurred unless the victim is moved to admit that the report is false. However, as in the false burglary or robbery complaint, certain characteristics are found with greater frequency in false rape reports than in actual rape cases. In and of themselves, none of these characteristics is significant; but taken together, they indicate a potential that the facts may be different from those reported.

The key to any successful criminal investigation is knowing what to look for and how to construct a logical sequence of the investigative steps (Kirk, 1974; O'Hara, 1977). If at some point in a rape investigation the allegation becomes suspect, immediate efforts should be made to resolve this question. Both the potential for false imprisonment and the need for objectivity demand this. To continue to work a case when the truthfulness of the victim is suspect invariably results in a poor investigation and reduced cooperation, both now and in the future.

It is extremely important to remember that no single element is significant; only the combination of factors suggests the possibility that an allegation may be exaggerated or false.

The Initial Complaint

The manner in which a rape allegation comes to the attention of law enforcement authorities is significant. The issue of prompt vs. delayed report is debatable. Some investigators become suspicious when a report is somewhat delayed. However, several other variables are also important to consider, such as to whom the complaint is made. Some investigators become suspicious if the complaint is first made to friends, associates, or medical authorities along with requests for tests for pregnancy or venereal disease. Or they are suspicious of a false report if the complainant is indifferent to apparent injuries.

Nature of Allegation

The concept of rape is deceptively simple, and women who make false allegations may structure their complaints in a fashion that meets the requirements of rape but ignores its reality. False allegations may be suspected if the complaint contains less common elements, such as:

- Complainant states she cannot describe her assailant because she kept her eyes closed.
- Complainant alleges she was assaulted by more than one person but cannot offer descriptions.
- Complainant claims she offered vigorous resistance but was forcibly overcome.
- Assailant was a total stranger or someone she can only describe in vague and nonspecific terms.
- Complainant claims she received threatening notes or phone calls prior to or after the assault.
- Complainant was unable to describe details and sequence of the sexual activities to which she was subjected.

Evidence

Law enforcement authorities correctly place a premium on the evidence supporting an allegation because it often provides information needed for the prosecution of the case. Because of the nature of a rape case, evidence is particularly important. Moreover, the consistency or inconsistency of the evidence may suggest that a rape complaint has been exaggerated or is completely false. An absence of the kinds of evidence usually associated with rapes is sometimes as revealing in identifying false allegations as its presence is in establishing that a rape actually occurred. The types of evidence to be considered in a false allegation are:

- Complainant cannot recall where the crime took place even though she does not report being blindfolded, under the influence of drugs or alcohol, or moved from location to location.
- Crime scene does not support story (ground cover is not disturbed; no footprints where they should be; no signs of struggle when they should logically be present).
- Damage to her clothing is inconsistent with any injuries she reports (cuts or scratches inconsistent with tears or cuts in clothing).
- Complainant presents cut-and-paste letters allegedly from the rapist in which death or rape threats are made. Note or letter is identifiable with pseudo-victim (via handwriting analysis, indented writing, typewriter comparison, paper stock, or fingerprint comparison).
- Confirming laboratory findings are absent.

Injuries

The nature of the individual's injuries can provide a great deal of information about what did or did not happen. Women who make false rape allegations and attempt to support them with injuries tend to present a consistent picture in terms of the cues suggested below:

- Injuries were made either by fingernails or by sharp instruments usually not found at the scene. Fingernail scrapings of victim reveal her own skin tissue.
- Injuries are extensive but do not involve sensitive tissues (lips, nipples, genitals, etc.).
- Complainant reports seemingly painful injuries with an air of indifference.
- Complainant's statement alleges wounds were incurred while she attempted to protect herself, yet the location and angle of injury are inconsistent with defense wounds.

- Practice or hesitation marks are present (sometimes they appear as older marks, indicating earlier attempts or rehearsals).

Personality and Lifestyle Considerations.   In false rape allegations, extensive and important information on the complainant is often available. In general, this information suggests that the pseudo-victim has experienced numerous personal problems and that her ability to cope is seriously impaired. For example, in temporal sequence, the rape follows one or more escalating incidents revealing difficulties in her personal relationships:

- Complainant has a history of mental or emotional problems (particularly referencing self-injurious behavior, with hysterical or borderline features).
- Complainant has previous record of having been assaulted or raped under similar circumstances.
- Allegation was made after a similar crime received publicity (suggesting modeling or copycat motive in which the similarity to the publicized crime offers credibility).
- Complainant has extensive record of medical care for dramatic illnesses or injuries.
- Friends or associates report that the complainant's post-assaultive behavior and activities were inconsistent with her allegation.
- Complainant becomes outraged when asked to corroborate her victimization.
- Complainant tries to steer the interview into safe topics or those that tend to engender sympathy.

A Second Opinion

A second opinion, through the use of a second interviewer, is an important strategy when a false rape allegation is suspected. Another investigator is used only when there are serious questions concerning the truth of the report. Confronting a person suspected of making a false complaint is always a difficult matter. The critical issue is that, if the doubts are incorrect, the victim's trauma is greatly compounded. Such a confrontation also destroys any relationship that may have developed between the victim and the investigator. One way to handle this challenge to the victim's credibility without sacrificing the investigator's rapport with the victim is to introduce a second party — a person who can act as a buffer. The principal investigator needs to be available to the person alleging rape and should maintain a nonjudgmental, supportive, and sympathetic relationship with her. It is counterproductive for this person to voice any doubts as to the veracity of her report. Issues regarding unresolved inconsistencies, conflicts, or the lack of supporting data are made by an investigative supervisor or coworker, thereby maintaining the vital relationship between the complainant and the principal investigator.

The supervisor's style of confrontation should also be supportive; however, since false allegations are usually desperate attempts to protect self-esteem, any harsh challenges to the person's credibility increase her defensiveness. It is often effective to simply present doubts to the victim in a way that makes it clear they are based on the information she herself has provided. This decreases personal conflict while conveying an impression that investigators have been thorough and objective. It also allows for adjusting investigative hypotheses and gives the victim an opportunity to provide additional information without having to place herself in a psychologically threatening position.

The reaction of factitious victims to this approach varies. At the low end of the adaptation continuum, there is usually an emotional confession, mixed with both despair and relief. The amount of energy required to maintain her story is exhausting, and this becomes a time for her to cooperate and to seek solace. Exaggerators and malingerers often provide great detail as to how and why they masqueraded as a rape victim. For those who adhere to their statements in the face of overwhelming contradictory evidence, it may be advantageous to request they take a polygraph examination.

At the extreme upper end of the adaptation continuum, the complainant's distortions are internalized. For her own well-being, she needs to believe what she is saying because she is unconsciously terrified of losing control. Consequently, her denial is intensified no matter how the confrontation is handled. Predictably, she reacts with outrage. If the family is advised of the findings, they may be of great assistance in her eventual recovery. Unfortunately, because of the disordered lives of such individuals, they are often estranged from their families.

Summary

False accusation is a term frequently used and heard in discussions of interpersonal crime. Though simple on the surface, this concept becomes vague and complex under scrutiny. This chapter explored the concept of false allegation in the context of rape, which usually occurs in isolated places where there is no one to support or refute an individual's claims.

False allegations of rape sometimes are not recognized by investigators and are almost totally neglected in literature. The reason for this is obvious: these are acts that are designed to appear plausible. The key to understanding false allegations lies in determining how a false allegation helps the complainant manipulate, control, or mentally recoup her self-esteem. Therefore, it is the context in which the allegation occurs that provides the framework for understanding the dynamics of the problem. A final word of caution — even those who are emotionally prone to make a false allegation can be raped. Basic principles of police professionalism require that officers who investigate rapes remain objective and compassionate. If they do not, the veracity of the allegation may never be known; and the victim — for she is a victim in either case — may never receive the help and support she needs.

Acknowledgments

The authors thank the following for contributing case examples: Margaret Aiken, Eddie Grant, David Muram, M.D., Robin Jones, Patricia Speck, and Nola Mendenhall.

References

American Psychiatric Association (1994) *Diagnostic and Statistical Manual,* 4th ed., Washington, D.C., American Psychiatric Press.

Asher, R. (1951/1) Munchausen's syndrome, *Lancet,* 339–341.

Benedek, E. and Schetky, D. (October 1984) Allegations of sexual abuse in child custody cases. Paper presented at the annual Meeting of the American Academy of Psychiatry and the Law, Nassau, Bahamas.

Book of Genesis, Old Testament, *Holy Bible,* Chapter 39.

Burgess, A.W. and Holmstrom, L.L. (1974) *Sex Stress Situation, Rape: Victims of Crisis,* Bowie, MD, Brady Co.

Burt, M.R. (1980) Cultural myths and supports for rape, *J. Pers. Soc. Psychol.,* 38, 215–233.

Carney, M.W.P. (1980) Artifactual illnesses to attract medical attention, *Br. J. Psychiatr.,* 136, 542–547.

Carney, M.W.P. and Brown, J.P. (1983) Clinical features and motives among 42 artifactual illness patients, *Br. J. Med. Psychol.,* 56, 57–66.

Faller, K. (1984) Is the child victim of sexual abuse telling the truth?, *Child Abuse Neglect,* 8, 473–481.

Feldman, M.D., Ford, C.V., and Stone, T. (1994) Deceiving others/deceiving oneself: four cases, *South. Med. J.,* 87(7), 736–738.

Ford, C.V. (1973) The Munchausen syndrome: a report of four new cases and a review of psychodynamic considerations, *Psychiatr. Med.,* 4(1), 31–45.

Gawn, R.A. and Kauffmann, E.A. (1955) Munchausen syndrome, *Br. Med. J.,* 2, 1068.

Goodwin, J., Sahd, D., and Rada, R. (1978) Incest hoax: false accusations, false denials, *Bull. Am. Acad. Psychiactr. Law,* V(3).

Green, A. (1986) True and false allegations of sexual abuse in child custody disputes, *J. Am. Acad. Child Psychiatr.*, 25(4), 449–456.

Grinker, R.R. (1961) Imposture as a form of mastery, *Arch. Gen. Psychiatr.*, 5, 53–56.

Hodge, D., Schwartz, W., Sargent, J., Bodurtha, J., and Starr, S. (1982) The bacteriologically battered body: another case of Munchausen by proxy, *Ann. Emergency Med.*, 4, 205–207.

Kanin, E.J. (1994) False rape allegations, *Arch. Sexual Behav.*, 2(1), 81–92.

Katz, S. and Mazur, M. (1979) *Understanding the Rape Victim*, John Wiley & Sons, New York.

Kilpatrick, D.G., Veronen, L.J., and Best, C.L. (1985) Factors predicting psychological distress among rape victims, in *Post-Traumatic Therapy and Victims of Violence*, New York, Brunner/Mazel, pp. 113–141.

Kirk, P.O. (1974) *Crime Investigation*, 2nd ed., John Wiley & Sons, New York.

Kurlandsky, L., Lukoff, J.Y., Zinkman, W.H., Brody, J.P., and Kessler, R.W. (1979) Munchausen syndrome by proxy: definitions of factitious bleeding in an infant by cr labeling of erythrocytes, *Pediatrics*, 63(2), 228–231.

Ledray, L.E. (1994) Rape or self-injury? *J. Emergency Nursing*, 20(2), 88–90.

Lefer, H. (1992) Women and the truth: who says we're lying? *Elle*, 194–200.

McDowell, C. and Hibler, N. (1987) False allegations, in Hazelwood, R. and Burgess, A., Eds., *Practical Aspects of Rape Investigations: A Multidisciplinary Approach*, Elsevier, New York, 275–299.

McDowell, C. (1990) *Rape Allegation Checklist*, North Carolina Justice Institute Press, Raleigh.

McDowell, C. (1990) False alligators and fuzzy data: a new look at crime analysis, *Police Chief*, 44–45.

Macdonald, J.M. (1994) *Rape: Controversial Issues*, Springfield, IL, C. C Thomas, 84–107.

Meadow, R. (1982) Munchausen syndrome by proxy, *Arch. Dis. Childhood*, 57, 92–98.

Nadelson, T. (1979) The Munchausen spectrum: borderline character features, *Gen. Hosp. Psychiatr.*, 1(1), 11–17.

O'Hara, C.E. (1977) *Fundamentals of Criminal Investigation*, 4th ed., Springfield, IL, C. C Thomas.

Pankratz, L. (1981) A review of the Munchausen syndrome, *Clin. Psychol. Rev.*, 1, 65–78.

Peters, J. (1976). Children who are victims of sexual assault and the psychology of offenders, *Am. J. Psychotherapy*, 30, 398–421.

Riger, S. and Gordon, M.T. (1988) The impact of crime on urban women, in Burgess, A.W., Ed., *Rape and Sexual Assault, II*, Garland, New York.

Rosenfeld, A., Nadelson, C., and Krieger, M. (1979) Fantasy and reality in patients' reports of incest, *J. Clin. Psychiatr.*, 159–164.

Vaisrub, S. (1978) Baron Munchausen and the abused child, *J. Am. Med. Assoc.*, 239(8), 752.

Waller, D.A. (1983) Obstacles to the treatment of Munchausen by proxy syndrome, *J. Am. Acad. Child Psychiatr.*, 22(1), 80–85.

Child Molesters and Cyber Pedophiles — A Behavioral Perspective

11

KENNETH V. LANNING

Introduction

Children have been repeatedly warned about the dangers associated with strangers; but often they do not understand that sex offenders can be people they have come to know, either in person or online. Throughout history, nonfamily members who sexually exploit children have frequented the places where children gather. School yards, parks, and malls have been prime contact places. Offenders have also used technological advancements (cameras, telephones, automobiles, etc.) to facilitate their sexual interests and behavior. Starting in the 1990s, home computers, online services, and the Internet have provided new technological tools and points of contact.

Like most acquaintance molesters, individuals attempting to sexually exploit children through the Internet tend to gradually seduce their targets through attention, affection, kindness, and gifts. They are often willing to devote considerable amounts of time, money, and energy to this process. They will listen to and empathize with the problems of children. They will be aware of the music, hobbies, and interests of children. Unless the victims are already engaged in sexually explicit computer conversation, offenders will usually lower any inhibitions by gradually introducing the sexual context and content. Some offenders use the computer primarily to collect and trade child pornography, while others also seek online contact with other offenders and children.

Children, especially adolescents, are often interested in and curious about sexuality and sexually explicit material. They sometimes use their online access to actively seek out such material. They are moving away from the total control of parents and trying to establish new relationships outside the family. Sex offenders targeting children use and exploit these characteristics and needs. Adolescent children may also be attracted to and lured by online offenders closer to their age who, although not technically pedophiles, may be dangerous.

Illegal Sexual Activity

Computer-related sexual exploitation of children usually comes to the attention of law enforcement as a result of citizen/victim complaints, referrals from commercial service providers, and inadvertent discovery during other investigations. Increasingly, cases are also proactively identified as a result of undercover investigations that target high-risk computer sites or utilize other specialized techniques.

Sexual activity involving the use of computers that is usually illegal and therefore the focus of law enforcement investigations includes:

1. Producing or possessing child pornography;
2. Uploading and downloading child pornography; and
3. Soliciting sex with children.

In the vernacular of computer exploitation investigators, those who traffic in online child pornography are known as transmitters while those who solicit sex with children are known as travelers. Using the computer to solicit sex with children could include communicating with children as well as with law enforcement officers taking a proactive investigative approach and pretending to be children (or pretending to be adults with access to children). After using the computer to make contact with the child, other illegal activity could involve traveling to meet the child or having the child travel to engage in sexual activity.

Cases involving adolescents using the computer to solicit sex with other adolescents and to traffic in child pornography that portrays pubescent children are a problem area for the criminal justice system, especially the federal system. For purposes of illegal sexual activity and child pornography, the federal statutes and many local statutes define children or minors as individuals who have not yet reached their 16th or 18th birthdays. Therefore, such behavior may be technically illegal, but may not be sexually deviant.

Legal Sexual Activity

Usually legal sexual activity involving the use of computers includes:

1. Validating sexually deviant behavior and interests;
2. Reinforcing deviant arousal patterns;
3. Storing and sharing sexual fantasies;
4. Lying about age and identity;
5. Collecting adult pornography that is not obscene;

6. Disseminating indecent material, talking dirty, cybersex, providing sex instructions; and

7. Injecting yourself into the problem of computer exploitation of children to rationalize your interests.

Although many might find much of this activity offensive and repulsive — and special circumstances and specific laws might even criminalize some of it — it is for the most part legal activity.

Understanding Behavior

The investigation of child sexual exploitation cases involving computers requires knowledge of the technical, legal, and behavioral aspects of computer use. However, because each of these areas is so complex, investigators must also identify experts and resources available to assist in these cases. Exploitation cases involving computers are very challenging, but they also provide an opportunity to obtain a great deal of corroborative evidence and investigative intelligence. This discussion focuses primarily on the dynamics of offender and victim behavior in the computer exploitation of children.

Paraphilias and Sexual Ritual Behavior

Paraphilias are psychosexual disorders defined for clinical and research purposes in the *Diagnostic and Statistical Manual of Mental Disorders*, 4th Edition, commonly referred to as the *DSM-IV* (American Psychiatric Association, 1994). They are defined as recurrent, intense, sexually arousing fantasies, urges, or behaviors that generally occur over a period of at least 6 months and involve (1) nonhuman objects, (2) the suffering or humiliation of oneself or one's partner, or (3) children or other nonconsenting persons. Better known and more common paraphilias include exhibitionism (exposure), fetishism (objects), frotteurism (rubbing), pedophilia (child), sexual masochism (self pain), sexual sadism (partner pain), and voyeurism (looking). Less known and less common paraphilias include scatologia (talk), necrophilia (corpses), partialism (body parts), zoophilia (animals), coprophilia (feces), klismaphilia (enemas), urophilia (urine), infantilism (baby), hebephilia (female youth), ephebephilia (male youth), and many others.

In the real world, each of the paraphilias typically has:

1. Slang names (big baby, golden showers, S&M);
2. An industry that sells related paraphernalia and props (restraining devices, gags, adult-sized baby clothing);

3. A support network (North American Man Boy Love Association or NAMBLA, Diaper Pail Fraternity); and
4. A body of literature (pornography).

In fact, the paraphilias are the organizational framework or the Dewey Decimal System of pornography, obscenity, adult bookstores, and Internet sex chat rooms.

Paraphilias are psychosexual disorders and not types of sex crimes. They may or may not involve criminal activity. Individuals suffering from one or more of these paraphilias can just engage in fantasy and masturbate; they can act out their fantasies legally (consenting adult partners, objects), or they can act out their fantasies illegally (nonconsenting partners, underage partners). The choice is theirs.

Although any of the paraphilias could become elements of a computer child sexual exploitation case, pedophilia is the most obvious and the one best known to investigators dealing with these cases. It is important for investigators to understand that the diagnostic criteria for pedophilia require recurrent, intense, and sexually arousing fantasies, urges or behaviors involving *prepubescent* children, generally age 13 or younger. The absence of *any* of the key criteria could eliminate the diagnosis. For example, an individual with a strong preference for and repeatedly engaging in sex with large numbers of 14-year-olds could correctly be evaluated by a mental health professional as *NOT* a pedophile. In spite of this, some mental health professionals continue to apply the term to those with a sexual preference for pubescent teenagers.

The terms hebephilia and ephebephilia are not specifically mentioned in the *DSM-IV* and are rarely used, even by mental health professionals. They are, however, being increasingly used in forensic evaluations submitted to the court by defendants attempting to minimize their sexual behavior. Although sexual attraction to pubescent children by adults has the obvious potential for criminal activity, it does not necessarily constitute a sexual perversion as defined by psychiatry.

On an investigative level, the presence of paraphilias often means highly repetitive and predictable behavior focused on specific sexual interests that go well beyond a method of operation (MO). The concept of MO — something done by an offender because it works and will help him get away with the crime — is well known to most investigators. An MO is fueled by thought and deliberation. Most offenders change and improve their MOs over time and with experience.

The repetitive patterns of behavior of some sex offenders can and do involve some MOs but are more likely to also involve the less-known concept of sexual ritual. Sexual ritual is the repeated engaging in an act or series of acts in a certain manner because of a sexual need; that is, in order to become aroused and/or gratified, a person must engage in the act in a certain way. Some aspects of the MOs of sex offenders can, if repeated often enough during sexual activity, become part of the sexual ritual. Other types of ritual behavior can be motivated by psychological, cultural, or spiritual needs. Unlike an MO, ritual is necessary to the offender but not to the successful commission of the crime. In fact, instead of facilitating the crime, it often increases the odds of identification, apprehension, and conviction because it causes the offender to make need-driven mistakes.

Ritual and its resultant behavior are fueled by erotic imagery and fantasy and can be bizarre in nature. Most important to investigators, offenders find it difficult to change and modify rituals, even when their experience tells them they should or they suspect law enforcement scrutiny. The ritual patterns of sex offenders have far more significance as "prior like acts" than the MO of other types of offenders. Understanding sexual ritual is the key to investigating preferential sex offenders. The courts in this country have, however, been slow to recognize and understand the difference between MO and ritual.

Pedophiles

The general public, the media, and many child abuse professionals sometimes simplistically refer to all those who sexually victimize children as pedophiles. There is no single or uniform definition for the word *pedophile*. As previously stated, for mental health professionals, it is a diagnostic term referring to those with recurrent, intense sexually arousing fantasies, urges, or behaviors involving prepubescent children. Technically, pedophilia is a psychiatric diagnosis that can only be made by qualified psychologists or psychiatrists. Therefore, for many, the word is a diagnostic term — not a legal one.

What, then, is the difference between a child molester and a pedophile? For many, the terms have become synonymous. For them, the word pedophile is just a fancy term for a child molester. The media frequently makes no distinction and uses the terms interchangeably. The term pedophilia is being used more and more by law enforcement and prosecutors, especially in cases involving the use of computers. It has even entered their slang usage — with some talking about investigating a *pedo case* or being assigned to a *pedo squad*. Although Americans most often pronounce the *ped* in pedophilia as the *ped* in pedestrian (from the Latin for foot), the correct pronunciation is *ped* as in pediatrician (from the Greek for child).

All pedophiles are not child molesters. A person suffering from any paraphilia can legally engage in it simply by fantasizing and masturbating. A child molester is an individual who sexually molests children. A pedophile might have a sexual preference for children and fantasize about having sex with them; but if he does not act out, he is not a child molester. Some pedophiles might act out their fantasies in legal ways by simply talking to or watching children and later masturbating. Some might have sex with dolls and mannequins that resemble children. Some pedophiles might act out their fantasies in legal ways by engaging in sexual activity with adults who look, dress or act like children (small stature, flat chested, no body hair, immature, baby talk). Others may act out child fantasy games with adult prostitutes. A difficult problem to detect and address is that of individuals who act out their sexual fantasies by socially interacting with children (in person or via an online computer) or by interjecting themselves into the child sexual abuse or exploitation problem as overzealous child advocates (cyber vigilantes). It is almost impossible to estimate how many pedophiles exist who have never molested a child. What society can or should do with regard to such individuals is an interesting area for discussion, but it is beyond the role of prosecutors. People cannot be arrested for their fantasies.

All child molesters are not pedophiles. A pedophile is an individual who prefers to have sex with children. A person who prefers to have sex with an adult partner may, for any number of reasons, decide to have sex with a child. Such reasons might include simple availability, curiosity, or a desire to hurt a loved one of the molested child. The sexual fantasies of such individuals do not necessarily focus on children, and these people are not pedophiles.

Are child molesters of adolescent victims pedophiles? Are individuals who collect both child and adult pornography pedophiles? Is everyone using a computer to facilitate having sex with children or trafficking in child pornography a pedophile? Many child molesters are, in fact, pedophiles, and many pedophiles are child molesters. But they are not necessarily one and the same. Labeling all child molesters as pedophiles can be confusing. Often, it may be unclear whether the term is applied with its diagnostic or with some other definition. Most investigators and prosecutors are not qualified to apply the term with its diagnostic meaning.

Not everyone using a computer to facilitate having sex with children or trafficking in child pornography is a pedophile. In addition, there is no legal requirement to determine that a subject or suspect in a case is a pedophile, and often it is irrelevant to the investigation or prosecution. Such a determination may sometimes be useful in developing a variety of investigative approaches. To avoid confusion with a mental health diagnosis and possible challenges in court, however, use of the term pedophile by law enforcement and prosecutors should be kept to a minimum.

For the purposes of this discussion, the term pedophile is defined as a significantly older individual who prefers to have sex with individuals legally considered children. Pedophiles are individuals whose erotic imagery and sexual fantasies focus on children. They do not settle for child victims but, in fact, prefer to have sex with children. The law, not puberty, determines who is a child. A pedophile is just one example or subcategory of what is referred to as a preferential sex offender. The term *preferential sex offender* is merely a descriptive label used only to identify, for investigative and prosecutive purposes, a certain type of offender. The term does not appear in the *DSM-IV,* and it is not intended to imply or to be used for clinical diagnosis.

Typology

When distinctions between types of offenders need to be made, the use of a descriptive typology developed for criminal justice purposes is recommended. This discussion sets forth such a typology.

My original typology of child molesters was developed in the mid 1980s and was published and widely disseminated by the National Center for Missing and Exploited Children (NCMEC) in a monograph entitled *Child Molesters: A Behavioral Analysis.* It was revised in April, 1987 (2nd edition) and again in December, 1992 (3rd edition). It divided child molesters into two categories (situational or preferential) and into seven patterns of behavior. Although still useful, this old typology has several limitations and has been updated by a new typology that places sex offenders, not only child molesters, along a motivational continuum (situational to preferential) instead of into one of two categories.

At one end of the continuum are the situational sex offenders. They tend to be less intelligent and are over-represented in lower socioeconomic groups. Their criminal sexual behavior tends to serve basic sexual needs or nonsexual needs such as power and anger. Their behavior is often opportunistic and impulsive but primarily thought-driven. They are more likely to consider the risks involved in their behavior but often make stupid or sloppy mistakes. If they collect pornography, it is often violent in nature, reflecting their power and anger needs. Their patterns of behavior are more likely to involve the previously discussed concept of MO.

Situational sex offenders victimizing children do not have a true sexual preference for children. They may molest them, however, for a wide variety of situational reasons. They are more likely to view and be aroused by adult pornography, but might engage in sex with children in certain situations. Situational sex offenders frequently molest readily available children such as their own or any others living with them. Pubescent teenagers are high-risk, viable sexual targets. Younger children may also be targeted because they are weak, vulnerable, or available. Psychopathic situational offenders may select children, especially adolescents, simply because they have the opportunity and think they can get away with it. Social misfits may select children out of insecurity and curiosity. Others may have low self-esteem and use children as substitutes for preferred adults.

Table 11.1 Motivation Continuum

Nonsexual Needs	Deviant Sexual Needs
(Not either/or, but a continuum)[a]	
Situational Sex Offender	Preferential Sex Offender
1. Personality Disorders	1. Paraphilias
2. Less Intelligent	2. More Intelligent
3. Lower Socioeconomic Status	3. Higher Socioeconomic Status
4. Impulsive	4. Compulsive
5. Considers Risk	5. Considers Need
6. Sloppy Mistakes	6. Needy Mistakes
7. Violent Pornography	7. Theme Pornography
8. Thought-Driven	8. Fantasy-Driven
9. Varied Criminal Behavior	9. Focused Criminal Behavior
10. Spontaneous or Planned	10. Script
11. MO Patterns of Behavior	11. Ritual Patterns of Behavior

[a] Offenders are not strictly situational or preferential; there may be a crossover or blending of characteristics.

At the other end of the motivation continuum are the more preferential sex offenders. They tend to be more intelligent and are over-represented in higher socioeconomic groups. Their criminal sexual behavior tends to serve deviant sexual needs known as paraphilias. This behavior is often scripted and compulsive and is primarily fantasy-driven. Repeated fantasy creates need. They are more likely to consider their needs and therefore make needy mistakes that often seem almost stupid. When they collect pornography and related paraphernalia, it usually focuses on the themes of their paraphilic preferences. Their patterns of behavior are more likely to involve the previously discussed concept of ritual.

As this descriptive term implies, preferential sex offenders have specific sexual preferences or paraphilias. Those with a preference for children could be called pedophiles. Those with a preference for peeping could be called voyeurs, and those with a preference for suffering could be called sadists, etc. But one of the purposes of this typology is to avoid these diagnostic terms. Preferential type sex offenders are more likely to view, be aroused by, and collect theme pornography. Some preferential sex offenders without a preference for children do molest children in order to carry out their bizarre sexual fantasies and preferences with young, less threatening, less judgmental, and highly vulnerable victims. Some of these offenders' sexual activities with children may involve acts they are embarrassed or ashamed to request or do with a preferred adult partner. Such offenders, even if they do not have a sexual preference for children, are still preferential sex offenders and therefore engage in similar patterns of behavior.

There are many advantages to the use of this criminal justice descriptive typology. If there is a need to distinguish a certain type of sex offender, this typology provides a name or label instead of just calling them *these guys.* The label is professional in contrast to referring to them as *perverts* or *sickos* or worse. Because the terms are descriptive (not diagnostic) and probative (not prejudicial) they may be more acceptable in reports, search warrants, and testimony by criminal justice professionals. For example, the currently popular term *predator* might be considered too prejudicial for court testimony. The continuum concept also better addresses the complexity of and changes in human behavior. Using the term *preferential sex offender* instead of *preferential child molester* addresses the issue of applying it to offenders who collect child pornography without physically molesting children. The one term, preferential sex offender, eliminates the need for investigators and prosecutors to distinguish between child pornography collectors and child molesters, between pedophiles and hebephiles, and among numerous other paraphilias. How to recognize and identify such offenders will be discussed shortly.

Investigators or prosecutors might argue that it is their job to investigate or prosecute individuals who violate the law, and that whether that offender is a pedophile or a preferential sex offender is of little importance to them. There is no legal requirement to determine that a subject or suspect in a case is a pedophile or preferential sex offender. Often it is irrelevant to the investigation or prosecution. There are, however, clear differences between the types of individuals who sexually victimize children, and prosecutors handling these cases sometimes need to make such distinctions. Although there is not a single profile that will determine if someone is a child molester, preferential sex offenders tend to engage in highly predictable and recognizable behavior patterns. The potential evidence available as a result of the long-term, persistent, and ritualized behavior patterns of many sexual exploiters of children make these cases very easy for prosecutors.

Need-driven behavior equals mistakes. This is why a reasonably intelligent individual may:

- use his computer at work to download child pornography
- deliver his computer filled with child pornography for repair
- send his film with child pornography on it to a store to be developed
- appear in child pornography images he is making
- discuss engaging in serious criminal activity with a stranger he met on the Internet
- transmit identifiable photographs of himself to such an individual
- maintain incriminating evidence knowing investigators might soon search his home or computer

- give investigators permission to search his home or computer knowing it contains incriminating evidence
- agree to be interviewed.

Defense attorneys might argue that such behavior indicates that their clients are innocent, lack criminal intent, or are not criminally responsible. Why else would an intelligent individual do something so obviously stupid? Such behavior does not necessarily mean the offender is insane or not criminally responsible. Another explanation is much more probable — it is need-driven. The fantasy- or need-driven behavior of preferential sex offenders has little to do with thinking. It is more a matter of the *little head* telling the *big head* what to do. It is what makes preferential sex offenders so vulnerable to proactive investigations, even though the techniques used have been well publicized. If necessary, an expert could be used to educate the court concerning certain patterns of behavior.

Investigators and prosecutors should be aware of a cautionary statement that appears on page xxvii of the *DSM-IV* and reads in part that:

> It is to be understood that inclusion here, for clinical and research purposes, of a diagnostic category such as *Pathological Gambling or Pedophilia* (emphasis added) does not imply that the condition meets legal or other nonmedical criteria for what constitutes mental disease, mental disorder, or mental disability. The clinical and scientific considerations involved in categorization of these conditions as mental disorders may not be wholly relevant to legal judgments, for example, that take into account such issues as individual responsibility, disability determination, and competency.

Computer Offenders

Offenders using computers to sexually exploit children tend to be white males and usually fall into three broad categories:

1. Situational Offenders
   A. Normal Adolescent/Adult — Usually a typical adolescent searching online for pornography and sex or an impulsive/curious adult with a newly found access to a wide range of pornography and sexual opportunities.
   B. Morally Indiscriminate — Usually a power/anger-motivated sex offender with a history of varied violent offenses. Parents, especially mothers, who make their children available for sex with individuals on the Internet would also most likely fit in this category.
   C. Profiteers — With the lowered risk of identification and increased potential for profit, the criminal just trying to make easy money has returned to trafficking in child pornography.

When situational type offenders break the law, they can obviously be investigated and prosecuted; but their behaviors are not as long-term, persistent, and predictable as those of preferential offenders. They are a more diverse group.

2. Preferential Offenders
    A. Pedophile — offender with a definite preference for children.
    B. Sexually Indiscriminate — offender with a wide variety of paraphilic or deviant sexual interests.
    C. Latent — individuals with potentially illegal (but previously latent) sexual preferences who have recently begun to criminally act out when their inhibitions are weakened after their arousal patterns are fueled and validated through on-line computer communication.

The main difference between them is that the pornography/erotica collections of the sexually indiscriminate preferential offenders are more varied, usually with a focus on their particular sexual preferences or paraphilias, whereas pedophiles' collections focus predominately on children. Also, the sexually indiscriminate offender is less likely to directly molest children, especially prepubescent children. With an absence of prior criminal sexual activity, latent offenders present problems concerning what should be the appropriate prosecution and sentence. A thorough investigation and a good forensic psychological evaluation are helpful in evaluating such latent offenders.

3. Miscellaneous Offenders
    A. Media Reporters — individuals who erroneously believe they can go on-line, traffic in child pornography, and arrange meetings with suspected child molesters as part of an authorized and valid news exposé.
    B. Pranksters — individuals who disseminate false or incriminating information to embarrass the targets of their dirty tricks.
    C. Older Boyfriends — individuals in their late teens or early twenties attempting to sexually interact with adolescent girls or boys.
    D. Overzealous Citizens — individuals who go overboard doing their own private investigations into this problem. As will be discussed, investigators must be cautious of all overzealous citizens offering their services in these cases.

Although these miscellaneous offenders may be breaking the law, they are obviously less likely to be prosecuted. This category includes media reporters breaking the law as part of a bona fide news story. It does *not* include reporters, or any other professionals, who engage in such activity to hide or rationalize the fact that they have a personal interest in it. They would be situational or preferential offenders. Overzealous citizens could also include sex offender therapists and researchers engaging in this type of activity. *Only* law enforcement officers, as part of official, authorized investigations, should be conducting proactive investigations or downloading child pornography on a computer.

Although a variety of individuals sexually victimize children, preferential sex offenders are the primary sexual exploiters of children. They tend to be serial offenders who prey on children through the operation of child sex rings and/or the collection, creation, or distribution of child pornography. Using a computer to fuel and validate interests and behaviors, to facilitate interacting with child victims, or to possess and traffic in child pornography usually requires the above-average intelligence and economic means more typical of preferential sex offenders. The computer sex offenders discussed here tend to be white males from a middle-class or higher socioeconomic background. As computers become more commonplace, this will increasingly change; and there will be growing numbers of the more diverse situational sex offenders.

Recognizing Preferential Sex Offenders

An important step in investigating sexual exploitation of children is to recognize and utilize, if present, the highly predictable sexual behavior patterns of these preferential sex offenders. If the investigation identifies enough of these patterns, many of the remaining ones can be assumed. However, no particular number constitutes *enough*. A few may be enough if they are especially significant. Most of these indicators mean little individually; but as they are identified and accumulated through investigation, they can constitute reason to believe a suspect is a preferential sex offender.

You cannot determine the type of offender with whom you are dealing unless you have the most complete, detailed, and accurate information possible. The investigator must understand that doing a background investigation on a suspect means more than obtaining the date and place of birth or credit and criminal checks. School, juvenile, military, medical, driving, employment, bank, sex offender and child abuse registry, sex offender assessment, computer, and prior investigative records can all be valuable sources of information about an offender.

A preferential sex offender can usually be identified by the following behaviors:

1. Long-Term and Persistent Pattern of Behavior.
   A. Begins pattern in early adolescence.

      B. Is willing to commit time, money, and energy.
      C. Commits multiple offenses.
      D. Makes ritual or need-driven mistakes.
2. Specific Sexual Interests.
      A. Manifests paraphilic preferences (may be multiple).
      B. Focuses on defined sexual interests and victim characteristics.
      C. Centers life around preferences.
      D. Rationalizes sexual interests.
3. Well-Developed Techniques.
      A. Evaluates experiences.
      B. Lies and manipulates, often skillfully.
      C. Has method of access to victims.
      D. Is quick to use modern technology (computer, video) for sexual needs and purposes.
4. Fantasy-Driven Behavior.
      A. Collects theme pornography.
      B. Collects paraphernalia, souvenirs, videotapes.
      C. Records fantasies.
      D. Acts to turn fantasy into reality.

Investigators must not over- or under-react to reported allegations. They must understand that not all computer offenders are stereotypical pedophiles who fit some common profile. Keeping an open mind and objectively attempting to determine the type of offender involved can be useful in minimizing embarrassing errors in judgment and developing appropriate interview, investigative, and prosecutive strategies. For example, the fact that preferential offenders (as part of sexual ritual) are more likely to commit similar multiple offenses, make need-driven mistakes, and compulsively collect pornography and other offense-related paraphernalia can be used to build a stronger case.

    In computer cases, especially those involving proactive investigative techniques, it is often easier to determine the type of offender than in other kinds of child sexual exploitation cases. When attempting to make this determination, it is important to evaluate all available background information. The following information from on-line computer activity can be valuable in this assessment. This information can often be ascertained from the on-line service provider and through undercover communication, pretext contacts, informants, record checks, and other investigative techniques (mail cover, pen register, trash run, surveillance).

- Screen name
- Screen profile
- Number of files originated
- Number of files forwarded

- Accuracy of profile
- Length of time active
- Amount of time spent on-line
- Number of transmissions
- Number of files

- Number of files received
- Number of recipients
- Site of communication
- Theme of messages and chat
- Theme of pornography

A common problem in these cases is that it is often easier to determine that a computer is being used than to determine who is using the computer. It is obviously harder to do a background investigation when multiple people have access to the computer. Pretext phone calls can be very useful in such situations.

Exaggerated Example

An investigation determines that a suspect is a 50-year-old single male who does volunteer work with troubled boys, has two prior convictions for sexually molesting young boys in 1974 and 1986, has an expensive state-of-the-art home computer, has a main screen name of "Boylover" and one screen profile that describes him as a 14-year-old, has for the last five years daily spent many hours on-line in chat rooms and the alt.sex.preteen newsgroup (justifying and graphically describing his sexual preference for and involvement with young boys), and brags about his extensive pornography collection while uploading hundreds of child pornography files, all focusing on preteen boys in bondage to dozens of individuals all over the world. If such a determination were relevant to the case, these facts would constitute more than enough probable cause to believe this suspect is a preferential sex offender.

Knowing the kind of offender with whom you are dealing can go a long way in determining investigative strategy. For example, it might be useful in:

1. Anticipating and understanding need-driven mistakes.
2. Evaluating the consistency between victim statements and alleged offenders' traits.
3. Developing offender and victim interview strategy.
4. Determining the existence, age, and number of victims.
5. Recognizing where and what kind of corroborative evidence might be found.
6. Proving intent.
7. Determining appropriate charge and sentencing.
8. Assessing the admissibility of prior acts.
9. Evaluating danger at a bond hearing.
10. Explaining behavior patterns to a jury.
11. Determining suitability for treatment options.

12. Addressing staleness.
13. Utilizing expert search warrant.

With any of the preferential types of computer offenders, the characteristics, dynamics, and techniques (expert search warrant) previously discussed concerning preferential sex offenders should be considered.

Concerned Citizens

Many individuals who report information to the authorities about deviant sexual activity on the Internet must invent clever excuses for how and why they came upon such material. They often start out pursuing their own sexual/deviant interests but then decide to report suspected crimes to the police because the deviancy went too far, because they are afraid they might have been monitored by authorities, or because they need to rationalize their perversions as having some higher purpose or value. Rather than honestly admitting their own deviant interests, they make up elaborate explanations to justify finding the material. Some claim to be journalists, researchers, or outraged, concerned citizens trying to protect a child or help the police. In any case, what they find may still have to be investigated.

Investigators must consider that the concerned citizens reporting such activities may be individuals who:

1. Motivated by a need to rationalize or deny their deviant sexual interests, have embellished and falsified an elaborate tale of perversion and criminal activity on the Internet.
2. Regardless of their true motivations, have uncovered others using the Internet to validate and reinforce bizarre, perverted sexual fantasies and interests (a common occurrence) but who are not engaged in criminal activity.
3. Regardless of their true motivations, have uncovered individuals involved in criminal activity.

One especially sensitive area for investigators is the preferential sex offender who presents himself as a concerned citizen reporting what he inadvertently discovered in cyberspace, or he is requesting to work with law enforcement to search for child pornography and to protect children. Other than the obvious benefit of legal justification for their past or future activity, most do this as part of their need to rationalize their behaviors as worthwhile and to gain access to children. When these offenders are caught, instead of recognizing this activity as part of their preferential pattern of behavior, the courts sometimes give them leniency because of their good deeds. Preferential sex offenders who are also law enforcement officers sometimes claim their activity was part of some well-intentioned but unauthorized investigation.

Use of Computers

The great appeal of a computer becomes obvious when you understand sex offenders, especially preferential sex offenders. The computer could be a stand-alone system or one utilizing on-line service capability. Whether a system at work, at a library, at a cyber café, or at home, the computer provides preferential sex offenders with an ideal means of filling their needs to: (1) organize their collections, correspondence, and fantasy material; (2) communicate with victims and other offenders; (3) store, transfer, manipulate, and create child pornography; and (4) maintain financial records. The sex offender using a computer is not a new type of criminal; simply, a matter of modern technology is catching up with long-known, well-documented behavioral needs. In the past they were probably among the first to obtain and use, for their sexual needs, new inventions such as the camera, the telephone, the automobile, the Polaroid camera, and the video camera and recorder. Because of their traits and needs, they are willing to spend whatever time, money, and energy it takes to obtain, learn about, and use this technology.

Organization

Offenders use computers to organize their collections, correspondence, and fantasy material. Many preferential sex offenders in particular seem to be compulsive recordkeepers. A computer makes it much easier to store and retrieve names and addresses of victims and individuals with similar interests. Innumerable characteristics of victims and sexual acts can be easily recorded and analyzed. An extensive pornography collection can be cataloged by subject matter. Even fantasy writings and other narrative descriptions can be stored and retrieved for future use. Such detailed records can be useful in determining the ages of children in pornography images, identifying additional victims, or proving intent.

One problem the computer creates for law enforcement is determining whether computer texts describing sexual assaults are fictional stories, sexual fantasies, diaries of past activity, plans for future activity, or current threats. This problem can be compounded by the fact that there are individuals who believe that cyberspace is a new frontier where the old rules of society do not apply. They do not want this freedom scrutinized and investigated. There is no easy solution to this problem. Meticulous analysis and investigation are the only answers.

Communication

Many offenders are drawn to on-line computers to communicate and validate their interests and behavior. Validation is actually the most important and compelling reason why preferential sex offenders are drawn to the on-line computer. In addition to physical contact and putting a stamp on a letter or package, they can use their computers to exchange information and validation. Through the Internet, national and regional on-line services, or specialized electronic bulletin boards, offenders can use their computers to locate individuals with similar interests.

The computer may enable them to obtain active validation with less risk of identification or discovery. The great appeal of this type of communication is perceived anonymity and immediate feedback. They feel as protected as when using the mail but get immediate response as when meeting face to face.

Like advertisements in swinger magazines, computer on-line services are used to identify individuals of mutual interests concerning age, gender, and sexual preference. The offender may use an electronic bulletin board to which he has authorized access, or he may illegally enter a system. The offender can also set up his own underground on-line bulletin board or Internet site or surreptitiously participate in those of others.

In addition to adults with similar interests, offenders can sometimes get validation from the children with whom they communicate on-line. Children needing attention and affection may respond to an offender in positive ways. They may tell the offender he is a great guy and that they are grateful for his interest in them. In communicating with children, and in a few cases with adults, offenders frequently assume the identities of one or more children.

Validation is also obtained from the fact that they are utilizing the same cutting-edge technology used by the most intelligent and creative people in society. In their minds, the time, technology, and talent it takes to engage in this activity prove its value and legitimacy. Because of this validation process and the fueling of sexual fantasy with on-line pornography, I believe that some individuals with potentially illegal (but previously latent) sexual preferences have begun to criminally act out. Their inhibitions are weakened after their arousal patterns are fueled and validated through on-line computer communication.

Offenders' needs for validation are the foundation on which proactive investigative techniques (stings, undercover operations, etc.) are built and the primary reason they work so often. Although their brains may tell them not to send child pornography or not to reveal details of past or planned criminal acts to strangers they met on-line, their needs for validation often compel them to do so.

Child Pornography

Child pornography should always be viewed as a violation of the law and as possible corroboration of child sexual abuse. In a relatively short time and at minimal expense, almost anyone with an on-line computer can have a large collection of child pornography. A short time ago, it would have taken years and great expense to accumulate such a collection. These collections are increasingly stored on computers and floppy disks. Because of on-line computers, child pornography is now more readily available in the U.S. than it has been since the late 1970s.

An offender can use a computer to transfer, manipulate, and even create child pornography. With the typical home computer and modem, still images can easily be digitally stored, transferred from print or videotape, and transmitted, with each copy as good as the original. Visual images can be stored on hard drives, floppy disks, CD-ROMs, or DVDs. With newer technology, faster modems, digital cameras, and better computers, similar things can now be done with moving images. Increasingly available high-speed Internet connections are now making it possible to even transmit the most preferred child pornography format — high-quality, lengthy moving images (videotape and films).

The other invaluable modern inventions for pornographers, video cameras and recorders, are now being used with the computers. Multimedia images with motion, sound, and virtual reality programs can provide added dimension to pornography. The stored data and transmitted information can be encrypted to deter detection.

The ability to manipulate digital visual images may make it difficult to determine the ages of persons in them. Television commercials now make it appear that Paula Abdul is dancing with Gene Kelly, or that John Wayne is talking to a drill sergeant. Halfway through a well-known movie, a Lieutenant's legs are no longer visible. With computer graphics programs, images can be easily changed or "morphed." This is similar to the technology that is used to age the photographs of long-missing children.

In an attempt to deal with this problem, the Child Pornography Prevention Act of 1996 expanded the federal definition of child pornography to include not only a sexually explicit visual depiction using a minor but also any visual depiction that "has been created, adapted, or modified to *appear* (emphasis added) that an identifiable minor is engaging in sexually explicit conduct." Although this new law makes prosecution of cases involving manipulated computer images easier, it also means that it is no longer possible in every case to argue that child pornography is the permanent record of the abuse or exploitation of a child. This law is currently being challenged in a variety of cases and jurisdictions that will ultimately establish its constitutionality. If this law is found unconstitutional, only existing obscenity laws may apply to such manipulated/simulated child pornography.

An offender's collection is the single best indicator of what he *wants* to do. It is not necessarily the best indicator of what he *did* or *will* do. Not all collectors of child pornography physically molest children, and not all molesters of children collect child pornography. Not all children depicted in child pornography have been sexually abused. For example, some have been surreptitiously photographed while undressing and others have been manipulated into posing nude. Depending on the use of the material, however, all can be considered exploited. For this reason, even those who *only* receive or collect child pornography produced by others play a role in the sexual exploitation of children, even if they have not physically molested a child.

Computer offenders who *only* traffic in child pornography are committing serious violations of the law, without law enforcement having to prove that they are also child molesters. Such individuals can be considered preferential sex offenders because such behavior is an offense. Some computer offenders who traffic in child pornography, especially the sexually indiscriminate preferential sex offenders, may have significant collections of adult pornography as well. In some cases, they may even have far more adult than child pornography. Such offenders may not be pedophiles but can still be preferential sex offenders.

Maintenance of Financial Records

Offenders who have turned their child pornography into a profit-making business use computers the same way any business uses them. Lists of customers, dollar amounts of transactions, and descriptions of inventory can all be recorded on the computer. Because trafficking in child pornography by computer lowers the risks, there may be an increase in profit-motivated distribution.

Victims

Offenders can use the computer to troll for and communicate with potential victims with minimal risk of being identified. The use of a vast, loose-knit network like the Internet can sometimes make it difficult to identify the actual perpetrator. On the computer, the offender can assume any identity or set of characteristics he wants or needs. Children from dysfunctional families and families with poor communication are at significant risk for seduction. Older children are obviously at greater risk than younger children. Adolescent boys confused over their sexual orientations are at particularly high risk.

An individual with whom a child has regularly communicated online for months cannot be called a stranger by any reasonable definition, even if that individual has lied about his true identity. Many offenders, however, are reasonably honest about their identities, and some even send recognizable photographs of themselves. They spend hours, days, weeks, and months communicating with and listening to children. In the world of the Internet, someone you never met in person is not only not a stranger but can also be your best friend. Warning potential victims about online predators can communicate a false impression of the nature of the danger.

The child can be indirectly victimized through conversation (chat or instant messages) and the transfer of sexually explicit information and material. The child can also be evaluated for future face-to-face contact and direct victimization. The latest technology even allows for real-time group participation in child molestation by digital teleconferencing by computer.

Investigators must recognize that many of the children lured from their homes after on-line computer conversations are not innocents who were duped while doing their homework. Most are curious, rebellious, or troubled adolescents seeking sexual information or contact. Investigation will sometimes uncover significant amounts of adult and child pornography and other sexually explicit material on the computer of the child victim. Nevertheless, they have been seduced and manipulated by a clever offender and do not fully understand or recognize what they were getting into.

Investigators and prosecutors must understand and learn to deal with the incomplete and contradictory statements of many seduced victims. The dynamics of their victimizations must be considered. They are embarrassed and ashamed of their behaviors and rightfully believe that society will not understand their victimizations. Many adolescent victims are most concerned about the responses of their peers. Investigators must be especially careful in computer cases where easily recovered chat logs, records of communication, and visual images may directly contradict the socially acceptable version of events that the victims give.

Investigators who have a stereotyped concept of child sexual abuse victims — who are accustomed to interviewing younger children molested within their families or kidnapped by strangers — have a difficult time interviewing adolescents molested after on-line seductions. Many of these victims are troubled or delinquent children from dysfunctional homes.

Although applicable statutes and investigative or prosecutorial priorities may vary, officers investigating computer exploitation cases must generally start from the premise that the sexual activity is not the fault of the victim even if the child:

- Did not say no
- Did not fight
- Actively cooperated
- Initiated the contact
- Did not tell

- Accepted gifts or money
- Enjoyed the sexual activity

Investigators must also remember that many children, especially those victimized through the seduction process, often:

- Trade sex for attention, affection, or gifts
- Are confused over their sexuality and feelings
- Are embarrassed and guilt-ridden over their activity
- Describe victimization in socially acceptable ways
- Minimize their responsibility and maximize the offender's
- Deny or exaggerate their victimization

All these things do not mean the children are not victims. What they do mean is that children are human beings with human needs and not necessarily innocent. Sympathy for victims is inversely proportional to their ages.

When law enforcement officers are pretending to be children as part of authorized and approved proactive investigations, they must remember that the number of potential offenders is proportional to — and the appeal of the case is inversely proportional to — the age of the victim. Because there are far more potential offenders interested in older children, pretending to be a 15- or 16-year-old results in a larger on-line response. The resulting case, however, has far less jury appeal. Pretending to be a 5- or 6-year-old is unrealistic. Most on-line undercover investigators claim to be 12 to 15 years old. If an investigator can effectively pretend to be a 12- or 13-year-old, it makes no sense to pretend to be a 14- or 15-year-old. One alternative used by some investigators is to pretend to be an adult with access to young children.

After developing a relationship on-line, offenders who are arrested attempting to meet with children to engage in illegal sexual activity (or individuals they believe to be children) often claim that they were not really going to have sex. They claim the discussed sex was just a fantasy, was part of an undercover investigation, or was a means of communicating with a troubled child. In addressing this issue of intent or motivation, investigators must objectively weigh all the offender's behaviors (past history, honesty about identity, nature of communications, who was notified about activity, overt actions taken, etc.). Ultimately, a judge or jury decides this question of fact.

Summary

Investigators must be alert to the fact that any offender with the intelligence, economic means, or employment access might be using a computer in any or all of the above ways; but preferential sex offenders are highly likely to do so. As computers become less expensive, more sophisticated, and easier to operate, the potential for abuse will grow rapidly; and a more diverse population of offenders will use them to exploit children. Although child exploitation cases present many investigative and prosecutorial problems and obstacles, suspects using computers are more likely to have large amounts of corroborative evidence to be uncovered by investigators. Ritual behavior helps in many cases of sexual exploitation of children.

References

American Psychiatric Association (1994) *Diagnostic and Statistical Manual of Mental Disorders*, 4th ed., Washington, D.C.

Lanning, K. (1992) *Child Molesters: A Behavioral Analysis*, Monograph, 3rd ed., Arlington, VA, National Center for Missing and Exploited Children.

Collateral Materials in Sexual Crimes

12

ROBERT R. HAZELWOOD
KENNETH V. LANNING

Introduction

Over the years the authors have assisted investigators in better understanding the significance of materials seized from violent sexual offenders. Some materials, such as items stolen from rape victims, are routinely seized by the police when found in the possession of the offender. However, it has been found that the full significance of these and other materials is not recognized by investigators, prosecutors, or mental health professionals. Seemingly innocuous items such as newspaper articles (apparently unrelated to the crime), published books, real estate listings, and detective magazines may be very significant to the subject's crime and can provide a greater understanding of the sexual offender.

Traditional Evidence in Sexual Crimes

Any individual who has participated in the investigation and prosecution of a sexual criminal recognizes that various types of evidence play critical roles in the successful conclusion of a case. Therefore, it is necessary to set forth and define the types of evidence that may be encountered in such investigations.

Forensic Evidence

Forensic evidence may be defined as physical or trace evidence that can be scientifically matched with a known individual or item. Such evidence includes fingerprints, footprints, body fluids, hairs, and fibers. Forensic evidence, if properly obtained and examined, can be powerful and reliable evidence in any type of crime.

Circumstantial Evidence

Evidence falling within this category is defined as facts or circumstances that tend to implicate a person or persons in a crime. Examples of such evidence might include the fact that a suspect owns a vehicle similar to one reported to have been in the vicinity of the crime at the time it occurred. Perhaps the suspect is known to have made a threat against the victim or is known to have engaged in similar patterns of behavior observed in the crime under investigation and had the means, opportunity, or motive to commit the crime. Although usually not sufficient to obtain a conviction, in sufficient quantities circumstantial evidence can constitute a powerful case against an individual.

Eyewitness Evidence

Evidence of this type exists when one or more individuals claim to have witnessed the crime during its commission or to have seen the suspect in the vicinity of the crime. Although believed by many to be the best evidence, the reliability of such evidence has historically been debated and is the subject of innumerable studies and publications.

Direct Evidence

Direct evidence may be defined as tangible items that directly implicate an individual in a crime. Most commonly such materials include items *used in the crime* (handcuffs, gloves, mask) or items *taken from a victim or scene of a crime* (fruits of the crime) and found either in the possession of a suspect or in a location under his control (home, storage area, car).

Items taken during a sexual crime have been previously classified by Hazelwood (1983) as follows:

Personal — Items that belong to the victim and are generally of no intrinsic value (driver's license, photograph, lingerie). Such items serve to refresh the offender's recollection of the crime and are used in fantasy reenactments of the offense. Behaviorally, such items are referred to as trophies or souvenirs. Items in this category may or may not be retained by a sexual offender.

Evidentiary — Items taken that, if discovered by the police, could be used to implicate the criminal. Such items may include sheets containing seminal fluids, items with fingerprints on them, or a partially smoked cigarette. The offender is not likely to retain such items, but that possibility cannot be ruled out.

Valuables — Items that have an intrinsic value and are taken during the commission of a crime. Generally, the purpose of taking such material is financial gain. As with evidentiary materials, these items are not likely to be retained by the sexual offender unless he has a personal need for them (television or CD player).

Collateral Materials

Prior to beginning a discussion of collateral materials, the reader should be aware that in the early 1980s, co-author Lanning noted that preferential sex offenders were very likely to collect theme pornography and other paraphernalia related to their sexual interests. Focusing on child molesters, he began referring to the paraphernalia they possessed as *child erotica*. Lanning defined child erotica as "any material relating to children that serves a sexual purpose for a given individual." Child erotica is a broader, more encompassing, and more subjective term than child pornography. Lanning intended that the term child erotica include such items as fantasy writings, letters, diaries, books, sexual aids, souvenirs, toys, costumes, drawings, and non-sexually explicit visual images. He noted that this type of material might also be referred to as *pedophile paraphernalia*. These materials are usually not illegal to possess or distribute.

Because of the diversity of material that could be considered child erotica, there was no way to develop a comprehensive itemization. Consequently, Lanning divided such materials into categories defined by the material's nature or type (published, unpublished, pictures, souvenirs, trophies, and miscellaneous). However, many investigators began using the term child erotica to exclusively describe visual images of naked children that were not considered to be pornographic. Additionally, for many professionals, the term erotica implies that the materials were used only for sexual purposes.

Later, co-author Hazelwood applied the same concept to sexual offenders who acted out against adults and termed the materials found in their possession as *collateral evidence*. Instead of dividing the materials into categories according to nature or type as Lanning had done, Hazelwood divided the materials according to purpose or use. The authors agreed that the term collateral evidence was a better one, and the two approaches were subsequently reconciled for this chapter.

Webster (1995) defines *collateral* as situated or running side by side, or parallel. For the purpose of this article, collateral materials are defined as items that do not directly associate the offender with a crime but give authorities information pertaining to an individual's sexual preferences, interests, or sexual hobbies. It can be valuable as evidence of intent and/or as a source of intelligence. The finding of collateral material may also influence bail, a guilty plea, and the sentence eventually imposed on the offender.

Collateral materials may include materials with an obvious sexual bent, or they may seem benign in nature. Items categorized as collateral may, on occasion, also be classified as *direct* or *circumstantial* evidence. For example, lingerie taken from a rape victim may be sexually arousing to the offender (see Erotica below) and simultaneously be used to link him to the crime (*direct* evidence).

The authors have identified four categories of collateral materials: *erotica* (material that serves to sexually stimulate); *educational* (material providing knowledge about criminal endeavors, the investigative process, the judicial system, or mental health); *introspective* (material providing the criminal with insight into his sexual and/or behavioral disorders); and *intelligence* (materials gathered by the offender that provide him with information about future crimes or information gathered about the offender from third parties). It will not surprise the experienced investigator to learn that some materials may be categorized as more than one type of collateral materials. For example, a partially clothed and bound female depicted on the cover of a detective magazine may be sexually arousing (*erotica*) and the articles in the magazine may also provide information useful to the criminal in circumventing crime detection techniques (*educational*).

Types of Collateral Materials

Erotica

Erotica is defined as any material that serves a sexual purpose for a particular person. When attempting to identify erotica, one should not apply one's own preference for sexual stimuli but instead remain objective. For example, the average person is not sexually aroused by a length of rope; but for a person with a rope fetish, such materials can be extremely stimulating. Material suspected of being erotica must be viewed and evaluated in the context in which it is found. The investigator must use good judgement and common sense. For example, in a child molestation case, possession of an album filled with pictures of the suspect's own fully dressed children probably has no significance. However, possession of 15 photo albums of fully dressed children who are not related to the suspect may be very significant. Possession of his own child's underwear may not be significant, whereas a suitcase containing other childrens' underwear would be quite significant. For a more complete discussion of collateral materials as they pertain to child-related offenses, refer to *Child Molesters: A Behavioral Analysis* (Lanning, 1992).

In determining whether a certain item should be classified as erotica, the investigator should consider whether:

1. It behaviorally relates to the crime under investigation or to possible paraphilias (fetishism) not evidenced in the crime.
2. There is an abnormal amount of the material present and it serves no practical purpose (three sets of handcuffs).
3. The material was secreted.
4. The subject's financial investment in the material is large ($500 worth of pornography).

Common forms of erotica include fetish items; literature and visual images of both a sexually explicit and nonexplicit nature that relate to demographically preferred victims; sexual paraphernalia such as inflatable dolls, vibrators, and dildos; fantasy recordings to include writings, sketches, drawings, and audio/videotapes; records of crimes;* plans for future crimes; crime paraphernalia;** abused dolls (bound, burned, gagged, punctured, dissected, or painted); mutilated or altered pictures of people or animals; media accounts of sexual crimes; advertisements (for clothing, lingerie, adult movies, police paraphernalia); weapons collections; and personal items taken from known victims.**

Educational

This type of collateral material is defined as items that provide the subject with knowledge to enhance his ability to commit a sexual or non-sexual crime, circumvent or thwart law enforcement and/or crime prevention efforts, or manipulate the judicial or mental health process.

Contrary to popular belief, serial sexual offenders do not necessarily have less-than-average intelligence. Research (Hazelwood and Warren, 1989) refutes this belief and documents the fact that serial rapists generally have better-than-average intelligence.

Intelligent criminals often attempt to learn as much as possible about the crimes they are committing and resort to literature sources one would not normally associate with such individuals. In an interview with FBI Special Agent William Hagmaier immediately prior to Ted Bundy's execution, Bundy was questioned about the influence of pornography in his life. Bundy asked Hagmaier if he had read the article entitled *Detective Magazines; Pornography for Sexual Sadists* (Dietz, Harry, and Hazelwood, 1986). Hagmaier advised that he had not, and Bundy advised him to do so as it was very accurate.*** Edward Kemper, an infamous serial killer, was reported to have memorized the Minnesota Multiphasic Inventory. When co-author Hazelwood was attempting to introduce himself to a serial rapist responsible for more than 60 sexually sadistic rapes, the man stated, "I know who you are. When I was raping, I did a literature search on you. I've read everything you've written."

Types of educational materials commonly observed by the authors in such cases include fictional and non-fictional crime books; newspaper articles reporting sexual and non-sexual crimes; law enforcement and mental health journal articles; textbooks on psychology and/or criminal justice; published

---

* Records of crime would also be classified as direct evidence.
** Also direct evidence.
*** Personal conversation with Mr. Hagmaier, 1987.

court decisions; detective magazines; crime prevention materials; and audio/videotaped programs featuring experts on sexual crimes.

Introspective

This type of collateral is defined as materials that provide the offender with information or understanding about his sexual or personality disorders, behaviors, or interests. In conducting research on serial rapists, sexual sadists, and pedophiles, the authors were surprised at the attempts of the men to gain insight into and/or rationalize their deviant sexuality. For example, many pedophiles spend a substantial portion of their lives attempting to convince themselves that what they are doing is not totally out of the mainstream but just happens to be politically incorrect at this time. Other offenders may be troubled by what society defines as atypical or abnormal sexual behaviors and turn to publications, college courses, seminars and, in some cases, counseling for answers. Still others recognize that their preferences and behaviors are not normal and are attempting to better understand, and thus cope with, their deviances. Such actions do not minimize their responsibility for criminal behavior but provide useful information for sexual crimes investigators, particularly in developing interview strategies.

Introspective materials associated with sexual crimes include books and other publications on psychopathology; video/audiotapes of experts addressing the subject; self-help books; surveys in sexually-oriented magazines; and newspaper, magazine, and journal articles on sexual offender research.

Intelligence

This type of collateral material is defined as (1) information or items obtained by the offender in planning for future crimes, and/or (2) information gathered by law enforcement from third-party sources about the offender. Examples of intelligence are:

1. Materials possessed by the offender that indicate he has planned and collected information for the commission of future crimes. Such materials may include automobile license plate numbers; telephone numbers or addresses of potential victims; commercial or hand-drawn maps with notations or routes of travel; notes concerning the movements or schedules of other persons; surveillance photographs of people or locations; written scripts for victims; and lists of materials needed for the commission of a specific crime.
2. Information obtained from interviews of current or former sexual partners of the suspect. This may include spouses, lovers, or prostitutes. Hazelwood, Warren, and Dietz (1993) and Warren and Hazelwood (in press) have reported on the value of conducting such

interviews. In sexual crimes, the investigator is specifically interested
in obtaining facts and knowledge concerning the subject's sexual preferences, fantasies, habits, and dysfunctions. Also of interest are locations where he may have hidden additional materials, what stressors
were present in his life at the time of the crimes, and whether he
sexually behaved with the interviewee in a manner consistent with his
criminal sexual behaviors.

Case Study

Co-author Hazelwood consulted on the following case and subsequently
testified at the subject's murder trial. The facts of the case, the items seized
from the subject, and the discussions provide classification of the materials
as *Erotica, Educational, Introspective, or Intelligence.*

The victim, a pregnant 24-year-old housewife, was abducted from her
rural home. Her husband discovered her missing when he returned from
work and found his 22-month-old infant on the floor of their home. There
was no evidence of forced entry and no sign that a struggle had taken
place. The victim's car, a quilt, a telephone with a 20-foot cord, the bottom
half of a swimming suit belonging to the victim, and all of her panties
were missing.

The victim's car was found the following morning about $^1/_2$ mile from the
residence. Two days later, her decomposing body was discovered eight miles
from the point of abduction. She was dressed in the same clothing she'd
been wearing when her husband last saw her, and there was no indication
that the clothing had been disturbed. The autopsy revealed no evidence of
sexual assault, and the cause of death was determined to have been aspira-
tion due to two paper towels lodged in her throat. It was the opinion of the
investigators that the offender had not intentionally killed the woman.

Within four months, a 37-year-old man was identified as the person responsible for the crime. He was an unemployed well-digger, having recently been
fired. One year prior to the crime, he had drilled a well on the victim's
property. He was married, had two children, and resided in a single-family
residence in an adjacent county.

The man had served time in prison for burglary and had been released
approximately 3 years prior to the homicide. He was a high school graduate
and of average intelligence. Investigation determined that the subject had
committed a variety of crimes over a nine-month period of time before and
after the homicide. The following is a sequential listing of those crimes:

March: Harassing phone call to a woman.
May: Exposed genitals to a woman.
June: Obscene phone call to a woman.
August: Theft of woman's purse from a car.
August: Kidnap and murder (current case).
November: Fondling and battery of a woman.
November: Impersonation of a police officer and attempted abduction of
              a woman.
November: Theft of woman's purse from a car.
December: Theft of property from a business site.
December: Kidnap and rape of a 27-year-old woman.

The abducted rape victim was taken from her home, raped at an abandoned farmhouse, driven to a second abandoned farmhouse, and forced to model a variety of lingerie. She was raped a second time and then driven back to her neighborhood and released.

During a search of the killer's residence, the police seized a large volume of materials that included collateral and direct evidence. The following is a listing of those materials:

1. More than 2500 index cards containing information on women who had appeared either nude or in lingerie in *Gallery* or *Que* magazines. On each card, he had written a woman's first name, age, marital status, occupation, hobbies, the initials GND (Girl Next Door section of *Gallery*) or FNL (Friends and Lovers section of *Que*), and the month and year of the issue in which the photograph and demographic data appeared. In the upper right-hand corner of each card was a numerical rating (0–10) of the woman.

2. A spiral notebook containing information identical to that found on the aforementioned index cards.

3. Hundreds of articles of clothing to include panties, bras, nightgowns, swimsuits, slips, mesh tops, wraparounds, nightshirts, camisoles, and teddies. This apparel, purchased from a mail order firm specializing in such items, was estimated to be valued at $3,000. Several of the items had been placed in plastic baggies and identified to allow cross-indexing to the index cards and the spiral notebook.

Discussion: Items in 1, 2, and 3 are correctly classified as *erotica*. The subject's purpose in having this information was to allow him to have sex (masturbatory fantasy) with any of the women whenever he chose. The amount of time and money he spent purchasing, indexing, and maintaining this collection is indicative of the importance he attached to the material.

It is also quite obvious that the man had a lingeric fetish. The reader will recall that the murder victim's panties and bottom half of her bathing suit were taken and that the kidnap-rape victim was forced to model teddies.

4. Over 100 *Gallery* and *Que* magazines.

Discussion: These magazines are classified as *erotica*. They dated to within one month of his release from prison on burglary charges, indicating that his preoccupation with such material existed long before his known sexual crimes. Worth noting is the fact that he was particularly attracted to women who were not professional models. In the authors' opinion, such women were complementary to his fantasies in that he could mentally relate more closely to such women. It is also to be appreciated that he invested over $250 in the magazines even though he was financially stressed.

5. Handwritten notes detailing specific items of lingerie and their cost if ordered from the mail order firm. The amount of the anticipated purchases would have totaled over $7,000.

Discussion: These notes are *erotica*. Whether he purchased the items is not as significant as the paraphilic preoccupation to possess them.

6. A library book entitled *Rape; The Bait and the Trap* and a newspaper article on law enforcement tips to avoid sexual assault.

Discussion: Both of these items are classified as *educational* materials. They provide information on the crime of rape and what techniques the experts recommend to thwart it. The book is also considered *introspective* in that it contains information on the underlying motivations of rape.

7. Numerous newspaper articles relating to the unexplained disappearances of women and runaway teenage females. These articles included photographs, descriptive data, and investigative methodology. The police determined that the subject was not involved in any of the disappearances.

Discussion: These items are classified as *erotic* and *educational* materials. They depicted visual images of the missing women and teenagers and lent reality to masturbatory fantasies. They also gave an indication of the media coverage and police procedures in such cases.

8. Three newspaper articles pertaining to the disappearance, discovery, and autopsy of the murder victim. These articles were hidden in a paper bag behind a basement wall in the offender's home. None of the other materials were hidden.

Discussion: These media accounts of the crime are considered *educational* materials in that they allow the man to keep up with the investigation. Recognizing that some types of sexual killers use media accounts to relive the crime for masturbatory purposes, it might seem logical to also categorize the articles as *erotica*. However, it should be remembered that the offender did not intend for the victim to die and subsequently released another kidnap victim. Therefore, it is unlikely that he would use such materials for masturbatory behavior. These materials would also be considered *circumstantial evidence* in that they were hidden and related to the crime for which the man was a suspect. All other recovered materials were easily found.

9. Several newspaper articles dealing with non-criminal activities. They included the grand opening of a new drug store with an accompanying photograph of female employees with their names underlined; wedding announcements with photographs of the bride-to-be; the announcement of a surprise lingerie shower (he had underlined the word lingerie); a photograph of an English model in a bikini swimming suit.

Discussion: All of these items are classified as *erotica*. Additionally, with the exception of the model's photograph, the items are classified as *intelligence* gathered by the offender for a potential victim pool. He underlined the names of the drug store employees, had a photograph and identifying data on the bride-to-be in the wedding announcement, and knew the identity of the guest of honor at the lingerie shower.

10. Several drivers' licenses, license plate numbers, credit cards, and telephone numbers belonging to women.

Discussion: The drivers' licenses and credit cards are *direct evidence* as they are fruits of their thefts and therefore directly link him to those crimes. The drivers' licenses, license plates and telephone numbers are categorized as *intelligence* as they were information he had gathered on potential victims.

11. The quilt taken from the murder victim's home and the bottom half of the victim's bathing suit; because of the voluminous amount of lingerie present in the offender's home, the victim's panties (all of which were taken) could not be positively identified.

Discussion: The quilt and bathing suit bottom are *direct* evidence. The bathing suit bottom is also categorized as *erotica*. While it is entirely possible that the quilt also served to sexually excite the man, there is nothing to indicate that he had a fetish for such material and therefore that assumption cannot be made.

12. A hand-drawn map depicting the route to a 27-year-old woman's residence. Notations on the map set forth details on her breast size, age

of children, and type of car she owned. The investigators followed the map and determined that the man had dug a well on her farm property about one year earlier.

Discussion: The map and notations are categorized as both *intelligence* and *erotica*. It was learned that the killer had visited her farm on the pretext of checking the functioning of the well. However, when her husband unexpectedly drove up, the man hurriedly left the farm property.

As previously mentioned, there are two types of *intelligence* — information gathered by the offender for future crimes and/or victims, and information gathered from third parties about the offender. The wife of the subject was interviewed extensively and provided the following *intelligence*:

She said that she was well aware of her husband's preoccupation with female attire, particularly lingerie. He had often purchased teddies and nightgowns for her to wear and he became sexually aroused when she wore the items. He was a chronic masturbator and would do so openly at all times of the day. He would ejaculate into condoms and leave them lying about their home. When she confronted him with this behavior, he denied the condoms were his and accused her of having affairs.

His extensive collection of lingerie led her to believe that he was having affairs, and she began denying him sexual relations for fear of contracting AIDS. She also ceased wearing lingerie for his pleasure.

She gave information that showed he was experiencing several stressors (financial, marital, health, occupational, and sexual) at the time that the known criminal behavior began.

The value of such first-hand information in a sexual crime investigation cannot be overestimated. In this case, it confirmed one of the subject's paraphilias (fetishism); identified various stressors in his life; and revealed a dysfunctional marriage.

Summary

The authors have assisted investigators and prosecutors in better understanding the significance of materials found in the possession of sexual offenders. In addition to forensic, eyewitness, circumstantial and direct evidence, investigators should also be cognizant of *collateral materials*.

Collateral materials can include newspaper articles, literature, viewing materials, advertisements, personal notes, fantasy recordings, sexual paraphernalia, collections, and information obtained from consenting and/or paid partners.

Collateral materials can augment hard evidence for investigators in presentation of their cases for prosecution and by prosecutors in the utilization of expert testimony in the education of juries as to the significance and importance of the items.

References

Dietz, P.E., Harry, B., and Hazelwood, R.R. (1986) Detective magazines: pornography for the sexual sadist?, *J. Forensic Sci.*, 31(1), 197–211.

Hazelwood, R.R. (1983) The behavior-oriented interview of rape victims: the key to profiling, *FBI Law Enforcement Bull.*

Hazelwood, R.R. and Warren, J.I. (1989) The serial rapist: his characteristics and victims, *FBI Law Enforcement Bull.*

Hazelwood, R.R., Warren, J.I., and Dietz, P.E. (1993) Compliant victims of sexual sadists, *Austr. Fam. Phys.*, 22(4).

Lanning, K.V. (1992) *Child Molesters: A Behavioral Analysis*, 3rd ed., National Center for Missing and Exploited Children, Washington, D.C.

Warren, J.I. and Hazelwood, R.R. (In press) Relational patterns associated with sexual sadism, *J. Family Violence*.

Webster's School and Office Dictionary (1995) Random House Inc., New York.

Interrogations and False Confessions in Rape Cases [*]

13

RICHARD LEO

Introduction

Researchers and practitioners alike wonder why the innocent might confess to crimes that carry lengthy prison sentences or life imprisonment (Ofshe and Leo 1997b, 1997a; Kassin, 1997; Gudjonsson, 1992). Though social scientists have studied psychological interrogations and false confessions for almost a century, these questions have not been fully answered. This is largely because the process of interrogation has only recently been studied in a direct and detailed manner. Over the past three decades, researchers have undertaken a variety of types of studies (field, observational, laboratory, documentary) in order to advance scientific knowledge about how interrogation procedures influence suspects' perceptions and move them from denial to admission. The studies and records of interrogation that have accumulated now make it possible to empirically describe and analyze the psychological process of interrogation and its influence on a suspect's decision to confess (Ofshe and Leo, 1997a, 1997b).

Because the third degree has virtually disappeared, false confessions might seem not only aberrational but completely irrational. However, confessions by the innocent still occur and pose a serious problem for the American criminal justice system in general and law enforcement in particular. No responsible scholar or practitioner suggests that the police intentionally seek to obtain false confessions or that prosecutors deliberately convict the innocent. Indeed, there is little evidence that intentional abuses of power occur with significant frequency. Rather, it appears that a lack of proper training is often the primary reason that false confessions occur. Police are not always properly trained to avoid eliciting false confessions or to recognize their varieties and distinguishing characteristics. This chapter briefly documents the process of interrogation and explains why false confessions, like truthful ones, can be understandable responses to certain interrogative strategies.

[*] This chapter was prepared with the assistance of Natasha Elkovich.

Causes of False Confessions

Through the 1930s it was not uncommon for police to rely on physical coercion and psychological duress to extract confessions (Hopkins, 1931). In the last 70 years, however, more subtle and sophisticated psychological methods have replaced the interrogation techniques of the past. Consequently, it is no longer as obvious why the innocent would falsely confess (Wrightsman and Kassin, 1993; Gudjonsson, 1992). With the decline of the third degree, the phenomenon of false confessions has become counter-intuitive (White, 1997).

Most people do not appear to know that the phenomenon of false confessions even exists (Kassin and Neumann, 1997; Johnson, 1997, Ainsworth, 1995) and believe in what the author calls the *Myth of Psychological Interrogation* — that an innocent person will not falsely confess unless he is physically tortured or mentally ill (Johnson, 1997; White, 1997; Ainsworth, 1995). Contemporary methods of psychological interrogation can and sometimes do result in false confessions obtained from cognitively and intellectually normal individuals. The central issue for researchers and practitioners is not whether false confessions exist, but why they occur and what can be done to prevent them.

The Police Interrogation

After identifying a suspect, investigators meet with that person to elicit information. The detective may intend that the meeting is only for an investigative interview, or that it is the first step of an adversarial interrogation. The use of an interview format allows the investigator to better develop rapport, to lead the suspect to believe that he is helping authorities solve the crime (Leo, 1996b), and to perceive that the questioning is non-threatening (Leo and White, 1999). If it is decided to move from an interview to an interrogation, the elicitation of a *Miranda* waiver typically signals the transition.

Many suspects, whether innocent or guilty, do not appreciate the significance of the *Miranda* warnings and may waive their rights without giving the content of the warnings much thought. A guilty person may believe that, if he does not waive his rights, the police will arrest him; and, after waiving his rights, he may attempt to misdirect the attention of the police and attempt to learn what evidence they possess. An innocent person, on the other hand, may believe that he is not in any jeopardy by waiving his rights. (Ofshe and Leo, 1997b).

Modern interrogation techniques and strategies are designed to break through the resistance of a rational person who knows he is guilty, convince him to stop denying his culpability, and persuade him to confess (Ofshe and Leo, 1997b, 1997a) (Inbau, Reid and Buckley, 1986). Officers conducting the interrogation elicit the decision to confess by influencing the suspect's perception of (a) the nature and gravity of his immediate situation, (b) his available choices or alternatives, and (c) the consequences of each of these choices (Ofshe and Leo, 1997b). The detective labors to persuade the suspect that he has few options but to confess and that the act of admitting culpability is the optimal and most sensible course of action.

Step 1: Shifting the Suspect from Confident to Hopeless

American police interrogation is essentially a two-step process (Ofshe and Leo, 1997b, 1997a). The goal of the first step is to cause a guilty party to perceive his situation as hopeless. The officer seeks to accomplish this by leading the suspect to believe that he has been caught; that his guilt can be objectively demonstrated to the satisfaction of any reasonable person; that this fact is indisputable and cannot be changed; and that there is no way out of this predicament.

Presuming the person is guilty, the officer is likely to rely on several well-known interrogation techniques to successfully communicate the message that the suspect has been caught and that his situation is hopeless. The detective may repeatedly accuse the person of having committed the crime and express unwavering confidence in the suspect's guilt, ignoring any assertions of innocence by the person. This may result in the suspect's belief that he has the burden of proving his innocence. If the person offers an alibi, the officer may attack it as inconsistent, implausible, or contradicted by the evidence.

The most effective technique used to convince the suspect of his hopelessness is to confront him with what appears to be objective and irrefutable evidence of his guilt. American law allows the police to state that they have physical or trace evidence, eyewitnesses, or even polygraph results that support their position of the suspect's guilt, when in fact such evidence may not exist. The purpose of doing so is to convince the suspect that his guilt will be established beyond any reasonable doubt and that his best option is to confess.

Step 2: Offering the Suspect Inducements to Confess

In the second phase of interrogation, the detective seeks to convince the suspect that the only way to improve his situation is by admitting to the offense and to persuade the person that the benefits of admitting guilt clearly outweigh the costs of continuing to assert innocence (Ofshe and Leo 1997b). To accomplish this, the officer may present the suspect with incentives which communicate that he might receive some personal, moral, legal or other benefit if he confesses to the offense. These inducements can be arrayed along a continuum and for analytic purposes have been classified into three categories: *low-end*, *systemic*, and *high-end* inducements (Ofshe and Leo, 1997b, 1997a).

Low-end inducements refer to self-image, interpersonal and/or moral appeals that suggest the suspect will feel better or improve his social standing if he confesses (Ofshe and Leo, 1997b). They are intended to impact on the guilty person who is either (a) experiencing a troubled conscience or (b) vulnerable to moral persuasion. The officer suggests that if the suspect continues to deny his culpability, he will also continue to experience guilt and anxiety; however, once he accepts responsibility for his actions by confessing, his distress will be alleviated and his conscience, family, friends and associates will view him as a better person.

Systemic inducements are intended to focus the suspect's attention on the discretionary ability of criminal justice officials to positively influence his case (Ofshe and Leo, 1997b). The officer's goal is to have the suspect reason that his case may be more favorably acted on if he accepts responsibility, cooperates with authorities, and admits guilt. The detective may seek to further motivate the guilty party by claiming to be his ally and expressing a willingness to inform others of his willingness to cooperate if the person confesses.

High-end inducements may be observed when an overzealous or untrained officer inappropriately advises the suspect that he will receive less punishment, a lower prison sentence, or prosecutorial or judicial leniency if he confesses — and more severe treatment by the criminal justice system if he does not confess (Ofshe and Leo, 1997b).

Effective psychological interrogation is a gradual yet cumulative process. As the officer progresses through the two-step process, he works to structure a guilty party's perceptions about the nature of his immediate situation, the limited choices available to him, and what follows from these choices.

The Different Types of False Confessions

Kassin and Wrightsman (1985) first identified three conceptually distinct types of false confessions — *voluntary, coerced-compliant, and coerced-internalized.* Kassin and Wrightsman's typology or classification scheme offers a useful conceptual framework for scholars of interrogations and confessions (Gudjonsson, 1992). Synthesizing the existing research literature, Ofshe and Leo (1997a) extended and modified Kassin and Wrightsman's initial typology to include five distinct types of true and false confessions — *voluntary, stress-compliant, coerced-compliant, non-coerced persuaded,* and *coerced-persuaded.*

Voluntary False Confession

A voluntary false confession is offered either in the absence of police interrogation or in response to minimal police pressure. As Kassin and Wrightsman (1985) state, individuals volunteer false confessions in the absence of police questioning for a variety of reasons — a morbid desire for notoriety, the need to atone for real or imagined acts (Gudjonsson, 1992), a need for attention or fame, the desire to protect or assist the actual offender, an inability to distinguish between fantasy and reality, or a pathological need for acceptance or self-punishment (Kassin, 1997). High-profile crimes such as the Lindbergh kidnapping in the 1930s, the Black Dahlia murder in the 1940s, or the JonBenet Ramsey and Nicole Brown Simpson murders in the 1990s may attract hundreds of voluntary false confessions (Kassin, 1997). If police suspect that such a confession has been given, there are at least three indicia of reliability that can be used to reach a conclusion about the trustworthiness of the confession:

1. Does the statement lead to the discovery of evidence unknown to the police?
2. Does the statement include identification of unusual elements of the crime that have not been made public?
3. Does the statement include an accurate description of the mundane details of the crime scene that are not easily guessed and have not been reported publically?

Stress-Compliant False Confession

A stress-compliant false confession is given when the pressure of custodial questioning overwhelms the suspect and he comes to believe that the only way to end the experience is by confessing. (Ofshe and Leo, 1997a). There are three potential sources of stress during the interrogation; the environment, the detective's interpersonal style, and the techniques and strategies used during the process. During interrogations, detectives commonly (and legally) structure the environment to induce stress. They place the suspect in an unfamiliar setting, they separate him from others, and they control the pace, length, and intensity of the questioning. The officer's interpersonal style may be one that is alternately confrontational, demanding, and insistent. Finally, the techniques and strategies of the questioning officers may be designed to induce anxiety by attacking the suspect's self-confidence and appearing not to listen when he claims his innocence. Even though the suspect knows he is innocent, he may make a false confession because the prospect of continued interrogation is intolerable. If the officer suspects that the person making the confession is doing so simply to end the interrogation, he should attempt to obtain crime information from the individual that will corroborate the confession absent any contamination. Such information should be known only to the police and the true offender. If the suspect is unable to provide such information, the officer should confront the suspect about his motivation for confessing.

Coerced-Compliant False Confession

As Kassin (1997) states, "Coerced-compliant false confessions occur when a suspect confesses in order to escape or avoid an interrogation or to gain a promised reward." A coerced-compliant false confession is similar to a stress-compliant false confession insofar as the person knowingly confesses falsely in order to end the interrogation. However, coerced-compliant false confessions occur because of threats and promises made by the questioning officer; and the suspect consciously decides to confess in order to gain a reward or end the interrogation. (Ofshe and Leo, 1997a). Officers should be aware of the legal ramifications of engaging in verbal and non-verbal behavior that threatens the well-being of a suspect and should avoid engaging in such activities. Furthermore, officers should make no promises that they are not legally empowered to make.

Coerced-Persuaded False Confession

Such a confession occurs when the detective refuses to accept the suspect's report of having no memory of committing the crime. The detective uses intimidating techniques, and this causes the person to begin to doubt the reliability of his memory. In such cases, the suspect comes to believe that he probably did it, or logically must have committed the crime and falsely confesses to it. Because a person making a persuaded false confession lacks any memory or knowledge of having committed the crime, he confesses in hypothetical, tentative, or speculative language that he *could have,* he *probably did,* he *must have,* or he may have, reflecting his uncertainty and lack of knowledge (Ofshe and Leo, 1997b, 1997a). When it appears that such a confession is being made, the investigator should be careful to ensure that he does not assist the suspect in constructing the confession, and he should avoid filling in the blanks or answering the suspect's questions about the crime. The officer should also determine whether the information provided by the suspect could have been obtained from other police officers, the media, or the community.

Non-Coerced False Confession

The same structure, sequence, and logic occurs in this type of false confession as occurs in the coerced-persuaded type. (Ofshe and Leo, 1997a). The major difference is that the confession is given not because of any perceived coercion but because of other factors that result in the suspect temporarily believing that it is likely he committed the crime. Again, such confessions will be given in language such as he *may have,* or he *must have,* and the officer is once more reminded to not assist in the formation of the confession or provide information to the suspect.

The Consequences of False Confessions

While it is not presently possible to provide a valid quantitative estimate of the incidence or prevalence of false confessions (Kassin, 1997; White, 1997; Gudjonsson, 1992), it is well established that false confessions do occur within our society. However, because researchers, police, prosecutors, and the media may be unaware that a false confession has been elicited, false confessions are not easily discovered. Even when discovered, they are rarely publicized.

Historically regarded as a form of self-conviction, false confessions ultimately may lead to finding an innocent person guilty. In rare instances, a rapist is caught in the act (more common in movies than in real life), providing the most damning piece of evidence possible in such cases. A confession is also one of the most powerful, persuasive, and damning pieces of evidence in rape cases (Leo and Ofshe, 1998; Leo, 1996a; Kassin and Wrightsman, 1985). To anyone who believes in the American system of justice, false confessions can have results that are frightening.

A person who confesses is likely to be treated more harshly by those within the criminal justice system. An officer who obtains a confession is inclined to consider the case solved. Prosecutors tend to make the confession the centerpiece of their cases and are less likely to initiate or accept plea bargains (Leo and Ofshe, 1998). The defendants may have more difficulty in obtaining bail, and defense attorneys are more likely to pressure their clients to plead guilty because the risk of conviction is greatly increased. Even the triers of fact may become biased in favor of conviction when a confession is involved.

Conclusion

False confessions occur. A police interrogation is a stressful event for the suspect whether he is guilty or innocent. While acknowledging that false confessions are not the goal of the trained and professional interrogator, it is still incumbent on law enforcement officers to be alert to the possibility of false confessions for any number of reasons.

False confessions can be prevented, and it is imperative that all reasonable steps be taken to ensure they do not occur. One of the most important procedural safeguards to reduce the possibility of false confessions is a comprehensive training program for law enforcement officers who will be involved in the conduct of interrogations.

As a minimum, officers should be trained in the following three areas:

1. The existence, variety, causes, and psychology of false confessions — if officers are taught the logic, principles, and effects of psychological

interrogation methods, they will not only become more knowledge-able about false confessions but they will also be more effective in obtaining truthful ones.

2. The indicia of reliable and unreliable statements and how to distin-guish between them — it has long been a generally accepted principle in law enforcement that valid confessions are supported by logic and evidence. The proper way to assess the reliability of a confession is by analyzing the suspect's post-admission narrative (detailed discussion of the crime after an admission has been given) against the underlying crime facts to determine whether it reveals guilty knowledge and is, in fact, corroborated by existing evidence (Ofshe and Leo, 1997a).

3. Officers cannot reliably intuit whether a suspect is innocent or guilty based on their uncorroborated suspicions — police must base their opinions about an individual's guilt on much more reliable and con-clusive evidence and should ensure that they have done all within their power to corroborate the confession. True confessions most often provide information that leads to corroborating evidence, whereas false confessions, by their very nature, cannot do so.

Awareness that false confessions happen and reliance on objective standards for evaluating a confession are professional approaches to interrogation. A confession that cannot withstand objective evaluation should not be accepted. Defective confessions have the potential to mislead the investigator initially and the jury eventually, resulting in the conviction and incarceration of an innocent person.

References

Ainsworth, P.B. (1995) *Psychology and Policing in a Changing World*, John Wiley & Sons, New York.

Gudjonsson, G.H. (1992) *The Psychology of Interrogations, Confessions and Testimony*, John Wiley & Sons, New York.

Hopkins, E.J. (1931) *Our Lawless Police: A Study of the Unlawful Enforcement of the Law*, Viking Press, New York.

Inbau, F.E., Reid, J.E., and Buckley, J.P. (1986) *Criminal Interrogation and Confessions*, 3rd ed., Williams & Wilkins, Baltimore.

Johnson, G. (1997) False confessions and fundamental fairness: the need for elec-tronic recording of custodial interrogations, *Boston Univ. Public Interest Law J.*, 6, 719–751.

Kassin, S.M. (1997) The psychology of confession evidence, *Am. Psychol.*, 52, 221–233.

Kassin, S.M. and Neumann, K. (1997) On the power of confession evidence: an experimental test of the fundamental difference hypothesis, *Law Hum. Behav.*, 21, 469–483.

Kassin, S.M. and Wrightsman, L. (1985) Confession evidence, in S. Kassin and L. Wrightsman, Eds., *The Psychology of Evidence and Trial Procedure*, Sage Publications, Beverly Hills, pp. 67–94.

Leo, R.A. and White, W.S. (1999) Adapting to *Miranda*: modern interrogators' strategies for dealing with the obstacles posed by *Miranda*, *Minn. Law Rev.*, 84, 397–472.

Leo, R.A. and Ofshe, R.J. (1998) The consequences of false confessions: deprivations of liberty and miscarriages of justice in the age of psychological interrogation, *J. Criminology Criminal Law,* 88, 429–496.

Leo, R.A. (1996b) *Miranda*'s revenge: police interrogation as a confidence game, *Law Soc. Rev.,* 30(2), 259–288.

Ofshe, R.J. and Leo, R.A. (1997b) The decision to confess falsely: rational choice and irrational action, *Denver Univ. Law Rev.,* 74, 979–1122.

Ofshe, R.J. and Leo, R.A. (1997a) The social psychology of police interrogation: the theory and classification of true and false confessions, *Stud. Law, Politics Soc.,* 16, 189–251.

White, W. (1997) False confessions and the constitution: safeguards to prevent the admission of untrustworthy confessions, *Harv. Civ. Rights Civ. Liberties Law Rev.,* 32, 105–157.

Wrightsman, L. and Kassin, S. (1993) *Confessions in the Courtroom*, Sage Publications, Newbury Park, CA.

The Maligned Investigator of Criminal Sexuality*

14

KENNETH V. LANNING
ROBERT R. HAZELWOOD

Introduction

Richard Beck was an individual respected for his ability to solve the most difficult homicide cases. He was also known as an officer who didn't let departmental rules and regulations stand in the way of his investigations. After numerous warnings, the powers that be decided to teach Detective Beck a lesson. He would be reassigned to the Sex Crimes Unit! If that didn't teach him a lesson, nothing would.

He was called into the captain's office and given the bad news. This time the department had his attention. He tried to reason with the captain, explaining that he would reform his ways. The captain was unsympathetic. This time Detective Beck had gone too far, and even his excellent record wouldn't save him. He was being assigned to the Sex Crimes Unit to teach him a lesson.

This scene was presented in a television movie starring Richard Crenna entitled *The Rape of Richard Beck.* The intent of the film was to portray a macho male who, after becoming a rape victim, was forced to confront the resultant physical and emotional trauma experienced by such victims. Even though it was only a movie, the filmmaker's perceptions of individuals who investigate sexual crimes are worth noting.

A similar scene appeared in the Burt Reynolds movie *Sharky's Machine.* After being transferred from Narcotics to Vice, Detective Sharky finds that his long-time partner won't accompany him as he descends into the bowels of the building to his desk in a squad room filled with oddballs and misfits.

Unfortunately, these fictional accounts are not simply the products of writers' active imaginations; they mirror perceptions often shared by

---

* This chapter was originally published in the September 1988 issue of the *FBI Law Enforcement Bulletin.* Male pronouns are used at times when the female gender would be equally applicable. This is done in the interests of sentence structure and readability.

individuals in and out of law enforcement. Conversations with investigators, friends, family, and associates confirm that such attitudes exist about those who work in sexual crimes investigation, prosecution, research, or training. Sexual crimes also include sexual vice (prostitution and pornography).

An Analogy

At this point, a simple analogy is helpful. Investigating sexual crimes is like being a garbage collector. Everyone would agree that it is important that garbage be collected and removed. People are used to putting garbage by the curb, coming home from work and finding it gone, and otherwise giving little thought to the details of its disposal. The only time they become more interested is when their garbage is not picked up, or when a new landfill or incinerator is to be located near their homes, when toxic waste seeps into their drinking water, or when a garbage barge cannot find a place to unload its cargo. In other words, people are concerned with garbage collection only when it directly affects them; but few want their children to grow up to be garbage collectors. Those who do the dirty job of collecting garbage become dirty by association. Unfortunately, the same may be said of sexual crimes investigators.

Sex is probably the most talked about and least understood subject in the American culture, and those whose work involves the criminal aspects of sex are viewed like those who deal with the world's trash — they are often considered to be different or, in some cases, even dirty. This is unfortunate, but it is something with which the investigator must learn to cope. There will always be those inside and outside the department who cannot or will not appreciate the complexity or the seriousness of sexual offenses. Nor do they understand the emotional impact such work can have on the investigator.

Society's attitude toward child sexual abuse, child prostitution, child pornography, rape, and other sexual crimes can be summed up in a single word — *denial*. People do not want to hear about these problems and certainly do not want to deal with them. This is not only the attitude of the average citizen but also of government leaders, law enforcement administrators, and other investigators. Only when they, or someone they know, are victimized by a sexual criminal does this attitude change. Few people attend public presentations on sexual assault awareness or prevention, and most of those who do have been directly or indirectly victimized in a sexual manner.

When people are confronted with the publicity of such crimes, they have preconceptions that the offenders are different — certainly not people who may appear normal. Every time a pillar of the community is arrested for a sexual offense, local newspapers and television stations react as though it were a first-time occurrence. People need to recognize that it is not an amazing story when nice people commit sexual crimes; it is amazing that people are still surprised by it.

Criminal Sexuality vs. Sex Crimes

One of the major obstacles that an investigator faces when working sexual crimes is the title that is most commonly associated with such work — Sex Crimes Investigator. While with the FBI, the authors were responsible for a course of instruction dealing with sexual crimes. A much shorter version of the course had previously been taught by another person who had titled it *Sex Crimes*. Upon assuming responsibility for the course, the first order of business was to change the title to *Interpersonal Violence*. This was necessary because when students of any discipline attend a course entitled *Sex Crimes*, the reaction invariably is, *Oh boy, this is what I've been waiting for*, or *Let me tell you a joke you can use in class*, or *Here is where we get to see the dirty pictures*.

Why should a change of title make a difference in the attitude of the student? The answer lies in the power of the word *sex* — it simply overwhelms the word *crime*. When one hears *sex*, a range of emotions is evoked — from pleasure, ecstasy, and lust to love, warmth, and sharing. On the other hand, the word *crime* is associated with violence, anger, and fear. When one hears *sex crime,* what actually registers is *sex*. Therefore, it should not be surprising that a person meeting or dealing with an investigator involved in sex crimes may smile and say, *You're one of those, huh?*

The terms *criminal sexuality* or *sexual crimes* leave no doubt about the involvement of crime (violence, fear, or harm). The listener is more likely to register all of the feelings associated with crime rather than those associated with sex. Even the word *sexuality* has a more neutral impact than the word *sex*. Such a distinction may seem trivial to some; however, the power of words should never be underestimated. If the truth of this is doubted, notice the reactions of individuals as they pass a classroom with the topic *Sex Crimes* posted on the door.

The Investigator of Criminal Sexuality

What type of people investigate sexual crimes in America? How old are they? What are the amounts of experience in law enforcement, the educational levels, or the marital status of typical investigators assigned to such crimes?

LeDoux and Hazelwood (1985) conducted a nationwide survey of police officers to determine their attitudes and beliefs about the crime of rape. To the best of the authors' knowledge, this remains the only such study ever conducted. Information concerning the demographics of the respondents was captured during the study. Three thousand questionnaires were mailed to law enforcement agencies throughout the U.S., and usable returns were received from 2170, or 72%. Two hundred two of the respondents reported involvement in the investigation of sexual crimes. Data extracted from the study provide useful information about the individuals who are charged with investigating such crimes.

Ninety-two percent of the investigators assigned to sexual crimes were white males with a mean age of 38.2 years and 13.1 years of law enforcement experience. Eighty-one percent were married, and 54% had either attended college or obtained a bachelor's degree. Statistical analysis was performed to compare sexual crimes investigators with other responding investigators on the variables of age, experience, gender, race, marital status, and education ('t' or chi square tests were used as appropriate). The sexual crimes investigators were found to be older (38.2 vs. 35.9 years) and more experienced (13.1 vs. 11.3 years) than the other responding officers. There were no significant differences between the two groups in the remaining variables. Although slightly more female officers were assigned to sexual crimes investigations, the difference was not statistically significant.

It appears that sexual crimes investigators are not unlike other officers in law enforcement. Why, then, are they viewed as different? The authors believe that there are multiple reasons for which the investigators, their departments, and their fellow officers must equally share the responsibility. The remainder of this chapter will address what each must do to correct an incorrect perception.

The Investigator's Responsibility

The investigator of criminal sexuality is most responsible for influencing how others perceive him. If he does not approach his job in a professional manner, he cannot expect to be treated with respect. The authors have conducted a number of courses designed to teach others how to conduct programs on criminal sexuality, and in each one the first two hours were dedicated to the ethics involved. Future instructors are advised against the use of unnecessary slides (those without a learning objective), profanity, inappropriate jokes, or sexist remarks. It is the responsibility of the teacher to maintain a sense of decorum when speaking on such a potentially volatile subject.

Pictures, Profanity, and Jokes

The same advice can be applied to those who investigate such crimes. Many in law enforcement have encountered an individual who wants to share some dirty pictures recovered from a case. However, when the investigator does so, he confirms the suspicion that he is in the job because he likes dirty pictures. If the truth were known, the photographs were probably being shown for much the same reason a teenager takes that first drink or a normally modest person tells an off-color joke — to prove that he is not any different from his peers. However unfair, such behavior is guaranteed to be misconstrued.

The sexual crimes investigator must maintain absolute control over any pornography in his possession. Failure to do so may not only cause legal problems with the chain of custody but also personal problems for the investigator. No officer should allow himself to gain the reputation as a source of pornography for parties or officers working the late shift.

There is certainly nothing wrong with telling a joke, and most people will use some profanity during their lifetime. However, when the investigator earns a reputation as the premier dirty joke teller, or the most profane individual in the department, he has almost certainly compromised his position and demeaned himself in the eyes of his colleagues.

Confidentiality

Officers have an enormous responsibility to the victims of the crimes they investigate. The victims have a *right* to expect confidentiality about their identities and the information they provide the officers. The information they provide is intended for investigative and prosecutive purposes only! The victim did not mean for it to be shared with those not having a legitimate need to know. It is understood that certain information must be shared for case comparison and other sound reasons; however, the neighbor, bartender, service station attendant, or anyone else not involved in the investigation has no need to know what the victim was forced by a sexual criminal to do or say. The victim is the best source of information about the crime and the criminal. The victim's trust must not be violated.

The instructor must also remember to keep this in mind when using investigative evidence during a presentation. The possibility of revealing the identities of victims in crime scene photographs, sexually explicit pictures taken by offenders, or videotapes of victim statements must be carefully considered before using such material for educational purposes.

Professional Space

Whether the investigator realizes it or not, his office or professional space is also under the scrutiny of others. Some years ago, the authors entered the office of a person reputed to be an expert in criminal sexuality. Tacked to the wall behind this person's desk were a pair of black lace panties and a brassiere. On a side wall was a leather whip, beneath which was a sign that read, "Without pain, there is no pleasure." On the expert's desk was a statue of a robed figure. The person demonstrated to the authors that, by pushing the figure's head, an erect penis protruded from beneath the robe. Needless to say, this man's reputation as an expert was greatly diminished in the eyes of the authors. It is difficult to envision a victim entering that kind of environment and feeling comfortable discussing very personal and traumatic experiences. Even if one disregards the impact of such an environment on victims, what do his peers or visitors feel upon entering his office?

Expertise

The professional investigator of sexual crimes continually improves his knowledge of criminal behavior and related information. He seeks opportunities to become more proficient through readings, attendance at seminars, courses, or conferences. He remains familiar with recent research on offender typologies, motivating factors for sexual offenses, and the impact of sexual crimes on victims. He is not satisfied with what he has learned on the job, in a single book, or from a course taken several years ago. Every day brings new and startling information to this field, and education and training can only result in enhanced expertise and consequently better performance.

Terminology

The knowledge and use of professional terminology is essential for individuals who are involved in this type of work. The investigator of sexual crimes deals with physicians, lawyers, judges, mental health professionals, victims, and witnesses. Most of these people can be expected to use professional terminology.

While the value of being knowledgeable of street terms is recognized, it may not be appropriate for use during the interview of a sexual assault victim. For example, if it is believed that oral sex on the male may have occurred, the authors would suggest beginning with the term *fellatio* during the victim interview rather than initially asking about *head*, *face*, or a *blow job*. The investigator must also be familiar with slang for body parts and sexual acts in the event the victim or the offender uses such terms. It is important to determine the exact words used by an offender or the terms as understood by the victim. In short, the officer needs to know both slang and professional terms, but he also needs to know the appropriate times for using them.

The Department's Role

The attitude a law enforcement agency has toward sexual crimes is reflected in the officers it selects as investigators of such offenses. It is generally accepted among law enforcement that the elite investigative group is the homicide unit. Wherever sheriffs and police chiefs gather, they proudly discuss the number of homicides solved and how the best men and women are assigned to those units. Rarely is the same pride demonstrated in the discussion of those who investigate sexual crimes. Why is this?

One has to wonder why the solution rate of homicides (68.7% in 1997) is almost always greater than for rapes (49.9% in 1997) (Freeh, 1998). The victim of a murder is unable to provide verbal information about the crime or criminal; but in rape cases the victim is almost always able to give helpful information (age, weight, height, race, etc.) to the investigator.

Is homicide an easier crime to investigate because it is most often committed by a relative, neighbor, associate, or some other person known to the victim? If, in fact, homicide is an easier crime to solve, then should management assign the best investigators to those cases? On the other hand, if the reason for the higher solution rate *is* because the better investigators are assigned to homicides, then wouldn't the department and the public be better served by the assignment of an equally high-caliber investigator to sexual crimes?

A more difficult question might be: if children are among our most precious resources, then is not the investigation of child sexual abuse or child pornography more important than the investigation of many other crimes?

Selection of Investigative Personnel

Law enforcement agencies would do well to be selective in assigning officers to sexual crime investigation. Officers should be volunteers who are carefully screened *and* trained for this highly specialized work. This task is not for everyone, and such an assignment should never be considered a form of punishment. If investigative assignments to this field are considered to be disciplinary in nature, only the marginal performers or those in trouble will interact with women and children who are the victims of this intrusive and violent crime.

Management would do well to recognize that the officer selected to work with a sexual assault victim directly influences how quickly the victim recovers from the traumatic event. The sexual assault victim has experienced fear, anger, guilt, and humiliation; and the officer's ability to recognize and deal with these emotions affects the victim's well-being and self-esteem for a long time to come.

Investigators also must be able to interact with the offenders — those people who are viewed by society and their own peers as sick, disgusting, and repulsive. If an officer expects to be successful in this field, he must be able to isolate personal feelings of anger and disgust. Allowing one's feelings to interfere may result in case dismissal due to avoidable investigator error. The sexual crimes investigator must not only be able to control his emotions but also to occasionally do some great acting.

Investigators with a Hidden Agenda

An unpleasant reality of life is that there are people who are attracted to this type of work for reasons other than a sense of duty or concern for victims. Some officers become voyeuristic in their jobs, receiving a vicarious thrill from interviewing the victims or viewing the pornography associated with sexual crimes. They may ask rape victims to describe their assaults an unreasonable number of times, make copies of seized materials for their private use, ask the victims for a date, or even demand sexual acts from victims who are prostitutes.

There is an old joke that defines psychiatry as the study of the *id* by the *odd*. Some investigators may be drawn to this type of work because they are unable to confront their own sexual problems or concerns. They believe that, by investigating sexual crimes, they can better understand or even repress their own feelings or urges. This may be a *reaction formation* — a Freudian defense mechanism — defined as "preventing the awareness or expression of unacceptable desires by an exaggerated adoption of seemingly opposite behavior" (Coleman, Butcher, and Carson, 1984).

Still others are drawn to this type of work because of prior victimization. Former victims of child abuse or sexual assault should not automatically be excluded from investigating sexual crimes; however, they should be carefully evaluated to ensure that they are functioning as objective fact finders and not as recruiters for the brotherhood or sisterhood of sexual abuse victims. Still others may get involved in these cases as a way to get even with the opposite sex.

Finally, some enter this investigative field to enforce their own moral or religious values. Officers must remember that they are employed to enforce the penal code and not the Ten Commandments. Child molestation and rape are of professional interest to law enforcement investigators because they are crimes, not because they are sins. A personal code of ethics is an important asset to any investigator; however, personal moral values are the criteria by which the investigator should judge his own behavior and not the behavior of others.

The managers responsible for the selection of officers to work in sexual crimes will find that using common sense in the process goes a long way. The axiom, "the best prediction of future behavior is past behavior," is applicable here. Individuals who have had problems with the public, their peers, supervisors, or subordinates should not be selected for such work.

Recognizing and Monitoring the Investigator

The investigation of sexual crimes is emotionally and psychologically demanding. Any officer assigned to such work should be provided with support and recognition *and* should be monitored in a positive manner. If this *is* a dirty job that someone has to do, then that person needs adequate office space, secure facilities for sexually-related evidence, a private interview room for victims, and funds for training. Even more importantly, the person needs someone to talk to, an occasional pat on the back, a thank you — those simple signs of interest and recognition that cost no money, only time. By helpfully monitoring an investigator's work and attitude, a supervisor should be able to recognize if and when it is time to transfer an investigator to another work assignment.

Training

The department must not only ensure that an individual is qualified for such an assignment but should also take measures to enhance the skills of the person. Training should be given to the officer *prior* to the time he assumes investigative duties. All too often, an investigator is assigned to patrol or robbery detail one day and transferred to sexual assault investigations the next day. An investigator cannot hope to have an understanding of *criminal* sexuality from the ordinary experiences of life or even other law enforcement experiences. In some departments, officers desiring to attend job-enhancement training must do so on their own time, often working an extra shift or taking leave, and/or even paying for such training. Such an attitude sends a strong, and negative, message to the investigator.

Fellow Law Enforcement Officers

The importance of peer support in law enforcement cannot be overemphasized. What one's fellow officers say or think about him or his work affects his attitude, self-esteem, and performance. Investigators tell the authors that this is the one area that is most troublesome to them. Daily, these officers interact with women and children who have been emotionally and physically battered by the most horrific types of sexual assault. They deal with rapists, child molesters, pornographers, obscene phone callers, and exhibitionists — offenders who are looked upon with revulsion even by other criminals. They are expected to remain above it all; yet when they get back to the office, their fellow officers may refer to them in terms meant to be humorous — *pervert, diaper dick,* and *kiddie cop.* These terms not only offend and degrade the investigator but they also assault his sense of self-worth and raise questions about whether or not he wants to continue in the job.

    The authors have experienced the embarrassment of being introduced to others in law enforcement or members of related disciplines as the department's expert on *weenie waggers* or *our local pervert.* Such an introduction immediately places a person in the position of having to legitimize his work. He must now convince the person to whom he is introduced that he is involved in a serious and demanding task. While some may consider this trivial, it does have a negative impact on the person.

The respect of one's peers is extremely important; and, while the comments made by fellow workers may not have a malicious intent, the fact remains that such comments do not reflect respect or build self-esteem.

Child Sexual Abuse

There are special problems for the investigator who deals with crimes involving child victims. Investigators report that they successfully separate their work from their personal feelings in almost all cases except those involving children. Male police officers seem to have more of a problem with this than female officers. Both male and female officers are repulsed by, and strongly condemn, child sexual abuse, and they believe such cases should be aggressively investigated and prosecuted. However, the female officer is often more willing (reluctantly) to do the dirty job. The male officer frequently tries to avoid it, sometimes using the excuse that women are better suited for such cases.

The authors are aware of no evidence to indicate that women are better at interviewing children than men. Although special cases or circumstances may call for either a male or female investigator, it is the skill and training of the officer that is most important, not the gender. Women are often assigned to these cases not because they relate better to children but because they tend to be emotionally stronger and less likely to vehemently complain than males.

The investigator working with child sexual abuse and exploitation must learn to cope with an additional stigma within law enforcement. The officer who seizes adult pornography has seized material of some interest to normal people. The person seizing child pornography returns to his department with material that not only offends but also repulses fellow officers.

Even some supervisors have difficulty dealing with these cases. They frequently do not want to hear about the details of a case and sometimes seem to treat case files as though they were contaminated. It becomes obvious that there are some in law enforcement and other disciplines who would prefer to deny that the problem even exists.

Yet the officer must examine, catalog, and analyze the evidence. The job may take hours, days, or even weeks — a task involving something that other officers cannot or will not do. There are people who assume that if *they* cannot deal with a particular task, there must be something wrong with those who can. Initially such people may use jokes and humorous remarks as defense mechanisms. However, they may progress to deprecating remarks made behind the investigator's back, or a request that the material be examined and discussed someplace else, or even that the investigator be moved out of the squad room. In extreme cases, the point may be reached where the mental health and/or sexual inclinations of the officer are questioned.

Some seem inclined to believe that the sexual crimes investigator has an interest, other than professional, in the activity under investigation. Some want to believe that the vice officer is having sex with prostitutes or that the rape investigator is involved in some form of aberrant sex. The unasked question is, "How could anyone work that kind of case and be normal?"

To be labeled in such a way is bad enough if the work involves adult victims, but the implication that the child sexual abuse investigator has a perverted interest in children is especially devastating. There have been situations in which child abuse investigators have become the object of jokes revolving around a lack of interest in attractive adults of the opposite sex, playing with anatomically correct dolls, or receiving post cards picturing the Vienna Boys' Choir. Unfortunately, this seems to come with the territory; and investigators who overreact to such joking only invite more of the same. Occasionally, however, such joking can evolve to the point where it becomes intentionally malicious. Supervisors should be alert to such situations and be prepared to intervene if necessary.

The investigator should examine his own behavior to ensure that he is doing nothing to invite or encourage this type of behavior. If he is performing his duties in a professional manner, such joking does not last long and dies of its own heaviness.

When a colleague has a loved one who has been molested and advice is needed, it is amazing how quickly the joking ceases. The work that was previously the subject of ridicule suddenly becomes an important and serious area, and the investigator is viewed as a valued professional and colleague.

Officers working child sexual abuse may become isolated from their peer groups. While police officers are known for their socializing and shop talk with each other, they do not want to hear about child molesters and child pornography. This problem does not occur as frequently in situations where officers are assigned to child abuse units in larger departments or to specialized task forces. Those officers are in an environment where they can share experiences, vent their frustrations, and reinforce one another. This is an important secondary benefit of the task force concept of investigation.

Unfortunately, some officers do not feel comfortable talking about this type of work with spouses, family members, or friends. Some officers may be reluctant to admit that they work with the sexual abuse of children. Family members or friends can unknowingly add to the officers' feelings of isolation with questions or comments such as, *Are you still working that child stuff? Get a transfer to something else. Do you have to tell people what you do?*

The authors have received numerous phone calls and letters from police officers who actually have no specific questions but merely want to talk. A letter received from one officer demonstrates the effect such work can have on a person. It stated in part:

> I am currently assigned to forgery and auto theft. However, my first assignment as an investigator was in Juvenile/Sex Crimes. I can honestly say that was the most trying and stress-filled assignment to date.

> I know that your job is tough, unforgiving, and constantly supplied with sarcasm by other agents; when I worked sex crimes, my peers called me *diaper dick.* My warrants were taken in jest; vice seemed all-important. Which I find a terrible joke; in a robbery, all one goes without is money or jewelry, but in sex crimes with children, these peers don't realize that you're talking of a potentially ruined life!

Symptoms of Stress

Carole and David Soskis, former consultants to the FBI's Psychological Services Program, have stated that sexual crimes work involves a number of special stresses that must be managed appropriately if the investigator is to function well and maintain good health. The strong emotional reactions provoked by this material and the isolation and prejudice to which it may expose the investigator can make this work psychologically and socially toxic. As in medical settings, professionalism in this work means controlling the exposure and monitoring its effects. The investigator must be alert to the early warning signs of overexposure or stress.

James T. Reese (Hazelwood and Burgess, 1995) has categorized the early warning signs of stress as follows:

> The numerous symptoms that may relate to stress disorders can be grouped in three categories: (1) emotional, (2) behavioral, and (3) physical. The number of symptoms a person may exhibit is not important, but rather the extent of changes noted from the person's normal condition. Furthermore, the combined presence of symptoms determines the potency of the problem. Indicators range from isolated reactions to combinations of symptoms from the three categories. Finally, the duration, the frequency, and the intensity of the symptoms indicate the extent to which the individual is suffering.

> In the *emotional* category, symptoms include apathy, anxiety, irritability, mental fatigue, and over-compensation or denial. Individuals afflicted with these symptoms are restless, agitated, overly sensitive, defensive, preoccupied, and have difficulty concentrating. These officers overwork to exhaustion and may become groundlessly suspicious of others. They may be arrogant, argumentative, insubordinate, and hostile. Their feelings of insecurity and worthlessness lead to self-defeat. Depression is common and chronic.

Behavioral symptoms are often more easily detected than emotional ones, for the sufferers withdraw and seek social isolation. Such individuals are reluctant to accept responsibilities or tend to neglect current ones. They often act out their misery through alcohol abuse, gambling, promiscuity, and spending sprees. Much of their desperate behavior is a cry for help and should be recognized as such. Other indications could be tardiness, poor appearance, and poor personal hygiene, both at work and at home. These patterns can lead to domestic disputes and spouse/child abuse.

The *physical* effects of stress are extremely dangerous. The individual may become preoccupied with illness or may dwell on minor ailments, taking excessive sick leave and complaining of exhaustion during the workday. Among the many somatic indicators are headaches, insomnia, recurrent awakening, early morning rising, changes in appetite resulting in either weight loss or gain, indigestion, nausea, vomiting, and diarrhea. Such psychophysical maladies may be a direct result of excessive stress upon the officer.

Coping Strategies

The following coping strategies are recommended for officers involved in the investigation of criminal sexuality:

1. *Limit Exposure* — This can be accomplished in two ways. First, an investigator's life simply cannot become a 24-hour-a-day crusade. He needs to pursue outside interests, develop hobbies not related to his work, and find both family and personal time. On an occupational level, he should consider getting involved in cases other than those involving sexual crimes. Secondly, there are investigators who should probably not make a lifelong career of criminal sexuality. For some, promotion is a means by which their exposure to criminal sexuality is eliminated. For others, a transfer to a different category of case work may be the answer.

    The authors do not believe that there is a specific time limit to a person's career in sexual crimes investigations. However, each individual should monitor himself carefully and regularly consider whether the time has arrived to move on to another area of work.

2. *Humor* — A good sense of humor is an invaluable asset for any investigator of violent crime. However, it seems to the authors that sometimes the officers must choose between laughing in self-defense or crying with pity for the victims. Those who have no sense of humor may not be suited for this type of work. If a person known to be humorous begins to lose that attribute, it may indicate significant psychological stress. While much humor on the job may be gallows humor (joking about situations or occurrences that do not call for

humor), it can be an effective coping mechanism. James T. Reese accurately states, "Once it finds its way out of the locker room, however, and into the public eye, it is a clear sign of maladaption to stress" (Hazelwood and Burgess, 1995).

3. *Peer Support* — Seeking support from others who deal with the same kind of work is also effective. As previously discussed, this is probably easier for investigators in large departments or specialized units. Other officers can obtain support by participating in sexual crimes task forces, training, conferences, and/or by joining professional organizations. Today there are sexual assault investigators' associations in a number of states, and there are many interdisciplinary organizations with which the officer may affiliate.

4. *Physical Fitness* — Any attempt to manage stress must include the nurturing of good habits in physical fitness. Proper diet, regular exercise, and sufficient sleep are essential. Numerous books and tapes are available in libraries or book stores that discuss relaxation techniques and managing stress.

5. *Self-Satisfaction* — In light of the numerous problems that have been discussed, the reader might well ask why anyone would voluntarily become involved in such work. It is a question the authors have been asked many times and have even asked themselves. The answer is simply that the sense of accomplishment that can accompany this work leads to the feeling that these efforts do make a difference. Many law enforcement professionals who investigate rape, the sexual exploitation of children, and other violent crimes mention the positive feeling they get from helping real victims of crime. Little can duplicate an investigator's sense of satisfaction when the victim or relative of a sexual crime victim says thank you. However, the officer cannot expect expressions of gratitude from society or superiors. Officers must take pride in their work and obtain their satisfaction with the realization of what they have accomplished.

Summary

Individuals in and out of law enforcement often perceive that those who investigate, prosecute, research, or teach about sexual crimes are different or weird. Much of this attitude is due to society's inability to openly deal with human sexuality — especially deviant or criminal sexuality. The investigators, their departments, and their fellow officers all share responsibility for allowing this perception to continue.

Officers must approach their jobs in a professional manner; and the law enforcement agency must select, train, and support qualified individuals to investigate such crimes. The importance of peer support cannot be over-emphasized, and other officers within the department must learn to appreciate and respect the problems faced by those who investigate criminal sexuality.

The sexual crimes investigator must be alert to the early warning signs of toxic exposure or stress-related symptoms. By using appropriate humor, limiting exposure, maintaining good physical fitness, and seeking and accepting peer support, the investigators of criminal sexuality can turn a job perceived as dirty or strange into a rewarding experience and achieve a sense of accomplishment.

References

Coleman, J.C., Butcher, J.N., and Carson, R.C. (1984) *Abnormal Psychology and Modern Life*, 7th ed., New York.

Freeh, L.H. (1998) *Crime in the United States*, Federal Bureau of Investigation, Washington.

Reese, J.T. (1995) in Hazelwood, R.R. and Burgess, A.W., Eds., *Practical Aspects of Rape Investigation; A Multidisciplinary Approach*, 2nd ed., CRC Press, Boca Raton, p. 247.

LeDoux, J.C. and Hazelwood, R.R. (1985) Police attitudes and beliefs toward rape, *J. Police Sci. Admin.*, 13(3).

Section III: Forensics and Court

Physical Evidence in Sexual Assault Investigations

15

ROBERT P. SPALDING
P. DAVID BIGBEE

Introduction

Physical evidence in criminal investigations, whether associated with sexual assault or not, represents an important and often critical aspect of the overall picture to be presented to a jury. While the intent here is to discuss physical evidence related to sexual assault investigations, the principles discussed are applicable to evidence in many types of crimes. There are, of course, unique aspects to sexual assault evidence per se, but many of the principles discussed here are generally applicable to evidence as a whole.

Events associated with a sexual assault frequently result in various kinds of personal evidence including body fluids, hairs, and fibers deposited on various surfaces and objects. Such evidence is often transient and subject to adverse environmental conditions, or it may be overlooked due to its size, distribution, and even the level of perseverance exercised by the personnel looking for it. Tasks such as collecting the evidence, documenting it, packaging it, preserving it, and determining what is then to be done with it are important — no, critical — to the overall integrity of the investigation. Rapid advancement of technologies such as forensic DNA analysis has made the crime scene investigator's role more significant and complex in that the evidence often must be handled more carefully now than before these newer methods became available. The value of physical evidence may easily be affected by any and all personnel associated with it, from the first responding officer to the attorney who presents it in court. The need for open and frequent communication between all of these individuals is essential to a successful resolution of the case.

This chapter will not address the techniques and procedures of the crime laboratory used in the analysis of physical evidence, nor will it discuss the potential results available from different kinds of evidence typical in sexual assault investigations. In general, this chapter will deal with the type of evidence often encountered, its recognition, documentation, collection, packaging, and preservation to ensure maintaining its integrity. Actual case examples will be mentioned occasionally, particularly to illustrate how *not* to handle evidence. The sources of the evidence will be considered as well — the victim, the suspect, and the crime scene. The term *crime scene* in a sexual assault refers to all three sources mentioned, since the victim and the suspect are as much crime scenes as is the location at which the assault took place.

This and the following chapter are closely connected, since this chapter provides a basis for a better understanding of the material discussed in Chapter 16. The overall nature of the evidence and general principles governing its recovery are addressed in this chapter, while more detailed discussions of specific evidence and the methods and techniques of collection and handling are presented in Chapter 16.

At the outset, it is perhaps useful to consider the potential, the problems, and the misunderstandings associated with the handling of evidence from the crime scene through the courtroom process. Evidence does not magically find its way from the crime scene to the courtroom, nor does it become analyzed without the dedicated efforts of a number of people. Also, it does not find its way to court without a few glitches along the way.

Forensic science has become a well-recognized field today, probably owing in no small part to the fact that several notable cases have occupied the headlines of the nation's newspapers in recent years. Additionally, television programs abound that emphasize evidence analysis in criminal investigation. Evidence must be properly documented, collected, packaged, preserved, and secured by personnel knowledgeable in these procedures. The application of forensic science in an investigation truly begins in the initial stages of the crime scene investigation.

The history of evidence is critical to both its relevance to the case and its admissibility under the rules of law. During the progression from the crime scene to the courtroom, attention must be paid to the proper chain of custody, proper evidence handling, and proper packaging and preservation procedures. Improper handling may render the evidence useless through degradation. Sometimes it cannot be used at all because its whereabouts cannot be established at some point during the process. From the first responding individual at the crime scene to those responsible for maintaining the security of the evidence through the trial, the rule should be: if you do not know how to handle it correctly or have no legitimate need to be involved, then leave the job to the experts. No one wants to be in the shoes of the senior police officer who was elated to find that his crime scene personnel had developed several exceptional fingerprints that did not belong to anyone having normal access to the scene. He was elated, that is, until he found out that the fingerprints were his and that he had carelessly left them when he was doing his own inspection of the scene.

It is also possible for the layman, based on the presentation of results of a detailed study of the evidence, to conclude that the laboratory solved the case when, in fact, many dedicated individuals contributed to the final result. The events leading to trial often include the crime scene investigation, examinations of witnesses, suspects, and victims, as well as the evaluation of evidence, reconstruction of the events of the crime, and preparation of the case for court. The laboratory would not have had the evidence to examine if a lot of work had not been done before the evidence went to the laboratory. The successful presentation of a case in court encompasses the hard work of a number of individuals working together.

Some evidence simply draws attention to itself or is more provocative than other material collected at the scene. The nature of the specific items of evidence or their locations within the crime scene may become a point of disproportionate focus, displacing appropriate consideration of other evidence. The finding of a fingerprint, spectacular bloodstains spattered over a wall surface, the DNA analysis of body fluids from the scene, the presence of a bullet in a wall — all of these may receive attention to the extent that other evidence is largely ignored. Some disciplines may be completely ignored until trial preparation poses the *what about* and *what if* questions. It is important to realize that a complete evaluation of the evidence initiated early in the game will be far more productive than picking up the pieces as trial time draws near.

It is not uncommon for individuals to recall the events of a crime differently. While present at the same events and at the same time, victims, witnesses, or even suspects will not necessarily recall the events precisely the same way. A person's fingerprints in a particular room may disprove his statement that he or she was never in that room. Often such discrepancies and conflicts may be resolved with a complete evaluation and analysis of the physical evidence. Accordingly, highly skilled attorneys, aware of such potential in the evidence, may attack the evidence itself and/or the manner in which it was secured to prevent its effective use. Again, we come back to the integrity of the evidence and the requirement for complete, documented, and detailed evidence procedures.

Finally, it must be said that communication between the individuals involved in an investigation is critical. The crime scene investigator, the investigative case officer, the medical examiner, the emergency room physician, the prosecuting attorney, the forensic laboratory analyst, and others involved should be aware of the facts of the case and the importance of communicating changes in these facts as they develop. Often, after evidence is sent to a laboratory, the general attitude is to forget about that case for a while and get on with other things. With some kinds of evidence, this is not unreasonable. However, when the investigation develops new information that may affect decisions about the analytical strategy in the laboratory or the conclusions that may be reached concerning a reconstruction of the events of the crime, that information should be passed on to those analysts who can use it. A second example would involve evidence or information developed during the crime scene investigation which is important to investigators on the street or, similarly, information developed on the street that needs to be known by personnel at the scene. Communication of this nature is sometimes overlooked and should not be.

The Nature of Physical Evidence

A discussion of the ground rules is in order. What are the general principles, terms, and concepts that allow us to have a common understanding of what is important with regard to evidence and its collection, packaging, preservation, and presentation in court?

Physical evidence presents itself in a wide variety of forms, sizes and locations. Evidence can vary widely with respect to the degree to which it can be analyzed and matched with a particular known source. A simple study of a few cases readily establishes the diversity represented by the evidence. Indeed, while there are some types of evidence that are almost always associated with sexual assaults, there may be no end to the variety of items that, based on the circumstances of the case, may present a very real evidentiary significance. As is the case with any scientific discipline, the need for some means to categorize and identify this wide variety of materials is dictated by a simple requirement for organization.

Not only is it important to be organized about how we look at evidence from the perspective of investigators and those involved in the preparation of a case for trial, but the trial attorney must set before a jury of lay persons an array of ideas, items, materials and information that must tell a story and equip them to carry out their responsibilities, to determine guilt or innocence. The attorney must educate the jury not only in the saga of the case but, to some extent, in how the evidence was collected and analyzed and the meaning of that analysis. The presentation of the evidence in a clear and convincing manner is often essential to an attorney's case, whether defense or prosecution. A simple and organized system for identifying, describing and working with the evidence is necessary.

There is a major advantage in understanding how a forensic examiner approaches the examination of the evidence that arrives at the laboratory. If the crime scene investigator knows what is to be done, then attention can be devoted to the collection and preservation of that evidence in ways that get a maximum amount of information from it. With much of the evidence to be discussed here, known sources will be compared with questioned or unknown samples. Such a comparison, whether with DNA or fibers, will determine how closely the two sources match one another. Understanding these things, the investigator is better prepared to recognize types of evidence that are perhaps out of the ordinary but that may provide valuable information as well.

Several major principles pertinent to evidence, especially in sexual assault cases, should be dealt with at this point. They are:

1. The identification of evidence — the ways in which evidence may be identified.
2. General types of evidence.
   A. Class characteristic evidence — belonging to a general class of items.
   B. Individual characteristic evidence — having its own unique character.
      (1.) From persons.
      (2.) From things.
3. Evidence resulting from transfer — ways in which evidence may be distributed prior to collection.
   A. Direct.
   B. Indirect.
4. The evidence environment — understanding the variety of evidence and the relationships between the different evidence types within the scene.
5. Evidence/crime scene contamination — addition to or deletion of a portion of the evidence.
   A. Nature of the evidence environment.
   B. Personnel.
   C. Careless and/or inadvertent alteration of the scene.
   D. Packaging of the evidence.
   E. Laboratory environment.
6. Degradation of evidence — the effect of a hostile environment.
   A. Heat.
   B. Humidity.
   C. Ultraviolet (UV) light.

The Identification of Evidence

Identification in an everyday sense does not seem a complicated concept. There is nothing unique or surprising when we call a screwdriver a screwdriver or a shirt a shirt. This simple identity is based on observations of familiar objects. However, the term identification often takes on additional significance in the forensic laboratory. Different disciplines of study apply a unique meaning to the identification of the evidence, depending on its nature, its chemical form, the quantity, its condition, its source, and other considerations.

Identifications may be based on appearance, color, physical properties (such as crystal structure) or chemical properties (such as composition) determined by analysis. A bloodstain on a shirt looks like a bloodstain. To the forensic serologist or DNA analyst, it is an unknown stain until it is specifically identified as blood. This requires more than simple observation; it requires chemical testing. Further characterization is then effected through extensive analysis of the DNA in the blood. Intentional avoidance of a specifically identifying (and possibly wrong) description of a sample of evidence is a practice not foreign to the crime scene investigator. Many identifying statements have been made only to be proven wrong by testing, followed by embarrassing exposure in court.

Chemical identification of a controlled substance requires specific and sophisticated testing to sufficiently identify the substance according to the legal description for court presentation. Chemical identification of the layers in a chip of paint from the scene often provides sufficient information to distinguish the chips from other sources considered in the investigation, thereby avoiding wasted time and effort.

It is not uncommon for the forensic examiner to receive two items that may have, in fact, been joined as parts of a single object at some time in the past. Such fracture matches represent a specific and positive identification, as the nature of the match is based on the unique edges of the two pieces. Examples of these kinds of matches might include two pieces of glass or stone that fit together, or fragments of a shredded document, painstakingly searched and pieced together to produce the original.

While it may not be strictly within the realm of identification to discuss terminology used in describing evidentiary characteristics and relationships, it does seem fitting to mention the topic here. Terms like *consistent with, typical of, matches in all observable characteristics,* or *cannot be distinguished from,* often do not instill any great confidence in the reader of a report. However, it must be remembered that when these terms are used, they are the closest the laboratory examiner can get to an identification. While not always as limiting and specific as desired, the information often has value in the overall picture.

Certainly, additional examples of forensic identifications can be cited; however, the above should serve to illustrate the idea that identifications will, by necessity, vary in the degree to which an item is identified in the conventional sense.

General Types of Evidence

Class Characteristic Evidence

Class characteristic evidence is that which cannot be forensically identified with a specific source to the exclusion of all others. Examples include the conventional (non-DNA) analysis of hairs, blood, saliva and semen, fibers, soil, glass (excluding fracture matches), and minute wood particles. Forensic science has no current methods to positively associate such items with a single or unique source. Here, forensic examination of evidence is directed at giving as much information as possible about each feature exhibited by each item and about many different types of evidence in combination. The more material of different types that can be associated with a suspect (because these are considered independent events), the stronger the association becomes in the minds of the jurors. Class evidence can be presented in such a manner that there is almost a direct inference of positive or negative association between the suspect and the victim, particularly when a preponderance of evidence exists. For example, a witness may testify that the genetic markers and ABO blood type of semen found in the vaginal vault of the victim matches a blood sample from the suspect and that the chances of finding someone in the population at random with the same genetic profile is very small. Another expert witness may testify that a pubic hair from the suspect matches in all characteristics one taken from the victim. These two together are very damaging testimony to the defendant, even though they are both class characteristic evidence.

There can be problems associated with the use of class evidence, stemming mainly from an inability of the evidence to specifically point to an individual with sufficient definition. Difficulties in this regard can often be overcome when it is understood that a preponderance of evidence (even though class in nature) can be nearly as effective as a lesser amount of individual characteristic evidence (see below). A number of misconceptions regarding this type of evidence continue to plague investigations from time to time:

1. If an item does not amount to a positive identification (such as a fingerprint), it is not worth collecting. This narrow focus in thinking is self-defeating.
2. It is too hard and confusing to explain the significance of class evidence significance to a jury. Not true. One only has to consider some of the more recently publicized cases.

3. Because an item is class evidence, it is common and therefore not of significant value to the case. The significance of several individual items when recognized collectively becomes considerably greater, even though individually they may be common.
4. If evidence is not present in reasonable quantity, it is not worth collecting; or "If I can't see it, it isn't there." The rapid development of technology to deal with micro quantities of materials wiped out this excuse long ago.
5. The availability of forensic services that can take advantage of the full range of information available through class evidence is too limited to be worth the time and trouble. To a point this is true, but the length of time between evidence collection and trial is often much longer than necessary for such examinations. If analysis is begun soon enough, much can be done.

These ideas and attitudes usually serve to cover the investigation with a negative cloud of inefficiency and incompleteness. Particularly in recent years, technological advances in the examination and analysis of evidence, class and otherwise, make it all the more important that this potential source is not overlooked. It is not infrequent that a sexual assault scene offers little of value in fingerprints but has an abundance of class evidence. This potential should not be ignored.

Individual Characteristic Evidence

Evidence that can be positively identified with a specific source to the exclusion of all others is individual characteristic evidence. Evidence of this type is frequently found in lesser amounts than class evidence and may not be present at all. Examples include latent prints left by the friction ridges on the hands and feet, specific cuts and tear matches in clothing, fracture matches of broken items such as bottles, ash trays, imprints of body parts on hit-and-run vehicles matched to a victim (ears, noses, etc.), and, more recently, the DNA analysis of body fluids. The specific nature of individual evidence makes it desirable; and, as indicated earlier, there is a temptation to ignore that which is less definitive. But to rely on nothing but individual evidence, especially when additional class evidence is present, is an unwise choice at best.

It is not uncommon for an item of evidence to exhibit both class and individual characteristics. For example, the victim wore a shirt that was torn during an assault in the back seat of the suspect's vehicle. The victim may have related that the suspect tore a piece of fabric from the shirt during the attack. A section of fabric found in the vehicle in the specific location of the assault would be examined for loosely adhering debris characteristic of debris taken from the vehicle. This would usually be class evidence. Results of an examination of the section of fabric and comparison of it with the shirt from which it was thought to have come (involving the fabric structure, color, pattern, composition, and design) would, again, represent class evidence. However, an examination of the torn edges of the piece and the shirt to show that the two match down to the individual threads would represent individual evidence. Further, the identification of semen on both the shirt and the piece of fabric is class evidence, but subsequent analysis of the DNA to establish a match with the DNA from blood of the suspect represents individual evidence. To take the case one step further, DNA analysis of hairs taken from the shirt and microscopically matched to hairs from the suspect (class evidence) also disclosed the DNA profile of the suspect (individual evidence).

Forensic science has developed DNA analysis to the degree that it is possible to achieve an individual match when a sufficient number of characteristics are analyzed in the DNA from a particular sample. This makes the condition of the DNA (and thus the evidence) more important than ever, as discussed below under Evidence Degradation.

As one can see from the above, individual evidence can originate from two general sources. There are associations that identify the evidence as coming from a particular thing or a particular person. Both of these are illustrated in the above example. However, it should again be stated that the value of the evidence to the case can be modified by information discovered through investigation. If an individual had normal and frequent access to a location that became a crime scene and that person's fingerprints were found at the scene, the significance of that find is considerably less than if the individual had never been at the scene. Similarly, denial of ever having been at the scene by the individual when his fingerprints were found there makes the fingerprint evidence very significant. Thus, investigation and forensic examination of evidence go hand in hand and should not be divorced during the preparation of a case.

Individual evidence that establishes beyond a doubt that a particular person is the only source of the evidence is generally confined to four different areas: latent fingerprints, DNA, bite marks (forensic odontology comparisons) and hand writing/hand printing. There are numerous other valuable individual evidence areas, but it should be remembered that both class and individual evidence is important.

Evidence Resulting from Transfer

Two questions often asked by the crime scene investigator are:

1. What is here that tells me that the suspect brought something to or took something away from the scene?
2. What is here that tells me that the victim brought something to or took something away from the scene?

The concept implied here is that the investigation might be able to capitalize on the transfer of something during the commission of the crime that associates either the suspect or the victim with the scene and/or with each other. This concept of transfer is operative in our daily lives all the time. Walk across a newly installed carpet with freshly shined dress shoes on (particularly in a dry atmosphere). More than likely there are fibers from the carpet accumulated on the toes of your shoes. A parent wearing a fur coat and hugging a child very likely leaves hairs from the coat on the child's clothing. If the child then sits on a sofa with a textured fabric, some of the hairs from the fur coat may be transferred to the sofa. What we see in all of this is evidence of contact. In fact, individuals often leave what is often referred to as trace evidence at crime scenes. It is up to the crime scene investigator to find it.

Trace evidence encompasses such evidence as hairs, fibers, smears of semen and/or blood, glass, soils, or even vegetation. It is often present in such small quantities as to make it difficult if not impossible to see without the aid of specialized lighting techniques and other aids. While the necessity of such additional help presents more of a challenge, it is perhaps an advantage; for if the investigator has to work to find it, the suspect is likely to have missed it. The suspect may think to sanitize the scene with respect to normally observable evidence, but he will likely miss trace materials transferred to a victim, the scene or even him or herself.

Since one of the ultimate goals of crime scene investigation is the reconstruction of the events of the crime, it is important to recognize the opportunity that the transfer of trace evidence affords. To be able to determine that a transfer of evidence took place between two individuals followed by another transfer between one of them and a third person is of particular corroborative value when investigative information suggests that this scenario might have taken place. This illustration identifies two important aspects of transferred evidence — namely, the direct and indirect transfer of trace evidence (sometimes referred to as primary and secondary transfer).

Direct Transfer

The idea of direct transfer is easily grasped and routinely relied upon in investigations. The parent above transferred fur hairs to the child's clothing during the hug. Direct transfer. A bleeding victim brushes against a tree when leaving the wooded sexual assault scene, depositing blood on the tree and leaving evidence of her presence at the scene. An attacker leans against the still tacky paint at the sexual assault scene and gets paint on his shirt, leaves a fabric imprint in the paint, and leaves fibers from the shirt in the paint. A victim is wearing slacks stained with the soil from the scene of the assault. All are examples of direct transfer from the original source to another object. But the collection of transferred evidence may not have to stop there.

Indirect Transfer

Less frequently recognized is indirect transfer since it is less frequently encountered and still less often thought of during an investigation. The fur hairs from the parent's coat, transferred to and left on a sofa by means of the child sitting there, represents indirect or secondary transfer. In a case in the Washington, D.C. area, just such a transfer of hairs to the child from the mother's coat did take place, followed by further transfer of some of those hairs to the floor of the passenger side of the car belonging to the suspect who was later convicted of abduction with intent to defile. The child's body was not found.

This identification of indirect or secondary transfer is not only important from an evidentiary standpoint, but it can also indicate the need to expand a crime scene investigation or indicate other areas that should be searched for additional evidence. Locating trace evidence similar or identical to that found at the scene on the victim in locations associated with a suspect can be extremely valuable in the reconstruction of the events surrounding the crime with respect to movements of people and objects.

Trace evidence transferred is just that — evidence that has been transferred to its current location. Since it was transferred, it can be transferred again — away and gone — if the item of evidence is not properly protected and preserved to secure the trace evidence. Specifics of evidence documentation, packaging and preservation are dealt with in the following chapter, but the importance of these subjects is paramount.

The Evidence Environment

The term *evidence environment* is key to understanding the value of being able to present a preponderance of transferred evidence in an effective manner to a jury of lay persons. The word environment conveys interest in the surroundings from which a sample of evidence was taken. More than that, however, the evidence environment relates to the particular surroundings and the wide variety of unique characteristics and combinations of evidence that make it up.

As an example, if we examine a bedroom where a sexual assault upon the occupant is said to have taken place, we have only to consider all the types of materials and possible transfer evidence in various combinations that can be taken from this scene. Articles normally present within the room that might provide transferrable evidence include the carpet or small rugs, fabrics composing bed clothing and personal clothing, chair coverings, window treatments, cosmetics, various medications, and various hairs normally shed by and forcibly removed from the victim. Many of these sources may exhibit a combination of colors and fiber compositions. A plaid blanket might be composed of cotton, polyester, and acetate fibers of several colors, thereby providing a variety of fibers and colors to be transferred to a person coming in contact with the blanket. This whole picture presents the investigator with an opportunity to take advantage of evidence from these materials in recognizable combinations. Thus, evidence transferred to the clothing of the suspect may reflect the variety of colors and fibers in the blanket; and the blanket is only one item in the evidence environment. It follows, then, that more combinations of trace evidence common to the scene and the suspect create a stronger association between the two.

Taking full advantage of the evidence environment approach to crime scene investigation dictates recognition of several basic concepts:

1. Trace evidence is transient. In addition to being easily dislodged and lost, it generally originates in the environment most recently contacted. In collecting trace evidence from a carpet, then, the goal should be to remove the debris from the surface as opposed to energetically cleaning the carpet to remove all dirt, hair, fibers, stains and soil ground in by years of use.

2. The significance of the evidence is greatly enhanced by the presence of materials that are unique or particularly uncommon. Evidence sources that are extremely common have relatively little evidentiary value because they are so common. Fibers from a garment made from a yarn constructed of an unusual fiber with a dye color in very limited use is far more unique and of more evidentiary value than the fibers from a white cotton t-shirt in wide manufacture, for instance.

3. It is significant to show that multiple fiber types, compositions, and colors recovered from the suspect's clothing match known samples from the scene. Even more important is to relate the specific places within the scene from which this evidence originated to the actions of the suspect. This adds greatly to the weight of the evidence in court, not to mention the potential value in corroborating a witness's account.

4. The more transfers taking place, the more significant the association between the original source and the person or object receiving the transferred material — especially when the available evidence types and varieties are limited. The quantity of hair, fiber, blood, or semen evidence is important — greater amounts of the transferred material indicates a greater struggle or a more lengthy contact.

Effective employment of the environment concept is infrequent, at best. Crime scenes are frequently approached with the mindset that what is foreign to the scene is of value; and if it is normally present, it doesn't really have any great significance. Items normally present in an assault scene often are not categorized as known samples, thereby tying the hands of the forensic examiner since he will not be able to relate recovered fibers to the suspect. Forensic science is a study of comparisons between known and unknown samples. Having more knowns than needed is far better than not having what is actually needed. Transferred evidence, particularly if complicated, is difficult enough to present to a jury in a coordinated and well-organized fashion. A lack of known reference samples makes the job even more difficult.

Evidence/Crime Scene Contamination

Just as two key objectives in crime scene investigation are to secure and preserve the scene, a paramount goal in evidence handling is to insure that both the evidence and the scene do not become contaminated. At the scene, in the evidence room, en route to the laboratory, or even in the laboratory, it is the responsibility of all to handle the evidence in a manner that will not allow its contamination. Unavoidable alteration or contamination of the evidence may take place before the scene is discovered or secured, but from that point a priority should be to limit further contaminating influences. Some of these influences are discussed below:

1. The nature of the evidence environment.
2. The personnel.
3. Careless and/or inadvertent alteration at the scene.
4. The packaging of evidence.
5. The laboratory environment.

The Nature of the Evidence Environment

The natural environment of a crime scene is not normally one of order and neatness. In fact, it is more likely to be disorderly, even to the point of complete disarray. The actual condition of the scene may be one of squalor and grime. Cross contamination between items of evidence or sources of evidence at the scene is more than a casual possibility. In a scene with two persons freely bleeding, the opportunity exists for transfer of blood from one piece of evidence to another through careless handling. Contamination of evidence may occur if the suspect wipes the victim and then himself with a single towel, or if someone throws clothing into a pile. These possibilities are real and have occurred. When any information regarding contamination of evidence comes to light, it should be documented. A useful approach to limiting this kind of contamination is to insure that personnel are briefed on information collected during a thorough preliminary survey of the scene to identify such possibilities for contamination of evidence.

The Personnel

The basic principle of transfer tells us that anyone entering the scene is capable of inadvertently adding something to or removing something from the scene. When the evidence of concern is trace evidence, it is doubly difficult to maintain scene integrity. Therefore, the fewer personnel entering the scene, the better. Personnel who have no legitimate purpose should not enter the scene until documentation and evidence collection are complete. Those who have legitimate access should be aware of their potential to contaminate the scene.

Clothing worn by personnel engaged in the crime scene investigation is important. Any clothing that might add or remove trace evidence from the scene should be avoided. Clothing that can easily generate an electrostatic charge may pick up trace evidence, especially during periods of low humidity. A person might track material into the scene or step in blood and track it about the scene, creating false evidence or contaminating preexisting evidence. To deal with this, a department might, in addition to limiting access, require a specific uniform for crime scene operations. It is easy to secure samples from clothing of known composition for future laboratory elimination comparisons of cloth fibers.

Alternatively, a wide variety of lightweight, breathable, non-shedding disposable clothing is now commercially available for protecting both the scene and the wearer, depending on the environment to be entered. Articles include jump suits, jackets, pants, gloves, hoods, bootees, and various types of breathing apparatus. This clothing may be saved and maintained with the evidence when the scene is completed.

Careless and/or Inadvertent Alteration at the Scene

Individuals not accustomed to working at a crime scene or not observant enough to realize what they are doing can alter or even destroy evidence before it is even collected. In a particularly bloody double homicide, an individual who had authority but no need to be in the crime scene had to be reminded more than once to stop stepping on the shoeprint impressions in blood on the floor. Many additional examples can be mentioned, but it is important to limit scene access of personnel who have no real need to be there.

The Packaging of Evidence

Recovery of evidence at a crime scene involves marking the item followed by proper packaging. At this point, the container (also marked as to the identity, location, date, time, and name of the finder) should be sealed. Evidence should not be removed from the original packaging for viewing or display prior to being examined by laboratory forensic personnel. Doing so allows for contamination, loss of trace evidence, and makes it impossible to testify as to the precise source of trace evidence found on the evidence item. The integrity of the evidence is compromised.

Proper packaging also means that the evidence is protected against damage. A sexual assault evidence kit once received by one of the authors was packaged in two manila envelopes, one inside the other. Items of evidence included hair and saliva samples, a communication explaining the case, and a tube of blood. The blood tube had broken in the mail and stained much of the contents of the package, including the edges of the outside envelope. The sender can only be thankful the incident occurred several years before the current hazardous materials shipping regulations were established.

Packaging materials should not only protect the evidence but also serve to avoid contamination. Some cardboard containers may have residual cardboard dust and debris from manufacturing. Certain plastic vials contain vaporous plasticizers that may contaminate chemical evidence. Evidence packaging materials kept unprotected in the trunk of a vehicle can collect debris and contaminants from the trunk environment. An extended discussion of evidence containers is not the objective here, but the importance of proper packaging should not be overlooked.

The Laboratory Environment

This is one environment that, in recent years, has become considerably more secure in the handling of evidence. Recent emphasis on quality control and quality assurance procedures within the crime laboratory, along with laboratory certification procedures conducted by outside agencies such as the American Society of Crime Laboratory Directors (ASCLD), has resulted in the adoption of extensive routines for evidence security, storage, transfer, and handling. Still, the condition of the evidence (its packaging, documentation, etc.) can go a long way in supporting the laboratory to this end.

Anyone routinely forwarding evidence to a laboratory normally is in contact with the laboratory personnel and has an appreciation of why and how the evidence must be packaged. A person not normally involved in this aspect of the investigation should not hesitate to get questions answered and confusions cleared up by a simple telephone call to the lab where the evidence is to be sent. The need for communication becomes apparent again.

A specialized case involving evidence contamination and personnel safety bears mention. Because of an improperly packaged knife, there was inadvertent contamination of the evidence with the blood of the person in the laboratory opening the package. Packages containing improperly packaged knives or similar sharp instruments, or sealed with staples that have not completely closed, have caused injury to laboratory personnel in the past. This can present a contamination source not only with respect to the evidence but also presents a very real concern with regard to the transmission of disease to the individual. Proper packaging includes safe packaging as well.

Degradation of Evidence

Perhaps more devastating than the effects of contaminants is the possibility of degradation. A significant amount of sexual assault evidence is body fluid in nature. Blood, saliva, vaginal mucus, semen, and other body fluids may be involved. The biochemistry of these fluids is, by nature, fragile with respect to hostile environments and can be rapidly degraded by unfavorable influences such as high heat and humidity.

The effect of heat on this kind of evidence is much the same as frying an egg. The first and most immediate change seen is the whitening of the egg as the proteins present are completely and irreversibly altered with the application of heat. No such visible changes are likely to occur in body fluid evidence, but the same principles guide the thermal destruction of the substances the forensic laboratory examiner is going to look for in the sample. Sexual assault evidence should be stored in a cool environment. In some instances, this will mean a refrigerator, particularly for blood samples awaiting transport to the laboratory. Routine practices in many forensic laboratories call for storage of evidence associated with sexual assaults in large refrigerators or freezers.

Wet evidence (wet blood, semen, etc.) should be dried as soon as possible after recovery. This could include drying at the scene, if the items can be protected. The second enemy of the body fluid evidence is moisture. Evidence allowed to remain moist presents a natural environment for the growth of microorganisms that feed on the chemical substances which are of interest to the laboratory analyst. Packaging wet or moist evidence in plastic bags or airtight non-breathable containers promotes the conditions optimum for putrefaction and hastens the degradation of valuable biochemical information in the evidence. The result? Useless evidence even before it reaches the laboratory.

A third factor needs to be mentioned and has become even more important in view of the ultra-sensitive nature of some forms of DNA analysis. This is ultraviolet light (UV) and its potential effect on body fluid evidence. DNA is specifically susceptible to the effects of UV radiation, and samples that contain analyzable DNA should be protected from UV sources. Such sources include direct sunlight, some alternate light sources used in crime scene investigations, and black lights used in hospital emergency rooms for locating sexual assault evidence on victims. While short exposure is not likely to damage the evidence, prolonged exposure may damage the chemical integrity of DNA present.

Considerations Relating to the Victim, Suspect, and Assault Scene

As indicated above, it all starts with the collection of the evidence at the sexual assault scene. This, however, is only a beginning stage in the overall investigation. A variety of evidence comes from different sources and is collected using a number of different procedures. The assault scene is a primary source of evidence in a sexual assault investigation. Remember, there are really three crime scenes at a minimum, and all three may be encountered at different times and at different locations during an investigation. They are, of course, the victim, the assault scene, and the suspect. To achieve maximum efficiency in collecting evidence from these sources, protocols and guidelines tailored to each situation are of importance.

The Victim

The very nature of a sexual assault dictates that the victim is the focal point of the initial investigation. The nature of a sexual assault also dictates that investigators recognize that the victim will more than likely be emotionally distraught and may be physically injured. While it is not the intent of this text to deal with the psychology of the victim, it is natural for the victim to want to take steps to distance herself or himself from the experience. This may involve such actions as bathing, changing clothes, destroying the clothes worn during the assault, not telling anyone of the assault, or not revealing the more embarrassing aspects of the assault (oral or anal assault) to physicians and investigators. These actions will have the effect of destroying or limiting the evidence recoverable and thus the success of the investigation.

When a victim does report the assault, it may be by telephone. Whether this contact is made to medical or law enforcement personnel, it is the first opportunity to preserve potential evidence. The dispatcher, crisis center worker, nurse, physician, or whoever may take the call should be trained and prepared to reassure and counsel the victim to avoid taking any actions that might jeopardize his or her personal safety or the integrity/preservation of the evidence. Such actions as those mentioned above should be carefully discouraged. Valuable corroborative evidence such as blood, semen, saliva, hairs, and fibers, often present immediately after the assault, can be easily lost because of a shower or in the laundering of clothing.

Another frequent first contact occurs between a patrol officer and the victim. With good reason, the officer's first priority is the safety and well-being of the victim. Such concern may be exercised at the expense of the scene security and evidence integrity. If the potential value of the scene is not well understood at the outset by all those involved in the investigation, evidence may be limited, contaminated, or missing. Through extensive discussions with police officers involved in active investigations as well as those who attend classes at the FBI Academy in Quantico, VA, certain points surface with some regularity regarding scene investigation and evidence collection when the victim is first contacted. It is not uncommon for responding officers to be ill-equipped to deal with the handling of evidence or the actions of a distraught, emotionally abused victim. Sympathy for the victim may lead to allowing the victim to wash, bathe, change clothes, and possibly take other actions that may eliminate valuable evidence. In some cases, condoms worn by the suspect were thrown into a toilet and subsequently flushed by the victim after using the toilet. The condoms contained the only seminal fluid available from the assault. Not often enough is the victim asked about potential items of evidence within the scene and their location. Some agencies discourage the responding officer from becoming involved in the evidence process at all, leaving that up to the experts. Consequently, patrol officers may not consider physical evidence handling as part of their jobs.

The first responding officer should not make an effort to locate, collect, and preserve as much evidence as possible. He is not likely to be a one-person evidence team, and security of the scene is the primary objective at this point. However, it is equally inappropriate for the officer to consider the protection of the scene and evidence as "not my job."

In many jurisdictions, the victim is taken to a medical facility for an examination and collection of existing evidence. In such situations the victim normally is requested to bring an extra set of clothing to change into after the examination so that the clothes worn during the assault can be taken as evidence. There are times, however, when the victim may have to change clothes prior to transport to a hospital or similar facility. Privacy issues considered, the victim should disrobe over a clean white cloth or paper, preferably supplied by the officer. Each item of clothing should be packaged separately and marked appropriately for chain-of-custody purposes. The paper or cloth should be marked to identify the side facing the victim and folded to retain any trace evidence that became dislodged during the undressing process. Once secure, it should be packaged as another item of evidence. This process will more than likely involve more than one officer. A preferable approach is to take the victim to a hospital for examination and evidence collection.

Whether or not the victim is taken to a medical facility, consideration should be given to the possibility of collecting loosely adhering trace evidence (hairs, fibers, etc.) from the clothing before the clothing is removed and the evidence is lost. Ideally, photographs are taken and the evidence is documented as to location prior to collection. Removed materials should be immediately packaged and, as always, labeled to include proper documentation as well as chain of custody. The actual recovery of such evidence should be done with gloved hands to avoid any possible contamination of the evidence for purposes of such analyses as DNA. Highly sensitive procedures used in the analysis of DNA such as polymerase chain reaction (PCR) may be affected by residue from the skin of the person collecting the evidence. A good rule to keep in mind is that the less invasive an investigator can be with respect to the evidence, the better off he is. Thus, only trace evidence that is likely to be lost should be collected; the forensic laboratory is the best place to remove such evidence so that recovery possibilities are optimized.

In those cases where the victim is taken initially to the medical facility, the same clothing removal procedures are most likely employed by the medical personnel; and the clothing is separately packaged as before. Coordination with medical personnel as to how the evidence will be handled is essential. Careful documentation of the clothing, including photographs, effectively records damaged items and assists in demonstrating injuries suffered by the victim. There are times when the victim has suffered significant physical injury, and clothing must be cut off to allow immediate treatment. During these times, there is often no good recourse, and the clothing may end up piled in a heap. This is one of those situations where "you do the best you can with what you've got" (but document it!). The cutting and removal of clothing should be recorded and the clothing packaged as soon as possible. A laboratory examiner will not know if the hospital personnel or the suspect cut the clothing without documentation to explain it. An examination of the area where the victim's examination was conducted is advisable to recover any debris or residue left behind.

It is highly likely that the victim will be interviewed as part of the overall examination. The primary interest is the health and welfare of the victim; but if the medical personnel are aware of the requirements governing the use of evidence, a great deal of difficulty can be avoided. Cooperative efforts between the medical and law enforcement professions have been established in many jurisdictions, streamlining the process. The establishment of the SANE program (Sexual Assault Nurse Examiner) in many areas of the United States is an example of this collaborative effort. Additionally, the evolution of a wide variety of sexual assault evidence kits to guide the medical professional has improved the overall collection of evidence from the victim's person. These kits are the subject of a later section in this chapter.

The foregoing addresses investigation with regard to a living and generally ambulatory victim. Should the assault involve a deceased victim, the general evidence collection principles are the same since the evidence is generally the same.

The Suspect

A primary goal is the association of the victim, the suspect, and the crime scene. An obvious but important point is that the longer it takes to develop a suspect, the greater the chance for evidence to be disposed of or simply lost. Clothing may be disposed of, vehicles may be cleaned, and individuals may shower or alter their appearance. It must again be emphasized that the trace evidence — that which is likely to be overlooked — can often save the day in such situations. While the possibility of finding even the minute types of evidence diminishes over time, the potential should not be overlooked. The suspect is a crime scene as much as the victim is, although the passage of time may reduce the likelihood of recovering evidence from that scene.

Suspects developed shortly after the incident are the most likely to have valuable evidence associated with them. Every effort should be made to secure the suspect's clothing and any other personal items before an effort to destroy or dispose of potential evidence can take place. Not to be overlooked is the suspect's body. Medical assistance may be helpful in conducting a thorough examination of the suspect's body. Sexual assault evidence kits have been developed for use in examining suspects as well.

A suspect who is injured during the assault and has to seek medical treatment as a result presents an opportunity for evidence collection that is almost as valuable as evidence from the victim. Recovery of clothing (especially that matching any described by the victim), biological fluid samples (blood and saliva), hairs (head and pubic), records of the examination, photographs of the condition of the suspect to include scratches and marks possibly resulting from contact with the victim — all should be secured while the opportunity is available.

A far less desirable situation is that in which the suspect is not developed for an extended period of time after the assault. It is probable that the more commonly encountered evidence has been lost or destroyed by this time; but it is still important to recognize that the more easily overlooked the evidence, the more likely it is that some may remain available. Trace evidence such as hairs, fibers, soils, glass fragments, small stains of blood, or body fluids may have been overlooked in any efforts by the suspect to prevent association with the crime. Again, consideration of these possibilities should not be ignored. A semen stain on a pair of pants in the suspect's closet that contains both his DNA and that from the cells lining the vaginal canal of the victim is likely to be valuable evidence regardless of time elapsed.

Occasionally, the presence of disease presents an advantage in an investigation. While that statement may draw some attention, it is possible that during the assault the suspect infected the victim with a sexually transmitted disease. When a victim develops symptoms of a disease and it can be attributed to the assault, attempts should be made to identify the medical condition of the suspect. Legal actions are likely necessary since this kind of information may not be readily available.

Regardless of the time span between the assault and the identification of a suspect, collection of evidence from that suspect should not be ignored. It is not uncommon to see cases in which a sexual assault evidence kit executed on the victim is the only evidence collected. Armed with a confession, investigators may not see the need for collection of evidence from the suspect — until that confession is not admitted by the court or is retracted. The difficulties that potentially accompany the decision not to collect can be enormous and severely damaging to the prosecution of a case. Today's juries have come to expect evidence, and a preponderance of circumstantial evidence can be as effective or more so than a limited amount of specific individual evidence.

Sexual Assault Evidence Collection Kits

The role of physical evidence in sexual assault crimes is to associate the victim, the suspect, and, if possible, the crime scene. However, it should be recognized that a primary (and critical) role of the evidence is to show that sexual contact did, in fact, take place. It should also be understood that the science of forensic examinations is one of comparisons between known and unknown samples. For example, DNA from the semen on the victim's clothing might be compared with DNA from the blood of both the victim and the suspect, identifying the suspect as the semen donor. Pubic hairs found in the victim's panties might be compared with the known pubic hairs of the victim and those of the suspect, ultimately with the same result. Such comparisons are common and the normal course of business in a forensic laboratory. Accordingly, it is evident that the examination of the victim and, if possible, the suspect for significant evidence and known samples is critical to the investigation. A tool for achieving this objective is the sexual assault evidence collection kit.

Here too, the cooperative effort between the medical profession and law enforcement comes into play. Assuming all necessary medical attention has been extended to the victim, medical personnel have a valuable tool to guide them in the collection of evidence. Working together with an investigating officer who collects the evidence as it is recovered, evidence collection can be optimized, increasing the chances of valuable information resulting from the forensic examinations. This information may be inculpatory or exculpatory, but the combined effort of medical and law enforcement personnel goes a long way toward insuring the best evidence is secured. However, make no mistake, personnel (medical or law enforcement) poorly or improperly trained can mishandle the evidence to the point that it is useless or provides inconclusive results, irreparably damaging the case. Medical personnel may include emergency medical technicians or paramedics as well as the emergency room personnel. It is imperative that both are aware of the need for working together.

The extent to which a law enforcement officer is involved in the actual evidence collection process varies widely with jurisdiction; however, an officer should at minimum be the one to securely package the evidence and record its recovery for chain-of-custody purposes. In those areas where the officer has only to pick up the packaged evidence from the medical professionals, the burden of chain of custody and proper packaging of the evidence falls on the medical personnel. This may place the medical person in a position to have to testify about matters outside the realm of normal medical practice. With the two working together, communication can take place that would not be otherwise possible. From both investigative and medical standpoints, the value of working together should be evident. As this issue is one that can become a serious concern for all involved, it should be established as protocol prior to action time when a victim is actually involved.

This effort to work together has improved greatly over the last 25 years. The growing acceptance of prepared sexual assault evidence collection kits has resulted in an improved quality of evidence collected in sexual assault cases. These kits allow the documented recovery of evidence and provide forms to ensure a complete interview of the victim. The kits are often supplied by the investigating agency or, in some jurisdictions, maintained at the medical facility for use when needed.

Earlier versions of these kits were often assembled by trained personnel for local and state crime laboratories. In time, the commercial uses of the kits have been recognized; and they have been available for purchase through several crime scene equipment suppliers for several years. Some suppliers will tailor the kit to the purchaser's specific requirements and print the outside container with a specifically desired logo and chain-of-custody information. Kits are designed for ease of use and provide a systematic examination and collection process to insure maximum effectiveness. While the kits are designed with simplicity in mind, it is essential that personnel be trained in the legal and evidentiary aspects of their use. The actions of personnel carelessly or unknowingly using the kits incorrectly may result in lost or contaminated evidence. This responsibility for training in the legal and evidentiary aspects often falls to law enforcement.

While the content of the kits may vary somewhat, the documentation contained is often quite similar. These documents, all of which should be executed by the examining personnel, normally include forms to guide the medical examination and interview of the victim, a consent for the release of any evidence obtained from the victim, a similar form to allow release of victim-related information, and chain-of-custody documents to ensure complete records as to what was found and recovered. Use of these forms allows the recovery of sufficient medical information to assess the condition of the victim, determine the nature of the assault, and document the evidence recovery process and the subsequent chain of custody of the evidence collected. A point not to be overlooked is the question of recent consensual sexual activity of the victim. Recent consensual sexual activity may mean that a blood sample will have to be secured from the victim's partner for comparison purposes to eliminate any results (DNA) that individual may have contributed to the evidence.

Available sexual assault evidence kits contain a variety of materials and incorporate a number of procedures for evidence collection, depending on the age and sex of the individual being examined and the identity of the person as victim or suspect. During collection, the outsides of all containers should be marked with the identity of the individual from whom the evidence was recovered, the person packaging it, the date, the offense, the location of the examination, and any other administrative information deemed necessary. Where swabs or fluids are used, it is advisable to provide an unused and uncontaminated swab or fluid sample packaged separately for control purposes.

Generally kits will include many if not all of the following items, and the kit contents listed below should serve as a guide to tailoring a kit to a particular department's needs. As indicated above, some jurisdictions have designed and provided tailored kits to departments and hospitals, and some have taken advantage of commercial resources. Regardless of the source of the kit used, its contents should be well thought out and execution should be carried out by trained personnel.

Known Blood.   Approximately 5 milliliters (cc) of blood are drawn into a Vacutainer® tube for blood grouping and DNA analysis. A red-top tube (containing no preservatives) and a purple-top tube (containing EDTA as a preservative for DNA) are normally provided.

Known Saliva.   A known saliva sample is usually taken by having the individual expectorate on a piece of clean filter paper. Portions of the paper not stained with the saliva act as uncontaminated controls.

Head Hair Combing/Brushing.   The head of the victim is combed or brushed over a clean cloth or catch paper to recover any loosely adhering hairs or fibers. The comb or brush is then packaged along with the materials obtained. This is done before any known head hair samples are recovered. A separate comb or brush is supplied for each area sampled.

Known Head Hairs.   Approximately 25 hairs representative of the entire head area, color and length should be pulled rather than cut. This is normally done after the collection of head hair combings/brushings.

Pubic Hair Combing/Brushing.   The pubic area is combed or brushed with a new comb or brush over a clean cloth or catch paper to recover any loosely adhering hairs or fibers. The comb or brush is then packaged along with the materials obtained. This is normally done before any known pubic hair samples are recovered. A separate comb or brush is supplied for each area sampled.

Known Pubic Hairs.   Approximately 25 hairs representative of the area, color and length should be pulled rather than cut. This is normally done after the collection of pubic hair combings/brushings.

Combing/Brushing of Body Hair Regions Other than Head and Pubic. In the event an individual has an unusual amount of body hair, separate supplies for taking combings or brushings from these areas might be supplied/used. A separate comb or brush is used for each area sampled.

Vaginal Swabs.   Samples of vaginal contents are taken for identification and analysis of sperm cells and/or seminal fluid. A separately packaged control swab is usually provided.

Oral Swabs.   Samples of oral contents are taken for identification and analysis of sperm cells and/or seminal fluid. A separately packaged control swab is usually provided.

Anal Swabs.   Samples of the anal surfaces and contents are taken for identification and analysis of sperm cells and/or seminal fluid. A separately packaged control swab is usually provided.

Microscope Smear Slides Made from Swabs.   Slides are frequently made during the examination for immediate identification of sperm cells, confirming sexual activity has occurred. These slides are saved for later analysis if needed. Slide holders are usually provided for this.

Vaginal Aspirate.   The vaginal contents are sampled by irrigation with a sterile fluid such as saline. This is intended to recover semen not recovered by swabbing. The wash is normally placed in a test tube provided in the kit.

Oral Rinse (Wash).   The oral contents are sampled by irrigation with a sterile fluid such as saline. This is intended to recover semen not recovered by swabbing. The wash is normally placed in a test tube provided in the kit.

Nasal Mucus Sample. Sometimes, a gag reflex occurring in persons forced to commit fellatio results in semen or semen components being deposited in sinuses. A special tissue or cloth may be provided for recovering this material. Unstained portions of the tissue or cloth serve as control material.

Fingernail Scrapings. Wooden picks or scraping devices and tissues to collect debris are provided to allow removal of material (blood, hairs, fibers, etc.) that may have been deposited under the individual's fingernails. Each hand is done separately (sometimes each finger is done separately). The material collected is saved along with the scraping device. Debris samples should be packaged separately.

Clothing. Each item of the individual's clothing is separately and securely packaged and sealed in paper. Standard brown wrapping paper or sturdy paper bags are useful for this.

Penile Swabs. The surface of the penis is swabbed to collect blood or any other evidentiary material. A separately packaged control swab is usually provided.

Miscellaneous Debris Collection. Supplies (tissues, envelopes, containers, etc.) are usually provided to collect any unexpected or extra evidentiary material (blood, hairs, fibers, semen, etc.) found on body surfaces. Catch papers or cloths are often provided for the individual to stand on when undressing or to sit on during an examination to recover any evidence dislodged during the examination process.

Sheets/Body Bags. Sheets or body bags used to transport a deceased or injured victim to the hospital should be recovered without loss of any materials present in or adhering to them for the recovery of trace evidence by the laboratory.

The above discussion deals with typical items that can be expected in sexual assault evidence kits. Seldom do all commercially available or even locally prepared kits contain every one of these items. Below are several observations that should be of assistance in deciding what to have in a kit, whether it is purchased or assembled in-house.

1. Because the pubic region of the victim is often thought to be the only area involved, no head hair combing/brushing sample supplies are recovered. The trace evidence collection potential of head hair (fibers, suspect hairs, glass fragments, botanical material, etc.) is significant and should not be ignored.

2. Some victims are reluctant to discuss or admit any activity involving oral or anal ejaculation by a suspect. Accordingly, oral and anal sampling should perhaps be performed as a normal policy.

3. Catch papers/cloths may be overlooked in kit preparation. Evidence recovered by these means (often not seen until the evidence is subjected to close scrutiny by a forensic examiner) can be lost by simply not using such devices.

4. Fluid samples are particularly vulnerable to degradation by microorganisms. Such samples, if the volume is small, could be air dried, out of direct sunlight, and frozen. In any event, fluid samples should be sent to a laboratory as soon as possible. A common practice in many laboratories is to dry samples of known blood on clean washed cotton sheeting, after which the stain is kept refrigerated or frozen.

5. Examination of several commercial kits shows a specific order for the recovery of samples. The order follows the principle of collecting the most easily lost first and the least easily lost last. That order is not reflected above since the intent here is to present the types of samples and briefly discuss them. Designing a departmental kit should take advantage of the instructions that come in commercial kits.

6. Samples for analysis and diagnosis of sexually transmitted diseases may be secured during the execution of a sexual assault evidence kit. Since these specimens are submitted to a medical (and not a forensic) facility for analysis, the forensic laboratory should be notified immediately if any positive results for such diseases are observed and/or reported.

A review of several commercial catalogs reveals a wide variety of kits, in terms of contents, that can be procured. Kits can be specifically designed for the examination of victims (male and female), suspects, adults, and children. The nature of the assault and the victim will largely determine what is required for examination. It is often expeditious to have a general kit containing supplies to cover as wide a range of evidence collection situations as possible.

As with many investigative aids such as report forms, the sexual assault evidence kit is probably of most value in that it guides the process of evidence collection regardless of the individual examined or the circumstances of the assault. As indicated above, the victim, the suspect, and the scene should all be considered as crime scenes; and it is necessary to apply the same standard process to evidence collection wherever it may be located.

The Crime Scene

The terms *crime scene search* and *crime scene investigation* may mean the same thing to many. Indeed, it might be the opinion of some that crime scene search is merely a task of locating the evidence, bagging it, and leaving. In fact, given the level of sophistication that has developed in crime scene technology, forensic evidence analysis, and presentation of the case in the courtroom, this impression of crime scene activity is not only outmoded — it needs to disappear. The impression that all that is necessary is to go and pick up the evidence, put it in a bag, and go home is not only short-sighted but also displays a lack of understanding of what is required. Crime scene investigation is far more descriptive of what takes place today, and the experienced crime scene officer is well aware that an apparently simple matter can easily become a major operation.

As has been indicated in earlier sections of this chapter, the value of the evidence collected is often directly in proportion to the care exercised in its collection. Sloppy collection, documentation, and preservation procedures can mean evidence lost, useless for forensic examination, and/or inadmissible in court. Well-designed, routinely followed protocols employed at crime scenes may make a major difference in the amount, quality, and effectiveness of the evidence collected.

It has been said that the secret to good crime scene documentation is document, document and document! In the experience of one of the authors, crime scene documentation, while having experienced a drastic improvement during recent years, is an area where a great deal of room for improvement still exists. In cases received for analysis by one of the authors, this area often receives minimal attention at the scene.

Anyone familiar with the repeated use of a complex procedure can understand that careful adherence to the steps of the procedure leads to a job completed correctly. A step-wise process or protocol makes it possible to check one's work and be sure no part of the job is ignored. Crime scene investigation is no different. It should be looked at as a process, some steps of which may be eliminated but not without sufficient and recorded reason.

Another area of concern to crime scene personnel is that of focus. In the pressure associated with a high-profile case (or perhaps a not-so-high-profile case) it is not difficult for focus to shift to one aspect of the case. It has been pointed out that the victim, the suspect, and the scene are all crime scenes. It may happen, for instance, that the victim might become the focus of the investigation to the extent that the actual scene of the sexual activity becomes secondary and receives far less attention in terms of actual scene investigation. Both authors have received evidence in cases where little to no effort was expended at the location of the assault. While it may have happened for a variety of reasons, this kind of lack of attention may be inviting disaster.

General Stages of Crime Scene Investigation

After expressing so much concern about crime scene investigation protocol, it is in order to discuss a general procedure. The following is not intended to represent a panacea for all problems encountered in crime scene investigation; but it can, in most circumstances, be tailored to the needs of any particular crime scene. It should also be noted that there will be some overlap of stages, which if done properly will cause no difficulty. Some stages may continue throughout the entire scene investigation. Further, no suggestion is made that every step is always followed; but it is suggested that when something is not done, there should be a documented reason for it. It will be obvious that the foregoing addresses large-scale scenes; however, the procedure presented may be scaled down to accommodate smaller scenes. The very nature of the work requires that flexibility be an integral aspect of it. Trying to handle every crime scene in precisely the same manner will soon result in frustration. It should also be noted that many departments have well-established protocols that will probably be similar to what is below. As a step-wise approach, the following is offered:

1. Approach the scene.
2. Secure and protect the scene.
3. Conduct a preliminary survey.
4. Evaluate observed evidence.
5. Prepare a narrative description.
6. Photograph the scene.
7. Sketch the scene.
8. Conduct a detailed search for evidence.
9. Collect, preserve, and document the evidence.
10. Conduct a final survey.
11. Release the scene.

Approach the Scene

In many instances, the first responding officer will have the initial contact with the victim and the scene. While there are a number of cautions relative to the evidence, personal safety is a topic that needs priority attention. Crime scenes can offer a wide range of safety hazards that can result in injury to the victim or to the officer. Certainly most likely to be encountered in a sexual assault scene are biohazards such as blood-borne pathogens. A section is presented on this subject at the end of this chapter. However, officer safety in terms of mental preparation prior to arrival is something many fail to consider. Even seasoned officers in the face of extremely brutal and violent crimes have been taken by complete surprise on arrival. The emotional effects of processing the scene of a particularly brutal crime are often very unpredictable, and those who feel they can handle it may be rudely surprised. It is only good sense to prepare oneself mentally as to what might be ahead before arriving at the scene.

While the safety and well-being of the victim are of paramount importance and should be of first concern, our discussion here relates to evidence. We will therefore assume the victim is secure. A key point to remember in approaching a scene, then, is that the suspect (in many cases) will have already left the area. Identifying the departure route and the means taken as well as any evidence discarded along the way should allow the officer to avoid disturbing that area. Observing people, vehicles, and the overall area may provide details that will be valuable later on in the investigation. Initial officers on the scene should be especially alert to potential witnesses and any other sources of information that might be available.

Secure and Protect the Scene

Initially, it may be that sufficient personnel are not available to accomplish the level of security required or desired. It is critical to provide for the safety of personnel, and efforts should be made to insure the scene is adequately protected from contamination or unnecessary alteration. This twofold requirement cannot be successfully accomplished without some degree of careful thought and planning. In order to protect the scene, it must be secured. That means that the boundaries must be established. This may result in some disturbance of the scene but should be controlled as much as possible. The scene's initial condition as well as any significant alteration should be documented.

With the boundaries of the scene identified, establish control of the perimeter with assigned personnel; and use a single entry point to control who has access to the interior. Record the names of all persons entering and leaving the scene, and deny access to anyone not having legitimate activity within the perimeter. Uncontrolled access to the scene has resulted in courtroom difficulties on more than one occasion. A predefined agency policy determining who is to be in control and who should have scene access will very likely be helpful. There are additional comments on this above in the section titled Evidence/Crime Scene Contamination.

Conduct a Preliminary Survey

The purposes of a preliminary survey of the scene are to assess the requirements for conducting the investigation and to prevent an uncontrolled, confused processing of the scene. The individual in charge of the scene investigation should conduct a walk-through with a minimal number of other persons to determine the extent of the search area, methods and techniques to be used in the collection of evidence, to identify personnel and equipment needs, and to identify evidence that may be easily moved, destroyed, or altered. That evidence should receive special attention to ensure its successful recovery. The narrative description of the scene is logically started at this time (see below). It is also during this time that entry photographs normally are taken. Observations made at this time help to formulate a theory as to what happened and guide the evidence collection efforts.

Once the survey is completed, a briefing is held to inform the remaining personnel of what can be expected in terms of safety issues, evidence present, areas requiring special attention such as unique hiding places, the overall layout of the scene, and any special conditions that may require additional help such as electricians, plumbers, or public utilities personnel. Special equipment needed such as alternate light sources and other materials should be identified at this point and tasked out accordingly.

Evaluate Observed Evidence

The process thus far has emphasized planning and preparedness, and the need for prior planning continues. During the preliminary survey, evidence readily observed was noted for the purpose of preparing a collection strategy. Recognizing the types of evidence present and the possible attendant hazards at the outset allows formulation of a plan for collection and preservation. This also assists in the execution of a systematic, more intrusive search for evidence that will take place later. Recognition of unique or special situations where types of evidence may conflict with one another should take place now. As an example, it should be determined how blood on a surface exhibiting fingerprint ridge detail is to be handled. Such a situation incorrectly handled by enhancing the fingerprints with chemical processing may destroy the blood for further analysis — and collecting the blood without regard for the fingerprint ridge detail may destroy the detail needed for comparisons. In fact, such a situation was experienced by one of the authors when asked to identify blood on a door that had been treated with chemicals prior to any blood collection efforts. The result was that the blood could not be identified due to alteration by the chemicals applied.

Prepare a Narrative Description

Why prepare a narrative description of the scene if sketches, photographs, and finely detailed evidence notes will be prepared? Why not just take the photographs or do a really good sketch to tell the whole story? Because documentation of the scene in all three ways requires the individual to think and observe differently; and when this happens, a more complete picture of the scene is recorded. A narrative description is a primary but often ignored means of documenting the scene. The objective is to record the initial condition of the scene and the evidence (as found) for courtroom presentation. A narrative will record in general terms a verbal description of the scene, either as text or as tape recorded information. Video taping is also used and can be done with or without audio taping.

Generally, the preparation of a narrative begins with the most generally descriptive information and moves to the more complex without going into great detail. This is done for each area of the scene (room in the apartment, house, etc.) as a running description of the conditions and features of the scene. Narrative descriptions should systematically represent the scene and supplement both the photographs and the sketches.

Photograph the Scene

The importance of photography to the courtroom process of presenting a case cannot be overstated. Complete photography of a scene may result in some photographs not being used — but those needed will be available. Incomplete photography inevitably results in the lack of key photographs and an inadequately documented scene, often to disadvantage in court. An experienced photographer will take long-range, medium, and close-up views of the scene and the evidence, depending on the specific subject being photographed. Photographs taken during the preliminary survey should sequentially walk the viewer through the scene as the photographer walks through the scene. A photographic log is essential to record the photographs taken, as is the use of scales and identification placards or tags in photographs. Evidence should be photographed as found and from viewpoints that will allow a jury to understand where the evidence was located when it was found. The spatial relationship of the evidence to its surroundings should be evident from the photographs.

Unique forms of evidence may require extra effort to insure photographs are taken properly. Panoramic, overlapping photographs should be taken (preferably with the focal plane parallel to the subject surface) when evidence extends over large surfaces or areas, such as bloodstain patterns covering an expanse of wall. Castings of shoeprints or tool marks should be taken after photography of the impressions.

Ultimately, the photographs should tell the story of the crime. If the suspect entered through the kitchen door, drank some milk, proceeded to the bedroom, assaulted the victim, dragged her to the living room, assaulted her again and then left through the front door, sufficiently detailed photographs should be taken to illustrate this sequence of events for anyone to see. The photographs should focus on the location of the crime, the nature of the crime, the results of the crime, the evidence present after the crime, and the follow-up activity that occurred after the scene investigation. Exit photographs taken when the scene is released establish the condition of the scene and are useful in answering any claims of excessive damage or alteration of the scene during the investigation.

Photography of individuals (both medium and close-up with scales) such as the victim or the suspect can be used to record injuries that may corroborate a particular story being investigated. Scratches on the arms and face of a suspect who could not explain them after his mother was found beaten to death in their home represented significant evidence of his involvement in the struggle.

With the availability of hi-tech equipment, it is popular to videotape the crime scene. This type of documentation provides a new dimension to the ability to review the scene; but if done improperly, it can produce a result that is difficult to work with, at best. It is not the intent here to detail techniques and procedures for video work; however, some basic points may be mentioned. Tapes should be of good quality and kept in their boxes/sleeves when not in use. The videographer should be very familiar with the camera and its functions as well as familiar with basic techniques for properly covering an area and the details within that area. A preliminary survey specifically for video purposes may be helpful in planning the taping process.

Many law enforcement agencies currently are using digital cameras for various purposes. It is not recommended that digital cameras be used as the primary tool for crime scenes. Large-format film cameras (no smaller than 35 millimeter) are recommended. The current digital camera technology creates unclear and grainy images, especially when enlarged, and is less effective for jury presentation.

Sketch the Scene

Crime scene sketching is a method of crime scene documentation that is often neglected or inadequately performed. It is worth repeating: narrative descriptions, photographs, and sketches all complement and supplement one another and should not be used as substitutes for one another. Photographs record a three-dimensional scene in two dimensions. Distances between features in the scene can be distorted and detail can be lost when lighting is not properly controlled. Sketches can be used to record three dimensions and accurately reflect distances. Narrative descriptions (particularly recorded descriptions) can provide details that cannot be covered with sketches and photographs.

In its simplest form, a sketch is a depiction of the area of the crime showing the interrelationships of people, places and things. Locations of all (or nearly all) recovered evidence should be represented, and sketches can deal with unique situations and hard-to-photograph areas and subjects. A frequent concern of individuals is that they cannot draw. Sketching a scene need not (and seldom does) produce a courtroom-ready diagram the first time. Usually only a rough sketch is prepared, which is later refined and prepared for courtroom use. The critical point is that sufficient data must be collected to allow a final sketch to be made. Various methods for sketching and measuring dimensions at scenes are available and not difficult to learn. It is important to be aware that, in larger scenes, measuring to determine scene dimensions and evidence positions often requires more than one person.

With the ready availability of computers, a selection of inexpensive, user-friendly computer-assisted design (CAD) software for home design and land-scaping has become available in recent years, making professional-looking sketches much more within the reach of all jurisdictions. Basic to moderately complex sketches are a simple matter with these kinds of tools and moderate skill levels with a computer.

A relatively new and remarkably accurate concept for crime scene sketches is the use of standard commercial surveying equipment that uses specialized law enforcement software. This technology, which was used by the U.S. Bureau of Alcohol, Tobacco, and Firearms to assist local law enforcement at the Columbine High School in Colorado and the Westwood Baptist Church in Texas, can allow angles to be measured to within one inch at 100 yards and create exceptional crime scene sketches. Within hours, the equipment and software can produce small or large accurate sketches that show the locations of bodies and hundreds of pieces of physical evidence. This technique is especially useful in mass shootings or bombings in large spaces with a multitude of physical evidence to be recovered and locations to be accurately recorded.

Conduct a Detailed Search for Evidence

A primary aspect of the investigation process is the search for physical evidence of the crime. Continuing the mental preparation for the task at hand, one should consider three questions when beginning (two of which have been proposed before): *What evidence is there here to tell me that a crime was committed? What is present (or missing) to tell me that the victim was here? What is present (or missing) to tell me that the suspect was here?* An experienced crime scene investigator, while probably not reciting these specific questions when going into each scene, will often be guided along these general lines in the overall approach.

This stage of the investigation inevitably produces the greatest portion of the evidence recovered. Thus far it has been emphasized that planning is necessary for a successful investigation. In fact, it is at this point that a lack of planning can be most felt. The planning as to who is going to do *what, where,* and *when* helps to ensure the success of the effort. Additionally, there should be no unauthorized assumptions of new or unassigned duties. Normally the individual in charge of the scene investigation should not be looking for and collecting evidence. This individual should be looking out for the needs of the overall process and the individuals doing assigned tasks.

Specialized methods and techniques of evidence location, identification, and collection come into play at this point. Various methods for conducting a search are available, depending on the area to be searched. Many will agree that there is usually more than one way to do a particular job, and careful consideration should be given to the best way to accomplish that particular task. The objective is to collect the evidence in a manner that is least intrusive to the evidence itself. Photography of the evidence in place or as found is a basic need, and scales as well as identifying number placards or tags should be used. Logs contemporaneous with evidence collection and the photographs as they are taken should be kept. Chain-of-custody documentation for evidence recovered should be kept as well.

A particular point worthy of specific mention is that any activity or event outside the normal scope of routine crime scene investigative techniques should be documented. If a piece of evidence is inadvertently picked up by someone and then replaced in its original position, the event should be accurately documented. Any intended or unintended alteration of (or damage to) the crime scene should be carefully documented.

Collect, Preserve, and Document the Evidence

Documentation of evidence has been a continuing process thus far, and it does not stop here. Evidence in place has been recorded photographically, and measurements have been taken to locate it within the scene on a sketch. It is at this stage of the operation that consideration must be given to how an individual piece of evidence will be packaged for most effective preservation. Evidence may be contaminated, degraded, or lost if it is not properly packaged and preserved. This process of collecting, preserving, and finally documenting the evidence will go much more smoothly if a single person is designated as the evidence custodian and is responsible for logging and final sealing of the evidence containers. Others in the process must work with and not independently of that person.

Conduct a Final Survey

Like the preliminary survey and the preparation of the narrative, the final survey is an administrative task and falls to the individual in charge of the scene investigation. When the tasks of sketching, photographing, collection of evidence and documentation are completed and/or updated, a final survey should be conducted. All of the activities carried out thus far should be reviewed to ensure personnel are uninjured, no evidence has been missed, all documentation is complete to this point, and all available theories of the crime have been considered. Specific tasks and stages mentioned above should be reviewed with the individuals involved to ensure that nothing has been left undone. A walk-through should be conducted once more. A carefully conducted final survey has located many pieces of evidence including firearms and even bodies. In a homicide case involving the death of a mother by her son, the father's body was found in a freezer only after discussion as to whether a final survey was necessary (and the decision was to go ahead with it). While there was some sentiment toward releasing the scene without bothering with the survey, the more methodical viewpoint won. The aim here is to review the entire process to be sure all necessary tasks have been completed.

This, too, is the time for the final or exit photographs of the scene to be taken to document the condition of the scene at the conclusion of the scene investigation. An inventory of all equipment used should establish that none is about to be left behind.

Release the Scene

After a thorough review of the collected evidence and all prepared documentation, release of the scene should be considered. It should be noted that after the release, another warrant is usually required to re-enter the scene. If there are specialists or additional personnel who will be conducting examinations and have not been able to arrive on scene yet, the scene should not, if possible, be released until after this work has been accomplished. In particularly large scenes, it is important to be sure all personnel have completed their work and have been advised that release is imminent so that no one will be caught by surprise. Thus, this stage of the process is one in which all participate to one extent or another.

The individual in charge should be the person to release the scene and should document the date and time of release, the person to whom the scene was released, and who actually released the scene. Copies of paperwork including any warrant(s) and an inventory of evidence recovered are normally left behind.

It Does Not End There

The crime scene investigation is the search, recovery and documentation process. Following that, the recovered evidence and documentation must be secured, chain-of-custody documents completed, and decisions made by the forensic laboratory as to what evidence will be examined for what types of materials and characteristics. Information of immediate significance to investigators on the street should be communicated to them as soon as possible. A study of information gained through other avenues of investigation, coupled with the above and the results of forensic examinations, represents the final step in this sequence of events — reconstruction of the events of the crime.

Blood-Borne Pathogens

On March 6, 1992, the Occupational Safety and Health Administration (OSHA) of the U.S. Department of Labor released requirements for the handling of blood-borne pathogens by public service agencies including law enforcement agencies. The Blood-borne Pathogens Act included requirements that all law enforcement officers who might be handling blood and other bodily fluids be offered vaccinations against hepatitis B on a voluntary basis at no charge. Further, the act requires training and safety equipment to be provided to the officers.

Blood, semen, saliva, and other body fluids from either victims or suspects in sexual assault cases could be contaminated with infectious microorganisms capable of causing sickness or death. For those reasons, law enforcement officers should follow the so-called universal precaution when handling any body fluid from any source: assume it is infectious. The purpose of this chapter is not to go into detail regarding this act but to remind law enforcement that these requirements exist.

Bloodstain Patterns

The nature of a sexual assault usually does not involve a great deal of violence and spilling of blood. The sexual assault is not without violence, however; and in those crimes where there is bloodshed, the field of bloodstain pattern analysis may provide useful information to the investigation.

Bloodshed during a violent crime may create bloodstain patterns. It is not unusual for such patterns to record a wealth of information about the events that took place to create those patterns. A suspect, after beating the victim severely, may have blood on a shirtsleeve. If the suspect leans against a door frame and leaves a fabric imprint of the stain, the size, shape, and general characteristics of the stain as well as the nature of the fabric may provide information when compared with the shirt that specifically links the suspect with the scene through a transfer of wet blood. A spatter pattern on the front of a suspect's shirt might be explained by the claim that the suspect picked up the victim and held her to comfort her until help arrived. The story begins to take on a new light when it is recognized that the stains are of an impact nature (not contact stains) and would have been deposited on the shirt during the application of blows to a source of wet blood.

The following outline sets forth evidentiary material that may be critical to the successful bloodstain pattern examination/analysis of a violent crime scene. It is based on the ultimate goal of bloodstain pattern analysis — reconstruction. Not all of the listed materials apply to every case under investigation, and seldom are all of the materials available. However, assembling as much of this material as possible for an analyst greatly assists in the development of a reconstruction of the events of the crime. In many cases, the analyst will not be able to view the crime scene. Assuming that no analyst will be able to come to the scene and that the investigator is collecting evidence to send to an analyst, remember that the investigator is dealing with someone who has to gain a familiarity with the scene that is as good as or better than his but from the perspective of the blood patterns present. Be as thorough as possible in providing pertinent information to the analyst. Do not deny that person information that may help your case — it is *your* case. If there is a question, do not let it go — talk to the analyst.

1. Documentary evidence.
   A. Medical examiner's report of autopsy.
   B. Crime scene officer report.
      (1.) Initial observations on arrival.
      (2.) Evidence collected.
      (3.) Information concerning activities of suspect and/or victim.
      (4.) Crime scene investigator notes, administrative logs, etc.
   C. Reports of forensic laboratories, consulting firms, other experts, etc.
   D. Statement of victim, suspect and witness.
2. Photographic evidence.
   A. Copies of all photographs taken of the scene: victim, suspect and evidence.
   B. If 8×10 or larger color prints are not available, it may be expeditious to send the negatives to the analyst. Normally, small-format Polaroid® prints are not sufficiently detailed to provide necessary information.
   C. Videotape recordings of crime scene. Video is often used at crime scenes to gain overall spatial relationships between objects at the scene and perspectives not possible with still photography prints. Video, however, unless recorded with better-than-average equipment, is often not of sufficient quality to allow detailed analysis of small areas and specific stain patterns. Extreme care must be exercised regarding the microphone.
3. Graphic evidence.
   A. Crime scene sketches, diagrams, finished drawings, etc.
   B. Drawings of homes, blueprints or sales sketches from real estate agents, residential builders, building managers, architects, etc.
   C. Maps (hand drawn, road, topographic, satellite, etc.).
   D. Resources: U.S. Geological Survey, U.S. Army Corps of Engineers, state mapping agencies, etc.
4. Physical evidence.
   A. Typically the physical evidence which bears blood collected at and associated with the scene. Stains and stain patterns on clothing, weapons, and various items collected may provide useful information.

Summary

While evidence in sexual assault investigations is in many respects the same as that involved with other kinds of cases, the more specific issues of sexual assault impart a uniqueness that needs to be recognized. It is hoped that these issues have been adequately addressed here. With the exception of DNA evidence, most of the evidence dealt with in sexual assault investigations is class evidence, not individual. This makes the topic of evidence in general all the more important, as it becomes more critical to be able to present a preponderance of class evidence to the court even if it is class in nature. Challenges can be expected in the courtroom that will necessitate a well-established understanding of the evidence, its characteristics, and the procedures by which it was recovered, preserved, and maintained prior to presentation before the court. It has been the intent in this chapter to address the more important aspects of physical evidence in sexual assault investigations.

Evidence Recovery Considerations in Sexual Assault Investigations

16

ROBERT P. SPALDING
P. DAVID BIGBEE

Introduction

The tremendous number of possibilities regarding the identity, type and general character of evidence that may play a critical role in sexual assault investigations seems to grow with experience rather than to cap out. While this is really no different than in other violent crime investigations, one need only spend a moderate amount of time dealing with these cases to appreciate the variation and complexity of the evidence that can be important. Body fluids, fabric impressions, hairs, latent fingerprints, shoe prints, tire-tread impressions, cosmetics, bite marks, tool marks, fibers, cordage, paints, tape, glass, soil, and documents may seem a long list; but it is certainly incomplete in considering the types of evidence which may play vital roles. The wide variety of evidence makes it necessary for the investigator to avoid focusing on expected evidence in sexual assault cases. Such thinking can result in evidence overlooked and thus a potentially deficient investigation.

Despite that cautionary note, body fluids (blood, semen, and saliva), hairs, and fibers will be discussed here for several reasons:

1. They are frequently encountered in sexual assault cases.
2. Sexual assault evidence collection kits are designed to accomplish the collection of these types of evidence.
3. They will often corroborate the victim's testimony and may positively identify the subject.
4. They demonstrate close contact and sexual elements of the crimes committed.
5. They are difficult to see and easily overlooked.
6. The modern forensic laboratory is often well equipped to handle many examinations dealing with them.

In communicating with a laboratory, the investigator may hear terms such as *unknown, control, standard, known, questioned sample,* and so forth, depending on laboratory protocol. This discussion uses the terms *known, questioned,* and *control.* Questioned evidence is of questionable origin or about which a detailed history is unknown. Blood on a shirt, loose hairs in the crotch of a pair of panties, hairs on the floor of an automobile, the shirt, and even the panties are all questioned specimens. Questioned specimens are compared with possible sources later in the investigation.

Known samples are those whose origin is known and which can be used for comparison to questioned specimens or samples. Known samples are collected specifically with this purpose in mind, and care is normally taken to prevent alteration of any kind. Hair samples taken from the head and pubic region of the victim in an assault, as well as blood and saliva samples secured for later comparisons, are known samples. Questioned samples become of value to the investigation when they are compared with known samples to establish their probable or even specific source. Occasionally comparisons between questioned samples may be of value as well. Fibers of a particular nature identified on a person's clothing and on the floor of the location where the violation took place provide a link between the individual and the scene.

The explosion of technology in recent years has had its effect in law enforcement. Whether documenting the scene with computer-driven surveying equipment or searching for evidence with sophisticated lighting techniques, it still must be emphasized that proper training and careful use of such devices are key to successful recovery of evidence. As with any of the evidence-handling procedures discussed, ineffective evidence recovery or even loss of evidence may result from getting it done quickly rather than doing it right. It should also be pointed out that discovering and recovering evidence are two entirely different actions. A knowledge of the techniques for discovering evidence as well as those for proper recovery and preservation is important.

There are many procedures and techniques available to the investigator and the forensic laboratory. The investigator is well advised to be familiar with the policies of the laboratory to which the evidence will be forwarded, since the degree to which the field investigator is encouraged or allowed to conduct testing, however preliminary, varies between laboratories. A good rule of thumb to follow is to be the least intrusive as possible in securing the evidence. Remember, the laboratory has better controlled conditions to recover the small fleck of blood crust from that watch crystal than the investigator probably has. Magnification and special lighting techniques beyond those available to the field often make it advantageous for the laboratory to do the micro work. There is always the corollary to the rule, and it should be obvious that a hair or a small bloodstain that will most certainly be lost if not secured in a container should be collected and secured. However, if you have questions or are not sure of what to do or how to do it, call the laboratory with which you intend to work.

Safety is everyone's responsibility. With the increased awareness of blood-borne pathogens today, we should all be attentive to caring for our own safety as well as the safety of others. In discussing a situation with laboratory personnel, the need for routine and special safety requirements should be covered. Is there reason to believe that the victim/suspect had AIDS, hepatitis, or some other infectious disease? Basic safety practices should be considered such as proper disposal of sharp items (scalpel blades, etc.), use of protective gloves, and additional clothing to include eyes, nose, and mouth protection. Using a probe to search areas where visibility is poor (a paint stirrer works well) goes a long way toward preventing a needle in one's finger.

The following discussions regarding evidence assume that some of the basic minimums of documentation discussed in the previous chapter have been followed — namely, that the evidence has been properly photographed with a scale when necessary, that a photographic log has been kept, that an evidence log is being kept, and that the packaging to be used will secure the evidence to include proper labeling.

Recovery of Questioned Evidence

Hairs and Fibers

Hair and fiber transfer during violent interaction has been discussed in depth, and the recovery of foreign hairs and fibers at a scene or on an article of clothing has obvious potential to aid the investigation. In the forensic laboratory an examiner can identify hairs as being of human or animal origin and, if animal, can often determine the animal species of origin. Human hairs are often identifiable to racial origin (Mongoloid, Caucasoid, Negroid). Other characteristics such as color, body area of origin, chemical treatment, method of removal, damage, and presence of foreign material on or chemically in the hair, can often be established. The examination of physical and chemical characteristics of hair often allows conclusions that strongly associate the hair with a particular source individual. Identification of a particular hair as having come from a specific person is not normally possible at this time. This topic will be dealt with in more detail later.

Fibers are so frequently considered with hairs that it is possible to hear the term *hair-fibers*. The term is a misnomer and incorrect. Hairs are hairs and fibers are fibers. Fibers, however, can be as important as hairs in sexual assault investigations. Textile fibers are normally classified as either natural or synthetic as an initial step in forensic examinations. Specific color and a variety of other chemical, optical, and microscopic characteristics — as well as the presence of foreign substances indicative of a particular environment — might then be identified, making comparison with other recovered fibers possible. These comparisons are normally made with a known sample but could be made with a questioned sample as well. It should be noted that specific connection of a fiber to a particular fiber source (an individual garment or other fiber source) is not possible based on forensic comparisons.

Hairs are often easier to see and recover than fibers; but both can present difficulties, particularly when the scene is extensive and multiple areas are to be searched. Observations made during the preliminary survey should identify possible sources for these kinds of trace evidence so that known samples can be secured during the conduct of the overall scene investigation.

In general, the discovery of hairs or fibers at a scene involves either removing and securing the trace evidence or collecting the entire item to which the hairs and/or fibers are adhered. It is normally preferable to let the laboratory deal with the removal of trace evidence from a source item, but there are instances when it is advisable to remove and secure individual hairs and fibers to avoid loss or contamination.

Search Methods and Techniques

Many methods are available for identifying and securing hairs and fibers at scenes, none of which are universally effective. The following procedures/techniques are useful, depending on circumstance and environment and the investigator's knowledge and experience. The techniques fall into one of two categories: visual enhancement or mechanical recovery.

1. General unassisted visual search (naked eye)
2. Oblique light
3. Ultraviolet (UV) light
4. Vacuuming
5. Adhesive lifts
6. Combing/brushing
7. Fingernail scrapings and clippings
8. Lasers and alternate light sources

General Unassisted Visual Search

A general unassisted visual search is just that — a search with the naked eye to locate any trace evidence that may be available to find. Various colors and backgrounds make it difficult to see the evidence, so it is not, perhaps, the most effective method of discovering this kind of evidence. Still, to ignore one's senses is neither logical nor good judgment. The principle is simple —

if you do not look, you will not see evidence. It is at this point that one might find individual hairs or fibers clinging to a vehicle head rest or some other surface, just begging to be collected. If this is the only method available, it should be exercised thoroughly and carefully.

Oblique Light

When a beam of light is directed nearly parallel to a surface (a wall) such that the light plays across that surface, imperfections and irregularities will be highlighted due to the shadows they cast. This created contrast makes it easier to see minute detail and can help draw attention to such evidence as hairs and fibers. The same applies to small objects on a floor (cartridge cases, bullets, etc.). Any surface that may retain hairs or fibers can be searched in this manner, often to good advantage.

Ultraviolet Light

Ultraviolet or UV light is of value due to its excitation capabilities. When irradiated with UV light, certain chemical substances give off energy in the form of light, resulting in a phenomenon known as fluorescence. Simply said, certain fibers and fabrics will glow in the dark when exposed to UV light, based on the dyes and chemical treatments given the fibers and fabrics. The fluorescence makes it easier to see this kind of trace evidence. UV light is probably of more value in locating fibers than hairs, since hairs seldom fluoresce unless treated with cosmetics. UV is also of value when used with fluorescent fingerprint powders, but one should be very familiar with the use of such fluorescent powders. Because of the amplifying effect of the fluorescence under UV, a little powder goes a very, very long way.

UV light is not to be treated casually, and care should be exercised during its use. Ultraviolet lamps produce light in the UV region of the electromagnetic spectrum just at the edge of the visible light spectrum. Light is measured in units called nanometers (nm) ranging from 400 to 700 nm in the visible range, and the UV range is from 200 to 400 nm. The 200 to 300 nm region is referred to as short wavelength UV and the 300 to 400 nm region as long wavelength UV. The significance of this is that UV light (particularly the short wavelength UV) is responsible for sunburn, and extended exposure to a UV source can cause sunburn even if the user is working indoors. Because of its higher energy, short wavelength UV is especially dangerous. Eye protection (UV filtering goggles) is advisable when using either type of UV light. Extended use of UV at a scene can also result in sunburn since some surfaces reflect UV and direct it back toward the investigator. Additional protection such as long sleeves or more extensive protective clothing for exposed skin may be advisable. Use of UV should be approached with a knowledge of the hazards associated with it and appropriate precautions taken.

Some UV lights supplied for forensic work often have lamps that emit only the long wave UV because of the increased danger associated with the short wave. While this is an understandable safety precaution, it is often helpful to have a unit capable of giving off both wavelengths since not all fluorescence occurs in the long wave region. It is also advisable to invest in a quality instrument, since poorly constructed lamp housings and poor filters allow visible light to leak and defeat the effort of working in darkness.

Since the usefulness of UV depends on the fluorescence of trace evidence to make it stand out from the background, a fluorescing background represents a major obstacle to UV use. Bedding (sheets and similar large fabric items) fluoresce due to the detergents normally used in laundering them, and stains accumulated through normal use flouresce. A reasonable recommendation is to allow the laboratory to conduct the complete examination of such items for trace evidence.

Vacuuming

Vacuuming an area for the collection of hairs and fibers seems an attractive method, especially since it can be thorough and relatively quick. While this is true, there are a number of other factors that should be considered to insure the best possible results.

Vacuuming allows relatively easy coverage of large areas and objects, which means they do not have to be sent to a laboratory for processing. That is an advantage for everyone. Any area to be vacuumed should be carefully inspected visually to locate any evidence that may be disrupted by the vacuuming. A drop of blood crusted on some carpet fibers could be broken up and reduced to a powder that might never be recognized or recovered if the area is vacuumed without first securing the blood.

Several vacuum kits are commercially available for forensic use. Also available for use with these vacuums are specially designed filter canisters for the collection of hairs, fibers, and other trace evidence. Some are meant to be reused and thus require thorough cleaning of the canister between samples. Others are one-time-use canisters, which have the advantage of maintaining sample integrity both at the scene and when presented in the courtroom.

Vacuuming should be approached with a plan for the area to be covered. A 9- by 12-foot carpet should not be vacuumed with one sample canister. Rather, the carpet should be divided into segments, perhaps 3 feet by 4 feet or smaller, and a sketch should be maintained to identify locations where the samples came from. The same thinking applies to an automobile. Separate samples should be taken from different areas of the vehicle, depending on what is thought to have occurred. If the victim of an assault was forced to lie on the back seat floor with her head behind the driver's seat, that area of the floor should be vacuumed as a separate sample to both isolate any hairs coming from that location and to avoid filling the sample with unwanted debris from other areas of the vehicle. Vacuuming too large an area results in the collection of a ball of fluff and debris that takes a laboratory examiner far more time to examine. Procuring several smaller samples makes everyone's job easier and improves the chances of finding valuable hairs and fibers. While a somewhat unusual approach, vacuuming of body areas has been used with some success to collect foreign hairs and fibers.

Points to be especially careful about when vacuuming a scene include: (1) sample contamination due to poor cleaning of a filter canister after the previous use; (2) overusing the canister to collect too much material, thus making it difficult if not impossible for the laboratory examiner to extract significant evidence; (3) vacuuming too vigorously and collecting ground-in debris that has no relation to the crime; and (4) small tufts of fabric or fibers may become separated, distributing the fibers throughout the sample and reducing the sample's effectiveness. For example, a small piece of fabric torn from a suspect's shirt can become shredded into fibers during vigorous vacuuming. The victim's story of tearing the piece loose from the shirt is far more effectively corroborated by having the piece of fabric match the shirt in pattern and shape of the hole as opposed to having loose fibers that are merely consistent with having come from the shirt.

Adhesive Lifts

The adhesive lift technique simply involves using wide clear packaging tape of relatively low tack and systematically covering a portion of a car seat (not too large) to pick up any hairs or fibers adhering to the seat. People employ a similar technique by using a lint roller on clothing to remove debris. In fact, a lint roller is a convenient tool for accomplishing this technique. Once used, the tape lift is then secured to a plastic bag (sticky side to the plastic) or other clear material for packaging. The tape should not be folded over on itself. Avoid mounting the lift on paper or similar material because removal of the evidence is much more difficult. This procedure can be applied to a wide variety of surfaces to include fabrics, solid surfaces, and even body surfaces, although personal comfort may be an issue with traumatized victims.

The adhesive lift procedure is often more selective than vacuuming since it picks up only surface material, and usually the interest is in showing evidence of recent contact between the individuals involved in the crime. Vacuuming, if not carefully carried out, may collect debris and dirt ground into a carpet which may have been there for years and has no bearing on the violation. It would be impractical to tape the entire scene, and a methodical approach should be adopted based on the information available.

The investigator should be familiar with the needs and policies of the laboratory to which the evidence will be sent. Taping with high-tack tape may result in considerable difficulty in removing the evidence for examination, often resulting in broken hairs and/or fibers. Removal of evidence from the tape may require the use of chemicals to dissolve the adhesive. For this reason many laboratories prefer not to deal with adhesive lifts. Again, call the laboratory and talk with its staff.

Combing/Brushing

Violent contact between two individuals frequently results in a transfer of hairs and/or fibers. Such evidence, loosely adhering to the clothing of an individual, can be recovered under controlled conditions and used effectively for comparisons with known samples. In the case of sexual contact, specific areas of interest are the heads and pubic regions of the individuals involved. Recovering hairs and fibers from these areas often involves the combing or brushing of the body area over paper spread out to collect what is dislodged. The procedure need not be restricted to the head and pubic areas, and available information about the crime may dictate other body areas as well. It is also important that new combs be used on each body area and that samples taken from different body areas be packaged separately. Simple logic dictates that the combings or brushings be collected before known hair samples are taken from an individual.

Collection of hairs and fibers by combing or brushing is usually accomplished with a brush or fine-toothed comb, with the individual standing or bending so that the body area to be sampled is over a large piece of paper or material spread out for this purpose. In some cases, such as with an individual with especially long hair, it may be advantageous to have the person lie on the paper while samples are collected. The body area of interest is carefully combed or brushed to cause evidence to fall onto the paper. The paper is then carefully folded to retain the collected material and securely packaged with the comb or brush. This procedure is usually the method of choice in sexual assault evidence kits.

Occasionally, an advantage can be gained by pushing the teeth of a comb through a layer of cotton batting, making the cotton a collecting medium for the hairs or fibers. The white cotton collects and provides a good visual background for the material collected. This may be a useful alternative if collection paper is not available; but it can present problems since, during transit to a laboratory, the hairs and fibers collected may become worked into the cotton, making them difficult if not impossible to retrieve.

Fingernail Scrapings and Clippings

Fingernails can collect a variety of materials that can be useful as evidence. Many sexual assault evidence collection kits contain materials to collect fingernail scrapings and clippings. It is essential that the person taking these samples understands that contaminated hands or tools may influence DNA analysis results. It is therefore important to use clean equipment and fresh gloves to collect such samples. New materials should be used to collect the material from each hand, which should be packaged separately. It is also important to use care in collecting scrapings, as a careless move could be painful to the person providing the sample. As with combings, materials to collect these samples are normally supplied in sexual assault evidence collection kits.

Lasers and Alternate Light Sources (ALS)

The use of laser technology in forensic science has expanded rapidly over the last ten years — so much so that often the terms *laser* and *alternate light source* are thought to be synonymous. A detailed discussion of laser technology is beyond the scope of this writing; but the use of lasers and ALSs is increasing all the time, and it is important to distinguish between the two types of instruments.

Both lasers and ALS units detect body fluid stains, fibers, cosmetics, and various materials that contain chemical substances capable of fluorescence. Both lasers and ALS units can be useful in locating fingerprints when fluorescent fingerprint powder is used. In a recent nationally publicized kidnapping/child molestation/murder case, an ALS located the suspect's palm print on the bed frame of the victim in her home. The suspect had already become of interest to investigators; and, when confronted with the results of the palm print comparison with his own, he revealed the location of the victim's body, which had been the subject of searches for weeks.

A laser is a sophisticated instrument, from the apparently simple laser pointer used in classroom instruction to the high-energy industrial laser requiring water cooling equipment and special environmental housing. Forensic lasers produce an extremely high-energy beam of light that is specifically defined and capable of causing fluorescence in certain materials. The fluorescent effect is usually viewed through filtered goggles or lenses. A single instrument normally produces only one wavelength of light, and its intensity is capable of causing eye damage if the operator's eyes are not protected. Such instruments are usually quite expensive and often require accessory equipment (cooling system, etc.). This makes it difficult to take the instrument to a crime scene. As a result, most lasers are confined to laboratory use. Smaller units are available for scene use, but the expense is difficult to justify for many agencies.

An ALS, on the other hand, is a more portable instrument and is designed to be taken to the scene. They are far more economically feasible for most agencies, and many agencies have more than one. The Federal Bureau of Investigation has equipped each of its field office evidence response teams with ALSs. While the principle of operation is much the same as the laser, the ALS is a high-intensity white light source that has multiple filters, providing the investigator with several wavelengths of visible light for examining the scene. Any resulting fluorescence is viewed with filtered glasses or goggles; but the light, while high intensity, does not have the energy of the laser and does not pose the same potential danger to the eyes. Caution: any light source is potentially dangerous to the eyes, especially if one looks directly into the beam. Good sense should be a guide.

Most of the wavelengths in an ALS are in the visible range of the spectrum; however, a number of companies can build a UV source into the ALS if requested. The use of UV built into an ALS is little different from using the hand-held UV light discussed above, and the same precautions for eye protection apply. Whether the investigator has a laser or an ALS to work with, or even the hand-held UV light, it should be remembered that these devices are tools, not instruments that will solve all the problems of finding evidence at crime scenes.

Blood

Depending on the facts of any given case, blood can become a major evidence substance in sexual assault investigation. The conventional analysis of blood yields results which are class characteristic evidence. Results obtained with modern DNA analysis methods can be considered individual characteristic evidence. In the past, when DNA data bases worldwide were in their infancy, a DNA expert could only testify that DNA analysis either eliminated a subject or was consistent with a subject. More recently, if statistical criteria are met, a DNA expert can testify to a scientific certainty that blood, semen, or saliva came from a specific person. Different judicial jurisdictions may have various restrictions. Some crime laboratories conduct conventional blood groupings and do not have the capability for DNA analysis. The conventional analysis of blood by the forensic serologist is discussed briefly, followed by a detailed discussion of DNA analysis.

Conventional Forensic Analysis

Forensic laboratories must initially establish that an unknown substance is definitely blood and must differentiate between animal and human blood. The family of animal can often be identified when animal blood is encountered. Human blood can be further characterized by many genetically controlled grouping systems. This capability is based on the forensic identification of many complex chemical substances that exist in the cells and serum of blood. These substances include the well-known ABO blood group system as well as various protein and enzyme marker systems, divided into a limited number of types within each system. For example, in one enzyme system called esterase D (EsD), the population can be divided into six categories, and each member of the population will fall into one of these categories. Markers such as phosphoglucomutase (PGM), erythrocyte acid phosphatase (EAP), haptoglobin (Hp) and others exhibit similar distributions throughout the population and supplement the ABO system of blood grouping in the arsenal of forensic laboratory tools. Known blood samples can be compared with questioned blood based on these markers.

DNA Analysis

For more than two decades, the ability to resolve and detect polymorphic markers has made possible the genetic characterization of body fluid stains for forensic scientists. Although the polymorphic protein and enzyme markers used by many laboratories provide the potential for a high degree of discrimination among different individuals, this upper limit is rarely attained because of the instability of some of these markers in dried stains. Moreover, of the markers that retain their structure and activity in the dried state, the number of expressed or observed forms is limited. Thus, in practice, the individualization of many evidentiary stains cannot be carried out to any great extent given the present array of polymorphic markers used in conventional forensic serology.

In all life forms, from viruses to humans, the basis for variation lies in the genetic material called deoxyribonucleic acid or DNA. Every living organism, with the exception of some viruses that possess ribonucleic acid (RNA), has this chemical as its genetic blueprint. In every cell of a person, the DNA blueprint is identical — whether it is a white blood cell, a skin cell, a spermatozoon, or a hair root cell. This extremely complex chemical is made of five simple chemical elements: carbon, hydrogen, oxygen, nitrogen, and phosphorus. The five elements then combine to form sugar, phosphate, and nitrogenous base molecules to constitute what is called a nucleotide. The language of DNA consists of an alphabet comprised of only four letters. These letters stand for the four nitrogenous bases found in the nucleotide and thus in DNA: thymine, cytosine, adenine, and guanine (abbreviated T, C, A, and G). Even though this alphabet is very short, an enormous array of different sequences of nucleotides can exist in a single strand of DNA, which is normally hundreds of thousands to millions of nucleotides long. The chromosomes found in one human cell are composed of six billion nucleotides. For example, if we consider only ten positions in the chain, each of which could be occupied by any one of the four nucleotides, the number of possible combinations would be 1,048,576. Hundreds of thousands of nucleotides are linked together in a long chain of DNA in a specific sequence of the nitrogenous bases, which then combines with protein to become a chromosome.

Humans have 23 pairs of these chromosomes. One chromosome of each pair originates from an individual's mother and the other from the father. Because the many genes found on the chromosomes for each trait in humans are a combination of the maternal and paternal genetic material, variation is generated in the offspring. No two people, except for identical twins, even though born to the same parents, will be exactly alike. Two brothers, though they may be similar, are not physically or genetically identical; their DNA is different.

DNA is actually made up of two strands forming a double helix (similar to a spiral staircase in structure). The bases (A, G, T and C) pair with each other in a specific way; A always pairs with T and G always pairs with C on opposite strands of the helix. This is called complementary base pairing. Thus, if the sequence of one strand is known, then the sequence of the other strand can be determined. This is a fundamental principle behind all DNA testing.

When evidence bearing DNA source material such as blood or seminal stains is received in the laboratory, the process of DNA typing begins. There are several methods for performing DNA analysis, but the two most common are designated *restriction fragment length polymorphism* (RFLP) and *polymerase chain reaction* (PCR).

Restriction Fragment Length Polymorphisms (RFLP).   The intact DNA is chemically extracted from the sample, and then enzymes (restriction endonucleases) are added which act like molecular scissors to cut the DNA into fragments. The double-stranded DNA is then chemically divided so that single strands are now found. These DNA fragments are placed in a sieving gel and separated by size in a process known as electrophoresis. The separated DNA fragments are blotted from the gel onto a nylon membrane in a process called Southern Blotting.

At this point DNA probes are prepared and applied to the DNA on the membranes. These probes are single-stranded pieces of DNA which can bind via complementary base pairing with the target DNA. A single locus probe looks for only one area of the DNA molecule, whereas a multilocus probe looks for several areas at once. Before the probes are applied to the DNA, they are made radioactive by using an isotope of phosphorus. The radioactive DNA probe then combines with the specific DNA sequences found on the fragments in the membrane. Subsequently, X-ray film is placed in contact with the membrane to detect the radioactive probe pattern. This image, which may develop in several hours to several days, resembles the optically read bar codes seen on products in supermarkets. These images are visually evaluated by an examiner, who then uses computer-assisted image analysis to size them, which means to measure their length. The evidence stains are then compared to the known samples, and a determination of either a match or a no-match is made. The suspect is then either absolutely excluded as the stain donor, or a match is made. When a match is made, the frequency of the profile is determined by consulting the human data bases; and the probability of finding the same match at random is then calculated. Depending on how rare or common the DNA fragments are, the probability of a random match can range from very high, such as 1 in 10, to extremely low, such as 1 in 10 billion.

Recent developments in DNA technology have led to the use of the chemiluminescent probes as an alternative to the radioactively labeled probes. These probes rely on a chemical reaction that produces light (derived from the chemical reaction that fireflies use) and expose the X-ray film in a much shorter time than the radioactive probes. The films are then examined and analyzed in the same manner as above.

DNA typing procedures are especially useful in sexual assault cases. Conventional analysis cannot differentiate origins of similar blood group substances found in mixed seminal/vaginal secretion stains. Therefore, if the rapist and the victim have the same blood type, the scientist cannot determine from whom the blood group substance was derived. DNA analysis eliminates this problem. The technology can separate the DNA from the victim's vaginal tract and the semen from the rapist. Because semen normally contains a large number of spermatozoa, there is a correspondingly large quantity of DNA available for typing. Seminal fluid does not contain DNA; however, in seminal stains lacking spermatozoa, it may still be possible to obtain a DNA type from epithelial tissue or white blood cells present in the stain. For example, a rapist who has had a vasectomy is not likely to deposit spermatozoa but might deposit his epithelial cells in his semen.

Like seminal fluid, saliva does not contain DNA; but, again, there may be epithelial tissue or white blood cells present which can be typed for DNA. Even though a bloodstain may appear to be large enough for RFLP analysis, it should be kept in mind that red blood cells do not contain DNA. The DNA from bloodstains is contained in the white blood cells, which are much fewer in number than the red cells. Urine and perspiration do not normally contain DNA — but again, they may occasionally contain cellular material that can be used.

Polymerase Chain Reaction (PCR).   PCR technology is now being used in many laboratories in conjunction with, or as an alternative to, RFLP. This technology is capable of using minute amounts of DNA that are too small for RFLP analysis and chemically amplifying the DNA sequences until enough is obtained for analysis. This technology is particularly useful for DNA typing of saliva stains, small amounts of tissue, and the root cells from hairs. As previously mentioned, saliva does not contain DNA but does contain epithelial tissue and may contain white blood cells. An example where this technology is particularly useful is the DNA typing of saliva stains left on stamps, envelopes, cigarette butts, and chewing gum. In one case in the FBI laboratory, PCR technology was used to determine a DNA profile from the sweatband of a hat dropped at the scene of a homicide. Perspiration does not contain DNA, but the skin cells from the suspect had sloughed off onto the sweatband and provided the needed DNA. PCR technology is also very useful when body fluid samples are degraded.

Newer Technologies.   Another DNA technology currently being researched is the literal nucleotide sequencing of the DNA to produce a map. Recent news media reports indicate that great strides have been made in identifying the human genetic code. It will be recalled that the variability of sequence in the DNA molecule is what distinguishes each individual from another.

Certain laboratories, forensic and otherwise, are currently conducting analyses of another kind of DNA found in hairs (and other structures such as bone and teeth) called mitochondrial DNA. Mitochondria are small organelles found in cells that contain their own non-nuclear DNA. Most of the DNA subjected to forensic analysis originates in the nucleus of the body's cells. Mitochondrial DNA is found in the cells but outside the nucleus as well as in structures such as telogen hairs, bones, and teeth. Advantages associated with mitochondrial DNA include the fact that it exists in many more copies than nuclear DNA, it is highly variable from person to person, and is maternally inherited. This technology offers a chance for the forensic scientist to obtain a DNA profile from hairs that have been cut or broken off and are devoid of root sheath cells (pulled hairs). It is also used to assist in the identification of skeletal remains.

It is important to understand that, being maternally inherited, mitochondrial DNA is the same throughout a maternal line and therefore does not, at least at this time, provide the ability to identify a hair as having come from a single individual to the exclusion of all others.

Recovery of Blood Evidence

The collection of body fluids for DNA analysis is essentially the same as for conventional analysis, with a few exceptions that will be addressed later in this chapter.

Two main dilemmas face forensic laboratories in dealing with blood and other body fluid evidence (such as semen and saliva) when dealing with sexual assault cases:

1.   Blood is often mixed with contaminants and other body fluids, making forensic interpretations difficult and limited. In sexual assault cases,

serologists often observe test results indicating that, in fact, genetic markers apparently have been contributed by both victim and suspect. The forensic interpretation of this mixture can be confusing, especially when the laboratory results appear to be inconsistent with the facts of the crime. It is essential that any recent sexual activity of the victim be noted by the investigator and made known to the crime laboratory. Body fluids on clothing items (especially undergarments) can be trans-ferred and mixed with other body fluids. Therefore, it is important not only to know the date of the victim's last sexual contact but also to know whether the clothes worn after that contact were the same clothes worn after the sexual assault. Investigators often neglect to obtain this type of information, thus possibly hampering the laboratory.

2. Most blood evidence received by a laboratory is dried and may have been dried for extended periods of time. While it is true that drying a bloodstain arrests most of the degradative processes that normally take place, the breakdown does not stop; and aged, dry bloodstains continue to lose biochemical integrity with time. It should be evident, then, that more potentially probative data can be obtained from fresh dried blood than from dried blood aged for long periods. Timely submission to a laboratory is important.

The recovery of questioned blood evidence usually involves dealing with various sizes and conditions of stains. Additionally, these stains are found on items of different colors, textures, and composition. The person collecting the stains has to use good judgment in establishing the most appropriate manner in which to recover the evidence. Collection of questioned wet and dry blood samples is usually done by (1) recovering the entire item bearing the blood, or (2) separate removal of all or a portion of the blood exhibited on an object. A cardinal rule, however, is that body fluid stains, wet or dry, can be rapidly and severely degraded by conditions of high heat, humidity, and direct sunlight. Sunlight includes UV light, which degrades DNA. The less time the evidence is subjected to these influences, the better.

Wet Blood.   Wet blood samples should be recovered and immediately trans-ported to a crime laboratory or frozen under uncontaminated conditions for a short time before being taken to the laboratory. The only alternative to this is to take wet samples and dry them at the scene, which can be done if a protected location not subject to contamination can be established. It is usually difficult to collect bulky evidence in the field (clothing, bedding, carpet, tile, drywall) that bears wet blood. The personnel involved in field recovery of wet blood should determine whether the crime laboratory to which evidence will be sent can accommodate wet evidence. Some forensic laboratories require blood specimens in an air-dried condition because of the problems of properly storing massive amounts of damp evidence. Wet blood samples can also be hazardous to crime scene personnel since they are more likely to transmit contagious diseases, such as hepatitis B or AIDS.

A device that is beginning to see more use in police department evidence rooms is a drying hood or any facility dedicated to drying wet evidence. This equipment is available commercially or can be constructed with some ingenuity by departmental personnel. One department devised several effective drying compartments from portable shower stalls.

Eye droppers and syringes are convenient tools for removing wet blood, but the sample must be frozen or shipped to the laboratory immediately. It is almost impossible to air-dry blood in such devices, and separate eye droppers or syringes must be used for each sample collection in order to prevent cross-contamination. Because of these and other difficulties, it is best to avoid collecting wet blood in eye droppers, syringes, or similar articles unless it is to be dried on clean cloth soon after collection.

Another technique is the use of swabs, cotton cloth, cotton threads, or filter paper to absorb the wet stain. As much blood as possible should be concentrated on the gathering medium so that a dense stain results. Simply obtaining smears or small deposits of blood may not provide sufficient blood for forensic testing. Many times most of the blood is left on the source object, and the absorbent material permits only a limited blood examination, or possibly one of no evidentiary value. Most absorbent methods often collect surface dirt and other extraneous debris in addition to the blood.

When absorbent cloth can be used to collect blood or any other body fluid, residues of detergent and chemical additives (optical whiteners) should be rinsed from the cloth before it is used. These materials can detrimentally affect serological testing of biological fluids. Some laboratories boil a new bed sheet (already washed several times) for several hours before drying and cutting it into appropriate sizes to use for collection of stains. Individual threads removed from this cloth can be used when small stains must be absorbed. The thread can be gently maneuvered to concentrate the blood in a dense manner.

In summary, wet blood evidence imposes numerous disadvantages on the field investigator. Because of significant time span and evidence storage problems, it is recommended that wet bloodstains be collected, air-dried, and forwarded to the laboratory as soon as possible, or frozen until submitted. Drying allows the fixing of stains in a specific location, reduces the opportunity for intragarment and intergarment transfer, and reduces decay and disease possibilities.

Dried Bloodstains.   Dried bloodstains are often encountered as physical evidence in sexual assault investigations. Under most circumstances, it is advisable to submit the entire item that bears the stain for forensic analysis. Like wet blood, blood in the dried state should be protected from heat, moisture, direct sunlight, and possible contaminants. Airtight containers are not recommended because they tend to retain moisture.

Dried blood samples can be removed from articles when it is impractical to submit the entire article to the laboratory or when the stained area is large. Methods most frequently used for removing such blood are:

1. Removing the desired sample (stain) completely intact
2. Scraping the stain from the surface
3. Reconstituting the stain

Removing the desired sample (stain) completely intact is the best alternative. Cutting out the stained area with an appropriate tool is in many ways easier than undertaking other methods, especially when articles are large. Removing stains on various items such as concrete, drywall, and wood can require saws or similar tools, which produce dust and other particulate matter that can contaminate the blood evidence. In such cases, the stained area should be protected with paper, sections of plastic, or other suitable items before removal.

Scraping dried blood from an object often results in small dust-like particles and can lead to the loss of the sample. The blood becomes separated to a great extent, making it difficult for the laboratory to evaluate. Static electricity in the packaging materials can disperse a powder quite easily. Furthermore, many possible contaminant substances on the surface from which the blood is scraped can be mixed with the stain. When it is absolutely necessary to use the scraping technique, the stain should be disturbed to the least possible extent. It is suggested that a clean razor blade be used and submitted to the laboratory as a control specimen accompanying but protected from the removed stain.

The method of applying absorbent materials (swabs, cotton cloths, etc.) to a dried bloodstain typically will not remove any appreciable amount of sample. Therefore, it becomes necessary to reconstitute the dried stain so that it can be absorbed by the material of the swab. A common medium used to perform this task is distilled water. The absorbent material (swab) is wetted slightly in this liquid and applied to the questioned stain area. The questioned stain is then concentrated on the material to the greatest extent possible. Probably the most important drawback to this procedure is the dilution of the sample, which will almost always result in loss of probative genetic information. Further, a reconstituted bloodstain that is not analyzed or dried promptly is fertile ground for bacterial growth, which can degrade the sample. As with the scraping technique, surface contaminants are obtained and intermingled with the blood. The reconstitution of bloodstains is best avoided and used as a last resort.

There will be instances, however, when it is impractical to remove dried blood without using the reconstitution method. For example, in cases of sexual assault involving vaginal bleeding of the victim, it may be appropriate to swab the penis of the suspect for blood or other evidence. As indicated in the last chapter, sexual assault evidence kits often contain materials for this sort of evidence collection. Dried blood can be sampled by using a swab moistened slightly with distilled water. Circumstances will probably seldom allow penile sampling; however, the swabbing procedure should avoid the penile opening, unless blood is obviously present there. It is not recommended that penile swabbing be used routinely; instead, it should be limited to those instances in which blood is very likely to be present.

A major disadvantage of both the scraping and absorbent-material methods of recovery is the difficulty of dealing with the porous media. Blood deposited on such articles as concrete, unfinished wood, cardboard, and drywall can be absorbed; and much of the stain can collect below the surface. Scraping a porous object normally will remove only surface-level substances. Swabs, cotton cloth, etc., moistened with distilled water, can cause the stain, when reconstituted, to be further absorbed into the porous object. In such cases, it is best to simply cut out a piece of the surface bearing the stains and send the stains intact to the laboratory.

Control Samples.   The subject of control samples is relevant to any situation in which blood is removed from an article. Blood is chemically complex, as are the forensic tests used to characterize it. Many substances common to everyday life (detergents, deodorants, fruit juices, plant materials) are capable of interfering with certain blood examination tests. It is a great advantage for the laboratory to know whether such substances are present in the area where a bloodstain has been deposited. Whenever a stain is recovered from an object or area that will not be sent intact to the laboratory, an unstained control sample taken adjacent to the questioned stain should be obtained. A prime example would be the removal of a stain from a wall-to-wall carpet. If the stain is approximately the size of a quarter, it would be satisfactory to cut out a four-inch square section of carpet bearing the stain. The unstained area surrounding the suspected blood could be tested by the laboratory to determine whether substances that could hinder examination are present. Also, in instances where swabs, cotton cloth, or filter paper are applied to the collection of bloodstains, control samples of these gathering agents from the same source as those used for actual collection should be retained and submitted to the crime laboratory.

One of the problems in the effective recovery of blood evidence is deciding how much blood should be removed when a large amount is present. While bloodstains that appear to be probative in the investigation should be secured as evidence, it may be impractical to remove all the blood that is present. Violent physical contact may result in bleeding by both suspect and victim at the scene. Bloodstains in the crime scene, then, may have come from the victim, the suspect, or it may be a mixture of blood from both persons. It is not possible to distinguish between different blood types simply by looking at stained areas. However, it is possible to see that blood has been deposited at several different points. Each area where the stains appear to be separated should be sampled.

Bloodstains indicating the apparent path a blood source has taken through the scene or identifying the location from which blood came can provide valuable information in reconstructing a crime. In some instances, a determination can be made as to the position of the person who was bleeding. This determination can assist in identifying possible areas from which samples are to be taken. However, the interpretation of bloodstain patterns involves a detailed examination of the configuration of individual stains and stained areas, at the very least. Care should be taken not to disturb the stains by sampling until documentation and analysis appropriate for this interpretation have been completed.

Representative Samples.   The application of good judgment based on training and experience is almost always the final determinant regarding the successful collection of questioned blood samples. Still, one must avoid the tendency to take random samples without any attention to the amount of blood present or indications that the blood deposits are from more than one person. Often the patterns present at the scene can indicate the samples to be taken in a representative approach. It is important to note that the terminology in forensic science for properly recovering these specimens is *representative* as opposed to *random*.

Representative sampling involves collection of the blood evidence that is deemed to be probative based on the facts and circumstances of the case. Samples are taken by evaluating the size and location of stains in conjunction with the information provided by witnesses, the victim, and others. The location of a stain may be of more significance than its size; and based on comments above, the amount of blood to be taken per sample and how many samples should be recovered must be carefully considered.

By contrast, random sampling involves the recovery of blood evidence in a disorganized fashion. Here, there is no attempt to evaluate the relevant sampling areas before collection is accomplished; blood samples are taken in a more or less shotgun approach, and no logic is applied to evaluate the scene and what is there to tell the investigator.

Chemical Presumptive Tests.   Forensic laboratories have long made use of so-called preliminary tests for the presence of blood. These chemical tests react with the hemoglobin present in the blood of animals and humans and are used to determine whether a stain could be blood. Various substances, such as certain plant materials, have the potential of causing false positive reactions to these tests. Therefore, while these procedures do not establish that blood is unequivocally present, they do strongly indicate its presence. In the crime laboratory environment, preliminary (also sometimes referred to as screening or presumptive) blood tests are conducted under controlled conditions and are supplemented with a variety of other procedures to identify a stain as containing blood and to characterize it further.

There has been a marked increase in interest in the use of preliminary tests for blood at the field investigative level, primarily due to circumstances in which it would be advantageous to distinguish blood from other substances. Dried blood exposed to numerous environmental conditions can take on a variety of shapes and colors and be difficult to recognize. Similarly, minute spots of blood and diluted blood may escape detection if an individual collects only what looks like blood to the unaided eye.

There are a number of commercially available test kits that claim to be ultimate solutions to these problems. One that is becoming more frequently used is Hemastix™ (Miles Inc., Diagnostics Division, Elkhart, IN). Hemastix is designed for use as a blood detection device in urinalysis and consists of a plastic strip with a filter paper pad at the end. Sampling the stain with a moistened swab and touching it to the filter paper tab will produce a color change if blood is present. The test is simple and relatively economical. A second alternative that some prefer is to use chemical testing agents prepared by the crime laboratory for field analysis. This procedure better ensures the quality and reliability of results, since the test materials will more likely be freshly prepared. Some commercial kits can remain for extended periods of time either on supplier's shelves or shelves in the crime scene equipment room. It is incumbent on the investigator who is not a serologist to seek training and guidance in effective use of these tests from experienced personnel in a crime laboratory.

Like any other procedure, preliminary blood tests are to be used with care. The investigator should understand that the protocols used with these tests were developed based on sound scientific principles, and there are reasons for doing things as the instructions indicate. The following points are important:

1. It is possible to destroy or contaminate minute samples by overzealous and untrained conduct of a test.
2. When the suspected blood can be seen by the investigator, generally it should not be tested in the field. Instead, it should be protected and submitted to the laboratory for analysis.
3. In instances when the blood cannot be seen but is believed to be present, field testing is appropriate. This situation is common when an area that once contained blood has been washed or cleaned. However, if the investigator cannot visually observe the suspected blood, it may be that the laboratory can do a great deal with the evidence from a forensic standpoint.
4. Chemical components of the preliminary tests are subject to deterioration as a result of storage time and conditions. When deterioration has occurred, the tests are not reliable even when blood is present. Quality control of test materials must be maintained and may be a subject of testimony in court.
5. Many tests are suited for application in small areas at a time, making it time-consuming, expensive, and difficult to cover large areas or surfaces.
6. The tests can differ in their susceptibility to false positive reactions. Again, the investigator must consult a knowledgeable serologist as to the potential for these reactions.

Chemical Agents.   Chemical agents of various types are used for preliminary blood analysis. Some of those encountered are:

1. Ortho-tolidine
2. Phenolphthalein
3. Tetramethylbenzidine
4. Leuco malachite green
5. Benzidine
6. Luminol

The ortho-tolidine, phenolphthalein, and other tests (except Luminol) work fundamentally in the same manner. A portion of the suspected stain is swabbed and treated with the test chemical, and the result in the swab is visually examined for the appearance of a color reaction. The color (bluish-green for ortho-tolidine and reddish-pink for phenolphthalein) is indicative of the probable existence of blood in the location swabbed.

Luminol is a chemical test that operates somewhat differently. When Luminol comes into contact with blood in the proper chemical environment, it has the capacity to exhibit chemiluminescence. This means a positive result causes the stain to emit visible light that can be seen with the naked eye (no goggles or filters needed) in a darkened setting. The user then recovers the stained areas that respond for examination in the forensic laboratory. Luminol testing usually involves spraying of large areas suspected of containing blood. It is not recommended, however, that the entire crime scene be completely sprayed as a routine procedure. Because of the potentially destructive effect on substances in blood that are characterized during serological examination, the application of Luminol to suspected blood evidence normally is undertaken with caution. Using too much spray volume will dilute and diffuse the stains, making additional examination more difficult and photography of the chemiluminescence difficult if not impossible. It has been shown, however, that DNA is not affected by the application of Luminol. Usually this method is used when bloodstains are so washed out (previously cleaned up with a mop, for example) as to be nearly impossible to see with the naked eye. Luminol can also be used in identifying a specific unknown crime scene when there are a number of possible scenes in question.

Personnel applying the tests should know that some of the agents contain harmful chemical substances. Benzidine, which was once used widely (but is now seldom used), is now known to be carcinogenic. A number of chemicals that are related to benzidine are suspect. Luminol should be used in a well-ventilated area and not sprayed indiscriminately. This fact reinforces the point that the choice of a preliminary test should be made on an educated basis.

When used properly, preliminary blood tests can be effective, especially in locating blood that might otherwise go undetected. As with the other methods, tools, and techniques discussed thus far, however, preliminary tests should not be viewed as shortcuts to substitute for proven evidence collection procedures. These tests can become misused tools for those persons who are not willing to spend the time and energy required to conduct a quality search in a methodical manner.

Chemical Enhancement of Blood Evidence.   Extreme care should be used when trying to develop fingerprints in blood. Protein-based stains (coomassie blue, amido black, etc.), while enhancing the visibility of these prints, can destroy the blood proteins and make further blood testing impossible. In one case, a door from a murder scene was examined in the laboratory by one of the authors. Bloodstains on the door had fingerprints visible in the victim's blood. To enhance the prints, amido black was applied by crime scene investigators, making the ridge detail more visible and allowing the prints to be identified as the suspect's. As an afterthought, it was decided that a serologist should be present to testify to the presence of the suspect's fingerprint in the blood. Subsequent attempts to identify the amido black-treated bloodstains even as blood were unsuccessful, depriving the investigation of a useful bit of information and testimony.

One final point of concern dealing with blood evidence regards the handling or touching of stains, or even unstained areas, with bare hands. The sensitivity of many of the new technologies for DNA analysis makes it possible for evidence to be contaminated inadvertently with biological residue from the bare hands of an individual. In addition, one should be concerned about contracting infectious disease. The use of surgical-type gloves provides protection for both the evidence and the individual. Some prefer the practice of double gloving. Double gloving has its advantages, since a single glove layer can conform so tightly to the skin that dermal ridge detail may be left on a surface handled by the investigator. Two glove layers prevents this. Transfer of a print in this manner is rare, but it has happened.

Bloodstain Pattern Evidence.   The study of bloodstain patterns to determine the nature of the activities that took place at the scene during the crime has been of interest to forensic scientists since before 1900. Observations of the size, shape, and distribution of stains and stain patterns can often provide information that will either be useful in interviewing a suspect or result in a nearly complete reconstruction of the events that took place to create the patterns. The best approach in dealing with this type of evidence is to have an analyst visit and study the original scene. Prior to such a visit, it is to the advantage of all concerned to assemble as much of the bloodstain pattern evidence material as possible for the analyst to review.

The scope of this writing does not allow a detailed discussion of proper documentation of the bloodstain pattern crime scene. Such documentation — photographically, graphically, and narratively — can be and often is decidedly different from that of routine crime scene documentation and thus should fall to an individual with some training in the interpretation of bloodstain patterns. If such an individual is not available, this becomes one of those situations where "more is probably better," and lots of photography and notes with good sketches will be helpful.

Semen

The type of physical evidence most frequently associated with sexual assault investigations is semen. The presence of this male reproductive fluid confirms the occurrence of sexual activity and can assist in corroborating the victim's contention of rape. Semen, like blood, can be used for DNA analysis; and again, depending on the degree to which the DNA can be analyzed, an expert can testify to a scientific certainty that the semen came from a single individual. If the data are not sufficient, then semen becomes class characteristic evidence.

Conventional Semen Serology

The time-honored means of semen identification is the observation of sper-matazoa or sperm cells. When the victim is examined in the hospital environment, microscopic inspection of slides prepared from vaginal, oral, and anal swabs is normally a part of the protocol. Depending on the time elapsed since the violation, sperm cells may be motile (free moving) or dead. Such an examination is done by medical personnel at the emergency room during the execution of the sexual assault evidence kit. The presence of motile sperm cells provides evidence of recent sexual activity. Material from evidence sent to the forensic laboratory may also be examined for sperm cells, but it is unlikely that any observed will be motile. The most significant point here is that sperm cells will not, in most circumstances, remain motile in the vaginal tract for more than 72 hours. When time is an important element of the investigation, the observation of motile sperm cells is of value. Factors that affect this survival include drainage, the chemical environment in the vaginal canal, and cleaning efforts undertaken by the victim.

With the development of newer methods for use in the forensic laboratory, the labor-intensive identification of semen by sperm cell observation has given way to the identification of a protein normally present in high concentrations in semen known as prostate-specific antigen, or p30. The presence of p30 in significant levels is sufficient grounds to conclusively establish the presence of semen in a stain. Besides offering a time advantage, aspermic semen will still have p30; and its presence will not fail to be identified due to a lack of sperm cells. The technology in use for p30 identification is extremely sensitive and highly reliable.

Once semen has been identified, it can be analyzed to characterize chemical substances that will indicate the ABO blood type of the donor. Approximately 80% of the population exhibits detectable amounts of the chemical substances which define their ABO blood group in body fluids other than blood. These people are referred to as secretors. The usefulness of this is simply that semen in the crotch of a pair of panties from a group A victim containing group B blood group substances is valuable evidence, especially when the suspect is determined to be a group B secretor. If both individuals are group A secretors, however, then no distinction may be conclusively made through conventional serology. Known blood and saliva samples from an individual are normally required by the forensic laboratory to determine secretor status. Provision is usually made for the collection of these samples in sexual assault evidence kits.

Enzymes or genetic markers that normally exist in blood are also present in semen and exhibit the same genetically determined characteristics. A specific enzyme type identified in an individual's blood is consistent with that identified in the semen; and, as with blood, these enzyme types in semen are independent of the donor's ABO type.

DNA in Semen

DNA is found throughout the body, particularly in cells that have a nucleus. The same is true with semen, and DNA is mainly present in the sperm cell and occasionally epithelial cells that come from the lining of the male reproductive tract. Since vaginally recovered semen contains vaginal material, DNA from epithelial cells from the vaginal lining will probably be present as well. It would not be of value to recount a discussion of DNA and how it is recovered, analyzed, and interpreted; however, it is important to understand where one can expect to find DNA in these investigations and how it might affect the interpretation of analytical results.

Semen Evidence Recovery

Sexual assault evidence recovery kits are designed to target those areas where semen is likely to be after an assault. Consequently, swabs are provided for collection of vaginal contents as well as semen on the external genital area of the victim. The investigator should be aware that a victim, through embarrassment or for some other reason, may not be willing to admit that non-vaginal sexual activity took place. It is not uncommon to locate seminal material on external body surfaces, genital or otherwise, even when no penile penetration of the vagina took place. Accordingly, it is often wise during the execution of a sexual assault evidence kit to complete the collection of all the samples (oral, anal and vaginal) as a matter of routine protocol in spite of what the victim's story indicates. Obviously, such swabs and the microscope slides prepared with them should be packaged separately; and unused control swabs should be provided to the laboratory as well. Microscope slides are normally prepared and used by medical personnel to identify sperm cell motility during the examination of the victim at the hospital. The examination, if possible, should not involve any chemical materials placed on the swabbed slides. As always, body fluid evidence should be dried before packaging (slides, swabs, etc.).

Some sexual assault evidence kits include materials to detect deposits of seminal material in the nasal passages of the victim as a result of oral sexual contact. While not a commonly occurring event, seminal material deposited in the nasal passages after forced oral copulation has been successfully collected. The collection procedure simply involves the victim blowing her nose hard on material provided in the kit. This is certainly less distressing to the victim than other necessary methods of evidence collection. Should this method not be included in the kit available, a piece of clean white cloth (sheeting or the like) measuring approximately 6 inches square will suffice. The cloth, to be handled only by the victim, should be packaged after drying.

Semen deposited in the oral cavity is normally collected by the preferred method of swabbing. Such efforts may not be successful in collecting material lodged between teeth, under the tongue, and in hard-to-reach spots. Rinsing the mouth (with a minimal amount of fluid) in such situations may collect the residual material. The rinse is collected in a container, sealed, and sent to a laboratory as soon as possible. The sample should be frozen if any delay in transport is expected. Such samples are teeming with bacteria that are waiting to feast on the normal constituents of semen. The sooner the sample can be examined, the better the chances of finding some evidence of value. Normal mouth functions such as swallowing and spitting cause a much shorter survival time of semen in the mouth than in the vaginal canal; so oral examinations by medical personnel should be prioritized in an assault examination. It is noted that this type of sample goes against what has been said concerning the drying of body fluid samples prior to packaging, and expeditious handling is essential. As noted above, the preferred method is swabbing.

Sexual Assault Evidence at the Scene

A sexual assault is an event that naturally draws attention to the victim — as it certainly should. This attention takes the form of medical treatment, compassionate assistance, and evidence collection. At the risk of minimizing this important aspect of the investigation, it is suggested that there may be a wealth of evidence at the scene as well. A point was made in the last chapter about allowing one's focus to obscure one aspect or another of the investigation. This kind of focus is not fiction and should be avoided. Evidence in the form of semen, hairs (suspect and victim), blood, and other items frequently identifies the scene and provides direct connections between one or more of the individuals involved. Evidence of sexual activity and/or assault may be present on a wide variety of evidence at the scene, and concentrating efforts on the victim to the exclusion of the scene is often a grave error.

Semen or other stains may be present on carpets, clothing, or various other materials at the scene. As with blood, the preferred approach of taking the entire item, if possible, still stands. Large areas should be considered for vacuuming or other larger-scale methods of trace evidence collection (as previously indicated, sectioning of the area is important). If, during this process, it is anticipated that potentially valuable stained areas may be contaminated or disturbed, cover them with paper and tape or some other suitable protection. With such large items as a carpet, a stain may be cut out, leaving sufficient unstained carpet around the stain perimeter to provide control material. Again, drying is critical before packaging.

Given the methods discussed and the aids available to assist the investigator in collecting sexual assault evidence, inevitably there will be times when semen, like blood, must be collected as a substance from a surface — when the entire item bearing the stain, or a portion of it, cannot be taken. Recovery of dry samples can be accomplished by cutting, chipping, or scraping. Wet samples respond to collection by swabs, sections of cloth, or clean absorbent filter paper. Of concern is the recovery of seminal material from glass or painted surfaces when the item cannot be secured. Carefully scraping the material (all of it) from glass into a small container works. Painted surfaces can be scraped as well, and it may be possible to gouge out a section of the surface bearing the stain and surrounding paint to provide a control. Reconstitution of any dried body fluid should be a procedure of last resort. Difficulties with this have been discussed; and while it may be necessary in some cases, it is best avoided. Still the old rule applies — the less intrusive, the better. Keep the stain as much in its original condition as possible and be sure it is dry before packaging.

Locating Semen at the Scene

Equipment, tools, procedures, and techniques for presumptive identification are available to the investigator, although employed less frequently for semen than for blood. When the precise location of the scene is unknown, some assistance often makes the job of location easier. As with blood, it is possible to become too dependent on such techniques and equipment and to pass up the more thorough and tedious work of detailed crime scene investigation. Proper handling of the scene is not a time for shortcuts. The tools and techniques available to the crime scene investigator are simply aids.

With that caution, a discussion of some of the practical aspects of the use of an ultraviolet light (UV) or alternate light source (ALS) is in order. Neither of these light sources alone will identify semen.

Under the proper conditions, semen can be seen to fluoresce under UV or some of the wavelengths of an ALS. This fluorescence is not restricted to semen stains and can be useful in locating stains that should be taken for subsequent laboratory examination. Seminal fluorescence is not brilliant in many instances; and, with stains on a substrate (background) that has a fluorescent character of its own, a lightly fluorescing stain may even look darker than the material to which it adheres. Such a stain may be overlooked and should not be. With practice it becomes evident that there are numerous items, fabrics, threads, substances, forms of dust and debris, etc., that will fluoresce. Experience is a great teacher when it comes to these kinds of observations.

DNA and UV light.   DNA is sensitive to UV light. A portion of the protocol used in the laboratory analysis of DNA involves the use of UV light to disrupt the DNA structure under controlled conditions. The importance of this to the investigator is that UV can and does disrupt the native structure of DNA — and if stains at a scene are exposed to UV long enough, this disruption may be extensive enough to interfere with the successful analysis of the DNA. UV is useful, to be sure, but its extended use is to be viewed with caution.

As a precautionary note, the fluorescence does not identify semen — it only highlights it for collection and subsequent examination in the laboratory. This is exemplified by a case in which an investigator stated in a crime scene report that semen, in fact, was identified with the aid of the ALS on a particular item. Subsequent examination by the laboratory failed to confirm this observation; in fact, semen was clearly not identified on the item. Because identification of semen was key to the charge filed, the prosecutor was extremely reluctant to accept the report of the laboratory detailing the negative result and wanted to use the information based on the less certain procedure. Only after considerable discussion was the laboratory result accepted.

The discussion thus far has centered primarily on semen evidence recovered as an uncontaminated substance. In realistic terms, there are numerous cases in which semen is mixed with urine, blood, vaginal fluid, saliva, and other materials. Analytical difficulties can arise in the laboratory when a mixture of body fluids from two or more persons is subjected to conventional analysis. Conventional blood groupings and secretor testing, for example, can be dramatically affected. It is to our advantage, however, that newer DNA techniques have successfully separated DNA from semen and other body fluids, making it possible to identify DNA from the semen donor and the victim in a single stain.

Post-Event Alteration of Stains

The investigator should be aware of the ease with which stains on clothing can contaminate other portions of the same item or another item of clothing after collection, thus altering the evidence. Such situations can create conflict between the evidence and information available from individuals directly involved in the assault. In particular, wet stains (blood or semen) can be problematic in this regard. As an example, consider a shirt worn by an assault victim — stained with blood around the neck and shoulders resulting from a beating, and stained with semen around the lower portion of the shirt near the hem. Folding or bunching the garment places the stained areas in contact with unstained or even other stained areas. When the stains are wet, even greater opportunity for transfer exists. New stains or mixtures can be created. The extreme sensitivity of testing procedures used with DNA can mean detection of mixtures even with dry stains abrasively contacting each other. Such transfer of staining has been observed in several cases in the authors' experience, at least one of which was a subject of lengthy national news coverage. Care must be exercised in packaging evidence to prevent this. Layered packing paper or cardboard between layers of fabric often provides the necessary protection to maintain evidence integrity.

Saliva

The goal of conventional forensic analysis of saliva has generally been the determination of secretor status for comparison with results from the analysis of other body fluids such as semen. With the advent of DNA, however, the extreme sensitivity of techniques like PCR have made saliva far more useful. DNA from epithelial cells sloughed off the surfaces of the oral cavity and present in saliva has made the analysis of cigarette butts, stamps, envelopes, and a variety of other items of greater significance to the investigator.

The high concentration of water and low level of dissolved and solid substances make saliva more difficult to see than blood or semen, which have visible and physical characteristics (color, texture, etc.). Saliva can be present but can go unnoticed even on clean white paper. The situation is complicated by the fact that saliva stains are more often found in areas that have a propensity for contamination, such as ash trays. From an investigator's point of view, it is more natural for saliva to be present on surfaces due to actions such as spitting than it is for blood or semen, since these fluids are internal and not likely to be spread around as much. Saliva is not always easy to find; it can often be contaminated, and it is easier to rationalize its existence where it is found.

Saliva Recovery

Techniques used in the recovery of saliva samples at a scene are dictated by the nature of the stain and the nature of the surface on which it is found. Surfaces bearing saliva can be categorized as porous or nonporous.

> *Porous Surfaces:* Stains (wet or dry) on porous surfaces that can be removed along with ample surface area surrounding the stain should be recovered. Obviously, stains on surfaces that can be collected as the entire item should be collected in whole. Wet stains should be allowed to dry before packaging. Cutting out a 4- to 6-inch-square section of sheetrock with a saliva stain in the center is a prime example. The peripheral surface area can provide adequate control material for the sample. Surfaces such as unfinished wood, porcelain, paper, cardboard, and many more fall into this category. These surfaces present unique problems since wet body fluids (saliva more than blood or semen) can be absorbed into the substrate to the point where they are nearly invisible. It is not recommended that stains on such surfaces be collected by absorption onto dry swabs or reconstitution with moist

swabs. The first option divides the stain into two parts, and the second promotes its absorption into the substrate even more.

Nonporous surfaces: On occasion saliva appears on nonporous items such as painted surfaces, plastics, glass, and metal cans. The mouthpiece of an inflatable toy given to a child by her kidnapper contained sufficient saliva for typing in one case. Collection of the entire item and removal of a section of the surface bearing the stain along with ample material surrounding the stain are two preferred methods of collection. Nonporous surfaces bearing saliva stains may be susceptible to abrasive removal of the stain materials by packaging if the stain is not protected. The stain can be protected by pliable materials (cardboard or the like) secured to the item to provide cover for the stain. Contamination through handling with uncovered hands or inadvertent rubbing should be avoided. Remember that saliva is more useful to the investigator now because DNA is easily analyzed today.

The reconstitution approach has been mentioned, and it is no more a preferred method with saliva than with blood or semen. However, there are times when such an approach is necessary. When the item or an appropriate section of the item cannot be secured, collection of the stain may be the method of choice. The same precautions are as important with saliva as with other body fluids. Control swabs should be prepared and packaged separately. Wet saliva on items that cannot be moved or sectioned should be absorbed onto dry swabs along with controls and packaged as above.

Ash Tray Contents

Cigarette butts and other ash tray contents are encountered often enough to make them a specific topic for discussion. Cigarette butts, toothpicks, chewed matches, chewing gum, and any other ash tray contents that may bear saliva have, in the past, been recovered by simply placing all the items in a bag. In some cases, the ash tray has been dumped, ashes and all, in the bag. This is not recommended. Ashes will, in fact, present a hostile chemical environment to the saliva constituents and should be avoided. There are drawbacks to advanced technology and the ability to identify individuals through the traces of body fluids they leave behind — in this case, contamination. Items from an ash tray, excluding the ashes, should be separately packaged.

DNA in saliva is not only obtainable through cigarette butts; paper surfaces offer likely material for retaining fingerprints. Fingerprint development methods and sampling methods for conventional saliva testing have often been incompatible. In the past the investigator often had to choose one type of evidence or the other. Further, the quantity of sample necessary for conventional testing made it difficult to choose sometimes between latent fingerprints and saliva analysis. DNA technology has helped overcome the problem. Smaller samples needed for PCR analysis of DNA and more effective latent fingerprint development methods have improved the situation. If a problem as to which approach should be used arises, consult with the lab. Discussion with the laboratory on these matters is recommended to ensure getting the best information from the available evidence. The investigator should collect as many intact cigarette butts as possible while limiting contamination. Again, if an item is wet, dry it before packaging it in breathable materials.

Bite Marks

A great deal of attention has been given by both crime scene investigators and forensic pathologists to the role and nature of bite mark evidence in sexual assaults. Direct contact between the suspect's mouth and the skin of the victim often results not only in a bite mark but also in the presence of saliva in the immediate region of the mark. The recovery and forensic analysis of this saliva evidence can be of extreme importance, especially in cases where the bite mark alone does not exhibit sufficient clarity of detail for positive identification with the dental configuration of the suspect. While bite marks are likely sources of saliva, saliva may be deposited through licking, sucking, or nibbling such that no bruising or marks are left on the skin. The statements of the victim concerning the actions of the suspect are indicative of locations from which saliva may be recovered.

The first stage of utilizing saliva in bite mark cases is the recognition of the mark and immediate protection of that location from contaminating or destructive activity. Care should be taken to avoid touching the area of interest with the bare hands. After documenting the initial condition and location of the bite mark photographically (with and without a scale), the area should be protected to prevent abrasion or contamination while the person bitten, if deceased, is removed from the scene. When possible, the same applies to an ambulatory individual. The person should be advised to refrain (or prevented) from washing or touching the area, and steps should be taken to protect it with a small cover. As mentioned in the last chapter, liaison between hospital personnel and law enforcement in sexual assault cases is critical, since it is possible that medical personnel may have the first contact with the bitten individual and can protect the saliva from contamination or loss. Medical personnel should be made aware of the need to refrain from washing a bite mark unless it becomes necessary during medical treatment.

Saliva may be recovered from a bite mark by using swabs and/or cotton thread wetted with distilled water. The area adjacent to, but not part of, the bite mark should be sampled separately as a control. Special attention should be given to ensuring that the mark is not altered by the saliva collection procedure. Additionally, sampling from bloody areas of the mark should be avoided. Unstained swabs and/or cotton threads used for evidence collection should be retained as additional control samples.

In some instances of sexual assault, efforts by the suspect to bite the victim (or vice versa) may not necessarily result in a bite mark directly on the skin, due to intervening articles such as clothing, bed sheets, and pillowcases. Biting through a fabric article may result in a mark on the skin and the deposition of saliva on the intervening article. Investigators should be alert to this possibility, as the intervening item will be valuable for its saliva content.

Recovery of Known Evidence

Forensic science is a science of comparisons. Questioned physical evidence only has real meaning when compared with known samples from individuals thought to be involved in the crime. While great strides have been made in training and education in law enforcement in recent years, a lack of known standards required for comparisons continues to plague investigations. This may be due to the system, a lack of attention to detail, or any one of a number of other reasons; but the samples are still required for meaningful laboratory work to be done. Additionally, and importantly, the forensic scientist is hampered by the quality of samples collected. The following procedures are recommended with the intent of providing the best possible samples for laboratory comparison and, ultimately, the best possible results obtainable from the available evidence.

Known Hair Samples

When forensic samples are collected under circumstances controlled by the investigator, it is reasonable to expect the best of samples to be secured. Indeed, the success of the work that follows in the laboratory may depend on the technique of an investigator and thus the quality of these samples. As has been stated, questioned hairs will be compared with known hairs. So it is evident that, for a meaningful comparison to be accomplished, the known and questioned hairs must be from the same body area and should represent the variations in length, color, etc., present in that body area. This means that representative samples are important. Often, the forensic examiner can distinguish hairs as having originated from various areas, which generally are head, pubic, limb, beard or mustache, chest, axillary (under arm), and eye areas.

Head and pubic hair characteristics vary more from one person to another within the same racial group and possess a greater number of identifiable characteristics than hairs from other areas of the body. They are therefore most often of value in sexual assault cases. Hairs from other parts of the body, such as beard hairs, may present pertinent physical evidence; however, the bulk of hair identification deals with the head and pubic regions. This is reflected in the design of sexual assault evidence kits. Head hairs taken from five major areas on the head (top, back, left side, and right side) generally compose a complete sample. With pubic hairs, sample hairs are taken from the entire pubic region.

How Many Hairs?

Obviously one or two hairs enable comparisons to be conducted. There are, however, numerous characteristics exhibited in hair which the forensic examiner evaluates. It follows, then, that more than one or two hairs will be required. In fact, it is generally considered that 25 full-length hairs represent an adequate sample, with the five different areas of the head or the entire pubic area represented in the sample. Of course, if it is indicated by the available information that hair from other body areas is involved, a similar number of hairs from the appropriate area should be secured.

How Should They Be Collected?

While there may be some discomfort involved, the preferred procedure for taking known hairs is by pulling hairs from the area of concern. Removing hairs in this manner ensures that the entire length of each hair is available for examination. It is, possible, however, that pulling hairs from an individual is simply not possible under the circumstances. At such times, hairs should then be cut as close to the skin as possible, preferably at skin level; and the laboratory should be advised of the method of collection. It is not unusual for known hair samples to resemble sweepings from a barber shop floor because the hairs were cut at midshaft or even near the tip end. With a person whose hair has been chemically treated, this practice can result in a limited number of true characteristics represented in the sample. As a result, it is possible that an individual could be falsely excluded as a source for questioned hairs which actually came from him or her.

It may be advisable to supplement the collection process with a combing procedure as one would use to collect questioned hairs. If this seems like overkill, the following should explain. Hair growth involves three stages in humans. Anagen hairs are actively growing, catagen hairs are in a resting phase, and telogen hairs are dormant and ready to be shed by the body. All three stages are exhibited on an individual's head at any one time, and subtle morphological differences in the hair can be observed by a trained microscopist as these hairs progress from one stage to another. Hairs typically transferred between individuals during a sexual assault are telogen hairs, ready for discard by the body. Simply put, a combing procedure coupled with the normal pulling or cutting provides the most complete and best representative sample. Should the pulled/cut sample be consumed or inadequate, the combed sample is then used.

It should be evident from the above that hair comparisons are not as straightfoward as one might think. To provide further perspective to this, add the element of time. Suspect individuals identified soon after the violation probably do not have appreciable changes (the natural growth process or intentional alterations such as dying, bleaching, etc.) that alter their hair. Actions taken by an individual to alter his or her hair such as dying, bleaching, shaving the head, etc., can make it difficult if not impossible to obtain reliable known samples. Thus, it follows that known samples should be collected as soon after the violation as possible.

Elimination Samples

Those familiar with latent fingerprint examinations are aware of the value of elimination prints. Elimination samples of known hairs from individuals who may have contributed hairs to the scene may be useful and necessary. A victim engaging in consensual intimate activity and assaulted by a different person shortly thereafter may still retain hairs from the first encounter — and those might be recovered in questioned samples. The value of elimination known hairs is evident.

Animals

A final subject to be covered is animal hair. The presence of animal hairs on a victim may place that individual in an environment frequented by the animal (the suspect's pet) when the victim has no access to or reason to be around such hairs. Should a dog or cat become the source of known hairs, several points should be considered. Animals normally exhibit two distinct types of hairs — fur hairs and guard hairs. Fur hairs are short and fine and are close to the body. Guard hairs are longer, more coarse, and display most of what we see as the animal's color. Should known samples be necessary, it is important to secure samples representative of color and body area from the animal.

Known Fiber Samples

In most cases, the first known fiber sources considered are from the clothing of the individuals involved. There are obviously many other items composed of fibers which will likely be in the evidence picture, but clothing is often in the forefront. Indeed, the laboratory routinely takes cuttings representative of the fabric and fibers from clothing for known sample purposes. It has been the continuing theme of this chapter to encourage the collection and securing of the entire item bearing trace evidence whenever possible. Accordingly, under normal circumstances it is not recommended that sample swatches be cut from clothing articles; rather, the clothing item should be sent to the laboratory. Transfer of fibers between individuals often means that additional trace evidence (blood, semen, hairs, etc.) is transferred as well. To submit fiber samples by cutting and not submit the clothing is taking the chance that nothing of value is on the clothing. The investigator faced with exceptionally large amounts of clothing or other types of cloth items may wish to discuss the matter with the laboratory.

Many types of fibrous items and sources potentially important to an investigation escape notice by investigators, simply because of focus. The term *evidence environment* was mentioned in the last chapter. It was stated that the evidence environment relates to the particular surroundings and the wide variety of unique characteristics and combinations of evidence that are present. This applies to fiber evidence probably more aptly than any other evidence we consider. The wide variety of fibers that make up an environment can often only be appreciated if one takes time to look over the scene, considering nothing else. Accordingly, a useful approach may be to assign an individual to study the scene and secure samples of all realistic fiber sources.

Fiber Samples to be Taken

Taking fiber samples is more than simply cutting a chunk of fabric or carpet. Representative aspects may have to include fiber color, composition, degree of physical wear, soiling, and any variables that may be unique to the scene. Each fibrous item should be represented as the scene is to be completely sampled. In addition, the following questions should be considered before taking samples:

1. How many fibrous objects are present and what are the colors present?
2. What is the physical condition of these objects?
3. What is the best way to remove the samples?

What this tells us is that a single chair made of a variety of fibers may have to be sampled in several locations to account for color, degree of wear, stains on the fabric, and composition of fibers.

Taking the Samples

Samples taken should be intact pieces or swatches if possible, as opposed to tufts of fibers, so that the laboratory examiner can see the relationship of different fibers to one another and so that individual fibers can be removed by the examiner. Samples should include a sample of each color present in the article and any material to which the fibers adhere, such as the backing of a carpet. A pair of scissors, a scalpel, or any sharp instrument suffices as long as it is clean and does not contaminate the samples.

Known Blood Samples

The importance of taking known samples is further underscored by the fact that forensic science is a comparison science, and knowns are critical to that process. In this regard, blood is no different from hairs, fibers, saliva, or any other material from which a known sample may be taken. While the actual taking of the sample from an individual and its transport to a laboratory may be considered as the complete job, the following information is intended to dispel that notion.

The most logical individuals from whom to take known blood samples are the victim and the suspect. In second place are those who may represent sources of blood or body fluids at the scene or on the evidence but who are not involved in the events of the crime. In sexual assault cases, the most likely are consensual and (most importantly) recent sexual partners of the victim. Children of sexual assault victims who may have had a nosebleed on the bed clothing, or persons who may have left other body fluid evidence on potential evidence items, should be considered as candidates for known blood samples. The same philosophy that instructs us to take elimination fingerprints guides us here.

Equipment and materials for the collection of known blood samples is normally found either in a sexual assault evidence collection kit or supplied at the hospital where the emergency medical treatment is provided. The kits may be supplied by the hospital or the investigative agency. A wide variety of sexual assault evidence kits is available commercially. In some jurisdictions the kits are prepared by the state forensic laboratory to control uniformity and provide a statewide standard format.

Known blood samples for conventional serological analysis should be provided to the laboratory since they come from medical personnel and were not dried by an investigator on cloth or some other material. Unless specifically instructed on the procedure of preparing such a sample by laboratory personnel, this practice is inadvisable. Experience in the past has shown this practice to produce inadequate samples. Whole blood samples, if not sent immediately, should be refrigerated (not frozen) as a temporary storage measure before shipping to the laboratory. Any lengthy storage should be avoided before getting the blood to the laboratory as refrigeration will not preserve blood indefinitely. Refrigeration will preserve the blood and retard bacterial growth, biochemical breakdown, etc., but freezing will break up the cells, making some forms of analysis more difficult.

Typical clinical blood testing today usually involves taking blood by venipuncture and collecting it in test tubes with various colored rubber stoppers. The colors of the stoppers represent a code to medical and forensic personnel which identifies the types of chemical preservatives included by the manufacturer in the tube. The types of preservatives contained in each tube are intended for specific types of analyses in the clinical or forensic laboratory. Generally, the preferred preservatives today for forensic purposes are:

- For conventional serology: either a plain red rubber-topped siliconized tube with no preservative or a tube with a yellow top containing acid citrate-dextrose
- For DNA analysis: a tube with a purple- or lavender-colored top containing ethylenediaminetetraacetic acid (EDTA).

It is common for the laboratory to receive both a tube for conventional analysis and one for DNA analysis in a sexual assault kit, since the manufacturer will not know which is needed. If no tubes are included in the kits used, it is best to include both red- and lavender-topped tubes. As with many other aspects regarding evidence, any questions on preservatives should be directed to the laboratory.

Conventional serology and DNA are not the only uses for blood in the forensic laboratory. Blood samples taken for alcohol or drug analysis require that separate tubes be taken. The alcohol tube contains sodium fluoride (gray top), but the tube for drug analysis does not contain any preservative. Five milliliters (cc) of blood is a minimum desired amount.

Known Saliva Samples

Contrary to blood handling, the collection of saliva is done with the idea that the sample is dried before packaging and shipping. Secretor status examinations may be conducted on saliva, and DNA testing is possible as well. The normal constituents of saliva include a host of bacteria and sufficient nutrients to support them for some time. As a result, remaining wet at room temperature even for a short time allows biochemical degradation of substances to be identified by the laboratory examiner. Body fluid samples need to be separated from heat and humidity.

A simple and effective method of saliva collection involves preparing a stain on paper or cloth (filter paper is preferred). The substrate should be clean — free of detergents, cosmetic additives (such as those found on some tissues), and any chemical treatments. Laboratory filter paper can be relied upon to be clean (preferred), and coffee filters provide an adequate collection medium. Gauze pads can be used but are not preferred. The subject individual's mouth should also be cleaned by rinsing with water several times and allowing time for a normal flow of saliva to resume (30 minutes without eating or smoking). The individual should then expectorate into the center of the paper or cloth, creating a stain one to two inches in diameter, and leaving an unstained area around the periphery of the stain. After partial drying (but when the original stain outline is still visible), the stain should be circled with pencil (pen will run) to establish the stained/unstained boundary. After complete air drying, the paper or cloth can be packaged in a paper envelope.

An alternative procedure of saliva collection, and one used in some sexual assault evidence collection kits, involves the use of swabs. Swabs (3 or 4) are saturated with saliva in the individual's mouth and allowed to dry before packaging. Additional swabs are provided as unstained controls. This method can be executed with cloth patches by placing a swatch of cloth in the individual's mouth (with forceps) and allowing saturation of the cloth. The swatch should be flattened (to hasten drying) on a clean surface and allowed to dry before packaging. A second unstained swatch sample is packaged separately as a control.

Finally, many laboratories have shifted the full emphasis of their body fluid analysis to DNA. If this is the case, the laboratory may not require a saliva sample. Consult with laboratory personnel before collecting saliva samples if there is any question.

Marking of Evidence for Identification

A most important aspect of the introduction of evidence into the courtroom is the ability to demonstrate a complete and well-maintained chain of custody. Forensic science begins when the preliminary survey of the scene begins. A great deal of work follows to document the scene, collect the evidence, package it, and see that it is protected, preserved, and transported to a laboratory. The evidence then must be analyzed; and when it is returned from the laboratory, it must be kept under secure conditions until it can be produced in court. Failure to maintain this process and records may result in inadmissible evidence, thus negating much of the preceding work.

Admission of the evidence in court has several requirements:

1. Authentication by an individual knowledgeable about the evidence and the case: this individual is usually the person who found the evidence or observed its collection.
2. Demonstration of the integrity of the evidence: it must be shown that the evidence has not been altered or destroyed outside the limits necessary for laboratory examination.
3. Demonstration of an unbroken chain of custody: a complete accounting of the location and identity of persons possessing the evidence from the recovery to the appearance in court is required.

Direct and Indirect Marking

One of the means by which this is accomplished is the routinely accepted marking practice for identifying the evidence. Done properly, marking authenticates the evidence and clearly establishes who has handled the evidence from the scene to the laboratory to the courtroom, providing a chain of custody. It helps establish a timeline for the item in terms of location; and identification of individuals involved may help establish actions to which the evidence was subjected. Marking should be legible and suitable for clear identification of individuals who are part of the chain.

While evidence may come in various forms and cannot always be marked or identified the way we would like, every effort should be made to mark the evidence in some way for later identification. If possible, not only the item but the exterior of the packaging (container) should be marked as well. We might use direct marking — placing a mark directly on the evidence — or indirect marking, which refers to marking only the container or packaging that holds the evidence. Information used in marking the evidence typically includes the identity of the individual finding or securing the evidence, the date, and often an evidence item number relative to the case. Attempting to place too much information on the evidence will frequently alter the evidence. In most instances, extensive records of chain of custody are kept with, but not marked on, the evidence; and it is often an advantage later to make a notation in the evidence log as to how the item was marked.

What Should be Marked on the Evidence?

The packaging should be labeled with a description of the evidence, the location from which it was recovered, the identity of the person finding or securing the evidence, the date, a case number, and an evidence item number. A point of caution: it is easy to let numbers get out of hand at this point. In the experience of the authors, evidence is assigned a number at the scene, a number at the property room, a number when it is submitted to a laboratory (for reference in the letter detailing the case), a number assigned by the laboratory, a number assigned by the court for identification in the courtroom, and finally an actual exhibit number when it is accepted into evidence during the trial. If this seems difficult to accept as an actual occurrence, be assured — it did happen. The profusion of numbers facing witnesses on the witness stand was more than a mere difficulty.

The practice of placing information on tags that are attached to the evidence by tape, string, wire, or some other method is often useful but has its shortcomings. The tags offer space to record useful information and are considered by some to make it unnecessary to mark the evidence directly; but the potential for removal or loss of the tag — with the evidence appearing in court absent any documentation — is enough to suggest this method should be used with caution. The person recovering the evidence still has the responsibility to be able to identify it in court.

When it comes to marking and recovery, a useful practice is to have two individuals participate in the process. One person performs the tasks of recovery, packaging, and marking of the evidence as well as the container; and the second individual witnesses the process and initials the evidence and the container or packaging, thus providing a second person who can authenticate the recovery of the evidence in the absence of the primary recoverer.

Use of an Evidence Log

While documentation of the evidence begins long before the initiation of an evidence log, the log is not a document to be taken lightly and should always be executed when evidence is recovered. Its preparation should be contemporaneous with the collection of the evidence to ensure more complete recording of observations that might be of value later. The log provides documentation of the administrative information regarding scene operations (scene location, date, personnel working at the scene, case identity, etc.), a sequential recovery record of each item of evidence, where it was found, who found it, the roll of photographic negatives on which the item can be found, and details of packaging. Complete evidence log records eliminate many headaches in the preparation of a case for trial. Incomplete records are encountered frequently.

Chain of Custody

While the marking of the evidence begins the actual chain of custody, the documentation continues with the evidence log and the movement of the evidence on to the property room and any other locations to which it might be sent. Proper maintenance of chain records involves recording times, dates, identities, any other pertinent information regarding person-to-person exchanges, transport to another facility (the laboratory, the prosecuting attorney's office, etc.), and return from that facility. In the last chapter, it was said that the secret to good crime scene documentation is to document, document and document! Nothing has changed. The lack of proper documentation is a hindrance to effective use of the evidence during field investigation, pretrial conferences, and, ultimately, courtroom proceedings.

Materials Used to Package Physical Evidence

Throughout this and the last chapter, the concepts of evidence sensitivity to a hostile environment and the transient nature of the evidence have been emphasized. It is the preservation of the evidence that has been so carefully collected to which we now turn our attention. The simple idea of packaging an item and sending it to a laboratory for examination does not seem difficult, but nature and the legal system impose more stringent requirements. Improper packaging and subsequent handling can mean evidence that is degraded, contaminated, or lost completely. Evidence with its protective packaging absent or extensively damaged may be considered to be compromised in terms of its integrity and thus not admitted in court.

Small Evidence Items

The vast majority of evidence in sexual assault investigations generally presents few problems given the guidelines and rules set forth here. Be prepared. Assembling an adequate number of containers (boxes, tubes, plastic vials), envelopes, bags, wrapping paper, plastic bubble wrap, styrofoam peanuts, sealing tape, etc.) — and any other materials dictated by one's imagination — is of great benefit when such materials are needed at the scene. The old adage, "Prior planning prevents poor performance" is definitely applicable. Evidence encountered in sexual assault investigations often is small in size, consisting of hairs or fibers, fingernails torn loose, and other small items; and there are a lot of small packaging materials to be found (many available free). Some suggestions regarding choice of packaging materials that may be useful include:

1. *Boxes:* Get cardboard boxes from small pillbox size (round, square or matchbox types are useful) to boxes capable of holding various larger items of clothing. Information may be recorded on the exterior, and moisture is not sealed in. Commercial entities provide a number of specialized boxes for guns, knives, shoeprint casts, etc., depending on the department budget.
2. *Envelopes:* Envelopes come in many sizes and shapes from very small (1 inch × 1 inch) to the quite large envelopes used to contain X-ray films (11 inches × 14 inches or larger). Envelopes with clear windows enable viewing of the evidence and still allow passage of moisture. A selection of different sizes and types on hand will ease the job of keeping all the evidence straight.
3. *Bags:* There is a wide variety of bags available (paper, plastic, zip-lock, open-ended, etc.). Paper allows the evidence to breathe and not retain moisture, while plastic does the opposite. Paper bags should be inspected for dust debris from the manufacturing process that may present a contamination issue. Plastic has the additional and decided disadvantage of conducting static electricity. Small hairs, fibers, or scrapings can be difficult to retrieve or incompletely recovered for

analysis in the laboratory because of the static. Still, there are useful purposes for both paper and plastic; and one can count on needing one or the other or both at a scene. Remember, plastic should not be used for evidence that is the least bit moist.

4. *Wrapping Paper:* Normally obtainable in 24-inch and 36-inch widths, rolls of brown wrapping paper with tape to seal it properly are helpful. Commercial forensic supply businesses sell wrapping paper on rolls constructed with two sheets sealed at the edges, forming a large tube that can be used effectively to package items. A specialized wrapping paper technique involves the druggist's fold. Paper sizes of 3 inches × 5 inches, 5 inches × 7 inches, and 8 $^1/_2$ inches × 11 inches are easily obtainable and convenient to keep in a crime scene kit. A sheet is folded in thirds one way, opened, then rotated 90 degrees and folded in thirds again, forming a rectangular area in the center into which evidence can be placed. It is useful to label the exterior before inserting evidence and sealing, since a pen may push through the paper if it contains grainy material. Refolding the paper and sealing it with tape provides a useful package for small items.

5. *35mm Film Container:* A useful container that becomes available as the documentation of the scene progresses is the 35 mm film container. It is sturdy and capable of holding small items securely. The interior should be wiped out before placing evidence inside.

6. *Sexual Assault Evidence Kits:* Finally, it is advisable to have on hand several unused, sealed kits. As indicated, hospitals may stock them or the state laboratory may provide them; but having a few on hand at the department is helpful when one is not available from some other source.

The above containers and packaging are adequate for nearly all applications with small- to moderate-sized items of evidence. The issue of sealing is worthy of comment and is addressed later in this chapter.

Large Evidence Items

Packaging of large or bulky items normally presents more difficulties and often requires more ingenuity on the part of the investigator. Such items as bulky bedding, furniture cushions, car seats, and carpets may require extra effort to adequately package. The first question with such an item is whether to send it intact or to take a cutting of the appropriate area with sufficient material surrounding it. The practicalities of dealing with such items often necessitate the cut, chip, or scrape approach; but it is still important to keep in mind that good crime scene work goes hand in hand with good judgment. If the circumstances do not result in any loss of trace evidence by taking cuttings, then cut away. If recovery of hairs and fibers from a sofa back can be effectively accomplished by vacuuming or taping, then either of those methods may provide a useful approach. On the other hand, if an inspection of that sofa cushion or other large item discloses evidence that the laboratory can better recover, then it should be packaged and removed.

The need for good judgment bears additional comment. Some investigators fail to review the evidence and evaluate it in light of the available case information, particularly with a large amount of evidence. The result is a shipment of evidence to the laboratory that is basically all the evidence collected at the scene (in a case involving one of the authors, the evidence filled an entire evidence storage room). Clearly the investigators did not know what to do with it, so they took it all to the lab to figure out.

The other side of the coin is just as true. The forensic laboratory has a responsibility to recover evidence that the field investigator cannot recover. Does the suggestion to call the laboratory for discussion sound familiar? Communication goes a long way to make it easier for everyone involved in the investigation. Most of the time it is not necessary to provide the laboratory with all the evidence collected at the scene. Doing so can greatly expand the chain of custody and complicate the overall picture.

Handling large or bulky evidence items often presents a challenge at time of packaging and shipping. Personal ingenuity often plays a role in getting the job done; however, there is no easy way that will work all the time. The following suggestions relate generally to the packaging of large items and supplement those given previously for smaller items. What follows is important, even if the discussion seems repetitive:

1 . We have discussed why it is important to dry wet biological evidence, but larger items present a special problem since the drying process can take longer — especially if the item is saturated with blood, water, or some other fluid (some fluids never dry, such as oil). The likelihood of bacterial growth and putrefaction becomes significant, while rapidly moving air and direct sunlight have their negative effects as well. It was mentioned earlier that a dedicated drying area is the answer to a lot of situations; and, taking it a step further, a well-ventilated room dedicated to evidence handling and drying is a valuable asset. Such a room should be secure, should not allow opportunity for contamination, and should protect the health and safety of the personnel working nearby. Personnel entry and exit logs should be kept to comply with the need for chain-of-custody records.

2. While plastic packaging materials definitely are not recommended for evidence packaging (sealing in moisture and trapping condensation), there are times when the use of such materials is expeditious for

temporary storage and transport of wet evidence from the scene. Air drying evidence at the scene is usually difficult unless the items are small in number and size. Consequently, it may be advantagous to use plastic bags for transporting evidence to a drying facility. Any bags used should be dried and kept with the evidence, as trace evidence (hairs, fibers, etc.) may adhere to the plastic. This applies, again, to temporary storage and transport of wet evidence — not permanent packaging.

3. Excess handling of the evidence after recovery is to be avoided. Many investigators have worked high-profile cases where the evidence may have been spread out as a display for all to see, perhaps on a large table or an area of floor space. This compromises the integrity of the evidence, at best. The potential loss of critical trace materials should be understood. After securing the evidence package at the scene, the next individual to open it should be someone who can deal with the recovery of trace materials unless there is no anticipated need for such examinations to be conducted.

4. While in some circumstances there will be exceptions to this, a priority at the scene should be to ensure that every item of evidence is packaged separately. Packaging all the clothing from the victim or the suspect in the same bag carries the potential for loss of corroborating information from the evidence. Pubic hairs identified as microscopically identical to those of the suspect (or having DNA matching the suspect's) and found in the crotch of the individually bagged panties of the victim are far more valuable corroborating information than the same pubic hairs would be if found in a bag with all of the victim's clothing. In the latter instance, there is no way the hairs can be specifically tied to the panties; and thus the hairs could have been on the outside of the victim's clothing and not associated with a sexual assault. One important exception to this is when a large pile of clothing or bedclothes has to be recovered, and the separation increases the chance of loss of trace material. Packaging of multiple items in the same container would be in the best interests of the case. It is advantageous to document the arrangement of the items in such a pile as much as possible (*blue towel covering yellow sheet, which is on top of a pair of blue jeans and a t-shirt*). However, it is often best to separately package as much of the evidence as possible.

5. A matter that is not always evident is the potential for inter-item contamination associated with contact among items from the victim, the suspect, and the scene. Handling evidence from the different sources in the same area potentially transfers evidence such as hairs, fibers, or even dried blood in the form of dust. This is not a small

point and can be easily dealt with by secure packaging, cleaning evidence handling areas after handling each item, and avoiding placing items from the three different sources together in boxes.

Sealing evidence requires further attention. The simple use of tape from the desk in the office, the stapler, or a variety of packing tapes or wires is not strange to most experienced evidence handlers. The current emphasis on evidence integrity makes it important to consider better and safer ways of sealing evidence and ensuring the evidence has not been subject to unauthorized access. Specialized tamper-proof tape has become commercially available in recent years and is required in many agencies. This tape seals the package in most cases without difficulty; but when entry of the package is attempted, the tape tears, breaks, and does not release in its original condition. Resealing the package requires a second piece of the tape, showing that the original seal has been broken.

A second point relates to both personnel safety and contamination of the evidence. The use of ordinary staples to seal the folded-over top of a paper bag is a common practice. Staples are also used to attach tags and other identifiers to the packaging. Many laboratory examiners have been stabbed by incompletely closed staples. Some have even bled (unintentionally, obviously) on evidence contained in the package. Staples are best left off the list of sealing materials for evidence bags.

Having the needed materials on hand before going out to a scene is much better than dealing with lack of required materials. There are enough complexities in thoroughly processing the scene without having to worry about the lack of the right materials on hand.

Summary

Handling different types of physical evidence can represent a complex task. Specialized techniques that apply to the five major kinds of evidence have been set forth as suggestions and recommendations. The infinite possibilities that cannot be adequately anticipated make it incumbent on the crime scene investigator or other evidence-recovery party to evaluate each problem before action is initiated. Aspects to consider include the number of available personnel, evidence storage facilities, access to a crime laboratory, and requirements established by the laboratory for receipt of evidence from the field. Most of all, planning and cooperation are the prime elements of success. These words are used routinely to the point that they may seem overly emphasized. Nonetheless, as with all areas of human endeavor, these two factors can make the difference between poor, mediocre, and exceptional performance. Physical evidence utilization is no different.

The information provided in Chapters 15 and 16 includes methodologies that law enforcement and the criminal justice community can apply to the use and interpretation of physical evidence. Many elements must move cohesively toward the central goal of making correct sense of the evidence in the court.

One element, while only mentioned in passing, may actually be the one that truly makes the difference between success or failure. Even if a case has the best crew in terms of training, experience, and techniques of evidence processing, it can still be compromised by the attitude of each individual involved. Attention to detail and care are the key distinctions between merely handling the scene and a first-class job, and the difference is often a function of attitude. Even the best in funding, technique, administration, and organization cannot outweigh the detrimental effects of poor attitude.

Conscious and subconscious psychological reactions are the most difficult human aspects to predict and control. Law enforcement personnel are not any more immune than anyone else to the tragic effects of the brutality and violence so characteristic of sexual assault crimes. The emotional effects of dealing with these matters can result in good judgment replaced by frustration and confusion. If responses to the challenges of evidence collection or legal challenges to evidence become reactive and governed by personal feelings, the resulting turmoil can be reflected in a disorganized effort during both the investigation and trial. The human side of evidence collection and utilization should be understood and monitored in order to deal with these kinds of problems before they become serious. This one issue transcends the myriad components of forensic science and must be given appropriate attention in the investigation of sexual assault cases.

Acknowledgments

The authors would like to express sincere appreciation to Dr. F. Samuel Baechtel, Mr. Anthony Onorato and Unit Chief Melissa Anne Smrz of the FBI Laboratory, and Supervisory Special Agent Dale Moreau of the FBI's National Center for the Analysis of Violent Crime, for their assistance in the preparation of Chapters 15 and 16.

References

The following texts and resources are presented to supplement the material in Chapters 15 and 16. While this text has attempted to provide useful guidelines based on experience and scientific principles, the reader is encouraged to seek additional resources to gain the views of others as well as information beyond the scope of what is presented here. The current writing was narrowed somewhat in scope to focus on the topics at hand, and there are many more forms of evidence that can provide assistance to the investigator in sexual assault cases.

Bevel, T. and Gardiner, R.M. (1997) *Bloodstain Pattern Analysis with an Introduction to Crime Scene Reconstruction*, CRC Press, Boca Raton, FL.

Deedrick, D.W. (2000) Hairs fibers crime, and evidence, *Forens. Sci. Comm.*, 2(3), www.fbi.gov.

DeForrest, P., Gaensslen, R.E., and Lee, H.C. (1983) *Forensic Science: An Introduction to Criminalistics*, McGraw-Hill Book Company, New York.

Fisher, B. (1996) *Techniques of Crime Scene Investigation*, 5th ed., CRC Press, Boca Raton, FL.

FBI *Handbook of Forensic Services*, Federal Bureau of Investigation, Washington, D.C., available on CD or at www.fbi.gov/programs/lab/handbook/intro.htm.

Gerbeth, V. (1996) *Practical Homicide Investigation*, 3rd ed., CRC Press, Boca Raton, FL.

Handbook of Forensic Pathology (1990) R. Froede, Ed., College of American Pathologists, Northfield, IL.

MacDonell, H.L. (1997) *Bloodstain Patterns, Revised Edition*, Laboratory of Forensic Science, Corning, NY.

Moenssens, A., Starrs, J., Henderson, C., and Inbau, F. (1994) *Scientific Evidence in Civil and Criminal Cases*, 4th ed., Foundation Press, New York.

Olsen, R. (1978) *Scott's Fingerprint Mechanics*, C.C Thomas Publishing, Springfield, IL.

Saferstein, R. (1997) *Criminalistics: An Introduction to Forensic Science*, 6th ed., Prentice-Hall Inc., Englewood Cliffs, NJ.

Spitz, W. (1994) *Medicolegal Investigation of Death*, C.C Thomas Publishing, Springfield, IL.

James, S.H. and Eckert, W.G. (1999) *Interpretation of Bloodstain Evidence at Crime Scenes*, CRC Press, Boca Raton, FL.

Scientific and Legal Applications of Bloodstain Pattern Interpretation (1998) James, S.H., Ed., CRC Press, Boca Raton, FL.

Westveer, A. (1997) *Managing Death Investigation*, FBI Academy, Quantico, VA.

Prosecuting Rape Cases: Trial Preparation and Trial Tactic Issues

17

WILLIAM HEIMAN
Revised and Updated by
ANN PONTERIO and GAIL FAIRMAN

Introduction

The focus of this chapter is the preparation and presentation of rape cases for trial. The trial of a rape case, like any other criminal case, is a series of connected parts dependent on one another. A trial is a network of interrelated pieces, all making up a discernible pattern. Everything that is done in the preparation stage must serve a purpose in terms of setting up the closing argument. From the start of jury selection, 90% of the closing statement should already have been prepared mentally or on paper. The remaining 10% is filled in based on material that is unforeseen at the start and developed during the course of the trial.

Whether trying an identification case, consent case, or an imperfect victim case, the prosecutor should begin to educate the jury in his or her opening remarks, during the *voir dire*, and during the opening statement. In closing, he or she should tie together all of the pieces of the argument that were developed in the preparation stage and established through the other stages of trial.

Process of Trial

The process of trial is a series of specific phases described as preparation, jury selection, opening statement, defense opening, cross-examination, rebuttal, and closing arguments.

Preparation

The key to presenting a well-organized, logical, smooth-running case in court is careful and thorough preparation. A case can be destroyed if the trial attorney is surprised by damaging information in the midst of trial. The prosecutor should also use the preparatory period to organize the file and trial exhibits. Avoid fumbling with papers and exhibits throughout the trial

0-8493-0076-2/01/$0.00+$.50
© 2001 by CRC Press LLC

in order to gain the jury's confidence and to impress them with your preparedness, competence, and thorough knowledge of the case.

Preparation for a rape case should begin with the earliest encounters between the prosecutor and the rape victim and other witnesses. Usually this occurs at the preliminary hearing. At this early stage the prosecutor probably does not have a complete file but can begin preparing the victim to deal with anticipated cross-examination and can observe the victim on the witness stand to detect demeanor and articulation problems that can be smoothed out prior to trial. The prosecutor should also use this opportunity to identify any possible "prompt complaint" witnesses — witnesses to whom the victim reported the rape before the first report to police. These corroborating witnesses are usually permitted to testify by statutory exceptions to the hearsay rule.

The next step in preparing a case for trial is to gather all the statements made by the witnesses. For a rape victim, this may mean gathering as many as nine different partial or full statements. They could include: (1) the transcript of the telephone call to police emergency and the actual tape of the call, if preserved; (2) the brief interview by the first officer on the scene; (3) the nurse's interview at the hospital; (4) the examining physician's interview at the hospital; (5) the formal interview with the assigned investigator; (6) the notes of testimony from the preliminary hearing; (7) the notes of testimony for the pretrial motion to suppress; (8) any statements to prompt complaint witnesses; and (9) any statement given to a private investigator working on behalf of the defendant or on behalf of a third party who may have civil liability to the victim.

After obtaining and reviewing all of these statements, a list of the inconsistencies should be compiled concerning such issues as the physical details of the defendant's appearance, time of day, amount of alcohol or drugs consumed, etc. Reviewing these discrepancies with the victim and attempting to reconcile them as much as possible are essential. In most cases such differences can be found to have a logical explanation.

Without exception, the trial attorney should interview all potential witnesses personally. In order to avoid the risk of the trial attorney becoming a witness, the investigating officer should be present during preparation sessions. The investigator may be an important witness at trial if the witnesses report any threats or other contacts from the defense at the prep session. Additionally, in the event that one of the witnesses recants either at the prep session or later at trial, the investigator will be able to testify regarding the circumstances of the interview, including the witness' demeanor and statements, or to refute any allegations by the witness that he or she was threatened or intimidated by the prosecutor.

After the witnesses' statements are reviewed and the discrepancies are explored, the victim should be informed about the areas of cross-examination that will arise. All the sensitive, unpleasant, and embarrassing issues that will come out at trial must be thoroughly reviewed. A review of the actual sexual acts should be avoided to prevent the victim from losing a genuine emotional edge when she recounts these acts on the stand and to avoid her appearing blasé or overrehearsed.

It is important to review all other areas of her testimony about which it is likely that she will become emotionally upset or angry, such as drug or alcohol use or prior, admissible sexual contact with the defendant. This helps give her an awareness of these issues and prevents her from losing self-control or dignity on the witness stand. However, explain that if she feels as though she is going to break down and cry on the witness stand, it is all right to do so, and that she should take a moment to regain her composure.

Whenever possible the prosecutor should visit the scene of the crime. A thorough understanding of the physical setting helps the attorney in preparing witnesses and in cross-examining defense witnesses and may help explain apparent improbabilities in testimony. The attorney should try to observe the viewpoints of any eyewitnesses to understand the relevant lines of sight, obstructions, and lighting.

The trial attorney should be creative in the preparation and use of demonstrative evidence. The key rule in the area of demonstrative evidence is to provide the jury with clear, visible exhibits. Pictures should be enlarged or mounted on cardboard so that they can be seen and handled easily by the jury. During the preparation sessions with the witnesses, the photographs and any other physical evidence should be reviewed to ensure that the witness is not surprised at trial.

Try to learn as much as possible about the defendant in order to effectively cross-examine and to prepare for any defense. Subpoena and obtain any available material including prior criminal files, prison records, prison visitor logs, work or school records, and health records.

Once the case has been dissected and analyzed, it is time to put it together for trial. Make a list of the order of witnesses to be called. It is often effective to use an articulate prompt complaint witness or the first officer on the scene as the initial witness to set the scene for the jurors, and then follow with the victim. List the major points each witness is expected to make and any physical evidence they will identify. Review the information or bills of indictment to determine the bills on which you will move to trial. Deleting the minor bills will help the jury by simplifying the case and will help avoid a compromise verdict. The testimony of the witnesses on your list should cover all of the elements of all of the crimes that are moving to trial. Avoid duplicative witnesses who may contradict each other.

At this point, the case should be thought through carefully to pinpoint the areas in which there will be a serious issue with respect to admissibility.

Do the legal research and obtain cases that will support the theory of admissibility of evidence. If necessary, prepare a short memorandum on the point.

After the preparation is completed and the trial is ready to begin, the rule of thumb is to have, in outline form, 90% of the closing argument prepared. Rape trials are not won by "winging it;" they are won by careful, meticulous preparation.

Jury Selection and the *Voir Dire* Process

Voir dire is a preliminary examination of the witness to determine his or her competency and suitability as a witness. Entire books have been written on jury selection. Purported experts and psychologists have designed and employed personality profiles and all types of analyses in an effort to pick the perfect jury for one side or the other. As a word of caution, most experienced trial lawyers cannot agree on most issues in jury selection. For example, the two most experienced and successful trial lawyers in the author's office once gave a lecture on jury selection. The first attorney said that a prospective juror should be struck unless there is some specific positive reason to want him. The second attorney said if you are neutral about the person, take him. Obviously, there are few rules in jury selection that apply in all cases.

People who have roots and a stake in the community, the solid citizen types, are good pro-government jurors. Working people from high-crime neighborhoods are excellent jurors who understand the dynamics of crime and victimization. People from the victim's neighborhood or the area where the crime was committed may understand the particular problems in the case, such as why neighbors did not respond to screams or a struggle or why a witness might initially lie to officials.

Always be conscious of the nature of your particular case or victim in selecting jurors. Try to pick people who will identify or relate to your victim or to you and who will not identify with the defendant. Remember that the U.S. Supreme Court has ruled that peremptory strikes cannot be used to eliminate jurors solely on the basis of race or gender. See *Batson v. Kentucky*, 476 U.S. 79, 106 S.Ct. 1712, 90 L.Ed.2d (1986).

Avoid people who are on the fringes of society, who are drifting through life, who act and dress in a bizarre manner, or who answer questions inappropriately. Look for the mainstreamers and achievers in the group. Try to select at least two strong pro-government jurors who can control jury deliberations.

Avoid picking jurors who would be naturally antagonistic toward one another. The jury will have enough to discuss and argue about when they examine the case. It only takes one intransigent juror to hang a case.

The *voir dire* process varies among jurisdictions and among individual judges. It is therefore impossible to recommend any one style. However, the following are some factors to keep in mind:

1. *Voir dire* is the first time that you have any opportunity to influence the jury. Speak to them as much as the judge will allow. This will permit you to educate them about crucial points of law in your case and to establish a personal rapport. If the judge limits your opportunity to ask questions directly of a juror, try to establish eye contact as much as possible.
2. In the imperfect victim case, extract from the jurors a promise that they will follow the law, even if they do not agree with it.
3. Avoid embarrassing, humiliating, or insulting the jurors. They will not forgive you and they certainly will not forget.
4. If the case depends heavily on police work, explore the juror's feeling about law enforcement. A person who believes he has been mistreated by the police will likely use your trial to get even.
5. If a juror is obviously not acceptable, thank him or her politely and abort the questioning. Do not provide a forum for the juror to espouse ideas and possibly influence the others on the panel.
6. Show utmost respect at all times for the judge and the panel. Do not appear friendly to the defense counsel in front of the jury. Your tone should be dignified and professional. Any attempts at sarcastic remarks or humor are inappropriate in a rape trial. Be conscious of your behavior and the behavior of your witnesses in the hallways surrounding the courtroom if jurors roam in that area.
7. Always keep in mind the number of peremptory strikes that are left and the types of people remaining on the panel. A person who did not initially appear to be a good selection might begin to look great when you have only one strike left and the remaining group is even less promising.

Opening Statement

An opening statement is the first opportunity for a prosecutor to reveal to the jury the essence of the case. A prosecutor should create with words a clear image of the facts of the case for the jury. In preparing an outline of an opening statement, write down all of the strengths and weaknesses of the case. Foremost, be confident in presenting an opening statement. Bring out the best points and defuse the worst points of the case. Do not be afraid to address the weaknesses. Never apologize to the jury for the lack of evidence. (Juries, unlike judges, are unfamiliar with inadequacies of a case.) A prosecutor should strive for a fluid opening statement. Use language the jury will understand. While evidence in a trial may be introduced out of turn because of scheduling difficulties, you should structure an opening statement so that the evidence flows and is not confusing.

The following are some suggested guidelines for delivering an effective opening statement:

1. Speak slowly.
2. Reintroduce yourself. Tell the jury the main charge of rape. Do not outline every lesser included offense.
3. Be brief; avoid relating minute details or quoting specific conversation.
4. Personalize your victim. Do not address her by her first name; rather, say, "Donna Jones will tell you" or "Miss Jones cried for help."
5. Depersonalize the defendant. Refer to him as the defendant. Never refer to him as "that gentleman."
6. Promise the jury only what you know you will be able to deliver to them. If you are not sure that a certain witness will testify, do not tell the jury that the witness will definitely testify.
7. Do not tell the jury your entire case.
8. Focus in on the key and crucial issues of the case. If it is an ID case, urge the jury to pay particularly close attention to the victim's opportunity to observe her assailant.
9. If the victim is, for example, a drug user or met the defendant when she was frequenting a bar, be tactful but firm (without being insulting) in stating to the jury that the lifestyle of the victim is not the issue; remind the jurors of their solemn oath to be fair and impartial and not to prejudge the facts until they hear from the victim when she relates to the jury what happened to her. No woman should ever be made to feel apologetic or shameful as to the circumstances that led up to her rape.
10. Avoid law-school-esque phrases such as "I welcome the awesome burden of the commonwealth" or "the government will prove to you beyond a shadow of a doubt that the defendant committed this heinous, dastardly act." They may sound good on television shows, but they are less persuasive in a real courtroom before real jurors. On the other hand, telling the jury that they are about to begin their search for the truth has a good ring and is effective.
11. Save the dramatics, the flamboyance, and the clever phrases for your closing. Be controlled and straightforward in your delivery of the opening statement.
12. Most importantly, *be yourself.* No one style is better at communicating to juries than another. Your own style, whether it be soft spoken or

energetic, is something you cannot fake. Being comfortable with who you are and how you speak will make you credible to a jury.

Defense Opening

After a prosecutor opens to the jury, the defense may make an opening statement. The purpose of any opening statement is to inform the jury of the facts of the case and what each side intends to prove as evidence. Many defense openings are dramatic, mini-closing arguments that rehash reasonable doubt and state nothing of the facts of the case. While most judges give defense attorneys considerable leeway, do not sit there listening to a defense attorney take two bites of a closing argument; stand up and object. Do not get carried away and object continuously, but set the tone with an objection.

Cross-Examination

Cross-examination of the defendant or any of his witnesses is obviously a crucial part of the truth-seeking and fact-finding process. It is also fraught with danger for the prosecutor. An excellent book on this subject is Francis Wellman's *The Art of Cross Examination*. It provides valuable background and a foundation. The writings (and some video tapes) of Professor Irving Younger offer another excellent resource, particularly his famous piece, *Ten Commandments of Cross Examination*.

Following are some suggestions:

1. Avoid rehashing the witness' direct examination. Have specific areas of the direct examination in mind to challenge on cross. Repeating the direct examination is boring to the jury; and it allows the witness to emphasize the points a second time, which is very damaging to the prosecution's case.
2. Ask as many leading questions as possible. Have in mind the answer you are looking for. Don't ask the key question early on in cross-examination. Set up your cross with preliminary questions, then focus in on the key question the witness/defendant does not have an answer for. When your point has been made to the jury, do not ask another question along that line. Invariably, attorneys have a bad habit of asking one too many questions. It only gives the witness an opportunity to explain his or her previous answer.
3. Two traditional rules of cross-examination are never to ask questions to which you do not know the answer, and rarely ask a witness a question beginning with the word "why." There may be instances in which a question beginning with a "why" is appropriate; more often than not, it gives the defense witness another opportunity to tell his or her story.

4. Not all cross-examinations are hostile, heated retorts between a witness and a prosecutor. It depends on who the witness is, such as the defendant's grandmother, and what the witness says and how damaging it is to your case. A cross-examination may illustrate to the jury that, although the witness believes what he or she is saying, the witness is mistaken in that belief.

5. Often the hardest thing for a prosecutor to do is not to cross-examine a witness. Do not cross-examine a witness who does not hurt your case.

6. Before cross-examining the defendant, outline all possible avenues the defendant may take on the witness stand. The defendant can admit or deny sexual intercourse with the victim. If he admits sexual intercourse, then his defense is most likely to be consent. If he denies sexual intercourse, then his defense can be one of the following: the victim is mistaken in her identification of the defendant; the victim is fabricating the rape; the defendant has an alibi for his whereabouts at about the time of the (most often used word by the defense attorney during a trial) *alleged* occurrence.

7. Be prepared to cross-examine the defendant thoroughly depending on which avenue he chooses. (A prosecutor should always be prepared to cross-examine a defendant on the rare occasion when he testifies at a motion to suppress. Never give much credence to a defense attorney who tells you that the defendant will not be testifying at trial.)

8. Always know the extent of any prior sexual relationship the defendant had with the victim.

9. It is important to bring out questions to demonstrate to the jury the defendant's motive to lie on the witness stand.

10. Often an overlooked, important piece of cross-examination is cross-examining the character witness. In many jurisdictions, a defendant can introduce character only through reputation and not through specific good acts. Bring out any bias the character witness has such as being a family member or a close friend. If the witness is a co-worker, demonstrate how the witness only knows the defendant from work and not from any social setting. Ask the character witness when was the last time he or she spoke about the defendant's character in the community — before or after his arrest — and with whom. You may choose not to ask the defendant's mother any questions regarding character; and if you do, only ask one or two questions.

11. In preparing your victim for cross-examination, tell her not to be sarcastic in answering the defense attorney's questions.

12. Tell the victim that the defense attorney's tone may be sarcastic so that she will respond in a sarcastic fashion. The prosecutor's job is to not let this happen and object when the defense does this.

13. Have the witness remain as calm as possible and not show temper to the jury.
14. Tell the victim that when you object, she is to stop answering the question until the judge indicates otherwise.
15. Remind the witness to only answer the question and not to volunteer any additional information.
16. Explain to the witness that, if she does not understand the question, say she doesn't understand the question.
17. Know the terminology of the victim. A victim may not comprehend what words such as ripped and torn mean, as illustrated in the following exchange:

> **Defense attorney**: Are you telling this jury that my client ripped your panties off of you?
> **Victim**: He most certainly did.
> **Defense Attorney**: And he did it with as much force as he could muster, he ripped your panties apart in getting them off of you?
> **Victim**: I told you already that he did.

Defense attorney then argues to the jury that the jury heard from the witness that the defendant ripped her pants apart getting them off of her and introduces a report from the forensics laboratory that the panties are intact and show no tears. The victim, on the other hand, understood the expression "ripped" as being taken off forcibly, not actually "ripped apart."

This is nothing more than a game of semantics. Tell the witness that the defense attorney may use words that she is not familiar with and she may not understand their meaning. Tell her not to be embarrassed in saying to the attorney that she does not understand his question. Make the defense attorney rephrase it. Attorneys get flustered when they have to repeat or rephrase questions.

18. Every attorney must be comfortable with his or her style of cross-examination. Many prefer to stand through all of cross-examination; others prefer to stand when they make their key points. If time permits, discuss your cross-examination with fellow colleagues and ask for their input.

Rebuttal

The government's rebuttal to certain parts of the defense case is an explosive part of the prosecutor's package. Keep in mind the following points:

1. Rebuttal testimony should be very brief, pointed, direct, and specific. It should be aimed at challenging a specific point presented by the

defense. Avoid recalling a witness on rebuttal unless he or she has compelling evidence, to avoid the risk of opening the door on issues that are ancillary to the case.

2. Rebuttal evidence is particularly persuasive to the jury because it is usually the last evidence presented.

3. The jury already has a frame of reference in which they can evaluate the credibility of the evidence offered; they know what defense evidence is being directly challenged by the rebuttal evidence.

4. Documents and records make particularly strong rebuttal evidence. By presenting records, the prosecutor does not have to worry about credibility factors, which are present when a live witness is evaluated. The records are cold, unemotional facts that speak for themselves.

5. The way to present rebuttal evidence effectively is first to lock the witness into his testimony regarding a particular fact. Make sure the fact to be challenged is on the record in a clear, unambiguous manner. Then put on your rebuttal witness in as short and succinct a manner as possible — get in and get out. Examples of documentation of record that are particularly effective include time cards from work records proving that the defendant was not, in fact, at work when he said he was; records from a television station showing that the program the witness was supposed to have been watching that night was pre-empted, etc. The point is that when the jury has to evaluate a witness's testimony against a cold business record, they will invariably resolve any factual dispute in favor of the business record.

6. In rebutting an alibi defense, consider the alibi witnesses like links in a chain that is only as strong as the weakest link. You do not have to explode the entire testimony of every alibi witness. Search for the inconsistent part of one alibi witness's testimony and then argue to the jury that the entire alibi crumbles when the weak link in the chain breaks.

7. If the defendant testifies to materially different facts from those the victim has already testified to, you must decide whether to recall her in rebuttal. This may not be wise if she is an imperfect victim. However, if the defense raises a fact that the victim did not testify to (drug use, for example), it is incumbent on the prosecutor to bring the victim back on rebuttal to deny it. Be careful not to have the victim rehash her whole testimony on rebuttal. Raise the specific point and stop. This type of rebuttal is particularly effective as it gives the jury one last opportunity to see, hear, and evaluate the victim.

Closing Argument

The closing argument is a crucial part of every criminal trial. Countless cases are won or lost based upon the quality of the summation.

The first point to keep in mind is preparation. As mentioned above, you should have about 90% of your closing argument outlined in your head or on paper at the time you begin the trial; the remaining 10% of the content is based on materials that came to light during the course of trial.

The length of your closing varies with the length and complexity of the case. In general, however, anything under 15 minutes is probably too short; 30 to 45 minutes is a good period of time; and argument longer than an hour may very well be too long.

The following is a general outline of a closing argument in a rape trial:

1. Do not read your closing verbatim from a tablet or cards.
2. Speak *to* the jurors and not at them. Speak slowly; take your time. Jurors cannot understand or absorb your points if you rattle them off. Forget big legal words — they are not impressive.
3. Have a general outline with keywords to remind you of the areas to cover.
4. Answer the most offensive or fallacious arguments made by the defense attorney in his closing. Mention to the jury that before you begin the merits of your argument, you feel obliged to respond to a few comments made by your opponent that you cannot let pass. Avoid the trap of spending your whole time responding to the defense's argument.
5. Cover the main thrust of your case.
6. In an identification case, review the witnesses' opportunities to observe, one by one. In reviewing your notes from trial, write down every fact that helps you in identifying the defendant — distance, lighting, time period to observe, height, prior descriptions — and match these facts to the defendant. In a consent case, highlight issues such as the lack of a motive for the victim to lie and any other evidence in the case that supports her testimony.
7. Emphasize all corroboration of the rape victim's testimony. Review the key portion of each witness's testimony and point out how it adds to the government's overall case or how it supports the victim's testimony.
8. If the victim is an imperfect victim, argue that the jury has been summoned to decide the issue of rape, not to decide a popularity contest as to whether they like the victim as a person or approve of her lifestyle. Emphasize that negative opinions regarding the victim's lifestyle or personality are never an excuse for the defendant to have raped her.
9. Use the emotional aspects of rape — that the dignity of the person has been attacked.
10. It is helpful to have the victim sitting in the front row of the courtroom so that you can gesture toward her as you speak. Make sure to have

someone sit next to the rape victim such as a police officer or a rape crisis counselor.

11.   It is particularly important to stress the credibility of the testimony of the neutral or unbiased witness — the examining physician or the bystander stranger who obviously has no axe to grind. These unbiased corroborating witnesses lend strong support to the victim's credibility.

12.   Where the defense has offered evidence in the case, particularly if the defendant testified, remind the jury that they must evaluate this testimony by the same yardstick they used for the victim's testimony.

13.   Mention the defendant's strong motive to lie to avoid conviction, and pick apart any inconsistencies in his testimony. Appealing to the jury's collective common sense and logic is more effective than appealing to their passion. Usually in the "he said vs. she said" type of case, there is one witness or piece of evidence that can be indicative of which side is telling the truth.

After the facts have been analyzed in the closing and the jury has been urged to resolve credibility issues in favor of the victim and the government witnesses, mention the definition and elements of the crimes charge. Be deferential to the judge by stating to the jury that the judge will instruct them on the law, but you would like to take a few moments to discuss it and how it applies to the facts of this case. Often juries become bored and confused during the judge's charge when he or she reads legal definitions to them. If the prosecutor in his or her closing argument uses similar words without all the legalese attached, the juries will have a better understanding of the elements rather than only hearing the legal definition once. Carefully analyze any key issues of your case, such as the sufficiency of a "substantial threat" in an attempted rape case or the definition of sufficient force, and the lack of any requirement that the victim offer physical resistance in the face of a substantial threat. Remind the jury of their solemn oath to obey the law, even if they do not agree with or approve of it.

It is often useful to reserve until the end of your closing summary a discussion of how the crime occurred. Do not repeat the testimony. During the course of a trial, witnesses are not presented chronologically. There are many breaks and jurors can forget parts of the testimony. Summarizing the testimony in a coherent narrative gives the jurors a clearer understanding.

It is often effective to reserve the last section of the closing argument for a jurors' call to duty. Remind jurors that they represent the spirit and the conscience of the community and that all of us have a right to expect that they will act fairly and impartially and will seek justice. As always during the course of the trial, be proud to be a prosecutor and be proud to represent the interests of the victim and the community at large. Never apologize for the lack of evidence. If you are confident, then that confidence transcends to the jury.

Difficult Cases

Identification Issue Case

The identification issue case is the most straightforward type of rape case to try. The issue is not whether she was raped — it is whether the defendant did it.

The identification case is an excellent example of how the prosecutor should weave different parts of the trial into a coherent whole. Basically, the identification case breaks down into three distinct issues: (1) the victim's opportunity to observe the assailant, and barring some unusual physical characteristic, specifically his face; (2) the accuracy of the physical description made by the victim to the authorities; and (3) the identification or confrontation of the defendant by the victim, whether by photograph, in person, in a lineup, or in a one-on-one confrontation.

The first key to successfully prosecuting this type of case is the preparation session with the victim. Having all of the prior statements in hand, review with her in minute detail each opportunity she had to see the defendant during the commission of the crime. Focus on the victim's observations of the defendant's face. For each opportunity ask her the following questions: *How far from his face were you when you saw his face? What were the lighting conditions? What were you thinking of at the time?* List each and every specific opportunity and the surrounding information separately. These small, isolated chips of information must be ascertained. Work with the victim carefully and help her to recall every opportunity.

Also, at the preparation session you must review with the victim why she is certain it was the defendant who assaulted her. If the victim merely says, *Yes, the defendant,* when asked if she sees the person who attacked her in the courtroom, the jury won't know if *yes* means *I know that's him and I'll be positive until the day I die,* or whether the *yes* means *I guess that must be him. After all, they arrested him didn't they?* The prosecutor must review this question with the victim very carefully. She must be prepared to tell you at the end of your direct examination, and stress during cross-examination, the basis or reason why she is able to swear under oath the defendant and no one else attacked her.

During your opening statement to the jury, tell the jurors that, while they must pay close attention to all of the testimony, they should listen very carefully to the victim as she describes each and every opportunity to see the defendant's face. They should also note carefully the accuracy of her description to the authorities and her certainty during the identification confrontation that occurred.

The next important step occurs during direct examination of the victim. As soon as the victim mentions the presence of the assailant on the scene, immediately ask her if she sees the man she is describing physically in the courtroom. Indicate on the record that she has identified Mr. Jones, the defendant. From then on, she should refer to him as the "defendant."

As mentioned earlier, let the victim testify in a narrative, flowing form on her direct testimony. Interrupt her with specific questions only when necessary. You want the jury to hear her dramatic account of what happened in a narrative manner, without constantly being interrupted. After the victim has finished recounting the assault, ask her to go back to the point at which she first saw the defendant and tell the jury about that and about the first time that she saw the defendant's face. Take her through the accompanying detailed questions just as you reviewed them in the prep sessions. Then go through the same series of questions with each opportunity to observe. The effect of letting the victim describe the incident in narrative form and then filling it in with specific opportunities to observe is twofold: first, it organizes her opportunities to observe the defendant for the jury and makes it easy for you to argue the point in your closing; and second, it gives the jury two chances to hear the violent aspects of the victim's testimony as she explains her opportunities to observe the defendant. Emphasize any unusual features of the defendant that the victim noted and used in making her identification. The victim should also note any significant changes in appearance that may be efforts on the part of the defendant to conceal his identity and evidence a consciousness of guilt.

In closing, emphasize that the trauma of the assault has emblazoned the defendant's face into the brain of the victim. Argue to the jury that the case is not an identification case but a recognition case. Stress any consistent out-of-court identification and the absence of any misidentification. Review every opportunity the victim had to observe the defendant's face. The cumulative effect of listing every single opportunity impacts significantly on the jury. Argue that these many opportunities are the foundation of an accurate, reliable, in-court identification.

Consent Issue Case

The consent issue case presents several difficult problems for the prosecutor. The issue in the case is not whether the sexual activity occurred; most often the defendant will readily admit sexual contact with the victim. The issue is whether the act occurred by direct force or threat of force or whether it happened with the victim's consent.

One of the problems presented by this type of case is that extraneous issues find their way into the record about the prior relationship between the parties or the nature of the activities of the victim and the defendant prior to the assault. Rape Shield Statutes that preclude the introduction of evidence of prior sexual activity on the part of the victim do not usually preclude the evidence of a sexual relationship between the parties when consent is the issue. When you have this type of case, it is better to bring out the scope of the prior relationship in your opening statement and on direct examination rather than wait for the defense attorney to spring it on the victim on cross-examination.

When the facts show that the victim and the defendant were engaged in an unpopular type of activity prior to the assault, such as drug or excessive alcohol use, follow the suggestions outlined in the imperfect victim section of this chapter.

The key to successfully prosecuting the consent defense case is to corroborate the testimony of the victim with as much supporting evidence as possible. The following are suggestions for handling the consent issue type of case:

1. If the victim claims she was slapped, choked, or in some manner physically abused by the defendant, introduce evidence of her physical injuries from the medical records custodian, from the examining physicians, the first officer on the scene, or a prompt complaint or other witness. This documentation of her physical injuries, even minor scratches or bruises, becomes crucial in arguing to the jury in your closing that the victim's version of what happened can and should be believed.

2. If the victim claims she was screaming during the incident, it is important to bring in the neighbor or the person who heard her scream. This again corroborates the victim's testimony that the sexual contact was without her consent.

3. Any type of *res gestae* or excited utterance statement that is admissible is very valuable and should be introduced. (The legal term *res gestae* refers to the acts, circumstances, and statements that are incidental to the principal fact of a litigated matter and are admissible in the evidence in view of their relevant association with that fact.)

In a consent case where the victim has not suffered any trauma to her vaginal area, the defense attorney will try to argue to the jury during his closing that the lack of vaginal injury is consistent with the defendant's version of consensual intercourse. After all, he will argue, if the victim had been forced, she would have suffered some type of injury to her vagina. To a lay person this argument is persuasive. However, it is not valid. Therefore, in a consent case without vaginal trauma, consider bringing in an expert medical witness, preferably the examining physician, to educate the jury on this issue. The doctor should explain the female pelvic anatomy and how rarely visible bruises or tears are noted even in confirmed sexual assault cases. The medical expert should conclude by offering his expert medical opinion that the lack of trauma is entirely consistent with the victim having been forced to submit to intercourse.

Imperfect Victim Case

The imperfect victim is a label used to describe a victim who, by virtue of her background or lifestyle in general, or because of the particular activity in which she was engaged just before the rape, can be expected to elicit biased or negative feelings from the average juror. Examples include prostitutes, drug and alcohol abusers, and runaways.

The prosecutor should file a motion *in limine* (at the outset) before trial to obtain a ruling regarding any information concerning the victim's activities that is inadmissible and thus preclude a suggestive and improper defense question. Once the defense attorney asks a question in front of the jury regarding one of these unpopular activities, it is too late to object. The jury will suspect that you are trying to conceal some unpleasant facts and will not disregard the question regardless of how many times they are told that questions are not evidence. If you obtain a pretrial ruling in your favor, be sure to review the parameters with your witness to ensure that she does not open the door on the inadmissible and potentially damaging information through testimony.

Much of the unpopular information will be admissible, however; and because you will be unable to disguise the victim's unpopular activities or lifestyle, it is better to bring the matter to the jury's attention as soon as possible. You must be totally honest, without being apologetic, about the victim's imperfections throughout the trial. You must emphasize to the victim that, while she should not offer inadmissible information, she must be forthright no matter how bad she thinks the admissible information will make her seem to the jurors. The already imperfect victim cannot afford to be caught in an obvious lie by the defense. Additionally, the prosecutor can argue in closing that the victim was not concealing anything from the jurors in her quest for justice and use this point to highlight her credibility regarding the entire incident.

If the judge will permit you to participate in *voir dire*, it is crucial in this type of case to extract a promise from the jurors before they are selected that, notwithstanding the fact that they do not approve of the victim's lifestyle or of what the victim was doing before the rape, nevertheless, they will keep an open mind as they hear the testimony and not reach any conclusions until the appropriate time. Also, the jurors must promise that, like it or not, they will follow the law as it is stated by the judge in his charge.

One important benefit of bringing the unpopular facts out during *voir dire* is that you can judge whether the juror can be fair and impartial and will give the government a fair trial, notwithstanding the imperfect aspects of the victim. If the juror indicates that he cannot be fair or is hesitant in stating that he will be fair, it is obviously far better for the prosecutor to know that during *voir dire* rather than to accept a juror and run the risk of poisoning the other jurors during deliberations.

During the opening statement do not be afraid to state again the negative aspects of the victim. Be sure to remind the jurors of the promise they made when they were selected, both to you individually and on their oath, to keep an open mind and follow the law as the judge states it in his charge. As you present your case, at least the jury is not shocked when they actually hear the victim testify. Highlight any type of corroboration, as this evidence will be crucial when you argue, in closing, that the victim's testimony was credible and worthy of the jury's belief.

This is the type of case where it is particularly effective to use a witness other than the victim to set the stage. If an initial witness effectively describes a distraught, injured, or desperate victim seeking help, then the jury will be sympathetic to the victim from the start of the testimony and may be more forgiving of the unpopular aspects of her testimony.

When the victim testifies, be sure to bring out on direct examination the nature and extent of the unpopular activity, assuming, of course, that it is admissible and would be brought out on cross-examination. The purpose of this approach is to be up front with the jury and not hide any unpopular aspects of the victim's activities. This will "take the wind out of the sails" of your opponent by leaving no new material in these areas to develop on cross-examination. Use every piece of corroborating evidence available, including physical aspects of the scene, torn, dirty, or disheveled clothing, weather, and anything else a creative prosecutor can think of to hit hard that the victim is worthy of belief.

In closing argument, again remind the jury of the promise they made to be fair and impartial. Tell them that the issue in the case is not whether they approve of the victim's lifestyle or activities. Advise them that the only issue is whether the evidence proves, beyond a reasonable doubt, that the defendant assaulted her. Remind them of their oath to follow the law, whether or not they like or approve of it. Explain that when the judge defines the law they must follow and obey, they will hear nothing that says a drug addict cannot be raped or that it is a defense to the crime of rape that the victim had been drinking in a bar alone, etc. You must have the jury focus on the true issues in the case and move them beyond the imperfect aspects of the victim.

It is also effective in closing to point out that this type of flawed victim is easy prey or the perfect victim for the defendant, as she would be less likely to go to the police and less likely to be believed if she did. Remind the jury that she, as well as the defendant, is entitled to equal protection under the law.

General Policy Issues

The prosecutor's office should also set general policies to govern the handling of rape cases within the office and should use available resources to help to set policies with the law enforcement and civilian communities concerning rape cases.

In the category of policy issues external to the prosecutor's office, the prosecutor can have a direct impact by lobbying, primarily at the state level, for new statutes concerning issues ranging from mandatory minimum prison sentences for repeat offenders to the protection of the confidentiality of rape counseling records. Other external policy issues include dealing with members of the press who publish rape victims' names, pictures, and addresses; coordinating a sexual assault coalition in the local community made up of the treating hospitals, police departments, and rape crisis and victim counseling centers; and supporting in various ways the right of the rape crisis center to existence and financial viability.

In the category of internal office policies, the prosecutor should develop clearly defined standards for negotiating guilty pleas, nol-prossing charges (withdrawing from prosecution of cases), and administering polygraph tests to defendants or victims. There should be a regularly scheduled series of training sessions for the staff covering the legal, medical, and psychological issues involved in trying rape cases.

Summary

This chapter provides practical suggestions regarding the process of trial including preparation, jury selection and the *voir dire* process, opening statement, defense opening, cross-examination, rebuttal, and closing argument. Difficult cases include identification issue cases, the consent issue case, and the imperfect victim. The importance of general policies to govern the handling of rape cases within the prosecutor's office is discussed.

Forensic Examination of Sexual Assault Victims

18

KATHLEEN BROWN

Overview

Survivors of sexual assault require comprehensive, efficient, and sensitive care as soon as possible after the assault. Survivors have physical and emotional sequelae post-sexual assault that must be addressed. This chapter discusses physical sequelae and their treatment as well as collection of evidence from a victim of sexual assault. Examination post-sexual assault is necessary for identification and treatment of physical injuries and for the purpose of collection of forensic evidence. Examination and treatment of injuries have always been aspects of early intervention post-assault. Physicians are primarily responsible for this aspect, although few are specifically trained in forensic evidence collection related to sexual assault.

In order to help ensure comprehensive collection of evidence as well as treatment of injuries, sexual assault victims are now treated with a team approach. Identification and treatment of injuries have become pieces of a much larger picture in the immediate aftermath of sexual assault. The team approach requires representatives from rape care advocacy, law enforcement, prosecutors, a police crime laboratory, and a medical team that includes nurses or physicians who are trained in forensic evidence collection. The role of rape care advocacy in the period immediately after assault is to provide emotional support and information via accompaniment during interview and examination. Law enforcement is responsible for conducting the interviews and beginning the investigative processes. Prosecutors and the police crime laboratories provide guidelines for the collection of evidence. The police crime laboratory analyzes any evidence collected related to the crime of sexual assault. A specially trained nurse or physician interviews the victim, conducts an examination, and provides interventions.

Law enforcement, rape care advocacy nurses, and physicians must be available 24 hours a day, seven days a week. A team of rape care advocates, law enforcement personnel, and health care providers who are trained in caring for sexual assault survivors is therefore necessary. Every survivor of sexual assault should have access to a sexual assault response team in the immediate aftermath of the crime.

Access to the Sexual Assault Response Team

Victims of rape or sexual assault report the crime in a number of ways. The victim may call 911 to access the police. The victim may call a rape crisis hot line, or the victim may appear in the emergency room of a hospital accompanied by a family member or friend. Each point of access to the team must be prepared to receive the victim. Many victims do not report this crime, fearing revictimization by the legal system, the health care system, or both. Many victims are fearful of not being believed by police or health care providers. Many victims also fear retaliation by the offender if they report the crime. Department of Justice surveys reveal that rape and sexual assault are underreported crimes (U.S. Department of Justice, Bureau of Justice Statistics, Washington, 1996). It is important for team members to recognize victims' hesitancy to report. Creation of easy access to the team and appropriate, consistent, and caring initial responses to contact are crucial to victim reporting.

Calls to 911 should be received by trained personnel who follow protocols that help ensure victim safety and preservation of evidence. The 911 operators should evaluate the imminent danger for the victim and give her or him instructions as to how to preserve her or his safety until police can arrive on the scene. Instructions by 911 operators should also contain directions to be given to the victim to help preserve evidence. These instructions should include:

- Do not urinate or defecate if possible; if you must urinate, do not use toilet paper
- Do not eat or drink anything
- Do not gargle
- Do not change clothes
- Do not take a shower or bath
- Do not douche

Victims may reach the team via rape crisis center hot lines. Hot lines provide referrals 24 hours a day, 7 days a week. Trained personnel refer any victims of recent sexual assault to the emergency rooms that provide access to sexual assault response teams. Medical evaluation post-sexual assault is vitally important.

Victims may gain access to the team via direct entry to the emergency room. Victims may call a friend or relative after the assault. The assisting person may bring the victim directly to the emergency room. If this is the case, health care personnel will triage for injury and then activate the sexual assault response team including police, advocates, and a forensic examiner.

Preparation of personnel at all points of access to the team is an important team function. Whether the victim calls 911 or calls a hot line or goes directly to the emergency room, safety of the victim is the first priority followed by preservation of evidence and access to the sexual assault team.

Setting

Interview and examination within approximately 72 hours post-sexual assault are usually performed in an emergency department (ED) in a health care facility. It is not required that this be the setting; however, the 24-hour availability makes the ED the likely place for immediate care post-assault. The role of the health care facility in a sexual assault team is to ensure the medical safety of survivors of sexual assault. Every ED is equipped with emergency department physicians who can provide urgent care for survivors who require immediate medical attention. A prompt medical response to the arrival of the survivor to the ED is essential.

Medical intervention is required in many cases of sexual assault. Survivors may require interventions such as suturing of lacerations, treatment for fractures, or evaluation and treatment of head trauma. Safety of the survivor is always the number one priority. Necessary medical intervention precedes any evidence collection.

If interview and examination post-sexual assault are not conducted in an emergency room, careful triage for injuries must be performed prior to interview or forensic evaluation. A setting not in an emergency department should be reasonably close to emergency facilities for easy and quick access to medical care if necessary.

Role of the Forensic Examiner

A registered nurse or a physician who has been trained to provide comprehensive and competent care to sexual assault survivors in the immediate aftermath of the assault is an important member of the response team. This person's specialized training includes interview skills, assessment for injury skills, knowledge about collection of forensic evidence, and therapies for prevention of sexually transmitted diseases and pregnancy. Forensic examiners must have photography skills and must be prepared to testify in a court of law.

Sexual assault can occur any time and any place. The nurses or physicians trained to treat sexual assault survivors must provide 24-hour coverage. The providers must be able to reach the ED or other site where care is provided within an hour of the arrival of a victim. In an ideal setting, the victim, law enforcement, the rape care advocate, and the forensic examiner arrive at the ED simultaneously. More commonly the victim arrives at the ED accompanied by law enforcement, after which the rape care advocate and the forensic examiner are called.

Forensic Interview

As soon as reasonably possible after medical intervention ensures the safety of the victim, an interview and forensic examination are conducted. After injuries have been treated, a quiet place should be sought in which to conduct the interview, which need not be the examination room. The interview should be conducted in a secure area to prevent patients and personnel from overhearing details of the assault. Minimal interruptions during the interview are desirable. The interview must be conducted in a nonjudgmental fashion. (See Appendices A, B, and C.)

The purpose of the forensic interview is twofold. One purpose is to hear the victim's account of the crime in order to guide the forensic examination. For example, the forensic examiner must hear from the victim the time and location of the assault. Length of time since the assault identifies the type of evidence that may be retrieved. Location of the assault keys the examiner to the possibility of finding evidence particles that have transferred from the crime scene to the victim's body.

The forensic examiner must hear in detail the type of sexual activity involved in the assault. Examiners are looking for trace evidence that is often difficult to find without a clear history. For example, semen and saliva, even with the use of good lighting sources, are difficult to locate.

The examiner must know how control of the victim was obtained. If bindings were used, for example, the examiner will look for evidence of the restraint.

The second purpose is related to law enforcement, which also requires information from the victim. Law enforcement must know where the crime occurred and must locate the crime scene for further investigation. Law enforcement must hear and record the victim's account of the sex acts performed during the crime so that the assault can be coded appropriately. Information about the offender is necessary for appropriate investigation of the assault.

The victim's account of any injuries sustained during the assault is vital to the investigation. The survivor must describe any loss of consciousness, head blows, or any pain or bleeding that occurred during the assault. He or she must explain any physical force utilized during the assault as well as any use of restraints. Sex acts including penetration of the vagina, rectum, or mouth by a penis, finger, or object must be described. Any biting, licking, or kissing and any oral or genital contact must be described.

If the survivor is noted during the interview to have any physical or mental deficiency, the examiner must describe it. Utilization of members of the medical team to appropriately evaluate physical or mental disabilities may be required.

Law enforcement and the forensic examiner should interview the victim, preferably at the same time. Who leads the interview is a choice among team members, but conducting one interview has many beneficial effects. It is difficult for the victim to discuss the nature of the crime. Discussing non-consensual sex with total strangers is a difficult task indeed, and the victim does not wish to repeat her account many times. The rape care advocate may be present during the interview to provide support if the victim desires her/his presence. The advocate listening to the account may be desirable for future counseling sessions. Conducting one interview eliminates the need to repeat the account by the victim, and it also eliminates contradictory information given in a stressful time by a victim. An interview conducted by two members of the team can also help ensure comprehensiveness. Further questioning by law enforcement during the investigation process is often necessary, and victims should be advised of that possibility.

A format for the interview should be designed and approved by all members of the sexual assault response team. Consistency in interview questions helps ensure the quality and integrity of sexual assault investigation. Documentation of the facts of the case related by the survivor is the goal of the interview. The interview is recorded in a concise fashion, containing quotes from the survivor as much as possible. Interviewing prior to the examination cannot always be accomplished, but it is very desirable. The interview guides the examination process and it begins the investigative process.

Consent Issues

Consent from the victim must be obtained for examination and treatment. In a true medical emergency, consent is assumed and medical personnel proceed. When the survivor is able to consent, permission must be obtained for examination, for reporting the crime to law enforcement, and for taking photographs. (See Appendix B.)

The age for providing consent is frequently an issue in cases of sexual assault. Many victims of sexual assault are adolescents and may fall below the age of consent. Each state defines age for consent, what qualifies as emancipation, and exceptions for consent in minors without parental permission in areas such as the treatment of sexually transmitted diseases or treatment of pregnancy. Forensic examiners must explore the law describing consent in the state in which they practice. In most cases, it is advisable to obtain parental consent for examination and treatment. Parental consent for examination of an adolescent survivor of sexual assault is the beginning of a long-term involvement of parents in the healing process after the assault.

Consent to report to law enforcement is vital to investigation of the case and is strongly encouraged. Rape care advocacy is often helpful in explaining issues related to consent. Victims may refuse to consent for reporting the assault based upon a belief system that is not grounded in fact. Members of the advocacy groups use education as a tool to encourage reporting. If the survivor refuses to consent to report, examination and treatment are provided; but forensic evidence is not collected.

Photographs are an important component of evidence collection. Permission to photograph must be obtained prior to taking pictures with a camera or via a colposcope. Health care facilities usually have consent-to-photograph forms that may be located in the emergency room.

Obtaining consent may be delayed if the victim is intoxicated or drugged and cannot give consent. Urgent care is provided, and the interview and forensic evidence aspects are delayed until the victim is able to consent and cooperate for interview and examination.

History

Medical history must be obtained prior to physical examination and treatment. History must include chronic diseases, medications, allergies (particularly to medication), and immunizations received. Information on last menstrual period should be requested, as should method of birth control.

History of the last consensual intercourse must be obtained; the police crime laboratory analysis requires this information since fluid from consensual sex may be incorporated into the specimen submitted for evidence.

A history of events that occurred after the assault that may influence evidence collection must be obtained. These include bathing or showering, changing clothes, douching, gargling, urinating or having a bowel movement, and eating or drinking. (See Appendix C.)

Forensic Examination

The body of the victim is carefully inspected for any possible transfer of evidence from the crime scene to the victim or from the perpetrator to the victim. Common trace evidence found in the immediate aftermath of sexual assault may include hair and fibers, semen and saliva, blood and tissue, and bite marks. The body is systematically inspected for injury and presence of trace evidence. Any organized method of inspection is acceptable. The most common organizational method is head and neck, chest and abdomen, arms, back, and legs. Pelvic examination and inspection of the rectum and buttocks end the examination. All injury is described and photographed (see Appendix D). All trace evidence is collected and packaged in a systematic fashion after it has been dried. Evidence can be lifted with gloved hands, combing onto a piece of paper, scraping with a glass slide, reconstituting with moistened cotton swabs or pieces of gauze, or with forceps with plastic covers to protect the tips.

First, the procedure for forensic examination must be explained to the victim. This can be done by the rape care advocate, the forensic examiner, or both members of the team. Explanation is usually given after the interview is complete. A private and preferably quiet place for examination is desired. The examination must be complete and concise and conducted in a caring and sensitive manner. The rape care advocate may be present for the examination. Law enforcement should not be present during the examination. The forensic examiner may invite a parent or spouse or partner to be present during the examination at her or his discretion. Examination should take place in a private area that will remain free of interruption. No one should enter or leave the room during the examination period. This not only ensures privacy, it prevents contamination of evidence collection.

The examination begins with the overall appearance of the victim. The physical appearance of the victim is objectively described, and a photograph of the victim is taken prior to evidence collection. Two photographs — one front view and one side view — may be taken. It is advisable for the victim to hold a piece of paper with her/his name and date on it for inclusion in the photographs.

The demeanor of the victim is a question often asked in a courtroom setting. The examiner must objectively describe the victim's behaviors observed during the interview and examination. Crying should be noted along with the exact time during the exam or interview when the crying was observed. "The victim is observed to be oriented to person, place, and time" is an example of an objective observation. Aspects of a neurological examination including test of coordination can be objectively documented. The opinion of the examiner as to the demeanor of the victim should never be included in a forensic report. Statements such as "in no apparent distress" are non-objective and inappropriate in a forensic evaluation.

Consistency of the forensic examination post-sexual assault is important. Each examination should follow a format that has been reviewed by the sexual assault response team. Consistency in examination reduces the risk of forgetting a portion of the examination and also serves the examiner well in a courtroom situation. Objectivity of the examiner is vital to good testimony. A description to a judge and jury as to the examination procedure utilized with *every* victim of rape or sexual assault brings credibility to the examiner (see Appendices C and D).

Clothing

The survivor is asked, after overall appearance is documented in writing and via photographs, to undress over a white paper sheet. The clothing worn during the assault is placed within paper bags and submitted for analysis to the police crime laboratory. If the clothing worn during the assault is not the clothing the victim wears to the examination, submit the clothing she or he is currently wearing and request that law enforcement also submit the clothing worn during the assault to the police crime laboratory. The victim places each piece of clothing in a separate paper bag to prevent cross-contamination. Items of clothing usually sent for evidence collection are shirts, pants or skirts, and underwear. Coats and shoes are usually not sent unless there is evidence present. The sheet over which the victim undressed is also sent to the police crime laboratory within a paper bag. The purpose for sending the clothing is to allow the police crime laboratory to inspect each piece for transfer of evidence from the crime scene to the clothing or from the perpetrator to the clothing.

The police crime laboratory describes each piece of clothing and carefully inspects it for evidence transfer. The item most frequently found to contain transfer from the perpetrator to the victim's clothing is women's underwear. If a female victim changed her underwear before arriving in the emergency department, it is important for the underwear worn during and/or right after the attack be found and delivered to law enforcement.

Each item of clothing must be dry before it is sent to the lab. This may require hanging items to dry in the examination room while the examination is performed. At times, when an item of clothing is soaked in blood, drying must occur in the police evidence room. If this is the case, the item is placed within a biohazard bag for protection of the law enforcement officer. The wet item is then given to the law enforcement officer. The officer takes responsibility for freezing the item, drying the item, or taking it directly to the crime laboratory. If the clothing is dry after the forensic examination, the paper bags are sealed with evidence tape, identified, and passed on to law enforcement. Law enforcement may choose to examine the clothing for rips, tears, and stains prior to sealing the paper bags. If this occurs, the officer should wear gloves. If the victim is unable to undress herself or himself, the examiner should wear gloves while the clothing is removed. If clothing must be cut in order to be removed, cutting should not be done through rips or tears or stains.

Detection of Injury

The victim is then dressed in a patient gown and inspected for signs of bodily injury. Inspection must be done with good light sources. High-intensity lights and a Wood's lamp are most commonly utilized. Inspection should be done slowly and carefully with the history of the event in mind throughout. Any sign of trauma must be described and photographed. Bruising should be noted and dated. Any soft tissue injury, laceration, or contusion should be noted, photographed, described in the record, and drawn on a body map contained within the record.

Bruising occurs over time. Early on, a bruise appears as a reddened area. In time, it becomes black and blue. Arrangements for follow-up photography should be made with law enforcement after completion of the examination. The police laboratory should develop all photographs that require development. Forensic Polaroid photographs develop on site. Digital cameras can be utilized. All members of the sexual assault team must agree upon the use of digital photography.

Inspection for injuries obtained during the assault is vital to the investigation and most commonly begins with the head and neck area. Lacerations, abrasions, scratches, and bruises of the head and neck area are noted and photographed. The eyes are carefully inspected for petechaie and retinal hemorrhage. Petechaie can be related to anoxia, and retinal hemorrhage can be related to shaking as in shaken-baby syndrome. Any victim who lost consciousness during the assault and/or experienced head trauma requires appropriate medical evaluation and treatment. The nose and the ears are inspected with an otoscope for bleeding, swelling, or bruising. The backs of the ears must be inspected for signs of bruising. Mouth and lips are inspected for injury. Early bruising and petechaie have been observed in victims of oral sexual assault in the mouth and throat area. If the victim is punched in the area of the mouth, injury will be detected. Use of a Wood's lamp may assist in finding semen on the face. The teeth of the victim should be observed for integrity. Bruising of the neck is a common finding in victims of sexual assault. Control of the victim is frequently obtained via offender's hand on the victim's throat. Any indication of early bruising of the neck should be noted and photographed.

The body is then inspected for injury. The entire body is inspected for bruising, scratches, lacerations, abrasions, bite marks, and edema. If bondage was utilized during the assault, close attention must be paid to the legs and arms for early bruising or other signs of restraint. The breasts are commonly injured in sexual assault. The breasts must be carefully inspected for saliva, bite marks, bruising, scratching, and swelling. The inner thighs of the survivor must be carefully inspected for scratching and bruising. The inner thighs are also a common place for the discovery of semen. A Wood's lamp may assist in this discovery.

Collection of Forensic Evidence

Forensic evidence is collected from the survivor's body. Her or his body is inspected for hair, fibers, blood, semen, and saliva. The history of the event guides the examination for evidence. A Wood's lamp is often helpful in finding semen and saliva. Items such as hairs, fibers, grass, or sand are packaged on a piece of paper placed within an envelope or, if dry, in a film container. The container or envelope should not be airtight to retard growth and degradation. Dried blood found on the survivor's body can be scraped off with the side of a glass slide onto a piece of paper. The paper is folded druggist-style and placed within an envelope. If dried blood cannot be scraped off the body, it can be lifted with cotton swabs slightly moistened with sterile water. These swabs are then dried at room temperature and packaged in an envelope. Semen and/or saliva found on the body can be reconstituted with cotton swabs damp with sterile water that are then dried and packaged.

The survivor's head hair is combed through for any transfer of evidence from the crime scene or perpetrator. The hair is combed through onto paper, and both the paper and the comb are packaged into an envelope and sent to the police crime laboratory. Head hair is not pulled from the victim. Pulled head hair may be necessary for the investigation only if a hair with a root is obtained from the perpetrator as part of evidence collection. In that rare case, where a full head hair from the perpetrator is found, pulled hair from the victim is recovered for a control during the investigative process.

Fingernails are scraped looking for fibers, blood, and tissue, especially if the victim scratched the perpetrator. These scrapings are placed onto paper and placed into an envelope. Fingernail scraping from one hand should be kept separate from scrapings from the other hand. Fingernails may be clipped and the tips sent to the laboratory if the fingernail(s) are broken or injured during the assault.

A blood sample is drawn from the survivor. This blood sample becomes the known or reference source of DNA in the investigation.

The oral cavity is swabbed with cotton swabs. The area around the gums and teeth is the area of concentration. These specimens are analyzed for semen and sperm. The police crime laboratory may require that a slide be made of the oral secretions. Bite marks can be analyzed for identification. Any bite mark found on the body requires assistance from a forensic dentist. No attempt should be made to analyze a bite mark by a forensic examiner. The forensic dentist utilized by the team must be consulted.

DNA can be found in any human tissue or body fluid containing nucleated cells. The new methods for analyzing DNA require minimal amounts of substance. Careful searching of the body can reveal important forensic evidence that can be analyzed for the presence of DNA. DNA can be retrieved from samples of blood, flesh, seminal fluid, vaginal fluid, saliva, and hair with roots, perspiration stains, and dandruff in sufficient sample.

Examination of Genitalia

Examination of genitalia and rectal examination concludes the examination. The female victim should be appropriately draped and reclining on a gynecology table for this examination. A male victim can be examined on an examination table and should also be draped appropriately. The rape care advocate should be seated at the head of the exam table in order to provide support and education.

Inspection begins the genital examination. Colposcopy assists in the detection of injury (see Appendix D at the end of this chapter). The colposcope serves as a light source and as a source of magnification. The examiner carefully inspects the external genitalia using the colposcope to detect any injury. Common injuries found on external genitalia include tears, ecchymosis, abrasions, redness, and swelling (TEARS) (Slaughter et al.[1]). Many examiners utilize the acronym TEARS as a describing and charting mechanism. Photographs are taken via the colposcope. Inspection of external genitalia and orienting photographs, if they are to be taken, are done first. Photographs are taken before evidence is collected. The photographs will then demonstrate the appearance of the genitalia prior to collection of evidence. The number of photographs taken is a decision made by the team. A common approach is one or two orienting photographs of external genitalia that include the entire area followed by photographs centering on any injured area. In addition to being photographed, each area of injury should be described in the record and drawn on a body map within the record.

Toluidine blue dye can be utilized to enhance visualization of any injury to the external genitalia. The dye is liberally applied to areas of injury using swabs. Excess dye is then removed with a vinegar solution or with a water-soluble lubricant. The dye will "take" only in areas where the integrity of the tissue has been disturbed. Photographs of any injury are then retaken with the dye in place. If toluidine blue dye is applied to female victims, it should be placed on any sites of injury prior to insertion of the speculum.

Pubic hair is combed for any transfer of evidence. A clean comb is utilized, and the combing occurs onto a piece of paper. Both the comb and the results of the combing are sent to the police crime laboratory. The comb and the hair are folded into a piece of paper that is placed within an envelope. Any matted hair in the pubic region is clipped and sent in a piece of paper in an envelope to the laboratory. Pubic hair is not pulled at the time of examination. Pulled pubic hair may need to be collected at a later date in the unlikely event that a hair with a root from the perpetrator is recovered in evidence collection. If this occurs, a pubic hair with a root from the perpetrator is obtained; and a control pubic hair sample from the victim must be obtained. The low frequency of necessity for pulled pubic hair from the victim, coupled with the discomfort associated with the procedure, negates any recommendation that pubic hair be pulled in the immediate aftermath of sexual assault.

The external genitalia may be swabbed for semen. Swabbing can be done with moistened cotton swabs or with moistened gauze. If the victim is a male, the penis and scrotum should be swabbed.

Injury to the hymen may be detected in internal inspection prior to insertion of the speculum. Careful inspection of the hymenal tissue with labial retraction is required. In victims who have no sexual experience prior to the assault, good visualization of the hymen is necessary. Positions required for good visualization are lithotomy with legs in stirrups, and the knee-chest position. Firm but gentle retraction of the labia is required for visualization of the hymenal tissue. The colposcope can aid in identification of the tissue. The use of a Foley catheter for visual inspection of the hymen may be necessary in female victims with redundant hymenal tissue. In this case, a Foley catheter is inserted past the hymenal tissue. The balloon is then inflated with air or water. The inflated catheter is pulled back against the hymenal tissue and brings the tissue forward for observation. (See Appendix D.) Photographs are taken of any injury.

Internal genitalia of the female victim are inspected secondarily. Speculum insertion is required for internal inspection. Orienting photographs of the vaginal walls and cervix should be taken. One or two orienting or overall photographs demonstrate the appearance of internal genitalia prior to collection of evidence. Photographs of any areas of injury are then taken. Common injuries seen on internal examination are bruising, bleeding, and lacerations. The TEARS checklist can be utilized in the recording of injury to internal genitalia. Each injury should be photographed as well as described in the report and drawn on a body map within the record.

Vaginal swabbing is done after inspection. The vagina is swabbed with at least four cotton applicators. One applicator is inserted into the cervix. The other three are utilized to absorb any secretions visualized in the vagina. The swabs must stay in place for purposes of absorption for a few minutes. Any secretions noted on the speculum when it is withdrawn from the vagina are also swabbed. Secretions on the bottom blade of the speculum are derived from the surface area underneath the cervix. Swabbing the speculum allows for collection of secretions from this area. The police crime laboratory may request that a slide from swabs be made of the vaginal secretions. All swabs must be dried prior to packaging for the crime laboratory. Any slides made are allowed to air dry before packaging.

Inspection of vaginal secretions for sperm may be performed under a microscope. Presence and motility of sperm can be noted under the microscope. If a slide is prepared for identification of sperm, both the slide and the swab utilized to make the slide should be dried, packaged, and sent to the police crime laboratory. No evidence may be discarded. Visualization of sperm under the microscope permits corroboration of the victim's account of the assault in terms of time. If sperm can be identified as motile by the examiner, the ejaculation occurred within hours of the examination. Visualization of sperm does not identify the perpetrator, as DNA is capable of doing; therefore, the slide and the swabs utilized to prepare the slide must be submitted to the laboratory for further analysis. In a male survivor, external genitalia are inspected and photographed. The penis and scrotum are swabbed. The swabs are dried and packaged and sent to the police crime laboratory.

Rectal Examination

Rectal examination is performed after genital inspection and collection of evidence. Anoscopy is performed if the case involves known or suspected sodomy. Swabs for forensic evidence can be collected via the anoscope. Appearance of rectal bleeding indicates a need for anoscopy. The rectum is inspected in both the lithotomy and side-lying positions in all cases of sexual assault. The rectum is carefully inspected using gentle but firm retraction. Tears, bruising, and masses (rectal prolapse) have been noted post-rectal assault. The rectum is inspected utilizing the colposcope. Any injuries are photographed via the colposcope. Toluidine blue dye may be used to enhance visualization of perianal injuries. Swabs from the rectum are obtained in all cases of sexual assault.

The buttocks must be inspected before completion of the examination. The buttocks must be inspected for any injury such as bite marks or bruising. Evidence in the form of semen or saliva must be collected from the buttocks if present.

Proper Handling (Management) of Evidence

A drying box must be utilized or the examiner must design another method of drying swabs and pieces of gauze. A common method for drying in the absence of a drying box is individual test tubes, clearly identified, in a test tube rack. It is important that all material submitted to the police crime laboratory be dried at room temperature. Swabs must be kept separate from each other to prevent transfer of evidence during the drying process. The sources of the swabs must not be confused during the drying process.

All evidence collected must be labeled properly. Swabs must be placed in envelopes clearly marked *vaginal, oral,* or *rectal*. Each piece of evidence must be marked on the container (indirect marking) with description, name, number or other designation, person who recovered the evidence, and date. An evidence log should be part of the permanent record. Each piece of evidence collected should be marked on the evidence log.

A common way to organize the collection of evidence is via an evidence collection kit. Three companies make kits, and each kit organizes the collection slightly differently. The kits include envelopes marked with areas of collection such as vaginal swabs, rectal swabs, oral swabs, pubic hair combing, debris collection, fingernail scrapings, head hair combing, etc. Both the forensic examiner and the police officer should sign off the evidence log and the sexual assault evidence collection kit if one is utilized. The kit is sealed with evidence tape by the examiner and the law enforcement officer.

Any evidence collected during examination is turned over to law enforcement. (See Appendix E.) If the victim brings evidence to the examination that cannot be contained within an evidence collection kit, it is given to law enforcement. For example, if the victim brings a condom utilized during the assault to the examination, the condom is placed in a biohazard bag and given to the police officer. The kit, after evidence has been collected, is given to the officer. Clothing collected during the examination is given to the officer.

Chain of Custody

Chain of custody of evidence must be maintained throughout the examination. The purpose of chain of custody is to demonstrate that the evidence was never left unattended and was not subject to tampering. Evidence must be in the control of the forensic examiner or the law enforcement officer at all times or it must be under lock and key with minimal access to the key. The kit must be sealed and signed by both the officer and the examiner. The evidence log indicating what was collected (clothing, condom, tampon) and the kit should be signed and dated by both the officer and the examiner. Evidence must be collected properly, stored properly (at no more than 70 degrees), transported properly via the law enforcement officer, and properly documented as to its collection and transfer. Each sexual assault response team must develop procedures to ensure chain of custody of all pieces of evidence. Without meticulous procedure and documentation of procedure related to chain of custody, evidence cannot be utilized in a court of law.

Documentation

Adequate, concise, and well-organized documentation is a must in sexual assault cases. A clear and easy-to-use charting system is important for consistency among the examiners and for clarity in the prosecutor's office. Photographs should be developed by law enforcement. Colposcopic pictures are given to law enforcement at the completion of the examination as evidence. A photography log should be included in the record. Each picture taken, colposcopic pictures included, should be listed with a number and description of what has been photographed.

Body maps and maps of genitalia on which to draw injuries are recommended. At times, photographs do not develop well and drawings become necessary. A narrative account of the assault is recommended for inclusion within the chart. Documentation should be non-judgmental and draw few conclusions. Documentation should be legible and clear.

Commonly, prosecutors ask for the forensic examiner's opinion in writing as to consistency of findings with history. Forensic examiners typically conclude their documentation with a statement indicating consistency or inconsistency of physical findings with history from the victim.

Drug and Alcohol Testing

Many police crime laboratories are equipped to analyze blood and/or urine for toxicology. If the police crime laboratory does not have this capability, law enforcement may contract with a private laboratory capable of performing toxicology screenings. The decision to provide blood or urine for screening is made by law enforcement and the forensic examiner. The examiner may recommend screening based upon the interview of the victim and/or the neurologic evaluation of the victim.

If toxicology screening is to be obtained, a specimen should be collected and submitted to law enforcement under guidelines for chain of evidence. The specimen should be collected per laboratory rules for collection as soon as possible after entry into the health care system. The forensic examiner may choose to wait and watch the victim before the interview and examination are conducted, when neurologic testing indicates that obtaining consent due to intoxication is an issue. Drug and alcohol screening samples should be obtained prior to the waiting period for reasons of medical and forensic necessity. Full toxicology screening must be requested. The appropriate laboratory as indicated by law enforcement must perform analysis.

Therapy and Prophylaxis

Medical therapy is implemented as required. Suture of lacerations, treatment of fractures, and other medical therapies are priority and are implemented prior to evidence collection. Prophylactic treatment for sexually transmitted diseases (STDs) and prevention of pregnancy should be addressed in every case of female sexual assault. Male survivors of sexual assault require prophylaxis for STDs. The Centers for Disease Control (CDC) published a protocol for prevention of STDs post-sexual assault. Cultures are not taken in the immediate aftermath of sexual assault. Treatment is the current recommendation, with cultures performed at follow-up visits. Protocol for treatment of STDs is followed according to the CDC published standard with deviations for age, allergies, or pregnancy implemented throughout the guidelines.

Prevention of pregnancy is offered to all female victims of sexual assault. Prevention is achieved via emergency contraception published in *Contraceptive Technology*.[2] The victim is given 100 mcg of estrogen via birth control pills after completion of the examination and again in 12 hours. Progesterone-only tablets may be given to prevent pregnancy rather than a combination of estrogen and progesterone. An existing pregnancy must be ruled out prior to administration.

Follow-Up Care

Follow-up examinations for pregnancy testing, cultures for STDs, Hepatitis B vaccinations, healing of injuries, and anonymous HIV testing are recommended. Follow-up examination can occur in a private health care office or at a public health center. Arrangements for follow-up medical care should be made after interview and examination. Rape care advocates can be of great assistance in scheduling and helping the victims to maintain these appointments.

Post-sexual assault counseling is vitally important. The presence of rape care advocacy in the immediate aftermath of sexual assault sets the stage for follow-up counseling. During the forensic examination, the rape care advocate ensures the safety of the survivor and works toward keeping the forensic evidence collection process and the follow-up experiences as victim-focused and non-traumatic as possible. The rape care advocate does what the title suggests — advocates. She or he will follow the survivor after the assault.

The advocate may accompany the survivor for follow-up visits and screenings and accompanies the survivor in court. The advocate ensures that the survivor receives adequate counseling and support as long as is necessary post-sexual assault.

The forensic examiner should call the survivor within 48 hours of the assault. The purpose of the telephone call is to answer questions related to the examination and to provide reassurance to the survivor concerning her or his health. The objectivity of the forensic examiner is assured by termination of contact with the victim after the follow-up telephone call. The rape care advocate assumes the responsibility for long-term advocacy and counseling.

Discharge Instructions

Written discharge instructions related to completion of STD treatment and prevention of pregnancy are recommended. Discharge instructions should contain information about follow-up visits — where and when — and they should include information about 24-hour help lines and how to contact rape care advocacy centers. All findings of the examination should be explained clearly to the survivor, with written suggestions for any follow-up care that may be required.

Conclusion

Women and men, young and old, deserve compassionate, complete, and comprehensive care as soon as possible after sexual assault. The development of highly specialized teams composed of members from law enforcement, health care, and rape care advocacy helps ensure that all victims of sexual assault receive integrated, concise, and timely responses to sex-related crimes. The development of forensic examiners ensures interview post-sexual assault and collection of evidence that enhances investigation of sexual assault. Forensic examiners provide testimony in court as to evidence collected and injury detected. Every community should develop and maintain a sexual assault response team.

References

1. Slaughter, L., Brown, C., Crowley, S., and Peck, R. (1997) Patterns of genital injury in female sexual assault victims. *Am. J. Obstet. Gynecol.*, 176(3), 609–616.
2. *Contraceptive Technology,* 16th Edition, Irvington Publishers Inc., New York.

Appendix A

STATE OF NEW JERSEY
SEXUAL ASSAULT EXAMINATION REPORT
(PLEASE PRINT)

EXAMINATION INFORMATION:

Location of Examination_____

Case Number _____ Date _____ Time of Report _____

Name of Primary Examiner _____

Additional Personnel Present _____

_____

Investigating Agency(ies) _____

Investigating Officer(s) _____

PATIENT INFORMATION:

Name _____

Address _____

_____

Telephone _____ Social Security Number _____

Date of Birth _____ Race _____

The patient is the reported: ☐ Victim   ☐ Suspect

Appendix B

AUTHORIZATION
FOR COLLECTION AND RELEASE OF EVIDENCE AND INFORMATION

I, _____, freely consent
(Name of Patient)

to allow _____, and
(Name of Examining Nurse or Physician)

designated assistants to conduct a physical examination for purposes of identifying and treating injury and collecting evidence related to a reported sexual assault. This procedure has been fully explained to me, and I understand that this examination may include clinical observation for the presence of injury and the collection of specimens for laboratory analysis. I understand the nature of the examination and that information gathered may be used as evidence in a court of law.

I   do ☐   do not ☐   authorize the examiner, the examination facility and its agents to release the specimens, photographs, medical records, and related information pertinent to this incident to law enforcement officials.

I understand that if I do not authorize release at this time, the evidence and information will be secured for 90 days, pending my decision to proceed with notification of law enforcement authorities.

I hereby release and hold harmless the examiner, the examination facility, and its agents from any and all liability and claims of injury whatsoever which may in any manner result from the authorized release of such information.

_____
(Signature of Patient)

_____
(Signature of Parent or Guardian where applicable)

_____   _____
(Date)   (Signature of Witness)

Appendix C

MEDICAL HISTORY

HEIGHT _____ WEIGHT _____ Last Menstrual Period _____

Current Pregnancy? ☐ YES ☐ NO   If Yes, Weeks of Gestation _____

History of Medical Problems? ☐ YES   ☐ NO

Describe _____

_____

History of Hospitalizations? ☐ YES   ☐ NO

Describe _____

_____

Medications Currently in Use? ☐ YES   ☐ NO

List _____

_____

Medication Allergies? ☐ YES   ☐ NO

List _____

_____

Date of Incident _____ Time of Incident _____

Describe the Environment where the Incident Occurred _____

_____

_____

_____

Case Number

_____

Initials of Examiner

Patient's Description of Incident:

_____

_____

_____

_____

_____

_____

_____

_____

_____

_____

_____

_____

_____

_____

_____

_____

_____

(If more space is needed, document under "Additional Information")

Were restraints used? ☐ YES ☐ NO ☐ UNSURE

If yes, method: ☐ Suspect's hands ☐ Suspect's body ☐ Blindfold
☐ Bindings ☐ Other _____

If yes, describe restraint:

_____

_____

_____   _____
Case Number   Initials of Examiner

Indicate all acts which occurred during the incident:

ORAL CONTACT: YES NO ATTEMPTED UNSURE

Did suspect kiss, suck, lick or bite patient?   ☐   ☐   ☐   ☐
If yes, describe _____
Did suspect's mouth touch patient's genitals?   ☐   ☐   ☐   ☐
Did patient's mouth touch suspect's genitals?   ☐   ☐   ☐   ☐

GENITAL CONTACT:

Did suspect's penis contact patient's genitals?   ☐   ☐   ☐   ☐
Did suspect's penis enter patient's vagina?   ☐   ☐   ☐   ☐
Did suspect's fingers contact patient's genitals?   ☐   ☐   ☐   ☐
Did suspect's fingers enter patient's vagina?   ☐   ☐   ☐   ☐
Did a foreign object contact patient's genitals?   ☐   ☐   ☐   ☐
Did a foreign object enter patient's vagina?   ☐   ☐   ☐   ☐
If yes, describe object _____

ANAL CONTACT:

Did suspect's penis contact patient's anus?   ☐   ☐   ☐   ☐
Did suspect's penis enter patient's anus?   ☐   ☐   ☐   ☐
Did suspect's fingers contact patient's anus?   ☐   ☐   ☐   ☐
Did suspect's fingers enter patient's anus?   ☐   ☐   ☐   ☐
Did a foreign object contact patient's anus?   ☐   ☐   ☐   ☐
Did a foreign object enter patient's anus?   ☐   ☐   ☐
If yes, describe object _____
Did suspect wear a condom?   ☐   ☐   ☐   ☐
Did suspect ejaculate?   ☐   ☐   ☐   ☐
If yes, where? ☐ patient's mouth   ☐ patient's vagina   ☐ patient's anus   ☐ other
If other, describe location _____

_____   _____
Case Number   Initials of Examiner

PATIENT'S ACTIVITIES SINCE INCIDENT:

Urinated	☐ YES	☐ NO	Bathed or Showered	☐ YES	☐ NO
Defecated	☐ YES	☐ NO	Douched	☐ YES	☐ NO
Ate or Drank	☐ YES	☐ NO	Brushed teeth/gargled	☐ YES	☐ NO
Vomited	☐ YES	☐ NO	Changed Clothes	☐ YES	☐ NO

ADDITIONAL INFORMATION:

_____

_____

_____

_____

_____

_____

_____

_____

_____

_____

_____

_____

_____

_____

_____

_____

_____

_____

_____

_____

_____   _____

Case Number   Initials of Examiner

Appendix D

PHYSICAL EXAMINATION AND COLLECTION OF SPECIMENS

GENERAL INSTRUCTIONS

This examination outline has been designed to aid evidence collection by minimizing the potential for cross-contamination of anatomical sites and loss of trace evidence, while providing a tool to assess the needs of the patient.

All sections of the form should be completed fully, using the designation "N/A" for any sections not applicable to a particular case.

Gloves should be worn throughout the examination and collection procedures. Gloves should be changed to reduce the risk of cross-contamination.

All specimens should be labeled to include CASE NUMBER, EXAMINER'S INITIALS, and ANATOMICAL SITE of specimen collection.

All evidence should be dry before packaging. To dry swabs, place swab upright with cotton tip pointing upward to promote drying. For example, swab can be placed in a test tube rack or, after removing the stopper from a blood collection tube, place tube in a test tube rack or other device and place swab in tube. To avoid confusion, label swab and/or drying device to indicate anatomical site of each specimen. When swabs are *completely dry,* follow Instructions for Packaging Evidence at the end of this packet.

If an item of clothing is wet, place a plain piece of paper against the stain before folding and placing in a paper bag. Any paper bag containing wet clothing should be left unsealed to allow air circulation to promote drying.

FORENSIC EXAMINATION

Describe general appearance of patient and clothing: _____

_____

_____

DEBRIS COLLECTION: ENVELOPE 1

Specimens Collected: ☐ YES   ☐ NO

Carefully inspect patient's head, hands and other exposed skin surfaces, as well as outer surface of clothing, for any loose debris including grass, leaves, fibers, threads, etc.

Using one paper fold from the envelope marked "DEBRIS," carefully remove the loose material and place it inside the unfolded paper. Refold paper to retain material; seal using enclosed self-adhesive label, and indicate location on patient's body or clothing from which material was collected.

Repeat as necessary until all visible debris is collected.

Place sealed paper folds into envelope marked "DEBRIS," seal, and label envelope as indicated.

_____   _____

Case Number   Initials of Examiner

CLOTHING COLLECTION: ENVELOPE (BAG) 2

Specimens Collected: ☐ YES   ☐ NO

Are these the clothes worn at the time of the incident? ☐ YES   ☐ NO

If no, notify investigating officer and confer to determine which items should be collected.

Remove from kit and unfold the large piece of plain white paper; place it on the floor. Have the fully clothed patient remove shoes, then stand in the center of the paper.

Ask the patient to remove one article of clothing at a time. If the article of clothing has wet stains of potential biological material (blood, saliva, semen, etc.), lay flat to dry. If still wet at the end of the exam, place a piece of paper against the stain and fold carefully to avoid transfer of fluid to other parts of the clothing.

Place each item in a separate *paper* bag. Several bags are included in the kit, but additional bags may be needed. If so, any clean paper bag may be used.

The paper bag should be sealed and labeled as indicated.

Underpants should be collected in the bag marked "CLOTHING–UNDERPANTS," even if they are not the pair worn during or immediately after the incident. Vaginal secretions may accumulate, even if the patient has bathed or showered.

The paper on which the patient stood during the clothing collection should be carefully folded to retain any debris which may have fallen from the patient or clothing. This folded paper should be sealed with tape and labeled "Debris from clothing." Case number, date, and initials of examiner should be written on outside of folded paper.

SKIN SURFACE ASSESSMENT

Carefully perform a visual inspection of the patient's external skin surfaces. Locate, describe and, if equipment is available, photograph any evidence of injury or adherent foreign matter. Use anatomical diagrams on the next page to document a description of injuries including location, size, and appearance.

Were external injuries noted?   ☐ YES   ☐ NO

Were Photographs of external injuries taken?   ☐ YES   ☐ NO

If yes, describe photography equipment and indicate name of photographer:

_____

(Equipment)

_____

_____

(Photographer)

_____   _____

Case Number   Initials of Examiner

SKIN SURFACE ASSESSMENT

Utilize diagrams to document all injuries and findings including cuts, lacerations, ecchymosis, abrasions, redness, swelling, bites, burns, scars and stains/foreign material on patient's body. Distinguish pre-existing injuries from those resulting from incident. Record size, color and appearance of all injuries. If a Wood's Lamp is used to assist in visualizing secretions, denote areas of (+) Wood's Lamp findings with "WL."

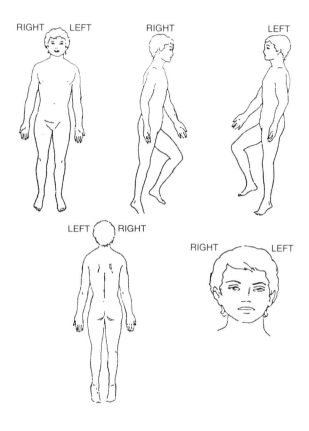

Case Number   Initials of Examiner

DRIED SECRETIONS: ENVELOPE 3

Specimen Collected: ☐ YES   ☐ NO

Was a Wood's (UV) Lamp used to assist in visualizing
dried secretions?   ☐ YES   ☐ NO

If visible areas of dried secretions are noted on external skin surfaces, with or without use of the Wood's Lamp, document findings on anatomical diagram on previous page.

Open swab packet and lightly moisten one swab using distilled water from dropper bottle in kit; gently rub swab over area of stain using a circular motion.

To collect a control specimen, moisten second swab and gently rub on skin surface approximately two inches from the skin surface from which dried secretion was collected.

Dry swabs as directed in GENERAL INSTRUCTIONS.

Repeat steps on all areas where secretions are noted.

BITE MARKS:

Were any bite marks noted?   ☐ YES   ☐ NO

If yes, document location of bite mark on anatomical diagram and, where possible, photograph bite mark with and without scale.

If available, confer with a forensic odontologist.

Collect a saliva specimen by using a lightly moistened swab to gently rub inside the parameters of the bitemark; collect a control swab from a skin surface approximately two inches from the bite mark.

EXAMINATION OF HEAD AND MOUTH

HEAD HAIR COMBINGS: ENVELOPE 4

Specimen Collected: ☐ YES   ☐ NO

Unfold white paper; hold this paper under the ends of the patients's hair and carefully comb the hair using the comb provided so that any debris in the hair will be caught on the paper.

Refold; place folded paper and comb in envelope marked "HEAD HAIR COMBINGS." Seal and label envelope as indicated.

HEAD HAIR CONTROL: ENVELOPE 5

Specimen Collected: ☐ YES   ☐ NO

DO NOT COLLECT head hair control sample if the patient and suspect work together or live together.

Unfold white paper; while wearing gloves, carefully pull 10 hairs from the *front* of the patient's head by grasping and pulling near the root. Only use tweezers to pull hairs if patient's hair is too short to grasp with gloved fingers. Place hairs on paper.

Repeat process collecting hairs from the *top, back, and both sides* of the head for a total of 50 hairs.

Refold paper and place in envelope marked "HEAD HAIR CONTROL;" seal and label as indicated.

_____   _____
Case Number   Initials of Examiner

ORAL SWABS AND SMEAR: ENVELOPE 6

Specimen Collected: ☐ YES   ☐ NO

Carefully inspect inner aspects of patient's lips, cheeks and throat for signs of injury.

Were any injuries noted?   ☐ YES   ☐ NO

If yes, describe _____

_____

Was photodocumentation of injuries done?   ☐ YES   ☐ NO

Open the swab packet from envelope marked "ORAL SPECIMENS," and grasp both swabs together by the shaft. Carefully swab the area between the cheek and gum with specific attention to the area behind the back molars on both the upper and lower teeth.

Remove glass slide from the envelope and use a pencil to label frosted end with CASE NUMBER and EXAMINER INITIALS and letter "O" for oral. Roll swabs on surface of glass slide using a single smooth stroke; *do not zig-zag*. Place slide in holder provided; place holder in envelope.

Label and dry swabs as previously instructed.

EXAMINATION OF HANDS:

Carefully inspect dorsal and palmar surface of hands for any signs of trauma. Document all findings on the anatomical diagram.

FINGERNAIL SWABS: ENVELOPE 7

Specimen Collected: ☐ YES   ☐ NO

Unfold white paper from envelope marked "FINGERNAIL SPECIMENS" and open swab packet.

Holding patient's hand over paper, use one swab lightly moistened with distilled water to carefully swab under the nails of the right hand, catching any loose debris on paper. Refold paper and seal using self-adhesive label provided. Indicate source of specimen.

Repeat this process using other paper fold and a fresh swab for the left hand.

Dry swabs as previously instructed.

_____   _____

Case Number   Initials of Examiner

GENITAL EXAMINATION

FEMALE

Utilize diagrams to document all injuries and findings including tears, ecchymosis, abrasions, redness, swelling, scars and stains/foreign material on patient's genitals. Distinguish pre-existing injuries from those resulting from the assault. Record size, color and appearance of all injuries. If a Wood's Lamp is used to assist in visualizing secretions, denote area of (+) Wood's Lamp findings with "WL."

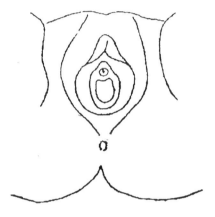

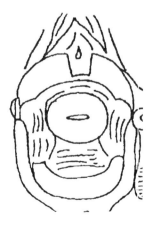

_____

Case Number

_____

Initials of Examiner

GENITAL EXAMINATION

MALE

Utilize diagrams to document all injuries and findings including tears, ecchymosis, abrasions, redness, swelling, scars and stains/foreign material on patient's genitals. Distinguish pre-existing injuries from those resulting from the assault. Record size, color and appearance of all injuries. If a Wood's Lamp is used to assist in visualizing secretions, denote area of (+) Wood's Lamp findings with "WL."

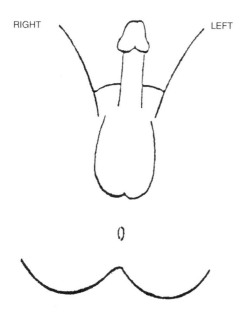

RIGHT   LEFT

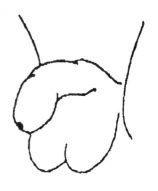

Case Number   Initials of Examiner

GENITAL EXAMINATION

PUBIC HAIR COMBING: ENVELOPE 8

Specimen Collected: ☐ YES   ☐ NO

Remove paper fold from envelope marked "PUBIC HAIR COMBINGS."

Ask patient to sit on unfolded paper so that the paper protrudes between the thighs; comb downward on pubic hair to dislodge any debris or loose hairs onto the paper. Fold paper to retain debris and place paper and comb in envelope; seal and label as indicated.

PUBIC HAIR CONTROL: ENVELOPE 9

Specimen Collected: ☐ YES   ☐ NO

Using a gloved hand, firmly grasp 5 pubic hairs close to the root and pull.

Place specimen on unfolded white paper; repeat procedure five times for a total sample of 25 hairs.

Refold paper and place in envelope marked "PUBIC HAIR CONTROL." Seal and label.

With patient in lithotomy position, carefully inspect entire genital area for signs of injury. Document positive findings on body diagrams of appropriate genitalia. If colposcopy equipment is available, use colposcope to examine for injuries and document any tears, abrasions, ecchymosis, redness or swelling noted.

Were injuries identified?   ☐ YES   ☐ NO

Was colposcopy used to assist visualization?   ☐ YES   ☐ NO

Was colposcopic photography done?   ☐ YES   ☐ NO

EXTERNAL GENITAL SPECIMEN: ENVELOPE 10

Specimen Collected: ☐ YES   ☐ NO

Open 2×2 gauze packet. Lightly moisten gauze with distilled water and gently wipe external genitalia. For male patients, wipe the surface of the glans and the shaft; for female patients, wipe the inner surface of the the labia minora with a downward motion. Place gauze on a flat surface to dry.

After drying, return gauze to envelope marked "EXTERNAL GENITAL SPECIMEN;" seal and label as indicated.

VAGINAL SWABS AND SMEAR: ENVELOPE 11

Specimen Collected: ☐ YES   ☐ NO

This step may be performed with a speculum in place, or "blindly" without the use of a speculum.

Using two swabs simultaneously, collect secretions from the vaginal vault (area below the cervix); roll swabs onto surface of a glass slide in one smooth motion; *do not zig-zag*. Label with CASE NUMBER, EXAMINER'S INITIALS and "V" for vaginal specimen. Return slide to holder and place in envelope marked "VAGINAL SPECIMENS."

Dry swabs as previously described.

_____   _____
Case Number   Initials of Examiner

CERVICAL SWABS AND SMEAR: ENVELOPE 12

Specimen Collected: ☐ YES   ☐ NO

This step should only be performed with the use of a speculum to ensure visualization of the cervix.

Using two swabs simultaneously, collect secretions from cervical os; prepare slide as indicated above, labeling with a "C" for cervix.

Dry swabs as previously described.

ANAL SWABS AND SMEAR: ENVELOPE 13

Specimen Collected: ☐ YES   ☐ NO

With the patient in the lithotomy, prone, or supine knee-chest or side-lying position, carefully evaluate the anus and buttocks for signs of injury. Document positive findings on appropriate genital anatomy diagram.

Using two moistened swabs simultaneously, gently rub swabs on anal folds and anal opening. Prepare slide as indicated, labeling with "A" for anal specimen. Return slide to holder and place in envelope marked "ANAL SPECIMENS."

Dry swabs as previously described.

DNA CONTROL SPECIMEN COLLECTION:

BUCCAL CONTROL SWABS: ENVELOPE 14

Specimen Collected: ☐ YES   ☐ NO

Ask patient to rinse mouth with water. Wait 30 seconds. Ask patient to swallow, then rub inner aspect of patient's cheek at least twelve times with two swabs simultaneously. Allow swabs to dry completely before packaging.

This has concluded the specimen collection process. The patient may be directed to perform any personal hygiene activities and to get dressed. Clean clothing should be made available to replace any items collected during the exam.

_____   _____

Case Number   Initials of Examiner

INSTRUCTIONS FOR PACKAGING SPECIMENS

After drying, swabs should be placed in corresponding swab boxes provided for each specimen. If additional swabs were collected from patient and no swab box is available for packaging, fully dried swabs may be placed in a plain envelope labeled with CASE NUMBER, INITIALS OF EXAMINER, and ANATOMICAL SITE of specimen collection.

Clothing bags should be sealed using tape, NOT STAPLES, documented on EVIDENCE RECEIPT FORM, and turned over to law enforcement or secured until transfer can be arranged. The sealed bag containing underpants may be packaged inside evidence kit box if space permits; all other clothing bags should remain outside of kit box. If wet clothing has been collected and packaged, the top of the bag should remain open and the police officer receiving evidence should been notified of wet contents.

All envelopes should be returned to the Evidence Kit box. As each envelope is placed in the box, indicate *presence of a collected specimen* by initialing on the line next to the corresponding specimen on the EVIDENCE RECEIPT FORM. Do not initial next to items of evidence that were not collected.

The white original of each document should be retained by the examiner as part of the examination site records, the yellow copy of each document should be given to the investigating officer, and the pink copy of each document should be placed inside the kit for use by laboratory personnel.

Upon completion of packaging, the Evidence Kit box should be sealed with red self-adhesive "Evidence Seals" that have been initialed by examiner.

Biohazard stickers should be attached to the Evidence Kit box and to any clothing bags that contain wet clothing.

The top portion of box top is to be completed by examiner.

If possible, the packaging of evidence should be observed by the law enforcement officer who will take possession as part of the chain of custody. If no law enforcement officer is available, packaged evidence should be stored in a locked, cool, dry location until release to law enforcement can be arranged.

ADDITIONAL NOTES:

_____

_____

_____

_____

_____

_____

_____   _____
Case Number   Initials of Examiner

Appendix E

SEXUAL ASSAULT EXAMINATION
EVIDENCE RECEIPT FORM

CASE NUMBER _____ DATE _____

Examiner should write initials next to each item of evidence collected from the patient. Any evidence collected that is not listed should be indicated in the area headed "Other Evidence." When possible, evidence should be packaged in the presence of the investigating officer.

ITEM OF EVIDENCE	INITIALS	ITEM OF EVIDENCE	INITIALS
DEBRIS		ORAL SWABS	
CLOTHING		ORAL SLIDE	
UNDERPANTS	_____	FINGERNAIL SWAB-LEFT	_____
OTHER CLOTHING		FINGERNAIL SWAB-RIGHT	_____
(LIST EACH ITEM SEPARATELY)		PUBIC HAIR COMBINGS	_____
_____	_____	PUBIC HAIR CONTROL	_____
_____	_____	EXTERNAL GENITAL SPECIMEN	_____
_____	_____	VAGINAL SWABS	_____
_____	_____	VAGINAL SLIDE	_____
_____	_____	CERVICAL SWABS	_____
DEBRIS FROM CLOTHING	_____	CERVICAL SLIDE	_____
DRIED SECRETIONS		ANAL SWABS	_____
(LIST EACH ITEM SEPARATELY)		ANAL SLIDE	_____
_____	_____	BUCCAL CONTROL SWABS	_____
_____	_____	OTHER EVIDENCE	
_____	_____	(LIST EACH ITEM SEPARATELY)	
_____	_____	_____	_____
_____	_____	_____	_____
_____	_____	_____	_____
HEAD HAIR COMBINGS	_____	_____	_____
HEAD HAIR CONTROL	_____		

_____   _____

SIGNATURE OF EXAMINER   SIGNATURE OF INVESTIGATING OFFICER

_____   _____

Case Number   Initials of Examiner

Section IV: Special Populations

The Sexual Crimes of Juveniles

19

JOHN A. HUNTER

Introduction

It is estimated that juveniles (typically defined as those under 18) account for up to one fifth of the rapes and one half of the cases of child sexual molestation committed in the U.S. each year (Sickmund, Snyder, and Poe-Yamagata, 1997). Generally consistent with overall trends in youth-perpetrated violence, juvenile sexual crime rose between 1985 and 1993 but has decreased since that time (OJJDP, 2000). Adolescent males commit the preponderance of these sexual crimes, although prepubescent children and females have been documented to engage in sexual aggression.

Concern about juvenile sexual perpetration has increased in recent years in response to incidence data and studies suggesting that juvenile offending may portend more chronic and insidious patterns of sexual aggression. The concern largely stems from retrospective studies of adult sex offenders indicating that 40 to 50% had a juvenile onset to their sexual offending (Marshall, Barbaree, and Eccles, 1991). While these studies have helped bring needed attention to the problem of juvenile sexual offending, the cited data may have led to an exaggeration of the likelihood that sexual aggression in childhood and adolescence leads to adult offending. At issue are the problems associated with retrospective data and sampling biases. A more accurate estimation of the number of juveniles who go on to offend as adults will come from prospective longitudinal studies.

Developmental Issues

An understanding of juvenile sexual offending necessitates some attention to examining causes. Clinical data have long suggested that many youthful sex offenders were sexually victimized before they ever began offending. Rates of sexual victimization in samples of adolescent male sex offenders range from 40 to 80% (Hunter and Figueredo, 2000). Rates appear to be even higher for prepubescent and female sex offenders (Mathews, Hunter, and Vuz, 1997).

Exposure to violence and pornography, problems with impulse control, and substance abuse are also linked to juvenile sexual offending.

Research suggests that early and prolonged exposure to interpersonal violence is particularly detrimental when it occurs in the absence of counter-balancing prosocial experiences. Juveniles who engage in delinquency and sexual aggression have not only been exposed to violence but also typically have not had close relationships with healthy male and female role models. Thus, they may be more vulnerable to the internalization of antisocial values.

Aggressive and delinquent youths often harbor the belief that aggression is an acceptable and effective means of resolving interpersonal conflict and achieving goals (Lochman and Dodge, 1994). Demonstrated deficits in self-efficacy and social competency are often coupled with a belief in the utility of aggression (Zigler et al., 1992). Therefore, these youths not only believe that aggression leads to interpersonal success, but they also perceive themselves as likely to fail if they employ alternative problem-solving strategies.

Juvenile delinquency and aggression may reflect a spiraling developmental trajectory. Youths who have a poor attachment to father, and who are exposed to antisocial behavior and violence, are more likely to have social competency deficits and engage in delinquency. Social competency deficits may in turn prevent them from forming and maintaining healthy interpersonal relationships and resolving conflict without violence — thus, there is an ever-growing dependency on aggression to resolve conflict.

Hunter, Figueredo, Malamuth, and Becker (2000) found support for the association between high-risk developmental experiences, personality characteristics, and sexual offending in adolescent males. Exposure to antisocial male role models is found to predict delinquent behavior and higher levels of egotism and antagonism. These personality traits in turn are predictive of negative, hostile attitudes toward females. The witnessing of male abuse of females, and abuse as a child (physical and sexual), predicts psychosocial deficits. Greater levels of psychosocial deficits were associated with offending against children. This research supports the belief that multiple developmental influences converge and act interactively and sequentially to produce sexual aggression in juveniles. Such research has implications for both prevention and intervention efforts.

Efforts to Classify

Juvenile sexual offenders appear to be a heterogeneous population representing different patterns of offending and various levels of risk and amenability to intervention. This heterogeneity has complicated legal and clinical decision making and led to efforts to create an empirically sound typology and decision-support tools.

Initial research efforts suggest that a meaningful differentiation can be made between those youths who sexually offend against younger children (5 or more years younger) and those who target peers and adults. In one of the first studies conducted in support of exploring this dichotomy, Hunter, Hazelwood, and Slesinger (2000a) compared 62 offenders against children to 64 offenders of peers and adults. Comparisons were made on victim selection and crime *modus operandi* using police investigative records.

Peer/adult offenders were found to be more likely to have female victims (93.7% vs. 67.7%) and to have selected victims who were either strangers or acquaintances (84.4% vs. 59.7%). They were also more likely to have committed their offenses in a public area, such as a park (28.1% vs. less than 10%) and to have acted in a group with other offenders (28.1% vs. 6.5%). This group of juvenile sex offenders was also more likely to commit a sex crime in association with other criminal activity (23.8% vs. 4.8%) and evidence higher levels of aggression and violence. With regard to the latter, 27% of the peer/adult offenders displayed moderate or greater physical force during the assault in contrast to 8.3% of the offenders against children. Similarly, 26.2% of the peer/adult offenders used weapons, in contrast to 16.1% of the offenders of children. Finally, within the small subset of juvenile sex offenders who murdered their victims, 85.7% offended peers and adults.

The above study provided guidance in further typology model development and testing. Hunter, Hazelwood, and Slesinger (2000c) collected extensive personality and crime *modus operandi* data on 206 adolescent male sex offenders from correctional and private treatment programs. As predicted, peer/adult offenders were more likely to have used weapons in the commission of the sexual crime; and they were found to have displayed higher overall levels of violence. Hypotheses that peer/adult offenders were less likely to be related to the victims and to have committed non-sexual offenses along with sexual offenses were also supported. This group of juvenile sex offenders was found to have less impairment in social competency than the offenders of children.

The above cited research group plans to continue to refine and test theoretical models for explaining differences between juvenile offenders against children and offenders of peers and adults. Study plans call for the identification of subtypes within major groupings of juvenile sex offenders as well as an extension of the study of personality traits to include psychopathy and sexual deviance.

Modus Operandi

Hunter, Hazelwood, and Slesinger (2000a) examined the *modi operandi* of juvenile sex offenders, including where the crimes were committed and how the offender gained control over the victim. Juveniles who offended against children most frequently committed their sexual offenses in the victim's residence (63.9%), followed by the perpetrator's residence (13.1%). Fewer than 10% committed their offenses in a public area. Most of these juvenile perpetrators either approached the victim without explanation or use of threat or force (over 40%), or used trickery or guile to gain victim compliance (about 25%). Threat to the victim or victim's family was evidenced in only 16% of the cases, and physical force or coercion was used in 12.5%.

Threat, intimidation, and coercion appeared to play a more prominent role in how offenders against children maintained control over the victims and maintained victim silence. Approximately one third of these adolescents used intimidation and 17.6% used physical force to maintain control; 29% threatened harm to the victim or his family if he revealed the sexual assault. Although the majority of the offenders against children did not display high levels of violence, their sexual assaults were quite invasive. Penis–vaginal rape was reported in 69% of the assaults of female children, and penis–anal rape was reported in 46.45% of the assaults of younger males.

Juvenile offenders against peers and adults committed their offenses in both the victims' residences (45.3%) and public areas (28.1%). Most frequently (40.4%), they would lie in wait for the victim and surprise him or her. A blitz attack, involving the immediate use of injurious force, was evidenced in 12.8% of the cases. Intimidation and force were commonly displayed as means of maintaining control over peer and adult sexual assault victims. Intimidation was used in nearly one half of the cases, a weapon in 29.2%, and injurious force (other than with a weapon) in 16.7%. Over one fourth of these victims were threatened with violence if the assault were revealed. The majority of the sexual assaults (63.5%) involved penis–vaginal rape, and penis–anal rape was evident in 19% of the cases.

Violent Juvenile Sex Offenders

While most juvenile sex offenders do not appear to be highly aggressive or violent, a subset of these youths engages in instrumental or gratuitous violence. As previously noted, these youths are more likely to target peers or adults than offend against children. However, even within the subpopulation that targets children, there are those youths who seriously injure or kill their victims.

Violence in juveniles has been studied as a function of personality and family characteristics. Youths low in social competency and those viewing aggression as an effective means of achieving interpersonal goals display higher levels of interpersonal violence than other youths. Similarly, those youths with long-standing difficulties with impulse control and affect modulation manifest higher levels of delinquency and aggression through-out childhood and adolescence (Caspi, Henry, McGee, Moffitt, and Silva, 1995; Block, 1995).

Many violent youths also appear to score high on measures of risk-taking and novelty-seeking (Sigvardsson, Bohman, and Cloninger, 1987; Krueger, Schmutte, Caspi, Moffitt, Campbell, and Silva, 1994). These traits may be related to psychopathy, a strong predictor of violence in adults (Harpur and Hare, 1994). Psychopathic adults have been described as shallow, callous, and lacking in remorse; and they often led unstable and anti-social lives. Psych-opathy may be manifested in childhood and displayed in the form of impul-sivity, insensitivity, and problem externalization (Lynam, 1998; Frick, O'Brien, Wootton, and McBurnett, 1994). Finally, a number of family factors have been associated with violence in youth, including parental criminality, harsh parental discipline, and authoritarian child-rearing attitudes (Far-rington, 1989).

Aggression in juvenile sex offenders has also been studied in relationship to crime scene characteristics. Hunter, Hazelwood, and Slesinger (2000a) found that victim difficulty better predicted level of violence than indices of environmental risk (risk of detection), alcohol/drug use during the crime, or degree of planning and control. Victim difficulty was computed for analytic purposes to reflect the effort required in gaining control over the victim based on the victim's gender, age, and level of resistance to the attack. The product of being a male victim, of an age representing greater physical prowess, and offering greater resistance to the assault predicted higher levels of perpetrator violence. In this study, both child and peer/adult victim resistance tended to result in a response of physical force from the adolescent perpetrator.

Hunter, Hazelwood, and Slesinger (2000b) extensively analyzed seven cases wherein the juvenile perpetrators murdered the victims. Peer/adult offenders committed six of these homicides. Only one of these victims (a nine-year-old boy) was a male, and none was related to the offender. The scenes of the crimes varied. Three of the victims were murdered in their homes, one in the home of the perpetrator, one in a convenience store, and two in outdoor locations. Based on review of police interrogation reports, it was concluded that in only two cases did the assailants immediately display violence. In the remaining cases, there was an escalation of violence. The perpetrators used weapons in six of the seven cases. The weapons were knives in two cases, a gun in one case, and blunt objects in the remainder. In two cases, it was apparent that the victims had been intentionally tortured. The sexual assaults involved penis/vaginal rape in three cases, penetration with a foreign object in two cases, cunnilingus in one case, and apparent penis/anal rape in another. In three of the seven cases, evidence suggested that the victims had been raped post-mortem. Three of the victims died of strangulation, two as a result of stabbing, one by gunshot, and one from massive internal bleeding. In two cases, there was evidence of overkill (much more violence than needed to end life).

Case No. 1

A 15-year-old Caucasian female was repeatedly bludgeoned with a large rock and assaulted with a wooden stick by a 15-year-old Hispanic male. The victim knew the assailant and had been seen leaving a party with him prior to the offense. According to the offender, he was engaging in consensual sexual intercourse with the victim when he experienced impotence and was subsequently ridiculed by her. The assailant stated, "I went nuts," and described beating the victim with his hands and then a rock. The victim was found with a sharp 11-inch wooden stick penetrating her vagina. The victim had died as a result of multiple cranial and internal injuries, including a perforated bladder. The assailant had no previous sexual or non-sexual arrest record.

Case No. 2

A 54-year-old white female was strangled, then raped post-mortem in her home by a 15-year-old black male. The assailant was an acquaintance of the victim and lived on the same street. The victim had allowed the adolescent to enter her home after he asked to use her dryer. The youth confessed to pretending to leave the victim's home, only to hide and attack the victim by surprise. He reportedly strangled her with a telephone cord before raping her and fleeing with about $2.25 in change and her car keys. The youthful murderer was apprehended four days later at his high school, where he had been keeping the victim's car.

Among violent juvenile sex offenders are isolated cases of emerging or fully developed sexual sadism. Sexual sadism is a paraphilia that involves sexual excitement and arousal to the psychological or physical pain, suffering, or humiliation of others. It is by nature chronic and persistent. Although seemingly rare, these cases reflect the potential for a pattern of violent and very dangerous sexual offending. The following case is presented to illustrate how sexual sadism can have an early developmental onset and portend a pattern of progressively more serious and violent sexual offending.

Case No. 3

"A" was 10 years old when he was first referred for residential treatment by his home state's department of social services. This referral was made with the support of his biological mother and stepfather following revelation that he had vaginally and anally raped his 4-year-old brother and 2-year-old sister. Notably, the younger brother had also been burned with an iron by the perpetrator. The local juvenile court had been notified of the assaults but had chosen not to become formally involved due to the perpetrator's age and familiarity with the family.

"A's" initial presentation was unremarkable. Like the majority of prepubescent youth engaging in sexual offending, he had a prior history of sexual victimization. He related that the adolescent male son of his babysitter had anally sodomized him when he was approximately 4 years old. This apparently happened on several occasions when he was spending the night at the babysitter's house while his mother was working. "A" related in therapy sessions that he always believed that his mother knew about his victimization but chose to do nothing about it. However, he freely admitted that he did not tell anyone about the abuse until much later and therefore there was no obvious reason why she should have known.

"A" did not seem different from other young children in the residential program and was judged to be responding well to treatment. He was generally compliant with therapeutic directives, was not a major behavior problem, and did reasonably well in school. His parents, although out of state, remained in close contact with "A" and participated in telephonic and face-to-face family therapy sessions. He verbalized a strong desire to not repeat his behavior, expressed remorse for the sexual offending, and demonstrated competence in taught self-control skills.

"A" was discharged after approximately 13 months of residential treatment to the custody of his mother. The discharge plan called for him to spend nights with his maternal grandparents to reduce the risk of sexual offending. His grandparents lived in the same neighborhood with his mother, and the plan permitted "A" to fully participate in family functions under adult supervision. Arrangements were also made for him to see a juvenile sex offender treatment specialist in a nearby town. However, his mother later admitted that she did not follow through on this recommendation.

"A's" mother contacted the residential treatment center approximately one year after his discharge and requested that he be re-hospitalized. She was distraught and revealed that "A" had sexually re-offended against his younger sister in an even more serious manner than previously. "A" presented for treatment the second time as a more surly, unremorseful, and less compliant 13-year-old adolescent.

Several months of intensive clinical work and case investigation were necessary before he revealed the full extent and motivations for his sexual re-offending.

"A" eventually revealed that he had deliberately tortured his then 4-year-old sister on numerous occasions by slapping and choking her, vaginally and anally raping her, pouring a caustic cleaning agent into her vagina, and forcing her to eat molded food and drink his urine. He reported that he had deliberately sabotaged the placement with his grandparents by non-compliance with rules so that he would be returned home and have access to his siblings.

"A" reported that his mother, in an attempt to keep him away from the younger children, locked him in his room at night and had his grandmother stay in the bedroom of the younger siblings. "A" confided that he had stolen his mother's house key when she was away and gone to a local hardware store where he had a duplicate made. At night, while his mother and step-father were away working, he would crawl out of his bedroom window (his door was locked from the outside) and enter the house through the front door (using his new key). He would then quietly wait until his grandmother fell asleep, whereupon he would enter his sister's bedroom, put his hand over her mouth, and carry her to his room. Once in his room, he would gag her with a t-shirt so that her screams could not be heard, and begin his nightly ritual of rape, sodomy, and torture. Following his abuse of his sister, he would return her to her bedroom unbeknownst to the still-sleeping grandmother. He would then re-lock his bedroom door, exit the house through the front door, and re-enter the house through his bedroom win-dow. This behavior continued nightly until the younger sister, previously too afraid to report the abuse because she had been threatened with death, finally in desperation confided to her mother what was happening.

"A" eventually revealed in therapy that he was sexually aroused by his sister's screams of pain and terror, and frequently masturbated to these thoughts. He stated that these urges had been present during his first residential stay, but he had not reported them to his therapist or the staff because he knew it would prevent him from being returned to his mother and deprive him of the opportunity to re-offend. He stated that he left the treatment center the first time with every intention of re-offending, and had not taken his treatment seriously. He said he targeted his sister because she was younger and less capable of verbalizing the abuse than his brother was. He calmly described how he planned and fully intended to kill his sister and family before being caught. His plan called for him to kill his sister by choking her. He then was going to set the house on fire and crawl out of his bedroom window, making it look as if he and his family had perished in the fire.

Investigative Issues

Detection

The author's clinical experience and available relevant research suggest that juveniles are generally not apprehended and brought to the attention of the police until after they have committed several sexual offenses. There are numerous reasons for this delay in detection. Victims are often young and may not report the offenses out of fear, confusion, or embarrassment. Parents of sibling victims may be hesitant to report the crimes because of concern as to what may happen to the youthful perpetrators or their families if external authorities become involved. Many adult and peer victims do not report their victimizations out of concern about potentially embarrassing and difficult social and legal consequences. Other victims may not know the assailant and can offer police only limited identifying information.

Because of the difficulty in detecting juvenile sexual offending, criminal investigators are likely to encounter juveniles who have been engaging in sexual offending for some time (whether or not the offending is limited to one victim). This may be even more likely if the offender is intelligent, socially skilled, and from a protective family system (Prentky and Knight, 1993). Obtaining a full and accurate report of the youth's history of offending is typically a significant challenge. This may be even more true today than it was ten years ago, given the more severe legal repercussions that youths potentially face when acknowledging criminal sexual behavior.

Guidelines for Interviewing Juvenile Sex Offenders

The investigator should expect that the juvenile will be resistant to acknowledging his sexual offenses. Aside from fear of legal consequences, many of the youths apprehended for the first time are embarrassed and confused about their sexual offending and its meaning. Even though the problem may have been present for some time, it is unlikely they have previously talked to anyone about it or spent much time attempting to understand it. Those with previous criminal justice experience may see acknowledgment of further criminal activity as a guarantee of correctional placement and hence are poorly motivated to cooperate.

It is generally prudent to interview alleged offenders following the interviewing of the victims, their families (in the case of child victims), and the offenders' families (when the victims and offenders are living within the same family system). Victims, including young children (Goodman and Saywitz, 1994) and their families, can provide valuable crime information that can subsequently be used in the interrogation of the juvenile perpetrators. The absence of investigator knowledge of crime details enhances the likelihood that the offenders will completely deny the allegations or minimize the seriousness and extent of the sexual offending.

Hunter, Hazelwood, and Slesinger (2000c) found that offender and victim reports of juvenile sexual crimes are frequently discrepant. These report discrepancies traverse both the nature of the assault and the *modi operandi* of the assailants. For example, in nearly 32% of the cases where the victims stated that vaginal intercourse had been attempted or completed, the adolescent perpetrators denied it. In 75% of the cases wherein the victims stated that force was used by the perpetrators, the perpetrators denied it. Similarly, 45% of the juvenile perpetrators denied the use of weapons when the victims had reported that weapons had been used. These data illustrate the importance of thorough interviewing of victims and their families in the investigation of juvenile sexual crimes and the filing of charges.

Effective interviewing of juveniles is a skill that requires attention to both *process* and *content* issues. The following guidelines are offered:

1. An interview is more productive when the youth fully understands the nature of the inquiry and how the information that he provides will be used. In particular, to the extent that he sees cooperation with the investigation as helping portray him in a more favorable light, and potentially making him eligible for less severe legal dispositions, he will be more likely to cooperate. Therefore, investigators should be as familiar as possible with how juvenile sexual offenders are processed and disposed by the local courts and share this information with the youth and his family. Especially helpful is the sharing of information about the opportunity for motivated youths and supportive families to receive specialized treatment services in lieu of correctional placement.

2. A youth needs to understand the seriousness of the inquiry, and confrontation may be necessary; however, interviews are generally more productive when conducted in a focused but even-handed manner. Investigators should convey an attitude of confidence and the expectation that the youth will cooperate because it is in his best interest to do so.

3. Questions should be posed in a straightforward manner, using language that the youth understands. Pedantic, esoteric, and legalistic terminology should be avoided. Such language is not only incomprehensible to most of these youths but also apt to increase their anxiety and resistance.

4. The investigation should include a focus on how and why the victim was *selected,* the method of gaining *access* to the victim, the means by which the perpetrator gained and maintained *control* over the victim, and whether and how he attempted to maintain *victim silence.* Questions should be specifically directed at determining whether intimidation or force was used and whether a weapon was employed.

5. In investigating sexual crimes, it is generally wise to first focus on the *behavioral* aspects of the crime. What did the perpetrator say and do; and how, in turn, did the victim respond? Questions can then be directed at the *thinking patterns or cognitions* of the perpetrator. What

was he thinking about before, during, and after the crime? Finally, questions can be directed at how the perpetrator *felt* (his emotions) before, during, and after the crime. The reverse of this order of questioning may result in social embarrassment and inhibit the youth from further revelations.

6. The investigator should attempt to develop a chronological sequencing of the sexual crimes of the youth. How old was the youth when he first began offending? Is there evidence of a consistent pattern to the offending as it relates to victim age, gender, and type of sexual perpetration? Is there evidence of a progression in the nature and seriousness of the offending over time? Particularly important is the determination of whether the behavior has become more violent over time. Also, of legal and clinical disposition relevance, is whether there is evidence that the sexual perpetrations reflect sexual compulsivity and paraphilic interests.

Mental Health Evaluations

Juveniles arrested for sexual crimes are often referred for mental health evaluations. Sometimes these referrals are made prior to adjudication in an attempt to help determine whether the youths are sex offenders or whether the problems are serious enough to warrant formal legal processing. The author cautions against such pre-adjudication mental health evaluations for the following reasons.

Mental health providers, including those with special training and experience in working with juvenile sexual offenders, enter into a realm of clinical and legal complexity when they attempt to conduct pre-adjudication evaluations. As discussed by Hunter and Lexier (1998), youths facing prosecution are placed in positions of double jeopardy when referred for these evaluations. Their conversations with the mental health evaluators are not confidential to the extent that they reveal information about the abuse of children or danger to self or others. If the youths, in the course of mental health evaluations, reveal unknown sexual crimes, or previously unknown details of sexual crimes of which they have been accused, they could be prosecuted on the basis of the divulged information. On the other hand, if youths refuse to talk to the clinicians about such matters, they may be construed as uncooperative and unmotivated for treatment. In the latter case, the court may use this information in support of the need for prosecution or perceive the youths as poor candidates for community-based treatment.

Criminal justice professionals should be aware that no psychological or psychophysiological tests, including the plethysmograph, are valid for determining whether an individual (juvenile or adult) is a sex offender or has committed a particular sexual crime. Therefore, mental health evaluators have no other way of determining the guilt of an individual accused of a sexual crime short of confession to the crime. The polygraph, though not typically considered a mental health evaluation tool, also has limitations for this type of inquiry. Aside from the issue of admissibility in court, its reliability and validity are potentially affected by a number of issues, including the subject's age, his mental status, his level of intelligence, and the examiner's level of training and experience in its administration and interpretation.

It is therefore recommended that mental health and other forensic evaluations be conducted post-adjudication and pre-sentencing. Mental health evaluations should be directed at helping determine the *nature of the sexual behavior problem* underlying the sexual crime, the individual's *level of dangerousness and risk for re-offending*, his *intervention needs*, and his *amenability to treatment*. This information should be submitted to the court prior to sentencing to aid in disposition decision-making.

Disposition Decision-Making and Management

Courts are faced with critical decisions about what to do with convicted juvenile sex offenders. Should they be committed to corrections or placed in a treatment program? Should treatment and management take place at the level of the community, or is institutionalization necessary to maintain community safety and adequately address the youth's needs?

These are obviously difficult questions that require careful consideration of statute guidelines and precedents, public opinion and community resources, and a thorough understanding of the youthful offender and his family. It is with regard to the latter that mental health, probation and parole, and social services professionals can make a contribution. Professionals tasked with making recommendations to the court may want to take into consideration the following:

1. The *type of offending* the youth has displayed — juveniles who offend against peers and adults are generally more predatory and violent. Many are not appropriate for community-based care.
2. The youth's level of *denial and accountability* regarding his sexual offending — research (see Hunter and Figueredo, 1999) supports the relevance of these attitudes at the time of clinical assessment. Youths steeped in denial and those blaming the victim or others for the sexual assault generally perform poorly in community-based treatment programs.

3. The individual's past *criminal record* for sexual and non-sexual offenses and his sexual offense history — those youths with more extensive criminal records and offending histories are at higher risk for re-offending. It should be remembered that non-sexual recidivism rates generally exceed sexual recidivism rates for juvenile and adult sex offenders.

4. Assessment of the presence of *paraphilic interests and arousal* and *psychopathy* — deviant sexual arousal and psychopathy are two of the most robust predictors of sexual recidivism in adults. Although more rare in juveniles, their detection should alert the evaluator to an increased risk for program failure and recidivism. Individuals high in sexual deviance and/or psychopathy are generally poor candidates for community-based treatment.

5. The extent to which the youths have *multiple psychological problems* and manifest problem behaviors in a variety of environments (home, school, community, etc.) — youths reflecting pervasive problems require more intensive services and supervision.

6. The level of *family support* for the youth and his effective management and treatment — the living environment of the youth is very important in shaping his attitudes toward treatment and willingness to comply with legal and therapeutic directives. Successful community-based management requires the cooperation and support of responsible caretakers. Caretakers must perform critical monitoring functions and be willing to work toward necessary systemic change.

7. The *identifications and peer affiliations* of the youth — youths with antisocial and delinquent affiliations are believed to be at higher risk for further criminal behavior.

8. The available *community resources* — effective community-based management requires comprehensive programming reflecting well-integrated criminal justice, mental health, and social services management efforts.

Effective Community Programming

The majority of juveniles who offend against children can be safely and effectively managed within the community. However, successful community management depends not only on the careful screening of referred youths but also on the development of a comprehensive system of care and management.

Programming for juvenile sex offenders should be conceptualized as a community-wide effort. Key stakeholders should have a voice in both the design and implementation of the program. This includes but is not limited to the juvenile and adult courts, the prosecutor's office, the public defender's office, the local schools, social services, and public and private mental health service providers. It may also include representatives from victim advocacy groups and parents of victims and offenders. All of these groups need to work together to ensure that the program fully responds to the needs of the community and operates in accordance with community safety standards.

It is particularly important that an effective interface be achieved between the criminal justice and mental health service delivery systems. In order to fully benefit from treatment, the juvenile must be willing to confront his problems and assume responsibility for his past and future behavior. Treatment requires the willingness of the youth to comply with therapeutic directives and sustain therapeutic diligence. Adjudication and ongoing court supervision and monitoring help ensure that the youth remains accountable for his behavior and fully committed to his rehabilitation plan.

One particularly effective strategy for motivating the youth to fully take advantage of the available help is to adjudicate and sentence him, then suspend the sentence contingent on successful completion of treatment. Under such arrangements, the court assumes a monitoring role; and hearings can be scheduled on a regular basis to review the youth's progress in achieving treatment goals. Recalcitrant youths or uncooperative families can be warned of the consequences of noncompliance, and probation can be revoked when necessary.

Probation and parole officers provide an important evaluative and supervisory function within the above-described framework. They help assess whether the youth and family are fully complying with therapeutic and court guidelines and whether the intervention plan seems to be working. They serve as an important conduit of information between the court and service providers and can assist in the identification of needed resources for the youth and family.

I support *social-ecological* models of intervention for juveniles with sexual behavior problems. These models (see Henggeler, 1999) are premised on the assumption that delinquent behavior is a product of the individual's interaction with the multiple social environments in which he functions, and that interventions should therefore be multisystemic in design and focus. Consistent with this model, interventions for juvenile sexual offenders should reflect an understanding of systemic influences (family, school, peer group) on the likelihood that the youth will sexually re-offend. Therapists working from this model seek to strategically involve a variety of important caretakers of the youth (parents, extended family members, teachers, etc.) in the implementation and evaluation of the treatment plan.

The treatment of juvenile sex offenders should also reflect an understanding of skills necessary to maintain control over sexual behavior and the formation of healthy interpersonal relationships. Therefore, therapeutic attention to the following is advised:

1. The enhancement of *social competencies* — rehabilitation is dependent on having the skills to form and maintain healthy interpersonal relationships. Most juvenile sex offenders can benefit from social skills and anger management training.
2. The fostering of *self-efficacy* and *self-esteem* — youths need to believe in their capacity to make positive life changes.
3. Improvement of *impulse control* and *judgment* — juvenile sex offenders can benefit from interventions designed to help them understand the thoughts, feelings, and events that led to their sexual offending and how to control urges to act out. Cognitive–behavioral methodologies designed to improve impulse control and judgment can be useful in helping them deal with both sexual and non-sexual impulse control problems (substance abuse tendencies).
4. *Male mentoring* and the instilling of a healthy sense of masculinity — mentoring by older, healthier, and successful males is important to the resocialization of juveniles who have engaged in sexual offending.
5. Education in *healthy sexuality.*
6. *Victim empathy* — a youth needs to understand and fully appreciate the impact that his behavior had on the victim and the victim's family.
7. *Relapse prevention* — each youth and his caretakers should have a comprehensive and well-conceived plan for preventing future sexual offending.

Although well-controlled treatment outcome studies have not yet been conducted with juvenile sex offenders, program follow-up studies suggest reason for optimism about the amenability to treatment of the majority of these youths. Sexual recidivism rates generally range from 7 to 13% over a period of 2 to 5 years (Hunter, 1999). Non-sexual recidivism rates are often higher (25 to 50%) (Becker, 1990; Kahn and Chambers, 1991). If outcome studies on adult sex offenders prove informative, sexual recidivism rates will be higher for those juvenile sex offenders who fail to complete treatment programs and those with lengthier histories of offending (Marques, Day, Nelson, and West, 1994).

The last case example illustrates how even severely sexually disturbed youths, with extensive psychiatric co-morbidity and limited intellectual capacity, can benefit from intensive intervention when motivation is sustained.

Case No. 4

"E" presented for treatment as a 16-year-old biracial male with a history of attempted rape, school failure, and out-of-control behavior within the home. Prior to admission, he had approached a female clerk in a clothing store with a knife and directed her to a back room where he intended to rape her. The assault was prevented by a customer entering the store and calling for help. "E" later confided to his therapist that he frequently fantasized of stalking women and violently raping them. His potential for sexual aggression had been in evidence for approximately one year prior to the attempted rape. He had attempted to fondle a female teacher providing him with home-bound instruction and had aggressively grabbed a female technician who had entered his room at the state psychiatric hospital where he initially had been placed for observation.

In addition to having a sexual behavior disorder, "E" was diagnosed in the residential sex offender program as suffering from paranoid schizophrenia, depression, and mild mental retardation. He verbalized feelings that women laughed and made fun of him, and he required a very high level of supervision to prevent aggression toward female staff. He was observed as challenging male authority as well and was prone to physical and verbal outbursts when frustrated. He frequently stated that he felt that his condition was hopeless and that he was destined to sexually re-offend and consequently spend the remainder of his life in prison.

An African-American family had adopted "E" at birth. His adoptive parents divorced when he was approximately 4 years old, following a lengthy history of paternal alcoholism and spousal abuse. "E" vividly described numerous incidents when he was a young child where he had witnessed his father verbally abuse and physically beat his mother. He verbalized wanting to rescue his mother from his father's abuse, but he was afraid of incurring his father's wrath and subsequently losing his affection if he attempted to intervene on her behalf. His mother described "E" as first displaying aggression toward her following an incident wherein he was reprimanded for running about the house in a boisterous and out-of-control fashion. When he refused to obey her, she threatened to spank him. At that point, he picked up her broom and threatened to hit her with it.

"E's" mother stated that he progressively became more difficult to manage in and out of the home as he got older. He reportedly had difficulty making friends as a child and became increasingly socially isolated over time. He ultimately had to be removed from school and placed in home-bound instruction after a long history of disobedience and behavioral disruption in the classroom. While in residential placement, "E" was aggressively treated with a combination of anti-psychotic, anti-depressant, and anti-androgen medications. He also received individual, group, and family therapies. "E" formed a very positive alliance with his male therapist and talked extensively of his uneasiness around females, his underlying sense of inadequacy and hopelessness, and his confused feelings about his father.

An attempt was made to involve his father in father-son therapy sessions. Upon arriving for the first session, his father commented to the therapist (in the presence of his son) that he did not see how boys in the program could be expected to make any changes in their sexual behavior when they were surrounded by so many scantily clad and sexually tempting females. (The females in the program were housed on different units, carefully supervised at all times, and subject to strict dress codes.)

These sessions came to an abrupt halt after "E" unsuccessfully attempted to process with his father how the early childhood witnessing of fights between his mother and father had frightened and confused him. The father immediately stood up, informed "E" that if he wanted to feel sorry for anyone that it should be for him, his father, not his mother. He angrily asserted that "E's" mother was a strong and aggressive person and that she had been the one who had inflicted injury on him, not the other way around. This assertion was made in spite of the fact that the father was approximately 6'3" tall and weighed 250 pounds, the mother was of average height and weight, and there was never the suggestion in "E's" reports that the mother had ever initiated any of these incidents. Much to the distress of "E" (and the therapist), the father stormed out of the session, never to return. According to "E's" mother, the father drove to her home to confront her about putting these ideas in his head and said that he was going to punish "E" for telling the therapist about these events by not visiting him.

"E" became progressively more attached to his individual therapist over time and began to verbalize that he saw the therapist as a father figure. Although he episodically became distraught and pessimistic that he could prevail in learning to control his aggressive sexual urges, aggressive outbursts became less frequent and intense over time. Anti-androgen medication appeared to be helpful in diminishing, and eventually eliminating, fantasies of wanting to attack and rape women.

Anti-psychotic medication appeared effective in improving the quality of his thinking and judgment, and anti-depressant medication helped improve his mood. "E" also responded well to special education and vocational training.

Due to the severity and clinical complexity of his problems, "E" required residential placement over a period of 5 years. The treatment plan included his very slow and progressive re-introduction into therapeutic environments that included females. Ultimately, he was able to interact with female staff and residents in a variety of therapeutic settings without displays of behavioral aggression or volatility, and he went on supervised community and family outings (with mother). He was also able to form a number of important and emotionally corrective relationships with female peers. Prior to discharge, he was placed in a transitional living environment within the residential program (group home-like setting). Discharge was not effected until he demonstrated behavioral and emotional stability for an extended period of time (24 months).

Discharge planning involved the careful coordination of services with his mother and his home community. He was ultimately placed in a group home for the chronically mentally ill in his home town operated by the publicly funded community services board. During the day, he attended a treatment program that included ample opportunity for social and recreational and vocational pursuits. He was able to visit with his family on weekends and holidays. A physician administered and monitored his medications, and he was provided with supportive counseling. At last contact with his therapist from the residential program, there had been no episodes of sexual aggression in the two years since his discharge from residential care.

References

Becker, J.V. (1990) Treating adolescent sexual offenders, *Prof. Psychol. Res. and Pract.*, 21(5), 362–365.

Caspi, A., Henry, B., McGee, R.O., Moffitt, T.E., and Silva, P.A. (1995) Temperamental origins of child and adolescent behavior problems: from age three to fifteen, *Child Dev.*, 66(1), 55–68.

Farrington, D.P. (1989) Early predictors of adolescent aggression and adult violence, *Violence and Victims*, 4(2), 79–100.

Frick, P.J., O'Brien, B.S., Wootton, J.M., and McBurnett, K. (1994). Psychopathy and conduct problems in children, *J. Abnormal Psychol.*, 102(4), 700–707.

Goodman, G.S. and Saywitz, K.J. (1994) Memories of abuse: interviewing children when sexual abuse is suspected, *Child and Adolescent Psychiatr. Clin. of North Am.*, 3(4), 645–661.

Harpur, T.J. and Hare, R.D. (1994) Assessment of psychopathy as a function of age, *J. Abnormal Psychol.*, 103(4), 604–609.

Henggeler, S.W. (1999) Multisystemic therapy: an overview of clinical procedures, outcomes, and policy implications, *Child Psychol. and Psychiatr. Rev.*, 4(1), 2–10.

Hunter, J.A. and Lexier, L.J. (1998) Ethical and legal issues in the assessment and treatment of juvenile sex offenders. *Child Maltreatment: J. Am. Prof. Soc. Abuse Child.*, 3(4), 339–348.

Hunter, J.A. and Figueredo, A.J. (1999) Factors associated with treatment compliance in a population of juvenile sexual offenders, *Sexual Abuse: J. Res.Treat.*, 11(1), 49–67.

Hunter, J.A. (1999) *Understanding Juvenile Sexual Offending Behavior: Emerging Research, Treatment Approaches and Management Practices*, Center for Sex Offender Management: U.S. Department of Justice, Washington, D.C.

Hunter, J.A., Hazelwood, R., and Slesinger, D. (2000a) Juvenile perpetrated sex crimes: patterns of offending and predictors of violence, *J. Fam. Violence*, 15(1), 81–93.

Hunter, J.A., Hazelwood, R., and Slesinger, D. (2000b) Juvenile sexual homicide, *FBI Law Enforcement Bull.*

Hunter, J.A., Hazelwood, R., and Slesinger, D. (2000c) Unpublished.

Hunter, J.A. and Figueredo, A.J. (2000) The influence of personality and history of sexual victimization in the prediction of juvenile perpetrated child molestation, *Behav. Modification*, 24(2), 241–263.

Hunter, J.A., Figueredo, A.J., Malamuth, N., and Becker, J.V. (2000) Juvenile sexual offender typology development: preliminary findings, in preparation.

Kahn, T.J. and Chambers, H.J. (1991) Assessing reoffense risk with juvenile sexual offenders, *Child Welfare*, 19, 333–345.

Krueger, R.F., Schmutte, P.S., Caspi, A., Moffitt, T.E., Campbell, K., and Silva, P.A. (1994) Personality traits are linked to crime among men and women: evidence from a birth cohort, *J. Abnormal Psychol.*, 103(2), 328–338.

Lochman, J.E. and Dodge, K.A. (1994). Social-cognitive processes of severely violent, moderately aggressive, and nonaggressive boys, *J. Consulting Clin. Psychol.*, 62(2), 366–374.

Lynam, D.R. (1998) Early identification of the fledgling psychopath: locating the psychopathic child in the current nomenclature, *J. Abnormal Psychol.*, 107(4), 566–575.

Marques, J.K., Day, D.M., Nelson, C., and West, M.A. (1994) Effects of cognitive-behavioral treatment on sex offender recidivism: preliminary results of a longitudinal study, *Criminal Justice Behav.*, 21(1), 28–54.

Marshall, W.L., Barbaree, H.E., and Eccles, A. (1991) Early onset and deviant sexuality in child molesters, *J. Interpersonal Violence*, 6, 323–336.

Mathews, R., Hunter, J.A., and Vuz, J. (1997) Juvenile female sexual offenders: clinical characteristics and treatment issues, *Sexual Abuse: J. Res. Treat.*, 9, 187–199.

OJJDP (2000). *OJJDP Statistics Briefing Book/Juvenile Arrest Trends by Offense: Forcible Rape* (retrieved from World Wide Web: http://ojjdp.ncjrs.org/ojstatbb/-qa258.html).

Prentky, R.A. and Knight, R.A. (1993) Age of onset of sexual assault: criminal and life history correlates, in G.C. Hall and R. Hirschman, Eds., *Sexual Aggression: Issues in Etiology, Assessment, and Treatment* (pp. 43–62), Washington, D.C., Taylor and Francis.

Sickmund, M., Snyder, H.N., and Poe-Yamagata, E. (1997) *Juvenile Offenders: 1997 Update on Violence*, Pittsburgh, PA, National Center for Juvenile Justice.

Sigvardsson, S., Bohman, M., and Cloninger, C.R. (1987) Structure and stability of childhood personality: prediction of later social adjustment, *J. Child Psychol. Psychiatry Allied Disciplines*, 28(6), 929–946.

Zigler, E., Taussig, C., and Black, K. (1992) Early childhood intervention: a promising preventative for juvenile delinquency, *Am. Psychol.*, 47(8), 997–1006.

Female Sex Offenders: A Typological and Etiological Overview

20

JANET I. WARREN
JULIA HISLOP

Introduction

When issues of sexual abuse and sexual exploitation are discussed, the common image is that of a male perpetrator forcing various degrees of nonconsensual sex upon a woman or a child. This type of exploitative sexuality is linked to violence in general and is found in all societies to be more often perpetrated by men than by women. The equally profound gender loading of paraphilic forms of sexual deviance disorders among men serves to highlight concerns about men acting in sexually dangerous ways. While these sexual stereotypes are factually true and thus correct in terms of generalized societal concerns, they also serve to camouflage the sexual exploitation and violence perpetrated by women against male and female children and, in some instances, against adults of both genders.

Attempts to scientifically and methodically classify the various forms of sexual deviance observed by the medical profession began with Krafft-Ebing, *Pschyopathia Sexualis*, published in Latin in 1886. It mentions women who were observed to submit to or request masochistic sexual contact, a classification referred to by Krafft-Ebing as "the association of passively endured cruelty and violence with lust." He references instances of "periodic insanity," in which the patient experiences "an abnormal intensity or a noticeable prominence of the sexual sphere." It also defines a condition defined as psychical hermaphroditism or "virginity," in which the woman experiences herself sexually to be a man. In addressing adult sexual attraction toward children, Krafft-Ebing references four cases, noting that they were all men; although he described a woman who sent her two daughters away, as she feared that she might sexually molest them.

The incestuous relationships present in some families began to be more explicitly explored in the context of psychoanalytic treatments, in which the nature of the interfamilial relationships was explored over a lengthy period. In this intimate, revealing context, it was found that some women were as capable as some men of initiating incestuous sexual relationships with their children. While these findings were imbedded in the ongoing controversy regarding unconscious fantasy and reality, it was clearly ascertained in some instances, as reported by the mother or the grown child, that these types of incestuous relationships did occur.

Chideckel (1935) wrote of sexual perversions in women, while Wulffen (1934) described women who were sexual criminals who engaged in exploitative and illegal sexual behavior, including several cases of sexual abuse against children. By the 1940s, Kinsey remarked that, "[o]lder persons are the teachers of younger people in all matters including the sexual. The record includes some cases of pre-adolescent boys involved in sexual contacts with adult females" (p. 176).

With the advent of empirical research, attention was directed to the statistical analysis of modal behavior. From this research came a number of paradigmatic descriptions of child molesters. Researchers differentiated between the fixated and regressed offenders (Groth and Burgess, 1977); the situational and preferential offenders (Lanning, 1985); and the interpersonal, narcissistic, exploitive, muted sadistic, non-sadistic aggressive, and sadistic types of child molesters recognized by the Massachusetts Treatment Center (MTC) taxonomy (Knight, 1988). In these paradigms, the etiological explanation of the behavior is attributed to psychodynamic, hormonal, characterological, biochemical, and structural anomalies as well as situationally provocative and inappropriate familial dynamics. Implicit but largely unstated in these paradigms is the assumption that the perpetrators of non-consensual sexual acts against children are men.

More recently, the attention of researchers has turned toward the sexual exploitation and sexual crimes perpetrated by women. The extent of this phenomenon is still unclear. However, in a retrospective study of 348 male sexual offenders, Groth (1979) found that, as children, 8.3% had been sexually abused by female adults and 4.3% by somewhat older female peers.

It is clear that there has been a cultural reticence to acknowledge that women perpetrate sexual abuse against children and, in some cases, the coercive rape of adults. In discussing female pedophilia, Mathis (1972) stated that it "comes to light either long after the fact, or if it is detected earlier, it is lightly dismissed." He added that "the usual case consists of a babysitter, maid, or female relative, who, if caught, is either discharged or strongly reprimanded, and that is that!" (p. 55).

Hislop (in press) discusses in some detail the reasons why the sexual abuse perpetrated by women seems to be more covert and less often prosecuted. For example, she observes that some male children do not recognize the sexual activity as abuse, identifying it as a normal part of a child's life or, alternatively, as a lucky score if it occurs outside the home with an older female partner. She further suggests that there are pressures against girls reporting that a female has sexually abused them. Not only does reporting require acknowledging the exploitative nature of the event but also its homosexual underpinnings. James and Nasjleti (1983) observe that, if the mother is the perpetrator of the abuse and she is the only caretaking adult in the child's life, there is additional resistance on the part of the child to create a crisis that could undermine his/her basic security and survival.

Several studies have documented this reticence of children to report female sexual abusers. Risin and Koss (1987) identified 216 college males who had been sexually abused in childhood, with almost one half abused by women. Eighty-one percent of these men had told no one about the sexual abuse. Rosencrans (1997) reported on nine cases of males who had been molested by their mothers. None had reported the abuse while they were children, and eight of the nine men described it as the most hidden aspect of their lives. Among 93 females who had been sexually abused by their mothers, Rosencrans (1997) found that over 95% of the women told no one about the abuse during childhood.

Rosencrans (1997) also found that, among these 93 women, 71% had also been sexually abused by someone else. Such a finding suggests that families characterized by maternal incest are at high risk for exposing children to other kinds of incest and to situations replete with the opportunity for sexual exploitation. Children in these situations may have particular difficulties establishing self-protection skills or the abilities to identify when adult/child interactions deviate from those that are generally considered acceptable.

A Typology of Female Sex Offenders

The Facilitator

Facilitators are women who consciously and intentionally aid men in gaining sexual access to children. These women often report having excessively dependent relationships with particular men and/or meet criteria for Cluster B character psychopathology — histrionic, borderline, narcissistic, and antisocial personality disorders. They may, for example, procure victims for adult males' sexual purposes (Warren and Hazelwood, in press), prostitute children, or involve a child in pornography. This pattern of abuse has been observed in a number of small samples of female offenders (Bouchard, 1994; Davin, 1999; Green and Kaplan, 1994; McCarty, 1986). In some such cases, these women also partake of the sexual exploitations of the children (Swink, 1989). A child assessed by one of the authors reported that her mother had actively allowed and encouraged the sexual molestation of the girl by the girl's uncle. The mother was also reported to have forced her children to watch pornography and to watch her engage in sexual encounters with an adult male.

The Reluctant Partner

The *reluctant partner* classification constitutes a category of women who offend within the context of a long-term relationship or marriage that is often abusive in nature. While it has been observed that this type of participation is generally coerced, some women who are initially coerced begin to offend independently over time (Faller, 1987; Mathews, Matthews and Speltz, 1989; Saradjian and Hanks, 1996). When describing these types of encounters, the women typically do not describe being motivated by feelings of affection for the victim (Larson and Maison, 1987) or by sexual arousal (Matthews, Mathews, and Speltz, 1991; Larson and Maison, 1987). Wolfe (1985) described the case of a woman who sexually abused with a partner; the woman had initially refused to participate, and was shocked by her partner with a cattle prod. These couples have been found to sexually abuse the women's own children as well as children they procure outside their immediate families. The Committee on Sexual Offences against Children and Youth (1984) documented the case of a female who was sexually victimized by her father and who later procured girls for her father and aided him in his offenses.

Researchers have commonly noted dependency (Hislop, 1999; Saradjian and Hanks, 1996; Travin et al., 1990) and the tendency to produce high scores on measures of femininity (Pothast and Allen, 1994) as traits commonly associated with sexual offending women in general. However, several researchers have commented upon the particular dependency of women who co-offend with males (Bouchard, 1994; Davin, 1999; Mathews, Matthews and Speltz, 1989; McCarty, 1986; Larson and Maison, 1987). Saradjian and Hanks (1996) also found that coerced co-offenders tended to have very low self-esteem and tended to deny the negative aspects of their relationships with their partners. Some were also found to have below-average intelligence (Bouchard, 1994; McCarty, 1986).

Faller (1987) described a category of polyincestuous female offenders who tended to act in concert with males and were more likely than other offenders to have histories of multi-generational, multiple-partnered incest histories. McCarty (1986) found that independent offenders tended to have been sexually abused by brothers, whereas it was more common for the co-offending women to have been abused by adult caretakers. While only preliminary, these findings suggest that different types of trauma may be associated with different dynamics of inappropriate sexual transgressions among women.

Hudson (1995) created categories of female sexual abusers based upon the results of psychological testing with the Minnesota Multiphasic Personality Inventory (MMPI). Of the 60 women she studied, all except six had offended against children rather than adults. Thirty-two had co-offenders, 15 did not, and for others the information was not available. On the basis of a cluster analysis of the scaled scores of the MMPI, Hudson described four subtypes of female sex offenders, two of which had less severe pathologies and two of which tended to have more severe forms of psychiatric impairments. There appeared to be no sustained relationship between the degree of pathology demonstrated by the women and whether they perpetrated alone or with partners.

The Initiating Partner

The *initiating partner* is a woman who wishes to sexually offend against a child. She either initiates the behavior in the context of her relationship with a partner or cajoles the partner into procuring for her the desired sexual experience that involves a generic or specific child. Saradjian and Hanks (1996) described a case in which a woman pressured her husband until he raped a 14-year-old girl while she watched. Faller (1987) reported on two cases in which the female took the initiative in co-offending cases. Myers (1992) described the case of a female who reported prepubescent sexual contact with a variety of men and women as a result of her parents having lived in a commune.

Sometimes the initiating partner offends with another woman. One such case was reported by Crewdson (1988), who described an incident in which a sexually abusive mother involved her son's maternal aunt (her sister) in his sexual abuse. Kaufman and his colleagues (1995) found that among 53 female offenders, 23% had offended with other females. Finkelhor and Williams (1988) found substantiated cases in day care centers in which both sexual offenders against the children were females. Of cases that they studied involving multiple sexual abusers, 17% involved females exclusively. Findings regarding day care centers during this period must, however, be viewed with some reservation given the proliferation of false allegations that appeared at that time.

Women who initiate violent sexual acts with co-offenders may also offend in the context of a group sexual assault. Lane (1991) reported on cases of juvenile females co-participating with other females in the forcible rape of same-age male and female peers. Sarrel and Masters (1982) described a case in which four women bound, threatened, and forced sex upon an adult male. Groth (1979) described cases in which women offended against adult male victims in groups of two or more.

Seducers and Lovers

The female *seducers/lovers* direct their sexual interest toward adolescents with whom they come in contact and with whom they initiate sexual contact in a manner that implies consent. These women often refer to the relationships as love affairs and minimize or deny the significance of the adolescent status of the partners. One case, highly publicized in the media, involved a teacher who not only became involved with a 13-year-old sixth grade student but also gave birth to his child in the course of the relationship. This woman was a married woman and mother of four children when this series of encounters occurred.

Larson and Maison (1987) described three women who reported having been in love with their victims; the victims were most commonly adolescents. The attachment to the victim was reported to be intense, as was the fear of abandonment. Saradjian and Hanks (1996) also described women who had offended against adolescents. The women offenders in their study reported that their relationships with the adolescents were among the closest relationships of their lives. The adolescents often did not concur that the relationships were close, and in some cases they described the abuse as sadistic.

The Psychotic

In addition to the women described above, there are also women who are severely mentally ill and who, in the course of their mental illness, inappropriately initiate sexual contacts often with their own children (Faller 1987; Sarajian and Hanks, 1996). One case evaluated by one of the authors involved a psychotic woman who believed that her 8-year-old daughter was attempting to seduce her boyfriend, that her daughter had been possessed by a demon, and that the daughter was the cause of her grandparents' deaths. These paranoid delusions led her to kill the child by inserting a knife into the child's vagina and then aggressively hitting the knife with a hammer.

The Pedophile

It is still unclear whether women can or do suffer from preferential, exclusive, and sustained sexual preferences for children as implied in the diagnosis of pedophilia. Cooper, Swaminath, Baxter and Poulin (1990) recently wrote about a 20-year-old female pedophile. Using extensive clinical, psychological, psychometric, and physiological arousal procedures, they found a profile that was interpreted as very similar to those of male incest perpetrators. The woman was diagnosed as suffering from borderline personality disorder and, on the photoplethysmograph, demonstrated polymorphous eroticism with sadistic, masochistic, and pedophilic elements. This case is reflective of the current thinking regarding paraphilic disorders in general. It is increasingly recognized that most paraphilic disorders cluster. Individuals commonly suffer from two or more paraphilic disorders, either simultaneously or over the course of their life spans.

Bouchard (1994), however, described the case of one woman categorized as a fixated pedophile on the bases of psychological testing and assessment. The woman was described as egocentric and lacking in emotional development, with little remorse or concern for others. She was noted to be clearly attracted to children.

Etiology of Female Sex Offending

Re-Enactment

Women who sexually abuse children are commonly found to have chaotic upbringings, with a large percentage having been sexually abused in childhood. Several case descriptions have noted extensive histories of sexual abuse or incestuous relationships in the histories of female sex offenders (Cooper and Cormier, 1990; Cooper, et al., 1990; deYoung, 1982; Freel, 1995; Higgs, Cavanan and Myer, 1992; Korbin, 1986; Marvasti, 1986; O'Connor, 1987; Sheldrick, 1991; Travin, et al., 1990). Emergent research, often on relatively small samples, is similarly identifying a pattern of early sexual abuse of the adult perpetrators. Saradijian and Hanks (1996) observed that the targeting, grooming, and silencing of victims by female abusers were often similar in method to those used upon them in their own childhoods.

Faller (1987) identified 19 of 40 women sex offenders in an evaluation and treatment sample as having histories of their own sexual victimization. McCarty (1986) found that 13 of 17 maternal offenders in an incest treatment program, for whom background data were available, had histories of childhood sexual victimizations.

Some researchers have examined groups of women who were not treated or evaluated, and they have found that similar percentages of females who engaged in sexually inappropriate behaviors with children have sexual abuse histories. Fromuth and Conn (1997) surveyed college women and found 22 who had sexual contacts with much younger children, primarily when they (the women) were children or adolescents. None had come to the attention of the police or mental health counselors. Seventy-seven percent of these undetected offenders had been sexually abused.

Hislop (1999) found that, when sexual abuse was experienced in the childhoods of women who had molested children, it was generally severe in nature. Thirty-two of the 43 female sexual offenders reported histories of childhood sexual abuse. The average age at which their own abuse began was $7^1/_2$ years. An estimated average of $7^1/_2$ years transpired between the first and the last incidents of such abuse. Fifty-eight percent of the 43 women had been molested by at least one relative or steprelative, while 20 of the women had more than one person sexually abuse them, ranging from two to seven offenders. Davin (1999) similarly found that the majority of her sample of 76 incarcerated female sex offenders had histories of childhood sexual abuse. Over 60% of the molestations against them were perpetrated by their male relatives. Several instances of sexual intercourse beginning before the age of 10 were found in these women's histories.

Early Trauma

Histories of childhood physical abuse and neglect and/or emotional abuse are also commonly noted among female sex offenders (Allen, 1991; Davin, 1999; Green and Kaplan, 1994; Hislop, 1999; Larson and Maison, 1987; McCarty, 1986; Saradjian and Hanks, 1996; Travin et al., 1990). Paiser (1992), who studied the female victims of female-perpetrated sex abuse, observed, "[t]he family in which sexual abuse occurs tends to exhibit certain interactional patterns that do not allow the victimized child to grow, separate, and move into relationships with the world at large." Larson and Maison (1987) similarly observed that poor relationships between the parents of the offenders; generations of abuse, instability and chaos; and drug and alcohol problems have all been identified in the family backgrounds of female sex offenders.

Personality Disorders

Research on male pedophiles indicates a relatively low level of character pathology as compared with groups of offenders charged with violent crimes against adults (such as rape). For example, Serin (1994) reported that only 7.5% of their sample of pedophiles were psychopaths as measured by the Psychopathy Checklist-Revised (PCL-R). In contrast, six studies have demonstrated elevations on the psychopathic deviance scale of the Minnesota Multiphasic Personality Inventory (MMPI) for males charged with incestuous relationships within their families. These types of findings suggest that sex offending represents a varied interplay between patterns of sexual arousal and personality functioning.

In many cases, personality factors among female offenders may exert a greater influence on the offending behaviors than the role of deviant sexual arousal. Among female sex offenders, the lack of the development of appropriate interpersonal boundaries during often chaotic childhoods may be particularly central to the development of the types of personality dysfunction associated with this type of criminal offending.

Green and Kaplan (1994) reported on a small sample of 11 incarcerated female child molesters; the average number of personality disorders for each woman was 3.6. The most common diagnoses were avoidant personality disorder (7 cases), dependent personality disorder (5 cases), and borderline personality disorder (5 cases). Also found were antisocial personality disorders (4 cases), passive-aggressive personality disorders (3 cases), obsessive-compulsive personality disorders (2 cases), histrionic personality disorders (2 cases), narcissistic personality disorders (2 cases), and a case of schizoid personality disorder (1 case).

Deviant Sexual Arousal

The case presented by Cooper et al. (1990) indicates that deviant sexual arousal can be detected among women on the photoplethysmograph (a device recently developed to empirically measure the degree of sexual arousal experienced by a woman in response to different types of sexual stimuli). However, the sexual attraction to children occurred in the context of polymorphous deviance and did not reflect an exclusive attraction to children — a pattern observed with some commonality among men. Hindman (2000) recently reported that, among a group of 21 women evaluated with a photoplethysmograph, only a small number demonstrated arousal to prepubescent bodies. Generally when this occurred, the women also showed indications of arousal to adults.

Mental Illness

It is clear that some women perpetrate sexual crimes against children as part of the distorted reality that arises from the more severe forms of mental illness, such as schizophrenia or bipolar disorder. Lawson (1984), for example, described the case of a 50-year-old woman with bipolar disorder who ran naked on the beach during a manic episode, shouting obscene remarks to young men along the way, suggesting that they were not up to the mark for failing to have intercourse with her.

Depression may also play a role in the offending behaviors. Woodring (1995) found evidence of depression and anxiety in the psychological testing of independent incarcerated female sex offenders. Saradjian and Hanks (1996) reported that, during the period of time in which independent female child molesters were offending, problems with depression and anxiety were uncommon — although women coerced into offending by a co-offending mate experienced consistent degrees of depression, anxiety, and suicidal ideation.

Perhaps not surprisingly, given the traumatic histories often found among sexually offending women, post-traumatic stress disorder is commonly diagnosed. Green and Kaplan (1994) reported that among 11 incarcerated female child molesters, eight exhibited post-traumatic stress disorder. Turner and Turner (1994) reported that of eight adolescent female sex offenders, three carried a diagnosis of post-traumatic stress disorder.

Drug and alcohol addiction may also play a role in the coercive sexual interactions that women have with others. The abuse of alcohol and drugs among maternal incest offenders and female sex offenders has been documented in several case studies. Wolfe (1985) found that of 12 female sex offenders, five were substance abusers. Faller (1987) found that of the 40 female child molesters in her study, alcohol was abused in 13 cases, drugs in six cases, and both in three cases. In an updated study in 1995, she reported substance abuse in 37 out of 72 females (about 51%). Of 65 female sex offenders in Allen's (1991) sample, 17% identified themselves as alcoholics and 26% indicated that they had used drugs. Saradjian and Hanks (1996) found that among women who abused alcohol and drugs, none offended against children exclusively when they were abusing substances, suggesting that drug and alcohol abuse, when present, may not be the primary contributor to the offending behavior.

Studies of female sex offenders generally indicate that the majority of these women do not have intellectual limitations, but in some instances that was the case. Faller (1987) found that 48% of the 40 female child molesters in her study had mental difficulties; of these, 33% were mentally retarded or brain damaged. In an updated study in 1995 covering a new total of 72 females, 16 (about 22%) were mentally retarded. In some cases, intellectual limitations may play a role in offending behavior. These cases may be over-represented in the literature, as these women may be among the more likely to be caught.

It is not uncommon for a child to understand that the parent is mentally ill and behaves inappropriately in many aspects of her behavior. The child may still feel protective of the parent's well-being, intent on keeping the parent in the home. When children are younger it is difficult for the authorities to be aware of the abuse that is occurring. As reported in a case study by deYoung (1982), one young man experienced his incestuous relationship with his mother as both special and private while also recognizing that she was mentally ill.

Role Replacement

Some researchers have observed cases in which the offenses against male children occurred in the context of family dynamics in which the children were placed in the role of spouses (Justice and Justice, 1979). Faller (1987) described several cases of single-parent females who lacked ongoing relationships with adult men. They placed the oldest children in the roles of surrogate partners with adult responsibilities, including sexual contact. Faller noted that in many of these cases the women were not married to the childrens' fathers and had children with multiple partners.

Revenge

In some instances, sexual behavior with children has been used to gain revenge toward an adult partner for abandoning the family, having sex with one of the other children, or for losing sexual interest in the adult partner.

Adolescent Curiosity/Exploitation

While not clearly documented in empirical studies, clinical experience with violent male offenders with chaotic and disturbed backgrounds has sometimes revealed the exploitation of male children by adolescent girls. In the majority of these instances, the female perpetrators come from chaotic homes, as do often the victims of the sexual encounter. The encounters reflect the poor judgment of the offenders and the wish to try out some behavior that has been presented to them in some other context. These instances seem to embody some element of adolescent curiosity with no amelioration of the behavior by a concern for the child.

Investigatory Significance

This emergent recognition of a previously under-reported form of criminal offending is important for law enforcement officials — both in widening their awareness of the types of sexual abuse that can and are being perpetrated against children and in alerting them to the role of women as both initiators and co-perpetrators in various kinds of sexual crimes. It is easy to overlook the role of a female accomplice in crimes that are being investigated and to underestimate the impact of this type of under-reported sexual abuse in the development of children who are raised in chaotic and exploitative family structures. In terms of prevention, the research is also making clear the need for resources to help children avoid this kind of abusive crime. Not only does it have long-term effects on the children, but it also serves as a contagion that follows the victims into the next generation with repetitious and cyclical traumatization of others.

References

Allen, C. (1991) *Women and Men Who Sexually Abuse Children: A Comparative Analysis*, Orwell, VT: The Safer Society Press.

Bouchard, V. (1994) Women who sexually abuse children: phenomenological case studies of 11 women. Doctoral dissertation, The Adler School of Professional Psychology, Chicago.

Chideckel, M. (1935) *Female Sex Perversions: The Sexually Aberrated Woman As She Is*, New York: Eugenics.

Committee on Sexual Offences Against Children and Youth (1984) Sexual Offenses against Children, Vol. 1, Ottawa: Canadian Government Publishing Centre.

Cooper, I. and Cormier, B. (1990) In Bluegrass, R. and Bowden, P. (Eds.), *Principals and Practice of Forensic Physchiatry*, New York: Churchill Livingston, pp. 749–765.

Cooper, A., Swaminath, S., Baxter D., and Poulin, C. (1990) A female sex offender with multiple paraphilias: a psychologic and endocrine case study, *Can. J. Psychiatr.*, 35, 334–337.

Crewdson, J. (1988) *By Silence Betrayed: Sexual Abuse of Children in America*, Boston: Little, Brown and Company.

Davin, P. (1999) Secrets revealed: a study of female sex offenders, In E. Bear, Ed., *Female Sexual Abusers: Three Perspectives*, Brandon, VT: The Safer Society Press.

de Young, (1982) *The Sexual Victimization of Children*, Jefferson, NC: McFarland & Company.

Faller, K. (1987) Woman who sexually abuse children, *Violence and Victims*, 2(4), 263–276.

Faller, K. (1988) The spectrum of sexual abuse in daycare. An exploratory study, *J. Fam. Violence*, 3(4), 283–298.

Faller, K. (1995) A clinical sample of women who have sexually abused children, *J. Child Sexual Abuse*, 4(3), 13–29.

Finkelhor, D. and Williams, L. (1988) Perpetrators, In D. Finkelhor, L. Williams, and N. Burns, Eds., *Nursery Crimes: Sexual Abuse in Day Care*, Newbury Park, CA: Sage Publications, 27–69.

Freel, M. (1995) Women who sexually abuse children, *Social Work Monographs*, Norwich: University of Hull, Monograph 135.

Fromuth, M. and Conn, V. (1997) Hidden perpetrators: sexual molestation in a nonclinical sample of college women, *J. Interpersonal Violence*, 12(3), 456–465.

Green, A. and Kaplan, M. (1994), Psychiatric impairment and childhood victimization experiences in female child molesters, *J. Am. Acad. Child Adolescent Psychiatr.*, 33(7), 954–961.

Groth, N. (1979b) Sexual trauma in the life histories of rapists and child molesters, *Victimology Int. J.*, 4(1), 10–16.

Groth, A.N. and Burgess, A.W. (1977a) Motivational intent in the sexual assault of children, *Criminal Justice Behav.*, 4(3), 253–265.

Higgs, D., Cavanan, M., and Meyer, W. (1992), Moving from defense to offense: the development of a female sex offender, *J. Sex Res.*, 29(1), 131–140.

Hindman, J. (2000) Understanding the male victim and the female perpetrator. Sixteenth National Symposium on Child Sexual Abuse. Huntsville, AL: The National Children's Advocacy Center.

Hislop, J. (1994) *Female Child Molesters*, Doctoral dissertation, California School of Professional Psychology, Fresno, CA.

Hislop, J. (1999) Female child molesters, In E. Bear, Ed., *Female Sexual Abusers: Three Perspectives*, Brandon, VT: The Safer Society Press.

Hudson, A. (1995) *Personality Assessment of Female Sex Offenders: A Cluster Analysis*, Doctoral dissertation, University of Oklahoma.

James, B. and Nasjleti, M. (1983) *Treating Sexually Abused Children and Their Families*, Palo Alto, CA: Consulting Psychologists Press, Inc.

Justice, B. and Justice, R. (1979) *The Broken Taboo: Sex in the Family*, New York: Human Sciences Press.

Kaufman, K., Wallace, A., Johnson, C., and Reeder, M. (1995), Comparing female and male perpetrators' *modus operandi*: victims' reports of sexual abuse, *J. Interpersonal Violence*, 10(3), 322–334.

Kinsey, A., Pomeroy, W., and Martin, C. (1948) *Sexual Behavior in the Human Male*, Philadelphia: W.B. Saunders.

Knight, R. (1988) A taxonomic analysis of child molesters, In *Human Sexual Aggression: Current Perspectives*, New York: Academy of Sciences, 2–20.

Korbin, J. (1986) Childhood histories of women imprisoned for fatal child maltreatment, *Child Abuse Neglect*, 10, 331–338.

Krafft-Ebing, R. (1886) *Psychopathia Sexualis: A Medico-Forensic Study*, Translation by H.E. Wedeck, New York: G.P. Putnam's Sons.

Lane, S. (1991) Special offender populations, In G. Ryan and S. Lane, Eds., *Juvenile Sexual Offending: Causes, Consequences and Correction*, Lexington, MA: Lexington Books, 299–332.

Lanning, K.V. (1985) *Child Sex Rings: A Behavioral Analysis*, Quantico, VA: National Center for Missing and Exploited Children.

Larson, N. and Maison, S. (1987) *Psychosexual Treatment Program for Female Sex Offenders, Minnesota Correctional Facility, Shakopee*, St. Paul: Meta Resources.

Lawson, W. (1984) Depression and crime: a discursive approach, In M. Craft and A. Craft, Eds., *Mentally Abnormal Offenders*, Philadelphia: Balliere Tindale.

Marvasti, J. (1986) Incestuous mothers, *Am. J. Forensic Psychiatr.*, 7(4), 63–69.

Matthews, R., Matthews, J., and Speltz, K. (1989) *Female Sexual Offenders: An Exploratory Study*, Orwell, VT: The Safer Society Press.

Matthews, J., Mathews, R., and Speltz, K. (1991) Female sexual offenders: a typology. In P.Q. Patton, Ed., *Family Sexual Abuse*, New York: Sage.

Mathis, J. (1972) *Clear Thinking about Sexual Deviations*, Chicago: Nelson-Hall Company.

McCarty, L. (1986) Mother-child incest: characteristics of the offender, *Child Welfare*, 65(5), 447–458.

Myers, K. (1992) The experiences of adult women who, as children, were sexually abused by an older, trusted female: an exploratory study, Master's thesis, Northhampton, MA: Smith College School for Social Work.

O'Connor, A. (1987) Female sex offenders, *Br. J. Psychiatr.*, 150, 615–620.

Paiser, P. (1992) Relational experiences of women survivors of female-perpetrated childhood sexual abuse, Doctoral dissertation, Boston: School of Professional Psychology.

Pothast, H. and Allen, C. (1994) Masculinity and femininity in male and female perpetrators of child sexual abuse, *Child Abuse Neglect*, 18(9), 763–767.

Risin, L. and Koss, M. (1987) Sexual abuse of boys: prevalence, and descriptive characteristics of childhood victimizations, *J. Interpersonal Violence*, 2(3), 309–323.

Rosencrans, B. (1997) *The Last Secret: Daughters Sexually Abused by Mothers*, Brandon, VT: The Safer Society Press.

Saradjian, J. and Hanks, H. (1996) *Women Who Sexually Abuse Children: From Research to Clinical Practice*, New York: John Wiley & Sons.

Sarrel, P. and Masters, W. (1982) Sexual molestation of men by women, *Arch. Sexual Behav.*, 11(2), 117–131.

Serin, R.C. (1994) Psychopathy and deviant sexual arousal in incarcerated sexual offenders, *J. Interpersonal Violence*, 9(1), 3–11.

Sheldrick, C. (1991) Adult sequelae of child sexual abuse, *Br. J. Psychiatr.*, 158 (Suppl. 10), 55–62.

Swink, K. (1989) Therapeutic issues for women survivors of maternal incest. Presented at the Association for Women in Psychology, National Conference, Newport, Rhode Island.

Travin, S., Cullen, K., and Protter, B. (1990) Female sex offenders: severe victims and victimizers, *J. Forensic Sci.*, 35(1), 140–150.

Turner, M. and Turner, T. (1994) *Female Adolescent Sexual Abusers: An Exploratory Study of Mother-Daughter Dynamics with Implications for Treatment*, Brandon, VT: The Safer Society Press.

Warren, J.I. and Hazelwood, R.R. (in press) Relational patterns associated with sexual sadism, *J. Fam. Violence*.

Wolfe, F. (March 1985) Twelve female sexual offenders, paper presented at "Next steps in research on the assessment and treatment of sexually aggressive persons (paraphilics)," St. Louis.

Woodring, H. (1995) An MMPI study of incarcerated female sex offenders, unpublished Master's thesis, Bucknell University, Lewisburg, PA.

Wulffen, E. (1934) *Woman as Sexual Criminal*, New York: American Ethnological Press.

The Serial Rapist

21

ROBERT R. HAZELWOOD
JANET I. WARREN

Introduction

> In the early 1990s, a mental health professional was alone in her single-family residence when she was captured by a masked offender. He bound her, using materials that he had brought with him, and then raped her in an excessively violent manner. During the rape, it became apparent that he was very knowledgeable about her personal and social life. Under threat of death, he forced her to attempt to explain his motivation for the crime. He also demanded that she describe for him her last sexual encounter. The victim described the rapist as articulate and physically and emotionally controlling. She was unable to identify his race with any certainty.

The Office of Juvenile Justice and Delinquency Prevention* (OJJDP) provided grant money for a collaborative effort by the National Center for the Analysis of Violent Crime (NCAVC) and Dr. Ann Wolbert Burgess of the University of Pennsylvania's School of Nursing to conduct research on serial rape. The study included interviews with 41 incarcerated serial rapists from every region of the U.S. (California, Maryland, Idaho, Louisiana, and Michigan) who had raped at least 10 times and who, as a group, were responsible for 837 sexual assaults and more than 400 attempted rapes. The rapists were incarcerated in prisons located in 12 states. The inclusion criterion of 10 rapes was established as it signified continuing success at eluding law enforcement, an aptitude that warranted further investigation. The study of multiple rapes by a single individual also allowed for an assessment of change over time on a number of important variables, such as the amount of force used, the sexual activities enacted, and the details of the *modus operandi*.

Members of the NCAVC (including Hazelwood and selected FBI Agents) conducted each of the 41 interviews. Prior to conducting the interviews, all available documentation was reviewed, including police investigatory

* This research was funded in part by grant #84-JN-AX-KO from the Office of Juvenile Justice and Delinquency Prevention to the University of Pennsylvania School of Nursing in conjunction with the FBI National Center for the Analysis of Violent Crime.

reports, victim statements, pre-sentence reports, medical and mental health records, and pertinent prison records. The interviews were open-ended and unstructured and ranged from $4^1/_2$ to $12^1/_2$ hours. They included a detailed review of the rapist's developmental, familial, sexual, marital, educational, employment, and military history as well as his current hobbies and pastimes. The interview also focused on the offender's pre-offense, offense, and post-offense behavior as well as any advice he might provide law enforcement regarding investigation, interrogation, and rape prevention. Following the interviews, a 70-page protocol was completed by the interviewers. While numerous studies of rape and rapists have been conducted over the years, to our knowledge this research represents the only body of information on this type of serial sexual offender.

Who is the serial rapist? At what age does he begin to assault, and how does he select his victims? In what other types of deviant sexual activities does he engage? Drawing from these interviews, this chapter outlines information about the serial rapist, his victims, and his criminal behavior. In assessing these data, it is important to remember that the data refer to a special category of serial rapist (10 or more victims) and may not be generalized to a more undifferentiated group of rapists.

Serial Rapist Demographics

The sample consisted of 35 white males, 5 black males, and 1 Hispanic male. At the time of the interviews, the subjects' ages ranged from 23 to 55 years, with a mean of 35.2 years. The mean ages of the subjects at the times of their first, middle, and last rapes were 21.8 years, 25.8 years, and 29 years respectively.

The youngest rapist interviewed also assaulted for the shortest period of time prior to his first arrest. That rapist, who will be referred to as Jess, was 20 years old when he was apprehended for a series of 12 rapes over a 3-month period.

Case No. 1

Jess advised that he had never consciously thought about rape until one month before he began his crimes. On that occasion, he and a male friend were discussing the friend's disappointment with a date the previous evening — one which had not culminated in sexual relations. The friend stated that he was so angry, he considered raping the woman. Jess asked why he didn't, and the friend stated that he wasn't willing to go to jail for sex. Jess reported that he thought about rape that evening and decided to commit one about a month later.

Although he was relatively young at the time, his method of obtaining victims was thoughtful. He would go to singles bars and wait until a woman over 40 years of age entered the bar unaccompanied. His rationale for selecting a victim of that age was that women over 40 had been raised during a time when it was believed that women who went to bars alone were looking for a sexual liaison. Jess was young and attractive, and therefore the women were flattered when he approached them. After spending time with the woman, he would suggest that they go to his place. If she agreed, he would ask himself, "I wonder what her face will look like when I tell her I'm going to rape her?" After leaving the bar, he would drive to an isolated area, stop the car, and tell her to take her clothes off saying, "I'm going to rape you." The victim would be incredulous, and he would strike her face, force her to remove her clothing, rape her, and leave her stranded.

Jess had no previous history of criminal activity prior to his arrest for rape. He was raised in an advantaged socioeconomic environment; from all accounts his family was close-knit, and his parents were involved in their children's lives. He was an outstanding athlete in high school and had been voted most popular student and senior class president.

Employment

Twenty (54%) of 37 who responded described their employment history as generally stable, 14 (38%) stated that it was unstable, and 3 (8%) characterized themselves as chronically unemployed. The respondents reported that, at the time of their most recent arrests, they had been employed at their last jobs for a mean of 2.4 years. They had held from 1 to 35 jobs, with a mean of 5.4 jobs during the previous 15 years.

The types of employment held by the rapists included unskilled jobs, skilled positions (cardiovascular technicians), and white-collar occupations (business managers). One of the authors has since interviewed a medical professional responsible for more than 50 stranger-to-stranger rapes. Of particular interest is the fact that the majority of serial rapists were generally stable in their employment; only a small minority were chronically unemployed. With few exceptions, the serial rapists were employed at the time they were committing their assaults.

Marital History

Twenty-nine (71%) of 41 respondents had been married at least once, with 14 of these individuals (34%) having been married more than one time. These findings confirm earlier studies[2] which suggest that the marital status of an individual, or the presence of consensual sexual relationships, is not directly related to whether a person commits rape. All but one of the rapists interviewed had participated in consensual sexual activities.

Case No. 2

"Phillip," a 45-year-old white male, had a master's degree and was earning a high salary as a white collar professional when he was convicted of multiple rapes. He reported that he had never had a consensual sexual relationship in his entire life. His first sexual encounter with a woman occurred when he was 16. He ran up behind a woman with a chloroform-soaked rag and held it over her mouth until she lost consciousness. When she fell, he became frightened that he had killed her and ran away. He went on to rape more than 40 women.

One of the serial rapists, "Mike," commented on the irony of raping when a consensual partner is readily available.

Case No. 3

Upon being released from prison after serving a sentence for rape, Mike obtained a job managing a business and moved back in with his wife of seven years. Prior to leaving work late one evening, he called his wife, suggested an intimate dinner, and hinted at sexual activities to which she responded positively. While driving home, he observed a woman driving alone. Pulling in behind her, he flashed his lights, and the victim, believing him to be a police officer, pulled over. He walked to her car, asked for her driver's license and registration, and requested that she accompany him back to his car. She did so, and he subdued and raped her.

After relating the details of the crime, Mike shook his head and said, "I mean, my God, there I was on my way home to have sex with my wife, and I ended up back here."

Military History

Twenty-one (51%) of the 41 rapists served in the Armed Forces. Of these, 18 were in the ground forces, and all were in the enlisted ranks. It is worth noting that the mean age of the men at the time of interview was 35.2, and therefore they were eligible for the draft that ended in 1972. As a result of the draft elimination, fewer rapists have military histories. However, in the authors' experience, when a military background is present, the discharge and criminal information presented in this chapter is found to be valid as it pertains to serial rapists.

Of 20 veterans, 10 received honorable discharges and 10 received other-than-honorable discharges. Information was not available on one veteran. Information on military performance was available for 18 veterans; nine of them reported that they had encountered occasional difficulties in the military. Eight veterans indicated that they had been charged with criminal offenses while in the service.

The large number of other-than-honorable discharges and the high incidence of noncriminal and criminal problems experienced by the interviewees are in keeping with a general pattern of antisocial behavior observed in the serial rapists' backgrounds.

Intelligence

In 33 instances, formal intelligence test scores were available for review. The serial rapists demonstrated unusually high levels of general intelligence. Only 4 (12%) scored below average, while 12 (36%) scored within the average range of intelligence. Seventeen (52%) scored above average (9 scored bright normal and 8 superior or very superior). In all, 88% of those tested scored average or better.

The educational levels of the men ranged from 5 to 17 years, with a mean of 11.3 years of formal education. Twenty-five (61%) of the 41 respondents had obtained GED or high school diplomas, and 9 (22%) held either an associate's or bachelor's degree.

"Ted" was one of the most intelligent rapists interviewed during the research. He had a measured Full Scale IQ of 139. Interestingly, he was the only individual who had never experienced a consensual sexual relationship.

Case No. 4

Ted was steadily employed, earned well over $30,000, and considered himself socioeconomically advantaged. The manner in which he committed his crimes evidenced a great amount of forethought. In preparing for a series of rapes, he would drive a great distance from where he resided or worked and select a residential area into which he would easily blend. Through peeping activities, he would select a minimum of six females who lived alone and would begin observing their homes in order to ascertain their patterns of behavior. He explained that he always maintained a minimum of six potential victims, and after raping one, he would select another to replace her. He did this in the event he was, for one reason or another, unsuccessful in his first attempt. On some occasions, after unsuccessfully attempting a rape, he would subdue an alternate victim and rape her while the police were responding to the first victim's complaint.

Ted was a very ritualistic rapist. Prior to entering the victim's residence, he would dress in his "going-in clothes," which consisted of work gloves, loose-fitting dark coveralls, oversized sneakers, and a ski mask. Using a glass cutter and a suction cup, he would noiselessly make entry through a patio door or window. After ensuring that the victim was asleep and alone, he would disconnect the telephone and light-emitting devices in her bedroom. He would then leave the residence, but prior to doing so, he would raise a window or leave the door ajar. Returning to his vehicle, he would change into his "rape clothes," which consisted of over-sized coveralls, tight-fitting surgical-like gloves, a differently sized pair of sneakers, and a ski mask. Upon approaching the home, he would check to see if the window or door had been closed. If it had, he would realize that the victim had awakened, and he would leave and go to another victim's home. If the window or door had not been closed, he would go to the victim's bedside and count to ten in increments of one half (one half, one, one and one half, two, etc.) He would then leap upon the victim, rape her, and depart within two minutes.

When questioned as to the meaning of this ritualistic behavior, Ted explained that he "was putting off the rape" because "that was the least enjoyable part of the whole thing." When asked why he didn't leave if that was the case, he stated, "Pardon the pun, but after all I had gone through to get there, it would have been a crime not to rape her."

In assessing the intelligence of these offenders, it is important to remain aware of problems inherent in relying too heavily upon documented intelligence test scores. The first rapist interviewed had a documented test score of 108. During the interview, it became obvious that the score did not accurately reflect the intelligence of the rapist. Commenting on this, the rapist advised that when first imprisoned, he was advised by older inmates to score intentionally low on such tests so that the authorities would not expect too much of him. At the interviewer's request, he agreed to be retested and scored 128, a full 20 points higher.

Formally measured intelligence may not always be the best indicator of ability to be a successful criminal. While the vast majority of the individuals included in this study were average or above average in intelligence, some scored below average, and yet they were very successful in eluding law enforcement. Street smarts, while not something that can be measured through standardized testing, is well recognized by both criminals and police. Perhaps it is best defined as the ability to survive by applying what has been learned through one's own experiences or the experiences of others.

Representative of this concept is the case of "Jack," an impulsive serial rapist who harbored a sincere and earnest hatred of women. Jack's measured intelligence was only 79 (Full Scale), yet he was a successful criminal because of his ability to anticipate and manipulate others.

Case No. 5

One sunny afternoon, Jack was walking across a food store parking lot and observed a woman placing groceries in her car. He approached the woman, shoved her into the front seat of her car, beat and raped her, and walked away. Following that crime, he left that city and traveled to his hometown. Aware that the FBI had a warrant for his arrest (under the Unlawful Flight to Avoid Prosecution Statute) and would surely be looking for him in his hometown, he entered a drug rehabilitation program. He did so knowing that these programs are immune from having to divulge the identities of the participants to law enforcement or any member of the criminal justice system. Even though he had no drug problem, he knew enough about drug addiction to be able to evidence the necessary symptoms.

After one month in the program, he decided that he wanted a woman and inquired as to when he would be allowed to leave the center unescorted. Upon learning he could not do so for at least six months, he stated, "I wasn't gonna wait no damn six months for a woman." He thought about it and decided to use a medical ploy to get away from the confines of the center. He feigned abdominal pains, knowing they were not easily diagnosed, and was taken to a hospital by a counselor. After being examined by a physician, he advised the counselor that he would have to take a series of tests, each test being on a different floor of the hospital. The counselor advised Jack that he would wait for him on the ground floor of the hospital.

Now on his own, Jack set out for the one location where he was guaranteed to find women — the restroom area. Observing a woman enter the lavatory, he followed her in, and seeing no one else was present, he took a paper towel from the dispenser. Using a marking pen and tape he had brought with him, he printed "Out of Order" on it and affixed it to the front of the restroom door. He then reentered the room and proceeded to assault the victim. Another woman, ignoring the sign, entered the restroom, at which time the victim screamed. The second woman ran out of the room and yelled that a woman was being assaulted, and a crowd gathered outside the door. Jack grabbed the victim by her hair, opened the door, and screamed at her, "If I ever catch you screwing around again, I'm not only gonna kill him, I'm gonna kill you too." Believing that Jack and the victim were involved in a domestic argument, the crowd parted; and Jack moved through them with the victim in tow. Fortunately for the woman, her doctor recognized her, and Jack ran down the stairwell and to his counselor. They returned to the treatment center, and Jack later fled to Canada.

Arrest History

The rapists reported diverse criminal histories, including a variety of property offenses, nuisance sexual offenses, and other sexual assaults. The authors dislike the term *nuisance* when associated with criminal sexuality. The word is commonly associated with sexual offenses such as window peeping, obscene phone calls, and exhibitionism. *Nuisance* is thought of as meaning

annoying, troublesome, or worrisome. It does not imply danger. The following case was consulted on by Hazelwood, and he later testified in the trial of
the offender.

Case No. 6

> A 17-year-old white female was found in a ditch with her blouse and bra
> pushed above her breasts and her pants open and slightly below her waist.
> She had been vaginally, anally, and orally assaulted by her killer. Her throat
> had been cut from ear to ear, resulting in a wound bordering on sub-total
> decapitation. She had been stabbed in the head, face, and the front and back
> of her torso. Because of contusions in the genital area, it was believed that
> a blunt force object had been used to penetrate her vaginally and anally.
>
> A young man was arrested and charged with her murder. He was linked
> to the case via DNA. It was a surprise to learn that he had no arrest history.
> During a meeting with the prosecutor and investigators, it was mentioned
> that, while he had no arrest history, he had made some obscene phone
> calls and had exposed himself to two college coeds while a teenager. The
> complaints had been referred to the juvenile division and had not been
> followed up.
>
> A 24-year-old woman had been one of the victims of the obscene phone
> calls, and fortunately she was able to recall in great detail what the caller
> had said. She advised that she had received in excess of 100 such calls and
> that in each one, the caller had said that he wanted to fuck her every way
> he could, he wanted to stab her until his arm got tired, he wanted to cut
> her open like a pig, and he wanted to use his gear shift on her.
>
> The young man was tried and convicted for these *nuisance* offenses, thereby
> allowing the woman who received the obscene calls to testify during the
> sentence phase of his murder trial.

What is essential for the investigator to understand about nuisance sexual
crimes is that the subject is acting out a fantasy and that he is masturbating
to that fantasy, thereby reinforcing the fantasy's arousal factor. In the case of
phone calls, what a caller says to the victim provides the investigator with
the fantasy of the caller. In Case No. 6, the fantasy involved rape, stabbing,
and cutting. These types of calls are hardly nuisance crimes. Investigators are
urged to determine what took place during a nuisance crime before automatically relegating it to the circular file. This issue will be addressed further
in this chapter.

Only one rapist had no prior arrests when he was apprehended for his
three-month spree during which he had raped 12 women (see Case No. 1).
The majority of the rapists (24, or 58%) had been institutionalized in either

correctional centers (46%) or mental facilities (12%) at least once prior to their arrests for their most current offenses.

When asked about previous sexual assaults, the respondents reported they had been convicted of a mean of 7.6 sexual assaults, although they were, in fact, responsible for a mean of 27.8 assaults. Prior sexual offenses committed by 38 of the respondents included rape only (37%), nuisance sexual offenses only (8%), a combination of rape and sexual nuisance offenses (42%), and other types of offenses (13%). The number of actual sexual assaults committed by the rapists ranged from 10 to 78. (According to the respondents, they also had been convicted of a mean of one sexual assault for which they were not guilty.) The most commonly reported nonsexual offenses included burglary and breaking and entering. This is not surprising in that police frequently arrest men they are convinced were intent on committing rape or other sexual assault, but lack the proof. Consequently, the police charge the offenders with the offense for which they have the necessary evidence.

The rapists were asked how they responded to being confronted by an arresting officer. The majority surrendered without resistance; and, when interrogated, nearly half admitted fully to the offense.

Residence

At the time of their crimes, most of the offenders were living in single-family dwellings, although a significant minority resided in apartments. In a small number of instances, the offender was institutionalized at the time of the offense. The majority of the rapists were living with others during their crimes; but during the first and last rape, nine (22%) out of 41 respondents were living alone.

These findings certainly contradict popular stereotypes that characterize the serial rapist as a lonely, isolated person who lives alone and has little or no contact with his family. Rather, in most cases, the rapist is more likely to be living with his parents or spouse at the time of the offense.

Use of Vehicle

The serial rapists frequently used vehicles in the commission of their crimes, to get to and from the scenes or to transport the victims. The types and ownerships of vehicles used by the rapists in their assaults were examined. In no instance was a stolen vehicle involved. In the majority of the assaults (62%), the perpetrators used their own vehicles. In only seven (8%) of the rapes the offenders used the victim's vehicles, while in six (7%) instances a borrowed vehicle was used by the rapist.

Sedans or hardtops were the most frequently used vehicle types (46%). The next most frequently used vehicle was a pickup truck (19%).

In 85% of the crimes, the vehicles were described as in good or better condition. At the time of the last assault, there were nine reports that the offenders' vehicles were equipped with a CB radio, police scanner, spotlight, or police antenna.

Personality Characteristics

The information presented here is based upon self-reported data and the observations of the interviewing FBI Agents. Not all serial rapists interviewed are represented by the descriptions set forth below.

The vast majority of the rapists could be described as neat and well-groomed men who obviously took pride in their personal appearances. They exhibited a range of emotions from cold and aloof to agitated and tearful. The largest proportion of them, however, were observed to be expressive, though guarded and controlled. The rapists indicated that they were not trustworthy individuals. They were, however, able to hide this aspect of their personalities when interacting with friends and associates.

They conversed in an articulate and conversational manner frequently punctuated with profanity. They used a precise and concise manner in an attempt to ensure that their thoughts were being conveyed and in order to maintain control.

When asked how their friends would have described them at the time they were committing the assaults, they responded with descriptions such as average, friendly, a leader, and willing to help out a friend. Further discussion brought out the fact that, while they tended to meet people easily, they eventually attempted to dominate the relationships. They displayed good senses of humor but were manipulative and cunning. While able to convince people of their abilities to achieve, they were impulsive and always seemed to be having one type of problem or another.

The rapists described themselves as being perceived by others as macho and suggested that they worked at maintaining this image through their dress, attitude, speech, and mode of transportation. They were intelligent and consequently tended to lead rather than follow.

While this was the image or "service personality" that others saw, many of the rapists related a sense of inadequacy, immaturity, and irresponsibility to the interviewers. As one rapist said, "I was expected to decide what my group was going to do or where we were going to go. I really didn't feel comfortable in that role and would have liked having someone else make the decision. I didn't see myself as others saw me."

Hobbies and Activities

Thirty-seven of the 41 rapists reported having pastimes or hobbies. Twenty-three of them reported outdoor activities, while 14 mentioned a variety of indoor interests. Of 35 pastimes reported, physically-oriented activities included fishing (12), hunting (7), swimming (5), and baseball (5). Non-physical types of activities included music, model building, reading, wood-working, coin or stamp collecting, chess, and antiques.

When asked what types of books and magazines they preferred to read, the respondents listed *Playboy*, *Penthouse*, other sex magazines, crime novels, and a variety of spy novels and science fiction books. Newspapers, *Time* Magazine, *Reader's Digest*, and entertainment magazines were also reported.

Developmental Characteristics

Socioeconomics

Table 1 summarizes various aspects of the rapists' family structures. As indicated, slightly over one half grew up in homes that were socioeconomically average (37%) or advantaged (17%). Approximately one quarter (27%) were raised in marginal but self-sufficient homes, while 20% were raised in sub-marginal homes and were, at times, on welfare.

The significance of these findings is that 54% of the serial rapists were brought up in average or above-average socioeconomic environments. While it is recognized that the results of this research cannot be generalized to the undifferentiated rapist population, these findings would seem to contradict long-held beliefs and theories that the majority of such individuals come from economically deprived families.

Parental Relationships

The rapists were asked questions about their relationships with their parents (see Table 1). When asked who was the dominant parental figure, 20 (50%) reported their mothers, 16 (40%) their fathers, and four (10%) named some other adult figures.

"Kenny" provides the reader with an example of a young man who was raised in an unusual interpersonal environment.

Case No. 7

When Kenny was 8 years old, his mother was convicted of murder; and he was sent to live with an aunt who had recently been released from prison for stabbing a man to death. The aunt was an alcoholic and chronic gambler, and all of the family's money went to support these activities. At the age of 14, he ran away from home and was taken in by a pimp. The pimp was in his mid-twenties and a college graduate. The man allowed Kenny to assist in his business by collecting monies from the female prostitutes in his "stable." Of interest is the fact that the pimp insisted that Kenny continue

Table 1   Family Structure of Serial Rapists

	Number	Percent
Assessment of Socioeconomic Level of Subject's Preadult Home (N = 41)		
Advantaged	7	17
Comfortable, average	15	37
Marginal, self-sufficient	11	27
Submarginal	8	20
Variable	—	—
Dominant Parental Figures (N = 40)		
Mother	20	50
Father	16	40
Other	4	10
Quality of Relationship to Mother or Dominant Female Caretaker (N = 39)		
Warm, close	14	36
Variable	12	31
Cold, distant	2	5
Uncaring, indifferent	4	10
Hostile, aggressive	7	18
Quality of Relationship to Father or Dominant Male Caretaker (N = 39)		
Warm, close	7	18
Variable	10	26
Cold, distant	12	31
Uncaring, indifferent	3	8
Hostile, aggressive	7	18
Evidence that Subject was Physically Abused by Parents/Caretakers (N = 40)		
Yes	15	38
No	25	62
Evidence that Subject was Psychologically Abused by Parents/Caretakers (N = 41)		
Yes	30	73
No	11	27
Evidence that Subject was Sexually Abused (N = 41)		
Yes	31	76
No	10	24

his education and not run the streets. The pimp stressed the value of education and advised that when Kenny could no longer work the girls, he could always fall back on his college degree. Kenny advised that while he was with the pimp, he never got into trouble with the law. Eventually, the man was arrested and sentenced to a long prison term; and unfortunately, Kenny returned to the streets.

Within the sample, only 14 (36%) of the men described their relationships with their mothers as warm or close. Twelve (31%) stated they had variable relationships, seven (18%) said their relationships were hostile or aggressive, four (10%) said they were uncaring or indifferent, and two (5%) described them as cold or distant.

Even fewer of the men (7, or 18%) described their relationships with their fathers as warm or close. Twelve of the respondents (31%) indicated that they were cold or distant, 10 (26%) reported they were variable, seven (18%) as hostile or aggressive, and three (8%) as uncaring or indifferent.

Childhood Abuse

Abusive behavior in the families of the serial rapists was well documented. As noted in Table 1, 15 (30%) of the rapists reported physical abuse. One man advised that his mother would "hit me with anything that was handy, a belt, a broom handle, iron, whatever." Scars on his back were evidence to the truthfulness of his statement. Another rapist explained that his mother caught him fondling his penis through his pants and reported it to his father. The father made the boy put his penis over the back of a chair and whipped it with a belt.

Thirty (73%) of the subjects described psychological abuse. However, obtaining this information was not always easy. One man, when asked if he had been emotionally abused as a child, replied negatively. Later however, when asked what his mother said to him when she was angry, he replied, "She would call me a bastard, son-of-a-bitch, asshole. Things like that."

In a separate analysis of the same 41 rapists, Burgess et al.[3] found that 31 (76%) of the men reported experiencing some type of unusual sexual experience in childhood or during their teen years. Eight (26%) of 31 subjects described being forced to witness disturbing sexual occurrences. Seven (22%) stated that they were fondled or were involved in the fondling of another, and 16 (52%) recalled being forced to submit to penetration of their bodies.[3]

"Ray," a progressively violent offender, was repeatedly raped by his father and later initiated by his father into raping women.

Case No. 8

Ray described his father as cold and distant until his father began anally raping him at the age of 9. From that stage of his life to the present, Ray described his father as hostile and aggressive. Ray's father raped him until the age of 12, and as his age increased, so did the aggressiveness of the assaults. He advised that when he reached 11 years of age, his father began taking him to bars where he would pick up women, take them to an isolated area, sadistically beat and rape them, and then force them into the back seat with Ray and tell them to "take care of my son." Ray would be told by his father what part of the victim's body he was to hit, bite, pinch, or pull. He stated that at the age of 12, he began anticipating his father being finished with the woman so that he could gain access to her. Ray maintained that he believed that this was the way men and women had sex until he was 14. He continued to rape with his father until, at the age of 16, his father raped Ray's girlfriend.

Sexual Development

Table 2 summarizes aspects of the rapists' sexual development as well as various components of their current sexual adaptations. Of etiological significance is the fact that 76% of the men reported either observing disturbing sexual acts or being sexually abused. This is alarmingly high when compared to percentages associated with the general population.[4]

Interestingly, while being interviewed, many of the rapists failed to define their sexual experiences as abuse, initially indicating that they had not been

Table 2   Serial Rapists Sexual History and Current Sexual Behaviors

Childhood or Adolescent Sexual Trauma	Number	Percent	Total Respondees
Witnessing sexual violence of others	8	28	32
Witnessing disturbing sexual activity on part of parents	17	44	39
Witnessing disturbing sexual activity on part of other family members or friends	9	25	36
Physical injury to sexual organs; venereal disease	5	14	36
Multiple sexual assaults	11	31	35
Sex stress situations (punitive parental reaction to masturbation)	17	46	37
Adult Sexual Behavior			
Marked inhibition/aversion to sexual activity	4	10	40
Compulsive masturbation	21	54	39
Exhibitionism	12	29	41
Voyeurism (peeping)	27	68	40
Fetishism	16	41	39
Cross-dressing	9	23	39
Obscene phone calls	15	38	40
Prostitution (or pimp)	6	15	41
Sexual bondage	10	26	39
Collected detective magazines	11	28	39
Collected pornography	13	33	39

sexually abused. However, when they were subsequently asked at what age and with whom they had their first sexual encounters with another person, evidence of sexual abuse became evident.

Case Nos. 9 and 10

"Fred," one of the rapists who initially denied being sexually abused, advised that, when 7 years old, he went to a movie. A man sat next to him and attempted to fondle him. He moved to another part of the theater, and the man followed him and offered him $2 to allow the activity. The boy agreed and continued to meet the man each weekend for a full year. The initial encounter bothered the boy enough to cause him to change seats; but as an adult, he rationalized it as a way of making money.

Another rapist explained that at age 8, his parents hired a 17-year-old female to babysit and she "taught me how to go down on women." As an 8-year-old child, the experience had to be frightening; but as an adult, he considered it a score.

This inconsistency in reporting reflects certain cultural biases in defining the sexual abuse of young males by older females. The detrimental effect of this type of experience, however, has been discussed by Katan,[5] who suggests that these early sexual experiences lead to an over-stimulation of the child's coping abilities and predispose him to interpret the acts as aggressive rather than sexual. Burgess et al.[3] discuss these dynamics in terms of Freud's conceptualization of the repetition compulsion. They suggest that the abused child begins to fantasize and then re-enact the sexual aggression as the perpetrator rather than the victim in an attempt to master the earlier trauma.

Earlier studies suggest that many rapists practice a variety of sexual perversions. When the serial rapists were asked about their past or present sexual behaviors, 27 (68%) reported that they began with window peeping during childhood or adolescence (see Table 2). (The reader will recall the earlier discussion of nuisance sexual offenses.) Most of the literature reports peeping as a nuisance sexual offense and generalizes that peeping toms are not dangerous. It is not the authors' intent to state that all window peepers will become serial rapists, but rather to acquaint the reader with the fact that 68% of the subjects in this study began with such activities.

"Troy" began his peeping as an adolescent, an activity that unexpectedly escalated into rape and murder three years later.

Case No. 11

Troy, one of the interviewees, began window peeping at the age of 14. At 17 years of age, he spied on a 24-year-old woman and found her especially appealing. He began to focus his voyeuristic activities on her and eventually observed her making love to her boyfriend. This so enraged him that he made the decision to rape the woman. After she had gone to sleep one evening, he entered through an unlocked window and jumped on her. She awoke and began screaming. In a panic, he grabbed a handful of tissues from a bedside table, pushed them into her mouth, and accidentally suffocated her. Five days later, he was arrested for voyeurism in the same neighborhood. He was not questioned about the death because he was "just a peeper." Seven years later, he confessed to the unsolved crime; but he was not believed until he provided information about the death scene that only the killer could have known.

Sixteen (41%) of the serial rapists reported fetishism, and 15 (38%) reported having made obscene phone calls. Thirteen (33%) collected pornography, 11 (28%) collected detective magazines, 10 (26%) were involved in sexual bondage, nine (23%) had cross-dressed, and six (15%) had engaged in prostitution as either a prostitute or pimp.

The investigative value of such information is in the development of questions about suspects when interviewing former wives or girlfriends about the offenders' sexual behaviors. It will also prove useful when preparing search warrants for a suspect's residence, workplace, or automobile in that a significant proportion of the men collected pornography relevant to their diverse sexual interests.

Chronic Behavior Patterns

The rapists were questioned about certain chronic behavior patterns that might have characterized their behaviors either as children or adolescents. A variety of delinquent behaviors were reported by more than half of the rapists.

Stealing and shoplifting were reported by 27 (71%) out of 38 who responded. Many rapists advised that a great number of their thefts occurred through break-ins of homes within close proximity to their own residences. These early experiences may account for why they were so adept at entering the homes of rape victims.

Temper tantrums, hyperactivity, and alcohol abuse also had high occurrence rates, with 63% of the sample reporting each behavior. Isolation or withdrawal occurred in 24 (62%) out of 39 of the cases, and 22 (55%) out of 40 respondents advised that they were assaultive to adults. One rapist recalled attempting to hit his female teacher over the head with a chair in the third grade. Chronic lying was reported by 20 (54%) out of 37 of the subjects.

These findings are in keeping with earlier studies. When Rada[2] asked 20 incarcerated rapists whether their parents considered them to be disciplinary or behavioral problems, 65% responded in the affirmative, 75% admitted to stealing, 55% to temper tantrums, 50% to frequent fighting, and 40% to truancy and suspension from school.

Hellman and Blackman[6] discuss the oft-cited hypothesis that enuresis, fire setting, and cruelty to animals are the triad of behavior patterns in childhood or adolescence that may be useful in predicting violent behavior in adulthood. In the current study, these behaviors were reported by 32%, 24%, and 19% of the respondents, respectively.

In terms of pre-adult institutionalization, 15% of the rapists reported residing in an orphanage, 41% in a detention center, 8% in a foster home, 26% in some sort of mental health facility, and 4% in a boarding or military school. These findings suggest that a significant number of serial rapists were identified at an early age as either delinquent or emotionally disturbed.

Victims of the Serial Rapists

Demographics

The serial rapists were asked a variety of questions about the victims of their first, middle and last sexual assaults (total of 123 victims).

The average ages of the victims for the first, middle, and last attacks were 22.8, 26.1, and 24.4 years, respectively (see Table 3). The victims of the serial

Table 3 Demographic Characteristics of Victims

	First Rape		Middle Rape		Last Rape	
	N	%	N	%	N	%
Age						
0–10	—	—	—	—	5	12
11–17	7	17	6	15	4	10
18–25	15	37	15	38	13	32
26–33	14	34	14	35	11	27
34–41	4	10	4	10	7	17
41+	1	2	1	2	1	2
Race						
Caucasian	36	88	39	95	38	93
Black	3	7	2	5	1	2
Hispanic	—	—	—	—	1	2
Asian	1	2	—	—	1	2
Native American	1	2	—	—	—	—
Sex						
Female	40	98	41	100	40	98
Male	1	2	—	—	1	2

Note: N = Number.

rapists were predominantly white; of the 123 victims, 113 were white, 6 black, 1 Hispanic, 2 Asian, and 1 Native American. In this study, white rapists did not cross the racial line in their crimes against women, whereas the black offenders raped white and black women. The youngest victim in this study was 5 years old, and the oldest victim was 65.

While the overwhelming majority of victims were adult females, there were a significant minority of child (19%) and same-sex victims (2%). One example of same-sex rape occurred in a prison environment.

Case No. 12

"Tony," a white male, was serving time for raping a woman. Upon entering prison, he became the lover of an older white inmate. The older man ordered him to rape a young black male and told him that, if he failed to do so, he would be given to other inmates sexually. On two separate occasions, Tony was used in this manner.

Children were the victims of the serial rapists in 22 (18%) instances. They were the children or stepchildren of the offenders, neighbor children, or total strangers.

As summarized in Table 4, most of the victims were strangers to the offenders. In only 10 (8%) instances, the rapists reported raping acquaintances, four (3%) raped neighbors, and two (2%) raped a friend or date. The rapists included in this study were selected because of their success in committing a large number of crimes over time. It is the authors' opinion that one of the primary reasons they were so successful is that they generally selected strangers as their victims. Combining the victims' fear with the fact that their attackers were complete strangers was a strong impediment to providing necessary identification to the investigator.

Isolation of the Victim

The majority of victims (87, or 79%) were alone at the time of the assault. Of the 23 victims who were not, four (13%) were with their children, two (2%) with a female friend, two (2%) with a parent, two (2%) with a spouse, and three (3%) with some other individual. There were co-victims in only seven cases; four females, two males, and one incident with co-victims of each sex.

The scene of the sexual assault was relatively consistent. In 59 assaults (50%), the rapists reported that the assaults occurred in the victims' homes. In seven assaults (6%), the offenses occurred in a street or alleyway, while in seven (6%) instances, they occurred either in a parking lot or on a highway. Less often, the assaults occurred at the subject's residence, public facilities, or at the victim's place of work.

Table 4   Victim Characteristics and Victim Selection

	Yes %	No %
Reason for Selecting Victim		
Availability	98	2
Gender	95	5
Age	66	34
Location	66	34
Race	63	37
Physical characteristics	39	61
Other specific reasons	31	69
No special reason	25	75
Clothing	15	85
Vocation	7	93

	First Rape		Middle Rape		Last Rape	
	N	%	N	%	N	%
Relationship to Victim						
Stranger	38	80	35	85	36	88
Acquaintance	3	7	5	12	2	5
Other	2	5	—	—	1	2
Date	1	2	—	—	—	—
Friend	1	2	—	—	—	—
Neighbor	1	2	1	2	2	5
Scene of Sexual Assault						
Victim's residence	21	52	20	53	18	45
Street/alleyway	4	10	1	3	2	5
Other	11	28	10	26	15	38
Parking lot	1	2	1	3	1	2
Subject's residence	2	5	3	8	1	2
Public facilities	1	2	—	—	1	2
Subject's workplace	—	—	1	3	—	—
Highway	—	—	2	5	2	5

Note: N = Number.

As noted, the victim's residence was the scene of the assault in half of the rapes (50%). As mentioned earlier, 71% of the men had been involved in stealing as children and adolescents, and many of them had done so by breaking into homes. Having this experience, they no doubt felt more comfortable in gaining access to residences. Many of the rapists selected their victims through peeping activities or following intended victims to their homes. Consequently, the offender learned the habits of the victim in her home (visitors, phone calls, sleeping hours, hours away from home). In several instances, the rapist entered the victim's home while she was absent and familiarized himself with the residence.

Selection Criteria

Many reasons were cited by the rapists for selecting their victims, as indicated in Table 4. Forty (98%) out of 41 men emphasized the availability of the victim, while 27 (66%) also cited the importance of location. Both of these reasons are closely related and signify that the victim was chosen more for her vulnerability than any particular personal characteristic.

Gender was the primary criterion for singling out victims, as cited by 39 (95%) of the men. Victims' ages were cited in 27 (66%) cases and race in 26 (63%) instances. Physical characteristics of the victims were reported as significant by 16 (39%) of the rapists and clothing (or dress) by six (15%) of the respondents. Rather disconcertingly, 10 (25%) of the rapists advised that there were no special reasons for the persons targeted for attack.

According to these data, the serial rapist apparently does not engage in specific or symbolic consideration in selecting his victim. The various accounts suggest that the victim was not selected because she reminded the offender of a significant person in his life; rather, the victim's availability, gender, age, location, or race were cited as the determining factors.

The Criminal Behavior of the Serial Rapist

Premeditation

The majority of the sexual attacks (55 to 61%) were premeditated across their first, middle, and last rapes, while fewer rapists reported their crimes as impulsive (15 to 22%) or opportunistic (22 to 24%). Although no comparable data on serial rape are available, it is probable that the premeditation involved in these crimes is particularly characteristic of these serial rapists. It is also probable that this premeditation is reflective of their preferential interest in this type of crime and largely accounts for their ability to avoid detection.

Method of Approach

There are three different styles of approach rapists frequently use: the con, the blitz, and the surprise.[1] Each reflects a different means of selecting, approaching, and subduing a chosen victim.

Case No. 13

Earl, a white male who raped more than 25 women, would sit in an upscale hotel lobby and wait for a woman to register. He would follow her, obtain her room number, and then return to the lobby. He would call her room, claim he was with maintenance, and tell her that a repairman was on the way to her room because the previous tenant had reported a thermostat problem. He would then go to her room, gain access, and rape and rob the victim.

As in the case presented above, the con approach involves subterfuge and is predicated on the rapist's ability to interact with women. With this technique, the rapist openly approaches the victim and requests or offers some type of assistance or direction. However, once the victim is within his control, the offender may suddenly become more aggressive.

The con approach was used in eight (24%) of the first rapes, 12 (35%) of the middle rapes, and 14 (41%) of the last rapes. Various ploys used by the offenders included impersonating a police officer, providing transportation for a hitchhiking victim, offering assistance, and picking up women in singles bars.

Case No. 14

Jack, a 32-year-old white male, would hide in the forest adjacent to a jogging trail popular with residents of a nearby apartment complex. He would wait until a single woman came along; and, as she passed his hiding place, he would jump behind her and strike her in the back of the head with his fist. He would then lead the stunned and disoriented victim deep into the woods and sexually assault her.

In a blitz approach, the rapist uses an immediate and direct application of injurious force against his victims. The attacker may also use chemicals or gases but most frequently uses his ability to physically overpower a woman. Interestingly, despite its simplicity, this approach was used in 23% of the first rapes, 20% of the middle rapes, and 17% of the last rapes. Even though it is used less often than either the con or surprise approach, it results in more extensive physical injury to the victims.

Case No. 15

Sean, a white male who raped more than 30 women, was arrested in the bed of one of his victims as he slept. He had captured the woman as she entered her car at her workplace. He had been hiding in her back seat. When she got in the car, he placed his hand over her mouth and held a knife to her throat, explaining that if she did as she was told, he wouldn't hurt her. He forced her to drive to her residence, where she lived alone. He raped her repeatedly and then fell asleep.

The surprise approach, in which the assailant waits for the victim or approaches her after she is asleep, presupposes that the rapist has preselected his victim through unobserved contact and knowledge of when the victim is alone. Threats and/or the presence of a weapon are often associated with this type of approach; however, there is generally no physically injurious force applied.

The surprise approach was used by the serial rapists in 19 (54%) of the first rapes, 16 (46%) of the middle rapes, and 16 (44%) of the last rapes (percentages vary due to the number of rapes). This is the most frequent means of approach and is used most often by men who lack motivation or confidence in their abilities to subdue victims through physical violence or subterfuge.

Controlling the Victim

How rapists maintain control over victims is primarily dependent on their motivations for the sexual attacks. Within this context, four control methods are frequently used in various combinations during a rape: (1) intimidating physical presence; (2) verbal threats; (3) display of a weapon; and (4) use of physical force.

The men in this study predominantly used a threatening physical presence (82 to 92%) and/or verbal threats (65 to 80%) to control their victims. Substantially less often, they displayed a weapon (44 to 49%) or physically assaulted the victim (27 to 32%). When a weapon was displayed, it was most often a sharp instrument such as a knife (27 to 42%).

One rapist explained that he chose a knife because he perceived it to be the most intimidating weapon to use against women in view of their fear of disfigurement. Firearms were less frequently used (14 to 20%). Surprisingly, all but a few of the rapists used bindings located at the rape scenes. One exception was an individual who brought pre-cut lengths of rope, adhesive tape, and handcuffs to the scenes of his rapes.

Use of Force

The amount of force used during a rape provides valuable insight into the motivation of the rapist and must be analyzed by those investigating the offense or evaluating the offender. The majority of these men (75 to 84%) used minimal or no physical force across all three rapes.[7] Minimal force is defined as non-injurious force utilized more to intimidate the victim than to punish.

Case No. 16

John began a career of 18 rapes at the age of 24. He estimated that he had illegally entered over 5,000 homes to steal female undergarments. He advised that he had no desire to harm his victims and stated "… raping them is one thing. Beating on them is entirely something else. None of my victims were harmed and for a person to kill somebody after raping them, it just makes me mad."

Force resulting in bruises and lacerations, extensive physical trauma requiring hospitalization, or death increased from 5% of the first rapes, to 8% of the middle rapes, and to 10% of the last rapes. Two victims (5%) were murdered during the middle rapes, and an additional two (5%) were killed during the last rapes.

Case No. 17

> Phil, an attractive 30-year-old male, described stabbing his mother to death when she awoke as he was attempting to remove her panties and bra. He had been drinking and smoking marijuana with her for a period of time prior to the attempted rape. She had fallen asleep, and he began having fantasies of sex with her. He began attempting to undo her bra when she awoke and asked him what he was doing. He told her that he wanted to fuck her and she slapped him. He responded by stabbing her twice.

Most of the rapists in this study did not increase the amount of force used across their first, middle, and last rapes.[7] However, ten of the 41 rapists, termed *increasers*, did use progressively greater force over successive rapes. The increasers raped a mean of 40 victims as opposed to 22 victims by the non-increasers; and they committed a sexual assault every 19 days as opposed to the non-increasers, who raped on the average of every 55 days.

Victim Resistance

Victim resistance has been defined as any action or inaction on the part of the victim that precludes or delays the offender's attack.

The rapists reported that their victims verbally resisted them in 53% of the first assaults, 54% of the middle attacks, and 43% of the last rapes. Physical resistance occurred in only 19%, 32%, and 28% of the first, middle, and last rapes, respectively. The relatively low incidence of passive resistance (28% in the first rape, 17% in the middle rape, and 9% in the last rape) most likely reflects the rapists' inabilities to discern this type of resistance.

In previous research, no relationship was found between verbal and/or physical resistance and the amount of physical injury sustained by the victim.[7] Interestingly, however, the degree of the rapists' pleasure and the duration of the rape increased when the victim resisted.

In this study, the offenders reacted to resistance in the first, middle, and last rapes by verbally threatening the victim (50 to 41%). Compromise or negotiation took place in 11 to 12% across the rapes; and physical force was used in 22% of the first rapes, 38% of the middle rapes, and 18% of the last rapes. The rapists also reported six incidents in which they left when the victim resisted; however, it is not clear at what point in the attack the resistance occurred.

Sexual Dynamics of the Rape

The sexual acts in which the victim was forced to engage remained relatively constant across all three rapes. The most common acts were vaginal intercourse (54 to 67%), fellatio (29 to 44%), kissing (8 to 13%), and fondling (10 to 18%). Anal intercourse (5 to 10%) and foreign object penetration (3 to 8%) were reported less often. In assessing changes in behavior over the first, middle, and last rapes, there appears to be a trend wherein the rapist's interest in fellatio increases while his interest in vaginal intercourse decreases.

The amount of pleasure that the rapist experienced during the three assaults was measured with the query: "Think back to the penetration during the rape. Assuming '0' equals your worst sexual experience and '10' equals your absolute best sexual experience, rate the amount of pleasure you experienced." The majority of rapists reported surprisingly low levels of pleasure (3.7). However, the types of contact that resulted in higher scores differed widely.[7] One rapist reported appreciation for his victim's passivity and acquiescence, while another referred to the pleasure experienced in the rape-murder of two young boys as off the scale.

Case No. 18

> Paul had raped adult women and adolescent girls and brought his criminal career to an end with the rape and murder of two 10-year-old boys. When asked to rate the sexual experiences, he advised that he would rate the adult and adolescent females as "0" and the preadolescent girls as "3." He then stated, "When you're talking about sex with 10-year-old boys, your scale doesn't go high enough."

Verbal Interaction with Victims

Across the first, middle, and last rapes, the majority of serial rapists (78 to 85%) usually conversed with the victims only to threaten them. Much less frequently, their conversations were polite or friendly (30 to 34%), manipulative (23 to 37%), or personal in nature (23 to 37%). In a minority of instances, the rapist reported being inquisitive (15 to 20%), abusive or degrading (5 to 13%), or silent (8 to 13%). It appears that serial rapists use verbal threats to subdue their victims, and only after they believe they have gained control do they move on to other modes of conversing or interacting.

Sexual Dysfunction

In a study of 170 rapists, it was determined that 34% experienced some type of sexual dysfunction during the rape.[8] The data on these serial rapists are strikingly similar. In the first rape, 38% of the subjects reported sexual dysfunction, 39% in the middle rape, and 35% during the last assault. This type of information can prove helpful to the investigator in associating different offenses with a single offender; the nature of the dysfunction and the means used by the rapist to overcome the dysfunction are likely to remain constant over a number of rapes.

Evading Detection

Considering the rapists' aptitudes for avoiding detection, it is surprising to note that very few of the serial rapists employed specific behaviors designed to preclude identification. The majority of rapists (61 to 68%) did not report dressing in any special way for the offenses. Interestingly, disguises were reported in only 7 to 12% of the offenses, suggesting that other means of evading detection were used by these particular offenders.

Alcohol and Other Drugs

Rada reports that rape is commonly associated with the use of alcohol and drugs.[9] The data on these rapists suggest a somewhat different relationship between the use of alcohol and/or drugs and serial sexual offending. Approximately one third of the rapists were drinking alcoholic beverages at the time of the first, middle, and last offenses; and 17 to 24% of the respondents reported using drugs. In a majority of these cases, these figures reflect the offenders' typical consumption patterns and not an unusual increase in substance abuse. The relative absence of alcohol involvement in the crimes may be one reason the offenders were so successful at eluding detection.

Post-Offense Behavior

The serial rapists were also asked about changes in their behavior following their assaults. The most frequent changes after each of these crimes included feeling remorseful and guilty (44 to 51%), following the case in the media (28%), and an increase in alcohol/drug consumption (20 to 27%). Investigators should also particularly note that 12 to 15% of the rapists reported revisiting the crime scene, and 8 to 13% communicated with the victims after the crime.

Summary

The findings reported in this chapter were obtained from the extensive interview of 41 men responsible for the rapes of 837 victims. The interviews were conducted by FBI Agents assigned to the Behavioral Science Unit of the FBI Academy.

Many characteristics of the rapist population studied appear relatively normal. Rather than being an isolated, poorly functioning individual, the serial rapist more often than not comes from an average or advantaged home. As an adult, he is a well-groomed, intelligent, employed individual who is living with others in a family context.

The greatest pathology is reflected in the serial rapists' developmental histories. Few of the men described close relationships with their mothers or their fathers. A significant number of them had been institutionalized at some point in adolescence, and an exceedingly high proportion reported sexual abuse during childhood or adolescence.

Interestingly, the majority of victims were strangers; and, in almost half of the cases, the women were assaulted in their own homes. This, as well as the rapists' recognition of availability as an important factor in victim selection, highlights the potential significance of prevention programs. Most serial rapists are not carefully stalking a particular woman. Rather, the choice of victim depends on general proximity, the availability of the woman, and access to her residence.

The majority of rapes committed by these men were premeditated, and the surprise approach was used most often in initiating contacts with the victims. The serial rapists relied primarily on threatening physical presence to maintain control over their victims. The victims resisted their attackers in slightly over 50% of the offenses, and the most common reaction to this resistance was verbally threatening behavior. Slightly over one third of the men suffered sexual dysfunction during their attacks, and their preferred sexual acts were vaginal rape and fellatio. The serial rapists tended not to be concerned with protecting their identities, and approximately one third of them had consumed alcohol prior to the crime. The most common post-offense behaviors reported by the rapists were following the case in the media and increasing their alcohol and drug consumption.

The material presented in this chapter, while not generally applicable to all rapists, can be helpful in learning more about serial sexual offenders and their offense behaviors.

References

1. Hazelwood, R.R. and A.W. Burgess, 1987. An introduction to the serial rapist: research by the FBI, *FBI Law Enf. Bull.*, 58, 16–24.

2. Rada, R., 1978. *Clinical Aspects of the Rapists*, New York, Grune and Stratton.

3. Burgess, A.W., R. Hazelwood, F. Rokous, and C. Hartman, 1988. Serial rapists and their victims: reenactment and repetition. In R. Prentky and V. Quinsey, Eds., Human sexual aggression: current perspectives, *Acad. Sci. Ann.*, 528, 277–295.

4. Risin, L. and M. Koss, 1988. The sexual abuse of boys: frequency and descriptive characteristics of the childhood victimizations. In A.W. Burgess, Ed., *Traumatization of Children*, New York, Garland Press.

5. Katan, A., 1973. Children who were raped, In R.S. Eissler, Ed., *The Psychoanalytic Study of the Child*, pp. 208–224, New Haven, Yale University Press.

6. Hellman, D. and N. Blackman, 1966. Enuresis, fire setting and cruelty to animals: a triad predictive of adult crime, *Am. J. Psych.*, 122, 1431–1435.

7. R. Hazelwood, R. Reboussin, and J. Warren, 1989. Serial rape: correlates of increased aggression and the relationship of offender pleasure to victim resistance, *J. Interpersonal Violence*, 465–78.

8. Groth, A. and A.W. Burgess, 1977. Sexual dysfunction during rape, *New Engl. J. Med.*, 14, 764–766.

9. Rada, R., 1975. Psychological factors in rapist behavior, *Am. J. Psychiatr.*, 132, 444–446 and R. Rada, 1978. Psychological factors in rapist behavior, In R. Rada, Ed., *Clinical Aspects of the Rapist*, pp. 21–85, New York, Grune and Stratton, New York.

The Criminal Sexual Sadist* 22

ROBERT R. HAZELWOOD
PARK ELLIOT DIETZ
JANET I. WARREN

Introduction

Any investigator who has taken a statement from a tortured victim or worked the crime scene of a sexually sadistic homicide will never forget the experience. Human cruelty reveals itself in many kinds of offenses, but seldom more starkly than in the crimes of sexual sadists.

This chapter describes the more commonly encountered actions of sexual sadists and differentiates sexual sadism from other cruel acts. It also describes the common characteristics of sexually sadistic crimes and offers investigators suggestions that they should follow when confronted with the crime of the sexually sadistic offender.

What is Sexual Sadism?

Sexual sadism is a persistent pattern of sexual excitement in response to another's suffering. Granted, sexual excitement can occur at odd times even in normal people; but to the sexually sadistic offender, the suffering of the victim is sexually arousing.

The writings of two sexual sadists graphically convey their desires. They write:

> … the most important radical aim is to make her suffer since there is no greater power over another person than that of inflicting pain on her to force her to undergo suffering without her being able to defend herself. The pleasure in the complete domination over another person is the very essence of the sadistic drive.

Of his sexually sadistic activities with a victim he killed, another offender writes:

> … she was writhering [sic] in pain and I loved it. I was now combining my sexual high of rape and my power high of fear to make a total sum that is

---

* Reprinted with permission of the *FBI Law Enforcement Bulletin*.

now beyond explaining … I was alive for the sole purpose of causing pain
and receiving sexual gratification … I was relishing the pain just as much
as the sex …

Each offender's account confirms that the suffering of the victim, not the
infliction of physical or psychological pain, is sexually arousing. In fact, one
of these men resuscitated his victim from unconsciousness so that he could
continue to savor her suffering. Inflicting pain is a means to create suffering
and to elicit the desired responses of obedience, submission, humiliation,
fear, and terror.

Physical and Psychological Suffering

Specific findings uncovered during an investigation determine whether the
crime involved sexual sadism. The critical issues are whether the victim
suffered, whether the suffering was intentionally elicited, and whether the
suffering sexually aroused the offender. This is why neither sexual nor cruel
acts committed on an unconscious or dead victim are necessarily evidence
of sexual sadism; such a victim cannot experience suffering. For this reason,
postmortem injuries alone do not indicate sexual sadism.

Rapists cause their victims to suffer, but only sexual sadists intentionally
inflict that suffering, whether physical or psychological, to enhance their own
arousal. Neither the severity of an offender's cruelty nor the extent of a
victim's suffering is evidence of sexual sadism. Acts of extreme cruelty or
those that cause great suffering are often performed for nonsexual purposes,
even during sexual assaults.

Sexually Sadistic Behavior

The behavior of sexual sadists, like that of other sexual deviants, extends
along a wide spectrum. Sexual sadists can be law-abiding citizens who fantasize but do not act or who fulfill these fantasies with freely consenting
partners. Only when sexual sadists commit crimes do their fantasies become
relevant to law enforcement.

Sadistic Fantasy

All sexual acts and sexual crimes begin with fantasy. However, in contrast
with normal sexual fantasies, those of the sexual sadists center on domination, control, humiliation, pain, injury, and violence, or a combination of
these themes, as a means to elicit suffering. As the fantasies of the sexual
sadists vary, so do the degrees of violence.

The fantasies discerned from the personal records of offenders are complex and elaborate. They involve detailed scenarios that include specific methods of capture and control, locations, scripts to be followed by the victim, sequence of sexual acts, and desired victim responses. Sexual sadists dwell frequently on these fantasies, which often involve multiple victims and sometimes include partners.

Case No. 1

One offender, who is believed to have kidnapped, tortured, and murdered more than 20 women and young girls, wrote extensively about his sexually sadistic fantasies involving women. These writings included descriptions of his victim's capture, torment, and death by hanging. At the time of his arrest, photographs were found depicting the subject in female attire and participating in autoerotic asphyxia. The offender had apparently acted out his fantasies on himself and others.

Sadism toward Symbols

Some individuals act out their sadistic desires against inanimate objects, most often dolls, pictures, and clothing, but sometimes corpses. As in the case of fantasy, the suffering in such activity is imagined.

Case No. 2

A female doll was found hanging outside an emergency room of a hospital. Around its neck was a hangman's noose, and its hands were bound behind its back. Needles penetrated one eye and one ear. Burn marks were present on the doll, and cotton protruded from its mouth. Drawn on the chest of the doll were what appeared to be sutures. An incision had been made between the legs, creating an orifice to which hair had been glued and into which a pencil had been inserted. Nothing indicated that a crime had occurred.

Although it is commonly believed that sexual sadists are cruel toward animals, it has not been determined that such cruelty is related to sexual sadism. Violent men were often cruel to animals during childhood, without sexual excitement. Cruel acts toward animals may reflect nonsexual aggressive and sadistic motives or may be sacrifices demanded by religious rituals or delusional beliefs. Someone who is sexually excited by an animal's suffering is probably both a sexual sadist and a zoophile (one attracted to animals).

Consenting or Paid Partners

Sexual sadism may also be acted out with freely consenting or paid partners who specialize in role-playing the submissive for sexually sadistic clients. The nature of the acts varies from simulations of discomfort to actions that result in severe injury. A consenting partner turns into a victim when her withdrawal of consent goes unheeded or when an act results in unexpected injury or death. This is when such acts come to the attention of law enforcement.

Some sexual sadists cultivate compliant victims (Hazelwood, Warren, and Dietz, 1993; Warren and Hazelwood, in press) — those who enter into a voluntary relationship but are manipulated into sadomasochistic activities for an extended time. These victims are wives or girlfriends who underwent extreme emotional, physical, and sexual abuse over months or years of a relationship that began as an ordinary courtship. In these instances, the offenders shaped the behavior of the women into gradual acceptance of progressively deviant sexual acts, and then, through social isolation and repeated abuse, battered their self-images until the women believed they deserved the punishments meted out by their lovers.

Case No. 3

> A woman in her thirties advised authorities that she had been coerced into an emotionally, physically, and sexually abusive relationship over an 18-month period. At first, she considered the offender to be the most loving and caring man she had ever known, and she fell deeply in love. Having occasionally used cocaine in the past, she was receptive to his suggestion that they use cocaine to enhance their sexual relations. Eventually, she became addicted. After 6 months together, he began to abuse her sexually. This abuse included forced anal sex, whipping, painful sexual bondage, anal rape by other males, and the insertion of large objects into her rectum. This abusive behavior continued for a full year before she made her initial complaint to the police.

These cases pose special problems to investigators because it appears as though the complainant consented to the abuse. However, the transformation of the vulnerable partner into a compliant victim resembles the process by which other abusive men intimidate and control battered women into remaining with their abusers. (See Chapter 23 for a more complete discussion.)

Behavior Patterns Confused With Sexual Sadism

Many crimes involve the intentional infliction of physical and psychological suffering. Sexual sadism is only one of the several motives for such crimes. To avoid misinterpretation, investigators should be aware of those behavior patterns that appear to be sexually sadistic but which, in fact, arise from different motives and contexts.

Sadistic Personality Disorder

Persons with this condition usually exhibit cruel, demeaning, and aggressive behavior in both social and work situations, most often toward subordinates. They tend to establish dominance in interpersonal relationships and convey a lack of respect or empathy for others. Such individuals are often fascinated by violence, take pleasure in demeaning, humiliating, and frightening others, and may enjoy inflicting physical or psychological abuse. In this condition, it is not the purpose of these behaviors to become aroused.

Case No. 4

A woman left her husband because of his verbal abuse, control over her relations with family members, intimidating behavior, and violent outbursts when drinking. Vengeful that she left him, he lured her back to the apartment under the pretext of dividing their possessions. He then attempted to tie her to the bed, beside which he had arranged a variety of torture instruments. In the ensuing struggle, he told her of his plans to kill her as he stabbed her repeatedly. She eventually persuaded him that she wanted to reconcile and convinced him to summon medical assistance, whereupon he was arrested.

The husband did not have a history of sexual offenses or deviations, nor did he show evidence of sexual sadism during the psychiatric examination. He denied any sexual arousal in response to the suffering and had no sexually sadistic fantasies. Although it is possible that the husband was a sexual sadist who only showed this tendency when he attacked his wife, the absence of evidence noting a persistent pattern of sexual arousal in response to suffering precluded this diagnosis.

Cruelty during Crime

While many crimes contain elements of cruelty, the acts are not necessarily sexually sadistic in nature.

Case No. 5

Two men who escaped from a state prison captured a young couple and took them to an isolated area. After repeatedly raping the woman, they severely beat the couple and locked them in the trunk of their car. They then set the car on fire and left the couple to burn to death.

Although these men intentionally inflicted physical and psychological suffering on their victims, there was no indication they did so for sexual excitement. They beat the couple after the rape and left as the victims were screaming and begging for mercy. Sexual sadists would have been sexually stimulated by the victim's torment and would have remained at the scene until the suffering ended.

Pathological Group Behavior

Cruelty often arises in offenses committed as a group, even where the individuals have no history of cruelty.

Case No. 6

> A group of adolescents attacked a mother of six as she walked through her neighborhood. They dragged her into a shed where they beat her and repeatedly inserted a long steel rod into her rectum, causing her death. Some of her attackers were friends of her children.

Most likely, the participants in this attack tried to prove themselves to the others by intensifying the acts of cruelty.

Sanctioned Cruelty

History is replete with reigns of terror during which powerful institutions sanctioned atrocious behaviors. Consider the rape and plunder of defeated populations during the Crusades of the Middle Ages, or the execution of women during the Salem witch hunts in colonial America. One of the most notorious times of cruelty occurred in the 20th century, when millions of people fell victim to the Nazis.

Case No. 7

> Commandant Koch, who headed the concentration camp at Buchenwald, punished a man who tried to escape by confining him in a wooden box so small he could only crouch. He then ordered that small nails be driven through its walls so that he could not move without being pierced. This man was kept on public display without food for two days and three nights until his screams ceased to sound human (Manvell and Fraenkel, 1967).

In all likelihood, sexual sadists volunteered to perform such deeds, but the widespread deployment of such tactics was politically and racially motivated.

Revenge-Motivated Cruelty

Cruelty is often evident during acts that are inspired by an obsessional desire for revenge, either real or imagined.

Case No. 8

A physician married a showgirl and came to believe that she was unfaithful, even though there was no evidence to substantiate this. Eventually, his obsession overcame his logic; and he decided to ensure that no man would ever take her away from him. After lashing her to a table, he poured sulfuric acid over her body and face. She survived for 84 days in agony before succumbing to her injuries.

The offender in this case wanted to punish his wife and make sure that she would not be desirable to any man. His act was not designed to gratify him sexually.

Interrogative Cruelty

Torture during interrogation may involve sexual areas of the body, which is sometimes misinterpreted as being sexually sadistic in nature.

Case No. 9

A government agent was captured in another country. During his months in captivity, he was continually subjected to physical torture, including beatings with clubs and electrical shocks to all parts of his body, including his genitals.

The victim was tortured in this manner to obtain information concerning his government's activities in that country, not to enhance sexual arousal.

Postmortem Mutilation

The intentional mutilation of a victim after death is often mistakenly attributed to sexual sadism. However, in a majority of these cases, the offender kills the victim quickly and does not try to prolong suffering, which is in total contrast to the actions of the sexual sadist.

Case No. 10

A father bludgeoned his adult daughter to death. After her death, he attempted to dispose of the body. On the day of his arrest, he bought a food processor. Investigators found portions of her remains in the bathtub, the kitchen sink, in pots boiling on the stove, and in the refrigerator.

The man killed his daughter either in self-defense or because of his frustration over her disruptive and hostile behavior caused by her chronic mental illness.

His actions were not intended to provide sexual satisfaction by seeing his daughter suffer.

Study Conducted

The authors studied 30 sexually sadistic criminals, 22 of whom were responsible for at least 187 murders (Dietz, Hazelwood and Warren, 1990). Most of these cases had been submitted to the FBI's National Center for the Analysis of Violent Crime (NCAVC). Sources of information for the study included police reports, crime scene photographs, victim statements, statements by family members, confessions, psychiatric reports, trial transcripts, pre-sentence reports, and prison records. The authors also reviewed evidence created by the offenders (such as diaries, photographs, sketches, audio tapes, videos, calendars, and letters). These materials, which recorded their fantasies and represented memorabilia of their crimes, provided windows into the minds of sexually sadistic offenders.

In addition, five of the 30 offenders were interviewed by the authors. When interviewed, these men revealed less about their sexual desires than they had in their writings and recordings of the offenses. This is consistent with our experience when interviewing subjects during ongoing investigations — offenders speak much more readily about their violent acts than about their sexual acts or fantasies.

Each of the 30 sexual sadists studied intentionally tortured their victims. Their methods of physical torture included the use of such instruments as hammers, pliers, and electric cattle prods, and such actions as biting, whipping, burning, insertion of foreign objects into the rectum or vagina, bondage, amputation, asphyxiation to the point of unconsciousness, and insertion of glass rods in the male urethra, to name a few.

Some offenders used a particular means of torture repeatedly. Such actions could constitute an offender's signature, which could show similar crimes were the work of a single offender. However, the absence of a common feature among crimes does not eliminate the possibility of a single serial offender, for he may be experimenting with various techniques in search of the perfect scenario; or he may be attempting to mislead investigators.

The 30 sexual sadists also inflicted psychological suffering on their victims. Binding, blindfolding, gagging, and holding a victim captive all produce psychological suffering, even if not physically painful. Other psychological tactics included threats or other forms of verbal abuse, forcing the victim to beg, plead, or describe sexual acts, telling the victim in precise detail what was intended, having the victim choose between slavery or death, and offering the victim a choice of how to die.

Offender Characteristics

All 30 of the sexual sadists in the study were men, and only one was non-white. Fewer than half were educated beyond high school. Half used alcohol or other drugs, and one third served in the Armed Forces. Forty-three percent were married at the times of the offenses.

Sexual deviations are often associated with other sexual abnormalities, as this study confirmed for sexual sadism. Fifty percent of the men participated in homosexual activity as adults, 20% engaged in cross-dressing, and 20% committed other sexual offenses such as peeping, obscene phone calls, and indecent exposure.

Case No. 11

As a teenager, one sexual sadist peeped throughout his neighborhood, masturbating as he watched women undress or have sex. At home, he masturbated repeatedly to fantasies in which he incorporated what he had seen while peeping. As a young adult, he made obscene telephone calls, which led to his first arrest when he agreed to meet a victim who had informed the police.

He later exposed himself to a series of victims, which he eventually explained was for the purpose of eliciting their "shock and fear." He followed women home from shopping malls, determined how much cover was available for peeping and entering the residence, and eventually raped a series of women. In his early rapes, he depended on opportunity, but later carried with him a rape kit, which consisted of adhesive tape, handcuffs, pre-cut lengths of rope, and a .45 caliber handgun. He became progressively violent in his sexual assaults, torturing his victims by beating, burning, and pulling their breasts. His violence escalated to the point that he so severely pummeled one victim that she lost both breasts. He forcibly raped more than 50 women and was contemplating murder when he was finally apprehended.

Investigators should not be misled by the fact that the sexual sadist may have been involved in what are commonly referred to as nuisance sexual offenses. A history of such activity is common, but not universal, among sex offenders of all types. It is a myth that individuals who engage in nuisance offenses have no propensity for violence (Hazelwood and Warren, 1989).

Crime Characteristics

Careful planning epitomizes the crimes of the sexual sadist, who devotes considerable time and effort to the offenses. Many demonstrate cunning and methodical planning. The capture of the victims, the selection and preparation of equipment, and the methodical elicitation of suffering often reflect meticulous attention to detail.

The overwhelming majority of offenders studied by the authors used a pretext or ruse to first make contact with the victims. The sexual sadist offered or requested assistance, pretended to be a police officer, responded to a classified advertisement, met a realtor at an isolated property, or otherwise gained the confidence of the victim.

Almost invariably, the victims were taken to locations selected in advance that offered solitude and safety for the sadist and little opportunity of escape or rescue for the victims. Such locations included the offender's residence, isolated forests, and even elaborately constructed facilities designed for captivity.

Case No. 12

A white male entered a respected modeling agency and advised that he was filming a documentary on drug abuse among pre-adolescents. He made arrangements to hire two young girls from the agency, and two elderly matrons accompanied them as chaperones. He drove to his trailer and, at gunpoint, bound the women and placed the girls in a plywood cell he constructed in the trailer. The cell contained beds and additional mattresses for soundproofing. He murdered the women, placing their bodies in garbage bags. He terrorized the girls for more than two days before they were rescued.

Twenty-three (77%) of the offenders used sexual bondage on their victims, often tying them with elaborate and excessive materials, using neat and symmetrical bindings, and restraining them in a variety of positions. Eighteen (60%) held their victims in captivity for more than 24 hours.

The most common sexual activity was anal rape (22 offenders), followed in frequency by forced fellatio, vaginal rape, and foreign object penetration. Two thirds of the men subjected their victims to at least three of these four acts.

Sixty percent of the offenders beat their victims. Twenty-two of the men murdered a total of 187 victims; 17 of them killed three or more people. The manner in which they killed varied.

Case No. 13

Two men, who offended as a team, used a variety of methods to kill a series of victims. One victim was strangled during sex. Another was injected in the neck with a caustic substance, electrocuted, and gassed in an oven. A third victim was shot.

Twenty-nine of the 30 men selected white victims only. Eighty-three percent of the victims were strangers to the offender. While the majority of the men

selected female victims, one fourth attacked males exclusively. Sixteen percent of the men assaulted child victims only, and 26% attacked both children
and adults.

Evidence of Crime

These offenders retained a wealth of incriminating evidence. More than half
of the offenders in the study kept records of their offenses, including calendars, maps, diaries, drawings, letters, manuscripts, photographs, audio tapes,
video tapes, and media accounts of their crimes. For the most part, these
secret and prized possessions were hidden in their homes, offices, or vehicles,
kept in rental storage space, or buried in containers.

Forty percent of the men took and kept personal items belonging to their
victims. These items, which included drivers' licenses, jewelry, clothing, and
photographs, served as mementos of the offense; and some of the offenders
referred to them as trophies of their conquests. However, none of the offenders retained parts of their victim's bodies, though some kept the entire corpse
temporarily or permanently.

Investigating Crimes of the Sexual Sadist

The law enforcement community's legitimate concern rests with the criminal
sexual sadist, who can be a noteworthy adversary. The sexual sadist is cunning
and accomplished at deception. He rationalizes his actions, feels no remorse
or guilt, and is not moved by compassion. He considers himself superior to
society in general and law enforcement in particular. And, while he envies
the power and authority associated with the police, he does not respect them.

Sources

Invaluable sources of information about suspects in sexual offenses are their
former spouses and/or girlfriends. As noted previously, sexual sadists sometimes force sexual partners to become compliant victims (Hazelwood, et al.,
1993). However, because of the embarrassing nature of the sexual acts
involved, these individuals are often reluctant to divulge information.

Search Warrants

Because offenders retain incriminating evidence and crime paraphernalia,
these items should be listed in search warrant applications. This would
include the records and mementos described previously as well as photographic equipment, tape recorders, reverse telephone directories, and weapons or other instruments used to elicit suffering. Pornography, detective and

mercenary magazines, bondage paraphernalia, women's undergarments, and sexual devices are other materials commonly collected by sexual sadists.

Interviewing the Sexual Sadist

Sexual sadists are masters of manipulation. Therefore, the investigator must be well prepared before conducting the interview. The investigator must know the suspect intimately and be aware of his strengths and weaknesses. Premature interviews of primary suspects often fail.

Despite their seeming sophistication, sexual sadists are likely to consent to interview, even after being advised of their rights. These offenders often have an exaggerated self-image and consider themselves intellectually superior to the police. They believe they are in no danger of divulging detrimental information about themselves. More importantly, they expect to learn more information from the officer than they provide during the interview. From the questions asked, they hope to determine how much the investigator knows and the current status of the investigation.

The interviewer should be of detective status or above, preferably older than the suspect, and superior to him in physical stature, personality, and intelligence. The interviewer must appear confident, relaxed, and at least as calm as the suspect. Any personal feelings about the crime or the suspect must be suppressed. The interviewer should not attempt to become friends with the suspect, as this will cause him to lose respect for the interviewer and provide him with an opportunity to manipulate the conversation. Instead, the interview should be conducted in a formal and professional manner.

Because these offenders enjoy attention, the interviewer should be prepared for an exhausting and lengthy interview. Questions should be thought out in advance and structured in such a way that the offender cannot evade a line of questioning with a simple "no" answer. For example, rather than asking the suspect if he likes to torture women, it is preferable to ask him his favorite instruments for torturing women. Posing questions in this manner reflects the interviewer's knowledge, does not provide additional information to the suspect, and may facilitate incriminating disclosures by the subject.

Above all, the suspect must not be allowed to provoke anger. In all likelihood, he will probably attempt to shock or antagonize the interviewer; and if the interviewer yields to human emotion, the suspect will score a significant victory.

Summary

Sexually sadistic offenders commit well-planned and carefully concealed crimes. Their crimes are repetitive, serious, and shocking, and they take special steps to prevent detection. The harm that these men wreak is so devastating and their techniques so sophisticated that those who attempt to apprehend and convict them must be armed with uncommon insight, extensive knowledge, and sophisticated investigative resources.

References

Dietz, P.E., Hazelwood, R.R., and Warren, J.I. (1990) The sexually sadistic criminal and his offenses, *Bull. Am. Acad. Psychiatr., Law*, 163–178.

Hazelwood, R.R. and Warren, J.I. (1989) The serial rapist: his characteristics and victims, *FBI Law Enf. Bull.*, 18–25.

Hazelwood, R.R., Warren, J.I., and Dietz, P.E. (1993) Compliant victims of sexual sadists, *Aust. Fam. Physician*, 22(4).

Manvell, R. and Fraenkel, H. (1967) *The Incomparable Crime: Mass Extermination in the Twentieth Century — The Legacy of Guilt*, Putnam, New York.

Warren, J.I. and Hazelwood, R.R. (In press) Relational patterns associated with sexual sadism, *J. Fam. Violence*.

Sexual Sadists: Their Wives and Girlfriends

23

ROBERT R. HAZELWOOD

Introduction

Marie, an attractive young college woman, began dating a young man during her freshman year. No one could really understand why they were dating. He was younger than she and certainly less attractive physically. She was a cheerleader and very popular, while he was a rather quiet person who participated in practically none of the school's activities. He had pursued her relentlessly since they were both in high school, and she had repeatedly rejected him. The young man came from a wealthy family, and he unsuccessfully tried to use his wealth to influence the woman. Eventually, however, she became impressed with his singular dedication to her and consented to a date, beginning what would become four years of apparent happiness and love — with one notable exception. One evening they went to a party; and for the first time in their relationship, he became intoxicated. When they returned to his apartment, he insisted on sex and forced himself on her after she complained about his intoxicated state. Because it was the only time in their relationship that he had exhibited such behavior, she accepted his apology.

They married after another year passed. His parents provided them with a very large and expensive home on a lake about 150 miles from their family and friends. Within 3 days of their marriage, their entire relationship changed. Sexually, he was infrequently interested in normal activities. Instead, he would force her to undress, beat her vagina with his fists, and masturbate onto her face and body. He would berate her verbally, using profanity and sexual slang to describe her as a person and to express his fantasy of having her raped by several of his friends while he watched. A year later, she had a child. She left him after $2^1/_2$ years — he brought his girlfriend home and wanted Marie to engage in sex with both of them.

The author was introduced to Marie by her treating psychologist. She had obtained a divorce and was in counseling in an attempt to cope with the residual emotional trauma. She was primarily interested in obtaining an answer to the questions, "What was wrong with me? How could I have allowed this to happen? Were there any warning signs that I was oblivious to during the dating relationship?" Fortunately, this young mother was counseled by a woman who not only had experience in dealing with battered spouses but, more importantly, was familiar with the paraphilias in general and sexual sadism in particular. Furthermore, she was knowledgeable about the current research on sexually sadistic men and their relationships with wives and girlfriends (Dietz, Hazelwood, and Warren, 1990; Hazelwood, Dietz, and Warren, 1992; Hazelwood, Dietz, and Warren, 1993; Warren, Hazelwood, and Dietz, 1996; and Warren and Hazelwood, in press).

Genesis of the Research

In 1990 I attended a presentation by Christine McGuire and Chris Hatcher on a crime that was recounted in the book entitled *The Perfect Victim* (McGuire and Norton, 1988). This case involved Cameron Hooker and his wife Janice, who had captured a young college student named Coleen Stans and kept her in sexual slavery for seven years before releasing her. McGuire, a career California prosecutor, had tried the case; and Chris Hatcher, a forensic psychologist (now deceased) had been one of her star witnesses. As they told the terrifying story of how Stans had been confined in a box beneath the couple's bed, physically tortured by Cameron Hooker, forced to sign a slave contract, and essentially became brainwashed, the attentive audience was completely silent. Following the lecture, one of the attendees asked me if I would like to interview Stans. I responded that I would rather interview the wife, Janice Hooker, to learn about what kind of person she was, what kind of person her husband was, what the nature of their relationship was, and why she had participated in such aberrant behavior. I saw an opportunity to learn about sexual sadism from a group that had not been queried before — the wives and girlfriends of the sadistic men.

In 1991 Dr. Park Dietz, Dr. Janet Warren, and I began the research that would eventually result in the interview of twenty women, including Marie (see Introduction), and would study the relational patterns of the sexual sadist and his spouse and/or girlfriend. These were the most interesting and emotionally draining interviews we had ever conducted. These women had lived and been intimate with the most cruel, intelligent, and, in some cases, criminally sophisticated sexual offenders confronting criminal investigators today.

Methodology

The research team developed an interview protocol (coded for data entry) over 70 pages long and containing more than 450 questions for the women.

The protocol was designed to capture information about the women's development from childhood and continuing into adulthood, what they knew about the childhood and development of their sadistic mates, how their relationships began and developed over time, their continuing relationships, and how/why the relationships were terminated. The interviews were conducted in an unstructured manner by at least two people. All were recorded by audiotape, but none were videotaped.

Eighteen of the participants were identified by law enforcement or mental health professionals who were aware of the research; and the two other women (incarcerated at the time), sought me out for inclusion in the project. Statements of confidentiality were executed prior to the interviews. The interviews ranged in length from $4^1/_2$ to 15 hours. The audiotaped interviews were transcribed, and the data from the protocols were entered onto computer.

The Women

While these women have been referred to as compliant victims (Hazelwood, Dietz, and Warren 1993), that term is designed to reflect the acquiescent nature of the women's cooperation in their own and others' victimizations. It is not intended to excuse the women's criminal behavior in those instances in which they became accomplices to sexually violent crime (Warren and Hazelwood, in press).

Twenty women were extensively interviewed. Of that number, only three had arrest histories prior to meeting the men, and those crimes involved minor theft. Four of them had contacts with mental health professionals prior to becoming involved with the sadistic males, but since leaving the men, all but one have been in therapy. Nine of the women had been sexually abused as children, and six had been physically abused. The formal education of these women ranged from 11 to 18 years, and they were employed in a variety of occupations including professional (elementary school teacher, fire system engineer), skilled (secretary), and unskilled (waitress) positions. Only two used drugs before meeting the men.

Their Relationships with the Men

Thirteen of the women married the sadistic males, and the remaining seven dated the men exclusively for a period of time. During their associations with the men, 18 of the women were physically abused; and all were emotionally battered. The women were convinced to engage in a variety of deviant sexual practices including bestiality, sex with other men and women, whipping, bondage, and hanging. If proper rapport is established with the women, one can expect to be informed of painful and horrendous behaviors that have been directed toward the wives of sexual sadists. It is imperative not to express judgment or shock at the revelations.

Seven of the men to whom these women were married killed at least 19 people, and four of the women were present during some of the crimes. All four of the women were charged with crimes against persons.

Case No. 2

Stephanie dated a sexually sadistic male for a number of years even though she was aware that he was dating other women. She remained faithful to him even when he became engaged to a woman named Lucy. She was so devoted to him that he felt comfortable in enlisting her assistance in Lucy's murder. He brought Lucy to Stephanie's home; and, after forcing Lucy to disrobe and engage in diverse sexual activities in the presence of Stephanie, he killed her. Together, they buried her body in Stephanie's back yard. The disappearance of Lucy was not solved for two years.

A fifth woman was charged with being a co-conspirator in the murder of her husband.

Case No. 3

Mary had been married for more than 10 years to a sexual sadist who had battered her physically, emotionally, and sexually. He had forced her to have sex with the family dog on several occasions, and she had been raped twice by different men who had been hiding in her home when she returned from shopping. Both times, the rapist had informed her that he had been hired by her husband to rape her. Each time, she called her husband to tell him of the assault, and he had only laughed and warned her not to call the police. On the evenings of both occasions, her husband forced her to masturbate him while recounting the rape in detail. He also used very large dildos and burned her with cigarettes and an electrical cattle prod.

After several years of this abuse, Mary confided in a female friend who convinced her to retaliate by allowing the friend to enlist male acquaintances to beat him up. Mary agreed to this, and one evening three men kidnapped the husband as he returned home from work and severely beat him with baseball bats. They then poured gasoline over the unconscious man and set him afire. He died, and Mary was convicted of being a co-conspirator in his murder.

The women left the men primarily for two reasons; fear for their lives and/or fear for their children's welfare.

Case No. 4

Clarissa, who was married to a sexual sadist for seven years, was forced to dress in a manner designed to sexually expose her body. He took her to swinger clubs and forced her to approach and proposition men and women for sex. This man had a fantasy of torturing and murdering women, and she was forced to participate in the fantasy as the victim. After six years of marriage, she had a baby, and he allowed her five days to recuperate before he resumed the sexual abuse. One day he began beating her with his fists; and the child, who was lying on a couch, began crying. She picked the baby up and attempted to comfort her. The husband grabbed the 1 ½-year-old girl by the arm and threw her back on the couch, stating "That fucking kid isn't going to help you." A short time later, he was eating his breakfast; she got a shotgun from the closet, held it a short distance from his head, and considered shooting him. She put the gun away after considering the probable consequence of going to prison and having to leave her baby. When he left for work, she took her child and went to an underground battered spouse shelter, where she remained for three months. She has since obtained a college degree and remains in contact with the author.

The Transformation of the Women

How is it that such apparently normal women not only became involved with sexually sadistic men and were convinced to participate in sexual activities well beyond their range of experience but, in some instances, engaged in violent criminal acts with the men against others?

It is important to understand that the ritualistic (see Chapter 6) and heterosexual sadist inherently believes that all women are evil — that they are all bitches, whores, and sluts. Consequently, if and when these men set out to prove this hypothesis, they do not select prostitutes or drug addicts to become their wives or girlfriends — with those types of persons, their theory is already proven. Instead they select nice, middle-class women who are apparently normal.

As the research interviews were accomplished and the team studied the results, they noted a patterned method used by the men to induce the women into compliance in their victimization. This process consisted of five easily identifiable steps — identification, seduction, reshaping of the sexual norms, social isolation, and punishment. This five-step procedure was reported by Hazelwood, Dietz and Warren (1993).

Selection of a Vulnerable Woman

Extrapolating from the behavior described by the women, it appears that the sexual sadists had developed an ability to identify a naive, passive, and vulnerable woman. The majority of the women reported feeling badly about themselves when they were initially approached by the sadists, due to situational factors such as the breakup of a relationship or as a result of more chronic problems with self-esteem. The sexual sadists seemed able to assess this vulnerability and exploit it to manipulate these women toward interpersonal scenarios that would meet their needs for dominance, control, and sadistic sexual behavior. It seems likely that these men had attempted such activities with other women and failed.

Seduction of the Woman

The women reported that their partners were initially charming, considerate, daring, unselfish, and attentive. They gave the women gifts unexpectedly and were constantly attentive to their desires. As one woman said, "He couldn't do enough for me." Another woman, who was experiencing marital problems, advised that the man she became involved with was available to her day or night for advice or just to listen. The women all fell for the men relatively quickly, even though they recognized a sinister side. In all of the cases, the men related to the women in a romantic, seductive manner that was the antithesis of their eventual degradation and abuse. Like pedophiles, the sadists continued in this phase until they were confident in their abilities to manipulate and use the women in ways that were sexually gratifying. They cultivated the women's genuine affections before initiating the next steps.

Reshaping the Sexual Norms

The time devoted to the shaping of the woman's sexual behavior depended on the vulnerability and susceptibility of the woman. Typically, the sexual sadist persuaded the woman to engage in a sexual activity that was beyond her normal sexual repertoire. Once she had participated in such an act, the sadist then used positive reinforcement (gratitude, compliments, or attention) or negative reinforcement techniques (pouting, ignoring, or rejection) to obtain her compliance for progressively deviant activities. Over time, what began as atypical sexual behavior became routine in their relationship. The men eventually relied on threats and violence to maintain compliance of the women in such activities.

Social Isolation

Having shaped the women's sexual behaviors, the sadists moved into the fourth phase of social isolation. The men gradually became overly possessive and jealous of any activities that did not center on them, and they alienated any acquaintances who were not their own friends.

Restrictive measures were used so that the worlds of these women became increasingly circumscribed, and their circles of confidants eventually dissipated.

Punishment

The fifth and final step in the transformation involves physical and psychological punishment. Having met, seduced, and transformed a nice woman into a sexually compliant and dependent individual, the sadist has validated his theory of women. The woman is now a subservient, inferior being who has allowed herself to be re-created sexually and has participated in sexual acts that no decent woman would engage in, thereby confirming that she is a bitch and deserving of punishment. Several of the men called the women evil.

Investigative Significance of the Research

Prior to becoming involved in any research project, one question must be answered affirmatively by the author — is it going to be of practical value to law enforcement? If research data will not help law enforcement in better understanding, investigating, interviewing, or prosecuting criminals, then there is no point to the project. This philosophy has proven beneficial over the years and has resulted in some lasting benefits to the criminal justice system. Having said that, it is helpful to inform the reader how this research can be of practical value to criminal investigators. The value lies in making the investigator aware of an often overlooked source of information and in better preparing him to effectively interact with these women.

Any experienced investigator will agree that there are three primary sources of information about a criminal — the offender, those who know him, and his behavior.

Behavior

The best source of information about an offender is his criminal behavior. Behavior does not lie. If the investigators are trained to recognize and capture significant behaviors, they are well on their way to understanding the sexual lawbreaker. Trying to understand the sexual offender without examining his criminal behavior with the victim is like asking a student to write a report on one of James Michener's excellent books but not allowing that student to read the book or any information about the book.

What an offender says to a victim, the type and sequence of sexual acts, and the amount of physical force he employs are very good indicators of what is going on in his mind. He is going to say and do those things he finds sexually gratifying.

The Criminal

When lecturing on sexually violent offenders, I often begin by asking the audience what is the *least* reliable source of information about offenders. The answer is self-reported information, or information provided by the criminals about themselves. Criminals lie. They exaggerate their accomplishments, they minimize their criminal behaviors, they deny responsibility, they project blame for their failures, and then they rationalize why they lied! And yet many professionals, including mental health, social workers, researchers, and even law enforcement, depend on what the *criminals* tell them in arriving at opinions about the *criminals*. Invariably I am asked, in a classroom or by an opposing attorney, whether I *ever* believe criminals? The answer is yes — with qualification. If what the offenders say can be validated with evidence, reliable witnesses, or behaviors, then I will believe them.

Former Wives and Girlfriends

The former wife or girlfriend is an excellent source of information. While their information is not on a validity level with the offender's behavior, these women can nevertheless provide invaluable information to the investigator or researcher.

This specifically addresses a *former* relationship. Legal ramifications aside, the current wife and/or girlfriend will probably be averse to speaking with investigators. While former sexual partners are much more likely to participate in interviews, investigators should be on guard against the inclination of a former partner to exaggerate or lie out of a desire to obtain revenge for the wrongs suffered at the hands of the sadistic male. The potential for lying or exaggerating can be minimized if the investigator thoroughly prepares and remains alert to the surfacing of anger or hostility during the interview.

Perseverance is the key word in dealing with these women. They have access to information that deals with the most private and potentially damaging behaviors of the sexual criminal — his own sex life. Among other things, former sexual partners can tell the investigators about the fantasies of the offenders, any paraphilic interests, types and locations of collections, record-keeping habits, paraphernalia for use in crimes, what makes them happy or sad, what they fear, what threatens them, what their strengths and weaknesses are, where they hide things, where and how they might travel as fugitives, the types of personalities (investigators) they would be most likely to cooperate with, and when (during the day or night) they are most vulnerable to interrogations.

If the investigator is familiar with the type of person such an offender would be attracted to and what that woman may have experienced in her life and at the hands of the man, the officer will be better prepared to obtain significant information from that woman.

Summary

Twenty former wives and girlfriends of sexually sadistic men were identified and extensively interviewed. Three of these women had committed minor thefts, and four had some contact with the mental health community prior to meeting the men. Four of these women assisted their husbands in committing murders, and one woman was convicted of conspiracy in the murder of her husband. All of the women were sexually and emotionally battered by the men and were convinced to engage in a variety of deviant and often painful sexual activities.

The sexually sadistic men engaged in a patterned method to transform these apparently normal women into compliant victims. This transformation process involved the selection, seduction, reshaping of sexual norms, social isolation, and physical and emotional punishment of the women.

There are three primary sources of information about an offender; the criminal himself, his former wife or girlfriend, and his behavior. The woman who was formerly involved in the life of the offender can be an excellent source for the investigator, and it is incumbent on him to learn as much as possible about that woman and what she has experienced to better enable him to effectively interact with her.

References

Dietz, P.R., Hazelwood, R.R., and Warren, J.I. (1990) The sexually sadistic criminal and his offenses, *Bull. Am. Acad. Psychiatr. Law*, 18(2).

McGuire, C. and Norton, C. (1988) *Perfect Victim*, Dell Publishing, New York.

Hazelwood, R.R., Dietz, P.E., and Warren, J.I. (1992) The criminal sexual sadist, *FBI Law Enforcement Bull.*

Hazelwood, R.R., Dietz, P.E., and Warren, J.I. (1993) The compliant victims of sexual sadists, *Aust. Fam. Phys.*, 22(4).

Warren, J.I., Hazelwood, R.R., and Dietz, P.E. (1996) The sexually sadistic serial killer, *J. Forensic Sci.*, 41(6).

Warren, J.I. and Hazelwood, R.R. (In press) Relational patterns associated with sexual sadism, *J. Fam. Violence.*

Sexual Predators in Nursing Homes

24

ANN WOLBERT BURGESS
ROBERT A. PRENTKY
ELIZABETH B. DOWDELL*

Introduction

Over the past decade, the diversity of the expression of sexually coercive and aggressive behavior has been recognized in numerous studies that have focused on many subgroups of sex offenders, including abuse reactive children,[1-4] juvenile sexual offenders,[5] female sexual offenders,[6-9] impaired professionals,[10-12] and even such specific subgroups as stalkers.[13,14]

The one remarkable omission has been empirical focus on the rape of the elderly. These highly vulnerable, often incapacitated individuals appear to represent yet another category of hidden victims of sexual assault. Although there are no reliable incidence data on the sexual assault of the elderly, prevailing educated opinion is that "underreporting is significantly higher in this age group compared to other groups."[15] The only identified published article that looked at offenders who sexually assaulted elderly women was a 1988 study by Pollock.[16] Pollock compared five sex offenders who assaulted women age 60 or older with seven offenders who assaulted younger women. By and large, the five men who assaulted older victims were more violent, more brutal, and more sadistic. Indeed, three of the victims were murdered or thought to be dead, and in the other two cases the victims were badly mutilated. Pollock concluded that the greater evidence of psychotic features among those who assaulted the elderly suggested more severe psychopathology in that group. In a larger study that focused on the elderly victims of sexual assault, Muram, Miller, and Cutler[17] compared 53 victims, age 55 or older, with 53 victims, age 18 to 45. The older victims were far more likely to sustain genital injuries than the younger victims (51% vs. 13%, respectively).

This chapter represents our initial attempt to explore the natures of those perpetrators who target highly vulnerable, typically elderly adult females for sexual assault. We examined a convenience sample of 18 offenders who

* This chapter reprinted from Burgess, A.W., Prentky, R.A., and Dowdell, E.B. (2000) Sexual predators in nursing homes, *J. Psychosoc. Nsg.*, 38(8), 26–35.

487

sexually assaulted residents of nursing homes and other 24-hour care facilities. A prior report focused on the 20 victims of these perpetrators.[18] In this descriptive study, we attempt to portray the offenders clinically and discuss the cases in terms of legal and policy issues.

Method

Twenty cases were reviewed from the files of Dr. Burgess. Files included employee reports, in-service records, reports of abuse to human service agencies, depositions of nursing home administrators and staff, expert forensic evaluations, police reports, and trial testimony and criminal justice dispositions for cases reported to law enforcement. A videtape of a suspect was available in one case. Consents to review the files for the purpose of abstracting aggregate data were provided by the families and/or attorneys representing the residents.

The files were reviewed and data abstracted. Variables were coded directly from the file data. Coded variables fell into three discrete categories: (1) demographics (sex, race, age, and marital status), (2) dynamics of the offense (style of approach, control of victim, resistance, number of assaults, number of victims, sexual acts), and (3) forensics (laboratory results, legal outcome).

Sample

Of these twenty cases, 18 perpetrators had been identified. Of the 18 known offenders, 15 were employees of the nursing homes and three were residents of the homes. Of the 15 employees identified as perpetrators, six were Black, eight were Caucasian, and one was Hispanic. The three resident perpetrators were Caucasian and abused Caucasian residents. The two unknown suspects were determined to be staff members but were never identified. Of the 15 employee offenders, 13 were nursing aides, one was a respiratory therapist, and one was a maintenance worker. Of the nursing aide perpetrators, all were male except one. The ages of all offenders ranged from 16 to 83 years.

Of the three resident perpetrators, one was transferred to another nursing home, one remained on his wing, and one was transferred to another wing of the same nursing home. Three identified suspects immediately left the state. Eleven of the employee perpetrators were arrested. Three plea bargained to lesser charges. Five were sentenced, and three cases are pending. One suspect was acquitted — an aide who had prior convictions for child sexual assault. A year later he was charged with sexual assault of a minor. Three aides and one respiratory therapist resigned and were not investigated by police.

The files were highly variable in the amount and quality of data available for coding. Although there were 20 victims in the initial sample, complete data sets were available on only eight of the perpetrators. Reliable data were obtained for 10 to 15 men for most of the variables. Despite the obvious limitations in the number of subjects available for analysis on most of the variables, inferential statistics were not utilized. Thus, the data are reported in descriptive terms. Clearly, the purposes of this preliminary study are to highlight a potential area of empirical neglect in the sexual assault domain and to report our findings on a small convenience sample. To the best of our knowledge, no prior attempts were made to examine in any systematic way sexual offenders who target very elderly and/or incapacitated victims.

Results

Dynamics of the Offense

Victimology

Victims may be categorized as low, moderate, or high risk in relation to their exposure to crime-threatening situations. Low-risk victims are not normally exposed to predator danger and are usually sought out by offenders. In contrast, high-risk victims' lifestyles or employment consistently expose them to danger from criminal elements.[19]

All victims in this sample were highly vulnerable by virtue of incapacitation, dementia, and fragility. They were residing in a 24-hour care facility, and only five were able to walk without assistance. It was thus not surprising that 16 of the assaults occurred in the residents' own beds (despite assignment of roommates). One resident was molested in her wheelchair, and three of the residents who could walk were assaulted in a bathroom, an empty classroom, and a closet. Two residents were taken from the secure unit to another part of the nursing home.

One could argue that risk level should vary depending on the number of staff available. The nursing homes all operated on three shifts, with the day shift employing the highest number of nurses and nursing aides. For those cases in which the times of the assaults were known, the offenses occurred either during the evening or night shifts and before the day shift staff arrived.

Style of Approach

Offenders can be categorized by the method of approach and control exerted on the intended victim. Three approach styles have been described: (1) con — verbal manipulation or coercion to gain the victim's confidence, (2) blitz

— injurious force used to physically control the victim, and (3) surprise — threats but no force; the intended victim is typically approached when incapacitated or unsuspecting.[19] The confidence method was used only in cases where the victim was ambulatory (*Let's go for a walk. It's time for your bath. We're going to a party.*). Extensive physical injury was noted in one victim, suggesting a blitz-style assault. The remaining cases could be categorized as the surprise style, where there was no physical force and the victim was sleeping or incapacitated. Two cases were known to involve threats.

Control of Victim

The manner in which an offender maintains control of his victim may occur in a variety of ways: mere presence, verbal threats, display of a weapon, and use of physical force.[19] Mere presence was the primary method of control exercised by this group of offenders. Given the frailty of the victims, control strategies employing greater force were unnecessary. One victim reported, however, that she was threatened with a knife; and the wrists of another victim had been secured.

Victim Resistance

When confronted with the offender, the victim may either comply or resist. When there is resistance, the offender may cease his demand, ignore the resistance, compromise, flee, or use additional force. Two victims of residents were overheard telling the offenders to stop. In both cases, staff did not intervene, and the offenders completed the sexual assaults. In one case, a resident reported hearing her roommate gagging; and in three cases the victims reported that they screamed but no one came.

Multiple Assaults

In ten cases there were verifications of multiple assaults on the same victim. Verifications derived from the offenders or the victims. In three additional cases multiple assaults were suspected (where venereal warts were detected). One 33-year-old woman, semi-comatose from a gunshot wound to the head when she was 19, was found to be six months pregnant. An investigation of this case revealed that six male aides were having routine sex parties in her room. DNA revealed the father of her baby.

Multiple Victims

There was only one confirmed case in which the offender (female) had multiple victims (two). She was arrested on one case because the assault was recorded on videotape. A second offender (unidentified male) was believed to have assaulted two victims. Both victims (ages 16 and 79) resided on the same floor, and both developed venereal warts within months of each other.

Types of Sexual Acts

Although the type and nature of the sexual act(s) performed in an assault are often critical in attempting to understand motivation, obtaining this information was difficult because many of the victims suffered from dementia and were unable to communicate what happened. Despite the almost uniform lack of reliable self-reported data, physical evidence clearly indicated the nature of the physical and sexual abuse in many cases.

In five cases, it was possible to reliably code the presence of preexisting sexual fantasy, suggesting a degree of planning and premeditation. In one case, for instance, a 31-year-old nursing aide was observed by another nursing aide at the bedside of a 95-year-old resident. The offending aide had his pants down and his penis exposed. He admitted that he was attempting sexual intercourse. He said that when he changed the victim, she asked to have her back scratched or her legs rubbed and that she would moan, which sexually aroused him. In one case involving fondling, a male resident was observed in the dining hall to have his hand inside the top part of the nightgown of another resident.

In four other cases, it was possible to code the presence of expressive aggression and sadism. In one case, a victim described a respiratory therapist who twisted her nipples and inserted his hand into her vagina. In another case, a videotape captured a female perpetrator prodding and poking a resident in all parts of her body, including her pelvic region, with a hanger. The physical findings reported in the nursing notes included bruises to left mid-thigh and inner upper right thigh, excoriated skin in the perineal area with bright blood, bright blood to mouth near reddened area to left side, and chest discomfort and bruising. In a third case, over a two-week period a male nursing assistant forcibly sodomized a male resident and forced the victim to swallow his semen. The ambulance attendants who had arrived to transport this 73-year-old victim said he was dazed and bleeding profusely. A fourth case included penetration with a foreign object (shower head inserted into vagina during perineal care).

Case No. 1

A nursing aide walked into a resident's room and observed a nursing aide (TM) with his penis exposed and making humping movements on an 82-year-old woman. The woman was lying across the bed without underwear. TM stated to the police that "I went into the woman's room to change her brief, and I thought of having sex with her. Then I unzipped my pants and began having sex, and someone walked into the room." His statement to the nursing assistant who caught him with his pants down was that he was looking for a bed sore.

Records on TM, a 16-year-old, noted that in elementary school, a family doctor diagnosed him with attention deficit disorder, prescribed Pamelor, and said his problems were due to depression. At age 13, he became sexually active with a 16-year-old girl who was living with his family and raising her 1-year-old child. The girl became pregnant by TM, who testified that he was working 50 to 60 hours a week to pay child support as well as attending high school. Cognitive testing revealed an average IQ (107).

The records also revealed sexual abuse by a male cousin when TM was age 5. At the time of the assault he lived in a trailer with his parents and four younger siblings. His father had frequently been charged with DWI. TM had no prior criminal record. The nursing home had received complaints that TM used frequent sexualized language, but he received no reprimand. TM was convicted and sentenced to seven years for the rape, although he continued to deny the act.

Case No. 2

An 89-year-old widow with Alzheimer's disease was given a sexual assault examination after her son noticed severe bruising to her pelvic area and a purulent vaginal discharge. Two suspects were identified. The first, a maintenance supervisor, was known to make sexual advances to residents. There were two reports that said he had made advances; and one resident, whom he offered to drive somewhere, had to flee his car. He was hired after being fired from another facility for "having sex with a mentally ill resident." His son was seen at the nursing home looking for his father the day before the bruising was noted. The son had been fired for having sex with residents at another nursing facility.

Case No. 3

CW, an 83-year-old resident of a nursing home, was observed closing the door after following a 76-year-old Alzheimer's disease patient into her room. Two nursing aides watched CW digitally penetrate the victim, lie on top of her, and put his face into the woman's genital area while the woman cried, "Stop. It hurts."

CW told the police that he "went into the lady's room, because an aide told me she had a room to herself and wanted to show it to me." He was just helping her take down her pants when she grabbed his private area and pulled him down on her and was grinding. She told him that he was hurting her leg so he got off her, inserted his finger into her vagina because he thought she wanted him to (she was saying "help me"). He asked her if she climaxed, and she said she did. He also claimed he was not aware of what was going to happen when he entered the room and that he thought he was set up.

The police report indicated that a physician said CW had no prostate, implying that he was impotent. The police report also noted that CW used a walker or wheelchair to get around, and that his mind was in good working order for his age. Although CW was known to hit other residents, he was allowed free access to most areas of the facility.

Case No. 4

JG, a 33-year-old, six-foot, 200-pound man with a felony history and an outstanding health warrant for gonorrhea, applied to be a nurse's aide. Under state law, the facility was required to request a criminal history check, which it did, mistakenly classifying him as a female. A state record check of a female by the name of JG revealed no criminal history. Three weeks after JG was hired, he was fired by the assistant director of nurses for repeatedly slapping a frail and helpless 87-year-old female resident.

After some time out of state, JG returned and applied to another facility within the same nursing home system. The required criminal check was done, but the facility submitted a form with JG's name written by hand. The first letter of the last name apparently looked like a C instead of a G. Again, the incorrect name was clear of any criminal record, and JG was hired. The offense that came to staff attention occurred about a month after he was hired. While in a shower stall, JG raped a 63-year-old semi-paralyzed woman, then returned her to her bed. Two nursing aides were alerted to a substance appearing to look and smell like semen, and they reported their findings to the nursing supervisor. The resident was taken to the hospital emergency room. A sexual assault examination revealed bruising to her left thigh and vaginal area, which was tender to the touch and included a brown mucous discharge. According to the victim, she was assaulted several times and was told by the offender to shut up when she screamed and that he would kill her if she told anyone. JG told the detective that he and the resident-victim were close. JG said that he discussed his personal problems with her, that he called her mama, and that he was sorry he could not make his penis bigger. He admitted that he digitally penetrated her and inserted a shower head.

Case No. 5

An 83-year-old female resident was observed being led out of a locked Alzheimer's unit by MO, a 42-year-old maintenance employee. A search ensued, and the resident was located in an area far removed from her unit. She was fatigued, nonverbal, disoriented, barefoot, and disheveled (clothes unbuttoned). She was taken for a sexual assault examination.

MO said the resident asked him to take her for a walk but that she had to go to the bathroom, so he helped her remove her pants. MO said she started giving him a sob story, that she appreciated his taking care of her, how her husband had died, and how she didn't feel whole. She didn't feel that she had time to play a last time before she died; she felt she was a nobody. MO said he kept trying to wrestle with her to get her clothes back on, but she kept on kissing. He got her up and then "It just happened; we had intercourse. I had to. I couldn't control it. I didn't ejaculate. I left her and she got up and she was satisfied. She grabbed me by the arm and she walked back pretending that it wasn't nothing. I unlocked the door and let her in. She said she hoped I'd come by to see her tomorrow." DNA evidence matched MO to the victim.

After identifying his real name, it was revealed that MO had a lengthy criminal history and that he was on probation at the time of hire. MO told police that he was angry at his girlfriend, that he had been to her house and asked for sex but that she would not give it to him because she had a yeast infection. She drove him to work and "kicked him out of the car." MO's girlfriend, who also worked at the nursing home, told police that she saw MO on her unit later that afternoon holding the hand of a blond-haired woman wearing a purple outfit.

Case No. 6

Staff observed a 68-year-old male resident (AB) with his hand under the dress of a 91-year-old resident in the dining room. Staff intervened, and family and nursing staff were notified. When AB was interviewed, he denied touching the woman in an inappropriate way. The consulting physician would not agree to a psychiatric consultation but did order medication to curb inappropriate behavior.

An investigation revealed that AB had a history of periodic aggressive episodes and disruptive behavior toward nursing staff. However, there was no evidence of aggressive or otherwise inappropriate behavior toward other residents until the episode with the 91-year-old woman.

Case No. 7

A 55-year-old married mother diagnosed with amyotrophic lateral sclerosis reported, using a communication board, that a short, fat bearded man came to treat her. He pulled the privacy curtains around her bed. He lifted up her hospital gown, touched her breasts, twisted her nipples, spread her legs apart, and inserted two fingers into her vagina. She was unable to scream, cry out for help, or fight him off due to her paralyzed condition. This happened two days in a row. The offender, a respiratory therapist, consistently denied that anything had happened. He had no prior criminal record. He pled *nolo contendere* in the criminal case. At the Department of Public Health Services hearing, which handled licensing issues, he received several restrictions on his license.

Taxonomic Heterogeneity

Although it is clearly impossible to draw any conclusions about the taxonomic characteristics of men who sexually assault elderly women based on the very small sample examined in this study, several observations are noteworthy.

First, and most importantly, the four offenders with sufficient background data to permit tentative classifications using the Massachusetts Treatment Center Rapist Classification, Revision 3 (MTC:R3)[20] were all different. TM was classified as a Type 7 (sexual, non-sadistic, low social competence). JG was classified as a Type 8 (vindictive, low social competence). MO was classified as a Type 2 (opportunistic, low social competence). The respiratory therapist in the last case was tentatively classified as a Type 5 (muted sadistic). Thus, based on this small sample, we first conclude that the ages of the predators and motives for sexual assault of the elderly are varied. Second, however unlikely it may seem, at least two of the offenders in our sample had long histories of criminal offenses; and a third offender had a prior history of sexual assault. All three were hired by the nursing homes despite criminal checks. Third, prior employment history is not always checked. In one case, out of ten prior nursing home employments, the offender had been fired from seven. Fourth, if there were any commonalities among the offenders, they fell into two categories: (1) all of the offenders were classified as low in social competence, and (2) all of the offenders exploited victims who were frail and defenseless.

Discussion

Two principal areas of concern are beginning to emerge from our initial inquiry into nursing home sexual assault. The first area concerns victimology, and the second is liability. Victimology was addressed in greater detail in our companion report on the victims of nursing home sexual assault.[18] In brief, the victims of these crimes are, not surprisingly, quite advanced in age and suffering from some degree of dementia. As a result, not only is the examination and assessment process quite difficult, often conducted in the absence of a coherent victim report and in the presence of victim resistance (from confusion and fear, victims resist routine physical examinations after rape), but the treatment and recovery process is immeasurably more difficult. Indeed, 11 of the 20 victims died within 12 months of the rape — not from physical injuries associated with the assault but from the impact of the trauma on a very frail constitution. The unique examination and recovery problems associated with these elderly victims were discussed in detail by Hicks and Moon.[15] It is imperative that alternative methods for examining and treating these frail, often elderly victims be developed, that nursing home policies and procedures incorporate these new methods, that all caregivers employed by nursing homes be properly trained in identifying and responding to cases of sexual assault, and that the medical personnel who respond to these victims be properly trained in more effective, humane methods of examination.

The second principal area of concern involves first- and third-party liability. Over the past two decades, an increasing number of suits have been brought by rape victims or their families against employers and property owners whose negligence in the face of foreseeable risks may have contributed to a sexual assault.[21] Liability may be imposed for punitive damages when it has been determined that the defendant acted with utter indifference or conscious disregard for the safety and welfare of the plaintiff.[21] In sum, "third-party liability for rape and sexual assault is clearly based upon the fact that such crimes are frequently caused or encouraged by the failure to protect against a known and identifiable risk of harm."[21]

All of the cases examined in this study raised such fundamental premises liability issues. Of the 18 known offenders in this study, 15 were employees and three were residents. For the three resident-offenders, the nursing homes had knowledge that these individuals committed prior offenses against other residents. In the male-on-male case, the nursing home had knowledge for three years that the offender was known to seek out males and assault them. The offender was allowed to sexually assault the victim for over 30 minutes. The nursing home staff labeled the victim a homosexual, said he was a willing participant despite his screams to "get away," and laughed at him. The fact that the victim lived with his parents for 62 years (running their farm) was interpreted as an indication of his homosexuality. In another case, an 83-year-old resident-offender was known to assault other residents and allowed free access to areas of the center wherein he could target vulnerable victims. The staff failed to take precautions to ensure that residents would not be placed in potentially dangerous situations.

The majority of the offenders were employees of the nursing homes, raising the obvious issue of negligent hiring practices. In the context of the cases reviewed here, it was not unusual to hear of rapid staff turnover and staff shortages as the reasons individuals were hired on the spot. One administrator said he did not use pool staffing to cover staff shortages because "They were not worth a darn and they cost too much." The pressure to fill high-turnover positions increases the likelihood of shortcuts and "false positive" hiring decisions. Although background checks identify with reasonable reliability potential employees with prior convictions, in one very serious case (JG), two checks revealed nothing because of input error (the first time he was coded as female and the second time the letter C was substituted for the letter G).

In a number of cases, background checks were unnecessary to reach a highly defensible conclusion that a candidate was inappropriate based on past conduct. In one remarkable case, a maintenance supervisor was hired despite three reports that he had made advances toward residents and had been fired from another facility for having sex with a mentally ill resident. In another case, a 23-year-old female aide, caught on videotape beating a resident with her hands and a coat hanger, had a prior arrest that was not questioned during the hiring interview. She answered on her employment application that she had been convicted of a crime and fined. Her references were not checked. This aide had told the victim's daughter that she thought someone was abusing her mother and had taken an in-service class on elder abuse two days before the videotape caught her. In another similar case, an aide had been fired from one nursing home for gross insubordination. He was subsequently hired by another nursing home despite a conviction for aggravated assault on his application. Gaps in employment were not checked, nor were references. No orientation checklist was completed. As a new graduate of the nurse's aide program, he failed the course in perineal care. His criminal record revealed two prior arrests on sex charges. Three months before he was fired for sexually assaulting a resident, he was written up by his supervisor for fraternizing with a minor while on duty, and then yelled and swore at the supervisor. The supervisor recommended that he be fired, but he was not. Another staff member observed him slapping residents on their backsides and saying, "Baby has a butt."

In four cases where background checks were not done, the employees had histories of prior convictions. In perhaps the most serious omission, an offender who used an alias had a long and serious criminal record that was unknown to the nursing home. He had been sentenced to five years for forgery and theft of an automobile. Probation was reduced to five years and revoked due to theft of an automobile. He returned to prison as a parole violator with a new eight-year conviction for unauthorized use of a motor vehicle. He returned again as a parole violator with another new conviction for auto theft and a 15-year sentence. He was then sentenced to 30 years for delivery of a controlled substance and was on probation working at the nursing home when the rape occurred. At least one nursing home demonstrated a general acceptance of the risks associated with the hiring of staff with criminal records and inattention to the state requirement that criminal history be checked. In one year 46% of the male employees had criminal records, and approximately 25% of the records included felony convictions.

Summary

There are no reliable incidence data on the magnitude of gerophile sexual assaults. Nursing home rape has similarities to other types of rape. There is the potential for multiple assault of the same victim (a dynamic noted in incest cases) and for multiple offenders (a dynamic noted in group rape cases).[22] It is evident from our initial look at the victims and perpetrators of these assaults, however, that the intervention and management problems are unique; and focal empirical inquiry into this area is important. As we pointed out in our small sample, the perpetrators of these crimes appear to be tax-onomically heterogeneous. It is critical to appreciate that no single motive drives these assaults. There appear to be essentially two entirely separate risk groups. One group is comprised of younger perpetrators who are hired as employees of these homes, and the second group appears to be the elderly residents of these homes. Both groups present different identification, inter-vention, and treatment problems that need to be further studied.

References

1. Elliott, C.E. and Butler, L. (1994) The stop and think group: changing sexually aggressive behavior in young children, *J. Sexual Aggression*, 1, 15–28.

2. Greenfeld, L.A. (1996) Child victimizers: violent offenders and their victims, U.S. Department of Justice, Washington.

3. Loar, L. (1994) Child sexual abuse: several brief interventions with young perpetrators, *Child Abuse Neglect*, 18, 977–986.

4. Barbaree, H.E., Marshall, W.L., and Hudson, S.M. (1993) *The Juvenile Sex Offender*, Guilford Press, New York.

5. Pithers, W.D., Gray, A., Busconi, A., and Houchens, P. (1998) Children with sexual problems: identification of five distinct child types and related treat-ment considerations, *Child Maltreatment*, 3, 384–406.

6. Adshead, G., Howett, M., and Mason, F. (1994) Women who sexually abuse children: the undiscovered country, *J. Sexual Aggression*, 1, 45–56.

7. Anderson, P.B. and Struckman-Johnson, C. (1998) *Sexually Aggressive Women: Current Perspectives and Controversies*, Guilford Press, New York.

8. Elliott, M. (1993) *Female Sexual Abuse of Children*, Guilford Press, New York.

9. Larson, N.R. and Maison, S.R. (1995) Psychological treatment program for women sex offenders in a prison setting, *Acta Sexologica*, 1, 81–138.

10. Abel, G.G., Barrett, D.H., and Gardos, P.S. (1992) Sexual misconduct by physicians, *J. Med. Assoc. Ga.*, 81, 237–246.

11. Haywood, T.W., Kravitz, H.M., Wasyliw, O.E., Goldberg, J., and Cavanaugh, J.L. (1996) Cycle of abuse and psychopathology in cleric and noncleric molesters of children and adolescents, *Child Abuse Neglect*, 20, 1233–1243.

12. Loftus, J.A. and Camargo, R.J. (1993) Treating the clergy, *Ann. Sex Res.*, 6, 287–303.

13. Meloy, J.R. (1996) Stalking (obsessional following): a review of some preliminary studies, *Aggression Violent Behav.,* 1, 147–162.

14. Burgess, A.W., Baker, T., Greening, D., Hartman, C.R., Burgess, A.G., Douglas, J.E., and Halloran, R. (1997) Stalking behaviors within domestic violence, *J. Family Violence,* 12, 389–403.

15. Hicks, D.J. and Moon, D.M. (1984) Sexual assault of the older woman, in *Victims of Sexual Aggression: Treatment of Children, Women and Men,* Stuart, I.R. and Greer, J.G., Eds., Van Nostrand Reinhold, New York, 180–196.

16. Pollack, N.L. (1988) Sexual assault of older women, *Ann. Sex Res.,* 1, 523–532.

17. Muram, D., Miller, K., and Cutler, A. (1992) Sexual assault of the elderly victim, *J. Interpersonal Violence,* 7, 70–76.

18. Burgess, A.W., Dowdell, E.B., and Prentky, R.A. (2000) Sexual abuse of nursing home residents, *J. Psychosocial Nursing,* 38(6), 10–18.

19. Hazelwood, R.R. and Burgess, A.W. (1995) *Practical Rape Investigation,* CRC Press, Boca Raton.

20. Knight, R.A. and Prentky, R.A. (1990) Classifying sex offenders: the development and corroboration of taxonomic models, in *The Handbook of Sexual Assault: Issues, Theories, and Treatment of the Offender,* Marshall, W.L., Laws, D.R., and Barbaree, H.E., Eds., Plenum, New York.

21. Loggans, S.E. (1985) Rape as an intentional tort, *Trial,* 45–55.

22. Prentky, R.A. and Burgess, A.W. (2000) *Forensic Management of Sexual Offenders,* Kluwer Academic/Plenum, New York.

Index

I